CONTRACT FORMATION
LAW AND PRACTICE

CONTRACT FORMATION

Law and Practice

MICHAEL FURMSTON
G J TOLHURST

CONTRIBUTOR: ELIZA MIK

OXFORD
UNIVERSITY PRESS

OXFORD

UNIVERSITY PRESS

Great Clarendon Street, Oxford OX2 6DP

Oxford University Press is a department of the University of Oxford.
It furthers the University's objective of excellence in research, scholarship,
and education by publishing worldwide in

Oxford New York

Auckland Cape Town Dar es Salaam Hong Kong Karachi
Kuala Lumpur Madrid Melbourne Mexico City Nairobi
New Delhi Shanghai Taipei Toronto

With offices in

Argentina Austria Brazil Chile Czech Republic France Greece
Guatemala Hungary Italy Japan Poland Portugal Singapore
South Korea Switzerland Thailand Turkey Ukraine Vietnam

Oxford is a registered trade mark of Oxford University Press
in the UK and in certain other countries

Published in the United States
by Oxford University Press Inc., New York

British Library Cataloguing in Publication Data

Data available

Library of Congress Cataloging in Publication Data

Typeset by Glyph International, Bangalore, India
Printed in Great Britain
on acid-free paper by
CPI Antony Rowe

ISBN 978–0–19–928424–5

1 3 5 7 9 10 8 6 4 2

1006085004

PREFACE

One of the authors lived for many years near the small Somerset town of Cheddar where his children went to school. Cheddar is famous worldwide for its cheese and more locally for its gorge and caves, the product of floods thousands of years ago. In the 1980's bones thousand of years old were found in the caves. DNA tests on local residents showed that one of the history teachers of the children was related and that very likely his family had been living locally for two thousand years. If there were similar tests for books they would certainly show a connection to Contract Formation and Letters of Intent written by Michael Furmston, Takao Norisada, and Jill Poole in 1977. The present book is a new book but it certainly owes a debt to its predecessor. It had originally been planned that this book would be written by Jill Poole and Michael Furmston but Jill's other commitments eventually made this impossible. Michael was greatly relieved at the willingness of Greg Tolhurst to step into the breach. Greg and Michael would like to record their gratitude to Jill and Takao for their contribution to the project.

One of the authors has spent most of his life teaching in British Law Schools but is now teaching in Singapore and has for many years visited Australia to teach. The other has worked in England but has spent most of his life in Australia. The book contains discussion of many cases from England, Australia, Canada, New Zealand and Singapore. The authors do not think the laws of these countries are identical. Clearly they are not. Blind obedience to the House of Lords has gone. (Like the House of Lords itself). Nevertheless we feel that in this field all the systems have so much to learn from each other that no one should retreat into an island of their own. For similar reasons we have made extensive references to developments in the United States.

The problems of contract formation have also been considered by the great Civil Law Systems. Neither of us is competent to give an account of these systems but we have thought it right to refer to the treatments of the topic in the Vienna Convention, the Unidroit Principles for International Commercial Contracts, the principles of European Contract Law and the Draft Common Frame of Reference. The appearance of these works suggests that in this area at least the gaps between common law and civil law are not impossibly wide.

There are many debts of gratitude which should be acknowledged. Greg Tolhurst would like to thank Professors John Carter and Elisabeth Peden for their help as well as Rachel Miller and Jack Geng for their valuable research assistance. Angie Choo Kum Woon has provided invaluable support to Michael at all times. The families of both authors have provided endless encouragement as have Rachel Mullaly and Anna Krzyzanowska at OUP.

Michael Furmston
G J Tolhurst

CONTENTS—SUMMARY

---

* Chapter 6 was written by Eliza Mik.

CONTENTS

TABLE OF CASES

TABLE OF INTERNATIONAL TREATIES, CONVENTIONS, AND OTHER INSTRUMENTS

TABLE OF NATIONAL LEGISLATION

1

FORMATION AND THE CONCEPT OF AGREEMENT

A. Introduction

For any law student undertaking a course in contract law, the first substantive topic studied **1.01** is that of contract formation. There is a certain logic to this because many other topics in a contract law course, such as construction, performance, breach and damages, depend on there being a contract in existence. The topic is also a nice introduction into contract law reasoning with many of the famous and entertaining cases contained in it. It is also considered by many students to be the easier part of the course seemingly made up of a lot of easy to understand rules that need to be applied to the facts of a case. It would then come as a surprise to many to learn that perhaps the most litigated area of contract law is that of formation. In particular the formation issue that takes up most of the courts' time is that of agreement.

For a contract to exist a number of requirements must be made out. The parties must come **1.02** to an agreement, they must intend to contract, the agreement must be supported by valuable consideration and any formalities, such as the need for the contract to be evidenced in writing, must be satisfied. The concern of this book is with the requirement of agreement. As noted above, this issue takes up most of the courts' time in formation disputes. However, given that that issue is closely connected to the requirement of an intention to contract, this too is discussed in this book. The approach taken in the book is to look at the topic of agreement from the perspective of principle. The rules governing the formation of contracts are not difficult rules to state. However, they are difficult to apply and this, together with a failure to involve lawyers early on in any transaction, may be the basis for so much litigation in this area. It is difficult to provide comprehensive legal advice on any given set of facts and so both sides will tend to feel that they have a good case. This is perhaps a natural consequence when an issue largely depends on the intention of the parties.

1.03 Because our approach is one of principle we have not attempted to cite all the judgments that are handed down each year on this topic. Most of those judgments are not nor will ever be reported and there appears little point in a doctrinal driven work to give endless examples of a principle in practice when the issue before the court depends on the facts of each case.[1] Moreover, such a text would be out of date within a few hours of publication. This is particularly so in a text that attempts to look at as many jurisdictions as this one. In addition, given the amount of unreported cases now available online, any lawyer who has a formation issue coming across his or her desk can log into an electronic database and find a case with similar facts in a very short period of time. Of course reasoning through facts is not the best approach to legal research and such research will usually result in finding an unreported decision of a single judge that may or may not be in line with the leading cases and may be overruled at any time.

1.04 The approach to this text is to start with the leading decisions on a topic to discover a principle of contract formation and how that principle operates which is then followed by examples which we believe apply the principle in the way the highest authority has explained it.

1.05 This is principally a work on English law for English practitioners. For that reason it is necessary to discuss the leading English authorities. However, the practising English commercial lawyer is well versed in the classic English cases and to provide a different perspective from that found in most standard contract texts we have included a lot of cases from other jursidictions. We were able to do this because the principles of contract formation are remarkably similar across many borders. When they are different they provide interesting contrasts. Very often a perceived difference can be accomodated under current common law principles should the need to change arise. In addition to comparative case law content we also discuss approaches to formation issues under the Restatement (2d) Contracts, the Uniform Commercial Code, the Unidroit Principles of International Commercial Contracts 2004, the Principles of European Contract Law and the Draft Common Frame of Reference.

1.06 For the most part, as the principles of formation are common throughout the jurisidictions discussed in the text we have not dealt with the law in each of these jurisdictions separately but have taken the liberty of using what we think are good case examples of a particular principle in operation from any of those jurisdictions. Separate treatment is given where there is some difference of approach.

B. The Objective Theory of Contract and Formation

1.07 Throughout the law of contract is the guiding principle of the objective theory of contract.[2] That theory has particular emphasis in the area of contract formation and is discussed in more detail in the text in those areas where it is relevant. In general terms whether or not

---

[1] This is not meant to suggest that someone with a lot of time, research assistants and a love of facts might not make some important empirical findings by reading through all these cases.

[2] See Spencer, 'Signature, Consent, and the Rule in *L'Estrange v Graucob*' [1973] CLJ 104; Howarth, 'The Meaning of Objectivity in Contract' (1984) 100 LQR 265; Vorster, 'A Comment in the Meaning of Objectivity in Contract' (1987) 103 LQR 274; de Moor, 'Intention in the Law of Contract: Elusive or

the parties have agreed to enter into a contract is determined on an objective basis.[3] However, the objective theory of contract is not a form of detached 'fly on the wall' objectivity. The focus of the theory is that of a reasonable person in the position of the parties.[4] Often this is expressed as a quest for the presumed intention of the parties. As noted by others this approach is one of commercial convenience, a purely subjective approach to contract formation is not workable.[5]

The objective theory dictates that when determing whether or not a statement made by a person was intended to form the basis of a contract, it is construed by reference to a reasonable person in the position of the party to whom the statement is directed. Thus, when trying to determine whether a statement was intended to be an offer, it is construed by reference to a reasonable person in the position of the offeree.   **1.08**

To some extent the approach to finding intention is purely objective as the available evidence is what the parties said or did.[6] It is generally not possible to put to the parties a direct question as to what was their intention. Nevertheless, the subjective beliefs of the parties are relevant.[7] Although the law is not concerned with the subjective belief of a person making a statement, it may be concerned with the subjective beliefs of the person to whom it is addressed. A useful starting point is a simple example. Assume it is alleged by B that A made an offer to B which B accepted and that A wishes to argue that his or her statement to B was not an offer. The starting point is to ask whether a reasonable person in the position of B would have construed the statement as an offer? If the answer to that is 'yes' then one turns to the subjective beliefs of B. If there is evidence that B did not believe that A was making an offer then the court will take cognizance of that and rule that there was no offer.[8]   **1.09**

Illusory?' (1990) 106 LQR 632; Perillo, 'The Origins of the Objective Theory of Contract Formation and Interpretation' (2000–2001) 69 Fordham L Rev 427; Solan, 'Contract as Agreement' (2007) 83 Notre Dame L Rev 353; Goddard, 'The Myth of Subjectivity' (1987) 7 Legal Studies 263; Farnsworth, *Farnsworth on Contracts* (3rd edn, Vol 1, Aspen Publishers, New York, 2004) § 3.6, p 208ff; Beever, 'Agreements, Mistakes, and Contract Formation' (2009) 20 KCLJ 21. See also *Ricketts v Pennsylvania R Co* 153 F 2d 757, 760ff (1946).

[3] *Smith v Hughes* (1871) LR 6 QB 597, 607. Contrast the position under civil law, see Nicholas, *The French Law of Contract* (2nd edn, OUP, Oxford, 1992), 32ff.

[4] Although the expression 'a reasonable person in the position of the parties' is a convenient expression it is more appropriate to contract construction where a document must be taken to represent the agreement and understanding of both parties.

[5] Peel, *Treitel, The Law of Contract* (12th edn, Thomson, Sweet & Maxwell, London, 2007) para 1-002.

[6] *Norwich Union Fire Insurance Society Ltd v WM H Price Ltd* [1934] AC 455, 463.

[7] Once there is a concluded contract, the terms must be treated as if agreed to by both parties. Therefore, in interpreting those terms the court must give to it a meaning that represents the intention of both parties. That this is the required approach is implied by the fact that in interpretation the court is not simply determining the meaning of terms but the legal effect of the terms and so the parties are generally taken to have meant what they said. Therefore, as noted above, the construction given will be one that represents the understanding of a reasonable person in the position of the parties, *Kell v Harris* (1915) 15 SR (NSW) 473, 479. It would not be sufficient for A (a party to a contract) to argue that a particular meaning should be given to a term because A subjectively believed it had that meaning and the other party (B) knew of A's belief. It would be necessary for A to prove that B assented to that meaning.

[8] *Air Great Lakes Pty Ltd v KS Easter (Holdings) Pty Ltd* (1985) 2 NSWLR 309, 330–1. See also *OT Africa Line Ltd v Vickers plc* [1996] 1 Lloyd's Rep 700. Such evidence may include the conduct of B and the course of negotiations. See further 4.62. Similarly if an offeror is aware that the offeree does not intend to accept, it will not be sufficent proof of the existence of a contract that objectively viewed the offeree's conduct might

1.10   The relevance of the subjective state of mind of the parties as set out in the above parargraph is well accepted. It is a negative formulation of the relevance of subjective belief. In the example the statement by A will be an offer if a reasonable person in the position of B would construe it as an offer unless B is aware that A did not intend to make an offer. There is no doubt that in practice this is the principal situation where the issue of subjective belief arises, that is, where one party wishes to contest the existence of a contract by showing that the other party was aware that the first party had no intention to contract. Nevertheless, there has been a long debate as to whether this represents a full statement of the relevance of subjective belief or whether it is necessary for B, in the example, to hold the positive belief that A was making an offer. It is suggested that this latter positive formulation reflects the need for a consensus—the requirement that each party intends to contract on the same terms as the other party—and an intention to contract. It also sets the limits on the concept of consensus, it is one sided, the law is not concerned with the subjective belief of the person making a statement. Thus, in *Smith v Hughes*,[9] Blackburn J said:[10]

> If whatever a man's real intention may be, he so conducts himself that a reasonable man would believe that he was assenting to the terms proposed by the other party, *and that other party upon that belief* enters into the contract with him, the man thus conducting himself would be equally bound as if he had intended to agree to the other party's terms.

1.11   Similarly in *Paal Wilson & Co A/S v Partenreederei Hannah Blumenthal*,[11] Lord Diplock said:[12]

> To create a contract by exchange of promises between two parties where the promise of each party constitutes the consideration for the promise of the other, what is necessary is that the intention of each *as it has been communicated to and understood by the other* (even though that which has been communicated does not represent the actual state of mind of the communicator) should coincide.

1.12   In the same case Lord Brightman stated:[13]

> To entitle the sellers to rely on abandonment, they must show that the buyers so conducted themselves as to entitle the sellers to assume, *and that the sellers did assume,* that the contract was agreed to be abandoned sub silentio.

---

evidence an acceptance, see *Airways Corp of New Zealand Ltd v Geyserland Airways Ltd* [1996] 1 NZLR 116; *Transpower New Zealand Ltd v Meridian Energy Ltd* [2001] 3 NZLR 700.

   [9] (1871) LR 6 QB 597.

   [10] (1871) LR 6 QB 597, 607 (emphasis added).

   [11] [1983] 1 AC 854.

   [12] [1983] 1 AC 854, 915. See also *Maple Leaf Macro Volatility Master Fund v Rouvroy* [2009] 1 Lloyd's Rep 475, 512 per Andrew Smith J suggesting that in addition to there being no contract if one party knew or had reason to believe that the other party did not intend to contract, there will be no contract if one party formed no view one way or the other as to the other party's intention. Cf the analysis of this situation in Peel, *Treitel, The Law of Contract* (12th edn, Thomson, Sweet & Maxwell, London, 2007) para 2-003. In *Excomm Ltd v Guan Guan Shipping (Pte) Ltd (The Golden Bear)* [1987] 1 Lloyd's Rep 330, 341 Staughton J said: 'For my part I cannot see why it should in practice make any difference whether on the one hand the respondent in fact assumed that the claimant was offering to abandon the reference, or on the other hand, he would have made that assumption if he had thought about the case at all. Indeed the older a case is, the less likely it is that the respondent will give it consideration from time to time. When the case is so old that he has ceased to consider it at all, a fortiori the doctrine of abandonment should apply.'

   [13] [1983] 1 AC 854, 924.

These statements are not meant to suggest that for a contract to exist there is a need for B **1.13** in our example to prove that he or she held a positive belief that A intended to make an offer. If there is no evidence led by A to the contrary that belief will be presumed. This presumption is very important to contract formation. For example, assume A in London agrees to pay £100 to the the first person who runs from Cambridge to London. Next assume B runs from Cambridge to London and is the first person to do so after publication of the offer. That fact alone is not sufficient to bring about a contract. Nevertheless, the law is such that so long as B had knowledge of the offer and carries out the act of acceptance there is a presumption that B arrived in London in reliance on the offer. However, it is open to A to show that B did the act without intending to accept the offer.

In addition, a party will be estopped from giving evidence as to their own state of mind in **1.14** order to resile from a contract. For example, assume the situation is that A makes an offer to B which is accepted by B in circumstances where a reasonable person in the position of A would construe B's statement as an acceptance. It is not possible for A to seek to resile from the contract by attempting to lead evidence that he or she did not subjectively believe B was accepting. A has acted in a way that a reasonable person 'B' would interpret as suggesting an intention to contract and is estopped from resiling from that position unless A can prove that B did not rely or could not have relied on the representation implied from A's conduct because B knew that, in fact, A did not intend to contract.[14] Thus in *Smith v Hughes*,[15] Blackburn J said:[16]

> I apprehend that if one of the parties intends to make a contract on one set of terms, and the other intends to make a contract on another set of terms, or, as it is sometimes expressed, if the parties are not ad idem, there is no contract, unless the circumstances are such as to preclude one of the parties from denying that he has agreed to the terms of the other.

This concept of 'estoppel' pervades contract formation and prevents a person leading **1.15** evidence of their state of mind even though such subjective intent may form part of contract formation theory at some level. It follows that in the result the positive formulation of the relevance of subjective beliefs will not in practice produce different results from the negative formulation.

There is yet another debate concerning the subjective beliefs of the parties. As noted above, **1.16** the relevance of these subjective beliefs is well accepted but there has been a long debate as to whether they operate as an exception to the objective theory of contract and effectively render the theory a fiction or whether they are captured by it. For many, as noted above, the objective theory is a theory of convenience and 'applies only where serious inconvenience would be caused by allowing a party to rely on his "real intention"'.[17] However, for others because the objective theory operates by reference to a reasonable person in the position of the parties that reasonable person must take on the characteristics of the parties including

---

[14] This is not an adoption of a reliance theory of contract and the 'estoppel' operates upon the giving of a counter-promise. Cf the formulation of estoppel by Lord Brandon in *Paal Wilson & Co A/S v Partenreederei Hannah Blumenthal* [1983] 1 AC 854, 914.

[15] (1871) LR 6 QB 597.

[16] (1871) LR 6 QB 597, 607.

[17] Peel, *Treitel, The Law of Contract* (12th edn, Thomson, Sweet & Maxwell, London, 2007) para 1-002.

their background and knowledge and this brings within the objective theory those subjective beliefs to the extent that they are relevant and admissible.[18]

C. The Concept of Agreement

1.17 It is a general principle of contract formation that the parties must have reached an agreement. This has traditionally been expressed as a requirement that there be a consensus *ad idem*. As noted above there are limits in the extent to which the common law requires a consensus.[19] The objective theory of contract necessarily dictates that there is no requirement of a true subjective meeting of the minds.[20] As a general proposition the requirement of an agreement necessitates that the parties agree the terms of bargain, that those terms be certain and complete and that the bargain is informed by an intention to contract as well as an intention to immediately assume legal obligations.

1.18 This description of an agreement raises numerous issues in practice that are the subject matter of this text. For example, what is the impact of an agreement made 'subject to contract'? What is the legal significance of an 'agreement to agree'? It will be seen that modern courts are changing the way some of these issues are dealt with. For example, it has long been stressed that the courts should not be the destroyer of bargains but should seek to give effect to transactions entered into by commercial people: in short the courts should 'oil the wheels of commerce' and not 'put a spanner in the works'.[21] On this basis courts have long sought to uphold contracts despite any difficulties that might arise.[22] But today that has been given new meaning whereby courts are emphasizing the need to give effect to the overall expectation of parties that there will be a contract even if in doing so that might contradict a term of the agreement.[23] At the same time the courts maintain the principle that they will not make a contract for the parties and this sets an upper limit on what a court can do.

1.19 The traditional method for discovering the existence of an agreement is that of offer and acceptance. Courts are quick to point out that offer and acceptance are merely tools that can be used to determine whether an agreement has been reached, they are not exhaustive and in many situations may be unworkable and innapropriate.[24] This is true and the

---

[18] See generally McLauchlan, 'Objectivity in Contract' (2005) 24 Uni Qld L Jnl 479, 484. However, where the issue is one of construction the background facts that are taken into account are those known to both parties and inform the objective interpretation of the contract, see *Toll (FGCT) Pty Ltd v Alphapharm Pty Ltd* (2004) 219 CLR 165, 179.
[19] See 1.10.
[20] However, this would be sufficient if it could be proved.
[21] Goff, 'Commercial Contracts and the Commercial Court' [1984] LMCLQ 382, 391. See also *Homburg Houtimport BV v Agrosin Private Ltd (The Starsin)* [2004] 1 AC 715, 749.
[22] *York Air Conditioning and Refrigeration (A/sia) Pty Ltd v Commonwealth* (1949) 80 CLR 11, 26; *AG v Barker Bros Ltd* [1976] 2 NZLR 495, 498; *Toyota Motor Corporation Australia Ltd v Ken Morgan Motors Pty Ltd* [1994] 2 VR 106, 130, 201; *Barrett v IBC International Ltd* [1995] 3 NZLR 170, 173.
[23] *Fletcher Challenge Energy Ltd v Electricity Corporation of New Zealand Ltd* [2002] 2 NZLR 433, 462–5. See further 11.06.
[24] *New Zealand Shipping Co Ltd v AM Satterthwaite & Co Ltd (The Eurymedon)* [1975] AC 154, 167. See also *Boulder Consolidated Ltd v Tangaere* [1980] 1 NZLR 560, 562; *Meates v Attorney General* [1983] NZLR

existence of many commercial agreements is proven by the execution of a formal contract with any formation issue going before a court being one of certainty and completeness. Moreover, it is possible to prove a contract by conduct without reference to offer and acceptance if all the essential elements of a contract are made out.[25] Such conduct must prove the parties intend to be bound by the agreed terms.[26] It is not enough that the conduct is consistent with there being a contract.[27] Despite this, any basic search of formation cases will show that the tools of offer and acceptance remain the primary method used to determine the existence of an agreement where there is no executed contract. Therefore, they are the subject of detailed discussion in this book.[28]

D. Contract Formation: An Issue of Fact or Law?

As a general statement whether or not the parties intended to contract is an issue of fact and may be proven by reference to relevant extrinsic evidence which includes pre and post contract conduct.[29] Despite this, there are many statements made in the cases to the effect that the issue is one of construction and involves a question of law.[30] Usually such statements are made where the alleged agreement is in writing.[31] These are dealt with in more detail in the text in the context in which they arise. However, a couple of introductory remarks can be made here.

1.20

The process of construction is concerned with the meaning and legal effect of the terms of a contract. Where there is a true issue of construction this will impact on the evidence available. As a general rule access to prior negotiations in construing a contract is limited and access to post-contractual conduct prohibited.[32] On one level this process of construction is distinct from determining the terms of a contract. However, it has been said that the less comprehensive an agreement is the more a court must draw inferences in order

1.21

308, 377; *Vroon BV v Foster's Brewing Group Ltd* [1994] 2 VR 32, 83; *Pobjie Agencies v Vinidex Tubemakers* [2000] NSWCA 105, [24]. See further Lucke, 'Striking a Bargain' (1960–62) 1 Adelaide l Rev 293.

[25] *Integrated Computer Services Pty Ltd v Digital Equipment Corp (Australia) Pty Ltd* (1988) 5 BPR 11,110, 11,117–18.

[26] *Kriketos v Livschitz* [2009] NSWCA 96.

[27] *Adnunat Pty Ltd v Olivetti Concrete Lifting Systems Pty Ltd* [2009] FCA 499, [39]. See further 2.02ff.

[28] See further *Gibson v Manchester City Council* [1979] 1 WLR 294, 297.

[29] *Hussey v Horne-Payne* (1879) 4 App Cas 311, 316; *Howard Smith & Co Ltd v Varawa* (1907) 5 CLR 68, 78; *Barrier Wharfs Ltd v W Scott Fell & Co Ltd* (1908) 5 CLR 647; *B Seppelt & Sons Ltd v Commissioner for Main Roads* (1975) 1 BPR 9147; *Allen v Carbone* (1975) 132 CLR 528, 533; *Australian Energy Ltd v Lennard Oil NL* [1986] 2 QdR 216; *Hughes v NM Superannuation Pty Ltd* (1993) 29 NSWLR 653, 670; *Elmslie v FCT* (1993) 118 ALR 357, 368–9; *Brambles Holdings Ltd v Bathurst City Council* (2001) 53 NSWLR 153, 163–4; *Kriketos v Livschitz* [2009] NSWCA 96.

[30] Eg *Hillas & Co Ltd v Arcos Ltd* (1932) 147 LT 503, 513–14.

[31] *Woodside Offshore Petroleum Pty Ltd v Atwood Oceanics Inc* [1986] WAR 253; *Australian Broadcasting Corp v XIVTH Commonwealth Games Ltd* (1988) 18 NSWLR 540.

[32] *James Miller & Parnters Ltd v Whitworth Street Estates (Manchester) Ltd* [1970] AC 583; *Chartbrook Ltd v Persimmon Homes Ltd* [2009] 3 WLR 267. See also *Bruner v Moore* [1904] 1 Ch 305; *Australian Energy Ltd v Lennard Oil NL* [1986] 2 QdR 216; *Hide & Skin Trading Pty Ltd v Oceanic Meat Traders Ltd* (1990) NSWLR 310. See further *Brambles Holdings Ltd v Bathurst City Council* (2001) 53 NSWLR 153, 163, 164. For a powerful critique of this view and the inconsistency between construction and contract formation, see McLauchlan, 'Contract Formation, Contract Interpretation, and Subsequent Conduct' (2006) 25 Uni Qld L Jnl 77.

to determine the intention of the parties and here resort may be had to the words or conduct of the parties.[33] This represents a technique of identfying the terms of a contract by construction. Terms may be implied by construction and so it is not entirely possible to distinguish between these processes and, moreover, the identification of the terms of a contract is intimately tied to issues of contract formation. It follows that there will be aspects of formation that are dealt with as issues of construction.

1.22 Very often where statements are made in the context of contract formation that the issue is one of construction, the court will nevertheless have regard to extrinsic evidence which suggests that any reference to construction was not meant in a technical sense.[34] Nevertheless, some issues around contract formation are clearly issues of construction. For example, if a court is determining whether a term is void for uncertainty, that will be an issue of construction.[35] However, where the issue is whether or not the parties intended to contract that is an issue of fact. Here the court can have regard to all the circumstances to determine whether the parties have entered into a contract. Thus, the whole of the communications between the parties must be looked at to determine whether there is an offer and acceptance.[36] As already noted, this process is related to the identification of the terms of a contract and extrinsic evidence is allowed to determine the terms of a contract.[37]

1.23 Often issues of formation and construction can become blurred when the agreement is in writing and many cases have referred to questions of formation as being questions of mixed law and fact.[38] Thus, if on construction a term is found to be void then whether or not it can be severed has been said to turn on construction,[39] but, at the same time, whether or not the parties intended to contract if that term was found to be void goes to the intention to contract and is an issue of formation. A practical example of where both processes are relevant to contract formation would be the approach to a 'subject to contract' clause. When a court is confronted with such a provision it must decide whether the clause impacts on the formation of a contract or its performance. Such a clause may evidence a lack of

---

[33] *Allen v Carbone* (1975) 132 CLR 528, 532; *Trawl Industries of Australia Pty Ltd v Effem Foods Pty Ltd Trading as 'Uncle Bens of Australia'* (1992) 27 NSWLR 326, 344.
[34] See *Marek v Australasian Conference Association Pty Ltd* [1994] 2 Qd R 521, 529; *Elmslie v FCT* (1993) 118 ALR 357, 367–9; *The Commercial Bank of Australia Ltd v GH Dean & Co Pty Ltd and Dean* [1983] 2 Qd R 204, 209; *B Seppelt & Sons Ltd v Commissioner for Main Roads* (1975) 1 BPR 9147.
[35] *Kell v Harris* (1915) 15 SR (NSW) 473, 479.
[36] *Hussey v Horne-Payne* (1879) 4 App Cas 311, 316; *Pagnan SpA v Granaria BV* [1986] 2 Lloyd's Rep 547.
[37] *R W Cameron & Co v L Slutzkin Pty Ltd* (1923) 32 CLR 81; *Sinclair Scott & Co Ltd v Naughton* (1929) 43 CLR 310; *Hope v RCA Photophone of Australia Pty Ltd* (1937) 59 CLR 348, 362–3. See further *Interway Inc v Alagna* 407 NE 2d 615, 618-19 (1980) ('The determination of the intent of the parties to a contract may be a question of law or a question of fact, depending on the documents presented … If [the] language is ambiguous, then the determination of its meaning is a question of fact … However, if the language is unambiguous, then the construction of the alleged contract is a question of law … If the trial court finds that the agreement is ambiguous, then "parol evidence is admissible to explain and ascertain what the parties intended." … However, if the trial court classifies the writings as unambiguous, then the intention of the parties must necessarily be determined solely from the language used in the document.')
[38] *Covington Marine Corp v Xiamen Shipbuilding Industry Co Ltd* [2006] 1 Lloyd' Rep 745, 756. Cf *G Percy Trentham Ltd v Archital Luxfer Ltd* [1993] 1 Lloyd's Rep 25.
[39] See 11.124.

an intention to contract. This is a question of fact. Once a decision on that issue is made, then, assuming there is an intention to contract, it is still necessary to construe the clause to determine whether the parties intended to immediately assume legal obligations or not, and if they did, whether performance is or is not suspended until execution.

2

OFFERS AND INVITATIONS TO TREAT

A. General Considerations

The technique of analysing transactions in terms of offer and acceptance to determine **2.01** whether there is an agreement appears to have been adopted by all developed legal systems and not surprisingly therefore features in the universal systems which are now appearing.

So the Unidroit Principles for International Commercial Contracts provide: **2.02**

ARTICLE 2.1

(Manner of formation)

A contract may be concluded either by the acceptance of an offer or by conduct of the parties that is sufficient to show agreement.

In most cases where there is a dispute as to whether there is a contract it makes sense to **2.03** analyse what the parties have done to see whether one of them has made an offer and then to look to see whether the other party has accepted that offer. This will solve a lot of disputes but it is not always either necessary or appropriate.

An obvious example is the way in which house purchase transactions are commonly carried **2.04** out in the English practice. The potential buyers and sellers typically negotiate about the price often with help from an estate agent but usually without legal help. Once a price has been agreed there is a deal but not a contract. Most buyers and sellers will know that it is usual to hand matters over to lawyers. At this stage, many will have little idea why and will not know that since 1989 English law has required such contracts to be in writing (this Act has made little practical difference to what happens). The solicitors will agree to the form of words which are to be used for the sale; two copies of the contract will be produced and one will be signed by the seller and the other by the buyer. At this stage there will still be no legally binding contract. The contract comes into existence by the process of exchange. The seller's copy is passed to the buyer and the buyer's to the seller. Each party now has a copy of the contract signed by the other party (at one time the contracts would have been physically exchanged; now the exchange is often telegraphic or electronic).[1] No one doubts that there is a contract but it is very hard to say, who is the offeror and who the offeree.

2.05 Another example is provided by the decision of the House of Lords in *Clarke v Dunraven*.[2] In this case a collision took place during a yacht race. The owners of the yachts had entered the race by completing the entry form provided by the organizers and had no dealing with each other. Each yacht owner had clearly made a contract with the organizer but the House of Lords held that there was also a contract between the competitors so that their duties to each other were governed by the race rules and not by the general law.

2.06 It is worth considering why this was a sensible and appropriate decision. There was no doubt that there was a contract between each of the competitors and the organizing committee. This meant that if one of the competitors broke the sailing rules this would be a breach of the contract between the competitor and the organizers but the organizers would not have been able to recover in a contract action damages for loss suffered by another competitor[3] and if this were the only contract privity of contract would be an obstacle to another competitor bringing a contract action (on the facts a tort action would have been much less satisfactory). In common sense terms it makes obvious sense to treat all the competitors as having agreed with each other to follow the rules.

2.07 Multi-party contracts are in fact quite common though they are not much discussed in the books. In some cases, such as partnerships, it will be normal for all the parties to enter into an explicit contract with all the others. But in the case of informal associations and clubs, members will often only deal with the secretary or the committee. Nevertheless in such cases *Clarke v Dunraven* may well provide support for finding a contract between the members.

2.08 It is clear then that there will be cases where objectively speaking it is clear that there is agreement but difficult to analyse what has happened in terms of offer and acceptance. The problems which are discussed in Chapters 7 and 8 exemplify this.

2.09 Nevertheless there are cases where offer and acceptance is the appropriate technique. Drawing the line can obviously be a problem. An instructive English case is *Gibson v Manchester City Council*.[4] In this case the council decided to sell some council houses to their tenants. Later, after an election, control of the council changed and the policy was reversed. It became necessary to decide which transactions had crossed the line into binding contracts. In Mr Gibson's case he had received a letter from the council indicating that they might be willing to sell and at what price and inviting him to return a form. He had returned the form but it had not been actioned when the policy changed.

---

[1] An excellent discussion of the reason for telephonic exchange will be found in *Domb v Isoz* [1980] 1 Ch 548.

[2] [1897] AC 59.

[3] *McAlpine v Panatown* [2001] 1 AC 518.

[4] [1979] 1 All ER 972, [1979] 1 WLR 294.

The majority of the Court of Appeal held that there was a contract.[5] In a characteristic **2.10** judgment Lord Denning MR argued for looking at the question of whether there was a contract in a broader setting. The House of Lords disagreed.[6] In an equally characteristic speech Lord Diplock affirmed the traditional analysis. The council's first letter was no more than an invitation to treat and Mr Gibson's reply was at most an offer which had not been accepted.

As a matter of orthodox contract law this seems clearly correct. In the range of possible **2.11** negotiations Gibson was well towards the simple end. Lord Denning's judgment reflects a feeling that councils should not behave like this. But if that is to stand it needs a quite different conceptual basis.

There is a group of New Zealand cases which have taken what has been described as a global **2.12** approach.[7] An interesting example is *Aotearoa International Ltd v Scancarriers A/S*[8] The defendants, a firm of shipowners, sent to the plaintiff, a firm of exporters, a telex agreement to a 'promotional rate' for cargo of US$120 per ton and saying that shipping rates would be held for six months. After two shipments the defendants refused to accept any more bookings from the plaintiffs.

The New Zealand Court of Appeal held, reversing the trial judge, that there was a binding **2.13** contract to ship goods at the specified rate. This was justified on the basis that the telex had to be construed in the light of matters which could be included into it on the basis of an objective view of its contents. The Privy Council disagreed and Lord Roskill[9] said:

> It is not correct in principle, in order to determine whether there is a legally binding bargain, to add to those terms which alone the parties have expressed, further implied terms upon which they have not expressly agreed and then by using the express terms and the implied terms together thereby create what would not otherwise be a legally binding bargain.[10]

B. Identifying an Offer

What constitutes an offer[11]

An offer is defined by Anson[12] as 'an intimation, by words or conduct, of a willingness to **2.14** enter into a legally binding contract, and which in its terms expressly or impliedly indicates that it is to become binding on the offeror as soon as it has been accepted by an act,

---

[5] [1978] 2 All ER 583, [1978] 1 WLR 520.

[6] [1979] 1 All ER 972, [1979] 1 WLR 294.

[7] Burrows, Finn and Todd, *Law of Contract in New Zealand* (3rd edn, Lexis Nexis NZ Ltd, Wellington, 2007) 35–7.

[8] [1985] 1 NZ LR 513.

[9] [1985] 1 NZLR 513.

[10] *Aotearoa International Ltd v Scancarriers A/S* [1985] 1 NZLR 513 (HC, CA and PC) at 556. For further discussion of what Lord Roskill meant see 11.119ff. As McLauchlan (2002) 18 JCL 153, 165–6 reminds us, the Courts often imply terms into agreements so as to provide sufficiently certain terms (see para 3.7.6). The Courts should not imply onerous terms which create a bargain to which one or both parties would not have assented.

[11] Section 2(a) of the Malaysian Contracts Act 1950 refers to a 'proposal' rather than an offer.

[12] Beatson, *Anson's Law of Contract* (28th edn, OUP, Oxford, 2002) 32.

forbearance or return promise on the part of the person to whom it is addressed'. Treitel considers that an offer is 'an expression of willingness to contract on specified terms, made with the intention that it is to become binding as soon as it is accepted by the person to whom it is addressed'.[13]

2.15 It is therefore necessary to look at all the circumstances to determine whether the alleged offeror has reached a point of making it clear that all that is needed is for the other to accept his terms.[14] *Harvey v Facey*[15] involved an exchange of three telegrams. The first was sent by the potential buyer and stated 'Will you sell us Bumper Hall Pen? Telegraph lowest cash price'. The second telegram was a reply by the owner stating 'Lowest price for Bumper Hall Pen £900'. The potential buyer purported to accept this in the third telegram. The Judicial Committee of the Privy Council held that there was no contract since the second telegram did not constitute an offer to sell. It merely indicated the lowest price if the vendor did decide to sell. The third telegram was therefore an offer by the potential buyer but it was not accepted by the owner.

2.16 It is important to consider both the language used in the document and the general context in determining whether an offer has been made. *Harvey v Facey* concerned a potential sale of a piece of land where matters other than price will be important.[16] If a document does not indicate a 'willingness to become bound upon acceptance', it will not constitute an offer but is classified as an invitation to contract or an invitation to treat.[17]

In the United States the expression 'preliminary negotiations' is generally used instead of 'invitation to treat'. The second edition of the American Restatement of Contracts distinguishes between an offer and preliminary negotiations as follows:

§ 24. Offer defined

An offer is the manifestation of willingness to enter into a bargain, so made as to justify another person in understanding that his assent to that bargain is invited and will conclude it.

---

[13] *The Law of Contract* (12th edn, 2007) 9.

[14] In *Australian Woollen Mills Proprietary Ltd v The Commonwealth* (1955) 93 CLR 546 it was claimed that the Commonwealth had made an offer to pay a subsidy when it had announced its decision to pay such a subsidy and that this 'offer' had been accepted by the plaintiff manufacturer on purchasing wool. However, the Privy Council held that there was no contract to pay a subsidy since the Commonwealth had only issued a statement of government policy which was not an offer capable of being accepted.

[15] *Harvey v Facey* [1893] AC 552. See also US case of *Owen v Tunison* 131 Me 42,158 A 926 (1932), where 'it would not be possible for me to sell unless I was to receive $16,000 cash' was held not to be an offer. Similarly, see the Irish decision of *Boyers & Co v Duke* [1905] 2 IR 617 where a statement of lowest price was not an offer.

[16] This is illustrated by the decision of the Court of Appeal in *Clifton v Palumbo* [1944] 2 All ER 497. The letter in question stated 'I am prepared to offer you ... my Lytham estate for £600,000'. This was held to be a preliminary statement as to price and not an offer. The complexity of the estate was a factor indicating that further negotiations were required. Compare *Bigg v Boyd Gibbins Ltd* [1971] 1 WLR 913, [1971] 2 All ER 183.

[17] Invitations to treat are sometimes referred to as 'offers to negotiate offers to receive offers—offers to chaffer' (per Bowen LJ in *Carlill v Carbolic Smoke Ball Company* [1893] 1 QB 256, 268).

§ 26. Preliminary negotiations

A manifestation of willingness to enter into a bargain is not an offer if the person to whom it is addressed knows or has reason to know that the person making it does not intend to conclude a bargain until he has made a further manifestation of assent.

Here also the distinguishing factor is the intention to make the 'offeree's' assent conclude **2.17** the contract. Such intention must be judged objectively rather than subjectively so that the courts examine the external manifestation of intention rather than a person's actual intention. This approach is expressed in the words of Lord Denning MR in *Storer v Manchester City Council*:[18]

> In contracts you do not look into the actual intent in a man's mind. You look at what he said and did. A contract is formed when there is, to all outward appearances, a contract. A man cannot get out of a contract by saying: 'I did not intend to contract', if by his words he has done so. His intention is to be found only in the outward expression which his letters, convey. If they show a concluded contract that is enough.

Thus it is a question of what the addressee is justified in believing as a result of the conduct **2.18** of the 'offeror'. Treitel[19] states that there will be an offer if the conduct of the 'offeror' 'is such as to induce a reasonable person to believe that he [the offeror] intends to be bound, even though in fact he has no such intention'. However, the addressee would not be justified in considering a communication to be an offer if he knows that no offer is intended. That is, although the fundamental approach is objective, the position is different if there is reliable evidence that the offeree knew that the offeror did not intend to make an offer. In that case there will not be an offer.[20]

Section 26 of the American Restatement (2d) Contracts, expressly provides that there is no **2.19** offer if the addressee knows or has reason to know that there is no intention to be bound.

The technique of offer and acceptance is used by civilian systems just as much as common **2.20** law systems though the application is not necessarily exactly the same.

Because both common law and civil law systems are accustomed to the analysis it has not surprisingly found its way into international conventions. The provisions of the Vienna Convention, the Unidroit Principles for International Commercial Contracts and the Principles of European Contract Law appear in the later discussion. The most recent such provision is in the Draft Common Frame of Reference, article 4.201 of which provides:

II.—4:201: Offer

    (1) A proposal amounts to an offer if:
        (a) It is intended to result in a contract if the other party accepts it; and
        (b) It contains sufficiently definite terms to form a contract.
    (2) An offer may be made to one or more specific persons or to the public.
    (3) A proposal to supply goods from stock, or a service, at a stated price made by a business in a public advertisement or a catalogue, or by a display of goods, is treated, unless the

---

[18] [1974] 3 All ER 824, 828.
[19] *The Law of Contract* (12th edn, 2007) 10.
[20] For further discussion see 1.09.

circumstances indicate otherwise, as an offer to supply at that price until the stock of goods, or the business's capacity to supply the service, is exhausted.

Requirements of a valid offer

2.21   The intention on the part of the 'offeror' to make the 'offeree's' assent conclude the contract is determined by examining the language used. In particular, it is necessary to assess the extent of commitment evinced, the certainty of the terms used and the specification of the addressees.

Commitment

2.22   Schlesinger cites 'use of non-committing language in the proposal' as one factor indicating that an offer has not been made, and continues: 'This factor can come into play in one or both of two ways: either the words of commitment are weak, e.g., "we quote ...", or they are coupled with words suggesting a denial of commitment. Of course, if the language is clearly enough non-committing or anti-committing, this is no longer merely a factor, but determinative.'[21]

(a) Weak words of commitment

2.23   This factor is apparent in the American decision of *Moulton v Kershaw*.[22] Kershaw, dealers in salt, had written a letter to Moulton in the following terms: 'we are authorised to offer Michigan fine salt, in full car-load lots of 80 to 95 bbls., delivered at your city, at 85c. per bbl., to be shipped per C & N.W.R.R. Co. only. At this price it is a bargain, as the price in general remains unchanged. Shall be pleased to receive your order.' On receiving this letter Moulton immediately sent the following reply by telegram: 'Your letter of yesterday, received and noted. You may ship me two thousand (2,000) barrels Michigan fine salt, as offered in your letter. Answer.' When Kershaw refused to deliver Moulton claimed damages for breach of contract alleging that the letter constituted an offer to sell him any reasonable quantity of salt he might order and that he had accepted this offer by telegram. However, the court held that the letter was not an offer and therefore no contract had resulted. As Taylor J stated:

> The language is not such as a business man would use in making an offer to sell to an individual a definite amount of property. The word 'sell' is not used. They say, 'we are authorised to offer Michigan fine salt,' etc, and volunteer an opinion that at the terms stated it is a bargain. They do not say, we offer to sell to you. They use general language proper to be addressed generally to those who were interested in the salt trade.[23]

2.24   Another American example of the lack of commitment evidenced in the language used is *Nebraska Seed Co v Harsh*.[24] A farmer, Harsh, had written a letter to the Seed Company in the following terms: 'I have about 1800 bu. or thereabouts of millet seed of which I am mailing you a sample. This millet is recleaned and was grown on sod and is good seed. I want $2.25 per cwt. for this seed f.o.b. Lowell.' The plaintiff company immediately sent

---

[21] Schlesinger, *Formation of Contracts* (Vol. I, Oceana Publications Inc, New York, 1968) 329.
[22] 18 NW 172 (1884), 59 Wis 316.
[23] Ibid., at 174.
[24] 152 NW 310 (1915), 98 Neb 89.

a reply by telegram stating: 'Accept your offer. Millet like sample two twenty-five per hundred. Wire how soon can load.' They also sent a letter to confirm. The Supreme Court of Nebraska held that Harsh's letter was not an offer. Morrissey CJ referred to the fact that Harsh had used only general language, in particular the words 'I want $2.25 per cwt. for this seed f.o.b. Lowell' rather than 'I offer to sell to you'. He continued: 'The letter as a whole shows that it was not intended as a final proposition but as a request for bids.'[25]

The importance of the language used in indicating commitment is also demonstrated by English case law, an example of which is the decision of the House of Lords in *Gibson v Manchester City Council*[26] discussed earlier. This can be contrasted with the language used in the correspondence in *Storer v Manchester City Council*,[27] a case which also involved the question of the sale of council houses to tenants. The town clerk had used the following language: 'I understand you wish to purchase your council house and enclose the agreement for sale. If you sign the agreement and return it to me I will send you the Agreement signed on behalf of the corporation in exchange.' The Court of Appeal held that, having regard to the language used, it was the council's intention that it would become contractually bound when the tenant signed and returned the agreement for sale. **2.25**

(b) Words expressly denying a commitment

The proposer may use language which reserves the power to conclude the contract to the proposer himself. This clearly indicates that the proposal is not an offer because there is evidently no intention to allow the addressee's consent to conclude the contract. Examples of wording which expressly deny any commitment include **2.26**

> [This quotation] shall become a contract upon, but not before, acceptance by the Home Office of our company ...[28]

and

> This offer is subject to formal approval by our Board of Directors.[29]

Such clauses enable a company to check proposals made by officers. In *International Filter Co v Conroe Gin, Ice and Light Co*[30] a proposal had been made by the plaintiff's travelling solicitor, Waterman, which contained the following clause: **2.27**

> This proposal ... becomes a contract when accepted by the purchaser and approved by an executive officer of the International Filter Company, at its office in Chicago.

---

[25] Ibid., at 311.

[26] [1979] 1 WLR 294, [1979] 1 All ER 972. See discussion above at 2.9. See the Singapore decisions of *Kwong Kum Sun (S) Pte Ltd v LMn Soon Siew* [1984] 1 MLJ 150 and *Pac-Asian Service Pte Ltd v Westburne International Drilling Ltd* [1987] 1 MLJ 283. In Malaysia see *Abdul Rashid Abdul Maiid v Island Golf Properties Sdn Bhd* [1989] 3 MLJ 376. But cf *Diamond Peak Sdn Bhd v Tweedie* [1980] 3 MLJ 31 and *Tan Geok Khoon + Gerard Francis Robless v Paya Terubong Estate Sdn Bhd* [1988] 2 MLJ 672.

[27] [1974] 3 All ER 824.

[28] *West Penn Power Company v Bethlehem Steel Corporation* 236 Pa. Super. 413, 348 A. 2d 144 (1975).

[29] *Pennsylvania Company v Wilmington Trust Company* 166 A. 2d 726 (1960). See also Art 2.2 of the Unidroit Principles of International Commercial Contracts, Illustration 2, 'agreement is not binding until approved by A's Board of directors'.

[30] 277 SW 631 (1925).

The defendant, addressee, had indicated its acceptance on the proposed document which had then been forwarded to the plaintiff company's Chicago office. It was endorsed by the president of the company: 'OK Feb 13, 1920, P N Engel.'

Subsequently, a dispute arose as to whether a contract existed. It was held that the defendant had made an offer when the proposal was approved and that an enforceable contract came into existence when the president of the plaintiff company endorsed it at their Chicago office.[31]

2.28 By contrast, the use of the words 'for immediate acceptance' has been held to indicate a strong commitment and intention to be bound. In *Fairmount Glass Works v Grunden-Martin Goodenware*[32] a prospective purchaser had requested details of lowest price, cash discount and terms of sale 'for ten car loads of Mason green jars' and the defendant, seller, had replied: 'We quote you Mason fruit jars ... pints $4.50, quarts $5.00, half gallons $6.50, per gross, for immediate acceptance; and shipment no later than May 15, 1895; sixty days' acceptance, or 2 off, cash in ten days.' The buyer had sent a telegram entering an order in accordance with the quotation and subsequently argued that a binding contract had resulted.

Hobson J considered that the defendant's reply was more than a simple quotation because the words 'for immediate acceptance' indicated the defendant's intention to sell at those prices if accepted immediately. Consequently it was an offer which the plaintiff had accepted.

2.29 An expression which negatives commitment is not required to be inserted in any advertisement inviting bids or inviting tenders for the supply of goods or services. Such an advertisement is merely an invitation to treat so that each bid or tender submitted represents an offer and it is for the person requesting the bids or tenders to accept whichever he chooses. This is because, in general, the requester is under no obligation to accept the most competitive bid. Authority for this is provided by the leading English case of *Spencer v Harding*,[33] which concerned an action brought by the highest bidder who was not awarded the goods advertised.

The advertiser had sent out a circular in the following terms: 'We are instructed to offer to the wholesale trade for sale by tender the stock in trade of Messr G. Eilbeck and Co ... which will be sold at a discount in one lot.' Willes J rejected the argument that this amounted to a promise to the highest bidder. However, he expressly stated that if the circular had stated 'we undertake to sell to the highest bidder' the circular would have amounted to an offer which would be accepted by conduct, ie being the highest bidder.[34]

---

[31] There was no requirement to notify this acceptance since the proposal had indicated that the approval alone would conclude a contract.

[32] 106 Ky. 659, 51 SW 196 (1899).

[33] (1870) LR 5 CP 561. See also the Australian case of *Meudell v Mayor etc of Bendigo* (1900) 26 VLR 158.

[34] (1870) LR 5 CP 561, at 563. For further discussion of Contracts by Tender, see Chapter 5.

Certainty of terms[35]

The certainty of terms is one factor used to determine whether a proposal is an offer or an **2.30**
invitation to receive offers. However, it is difficult to draw the line between offers and invitations to treat from this standpoint alone, and this is especially so in sale of goods cases,
where 'even though one or more terms are left open, a contract for sale does not fail for
indefiniteness if the parties have intended to make a contract and there is a reasonably
certain basis for giving an appropriate remedy'.[36] In such cases those terms which are not
fixed between the parties are implied by statute, ie in accordance with the Uniform
Commercial Code (UCC) in all the states of the United States except Louisiana, and in
accordance with the Sale of Goods Act 1979 in England.

It is, however, possible to say that a proposal is very likely to be held to be an invitation to **2.31**
treat if it does not limit quantity.[37] In both *Moulton v Kershaw* and *Nebraska Seed Co v
Harsh*[38] uncertainty of quantity was also considered important in concluding that no offer
had been made.

In *Moulton v Kershaw* the proposal contained only the words 'full carload lots of 80 to
95 bbls.' and did not specify how many cars. In *Nebraska Seed Co v Harsh* only the
approximate quantity of stock was communicated via the words 'I have about 1800 bu.
or thereabouts of millet seed.'

However, in *Fairmount Glass Works v Grunden-Martin Woodenware Co*[39] a proposal which **2.32**
did not state a quantity was held to be an offer by considering the terms of the buyer's previous inquiry. This previous inquiry had requested terms for 'ten car loads' so that a definite
quantity had been specified.

The courts are generally reluctant to interpret a proposal which does not specify the quan- **2.33**
tity as an offer because 'such an interpretation would expose its maker to the risk of liability
for performance far beyond the maker's means',[40] ie he might find himself bound to supply
goods in a quantity that he did not possess.

Such risks are removed and a proposal can be interpreted as an offer 'if the proposal specifies **2.34**
a range or an upper limit within which the recipient may make a selection, or if such a restric-
tion can be read in from usage, course of dealing, or under a standard of reasonableness'.[41]

---

[35] See further Chapter 11 on Certainty.
[36] UCC § 2-204(3). See also the Unidroit Principles, Arts. 1.8, 5.6, 5.7, 6.1.1, 6.1.6 and 6.1.10.
[37] See for example the South African case of *Crawley v Rex* 1909 TS 1105 (price specified but failed to
specify the quantity involved in each sale). In *Kelly v Caledonian Coal Co* (1898) 19 LR (NSW) 1 a statement
of the price at which coal would be supplied for a period was not an offer to supply because there was no reference to the quantity to be delivered.
[38] See nn 22 and 24.
[39] See n 32 above.
[40] *Farnsworth on Contracts* (3rd edn, Vol I, 2004) 259.
[41] Ibid. 'Usage' and 'course of dealing' are defined in the American Restatement (2d)
Contracts, as follows:

§ 219. Usage
Usage is habitual or customary practice.
§ 223. Course of dealing

A standing offer such as that in *Great Northern Railway Co. v Witham*[42] can be cited as a good example.

In this case the defendant had sent a written tender offering 'to supply the Great Northern Railway Company, for twelve months from the 1st of November, 1871, to 31st of October, 1872, with such quantities of each or any of the several articles named in the attached specification as the company's store-keeper may order from time to time, at the price set opposite each article respectively'.

This tender was held to be a standing offer which was converted into a series of contracts by the subsequent orders of the company. Brett J stated:[43] 'I think it would be wrong to countenance the notion that a man who tenders for the supply of goods in this way is not bound to deliver them when an order is given.'

Specified addressees

2.35   Advertisements placed via the mass media announcing that goods are for sale are addressed to unspecified addressees and are generally not interpreted as offers. The same is true of catalogues, price lists or circulars sent to general customers. The reason given for this is the so-called limited stocks argument used by Lord Herschell in *Grainger and Son v Gough*,[44] namely the danger that a seller could face an unfair burden of being obliged to supply a quantity of goods in excess of his stock held if he received a large number of orders.[45] Conversely, if an advertisement is addressed to a limited number of people or is only capable of acceptance by a limited number of people, then it may be interpreted as an offer.[46]

---

(1) A course of dealing is a sequence of previous conduct between the parties to an agreement which is fairly to be regarded as establishing a common basis of understanding for interpreting their expressions and other conduct.

(2) Unless otherwise agreed, a course of dealing between the parties gives meaning to or supplements or qualifies their agreement.

[42]   (1873) LR 9 CP 16. See, for example, *Re Webster* (1975) 132 CLR 270.

[43]   (1873) LR 9 CP 16, at 20

[44]   [1896] AC 325, 334. Clearly this rule is in the interests of sellers and it is the buyer who makes the offer to purchase. King, 'Reshaping Contract Theory and Law: Death of Contracts II' (1994) 8 JCL 16, 33–4, makes the point that this position is based on classical contract law but that, if a model emphasizing 'fairness in the relationship of the parties' were to be developed, the result might well be different in specific cases. King uses the example of an advertisement which induces the buyer to undertake a long journey to reach the store which he argues would render the advertisement binding on an application of a fairness theory.

[45]   It is interesting to compare this position with that adopted in the final draft of the Commission on European Contract Law's Principles of European Contract Law. These Principles contain a provision which would, in certain circumstances, presume an advertisement or brochure of this kind to nevertheless be an offer. Article 2:201 states: 'A proposal to supply goods or services at stated prices made by a professional supplier in a public advertisement or catalogue, or by a display of goods, is presumed to be an offer to sell or supply at that price until the stock of goods, or the supplier's capacity to supply the service, is exhausted.'

[46]   In *Carlill v Carbolic Smoke Ball Company* [1893] 1 QB 256 although the advertisement was addressed to the whole world, it was only capable of acceptance by those who performed the conditions specified. The same is true of the so-called 'reward' cases. See also *Bowerman v Association of British Travel Agents Ltd* [1996] CLC 451, where the Court of Appeal held that a notice displayed on the premises of tour operators who were ABTA members constituted an offer by ABTA which was accepted by those booking a holiday with an ABTA member. There was therefore a direct contractual relationship between ABTA and the customer of a failed ABTA tour operator.

In *Lefkowitz v Great Minneapolis Surplus Store*[47] the following advertisement had been **2.36**
placed in a Minneapolis newspaper: 'Saturday 9 A.M. Sharp/ 3 Brand New/ Fur Coats/
Worth to $100.00 1 First come/ First served/ $1 Each.' This was held to amount to an offer
which was accepted by the first person on Saturday to offer the stated purchase price at the
seller's place of business. Thus the use of the words 'first come, first served' limits the number who can accept. By analogy, price lists can be offers when the proposals in them are
qualified by language such as 'subject to prior sale' or 'while they last'.[48]

As has already been noted,[49] it is not the 'offeror's' actual intention which determines **2.37**
whether an offer has been made, but what the offeree reasonably understands that intention to be. Although price lists are generally assumed to be distributed among a large number of customers, letters are not. If letters containing the same proposal are to be sent to a
large number of persons, it is sensible to draw attention to this fact so that it is clear that an
offer is not intended. One way to achieve this is to expressly state: 'I am writing to several
people, including yourself, who have previously expressed an interest ...'[50]

The cases on price lists, catalogues, displays in shop windows and so on are often discussed **2.38**
as if particular transactions are being characterized as a matter of law as being or not being
offers. This is not always correct.

Most common law systems most of the time say that display in a shop window is not an
offer but this was not the result in the *Lefkowitz* case. The usual rules are sensible (though
the opposite rule applies in French law) because shopkeepers do not usually put goods in
shop windows for the purpose of selling the goods displayed but of encouraging shoppers
to seek to buy identical goods. So in many cases the argument that the shopkeeper has only
a limited supply has force.

Similarly if I received a catalogue from a second-hand book seller, I know that he will only
have one copy of most of the books and that offers are made by customers. The position is
not necessarily the same if a law publisher invites me to buy their latest monograph, the
chance of them being submerged with orders may be thought vanishingly small.

English Law appears to have adopted the position that display in a self-service store is an **2.39**
invitation to treat and not an offer. This cannot be explained on the exhaustion ground since
if the display is the offer, the offer is withdrawn as soon as there are no more goods displayed.
In the leading case Lord Goddard said that if the display were an offer there would be a
contract as soon as the goods are put in the shopping baskets or trolley. This seems very
doubtful since many shoppers change their minds and put things back on the shelves. So
applying an objective test putting goods in the basket would not be an acceptance.

---

[47] 251 Minn. 188, 86 NW 3d 689 (1957).

[48] *Farnsworth on Contracts* (3rd edn, 2004) 261. See also *Harris v Time* 191 Cal. App. 3d 449 (1987),
although in *Chang v First Colonial Savings Bank* 242 Va. 388, 410 SE 2d 928 (1991) it was recognized that
this was a 'very narrow and limited exception' to the normal rule on newspaper advertisements (per Hassell J
at 930).

[49] See 1.07.

[50] *Mellen v Johnson* 322 Mass. 236'76 NE 2d 658 (1948) where it was held that the use of such words
meant that the 'recipient could not reasonably understand this to be more than an attempt at negotiation', per
Wilkins J at 659.

2.40 It seems clear that the best solution is that the contract is made at the checkout though it can be argued whether the shopper approaches as acceptor or offeror. Despite the millions of such transactions daily, there seems to be no litigated example anywhere of the shop-keeper refusing to sell at this point. The cases which have been litigated involved either criminal law questions where the shopper has, for instance, switched price labels or cases of bottles exploding after being put in the trolley. In the latter case there will usually be tort liability on the manufacturer but no contract liability on the shop unless, contrary to the argument above, one holds that putting the goods in the basket is an acceptance.

The cases of auction and tenders are more complicated and are discussed more fully in Chapter 5.

Conclusion

2.41 It is clear that whether a proposal constitutes an offer turns not on the actual intention in the proposer's mind, but on the apparent intention which the addressee is justified in concluding from the proposer's external manifestations. If the external manifestations do justify the addressee in judging a proposal to be an offer then the proposer cannot argue that it was not his intention to make an offer.

2.42 The language used in the proposal is the most decisive factor when examining what the addressee is entitled to conclude. The level of commitment is important and language which expressly denies any commitment can be determinative. However, this language of commitment has to be interpreted in its context so that 'just as the word "offer" does not necessarily mean that an offer is intended, so the word "quote" may be used in an offer' (American Restatement (2d) Contracts, § 26, Comment c).

2.43 Case law suggests that the courts are reluctant to characterize a proposal as an offer in doubtful cases.[51] In *United States v Braunstein*[52] Medina J stated: 'It is true that there is much room for interpretation once the parties are inside the framework of a contract, but it seems that there is less in the field of offer and acceptance. Greater precision of expression may be required, and less help from the courts given, when the parties are merely at the threshold of a contract'.[53] A further warning was given by Foster J in *Lyman v Robinson*[54] that 'care should always be taken not to construe as an agreement letters which the parties intended only as preliminary negotiations'.

2.44 The United Nations Convention on Contracts for the International Sale of Goods 1980 (CISG) (the 'Vienna Convention')[55] so distinguishes expressly between proposals which have specified addressees and open proposals.

---

[51] See for example the South African decisions of *Efroiken v Simon* 1921 CPD 367 and *Gerhardt v State President* 1989 2 SA 499.

[52] 75 F. Supp 137 (1947).

[53] Ibid., at 139. Medina J (at 140) referred to the fact that the Privy Council had not construed the defendant's telegram in *Harvey v Facey* [1893] AC 552 as an offer despite the fact that it would have taken 'but little interpretation' to construe it as such.

[54] 14 Allen 254 (*Moulton v Kershaw* 18 NW 172 (1884), 174).

[55] The Convention has been adopted in a number of jurisdictions including Australia and the US but not the UK. It applied to international contracts for the sale of goods and so has no application where the

ARTICLE 14

(1) A proposal for concluding a contract addressed to one or more specified persons constitutes an offer if it is sufficiently definite and indicates the intention of the offeror to
be bound in case of acceptance. A proposal is sufficiently definite if it indicates the
goods and expressly or implicitly fixes or makes provision for determining the quantity and the price.

(2) A proposal other than one addressed to one or more specific persons is to be considered merely as an invitation to make offers, unless the contrary is clearly indicated by
the person making the proposal.[56]

Therefore, where a proposal is addressed to specific persons it will constitute an offer if it is
'sufficiently definite', which is defined in Article 14(1) as turning upon certainty of the
terms. However, it is not clear whether the requirements specified are mandatory or merely
indicate one way in which the proposal can be sufficiently definite.[57]

The other requirement is that such a proposal must indicate the offeror's intention to be **2.45**
bound by acceptance. This intention is to be determined in accordance with Article 8(1),
which is essentially subjective in nature since statements or conduct by a party 'are to be
interpreted according to his intent where the other party knew or could not have been
unaware what that intent was'.[58]

The Unidroit Principles of International Commercial Contracts (1994)[59] provide for **2.46**
agreement on the traditional basis of offer and acceptance but also accept that conduct
which is sufficient to show the parties' intention to be bound by agreement may suffice
(Article 2.1), for example, if both parties have begun to perform. The approach to contract
formation in the Vienna Convention follows the traditional analysis on the basis that 'to
have attempted a different analysis would have added greatly to the difficulties of drafting'.[60]
The definition of an offer in Article 2.2 of the Unidroit Principles uses the same criteria of
'definiteness' and 'intention to be bound' on acceptance as the Vienna Convention.
Although there is no explicit mention of the criteria of definiteness which exists in

---

sale contract is purely domestic (see Arts. 1–6 for its sphere of application). Article 6 provides that the parties
may exclude the application of the Convention or derogate from or vary the effect of any of its provisions
(subject to Art. 12). See Blanca and Bonell, *Commentary on the International Sales Law, The 1980 Vienna Sales
Convention* (Guiffre, Milan, 1987).

[56] Honnold, *Uniform Law for International Sales Under the 1980 United Nations Convention* (2nd edn,
1991), para. 137, argues that if a catalogue is mailed to 500 prospective buyers with each envelope being
addressed to a specific person it should be governed by Art. 14(2) since the catalogue is not restricted to the
addressee.

[57] Nicholas (1989) 105 LQR 201, 213, argues that the more natural interpretation is that these requirements are mandatory and suggests that 'the word "only" is to be read into the sentence after the word
"definite"'.

[58] In other cases Art. 8(2) provides that such statements are 'to be interpreted according to the understanding that a reasonable person of the same kind as the other party would have had in the same circumstances'.
See Feltham [1981] JBL 346, 349. Article 8(3) provides that in determining intent or the understanding of a
reasonable person consideration is to be given to all relevant circumstances including the negotiations, usages
and any practices established between the parties together with their subsequent conduct.

[59] International Institute for the Unification of Private Law. See M J Bonell, *An International Restatement of
Contract Law, The Unidroit Principles of International Commercial Contracts* (Transnational Juris Publications
Inc, 1994).

[60] Nicholas (1989) 105 LQR 201, at 212.

Article 14(1) of the Vienna Convention, the commentary to Article 2.2 makes reference to the fact that 'even essential terms, such as the precise description of the goods or the services ... the price to be paid for them, the time or place of performance etc., may be left undetermined in the offer without necessarily rendering it insufficiently definite'. It is therefore less prescriptive and instead the determining factors are the parties' intentions to enter into a binding agreement and whether any missing terms can be filled in accordance with the interpretation provisions and other articles contained in the Unidroit Principles. Thus there is a greater degree of flexibility on this point evident in the Unidroit Principles.

Communication of offer

2.47   An offer is not effective until it is communicated to the offeree. The formulation of this principle is identical in both the Vienna Convention (CISG) and the Unidroit Principles, namely: 'An offer becomes effective when it reaches the offeror.'[61] The Unidroit Principles also follow the CISG in attempting to address the question of when that important time occurs by specifically providing a definition of 'reaches'.[62] Such a definition would provide an answer to the current debate in English Law concerning what constitutes actual communication of an offer, acceptance or revocation sent by telex, fax or electronic mail since the message would be communicated on receipt by the addressee's machine.[63] It also avoids the practical difficulties which would result if it had to be shown that a particular communication specifically came to the attention of the individual addressee.

The need for the offer to be communicated in order to be effective is important in practice since an offeree can only validly accept if he acts in response to an offer of which he has knowledge so that acceptance cannot occur until there has been communication of the offer.[64] As Anson states:[65] 'A person who does an act for which a reward has been offered in ignorance of the offer cannot say either that there was a consensus of wills with the offeror, or that the act was done in return for or in reliance on the promise offered.'

2.48   This principle also appears in the American Restatement (2d) Contracts:

§23. Necessity that manifestations have reference to each other

It is essential to a bargain that each party manifest assent with reference to the manifestation of the other.

This would appear to be the reason why 'cross offers' do not result in a contract.[66] In *Tinn v Hoffmann and Co*[67] the majority of the Exchequer Chamber were of the opinion that the

---

[61]   Article 15(1) CISG and Unidroit Principles, Art 2.3.

[62]   '... an offer ... "reaches" the addressee when it is made orally to him or delivered by any other means to him personally, to his place of business or mailing address or, if he does not have a place of business or mailing address, to his habitual residence.' (Art. 24 CISG). Unidroit Principles, Art. 1.9(3) is a slightly simplified version of this in that it refers to oral receipt or delivery to the addressee's place of business or mailing address.

[63]   See Chapter 6, for further discussion of this debate.

[64]   *Fitch v Snedaker* 38 NY 248 (1868), *R v Clarke* (1927) 40 CLR 227. See Hudson 'Gibbons v Proctor Revisited' (1968) 84 LQR 503.

[65]   *Anson's Law of Contract* (2002) 49.

[66]   Cross offers occur where two identical offers are made which cross in the post.

[67]   (1873) 29 LT 271.

offer in one such 'cross offer' letter could not amount to an acceptance of the offer contained in the other.[68] Blackburn J stated:[69] 'The promise or offer being made on each side in ignorance of the promise or the offer made on the other side, neither of them can be construed as an acceptance of the other.' In any event, it appears that the 'cross offers' in *Tinn v Hoffmann* were probably not identical. The defendants had offered the plaintiffs 800 tons of iron but, following an inquiry from the plaintiffs about a lower price for a quantity of 1,200 tons, the defendants had sent a letter on 28 November offering a further 400 tons but at the original price of 69s per ton. The plaintiff's crossing letter agreed to take 800 tons and 400 tons 'making in all 1200 tons' at 68s per ton.

The same view on 'cross offers' is adopted in the United States.[70]

---

[68] *Cheshire, Fifoot and Furmston's Law of Contract* (15th edn, OUP, Oxford, 2007), 72, point out, however, that in the case of cross offers there is a coincidence of acts and a unanimity of mind and Honyman J in *Tinn v Hoffmann* considered that for this reason there ought to be a binding contract.
[69] (1873) 29 LT 271, 279.
[70] See the American Restatement (2d) Contracts § 23 comment *d*.

3

TERMINATION AND REVOCATION OF OFFERS

A. Termination

Introduction[1]

An offer may be terminated through lapse of time, the death of the offeror or offeree, the **3.01** failure of some condition or contingency, by rejection (or counter-offer), and by communication of a revocation of the offer.[2] The latter calls for separate treatment and is dealt with below. This first section deals with the other methods of termination.

Lapse of time

If an offer is stated to be open for acceptance for a certain period of time, it will remain open **3.02** for that period[3] and, unless there is a communication of a revocation in the meantime,[4] it will lapse at the end of that time.[5] This rule is of universal application and is adopted in

---

[1] The effect on an offer where there is some supervening incapacity of either the offeror or offeree is dealt with in standard contract texts in the context of capacity, see Peel, *Treitel, The Law of Contract* (12th edn, Sweet & Maxwell, London, 2007) para 2-069-2-073. See also Restatement (2d) Contracts § 48.

[2] Restatement (2d) Contracts § 36.

[3] *Nyulasy v Rowan* (1891) 17 VLR 663.

[4] Eg *King v Homer* (1913) 33 NZLR 222.

[5] *White Cliffs Opal Mines Ltd v Miller* (1904) 4 SR (NSW) 150 (offer by the New South Wales government was expressed to be open until 30 June 1902; an acceptance by way of cablegram was dispatched from London at 3.55 p.m. Greenwich time on 30 June 1902; held too late, New South Wales law governed the contract and at the time of dispatch it was 1.55 a.m. on 1 July 1902 in New South Wales, offer had lapsed). See also *Jacobsen Sons & Co v Underwood & Sons* 1894 1 SLT 578; *Spencer's Pictures Ltd v Cosens* (1918) 18 SR (NSW) 102. An option will also lapse at the end of its term, eg *8 Parriwi Road Pty Ltd v Raffan* [1970] 2 NSWR 431n, 433 (affirmed *8 Parriwi Road Pty Ltd v Raffan* [1970] 2 NSWR 428). See also Restatement (2d) Contracts § 41.

Article 18(2) of the United Nations Convention on Contracts for the International Sale of Goods (1980). However, Article 21 provides for later acceptance to be effective in two situations. First, if 'without delay the offeror orally so informs the offeree or dispatches a notice to that effect'.[6] Here it is the offeree who has caused the delay and he or she cannot therefore assume that there is a contract until it is confirmed by the offeror. Second, if 'a letter or other writing containing a late acceptance shows that it has been sent in such circumstances that if its transmission had been normal it would have reached the offeror in due time, the late acceptance is effective as an acceptance unless, without delay, the offeror orally informs the offeree that he considers his offer as having lapsed or dispatches a notice to that effect'.[7] The justification for such a rule is the need to protect the offeree's reasonable reliance on the fact that the acceptance ought to have arrived in time. Here the delay is not the fault of the offeree and he or she may reasonably believe that his or her acceptance has arrived in good time, the onus is on the offeror to take positive steps to inform the offeree that there is no contract. In both cases the offeror can decide whether he or she wishes there to be a contract or not depending on the market circumstances at the time when he or she is required to give notice. Honnold notes that 'the offeror will notify the offeree that the offer has lapsed if the change in conditions has made the transaction less attractive ... and will notify the offeree that he treats the reply as an acceptance if the change in conditions makes the transaction more favorable to him'.[8] Thus Honnold considers it to be 'an opportunity to speculate at the expense of the other party'.[9] Honnold's suggested solution is to construe Article 21(1) so that the late acceptance is not seen as indicating assent to the offer originally made because of the different circumstances prevailing when the acceptance is received. He also suggests that this would respect the need to promote good faith in international trade.[10]

3.03   Where no time is stated in an offer, then the offer remains open for a reasonable period of time and will lapse at the end of that period.[11] This too is adopted in Article 18(2) of the United Nations Convention on Contracts for the International Sale of Goods (1980). What constitutes a reasonable time depends on the circumstances.[12] The manner of

---

[6] Article 21(1).

[7] Article 21(2).

[8] Honnold, *Uniform Law For International Sales* (3rd edn, Kluwer Law International, The Netherlands, 1999) para 175.

[9] Honnold, *Uniform Law For International Sales* (3rd edn, Kluwer Law International, The Netherlands, 1999) para 175.

[10] Honnold, *Uniform Law For International Sales* (3rd edn, Kluwer Law International, The Netherlands, 1999) para 175.

[11] *Manchester Diocesan Council for Education v Commercial & General Investments Ltd* [1970] 1 WLR 241, 247. See also *Meynell v Surtees* (1855) 25 LJ Ch 257; *Ramsgate Victoria Hotel Co Ltd v Montefiore* (1866) LR 1 Ex 109; *North-West Co-operative Freezing & Canning Co Ltd v Easton* (1915) 11 Tas LR 65; *Barrick v Clark* [1951] SCR 177; *Ballas v Theophilos (No 2)* (1957) 98 CLR 193, 197, 199; *Cemco Leasing SpA v Rediffusion plc* [1987] FTLR 201; *Commonwealth v Newcrest Mining (WA) Ltd* (1995) 130 ALR 193, 243 per Beaumont (in dissent) (reversed without reference to the point sub nom *Newcrest Mining (WA) Ltd v Commonwealth* (1997) 190 CLR 513); *LJ Korbetis v Transgrain Shipping BV* [2005] EWHC 1345. See also *Kean v Dunfoy* [1952] NZLR 611 (vendor accepted deposit prior to contract being entered into, through error there was a delay in the purchaser communicating acceptance and a reasonable time elapsed before acceptance was communicated; held that the offer lapsed and there was no obligation on the vendor to communicate that he considered the transaction cancelled even though he held a deposit). See also Restatement (2d) Contract § 41(1) and (2).

[12] *Ballas v Theophilos (No 2)* (1957) 98 CLR 193, 197.

communication of the offer will be important. An oral offer generally may be expected to be replied to sooner than a written offer.[13] Article 18(2) of the United Nations Convention on Contracts for the International Sale of Goods requires such offers to be accepted immediately unless the circumstances indicate otherwise. By the same reasoning a quick response may be required where the offer is made by other instantaneous methods of communication.[14] The court will also take into account the nature of the market in which the parties are operating and whether it is a fast moving and variable market.[15] The nature of the subject matter of the contract is also relevant, if it is of a wasting nature, then the time frame will be shorter.[16]

Stipulations are often vague or ambiguous, for example, 'we will give you eight days to think over this offer', and 'reply within ten days'. When does the period begin: the date of the letter or the time of its receipt? And when does it end: the time of dispatch of acceptance or the time of its receipt? In *Caldwell v Cline*[17] an offer letter of 29 January 1929 stipulated 'we will give you eight days in which to accept or reject the offer'. This offer letter was received on 2 February and a telegram of acceptance was dispatched on 8 February, arriving on 9 February. The Supreme Court of Appeals of West Virginia held that the eight-day period did not begin until the letter arrived on 2 February. As a result the acceptance was received within the stipulated period. **3.04**

To prevent any confusion, a clear stipulation such as 'an acceptance must be received within eight days of the date of this letter' is advisable. *Housing Authority of Town of Lake Arthur v T Miller and Sons*[18] is authority for the fact that if, for example, acceptance is required within ten days of receipt of offer, the first day of the stipulated period is excluded whilst the last day is included. **3.05**

A stipulation such as 'by return' or 'immediately', which fails to limit the period, also ought to be avoided. In *Maclay v Harvey*[19] the offeror's letter requiring 'answer by return mail' was received on 22 March and it was held that the offeror was entitled to expect a reply sent on 23 March, or at the latest, on the morning of 24 March. Whilst in *TM James and Sons v* **3.06**

---

[13] It has been said that as a general rule an offer made orally in face-to-face conversation or by telephone will lapse when the conversation ends (see *Akers v J B Sedberry Inc* 39 Tenn App 633, 286 SW 2d 617 (1955)) unless the circumstances, including the conversation itself, indicate that it has survived. For example, the words 'we want to have time to check with our customers' can render the offer effective even after the conversation has ended, see *Testron Inc v Froelich* 223 Pa Super 506, 302 A 2d 426 (1973).

[14] *Quenerduaine v Cole* (1883) 32 WR 185.

[15] *Ballas v Theophilos (No 2)* (1957) 98 CLR 193, 197. See also *Manning v Carrique* (1915) 34 OLR 453, 25 DLR 840, where an offer to sell shares was considered to be no longer open the following day.

[16] *United Dominions Trust (Commercial) Ltd v Eagle Aircraft Services Ltd* [1968] 1 WLR 74. Where a right to renew a lease does not state a time within which it is to be exercised it has been held that its exercise will be effective if done prior to the expiration of the lease, see *Spectra Pty Ltd v Pindari Pty Ltd* [1974] 2 NSWLR 617. That time frame may be what is reasonable in such a case but it has also been suggested that this case is an example of where the rule requiring acceptance within a reasonable period of time does not apply because 'it is possible to imply a period of duration by reference to the circumstances, such as the occurrence of an event which is essential to the contract contemplated' see Carter, *Carter on Contract* (Butterworths, Sydney) § 03-120.

[17] 109 W Va 553, 156 SE 55 (1930).

[18] 239 La 966, 120 So 2d 494 (1960).

[19] 90 Ill 525 (1876).

Marion Fruit Jar and Bottle Co[20] an offer by telegram received on Saturday morning which included a request to 'wire immediately', was held to have lapsed before Monday morning.

3.07   It is important to note that the courts are not uniform in interpreting such words and must consider the circumstances of each individual case, in particular, the method of acceptance which is appropriate to the circumstances.

3.08   There are two views as to why an offer lapses after a reasonable period of time. In *Manchester Diocesan Council for Education v Commercial & General Investments Ltd*[21] Buckley J said:[22]

> First, it may be said that by implication the offer is made upon terms that, if it is not accepted within a reasonable time, it must be treated as withdrawn. Alternatively, it may be said that, if the offeree does not accept the offer within a reasonable time, he must be treated as having refused it ... The first of these alternatives involves implying a term that if the offer is not accepted within a reasonable time, it shall be treated as withdrawn or lapsing at the end of that period, if it has not then been accepted: the second is based upon an inference to be drawn from the conduct of the offeree, that is, that having failed to accept the offer within a reasonable time he has manifested an intention to refuse it. If in the first alternative the time which the offeror is to be treated as having set for acceptance is to be such a time as is reasonable at the date of the offer, what is reasonable must depend on circumstances then existing and reasonably likely to arise during the continuance of the offer; but it would be not unlikely that the offeror and offeree would make different assessments of what would be reasonable, even if, as might quite possibly not be the case, they based those judgments on identical known and anticipated circumstances. No doubt a court could resolve any dispute about this, but this approach clearly involves a certain degree of uncertainty about the precise terms of the offer. If, on the other hand, the time which the offeror is to be treated as having set for acceptance is to be such a time as turns out to be reasonable in the light of circumstances then existing and of circumstances arising thereafter during the continuance of the offer, whether foreseeable or not, an additional element of uncertainty is introduced. The second alternative, on the other hand, involves simply an objective assessment of facts and the determination of the question whether on the facts the offeree should, in fairness to both parties, be regarded as having refused the offer.
>
> It does not seem to me that either party is in greater need of protection by the law in this respect than the other. Until his offer has been accepted it is open to the offeror at any time to withdraw it or to put a limit on the time for acceptance. On the other hand, the offeree can at any time refuse the offer or, unless he has been guilty of unreasonable delay, accept it. Neither party is at a disadvantage. Unless authority constrains me to do otherwise, I am strongly disposed to prefer the second alternative to the first.[23]

---

[20]   69 Mo App 207 (1896).

[21]   [1970] 1 WLR 241.

[22]   [1970] 1 WLR 241, 247–8.

[23]   There is a move away from the use of implied terms in modern contract law. Courts today are more likely to resolve issues that were once dealt with on the basis of an implied term by using principles of contract construction, see 1.21 and 11.84n.

The above statement suggests that the explanation adopted may impact on what evidence is available to determine what is a reasonable time. However, generally, the circumstances at the time of the alleged formation will be taken into account.[24] **3.09**

A purported acceptance after the expiration of that reasonable period of time will not be effective as an acceptance,[25] but may, depending on the circumstances, constitute a counter-offer.[26] **3.10**

Delay in the communication of an offer

Suppose that an offer sent first class on Monday and stipulating that 'acceptance must be by return of post arriving not later than Wednesday' does not reach the offeree until Thursday. Can the offeree nevertheless accept it? It would seem not since: 'the offeror may have carelessly misaddressed the letter but as she was under no obligation to make any offer at all she may, without risk of liability, make an offer that cannot be accepted'.[27] **3.11**

The position in the United States is governed by section 49 of the Restatement (2d) Contracts, which provides that the offeree cannot accept if 'he knows or has reason to know of the delay, though it is due to the fault of the offeror'. However, 'if the delay is due to the fault of the offeror or to the means of transmission adopted by him, and the offeree neither knows nor has reason to know that there has been delay' the time within which the offeree can accept is extended by the delay.[28] **3.12**

Since a delay is normally apparent from the date of the letter or its postmark, in these circumstances the offeree will know or have reason to know of the delay and cannot accept the offer. **3.13**

Death of the offeror or offeree

It is often said that an offer lapses upon the death of the offeror.[29] This could be explained as a principled rule of law on the basis that an offer must be given by a living person or an **3.14**

---

[24] See *Khaled v Athanas Bros (Aden) Ltd* (1967) 1 BPR 9310; *Manchester Diocesan Council for Education v Commercial & General Investments Ltd* [1970] 1 WLR 241, 248. See also *Commonwealth v Newcrest Mining (WA) Ltd* (1995) 130 ALR 193, 243 per Beaumont J (in dissent) (reversed without reference to the point (1997) 190 CLR 513).

[25] *United Dominions Trust (Commercial) Ltd v Eagle Aircraft Services Ltd* [1968] 1 WLR 74; *Ballas v Theophilos (No 2)* (1957) 98 CLR 193. In the case of an offer for an allotment of shares which is accepted by the company after a reasonable time has expired, the offeror, if he or she has not previously withdrawn the offer, has been held to be required to repudiate the acceptance, see *Farmers' Mercantile Union & Chaff Mills Ltd v Coade* (1921) 30 CLR 113, 119, 124, cf 129ff per Starke J; *Ramsgate Victoria Hotel Co Ltd v Montefiore* (1866) LR 1 Ex 109, (1866) 35 LJ Ex 90; *Re Tasmanian Credits Ltd; Ex parte Pitt* (1930) 25 Tas LR 111.

[26] See further 4.11.

[27] Waddams, *The Law of Contracts* (5th edn, Canada Law Book, Toronto, 2005) para 99.

[28] *Chesebrough v Western Union Telegraph Co* 76 Misc 516, 135 NY Supp 583 (1912) affirmed 157 App Div 914, 142 NY Supp 1112 (1913).

[29] See *Meynell v Surtees* (1855) 25 LJ Ch 257, 259–60; *Dickinson v Dodds* (1876) 2 Ch D 463, 475; *Reynolds v Atherton* (1921) 125 LT 690, 695–6; *Spiro v Glencrown Properties Ltd* [1991] Ch 537, 544. See also Restatement (2d) Contracts § 48. See further Lucke, 'Striking a Bargain' (1960–62) 1 Adelaide L Rev 293, 306 discussing *Thomson v James* (1855) 18 Dunlop 1, 10. Generally, an option can be exercised after the death of the grantor; this result necessarily follows if the option is explained as a conditional contract but it

existing legal entity so it will cease to exist if that person or entity ceases to exist. However, it is probably only the first part of that statement that is true; once the offer is made, its continued existence may not necessarily depend on the continued existence of the offeror. Therefore, the notion that an offer lapses upon the death of the offeror is not so much a rule of law as a practical consequence of the death of the offeror because often the contract will become incapable of performance upon the offeror's death. However, that impossibility will not always arise where the contract would not have required the offeror to provide some personal performance. It follows that usually the issue of death gives rise to the same issue as revocation, namely, it needs to be communicated. This is the operable rule of law based on the objective theory of contract.[30] Thus, it is possible for an offeree to accept an offer after the death of the offeror so long as the offeree accepts the offer prior to hearing of the offeror's death.[31]

3.15   As regards the death of the offeree prior to acceptance, on one view, offers are inherently personal and so they cannot be accepted by the estate of the offeree if the offeree dies prior to acceptance. Similarly it has been said that an offer made to a living person ceases to be an offer if that person dies prior to accepting the offer.[32] However, it would appear that the preferred view is that the nature of an offer depends on construction, it may be personal and it may not. The fact that it is possible to make an offer to more than one person proves

is likely that that result would be the same even if the court were to subscribe to the view that an option is an irrevocable offer, see *Laybutt v Amoco Australia Pty Ltd* (1974) 132 CLR 57, 75–6; *Spiro v Glencrown Properties Ltd* [1991] Ch 537, 544–5. See also Restatement (2d) Contracts § 48. See further 3.44.

[30] It would appear to be the position in the United States that an offer is not capable of acceptance upon the death of the offeror. Farnsworth suggests this position is at odds with the objective theory, see Farnsworth, *Farnsworth on Contracts* (3rd edn, Vol I, Aspen Publishers, New York, 2004) § 3.18, p 308.

[31] *Fong v Cilli* (1968) 11 FLR 495. In addition, although a mere authority would be revoked upon death, a contract is not revoked upon death and obligations other than personal obligations can be enforced against the estate of the deceased party; where the contract requires some personal performance by the deceased the contract will be frustrated, see Furmston (ed), *The Law of Contract* (3rd edn, Butterworths, London, 2007) para 2.239, and see *Bradbury v Morgan* (1862) 1 H & C 249, 158 ER 877 (estate of guarantor liable under continuing guarantee for advances to debtor after the death of the guarantor and before the creditor had notice of the guarantor's death); *Coulthart v Clementson* (1879) 5 QBD 42 (continuing guarantee revoked upon notice of death of guarantor). See also *Harris v Fawcett* (1873) LR 8 Ch App 866; *Offord v Davies* (1862) 12 CB (NS) 748, 142 ER 1336; *Re Whelan* [1897] 1 IR 575. One explanation for this result in the case of a continuing guarantee is that it operates as a standing offer accepted from time to time when advances are made and therefore can be revoked prior to acceptance by communication. However, the decision in *Bradbury* appeared to assume a contract of guarantee was in place and this rationale cannot explain cases where a contract of guarantee is clearly in place, see O'Donovan and Phillips, *The Modern Contract of Guarantee* (English edition, Thomson, Sweet & Maxwell, London, 2003) paras 9-27–9-45.

[32] *Reynolds v Atherton* (1921) 125 LT 690, 695, CA (affirmed (1922) 127 LT 189). See also Restatement (2d) Contracts § 48. An option can be exercised by the personal representatives of the grantee unless it is, on construction, personal to the grantee such as by requiring the exercise of some personal skill of the grantee or expressed to be made to the grantee personally so that it is not assignable or is expressed to limit the time for its exercise to the life of the grantee, see *Carter v Hyde* (1923) 33 CLR 115 120–1, 124–5; *Laybutt v Amoco Aust Pty Ltd* (1974) 132 CLR 57, 75–6. See further *Kennedy v Thomassen* [1929] 1 Ch 426 (offer to purchase certain annuities by way of redemption; the formal acceptance was sent by the solicitor of the offeree after she had died but before the solicitor had notice of her death; it was held that the acceptance was not operative on the ground that the offeree's death determined the solicitor's agency).

this point.[33] It would then follow that a non-personal offer could be accepted by the personal representatives of the offeree.[34]

Failure of a contingency

An offer may be made subject to a condition or contingency.[35] To a certain extent all offers   **3.16**
are contingent as they are given by reference to a certain context and if there is a fundamental change to those circumstances—determined from the position of a reasonable person in the position of the offeree—the offer will lapse.[36] There are two principal forms.[37] The first is where an offer is expressed to subsist so long as a certain condition or contingency subsists. In such a case, the offer will lapse if that condition or contingency ceases to exist or if a reasonable period of time elapses and the offer is not accepted in that time.[38] The classic example is the right to renew a lease which is subject to the lessee, during the term of the lease, properly performing all its obligations under the lease.[39] The second form is where the offer is expressed to lapse upon the occurrence of a contingency. Such an offer will lapse if that contingency eventuates or if a reasonable period of time elapses before the offer is accepted.[40]

It is possible for a condition or contingency to prevent an offer being accepted, such as   **3.17**
where an offer is made subject to approval of the board of directors or a legal representative.[41] Alternatively, a condition or contingency may prevent an offer coming into existence.

---

[33] See also *Reynolds v Atherton* (1921) 125 LT 690, 695 (affirmed (1922) 127 LT 189) (offer made to the directors of a company for the time being).

[34] Furmston (ed), *The Law of Contract* (3rd edn, Butterworths, London, 2007) para 2.239; Carter, *Carter on Contract* (Butterworths, Sydney) § 03-140. Indeed in *Reynolds v Atherton* (1921) 125 LT 690 (affirmed (1922) 127 LT 189, 191), itself, which is the authority usually cited for a rule that an offer is made to a living person and ceases to exist if that person dies before acceptance, the ratio of the decision turned on a construction of the offer which was held to be made to the directors for the time being and this prevented it from being accepted by the survivors of the directors who held the position of director at the time the offer was made, see further Peel, *Treitel, The Law of Contract* (12th edn, Sweet & Maxwell, London, 2007) para 2-068.

[35] Restatement (2d) Contracts § 36(2).

[36] *Nielsen v Dysart Timbers Ltd* [2009] NZSC 43, [4] (this case concerned whether an offer to settle a matter was conditional upon an application to extend the time for filing an appeal remaining unresolved, Ellias CJ and Blanchard J said: 'in the absence of an express term in the offer, the level of change of circumstance which is required for it to lapse is that of a fundamental change, which may occur all at once or by gradual development. An offeree cannot reasonably expect to accept an offer if the basis on which it was made has fundamentally changed. Furthermore, because it was possible for the offeror to specify the events in which the offer would lapse and, normally, to revoke the offer at any time without having to give a reason, in determining what must be taken to be, or amount to, a fundamental change the Court should give less weight to the occurrence of any event which an offeror must have had in contemplation when making the offer, and about which the offeror chose to be silent. That silence when the offer was made, or when it could have been revoked, may indicate that the offeror did not regard such a matter as fundamental to the continuance of the offer.').

[37] See Carter, *Carter on Contract* (Butterworths, Sydney) § 03-130.

[38] See 3.02.

[39] See *Gilbert J McCaul (Aust) Pty Ltd v Pitt Club Ltd* (1957) 59 SR (NSW) 122. The condition or contingency may be implied, for example, where there is an offer to sell goods there is an implied condition that the goods will be in the same condition at the time of acceptance as they are at the time of the offer, *Financings Ltd v Stimson* [1962] 3 All ER 386. See also *Rice v Taylor* [1969] 1 NSWR 449, 453–4.

[40] See 3.02.

[41] Eg *Macquarie Generation v CNA Resources Ltd* [2001] NSWSC 1040.

In *Toyota Motor Corp Australia Ltd v Ken Morgan Motors Pty Ltd*,[42] J D Phillips J, gave the following example:[43]

> A is interested in buying B's horse which B has for sale. But A tells B that he will make an offer only on condition that he is first allowed to have his expert examine the horse. If B agrees, B agrees to the condition which A attaches to the making of an offer. And the same is true, even if A tells B at the outset that he has in mind an offer of $100. What has happened is that A and B have agreed upon a condition, but it is a condition upon the fulfilment of which A will make an offer. Until the condition has been fulfilled, A has not made any offer. That is not to deny that A cannot make an offer at the outset which is subject to a condition (either precedent or subsequent) about inspection of the horse, so that upon fulfilment of the condition the offer (or, if the offer has already been accepted subject to fulfilment of the condition, the contract) stands absolute and unqualified.

Rejection and counter-offer

3.18   It is often said that an offer will come to an end if it is rejected by the offeree or if the offeree makes a counter-offer.[44] A counter-offer is said to 'kill' the offer.[45] Of course a counter-offer is available for acceptance by the original offeror.[46] Such a rejection or counter-offer takes effect when it is communicated to the offeror.[47] It is therefore possible for an offeree to send a rejection and change his or her mind before that rejection is communicated to the offeror and send an acceptance that overtakes the rejection and is communicated first. No problem arises with that scenario as no party is burdened by this possibility.[48] However, it also follows in terms of general principle, that if the postal acceptance rule applies to the transaction, an acceptance posted after a letter of rejection would take precedence over the rejection if the rejection had not yet been received by the offeror at the time the letter of acceptance was posted. This result has been rightly criticized as being too harsh on the offeror who could innocently act on the letter of rejection.[49] It is doubtful that any judge today would blindly apply the postal acceptance rule to that situation.[50]

3.19   Counter-offers are generally made throughout the course of negotiations and often without the parties understanding the consequences of their actions. Thus, if A offers to sell B certain goods for £1,000 and B, who is happy to pay that price but first wants to see if he or she can get a better deal, offers £900, then, if A does not accept this, it is now too late for

---

[42] [1994] 2 VR 106.
[43] [1994] 2 VR 106, 184.
[44] Theoretically it is possible to make an offer that by its terms will not terminate upon an initial rejection or counter-offer.
[45] *Hyde v Wrench* (1840) 3 Beav 334, 49 ER 132; *Trollope & Colls Ltd v Atomic Power Constructions Ltd* [1963] 1 WLR 333, 337; *OTM Ltd v Hydranautics* [1981] 2 Lloyd's Rep 211, 214.
[46] See the Malaysian decisions of *Diamond Peek Sdn Bhd v Tweedie* [1980] 3 MLJ 31; *Tan Geok Khoon & Gerard Francis Robless v Paya Terubong Estate Sdn Bhd* [1988] 2 MLJ 672. In Singapore see *Fiscal Consultants Pte v Asia Commercial Finance Ltd* [1981] 2 MLJ 64.
[47] See United Nations Convention on Contracts for the International Sale of Goods (1980), Art. 17; Restatement (2d) Contracts § 40.
[48] Restatement (2d) Contracts § 40.
[49] Peel, *Treitel, The Law of Contract* (12th edn, Sweet & Maxwell, London, 2007) para 2-063. See further 4.113ff
[50] See 4.120.

B to accept A's offer to sell for £1,000 as that offer was terminated by the counter-offer.[51] More often than not, A will be happy to make the offer again either expressly or impliedly,[52] but otherwise, in this example A can, if he or she has changed their mind, walk away from the negotiations.[53]

In order to destroy an offer it is not necessary that a statement be a positive rejection of the terms of the offer. Statements that purport to be acceptances of an offer can have this effect.[54] It has been said that at common law a purported acceptance that varies or adds to the terms of the offer, whether that variation or addition would be classified as material or not, will vitiate the acceptance and kill the offer.[55] Moreover, unless implied by law,[56] even the addition of a term that would be considered standard in a particular industry would not constitute a valid acceptance and would destroy the offer.[57] But much depends on the terms of the offer. For example, it has been held that were a person submits a proposal for workers' compensation insurance it is not an all or nothing request, so that an acceptance by the insurer for a lesser period of insurance than that put forward by the insured in the proposal would still be an acceptance.[58] Whether or not a purported acceptance which does not comply with the terms of the offer can be considered a counter-offer is dealt with elsewhere.[59]

3.20

---

[51] *Hyde v Wrench* (1840) 3 Beav 334, 49 ER 132. See also *Tucker v Godfrey* (1862) 1 SCR (NSW) 292; *McIntosh v Brill* (1870) 20 UCCP 426; *Mooney v Williams* (1905) 3 CLR 1; *Poel v Brunswick-Balke-Collender Co of New York* 110 NE 619 (1915); *Turner Kempson & Co Pty Ltd v Camm* [1922] VLR 498; *Evans Deakin Industries Ltd v Queensland Electricity Generating Board* (1984) 1 BCL 334; *Union Carbide Corp v Oscar Mayer Foods Corp* 947 F 2d 1333 (1991); *Lark v Outhwaite* [1991] 2 Lloyd's Rep 132; *Custom Credit Corp Ltd v Gray* [1992] 1 VR 540, 551. It does not matter that the offer was expressed to be open for a period of time and the offeree both rejected and attempted to accept it in that time, the original rejection terminates the offer, *Baker v Taylor* (1906) 6 SR (NSW) 500. Cf *Brambles Holdings Ltd v Bathurst City Council* (2001) 53 NSWLR 153, 176 per Heydon JA. See further 4.40.

[52] See *Livingstone v Evans* [1925] 4 DLR 769 (here an offeree made a counter-offer to which the seller replied, 'cannot reduce price'; this was held to evidence an intention to keep the original offer open). See also *Re Cowan & Boyd* (1921) 49 OLR 335, 61 DLR 497.

[53] The party in the position of A must also be aware that if B's counter-offer is the offer that is on the table then any act evidencing acceptance by A will be an acceptance on B's terms, see *Mooney v Williams* (1905) 3 CLR 1.

[54] See 4.42.

[55] Examples of variations include, *Cross v Davidson* (1898) 17 NZLR 576 (agreement for sale of steamer, purchaser agreed to the seller's price but added in his telegram of acceptance a delivery date); *Turner Kempson & Co Pty Ltd v Camm* [1922] VLR 498 (here, amongst other additions there was introduced into the acceptance a variation to the description of the subject matter); *Bastard v McCallum* [1924] VLR 9 (here a letter of acceptance introduced a term giving the seller a right to suspend delivery); *Northland Airlines Ltd v Dennis Ferranti Meters Ltd* (1970) 114 Sol J 845 (here an offer to sell an aircraft required immediate payment and had no express time for delivery thus requiring delivery within a reasonable time; it was accepted that the delivery date was not important; however, it was held that the acceptance which required delivery within 30 days of contract was not an acceptance; in addition the acceptance introduced a term for payment on delivery); *Lark v Outhwaite* [1991] 2 Lloyd's Rep 132, 139 (here the incorporation of the words 'will not prejudice', introduced a small but significant variation); *Precision Pools Pty Ltd v FCT* (1992) 37 FCR 554, 560 (introduction of a date for performance). See further 4.40ff. Cf *Canadian Market Place Ltd v Fallowfield* (1976) 71 DLR (3d) 341; *The Master Sterlios Monvia Motorship Corp v Keppel Shipyard (Pte) Ltd* [1983] 1 MLJ 361.

[56] *Frampton v McCully* [1976] 1 NZLR 270, 276.

[57] *Jones v Daniel* [1894] 2 Ch 332 (here the acceptance introduced a term for a deposit in a contract for the sale of land). See also *Cullen v Bickers* (1878) 12 SALR 5.

[58] *Georgoulis v Mandalinic* [1984] 1 NSWLR 612.

[59] See 4.11 and 4.42.

3.21   It follows from what has been said above that whether or not the original offer is to be put 'back on the table' for acceptance after a rejection or counter-offer is for the offeror to decide and is determined as an issue of fact.[60] If in the example given the offeree, instead of seeking to accept the original offer after its rejection by way of oral communication or in writing, were to tender the £1,000, it would be a question of fact as to whether the offeror's taking of that sum were to give rise to a contract.[61] Moreover, if the circumstances were such that an offer was made and rejected and thereafter the offeree took the benefit of that offer, a court may conclude there is a contract rather than leave the offeror in all cases to his or her restitutionary claim.[62]

3.22   It has also been held that where an offer is made and the offeree makes an enquiry, this does not terminate the offer.[63] The typical example of an enquiry is a request for further information or a request for credit terms, that is, whether the offeror would allow the offeree to pay the price later or over a period of time.[64] Whether or not a statement is a rejection, counter-offer or enquiry is determined by reference to the presumed intention of the parties.[65] The circumstances surrounding the communications may be important in determining whether a statement is an enquiry.[66] Generally, to be an enquiry the statement must not contain words that in any way reject the offer, or, subject to what is said below, put any counter-proposal forward. Thus, a reply that does not insist upon a different price but is 'exploratory of the possibility of a reduction in [the] price' may be an enquiry.[67]

3.23   The notion that an enquiry does not terminate an offer does raise the important issue as to whether a rejection or counter-offer terminates an offer as a rule of law or as a matter of intention, the latter being determined as an issue of fact. There are statements that suggest

---

[60]   *Khaled v Athanas Bros (Aden) Ltd* (1967) 1 BPR 9310. See also *Livingstone v Evans* [1925] 4 DLR 769.

[61]   See *Harris v Jenkins* [1922] SASR 59. See also *Ackroyd v Smithies* (1886) 54 LT 130, 132; *Day v McLea* (1889) 22 QBD 610. See further Eisenberg, 'Expression Rules in Contract Law and Problems of Offer and Acceptance' (1994) 82 Cal L Rev 1127, 1151–2.

[62]   See *Brambles Holdings Ltd v Bathurst City Council* (2001) 53 NSWLR 153, 179 per Heydon JA.

[63]   Once the contract is formed, a request to renegotiate the terms of the contract cannot impact on its efficacy, see 4.02.

[64]   Eg *Stevenson Jaques & Co v McLean* (1880) 5 QBD 346 (offer to 'Sell for 40s nett cash, open till Monday'; reply, 'Please wire whether you would accept forty for delivery over two months, or if not, longest limit you would give'; held to be an enquiry, no words of rejection appear in the reply and it did not make any counter-proposal to be a counter-offer). See also *Simpson v Hughes* (1897) 66 LJ Ch 334; *Brambles Holdings Ltd v Bathurst City Council* (2001) 53 NSWLR 153, 194 per Ipp A-JA, with whom Mason P agreed.

[65]   Where the communication is written it is often said that that intention is determined by construction. Moreover, it has been held that in such circumstances the issue is a true issue of construction being a question of law, see *The Homeward Bound Extended Goldmining Co Ltd v Anderson* (1884) NZLR 3 SC 266, 270.

[66]   *Stevenson Jaques & Co v McLean* (1880) 5 QBD 346, 350. Trade practice may also be important, eg *Armstrong v The Wellington-Manawatu Railway Co Ltd* (1885) NZLR 3 SC 442 (in reply to a tender, the offeree sent a telegram stating, 'Your tender accepted—letter posted', it was held that this was not an unconditional acceptance on the basis that it was the mercantile custom of the industry that this meant that the full conditions were to be contained in the letter).

[67]   *Gibson v Manchester City Council* [1979] 1 WLR 294, 302. See also *The Homeward Bound Extended Goldmining Co Ltd v Anderson* (1884) NZLR 3 SC 266 (an acceptance of employment by the offeree in Victoria requested three weeks in order for him to get his affairs together to take up the job in New Zealand; it did not insist on this extension of time and was held to be an acceptance). See further *Powierza v Daley* [1985] 1 NZLR 558, 561; *JRM Furniture Holdings v Cowlin* 1983(4) SA 541. Cf *Cross v Davidson* (1898) 17 NZLR 576; *Tinn v Hoffmann & Co* (1873) 29 LT 271.

it is a rule of law.[68] However, where parties are negotiating a contract they will often expect a lot of hard bargaining on the price. If an offeror at the commencement of negotiations makes an offer to sell at a high price it will often be within the reasonable contemplation of the parties that despite much bargaining on that price, that price will still be available for acceptance so long as that acceptance is made in context, such as at the same meeting. This would often be the case even if initial words of rejection are used by the offeree.[69] It follows that if the effect of a rejection or counter-offer on an offer is determined by reference to intention, then the example given at the start of this section must not be taken too far.

An example that raises these points and which is often made in textbooks is where the offeree puts an alternative transaction to the offeror while trying to keep the original offer open. For example, the offeror offers to sell goods to the offeree for £1,000 and the offeree replies, 'I am considering your offer but in the meantime would you consider selling them for £900'.[70] In such a case, arguably the offeree's statement would not terminate the offer. Clearly in this example the offeree seeks to explore a price reduction—which would be an enquiry—but he or she also takes the extra step of stating an alternative price. If the notion that a rejection or counter-offer kills the offer is a rule of law and there exists nothing in between rejection, counter-offer and acceptance other than enquiry, then for the offeree in this example to be successful it is necessary for his or her communication to be classified as a mere enquiry. As noted above this is determined by reference to intention. It is suggested that in terms of effect, the better view is that whether or not a rejection or counter-offer terminates an offer is always determined by reference to intention. Indeed any statement made by the offeree must be interpreted by reference to a reasonable person in the position of the offeror.[71] It follows that it is dangerous to limit the labels that can be placed on such statements. Thus, a document that purports to be an acceptance will not be taken to be a rejection or counter-offer if an additional term in that communication is not intended to vary the terms of the offer.[72] It would also follow that it is not only enquiries that would keep an offer open. In certain circumstances a counter-offer will not terminate an offer and conceivably a rejection in some circumstances will not terminate an offer.[73] In the example

3.24

---

[68] Eg *Evans Deakin Industries Ltd v Queensland Electricity Generating Board* (1984) 1 BCL 334, 339 per Connolly J, cf 342–3 per McPherson J.

[69] See further Eisenberg, 'Expression Rules in Contract Law and Problems of Offer and Acceptance' (1994) 82 Cal L Rev 1127, 1158–9.

[70] Perillo (ed), *Corbin on Contracts* (Revised edn, Vol I, West Publishing Co, St Paul Minn, 1993)§ 3.39, p 516.

[71] Eg *Wilmott v Johnson* [2003] 1 NZLR 649 (an agreement executed in the name of a trust as purchaser was sent to the vendors for execution; the vendors executed the agreement and inserted the names of the trustees as purchasers and sent it back to the trustees for initialling; it was held that the vendors' action constituted a counter-offer; the request for initialling signalled to a reasonable person in the position of the purchaser that the vendors did not consider themselves bound until that initialling occurred; although there is no difference between contracting with a trust and with the trustees the vendor's action showed that the identity of the trustees was important to them; note however, the court at [35] suggested that the proper perspective was that of a 'third party observer').

[72] *The English and Foreign Credit Co Ltd v Ludovico* (1871) LR 5 HL 64; *Re Imperial Land Co of Marseilles; Harris' Case* (1872) LR 7 Ch App 587; *Clive v Beaumont* (1848) 1 De G & Sm 397, 63 ER 1121.

[73] *Brambles Holdings Ltd v Bathurst City Council* (2001) 53 NSWLR 153, 179 per Heydon JA ('If offer and acceptance analysis is not always necessary or sufficient, principles such as the general principle that a rejection of an offer brings it to an end cannot be universal.') It has been said that the line between enquiries

above the communication would not operate as a counter-offer as the words 'would you consider selling them for £900' is not a statement capable of acceptance.

3.25 Under section 38 of the Restatement (2d) Contracts, rather than evoking notions of offers being 'terminated' or 'killed' upon rejection, it deals with the 'power' to accept. The starting point for the effect of a rejection is that it terminates the offeree's power to accept. This rule seeks to protect the offeror who may act in reliance on such a rejection. However, this is subject to the offeror manifesting a contrary intention. So the terms of the offer itself may evidence an intention that a rejection will not terminate the offer. Similarly the offer will remain open under this section if the offeree merely rejects the offer for the present and evidences an intention to consider it further in the future.[74] The same approach applies to counter-offers.[75]

B. Revocation of Offers

General rule

3.26 An offer may be revoked any time prior to its acceptance.[76] Even if an offer is expressed to be open for a stated period of time it can be revoked prior to that time elapsing. For example, in *Routledge v Grant*,[77] the defendant had offered to purchase a house from the plaintiff and had required 'a definite answer to be given within six weeks from the 18 March 1825'. It was held that the defendant could revoke this offer at any time before acceptance, even though the time limit had not expired. Where the offer is a standing offer capable of

---

and counter-offers is a fine one, see *Powierza v Daley* [1985] 1 NZLR 558, 561. Arguably it is a distinction that can only be maintained if they are legal titles given to communications after determining the intention behind the communication. Thus, every statement that is not a counter-offer is an enquiry and vice-versa. But that will often give a fictional conclusion to the language used. See further Eisenberg, 'Expression Rules in Contract Law and Problems of Offer and Acceptance' (1994) 82 Cal L Rev 1160 ('[T]he line between a counter-offer, an inquiry, a request, and a statement that the offer will be held under advisement can be very unclear. If A offers to sell his car to B for $7,400, a response of "I'll pay you $7,100" is a counter-offer, and a response of "Will you take less?" is an inquiry. But what about "Will you take $900?," "How about $900?," or "At this time, I can only offer $900, but I will get back to you if things change?".').

[74] Comment *b*.
[75] Restatement (2d) Contracts § 39.
[76] *Payne v Cave* (1789) 3 Term Rep 148, 100 ER 502 (bidder at auction retracted bid prior to the fall of the hammer); *Re National Savings Bank Association (Hebb's Case)* (1867) LR 4 Eq 9 (offer to purchase shares; shares allotted by directors, offer retracted prior to communication of acceptance). See also *Dickinson v Dodds* (1876) 2 Ch D 463; *Metropolitan Milk Supply (Greater Brisbane) Ltd v Paulsen* [1933] St R Qd 53; *Barker v Caird* (1876) 14 SCR (NSW) 358; *Great Amalgamated Gold Mining Co Ltd v Morris* (1877) 11 SALR 9; *Re Provincial and Suburban Bank Ltd, Hall's Case, Gregory's Case* (1881) 7 VLR (E) 63; *Nyulasy v Rowan* (1891) 17 VLR 663, 670; *Goldsbrough Mort & Co Ltd v Quinn* (1910) 10 CLR 674, 678; *Veivers v Cordingley* [1989] 2 Qd R 278, 296. See further *Nunin Holdings Pty Ltd v Tullamarine Estates Pty Ltd* [1994] 1 VR 74 (acceptance revoked prior to taking effect; acceptance had been posted but terms of offer excluded postal acceptance rule). Under the United Nations Convention on Contracts for the International Sale of Goods (1980), Article 16(1) an offer may be revoked if the 'revocation reaches the offeree before he has dispatched an acceptance'.
[77] (1828) 4 Bing 653, 130 ER 920. See also *Dickinson v Dodds* (1876) 2 Ch D 463; *Bristol, Cardiff and Swansea Aërated Bread Co v Maggs* (1890) 44 Ch D 616; *Nyulasy v Rowan* (1891) 17 VLR 663; *Fraser v Morrison* (1958) 12 DLR (2d) 612; *Macquarie Generation v CNA Resources Ltd* [2001] NSWSC 1040; *GIO General Ltd v Allen* [2002] NSWCA 333.

acceptance from time to time, it may still be revoked as to the future acceptances even though there have been acceptances in the past.[78]

Need for communication

In order to revoke an offer, the revocation must be communicated by words or conduct to the offeree[79] or someone authorized to receive that communication.[80] The notice of revocation must be *received* by the offeree or that authorized person.[81] Where an offer, such as an offer for reward, is made to the public such as through a newspaper, radio, internet or television advertisement, then an effective revocation would require a notice of revocation to be advertised in the same way using the same media. If that is done the revocation will be effective even if the offeree did not see the notice of revocation.[82]

3.27

It is necessary that the external manifestations be interpreted as constituting a revocation but just as the word 'offer' need not be used in an offer, the words 'withdraw' and 'revoke' need not be used in a revocation. In the American case of *Hoover Motor Express Co v Clements Paper Co*[83] when the offeree had indicated that he was ready to discuss the matter, the offeror had replied 'well, I don't know if we are ready. We have not decided, we might not want to go through with it'. The Supreme Court of Tennessee held that this reply constituted a revocation. In general 'judicial reluctance to force an agreement on parties whose assent is not clearly shown produces a tendency to resolve doubtful cases in favor of finding revocations, a tendency analogous to the tendency to resolve doubtful cases against finding offers'.[84]

3.28

---

[78] Restatement (2d) Contracts § 47.

[79] *Byrne & Co v Van Tienhoven & Co* (1880) 5 CPD 344; *Henthorn v Fraser* [1892] 2 Ch 27. See § 4 of the Indian Contract Act 1872 and § 4(3) of the Malaysian Contract Act 1950 which contain identical provisions on communication of revocations. The communication is complete 'as against the person who makes it, when it is put into the course of transmission to the person to whom it is made, so as to be out of the power of the person who makes it' and, so that the revocation cannot be recalled once postponed, 'as against the person to whom it is made, when it comes to his knowledge'.

[80] *Financings Ltd v Stimson* [1962] 3 All ER 386. See also Restatement (2d) Contracts §§ 42, 43, 68. See further on the authority of a legal representative to accept a notice of revocation, *IVI Pty Ltd v Baycrown Pty Ltd* [2005] QCA 205.

[81] In the case of a communication by way of a letter to a business address, receipt (and thus communication) is generally taken to have occurred when that communication is or would have been opened in the ordinary course of business, see *Eaglehill Ltd v J Needham Builders Ltd* [1973] AC 992, 1011, see also *Brinkibon Ltd v Stahag Stahlund Stahlwarenhandels Gesellschaft MBH* [1983] 2 AC 34, 42, cf *NV Stoomv Maats 'de Maas' v Nippon Yusen Kaisha (The Pendrecht)* [1980] 2 Lloyd's Rep 56, 66 (for the purpose of service the moment of actual receipt may be the relevant time even if outside business hours). It also follows that in the case of an instantaneous method of communication, such as a fax, it is taken as communicated when it is received (which will be the same time it is sent), if that occurs in normal business hours, *Schelde Delta Shipping BV v Astarte Shipping Ltd (The Pamela)* [1995] 2 Lloyd's Rep 249, 252; *Tenax Steamship Co Ltd v The Brimnes (The Brimnes)* [1975] QB 929. As to what address may be used for communicating a revocation, see *Bernuth Lines v High Seas Shipping Ltd (The Eastern Navigator)* [2006] 1 Lloyd's Rep 537 (email). See also Restatement (2d) Contracts § 68. Cf 4.96.

[82] See *Shuey v United States* 92 US 73 (1875). See also Restatement (2d) Contracts § 46.

[83] 193 Tenn 6, 241 SW 2d 851 (1951).

[84] Farnsworth, *Farnsworth on Contracts* (3rd edn, Vol I, Aspen Publishers, New York, 2004) § 3.17, p 305.

3.29 The postal acceptance rule does not apply to revocations; a notice of revocation is not effective on posting.[85] Therefore, an offeree may accept an offer either by an instantaneous mode of communication or by posting a letter of acceptance even though a notice of revocation may at that time be in the mail system.[86] It also follows that the fact that the offeror does an act inconsistent with keeping the offer open would not constitute an effective revocation unless communicated.[87] For example, in the context of a sale of goods, if prior to acceptance the offeror/seller sells the subject goods to a third person, the buyer may still accept the offer if he or she has no knowledge of that act.[88] Where a notice of revocation is communicated at the same time as an acceptance is communicated the revocation takes precedence.[89]

3.30 It is not necessary that the person communicating the revocation has authority from the offeror to do so. The revocation will be effective so long as the offeree hears of the revocation and that there was a revocation in fact.[90] The leading case on this point is *Dickinson v Dodds*.[91] In this case an offer concerning the sale of certain property was expressed to be open for acceptance for a certain period of time. Prior to that time elapsing and prior to the offeree attempting to accept the offer, the offeree heard from a third party that the offeror was 'offering or agreeing' to sell the property to another person. This communication from a third party was considered sufficient to revoke the offer. The difficulty with the case is not so much with the recognition that a communication of a revocation can come from a person not authorized to make the communication but with the words, 'offering or agreeing' which arguably suggest a negotiation with a third party and not necessarily a clear revocation of the offer. Presumably it was the word 'agreeing' that weighed most heavily with the court.[92]

---

[85] Cf Gardner, 'Trashing with Trollope: A Deconstruction of the Postal Rules in Contract' (1992) 12 OJLS 170, 175, 188, 189 discussing some cases to the contrary.

[86] *Byrne & Co v Van Tienhoven & Co* (1880) 5 CPD 344; *Stevenson Jaques & Co v McLean* (1880) 5 QBD 346; *Henthorn v Fraser* [1892] 2 Ch 27.

[87] *Henthorn v Fraser* [1892] 2 Ch 27, 33. See also *Adams v Lindsell* (1818) 1 B & Ald 681, 106 ER 250; *Cartwright v Hoogstoel* (1911) 105 LT 628. Whether an offer is revoked by the promisor issuing a second offer will depend on whether the second offer evidences an intention to revoke the first offer. A mere inconsistency between the offers will not always evidence such an intention as it is possible for two inconsistent offers to be made to a promisee (eg one offering services for a fixed price and one for a variable price) allowing the offeree to choose which one he or she prefers, see *Pickfords Ltd v Celestica Ltd* [2003] EWCA Civ 1741.

[88] *Patterson v Dolman* [1908] VLR 354. See also *King v Homer* (1913) 33 NZLR 222.

[89] *Head v Diggon* (1828) 7 LJKB 36.

[90] Query whether the information must also come from a reliable source before the promisee would be bound by it, see Restatement (2d) Contracts § 43. Comment d expressly states that 'a mere rumour does not terminate the power of acceptance, if the offeree disbelieves it and is reasonable in doing so, even though the rumour is later verified'. Section 6(a) of the Malaysian Contracts Act 1950 refers to the necessity for communication of notice of the revocation to be made by the proposer to the other party. This is also the position in § 6(1) of the Indian Contracts Act 1872, although this Act pre-dates the decision in *Dickinson v Dodds*. The position in Singapore, however, is generally the same as in England, see *Banque Paribas v Citibank NA* [1989] 1 NKH 329. Arguably if the requirement of communication is to protect the offeree it is not necessary that it come from a reliable source.

[91] (1876) 2 Ch D 463. See also *Re Whelan* [1897] 1 IR 575; *Cartwright v Hoogstoel* (1911) 105 LT 628; *King v Homer* (1913) 33 NZLR 222.

[92] The judgments are heavily based on the need to establish a meeting of the minds between the two parties and have been criticized, see Furmston, *Cheshire, Fifoot and Furmston, Law of Contract* (15th edn, OUP, Oxford, 2007) 74.

Practical problems with the general principle

The ability of an offeror to revoke an offer any time prior to acceptance taking effect can **3.31** cause difficulties for the offeree both in the context of bilateral contracts and unilateral contracts.

Problems may arise in the context of bilateral transactions in circumstances where the **3.32** offeree needs time to consider the offer or needs to spend money in carrying out various investigations before deciding whether or not to accept or needs to enter into some other contract prior to accepting the offer. For example, a contractor, prior to putting in a bid for a contract may wish to obtain bids from potential subcontractors in order to cost the work. The terms of the contractor's offer will rely on the figures supplied by those potential subcontractors. At the same time the contractor would not want to enter into formal contracts with a subcontractor—unless the subcontractor agrees to the subcontract being subject to the award of the head contract as a condition subsequent—prior to being offered the contract. In such cases the potential exists for the contractor to be awarded the head contract and for the subcontractor to then revoke its offer prior to acceptance. This occurred in *James Baird Co v Gimbel Bros.*[93] Here the defendant subcontractor sent a bid to supply linoleum for a public building in Pennsylvania to a number of contractors who were likely to bid for the construction contract. One of those contractors was the plaintiff. The bid prices were stated to be for 'prompt acceptance after general contract has been awarded'. The plaintiff received this bid on 28 December. On the same day the defendant discovered that a mistake had been made in computing the bid prices so they were much lower than they should have been. The defendant sent telegrams to the recipients of its bid stating that the bid was revoked. In the meantime the plaintiff had put in a bid based upon the prices quoted by the defendant and the plaintiff's bid was accepted. The plaintiff argued that the defendant's offer implied that it was to be irrevocable if the plaintiff relied upon it in making its own bid; this obligation it was said flowed from the fact the defendant must have known the predicament the plaintiffs would be in if it withdrew its offer after the plaintiff had put in its bid.

Judge Learned Hand held that the offer could be withdrawn before notice of acceptance **3.33** was given; by its terms it was not accepted merely by the contractor putting in a bid. That is, it was not a unilateral contract, the bid was an offer that required a counter-promise by way of acceptance under a bilateral contract. The subcontractor's offer was expressed to be contingent upon being awarded the main contract and the prices were expressed to be

---

[93] 64 F 2d 344 (1933). Cf *Loranger Construction Corp v E F Hauserman Co* 376 Mass 757, 384 NE 2d 176 (1978) (here when the subcontractor refused to carry out work after the contractor had used the subcontractor's bid to get the main contract, the court held there was sufficient evidence for a jury to conclude that a contract had come into existence between the parties either as a bilateral contract when the subcontractor's bid was given to the contractor over the phone—the contract being conditional as neither party would be bound unless the main contractor was awarded the head contract—or as a unilateral contract where the act of using the subcontractor's bid was the acceptance or when the contractor, after winning the main contract sent a subcontract to the subcontractor to sign). Query whether it is possible to use this analysis where the main contractor does not name the subcontractor on whose bid it is relying. See further 3.74ff.

offered for 'prompt acceptance after the general contract has been awarded'.[94] Moreover, the plaintiff would not have expected that at this stage it could have been sued by the defendant for breach of contract if the plaintiff was awarded the head contract and then repudiated it. He also held there could be no promissory estoppel here because the subcontractor's bid was by its terms given for an exchange, that exchange being its acceptance not its use in making a bid for the main contract.[95] The plaintiff's reliance therefore could not ground an estoppel. The Judge rejected the argument that the bid could be regarded as an option under which the plaintiff could effectively choose to accept the defendant's bid if the plaintiff's bid was accepted or try to get a better bargain elsewhere.[96] In short the defendant ought not to be prevented from revoking its bid if there was no corresponding obligation placed on the plaintiff.

3.34 Whether or not such a situation might give rise to an estoppel is dealt with below.[97] Mention here should also be made of an action in tort. Where a subcontractor has been negligent in fixing the amount in the subcontract tender and the main contractor has relied on this in determining its own main contract tender figure—this all occurring before the subcontractor realized its mistake and revoked the quotation—then arguably the main contractor may have an action in tort if it suffered loss. That is, arguably the subcontractor is under a duty to ensure the information it gives is correct and that it is prepared to supply goods or services in accordance with its bid. This possibility has not yet been before the English courts but it was considered and rejected by Henry J in the New Zealand case of *Holman Construction Ltd v Delta Timber Company Ltd*.[98] Henry J went on to say that the law on offer and acceptance could not be qualified by any duty of care giving rise to liability in tort for breach on the basis that, although there was clearly no concluded contract, the main contractor was seeking to use the offer as giving rise to a damages claim under *Hedley Byrne & Co Ltd v Heller & Partners Ltd*.[99] He said that an offer 'is not a representation that a careful or even an honest assessment of the price asked has been made ... It is no more than the expression of an intention to become bound by contract if the offer be accepted.'[100] Henry J held that the loss to the main contractor was attributable to the fact that it had not accepted the subcontractor's offer before it had been revoked.

3.35 It has been suggested that under English law an argument based on negligence may be plausible in some circumstances with the duty of care arising by reason of reliance and that

---

[94] Kessler and Fine suggest that the philosophy underlying Learned Hand J's decision was the offeree 'has himself to blame for expense incurred in relying on an offer if he has failed to protect himself by dispatching an acceptance, securing a conditional contract or an option', see Kessler and Fine, 'Culpa in Contrahendo, Bargaining in Good Faith, and Freedom of Contract: A Comparative Study' (1964) 77 Harv L Rev 401, 422.

[95] Cf *Drennan v Star Paving Co* 51 Cal 2d 409, 333 P 2d 757 (1958), see below 3.69. See also Closen and Weiland, 'The Construction Industry Bidding Cases: Application of Traditional Contract, Promissory Estoppel and Other Theories of the Relations between General Contractor and Subcontractors' (1980) 13 J Marshall L Rev 565, 581–4, 587ff).

[96] 64 F 2d 344, 346 (1933).

[97] See 3.64ff. See also Chapter 5.

[98] [1972] NZLR 1081.

[99] [1964] AC 465.

[100] [1972] NZLR 1081, 1082.

recourse to an action in negligence is not an attempt to evade or circumvent the rules of offer and acceptance.[101] It may be sufficient to show that the main contractor wanted the tender in order to indicate the sort of figure it would have to pay for the subcontract work. On this basis there is a direct link between the negligence of the subcontractor in fixing the tender and the loss suffered by the main contractor who would otherwise have been able to engage another subcontractor in the market at a figure similar to that used in the subcontract. Thus, in these circumstances, the loss would be caused by the negligence and not by the revocation. In such an action it would, of course, be imperative that the subcontractor had been negligent in fixing the tender so that the figure quoted was hopelessly incorrect. The argument could not therefore be used to seek damages in other cases involving revocation of the subcontract tender.

Turning to unilateral contracts, here because acceptance requires the offeree to complete **3.36** the act of acceptance, general principle dictates that the offeror may revoke its offer anytime prior to the offeree completing that act.[102] It would not matter that the offeree has incurred time and costs in commencing the act of acceptance. Thus, if an offeror says to an offeree:[103] 'If you will go to York, I will give you £100', then even though the offeree may have commenced walking to York with the intention of accepting the offer, the offeror can revoke that offer any time prior to the offeree arriving in York.

Such a scenario arose on the facts in *Petterson v Pattberg*.[104] The defendant, the mortgagee, **3.37** had written to Petterson, the mortgagor, offering to discount the mortgage if the balance of the sum owing was paid in cash on or before 31 May 1924. On a day in the latter part of May, Petterson presented himself at the defendant's home and knocked at the door.

---

[101] Furmston, *Cheshire, Fifoot and Furmston, Law of Contract* (15th edn, OUP, Oxford, 2007) 347.

[102] The concept of unilateral contracts has been much criticized over the years, eg see Llewellyn, 'On Our Case-Law of Contract: Offer and Acceptance' (1938) 48 Yale LJ 1 (Part I), (1939) 48 Yale LJ 779 (Part II); Stoljar, 'The False Distinction between Bilateral and Unilateral Contracts' (1955) 64 Yale LJ 515; Carter, 'The Breach of Unilateral Contract' (1982) 11 Anglo-Am Law Rev 169, 172. For a defence of the concept see, Pettit Jr, 'Modern Unilateral Contracts' (1983) BU L Rev 551. See further Tiersma, 'Reassessing Unilateral Contracts: The Role of Offer, Acceptance and Promise' (1992) 26 UC Davis L Rev 1.

[103] The example is taken from *Great Northern Railway Company v Witham* (1873) LR 9 CP 16, 19 per Brett J. Cf Atiyah, 'Consideration: A Restatement' in *Essays on Contract* (OUP, Oxford, 1986), 200, suggesting there is no actual authority to support the assumption that the consideration for a promise in a unilateral situation has to be the complete performance of the act requested. See also *Jones v Padavatton* [1969] 1 WLR 328, 333, per Salmon LJ (appearing to suggest that acceptance might accrue over a period of time rather than occurring at a point in time).

[104] 248 NY 86, 161 NE 428 (1928). Prior to this decision the Maine Supreme Court appears to have come to the opposite conclusion in *Brackenbury v Hodgkin* 116 Me 399, 102 A 106 (1917). In this case the defendant widow promised the plaintiffs, her daughter and son-in-law, that if they moved to Maine and looked after her during her lifetime, she would leave her farm to them on her death. The couple moved to Maine and commenced caring for the defendant. Soon after there was a falling out and the defendant asked them to leave the house which they refused to do. The court held that the plaintiffs had accepted this offer by moving to Maine and beginning the task of taking care of the widow. However, the act of acceptance would appear to have been looking after the widow for the rest of her life which had not occurred, but it only did not occur because the widow prevented the plaintiffs from doing so. This appears to be a revocation of the offer? It is in such a context, that is, where the act of acceptance requires performance over what may be an extended period of time, that Denning LJ suggested that the offeror could not revoke the offer once the act of acceptance had begun, see *Errington v Errington* [1952] 1 KB 290, 295, see 3.88. Query whether the better approach to such cases is to leave the parties to a restitutionary remedy or otherwise construe the offer as requiring either an act or a promise which can be evidenced by commencing performance.

Without opening the door the defendant asked for the name of the caller and Petterson replied: 'It is Mr Petterson I have come to pay off the mortgage.' The defendant answered that he had sold the mortgage to a third party. Petterson then managed to persuade the defendant to open the door so that he could talk to him. When the defendant did this Petterson exhibited the cash and said he was ready to pay off the mortgage according to the agreement. The defendant refused to take the money and the plaintiff had to pay the full sum to the third party who had purchased the mortgage. The plaintiff claimed the discount amount with interest. It was held that communication of the revocation had been made before performance of the act requested, namely the act of tendering the cash balance, and therefore no contract had been made.

Circumventing the general principle

3.38 Having outlined the practical problems of the general principle, the next section outlines how it can be circumvented with options and firm offers, how other areas of law, principally the law of estoppel, may provide relief and finally arguments for and against reform of the general principle are discussed.[105]

Option contracts

3.39 The ability of an offeror to revoke an offer prior to acceptance is based on the premise that an offer, although incorporating a promise to assume a legal obligation, does not create a legal liability until the moment of acceptance. To prevent the revocation of an offer, valuable consideration must be given in return for an undertaking to keep it open.[106] Where consideration is given to keep an offer open for a period of time an option is created. The consideration may take the form of either a promise or an act such as a promise to pay a sum of money or the payment of a sum of money. What is required will depend on what the offeror requests or agrees to accept in return for the promise to keep the offer open.

3.40 The above statement appears to represent the law even though it ignores a vital doctrinal issue. There has been a long debate as to the doctrinal basis of an option.[107] There have been

---

[105] In addition to the methods discussed it should also be mentioned that one way courts can overcome some of the harshness in this area is, where possible, to prefer a construction that allows the contract to be characterized as a bilateral rather than a unilateral contract, see *Dawson v Helicopter Exploration Co Ltd* [1955] SCR 868, 874–5. See also *Davis v Jacoby* 1 Cal 2d 370, 34 P 2d 1026 (1934). See also Restatement (2d) Contracts § 32, 'In case of doubt an offer is interpreted as inviting the offeree to accept either by promising to perform what the offer requests or by rendering the performance, as the offeree chooses.' This is an application of § 30(2):'Unless otherwise indicated by the language or the circumstances, an offer invites acceptance in any manner and by any medium reasonable in the circumstances.'

[106] Cf the position in the United States under Restatement (2d) Contracts § 87, see 3.54.

[107] See *Braham v Walker* (1961) 104 CLR 366, 376. Judges have been split on which theory they prefer. In England, perhaps the leading adoption of the conditional contract theory was in *Griffith v Pelton* [1958] Ch 205, 225. English cases preferring the irrevocable offer theory include, *Helby v Matthews* [1895] AC 471, 479–80; *West London Syndicate Ltd v Inland Revenue* [1898] 1 QB 226, 238. For a discussion and analysis of the leading English cases, see *Spiro v Glencrown Properties Ltd* [1991] Ch 537, see further 3.44. In Australia see, *Laybutt v Amoco Australia Pty Ltd* (1974) 132 CLR 57, 75–6; *Goldsbrough Mort & Co Ltd v Quinn* (1910) 10 CLR 674, 678–9, 690–2; *Carter v Hyde* (1923) 33 CLR 115; *Ballas v Theophilos (No 2)* (1957) 98 CLR 193, 207–8; *Commissioner of Taxes (Qld) v Camphin* (1937) 57 CLR 127, 132; *Gerraty v McGavin* (1914) 18 CLR 152, 163. See also *Gilbert J McCaul (Aust) Pty Ltd v Pitt Club Ltd* (1957) 59 SR (NSW) 122; *Johnson v Bones* [1970] 1 NSWR 28; *Westminster Estates Pty Ltd v Calleja* (1970) 91 WN (NSW) 222; *O'Halloran Enterprises Pty Ltd v Williamson* [1979] VR 33; *Karaguleski v Vasil Bros & Co Pty Ltd* [1981] 1 NSWLR 267;

two competing views, the conditional contract theory and the irrevocable offer theory. Moreover, there is a strong view that neither theory is necessarily dictated by contract doctrine and so the matter ultimately rests on construction.[108] However, where an option does not expressly deal with the issue of its legal effect and is simply drafted as an 'option', this leaves its legal effect to be determined by the court.

In theory the distinction may be important. Taking the example of an option to purchase **3.41** certain subject matter, under the conditional contract theory a contract of sale is taken to exist between the vendor and purchaser but performance is suspended until the party with the benefit of the option exercises it. The 'condition' is a condition subsequent to the formation of the contract of sale.[109] An option in the form of an irrevocable offer consists of an offer to buy or sell coupled with a contract which contains a promise not to revoke the offer.

Arguably, the form an option takes should impact on its revocability. Under the condi- **3.42** tional contract theory, a sale contract exists subject to a contingency, it follows that any purported revocation could not be effective. In the case of an option in the form of an irrevocable offer there is no agreement for sale and doctrinally it would appear to follow that, aside from injunctive relief, any purported revocation prior to the exercise of the option would merely result in a breach of the contract that contains the promise not to revoke thus giving rise to a right to damages. Despite this, it would appear the courts will not recognize the legitimacy of any purported revocation and will treat the option as exercised by the optionee and then,[110] if appropriate, order specific performance of the contract that then arises under the irrevocable offer theory.[111] This result is understandable given that the expectation that the offer will remain open forms the very basis of any option.[112]

There is a further difficulty with the conditional contract theory. It is difficult to see how an **3.43** agreement for sale can exist if one of the parties (the grantee of the option) has not

---

Traywinds Pty Ltd v Cooper [1989] 1 Qd R 222, 226; *BS Stillwell and Co Pty Ltd v Budget Rent-A-Car System Pty Ltd* [1990] VR 589, 594–5; *Karaguleski v Vasil Bros & Co Pty Ltd* [1981] 1 NSWLR 267, 269.

[108] See *Carter v Hyde* (1923) 33 CLR 115, 122–3 per Isaacs J (note that the rest of the court held that the option was a conditional contract, even though, in form, it was an offer coupled with a promise not to revoke); *Braham v Walker* (1961) 104 CLR 366, 376; *Johnson v Bones* [1970] 1 NSWR 28, 36–76; *O'Halloran Enterprises Pty Ltd v Williamson* [1979] VR 33. See also *Tonitto v Bassal* (1990) 5 BPR 11, 258, 11, 272 (overruled without reference (1992) 28 NSWLR 564); *Nicholas v Wade* [1983] 1 VR 708, 710.

[109] Rossiter, *Principles of Land Contracts and Options in Australia* (Law Book Co, Sydney, 2003) para 3.4.

[110] In the case of a land dealing it may be argued that the reason the revocation is not effective is that the option creates an interest in land. However, usually that interest is based on there being a contract of sale in place as it is an equitable interest dependent for its existence upon the availability of specific performance, see *Laybutt v Amoco Australia Pty Ltd* (1974) 132 CLR 57, 72–6.

[111] The availability of specific performance will differ depending on the subject matter of the option. For example, an option to purchase land would attract the remedy while an option to purchase shares would not.

[112] See *Goldsbrough Mort & Co Ltd v Quinn* (1910) 10 CLR 674, 691; *Carter v Hyde* (1923) 33 CLR 115, 122ff. Cf *Laybutt v Amoco Australia Pty Ltd* (1974) 132 CLR 57, 72–6. See further *Westminster Estates Ltd v Calleja* (1970) 91 WN (NSW) 222; *Melacare Industries of Australia Pty Ltd v Daley Investments Pty Ltd* (1995) 9 BPR 17,079, 17,091–2; *Baugham v Rampart Resources Ltd* (1995) 4 BCLR (3d) 146, (1995) 124 DLR (4th) 252. See also Restatement (2d) Contracts § 37.

committed itself to buy or sell.[113] There is merely a promise to sell which is kept open by the presence of valuable consideration. Whether the ability of the optionee to obtain any form of equitable relief short of specific performance should give rise to a proprietary interest in the underlying subject matter is a distinct issue.

3.44   In *Spiro v Glencrown Properties Ltd*,[114] Hoffmann J said that an option creates a *sui generis* relationship and neither of the expressions 'conditional contract' or 'irrevocable offer' are apt to explain an option. He suggested that these expressions are merely used by way of metaphor or analogy to help explain the position, rights and obligations of the parties under an option. In his view they are not meant to carry their strict contractual law meanings in this context. It is difficult not to agree with this.

The 'firm offer' concept

3.45   The argument that an offeree must accept the risk that an offer might be revoked arguably has less force where the offeror indicates that the offer will remain open for a certain period. Of course much would depend on the circumstances in which the offer was made and 'less force' does not connote 'no force'. An issue then arises as to whether the law should adopt a notion of a 'firm offer'. In 1937, the Law Revision Committee in its Sixth Interim Report[115] recommended that such a promise should not be rendered unenforceable on the ground that it was not supported by consideration, but no action was taken on this recommendation. The Law Commission considered this matter again in 1975.[116] In a Working Paper, the Law Commission suggested that the proposal put by the Law Revision Committee in 1937 would cause hardship to offerors and sought to balance the interests of both parties by suggesting that a 'firm offer' ought to be binding if it was made 'in the course of a business' and involved a promise not to revoke for a period which did not exceed six years.[117] However, the Law Commission did not produce a report converting this suggestion into a proposal.

3.46   The results of a small survey into tendering practices in the building industry in the Cardiff area conducted by Richard Lewis gives some insight into the attitude of main contractors and subcontractors to revocable offers. The following represents a summary of some of his findings.[118] Lewis found that the majority of main and subcontractors who responded to the survey stated that bids were usually firm. There was evidence from subcontractors that sometimes a main contractor would specifically request a period of time during which the subcontractor's bid would remain firm.

---

[113] *Helby v Matthews* [1895] AC 471; *West London Syndicate v Inland Revenue Commissioners* [1898] 1 QB 226, 238; *WM Cory & Son Ltd v Inland Revenue Commissioners* [1965] AC 1088, 1106–7; *Murray v Scott* [1976] 1 NZLR 643. See further *Amoco Minerals Australia Co v Commissioner of State Taxation (WA)* (1978) 8 ATR 719; *West London Syndicate Ltd v The Commissioners of Inland Revenue* [1897] 1 QB 226, 238 (overruled on other grounds [1898] 2 QB 507).

[114] [1991] Ch 537, 542.

[115] Cmd 5449, para 38.

[116] Law Commission Working Paper No 60, *Firm Offers* (1975).

[117] Law Commission Working Paper No 60, *Firm Offers* (1975) paras 30–4.

[118] Lewis, 'Contracts between Businessmen: Reform of the Law of Firm Offers and an Empirical Study of Tendering Practices in the Building Industry' (1982) 9 Jnl of Law & Society 153, 162–7. See further 5.33.

There was also evidence that most of the main contractors had encountered revocations of **3.47**
subcontract bids. A minority said it was rare and one had not experienced it in 30 years.
However, the main contractors did not feel it necessary to take steps to ensure the reliability
of their subcontract bids before using them to compute their own main contract bid.

As regards the attitude of main contractors if the subcontractor did try to revoke, five of the **3.48**
nine main contractors responding considered that revocation could occur before the award
of the main contract, whilst six of them considered that after the award of the main contract
the subcontractor should be bound by the subcontract bid. Eight of the 11 subcontractors
also considered that after the award of the main contract they were bound by their subcontract bid, but this was due to moral compulsion or because of a fear of loss of business
reputation rather than due to the fact that they considered themselves legally bound.

Among the main contractors there was no mention of legal action against a subcontractor **3.49**
who revoked its bid but the overwhelming evidence was that they could bring pressure to
bear on subcontractors with whom they had a continuing relationship, for example, by
striking a subcontractor from the list of those asked to tender for work.

In addition, there was evidence that, far from being inconvenienced by the revocability of **3.50**
subcontract bids, the main contractors were able to take advantage of this and the fact that
they themselves were not bound even though they had relied on the subcontractor's bid in
making their own bid. There was evidence of 'bid shopping', that is, main contractors
disclosing subcontract bids to other subcontractors in an effort to put pressure on them to
undercut the quoted price, and 'bid peddling', where the initiative to disclose comes from
the subcontractors and the main contractor supplies the information to encourage a lower
offer. However, fears were expressed that this price cutting would lead to poor quality work-
manship. The survey also revealed that main contractors do not always use the subcontractor whose bid they have relied on but 'switch subcontractors'.

One way to prevent 'bid shopping' and restrict the ability of main contractors to switch **3.51**
subcontractors would be if the main contractor was legally bound to use the subcontractor
whose bid had been used in computing the tender. This would also mean that once the
main contractor had used a subcontractor's tender, that subcontractor could not withdraw
its bid. The questionnaire asked whether the main and subcontractors would support such
a proposal. The response was divided with about half of each group strongly rejecting it and
the rest only accepting it subject to serious qualifications. It would also be difficult to prove
that the main contractor actually used a particular subcontractor's quotation. Therefore
such a proposal would be difficult to enforce. In addition, the evidence was that the subcontractors had no great interest in seeking such a legal solution. They were concerned that
because the competitive tendering process obliged them to make more bids than they had
the capacity to carry out, they might find themselves irrevocably bound to carry out work
on too many contracts.[119] The second reason against non-revocation of bids was that it

---

[119] Subcontractors need to avoid a situation where they have either insufficient work or, conversely,
are over-committed. It is important therefore for them to calculate what percentage of tenders need to be
successful. Subcontractors accept the fact that they need to make sufficient bids to generate a comfortable
level of work and on this basis tendering costs are part of the accepted overheads borne by the tendering

would result in subcontractors taking precautions against incurring liability, for example, by limiting the period during which their tenders were to be open for acceptance or issuing bids subject to various qualifications. Further, if a subcontractor was legally bound and forced to continue with a contract, that subcontractor might cut corners and be uncooperative. There was a fear that the Law Commission's suggested approach on the question of irrevocability would increase disputes with consequential increases in costs in the building industry.[120]

3.52   Lewis concluded that 'it may ... be that the informal control methods that already exist make formal legal regulation unnecessary'[121] and that in practice revocation of a firm bid by a subcontractor is less of a problem than in theory. In practice it does not normally matter whether the particular subcontractor is bound or not provided that the price relied on by the main contractor is set at the correct level and assuming that there is more than one available potential subcontractor. Generally, main contractors do not want to tie down subcontractors as they can get another subcontractor. The real difficulties occur in practice where the subcontractor whose bid is relied upon has made a mistake so that the bid is too low and, having discovered the mistake, has withdrawn the bid.[122] Lewis suggests that in England it is assumed that the risk of not being able to find another subcontractor to match the bid relied on is placed on the main contractor. However, in America bid bonds can be employed to protect the main contractor against this risk with the bond being forfeited if the subcontractor seeks to withdraw his bid.

3.53   Waddams[123] suggests a compromise between the competing principles which he identifies as, on the one hand, a need to apply the ordinary tests of enforceability to a firm offer promise and, on the other hand, the need to protect reasonable reliance by the offeree. Waddams is against the full-scale enforceability of firm offer promises and prefers a more flexible remedy of limited enforcement, along the lines of section 87 of the American Restatement (2d) Contracts, in cases of reasonable reliance by the offeree. He states:[124]

> [T]here are good reasons for denying full-scale enforceability to such promises. It must be appreciated that a promise to hold an offer open, if enforceable, amounts to an option, and a marked change in prices may turn out to be very expensive to the grantor of an option. If such promises were to be enforceable just as bargained-for promises, an oral promise to hold

---

subcontractors. This position is implicit in the judgment of Bingham LJ in *Blackpool & Fylde Aero Club Ltd v Blackpool Borough Council* [1990] 1 WLR 1195, 1201–2. Cf Creason Jr, 'Another look at Construction Bidding and Contracts at Formation' (1967) 53 Virginia L Rev 1720, 1737.

[120]   In the United States there is further empirical evidence to suggest that in practice business people are not unduly inconvenienced by the revocability of firm offers which are not supported by consideration, see Schultz, 'The Firm Offer Puzzle: A Study of Business Practice in the Construction Industry' (1952) 19 Uni Chicago L Rev 237, 283–4. See also Sharp, 'Promises, Mistake, and Reciprocity' (1952) 19 Uni Chicago L Rev 286; Creason Jr, 'Another look at Construction Bidding and Contracts at Formation' (1967) 53 Virginia L Rev 1720.

[121]   Lewis, 'Contracts between Businessmen: Reform of the Law of Firm Offers and an Empirical Study of Tendering Practices in the Building Industry' (1982) 9 Jnl of Law & Society 153, 1682.

[122]   See *James Baird Co v Gimbel Bros* 64 F 2d 344 (1933), discussed above 3.32.

[123]   Waddams, *The Law of Contracts* (5th edn, Canada Law Book, Toronto, 2005) paras 126–7.

[124]   Waddams, *The Law of Contracts* (5th edn, Canada Law Book, Toronto, 2005) para 127 (footnotes omitted).

an offer open made by a private individual would expose the individual to the full panoply of remedies including specific performance and expectation damages. The desirability of such a conclusion is open to serious question, and it is for good reason that the courts have hesitated to treat firm offers as universally irrevocable. A sounder approach is, it is suggested, to recognize that a promise to hold an offer open is not a bargain but that it may be enforceable to a limited extent if justice so requires in view of the subsequent reliance of the promise.

Section 87 of the Restatement (2d) Contracts deals with options. Section 87(1)(a) makes **3.54** an offer binding as an option if it is in writing and recites a consideration for making the offer. Apart from the general writing requirement this is akin to the position in English law. Section 87(1)(b) makes an offer binding as an option if it is made irrevocable by statute. However, section 87(2) provides:

> An offer which the offeror should reasonably expect to induce action or forbearance of a substantial character on the part of the offeree before acceptance and which does induce such action or forbearance is binding as an option contract to the extent necessary to avoid injustice.

This provision allows for some flexibility where the offeree engages in acts of reliance which **3.55** are not acts of performance.[125] Comment *e* states:[126]

> Full-scale enforcement of the offered contract is not necessarily appropriate in such cases. Restitution of benefits conferred may be enough, or partial or full reimbursement of losses may be proper. Various factors may influence the remedy: the formality of the offer, its commercial or social context, the extent to which the offeree's reliance was understood to be at his own risk, the relative competence and the bargaining position of the parties, the degree of fault on the part of the offeror, the ease and certainty of proof of particular items of damage and the likelihood that unprovable damages have been suffered.

In the sale of goods context, in the United States the traditional rule has been replaced by **3.56** section 2-205 of the Uniform Commercial Code which provides:

> **§ 2-205. Firm offers**
>
> An offer by a merchant to buy or sell goods in a signed record that by its terms gives assurance that it will be held open is not revocable, for lack of consideration, during the time stated or if no time is stated for a reasonable time, but in no event may such period of irrevocability exceed three months. Any such term of assurance in a form supplied by the offeree must be separately signed by the offeror.

A number of requirements must be satisfied before such an offer can be binding. Firstly, the **3.57** offer must make it clear that it will be held open, for example, 'This offer remains open for

---

[125] Comment *e* states that this provision applies § 90 (see 3.68) to 'reliance on an unaccepted offer, with qualifications which would not be appropriate in some other types of cases covered by § 90'. If the offeree engages in acts of performance, the relevant provisions are §§ 45 and 62 Restatement (2d) Contracts. The comment then goes on to state: 'But circumstances may be such that the offeree must undergo substantial expense, or undertake substantial commitments, or forego alternatives, in order to put himself in a position to accept by either promise or performance. The offer may be made expressly irrevocable in contemplation of reliance by the offeree. If reliance follows in such cases, justice may require a remedy.' See further 3.69.

[126] See Farnsworth, *Farnsworth on Contracts* (3rd edn, Vol I, Aspen Publishers, New York, 2004) § 3.25.

seven days' or 'This offer is irrevocable for seven days'.[127] If it does not do so, then the offer will be revocable. Secondly, the assurance must be contained 'in a signed record'; this authentication is the essence of the provision.[128] This is necessary to show that it is 'the deliberate intention of a merchant'[129] to make the firm offer binding. The offer itself must be signed or, at the very least, the clause containing the assurance must be signed.[130]

3.58   Since the section is only 'intended to apply to current "firm" offers and not to long term options',[131] a time limit of three months is placed on the irrevocability of the offer. Even if an offer states that it will be irrevocable for a period in excess of three months, the offeror will only be bound for the first three months and can revoke after this time unless the firm offer promise is supported by consideration.[132]

3.59   The last sentence raises another point namely if an offer is stated to be firm for six months, can it be accepted after the three-month period has elapsed if it is not revoked after that time or does the provision result in an automatic lapsing after that three-month period. Arguably if the offer has not been revoked, the offeree should have the power to accept the offer. However, if the offer does not expressly stipulate a period and three months have elapsed, it 'becomes a question of fact for the trier of fact to determine under all the circumstances whether more than a reasonable time since the making of the offer has elapsed so that the offer is to be deemed revoked by the lapse of time'.[133]

3.60   Finally, under this provision an offer need not state the day when it loses its effect or the period during which it is to have effect. If, for example, the offer states that it is firm 'until the happening of a contingency which will occur within the three-month period, it will remain irrevocable until that event'.[134]

3.61   Article 15(2) of the United Nations Convention on Contracts for the International Sale of Goods (1980) allows an offer, even if it is irrevocable, to be 'withdrawn if the withdrawal reaches the offeree before or at the same time as the offer'.[135] The concept of withdrawal is distinct from revocation; a right to revoke an offer is a right that operates after the offer has become effective by communication to the offeree while a withdrawal takes place prior to the offer becoming effective. Once the offer is received the right to revoke it is governed by Article 16. Article 16(1) generally allows for revocation prior to the contract being

---

[127] In *EA Coronis Associates v M Gordon Construction Co* 90 NJ Super 69, 216 A 2d 246 (1966) the court held that the words 'we are pleased to offer ...' with no further stipulation, did not give the assurance required by § 2-205.

[128] Official Comment 2.

[129] Official Comment 2.

[130] A broad approach to what constitutes authentication by way of signature is intended to be adopted by the provision, see Official Comment 2.

[131] Official Comment 3.

[132] Since an offer must be communicated to the offeree, the three-month period would appear to run 'from the date of communication of the offer to the offeree', Lawrence, *Lawrence's Anderson on the Uniform Commercial Code* (Thomson, West, Eagan, MN, 2004), § 2-205: 23.

[133] Lawrence, *Lawrence's Anderson on the Uniform Commercial Code* (Thomson, West, Eagan, MN, 2004), § 2-205: 22.

[134] Official Comment 3.

[135] See also Unidroit Principles of International Commercial Contracts (2004), Art 2.1.3(2).

'concluded', if the revocation 'reaches the offeree before he has dispatched an acceptance'.[136] The general rule under this Convention is that acceptance is effective when it reaches the offeror.[137] It follows that it is 'only when the offeree orally accepts the offer, or when the offeree may indicate assent by performing an act without giving notice to the offeror, that the offeror's right to revoke the offer continues to exist until such time as the contract is concluded'.[138] Article 16(2) then goes onto state:[139]

However, an offer cannot be revoked:

(a) if it indicates, whether by stating a fixed time for acceptance or otherwise, that it is irrevocable; or

(b) if it was reasonable for the offeree to rely on the offer as being irrevocable and the offeree has acted in reliance on the offer.[140]

It has been noted that this formulation may be read in a different sense by common law **3.62** lawyers and civil law lawyers.[141] A common law lawyer would understand that an offer might say that it was irrevocable and that the effect of Article 16(2) would be that such an offer could not be revoked even though there was no consideration for the promise not to revoke. However, such a lawyer would not, even in the context of the Vienna Convention, necessarily assume that the offer indicated an intention that it be irrevocable by the mere fact that the parties had stated a fixed time for acceptance. Instead, the common law lawyer might well assume that stating a fixed time simply indicated the maximum period for which the offer was open for the purpose of the rules concerning lapse of offers. A civil lawyer, on the other hand, would start from the assumption that all offers for a fixed time were irrevocable and would be likely to read Article 16(2)(a) as simply saying that offers might be made irrevocable otherwise than by stating a fixed time for acceptance.[142]

---

[136] See also Unidroit Principles of International Commercial Contracts (2004), Art 2.1.4(1).

[137] Article 18(2). See also Unidroit Principles of International Commercial Contracts (2004), Art 2.1.6(2).

[138] Unidroit Principles of International Commercial Contracts (2004), Art 2.1.4(1) Comment 1. This Comment goes on to state: 'Where, however, the offer is accepted by a written indication of assent, so that the contract is concluded when the acceptance reaches the offeror (see Art 2.1.6(2)), the offeror's right to revoke the offer terminates earlier, ie, when the offeree dispatches the acceptance. Such a solution may cause some inconvenience to the offeror who will not always know whether or not it is still possible to revoke the offer. It is, however, justified in view of the legitimate interest of the offeree in the time available for revocation being shortened. As to the determination of the time of dispatch, see Art 2.1.8'. See also Principles of European Contract Law, Art. 2:202(1), 'An offer may be revoked if the revocation reaches the offeree before it has dispatched its acceptance or, in cases of acceptance by conduct, before the contract has been concluded under Article 2:205(2) or (3)'. See also Draft Common Frame of Reference II-4:202(1).

[139] See Honnold, *Uniform Law For International Sales* (3rd edn, Kluwer Law International, The Netherlands, 1999) paras 139–151.

[140] See also Unidroit Principles of International Commercial Contracts (2004), Art 2.1.4(2). Compare Principles of European Contract Law, Art 2:202(3) which states that a revocation will be ineffective if the offer is by its terms irrevocable, or if it states a fixed time for acceptance or if 'it was reasonable for the offeree to rely on the offer as being irrevocable and the offeree has acted in reliance on the offer'. The Draft Common Frame of Reference, II-Art 4:202(3) is in the same terms.

[141] See Nicholas, 'The Vienna Convention on International Sales Law' (1989) 105 LQR 201, 213.

[142] This ambiguity was not the result of an oversight, at the Convention a United Kingdom amendment to clarify this article in accordance with the common law interpretation was rejected. A similar West German amendment to clarify the article in the civil law sense was also rejected.

Honnold suggests that these views can be accommodated by adopting the position that where a fixed time of acceptance is stated there is a presumption of irrevocability.[143]

3.63 The difficulty presented by Article 16(2)(b) is that of deciding exactly when it is reasonable for the offeree to rely on an offer as being irrevocable.[144] Article 2.4(2)(b) of the Unidroit Principles of International Commercial Contracts (2004) is in identical terms and the commentary states that the 'reasonable reliance of the offeree may have been induced either by the conduct of the offeror, or by the nature of the offer itself'.[145] The latter is exemplified by an offer that requires the offeree to undertake expensive and costly investigations before acceptance. Illustration 4 indicates the circumstances which are envisaged for the application of this Article:

> A seeks an offer from B for incorporation in a bid on a project to be assigned within a stated time. B submits an offer on which A relies when calculating the price of the bid. Before the expiry of the date, but after A has made the bid, B informs A that it is no longer willing to stand by its offer. B's offer is irrevocable until the stated date since in making its bid A relied on B's offer.

Estoppel and the protection of reliance

3.64 In the context of this chapter the legal concept of estoppel, when operable, prevents a person from going back on a representation—being a promise—they have made.[146] It is necessary for the representation to have been adopted by the other party with the result that they have suffered some detriment by reason of that reliance or will suffer some detriment if the person making the representation was allowed to retract it.[147] It follows that estoppel may be relevant in the unilateral contract context where the offeree has begun the act of acceptance but not yet completed it prior to the offeror communicating a revocation of the offer. Arguably this also evidences its limits in that it may protect the offeree in such a case but does not protect the offeror who may be disadvantaged as the offeree is not obliged to complete the act of acceptance.[148] However, if it is a requirement that the party making the

---

[143] Honnold, *Uniform Law For International Sales* (3rd edn, Kluwer Law International, The Netherlands, 1999) para 143.1. The commentary to the Unidroit Principles appears to accept that whether a fixed time set for acceptance will evidence that the offer is irrevocable will vary between legal systems, see also Unidroit Principles of International Commercial Contracts (2004), Art 2.1.4(2) Comment 2a.

[144] See Honnold, *Uniform Law For International Sales* (3rd edn, Kluwer Law International, The Netherlands, 1999) para 144.

[145] Article 2.1.4 Comment 2b.

[146] As to whether the word 'representation' should be used to include promise, see *Equititrust Ltd v Franks* (2009) 258 ALR 388, 401. The doctrine does not necessarily mean that the person making the statement can never retract it. Often an estoppel will operate to suspend the enforcement of existing contractual rights and require the person making the representation to give some reasonable notice that he or she intends to resile from the representation.

[147] See further *Thompson v Palmer* (1933) 49 CLR 507, 547 per Dixon J (estoppel prevents 'an unjust departure by one person from an assumption adopted by another as the basis of some act or omission which, unless the assumption be adhered to, would operate to that other's detriment').

[148] See also the comments of Yetka J in *Holman Erection Co v Orville E Madsen & Sons Inc*, 330 NW 2d 693, 698 (1983) (Yetka J's comments overstate the position as they assume both that a main contractor needs protection and that subcontractors routinely make bids to all potential main contractors). See also *Seacoast Electric Co Inc v Franchi Bros Construction Corp* 437 F 2d 1247 (1971).

representation is only estopped from resiling from it where it would be unconscionable to do so, then that party is also protected.

In England the doctrine of promissory estoppel is a limited one.[149] It applies where the **3.65** parties are in an existing legal relationship and operates as a defence, it generally cannot ground a cause of action.[150] For example, if a lessor under a lease were to promise that during a certain period of time or while certain conditions exist, only half the rent is payable and if the lessee relies on that statement in circumstances where it is inequitable for the lessor to resile from the statement—such as where the lessor knows of the reliance—then the lessor will be estopped from acting inconsistently with the promise. The estoppel can operate to suspend a legal right and prevent the enforcement of strict legal rights. Thus, the lessee, in the example given, will have a defence to a suit for the arrears of rent that accrued during the relevant period of time or during the period in which the condition subsists.[151] But the lessee could not sue the lessor for breach of the promise. Often, in the context of this chapter, it will not be necessary for estoppel to ground liability. If estoppel can be used to prevent a person revoking an offer so that the offeree has a chance of accepting it, then any liability would flow from the formed contract. However, the need for a pre-existing legal relationship is problematic. Moreover, arguably access to a broad remedial regime would be necessary if estoppel is to be used as the tool that provides justice in this. For example, there will be cases where the appropriate course will be to prevent the party revoking the offer but in others the appropriate course might be to make the party resiling from the promise liable for breach of an express or implied undertaking not to revoke.[152] In some cases justice might dictate that the offer remains revocable but the party revoking may have to pay a price for that revocation. It is also important to note that not all reliance will give rise to an estoppel especially if a party accepts the risk of revocation.[153] Finally, being an equitable doctrine, the party seeking to assert an estoppel must do equity and could not delay in its acceptance of the offer.

In other countries promissory estoppel has been used where the parties are not in a pre- **3.66** existing legal relationship and allows the court a discretion to fashion an appropriate remedy.[154] For example, in the decision of the High Court of Australia in *Waltons Stores (Interstate) Ltd v Maher*,[155] the parties were in negotiations for a lease by Waltons of property owned by the Mahers. This would require the Mahers demolishing an existing structure on the land and constructing a new building. Negotiations were well advanced and

---

[149] Furmston (ed), *The Law of Contract* (3rd edn, LexisNexis, Butterworths, London, 2007) para 2.124.
[150] *Combe v Combe* [1951] 2 KB 215, 224. See also *Baird Textiles Holdings Ltd v Marks & Spencer plc* [2002] 1 All ER (Comm) 737 and see *Cobbe v Yeoman's Row Management Ltd* [2008] 1 WLR 1752, 1786.
[151] *Central London Property Trust Ltd v High Trees House Ltd* [1947] KB 130. See also *Hughes v Metropolitan Railway Co* (1877) 2 App Cas 439, 448; *D & C Builders Ltd v Rees* [1966] 2 QB 617, 624.
[152] See Law Commission Working Paper No 60, *Firm Offers* (1975) paras 42–50.
[153] Waddams, *The Law of Contracts* (5th edn, Canada Law Book, Toronto, 2005) para 160.
[154] See further Spence, *Protecting Reliance: The Emergent Doctrine of Equitable Estoppel* (Hart Publishing, Oxford, 1999), 30–1.
[155] (1988) 164 CLR 387. Cf *Austotel Pty Ltd v Franklins Selfserve Pty Ltd* (1989) 16 NSWLR 582. See generally Carter, Peden and Tolhurst, *Contract Law in Australia* (5th edn, Butterworths, Sydney, 2007), Ch. 7. For a powerful criticism of the analysis in *Waltons Stores (Interstate) Ltd v Maher*, see Handley, 'The Three High Court Decisions on Estoppel 1988–1990' (2006) 80 ALJ 724.

Waltons' solicitors sent the Mahers a draft lease. Some alterations were discussed between the solicitors on either side. The Mahers also informed the solicitors for Waltons that they had commenced demolition, that in order to have the building completed on time it was necessary to finalize the lease in the next couple of days and they did not want to do any more demolition work unless they were sure a deal was in place. The solicitors sent the Mahers another lease incorporating the changes discussed and informing them that they did not yet have sign off from their client for those changes but thought it would be forthcoming and they would get back to them the next day if there was any problem. The Mahers signed the lease and sent it back by way of exchange. Nothing more was heard from Waltons and the Mahers continued to incur costs. Finally Waltons had a change of heart and ended negotiations. At this time the new building was 40 per cent complete. Clearly there was no contract between the parties but the Mahers were ultimately successful in their claim against Waltons who were estopped from resiling from the promise.

3.67 For the majority of the High Court, Waltons were estopped from denying that there was an implied promise to complete the contract. The majority grounded the action in unconscionable conduct. There had to be a representation and reasonable detrimental reliance but in addition there had to be unconscionable conduct on the part of the representor. This could be evidenced by showing that the party estopped encouraged the other party to adopt the assumption 'that a contract will come into existence or a promise will be performed and that the other party relied on that assumption to his detriment to the knowledge' of the party estopped.[156] The knowledge requirement may operate as a limitation in a tender situation where the subcontractor who wishes to revoke its bid will often not know whether its bid was the one relied upon by the head contractor in its tender. However, it may be noted that if these elements are made out then, for the majority, this does not result in the promise being enforceable as a contract, rather there arises an equity in favour of the plaintiff and the court will fashion a remedy to do the minimum equity.[157]

3.68 In the United States, the 'binding' nature of a promise based on reliance is recognized by section 90 of the Restatement (2d) Contracts.[158] This provision provides:

§ 90. Promise reasonably inducing action or forbearance

(1) A promise which the promisor should reasonably expect to induce action or forbearance on the part of the promisee or a third person and which does induce such action or forbearance is binding if injustice can be avoided only by enforcement of the promise. The remedy granted for breach may be limited as justice requires.

3.69 Although this section gives the court a discretion to fashion an appropriate remedy,[159] it clearly gives effect to the promise and this is based upon detrimental reasonable reliance.

---

[156] (1988) 164 CLR 387, 406.
[157] See generally Carter, Peden and Tolhurst, *Contract Law in Australia* (5th edn, Butterworths, Sydney 2007), paras 7.19–7.22.
[158] See generally, Henderson, 'Promissory Estoppel and Traditional Contract Doctrine' (1969) 78 Yale LJ 343; Knapp, 'Reliance in the Revised Restatement: The Proliferation of Promissory Estoppel' (1981) 81 Columbia L Rev 52; Farnsworth, *Farnsworth on Contracts* (3rd edn, Vol I, Aspen Publishers, New York, 2004) §§ 2.19, 3.25.
[159] The importance of this remedial flexibility was noted above, see 3.65.

This enforcement of the promise distinguishes this provision from the approach taken in *Waltons v Maher*. Perhaps the most famous case in the United States on promissory estoppel in the context of this chapter remains *Drennan v Star Paving Company*.[160] In this case the main contractor, Drennan, was preparing to bid for a particular contract and had received a subcontract bid of $7,131 for the paving work from Star Paving. Drennan used this bid in computing his own bid and even listed Star Paving as the paving subcontractor. Drennan was awarded the contract but was then told by the subcontractor that a mistake had been made in computing their bid and the bid should have been $15,000. Drennan found another subcontractor to do the paving work and sued Star Paving for $3,817, the difference between their bid and the price paid to the actual subcontractor. Star Paving contended that they had made a revocable offer and had revoked it before acceptance.[161]

Like the situation in *James Baird Co v Gimbel Bros*,[162] the offer was not intended to give rise **3.70** to a unilateral contract when the contractor used the bid to put in its tender. However, Traynor J concluded that when Star Paving made their bid, which was the lowest, they reasonably expected that, if it proved to be the lowest, it would be used by Drennan. Their promise did induce action or forbearance by Drennan, since Drennan relied on this bid in making his own bid and reasonable reliance justified implying a promise not to revoke the offer.[163] Since Star Paving had reason to foresee this action in reliance, the 'subsidiary promise not to revoke [was] supported by foreseeable and injurious reliance in lieu of consideration'.[164] In giving his decision Traynor J drew an analogy between these facts and the approach taken in the United States to revocations of offers in the unilateral contract context. Under section 45 of the Restatement (2d) Contracts, an offer made in exchange for an act is irrevocable once the offeree has commenced the act of acceptance or tenders all or part of the consideration.[165]

---

[160]   51 Cal 2d 409, 333 P 2d 757 (1958). See also *Norcross v Winters* 209 Cal App 2d 207, 25 Cal Rptr 821 (1962); *Loranger Construction Corp v EF Houserman Co* 6 Mass-App Ct 152, 374 NE 2d 306 (1978). See further, Closen and Weiland, 'The Construction Industry Bidding Cases: Application of Traditional Contract, Promissory Estoppel and Other Theories of the Relations between General Contractor and Subcontractors' (1980) 13 J Marshall L Rev 565 (in this article the authors trace the history of American courts using estoppel and contract formation principles to deal with situations that arise in the context of tenders. The authors note the rise of estoppel after the decision in *Drennan v Star Paving Company* and in more recent years the use of formation techniques).

[161]   At the time of this decision, § 90 was in a different form to what it is today. Under the Restatement of Contracts (1932), § 90 provided: 'A promise which the promisor should reasonably expect to induce action or forbearance of a definite and substantial character on the part of the promise and which does induce such action or forbearance is binding if injustice can be avoided only by enforcement of the promise.' The requirement that the action or forbearance be of a 'definite and substantial' character has been deleted. The last sentence of the current provision gives the court an express discretion in fashioning a remedy. Note also that the current provision applies to a third person relying on the promise.

[162]   64 F 2d 344 (1933). See above 3.32.

[163]   It should be noted that the estoppel prevented Star Paving from resiling from the promise not to revoke which then allowed the contract to be formed upon acceptance and the normal remedies for breach of contract to then follow.

[164]   Kessler and Fine, 'Culpa in Contrahendo, Bargaining in Good Faith, and Freedom of Contract: A Comparative Study' (1964) 77 Harv L Rev 401, 424. If a subcontractor wishes, it can, in theory, include an express provision governing its right to revoke the bid. It was important in *Drennan v Star Paving* that the bid was silent on this question of the right to revoke.

[165]   Traynor J noted that the then comment *b* stated that the main offer implies a promise not to revoke upon part of the performance being provided. See further 3.32.

3.71   As noted earlier, in *James Baird Co v Gimbel Bros*[166] the plaintiff had sought to rely on this doctrine to argue that the subcontractor's bid was binding because it had been relied upon. However, Judge Learned Hand held that the doctrine could not apply where the parties were bargaining and the offer sought a return promise. The decision in the *Drennan* case is therefore particularly significant since the court concluded that reliance based liability, equivalent to promissory estoppel, could be applied in what would be a bilateral contract had the contract come into existence.

3.72   It follows that even where a return promise is required to form a contract there can be reasonable reliance on the offer to ground an estoppel. Moreover, the fact there is a large discrepancy between the bids put in by different parties does not of itself suggest that the party making the lowest bid has made a mistake especially if such variance is common in the industry.[167] But there will be circumstances where a subcontractor's bid is so low that there will have obviously been a mistake made. In such a case the main contractor's reliance on that bid would not be reasonable.[168] On the other hand, if a subcontractor is asked to check the bid because there appears to be a mistake, and then affirms it, reliance may well be reasonable.[169]

3.73   The main difficulty in using reliance as the protecting principle in this context is establishing that the reliance actually occurred. Unless the main contractor names the subcontractor within its own bid it will be difficult to determine, on the face of the documents, whether there has been reliance. In addition, the particular practices of the main contractor may be relevant in determining whether it can be said that there has been reliance. Some main contractors will seek a range of subcontract bids in order to have an idea of the correct subcontract price but intend to argue for bid reductions thereafter. However, some main contractors make use of particular subcontractors as a matter of general practice.[170]

The two contract approach[171]

3.74   An approach which would give clear contractual remedies where one party sought to revoke an offer would be to have in place an initial contract that prevented revocation. This idea has been developed by the Canadian courts. For example, in *R v Ron Engineering & Construction Eastern Ltd*,[172] the respondent tendered for certain work and later found it had made an error in its pricing; it was not an error that was discoverable on the face of the document. It then approached the appellant asking if it could put in a new bid. It argued that it did not at any time seek to withdraw the bid because that would trigger a deposit forfeiture provision which the respondent had had to pay when it first put in the tender. Rather the respondent argued that once the appellant was aware of the mistake the tender

---

[166] 64 F 2d 344 (1933).

[167] *Norcross v Winters* 209 Cal App 207, 25 Cal Rptr 821 (1962).

[168] *Robert Gordon Inc v Ingersoll-Rand Co* 117 F 2d 654 (1941).

[169] *C & K Engineering Contractors v Amber Steel Co Inc* 23 Cal 3d 1, 587 P 2d 1136 (1978).

[170] Although the main contractor may not tell the employer which subcontractor will be used, the main contractor may nevertheless be relying on a particular subcontractor's figures.

[171] This section is only concerned with the issue of revocation, this 'two contract' approach to tenders is dealt with in more detail at 5.33.

[172] (1981) 119 DLR (3d) 267, [1981] 1 SCR 111.

became incapable of acceptance. The appellant did seek to accept the bid and sent the respondent a contract to sign. Upon the respondent refusing to execute the contract the appellant entered into a contract with a third party and forfeited the deposit pursuant to the tender terms and conditions. In this case the court was able to hold that the placing of the tender, which complied with the terms and conditions specified in the 'General Conditions' and 'Information for Tenderers', was the act of acceptance creating a unilateral contract[173] under which the respondent could not withdraw the tender without incurring the forfeiture of the deposit under the tender terms and conditions.[174] The result is dependent on the bid being expressly or impliedly intended to be irrevocable as this is the term enforced once there is acceptance.[175] The court called this contract, 'Contract A' to distinguish it from 'Contract B' which the parties would enter into if the appellant decided to accept the respondent's bid. Moreover, the mistake was not one that impacted on the efficacy of the tender or the unilateral contract that arose upon the submission of the tender.[176]

In doctrinal terms, this analysis relies on there being a call for irrevocable tenders which is itself an offer. That offer is accepted when a tender or bid is made in accordance with the terms of the call for tenders. At that point the tender becomes irrevocable as a matter of contract law. If the tender is accepted the parties are then obligated under a term of Contract A to enter into Contract B. It would appear that Contract A operates like an option under the irrevocable offer theory except for the contractual obligation to enter into Contract B which is binding on both parties.[177]   **3.75**

---

[173] For the view that this contract is best seen as bilateral as it creates executory obligations on both parties, see Henley, 'Significant Developments in the Canadian Law of Tenders' (1991) 18 Can Bus LJ 382, 392ff; Seddon, *Government Contracts, Federal, State and Local* (4th edn, Federation Press, Sydney, 2009) para [7.14].

[174] This decision has been the subject of much critical analysis, see eg Nozick, (1982) 60 Can Bar Rev 345; Henley, 'Significant Developments in the Canadian Law of Tenders' (1991) 18 Can Bus LJ 382, 387–8; Percy, 'Radical Developments in the Law of Tenders: a Canadian Reformulation of Common Law Principles' (1994) 10 Const LJ 171, 174; Seddon, *Government Contracts, Federal, State and Local* (4th edn, Federation Press, Sydney, 2009) paras [7.14], [7.24], [7.25].

[175] *R v Ron Engineering & Construction Eastern Ltd* (1981) 119 DLR (3d) 267, 275, [1981] 1 SCR 111, 122–3. Cf *Town of Slave Lake v Appleton Construction Ltd* (1987) 53 Alta LR (2d) 177 (1987) 25 CLR 311.

[176] See also *Gloge Heating & Plumbing Ltd v Northern Construction Co Ltd* [1986] 2 WWR 649, (1986) 27 DLR (4th) 265 (when the practice is one of putting in bids just before the deadline, the offeree has little time to analyse the bids and discover if there is a mistake on the face of the document). Cf *McMaster University v Wilchar Construction Ltd* [1971] 3 OR 801, (1972) 22 DLR (3d) 9 (affirmed (1973) 12 OR (2d) 512n, (1977) 69 DLR (3d) 400n) (here the entire first page of a tender was missing and this was held to be an obvious mistake on its face and therefore sufficient to avoid the tender on the basis of an operative unilateral mistake). See also *Calgary (City) v Northern Construction Co* (1985) 42 Alta LR (2d) 1, [1986] 2 WWR 426 (aff'd (1987) 56 Alta LR (2d) 193, [1988] 2 WWR 193) (the mistake may impact on the efficacy of Contract B, the contract arising upon acceptance of the bid; query whether this necessarily follows in a contractor/subcontractor situation if the correct analysis is that Contract B arises automatically upon acceptance of the bid for the head contract, see *Peddlesden (MJ) Ltd v Liddell Construction Ltd* (1981) 32 BCLR 392, (1981) 128 DLR (3d) 360).

[177] The analogy with an option has been drawn in other cases, see *Gloge Heating & Plumbing Ltd v Northern Construction Co Ltd* (1986) 27 DLR (4th) 265.

3.76   The *Ron Engineering* approach has been extended to the relationship between a main contractor and subcontractor in *Peddlesden (MJ) Ltd v Liddell Construction Ltd*.[178] The facts of
this case were that the defendant main contractor used the plaintiff subcontractor's bid
when submitting for a general contract and listed the plaintiff as one of the subcontractors
it intended to use. The owners awarded the general contract to the defendant and the
defendant advised the plaintiff that it was awarded the subcontract. Later when becoming
aware that the plaintiff's 'bid bond' was not in order the defendant took the view that the
plaintiff's bid was therefore invalid and entered into a subcontract with a third party for the
work. The plaintiff subcontractor sued for damages for breach of contract and was
successful.

3.77   The court held that the fault in the bid bond was not fatal as it could be rectified and applying the principle under *Ron's* case, concluded that a unilateral contract came into effect
which bound the plaintiff when it sent in its bid and bound the defendant when it adopted
that bid as part of its tender subject to the acceptance of the defendant's tender for the
general contract.[179] They went on to hold that the acceptance of the tender for the general
contract automatically created Contract B between the plaintiff and defendant without the
defendant having to communicate that acceptance; this assumes the terms of contract B are
sufficiently certain.[180] Difficulties would arise using this reasoning where the bid is used by
the main contractor to formulate its tender but the subcontractor is not named as the
intended subcontractor.[181]

---

[178] (1981) 32 BCLR 392, (1981) 128 DLR (3d) 360. Cf *Calgary (City) v Northern Construction Co* (1985)
42 Alta LR (2d) 1, [1986] 2 WWR 426 (aff'd (1987) 56 Alta LR (2d) 193, [1988] 2 WWR 193). See also
Norcross v Winters 209 Cal App 2d 207, 25 Cal Rptr 821 (1962) (use by contractor of subcontractor's bid does
not operate as an acceptance of the subcontractor's bid giving rise to a contract between the parties, but it does
render the subcontractor's bid irrevocable).

[179] See also *Megatech Contracting Ltd v Ottawa-Carlton (Regional Municipality)* (1979) 68 OR (2d) 503.
See further Henley, 'Significant Developments in the Canadian Law of Tenders' (1991) 18 Can Bus LJ 382,
390ff. Of course it is possible to derive a contract out of the *use* of a bid with the bidder making the offer. See
Henley, 'Significant Developments in the Canadian Law of Tenders' (1991) 18 Can Bus LJ 382, 398ff; Closen
and Weiland, 'The Construction Industry Bidding Cases: Application of Traditional Contract, Promissory
Estoppel and Other Theories of the Relations between General Contractor and Subcontractors' (1980) 13
J Marshall L Rev 565, 597ff. See further Stoljar, 'The False Distinction between Bilateral and Unilateral
Contracts' (1955) 64 Yale LJ 515, 533, who in the context of discussing firm offers suggests that the firm offer
problem is 'wholly artificial' since it is based on the false assumption that the offeree (main contractor) cannot
accept the subcontractor's bid which in turn is underpinned by the view that contracts have to be bilateral
or unilateral. He suggests that a conditional acceptance could occur (that is, conditional on the award of the
contract to the main contractor). In his view there is no need to establish a separate branch of 'firm offer law',
since once the main contractor has 'used' the subcontractor's bid it would have accepted the offer and would
be liable to the subcontractor. Once reliance had occurred the subcontractor would also be liable on the
bid, whether firm or not. However, the obvious difficulty here seems to be the recurring problem of actually
establishing that reliance when the subcontractor is not named in the main contractor's bid.

[180] See also *Dave's Plumbing & Heating (1962) Ltd v Voth Brother's Construction (1974) Ltd* (1986) 21
CLR 276. See further *Moncton Plumbing & Supply Co Ltd v Brunswick Construction Ltd* (1983) 52 NBR (2d)
309.

[181] See generally Henley, 'Significant Developments in the Canadian Law of Tenders' (1991) 18 Can Bus
LJ 382, 393ff.

Finally, it should be noted that this 'unilateral contract' when created may give rise to bilat-   **3.78**
eral obligations.[182] The tenderer may not be able to now revoke its tender but depending
on the term of the call for tenders there may be obligations imposed on the party calling for
tenders. In particular this analysis allows for the creation of a 'process contract' under which
the party calling for tenders may have an express or implied obligation to properly consider
the tender submitted.[183]

Modification of the rules applying to unilateral contracts

It can be seen from the above discussion that the rule that an offer can be revoked any time   **3.79**
prior to the completion of the act of acceptance can cause hardship for an offeree who has
commenced performance and who is capable of completing performance. But should that
attract some legal modification of the rule so as to allow a contract law remedy or is it a risk
the offeree must accept unless some other area of law provides a remedy.[184] Not all commentators agree that such an offeree deserves protection, rather the proper focus is to look
at the nature of the contract in question and in the case of a unilateral contract arguably the
offeror should be entitled to receive the performance requested.[185] The offeror does not in
any way give up his or her right to revoke the offer at will and this is matched by the offeree
who can, at any time, stop the act of performance and prevent the contract coming into
effect.[186] An offeror may take a risk and act on the basis that a contract will come into existence when the offeree commences the act of performance in the same way that the offeree
takes the risk that the offeror will not revoke the offer once he or she has commenced the
act of performance.[187] Similarly, in *Mobil Oil Australia Ltd v Lyndel Nominees Pty Ltd*,[188]
the Full Federal Court of Australia in rejecting the view that 'it is universally unjust that an
offeror be at liberty to revoke once the offeree has "commenced" or "embarked upon"
performance',[189] identified the following factors as reasons for rejecting such a universal
position:[190]

> (i) The offeror may or may not know that the offeree has commenced performance;
> (ii) The offeree may or may not have an understanding that the offeror is at liberty to
> revoke and that any incomplete performance of the act of acceptance by the offeree
> will be at his or her risk;

---

[182] This may call into question the 'unilateral contract' analysis of this approach but similar results flow in
the case of an exercise of an option, see above n 173.

[183] *Hughes Aircraft Systems International v Airservices Australia* (1997) 146 ALR 1. See also Seddon and
Ellinghaus, *Cheshire and Fifoot's Law of Contract* (9th Australian edn, LexisNexis Butterworths, Sydney,
2008) para 3.35 and Seddon, *Government Contracts, Federal, State and Local* (4th edn, Federation Press,
Sydney, 2009) paras [1.10], [7.15]. See further 5.32.

[184] See Atiyah, 'Consideration: A Restatement' in *Essays on Contract* (OUP, Oxford, 1986) 205–6
(suggesting that the offeree in the commercial sphere is more likely to be taken as having accepted the risk that
the offeror may change its mind than the offeree in a domestic situation).

[185] Wormser, 'The True Conception of Unilateral Contracts' (1916) 26 Yale LJ 136.

[186] Wormser, 'The True Conception of Unilateral Contracts' (1916) 26 Yale LJ 136, 138.

[187] Wormser later altered his view to that in § 45 of the Restatement (2d) Contracts, see (1950) 3 J Legal
Ed 145,146. § 45 is discussed at 3.97.

[188] (1998) 153 ALR 198.

[189] (1998) 153 ALR 198, 224.

[190] (1998) 153 ALR 198, 224.

(iii) The notion of 'commencement of performance of the act of acceptance' or 'embarking upon the act of acceptance' is problematical and can lead to a result which is unjust to the offeror ...

(iv) The act called for by the offer may be detrimental to the offeree, or of some benefit to the offeree as well as to the offeror, as in the present case;

(v) Although the offeree is not obliged to perform, or to continue performing, the act of acceptance and is at liberty to cease performing at any time, *ex hypothesi*, the offeror remains bound, perhaps over a lengthy period as in the present case, to keep its offer open for completion of the act of acceptance, without knowing whether the offeree will choose to complete or not to complete that act;

(vi) The circumstances of the particular case may or may not, by reference to conventional criteria, suggest that the parties intended that the offeror should not be at liberty to revoke once the offeree had performed the act of acceptance to some extent.

3.80   On the other hand, Ballantine has stated:[191]

> It is true that an offer must be accepted according to its terms. But if the offeree assents to the offer and begins performance on the faith of it, we have all the essential elements of contractual obligation. It is true that the offeree assumes no obligation by beginning to perform. He may unquestionably stop performance half-way without liability, unless, indeed, he has induced the other party to change his position in reliance on his undertaking. But because completion of performance is still optional with the offeree it does not follow that the proposer may not be bound. He has not yet, it is true, actually received the full consideration requested. But that is always true of executory consideration in bilateral contracts ... It is sufficient 'consideration' or ground of enforcement of the defendant's promise that he has invited action by the offeree in reliance on the offer.

3.81   Ballantine considered that, where it would take time to complete the act called for, good faith and common honesty required that the proposal should become binding when performance was begun.[192] The doctrinal difficulty with this reasoning is that it does not distinguish between consideration in the formation of contract sense with consideration in the performance sense when applied to a restitutionary claim based on failure of consideration. In bilateral contracts the offeror has received the consideration he or she requested for the purpose of formation by being given the counter-promise by the offeree. That is not so in the case of a unilateral contract where the offeror, in order to protect him or herself from non-performance by the other party, does not request a counter-promise for the purposes of formation but rather the full performance of that promise. Moreover it neglects to consider the position of the offeror where two or more offerees may be competing for the contract and both commence performance. Is the offeror bound to put them on notice of each other?

3.82   By contrast Stoljar has argued that the harsh results and theoretical difficulties in this area 'stem solely from the intrinsic falsity of the unilateral-bilateral distinction'.[193] In his view

---

[191] Ballantine, 'Acceptance of Offers for Unilateral Contracts by Partial Performance of Service Requested' (1921) 5 Min Law Rev 94, 96–7.

[192] Ballantine, 'Acceptance of Offers for Unilateral Contracts by Partial Performance of Service Requested' (1921) 5 Min Law Rev 94, 97.

[193] Stoljar, 'The False Distinction between Bilateral and Unilateral Contracts' (1955) 64 Yale LJ 515, 518. See further n 179 above.

the true reason for contractual enforcement lies not in consideration but in the protection of expectation and reliance interests. In a bilateral contract the law protects the parties' expectations in advance of complete performance and in his view the law should accept the enforcement of 'reliance bargains' in the unilateral context.[194] Stoljar considered that the perceived need for complete performance to constitute acceptance in a unilateral contract context leads 'to serious error' since the interest then being protected is an interest in restitution rather than reliance.[195] This, he argued, confuses formation with fulfilment, obscures the real issue of enforcement of 'future bargains' and 'transforms into a virtual promise of a gift what is in fact a bargain-promise which causes the promisee to begin the performance of his exchange'.[196] He suggested the concern of formation is with the way 'enforceable bargains may be made *before* either party has rendered complete performance'.[197] Stoljar therefore concluded that reliance on the unilateral promise should constitute acceptance if the offer is designed to produce reliance so that reliance is justified. Thus, upon such reliance the promise becomes irrevocable so that 'we need none of the troublesome special doctrines which have been created to enforce part-performed unilateral contracts'.[198] Treitel has also suggested 'that acceptance is no more (or less) than an unqualified expression of assent to the terms of the offer by words or conduct; and that the question whether an inference of such assent can be drawn from part-performance is simply one of fact'.[199] Perhaps underpinning these ideas is the notion that unless the offer very clearly states that only acceptance by conduct will suffice, then acceptance can be either by way of promise or performance and in many cases the commencement of performance will imply a promise thus giving rise to a bilateral contract.[200]

If we put to one side the views that suggest there is no need to change the law to overcome **3.83** the harsh results that may occur in the unilateral contract context—there is only a need to better understand it—then if the law is to be changed, the most likely way in which this would be done would be to vary the revocation rule and prevent the offeror from revoking the offer once the offeree has commenced performance. Whether or not such a change necessarily means that part-performance under the law constitutes 'acceptance' is debatable. However, clearly complete performance would be required in order to call for the performance of the other party's promise.[201] This approach does find support in statements made in a number of cases. However, in each case the criticism that has been made of these statements is that unlike Stoljar's argument, the judges making them do not define the juristic

---

[194] Stoljar, 'The False Distinction between Bilateral and Unilateral Contracts' (1955) 64 Yale LJ 515, 519.

[195] Stoljar, 'The False Distinction between Bilateral and Unilateral Contracts' (1955) 64 Yale LJ 515, 520–21.

[196] Stoljar, 'The False Distinction between Bilateral and Unilateral Contracts' (1955) 64 Yale LJ 515, 535.

[197] Stoljar, 'The False Distinction between Bilateral and Unilateral Contracts' (1955) 64 Yale LJ 515, 521.

[198] Stoljar, 'The False Distinction between Bilateral and Unilateral Contracts' (1955) 64 Yale LJ 515, 525.

[199] Peel, *Treitel, The Law of Contract* (12th edn, Sweet & Maxwell, London, 2007) para 2.053. See also paras 2.054, 2.055, 2.056 discussing continuing guarantees, irrevocable letters of credit and estate agents' contracts.

[200] This preference for allowing formation by counter-promise is reflected in the Restatement (2d) Contracts §§ 30 and 32.

[201] See Peel, *Treitel, The Law of Contract* (12th edn, Sweet & Maxwell, London, 2007) para 2.053; Atiyah, 'Consideration: A Restatement' in *Essays on Contract* (OUP, Oxford, 1986), 199, 200.

basis for these statements.[202] The starting point is the Australian case of *Abbot v Lance*.[203] Lance owned certain rural properties and communicated to Abbott that he was willing to sell them for a certain price and on certain terms. Abbott wished to inspect the properties before offering to buy them and this would involve travel over a two-month period. It was agreed between the parties that if Abbott made an offer at the stated price and on the stated terms within this period then Lance would pay Abbott £100 as a 'forfeit' if he had sold the property to a third party in the meantime. The agreement also stated that if the properties were not sold and Abbott made an offer on the agreed price and terms then Lance bound himself to sell the property to Abbott at that price and on those terms. When Abbott was on his way to visit the properties he received a communication from Lance that they had been sold. Upon receipt of this communication Abbott returned home and made no offer to purchase the property. The court then had to decide whether he was entitled to the £100. The court held that he was entitled. It did not matter that he had not made an offer—which was a condition of the agreement—as Lance's conduct in selling the property rendered the act of making an offer useless. In giving its reasons for the result the court stated:[204]

> The agreement is certainly somewhat obscure ... But is appears to us in substance to be an agreement by the defendant to keep the offer open two months, if the plaintiff will go and inspect the stations, to sell them at the price named within that time, unless previously sold, in which case £100 is to be paid ...

3.84 The difficulty with this reasoning is that the first paragraph appears to set up two different types of contract, one akin to an option based on an irrevocable offer and the other an option based on a conditional contract. However, this arrangement could not be an option as the vendor retained full power to sell the properties.

3.85 McPherson J in *Vievers v Cordingly*,[205] in supporting a rule that prevents revocation once performance has begun, explained *Abbott v Lance* in the following terms:[206]

> the decision in *Abbott v Lance* is authority for propositions that, although as a general rule an offer may be retracted before acceptance, yet, if it takes the form of an offer in exchange for the doing of an act or acts, then: (1) acceptance takes place when the offeree 'elects' to do the relevant act or acts; and (2) the offer becomes irrevocable once the act or acts, which will constitute consideration for the offer, have been partly performed.

3.86 This explanation was doubted by the Full Federal Court in *Mobil Oil Australia Ltd v Lyndel Nominees Pty Ltd*.[207] As already noted the court here, for the reasons set out above, rejected the notion that there should be a strict rule that prevented revocation of an offer once the act of performance had begun. Of *Abbott v Lance* the court said:

> The decision itself can be supported if the contract is conceived of as a promise to pay £100 as compensation for the plaintiff's having embarked upon his inspection trip and been

[202] *Mobil Oil Australia Ltd v Lyndel Nominees Pty Ltd* (1998) 153 ALR 198, 225–8.
[203] *Abbott v Lance* (1860) 2 Legge 1283. See also *Aldwell v Bundey* (1876) 10 SALR 118, 128.
[204] *Abbott v Lance* (1860) 2 Legge 1283, 1284–5.
[205] *Veivers v Cordingley* [1989] 2 Qd R 278.
[206] *Veivers v Cordingley* [1989] 2 Qd R 278, 297–8 per McPherson J (with whom Andrews CJ and Demack J agreed). See also *Mobil Oil Australia Ltd v Lyndel Nominees Pty Ltd* (1998) 153 ALR 198, 225–6.
[207] (1998) 153 ALR 198.

62

deprived of the opportunity of making a *bona fide* offer within two months by the defendant's having previously sold to another. This view ignores the reference to a *bona fide* offer, but apparently this is exactly what their Honours did: they accepted that once the defendant had sold, he had made it impossible for the plaintiff to make a *bona fide* offer. It should be noted that the contract expressly reserved to the defendant the liberty to sell to another party subject to his paying £100 to the plaintiff.

In substance, the contract in *Abbott v Lance* was simply a promise to pay £100 as compensation for the plaintiff's time, trouble and expense in undertaking the inspection trip if the defendant should cause them to be wasted by selling to someone else, upon a condition that they would only be taken to have been wasted if the sale by the defendant occurred within two months and could be seen to have prevented the plaintiff from making, within that period, a *bona fide* offer to purchase.

The view of the case which we have advanced is consistent with the final, if characteristically tantalising, paragraph of the report.

This is clearly the best explanation of the result in *Abbot v Lance* in doctrinal terms even if **3.87** it necessarily puts aside the important aspects of the reasoning of the court in *Abbott v Lance*. However, it sidelines *Abbot v Lance* as an authority for a discrete rule modifying the revocation rule.[208]

The next relevant statement was made by Denning LJ in *Errington v Errington and Woods*.[209] **3.88** This case concerned a promise by a father to his son and daughter-in-law that if they continued occupying the subject property which was owned by the father and paid all the mortgage instalments on the house until the loan was repaid then he would transfer the property to them. The son and daughter-in-law did this until the father died. The father left all his property to his widow. The son and daughter-in-law then separated with the son going to live with his now widowed mother. The daughter-in-law stayed in the property and continued to make repayments. The widow unsuccessfully sought possession of the property. It was held that the son and daughter-in-law had a licence to occupy the property so long as they kept paying the instalments. The issue of whether they would have a right to a conveyance of the property once all instalments were paid was not before the court. He gave no analysis as to how he reached that conclusion. On the facts this is an overwhelmingly desirable result. In his reasoning Denning LJ (with whom Somervell LJ agreed) while recognizing that the son and daughter-in-law were not bound to pay the instalments nevertheless considered that the father could not revoke the offer once the couple 'entered on performance of the act'.[210]

---

[208] It must be accepted that *Abbott v Lance* is not strong authority for advocating a new rule because in the final paragraph of the judgment (*Abbott v Lance* (1860) 2 Legge 1283, 1285), the court stated: 'The present case does not affect the general proposition that an offer may be retracted before acceptance, because we consider that the part-performance of the journey constituted a sufficient consideration to give the plaintiff a right in the events that have happened.'

[209] [1952] 1 KB 290. See also *Ward v Byham* [1956] 1 WLR 496, 498; *Beaton v McDivitt* (1988) 13 NSWLR 162, 175 per Mahoney JA, 183–4 per McHugh JA.

[210] [1952] 1 KB 290, 295.

3.89 In *Daulia Ltd v Four Millbank Nominees Ltd*,[211] the plaintiffs, prospective purchasers of property, were told by the defendants that if they attended at the defendants' offices at 10 a.m. on the following day with a banker's draft for the deposit and their part of the contract engrossed and signed, the defendants would exchange contracts. When the plaintiffs duly complied and tendered the requested documents, the defendants refused to proceed. The Court of Appeal held, on the facts, that the act requested had been completed before the attempted revocation and therefore the offer had been accepted.[212] However, Goff LJ in *obiter* stated:[213]

> Whilst I think the true view of a unilateral contract must in general be that the offeror is entitled to require full performance of the condition which he has imposed and short of that he is not bound, that must be subject to one important qualification, which stems from the fact that there must be an implied obligation on the part of the offeror not to prevent the condition becoming satisfied, which obligation it seems to me must arise as soon as the offeree starts to perform. Until then the offeror can revoke the whole thing, but once the offeree has embarked on performance it is too late for the offeror to revoke his offer.

3.90 What these cases suggest is that there is some dissatisfaction with the rule in certain circumstances but that the courts are unlikely to 'fix' those circumstances with a complete overhaul of contract formation and the doctrine of consideration that was suggested by Stoljar.[214]

3.91 A way forward that might be more attractive to a court is the development of the idea of a side contract. As a matter of contract doctrine if the facts evidence an offer under a side contract not to revoke which is accepted upon the offeree commencing the act of acceptance under the main contract, then that side contract can be given effect to.[215] Arguably this method merely gives the offeree a right to damages if the offer is revoked,[216] but perhaps like options, if the court finds such a contract exists then even if it is in the form of an irrevocable offer, the court will hold the promisor to its promise.[217]

3.92 This approach has already been discussed above in the sections dealing with 'estoppel' and 'the two contract approach'. It remains to consider though whether it is likely to be used in England and whether its use would be widespread. It has been the subject of some criticism. Stoljar thought that this theory failed to state the basis for implying any subsidiary promise and failed to explain how the promisee 'accepts' the offer.[218] Corbin[219] stated that in many cases the notion that there was a term to keep the offer open would be a 'fiction' used to give

---

[211] [1978] 1 Ch 231. See also *Dickson Trading (S) Pte Ltd v Transmarco Ltd* [1989] 2 MLJ 408, 414.

[212] However, there was not a sufficient note or memorandum so the contract was not enforceable; there were also insufficient acts of part performance to overcome the writing requirement. Cf *Petterson v Pattberg* 248 NY 86, 161 NE 428 (1928).

[213] [1978] 1 Ch 231, 239.

[214] See 3.82.

[215] See McGovney, 'Irrevocable Offers' (1914) 27 Harv L Rev 644. See also Murdoch, 'The Nature of Estate Agency' (1975) 91 LQR 357.

[216] *Mobil Oil Australia Ltd v Lyndel Nominees Pty Ltd* (1998) 153 ALR 198, 224, 228.

[217] See 3.42.

[218] Stoljar, 'The False Distinction between Bilateral and Unilateral Contracts' (1955) 64 Yale LJ 515, 523n.

[219] Corbin, 'Offer and Acceptance, and Some of the Resulting Legal Relations' (1917) 26 Yale LJ 169.

effect to some policy consideration.[220] He thought that this fiction ought to be discarded and that it should simply be accepted that 'such offer shall be irrevocable after the offeree has begun the performance of the requested acts, unless the offeror expressly reserved the power of revocation'.[221] Corbin had no difficulty in accepting the idea that the offeror should be prevented from revoking, whereas the offeree could discontinue at any time, since the offeror did not bear a risk. The offeror was not bound to pay unless the act was fully completed. The offeree, on the other hand, did bear a risk in that it might later be discovered that performance was too expensive or too difficult.[222] In Corbin's view it was fair that the party bearing the risk should possess the privilege of revoking, whereas the party who did not bear any risk was deprived of that privilege.[223] Ballantine regarded this solution as 'needlessly complex and artificial'.[224] Treitel too has described it as 'artificial', and like Ballantine has suggested that it is 'more realistic to say that the principal offer itself is accepted by beginning to perform'.[225] In a different paragraph Treitel provides an example which shows why it may be necessary to bind both parties at an early stage and not leave the offeree with the way out that the 'promise not to revoke contract' provides. He states:[226]

> The distinction between the two types of contract [unilateral and bilateral] sometimes gives rise to difficulty, because a contract may be in its inception unilateral, but become bilateral in the course of its performance. For example, A may promise to pay B £1,000 for some service (such as repainting A's house) which B does not promise to render. Here B would not be liable if he did nothing; but once he began the work (eg by stripping off the old paint) he might be held to have impliedly promised to complete it, so that at this stage the contract would become bilateral and both parties would be bound by it.

If a contract containing a promise not to revoke is to be given effect to then that term must be incorporated using general principles. Arguably the implication of a promise not to revoke by either party in certain circumstances could be said to be necessary for business efficacy. But arguably what is occurring here is the implication of an offer which will give rise to a contract containing such a term and not merely the implication of a term into an existing contract.[227] Despite this, there is no doubt that a statement can contain more than one offer each to be accepted in different ways.[228] If that can be done expressly then it can

3.93

---

[220] Corbin, 'Offer and Acceptance, and Some of the Resulting Legal Relations' (1917) 26 Yale LJ 169, 195.

[221] Corbin, 'Offer and Acceptance, and Some of the Resulting Legal Relations' (1917) 26 Yale LJ 169, 195. He added (at 196): 'To this rule there should be added some such as the following: If the continuation of performance will increase the amount of the offeree's claim, the revocation shall be effective; in such case if the offeree can show with reasonable certainty that he would have performed in full, he shall be entitled to the same damages as if the contract had been a bilateral contract in the beginning.'

[222] Corbin, 'Offer and Acceptance, and Some of the Resulting Legal Relations' (1917) 26 Yale LJ 169, 196.

[223] Corbin, 'Offer and Acceptance, and Some of the Resulting Legal Relations' (1917) 26 Yale LJ 169 at 197.

[224] Ballantine, 'Acceptance of Offers for Unilateral Contracts by Partial Performance of Service Requested' (1921) 5 Min Law Rev 94, 97. His preferred approach is set out above, see 3.80–3.81

[225] Peel, *Treitel, The Law of Contract* (12th edn, Sweet & Maxwell, London, 2007) para 2.053. See above 3.82.

[226] Peel, *Treitel, The Law of Contract* (12th edn, Sweet & Maxwell, London, 2007) para 2.050.

[227] See further 11.119ff.

[228] See *Warlow v Harrison* (1858) 1 El & El 299, 120 ER 920; *Barry v Davies* [2000] 1 WLR 1962. Similarly an invitation calling for offers may itself contain an offer, for example, a call for tenders may state that the party making the call will bind itself to accept the highest tender, cf the analysis of Lord Diplock

be done impliedly. However, there would need to be found an intention on the part of the offeror to make the subject promise and that would depend on the facts of each individual case. Any alternative result would depend on the courts adopting the view that necessity required an implication at law that in the case of offers in the unilateral contract context there is a promise not to revoke which is accepted upon commencement of acceptance. But implication at law is generally used to imply a term into a certain class of contract and not to imply a term into every contract formed on a unilateral basis. The alternative, which would be to create a principle of contract law that such offers cannot be revoked once performance has begun, would constitute an infringement into the freedom not to contract and would need to be carefully explained in terms of policy.

3.94 The widespread use of the implied term approach seems to have been dismissed by the House of Lords in *Luxor (Eastbourne) Ltd v Cooper*.[229] The case concerned an offer to pay an agent a commission 'on the completion of the sale'. The House of Lords held that the offeror could revoke at any time prior to that event taking place despite the fact that the agent had sought out purchasers who were prepared to buy. The agent argued that he was entitled to damages of the commission amount because the offeror had broken an implied term that the offeror undertook not to do anything to prevent the agent earning his commission. The breach was in not concluding a sale with the purchaser introduced by the agent. In essence the agent was alleging that there was an implied term not to revoke the offer. However, the House of Lords refused to imply any such undertaking on these facts and expressed serious doubt as whether such a term could ever satisfy the business efficacy test for implication in fact involving, as it would, a vendor giving up all its freedom of choice.[230] Moreover, it was thought that such a term could not be implied in law into this type of commission agent's contract. Arguably in such circumstances the agent accepts the risk that the vendor may change his or her mind. However, in a case like *Errington v Errington and Woods*,[231] the risk that the father would change his mind is unacceptable.

---

in *Harvela Investments Ltd v Royal Trust Co of Canada (CI) Ltd* [1986] AC 207, 224 and see Diplock LJ's analysis in *United Dominions Trust (Commercial) Ltd v Eagle Aircraft Services Ltd* [1968] 1 WLR 74, 83–4. See also Tiersma, 'Reassessing Unilateral Contracts: The Role of Offer, Acceptance and Promise' (1992) 26 UC Davis L Rev 1. See further *Dickson Trading (S) Pty Ltd v Transmarco Ltd* [1989] 2 Malayan Law Journal 408. Similarly a call for tenders might contain an offer to properly consider each bid. This is termed a 'process contract'. The existence of such a contract depends on the facts of the case, see *Hughes Aircraft Systems International v Airservices Australia* (1997) 146 ALR 1; *Macquarie Generation v CNA Resources Ltd* [2001] NSWSC 1040; *State Transit Authority of NSW v Australian Jockey Club* [2003] NSWSC 726; *Dockpride Pty Ltd v Subiaco Redevelopment Authority* [2005] WASC 211; *Pratt Contractors Ltd v Transit New Zealand* [2005] 2 NZLR 433; *St George Football Club Inc v Soccer NSW Ltd* [2005] NSWCA 481. Such contracts are discussed in detail at 5.25.

[229] [1941] AC 108. See also *Snider v Wallis* (1960) 24 DLR (2d) 214; *Summergreene v Parker* (1950) 80 CLR 304, 322, 325. Cf *Baumgartner v Meek* 126 Cal App 2d 505, 272 P 2d 552, 554 (1954). See further *Christie, Owen & Davies Ltd v Rapacioli* [1974] QB 781. Ultimately when a commission is payable is dependent on the terms of the subject contract, see Reynolds, *Bowstead and Reynolds on Agency* (18th edn, Sweet & Maxwell, London, 2006) para 7.013ff.

[230] Atiyah considers the decision in *Luxor* to be the orthodox and prevailing authority on the question of revocation of a unilateral offer and to have been decided on the basis of considerations of justice on the facts of the case rather than consideration and that in the right circumstances (he gives the example of *Errington v Errington* [1952] 1 KB 290) such a promise could be implied, see Atiyah, 'Consideration: A Restatement' in *Essays on Contract* (OUP, Oxford, 1986), 200, 204–6.

[231] See 3.88.

Farnsworth[232] suggests two further construction devices which might be used, although **3.95** both are dependent upon the facts of each individual case. First, the offer might be interpreted as seeking a promise to carry out an act and, moreover, a promise to do that act might be inferred when the offeree commences the act of acceptance.[233] The decision in *Davis v Jacoby*[234] is an example. Here an offer had been made by an uncle requesting that a niece and her husband move house and look after the uncle's affairs and help care for his sick wife and asking, 'Will you let me hear from you as soon as possible?' The niece and husband did so respond. However, during transit to the uncle's home, the uncle committed suicide. Nevertheless, the niece and nephew took care of his affairs and cared for his wife until she died. It was argued that this was a unilateral contract that could not be accepted after the death of the uncle. The Supreme Court of California interpreted this as an offer requesting a promise in return and therefore giving rise to a bilateral contract which the niece and her husband had fully performed. As such, the offer was accepted by the letter sent in response agreeing to these terms.

Second, Farnsworth makes the point that it is also possible to interpret an offer as seeking **3.96** a series of acceptances by performance and therefore as constituting a number of unilateral contracts. This is the traditional standing offer. Farnsworth gives the following illustration: 'If, for example, A had said to B, "I will give you $100 for each time that you walk across the Brooklyn Bridge up to a maximum of $1,000".'[235]

Finally, mention must be made of the contractual approach adopted under section 45 of **3.97** the Restatement (2d) Contracts, which seeks to protect offerees who have begun performance of a requested act by means of an option contract device.[236]

§ 45 Option contract created by Part Performance or Tender[237]

(1) Where an offer invites an offeree to accept by rendering a performance and does not invite a promissory acceptance, an option contract is created when the offeree tenders or begins the invited performance or tenders a beginning of it.[238]

---

[232] Farnsworth, *Farnsworth on Contracts* (3rd edn, Vol I, Aspen Publishers, New York, 2004) § 3.24, p 356. Cf Ballantine, 'Acceptance of Offers for Unilateral Contracts by Partial Performance of Service Requested' (1921) 5 Min Law Rev 94, 96.

[233] This was referred to above at 3.82. See also *Dawson v Helicopter Exploration Co Ltd* [1955] 5 DLR 404.

[234] 1 Cal 2d 370, 34 P 2d 1026 (1934).

[235] Farnsworth, *Farnsworth on Contracts* (3rd edn, Vol I, Aspen Publishers, New York, 2004) § 3.24, p 357.

[236] See Farnsworth, *Farnsworth on Contracts* (3rd edn, Vol I, Aspen Publishers, New York, 2004) § 3.24.

[237] Reference here should also be made to § 62 which deals with the situation where the offer requires the offeree to choose between acceptance by promise and acceptance by performance. It states:

Effect of Performance by Offeree Where Offer Invites Either Performance or Promise

(1) Where an offer invites an offeree to chose between acceptance by promise and acceptance by performance, the tender or beginning of the invited performance or a tender of a beginning of it is an acceptance by performance.

(2) Such an acceptance operates as a promise to render complete performance.

Note that under this section the offeree undertakes to complete performance whereas under § 45 the offeree is under no such obligation. Note also that under § 32 in cases of doubt offers are interpreted as inviting either a return promise or an act.

[238] If performance by the offeree requires the cooperation of the offeror which is not forthcoming the offeree need only tender performance to bring the option contract into existence, Comment *d*.

(2) The offeror's duty of performance under any option contract so created is conditional on completion or tender of the invited performance in accordance with the terms of the offer.[239]

3.98   This provision only applies where the offer requires acceptance by performance rather than a promise. Such an offeree requires more protection than one who can bring a contract into being by providing a counter-promise.[240] The offer will become irrevocable, and the offeree is protected, as soon as performance of the requested act commences since 'the beginning of performance ... furnishes consideration for an option contract'.[241] This rule is 'designed to protect the offeree in justifiable reliance on the offeror's promise'[242] and therefore it will not apply if it is apparent that such reliance is unjustifiable, for example, if the power to revoke is reserved even after performance has begun or the power to refuse receipt of performance is reserved.[243]

3.99   An inevitable practical difficulty under section 45 relates to the point at which it can be said that performance has begun. The provision only applies to acts of performance and not to 'preparations for performance'.[244] Ultimately, this will turn on the construction of the terms of the offer. However, a number of relevant factors are identified by the commentary such as 'the extent to which the offeree's conduct is clearly referable to the offer, the definite and substantial character of that conduct, and the extent to which it is of actual or prospective benefit to the offeror rather than the offeree, as well as the terms of the communications between the parties, their prior course of dealing and any relevant usages of trade'.[245]

---

[239] The offeree is not bound to perform, the partial performance merely results in the creation of an option contract, see Comment *e*.

[240] Farnsworth, *Farnsworth on Contracts* (3rd edn, Vol I, Aspen Publishers, New York, 2004) § 3.25, p 362.

[241] Comment *d*.

[242] Comment *b*.

[243] Comment *b*.

[244] Comment *f*. Where the offeree has commenced preparing for performance and the offer is revoked he or she might be able to claim relief under the provision that protects reliance, see § 87(2) discussed above at 3.54.

[245] Comment *f*. § 45 can be relevant in the area of real estate brokerage transactions. Where an owner lists their property with more than one broker with the commission being paid to the broker who is successful in concluding the sale (so-called 'open listing'), then each broker's incentive is small and reliance on such an offer is not assumed to require protection under § 45. However, if an individual gives a broker the exclusive right to seek to sell his or her property for a period of time and the owner seeks to revoke that right when the broker has expended time and effort in trying to arrange a sale, then the broker may be able to recover its commission by relying on § 45, see *Baumgartner v Meek* 126 Cal App 2d 505, 272 P 2d 552, 554 (1954). See above n 229.

4

ACCEPTANCE

A. Introduction[1]

The clearest way to prove that the parties have reached an agreement is for them to execute **4.01**
a written contract. Once that is done then that document will evidence the agreement and
there is no need to look into earlier or later correspondence at least for the purposes of proving that an agreement has been reached.[2]

Where such a document does not exist it is then necessary to prove an agreement has been **4.02**
reached by using the tools of offer and acceptance or by showing that an agreement has
been reached by other conduct or communications. Where it is necessary to prove a contract by conduct all the circumstances must be looked at to determine whether the parties
intended to voluntarily assume legal obligations by assenting to be bound by some express
or implied terms. Relevant factors will include whether during negotiations either party

---

[1] This chapter deals with the general rules of acceptance. For the operation of the concept of acceptance in
the context of 'ecommerce', see 6.33ff.
[2] See *Remilton v City Mutual Life Assurance Society Ltd* (1908) 10 WALR 19. The document may not
represent all the terms agreed, and the enforceability of the 'agreement' will still depend on it evidencing an
intention to contract and being sufficiently certain and complete.

reserved the right not to be bound until execution of a written contract;[3] whether there was partial performance;[4] whether there is agreement on all essential terms;[5] whether the agreement is of a type that is usually committed to writing.[6] It is not sufficient that the conduct be consistent with a contract, it is necessary to show assent to the terms of a contract.[7] This chapter is concerned with acceptance and discusses the various rules governing acceptance. In general terms an acceptance involves the communication of an unequivocal assent to the terms of an offer.[8] Such 'assent' requires a commitment to the terms of the offer and not an acknowledgement of the offer or an expression of interest in the offer.[9]

4.03 In addition to determining whether or not an agreement has been reached, acceptance is important for two other reasons. First, a contract will come into existence at that moment in time when acceptance takes effect.[10] Subject to the terms of the contract,[11] and except where acceptance can and does occur by way of uncommunicated conduct,[12] this is when it is communicated or is otherwise taken to have reached the offeror.[13] Second, under English law a contract is formed at that place where it becomes effective as a contract.

---

[3] See 9.15ff.

[4] See 11.100ff.

[5] See 11.03.

[6] See *Winston v Mediafore Entertainment Corp* 77 F 2d 78 (1985); *Miglin Inc v Gottex Industries Inc* 790 F Supp 1245, 1250 (1992).

[7] See 1.19.

[8] Peel, *Treitel, The Law of Contract* (12th edn, Thomson, Sweet & Maxwell, London, 2007) para 2-015. See Restatement (2d) Contracts § 50(1). See also United Nations Convention on Contracts for the International Sale of Goods, Art 18(1), which provides that to constitute an effective acceptance the communication must indicate assent to the offer.

[9] Farnsworth, *Farnsworth on Contracts* (3rd edn, Vol 1, Aspen Publishers, New York, 2004) § 3.13, p 272. It is also necessary that the acceptance be given in return for a promise and, except in the case of a unilateral contract, must itself contain an express or implied promise. A difficult example is given in Perillo, *Corbin on Contracts* (Revised edn, Vol 8, Lexis Law Publishing, Virginia, 1999) § 31.6, p 68 ('Suppose that A writes thus to B: "I offer you my automobile for $5,000. You need not pay anything unless you wish to do so when you see the car. Please email acceptance." B faxes: "I accept your offer". Here, no contract has been made. B's satisfaction with the car or with the price is not a condition of B's duty to pay. There is no contract because B's fax acceptance makes no promise of any kind, either to be enforced against B or to constitute a consideration for A's promise to transfer the car.')

[10] Eg United Nations Convention on Contracts for the International Sale of Goods (1980), Art 23.

[11] Eg *Bowman v Durham Holdings Pty Ltd* (1973) 131 CLR 8 (here notice under an option was deemed to have been given by post 'at the time when such envelope would in the ordinary course of post be delivered'; in this case there was evidence that a letter posted before 5 p.m. on Friday would be delivered on Saturday morning if the addressee's office was open and retained by the postman if it was not; it was held that the clause took into account the practices of the postal service rather than the practices of the addressee; therefore the notice would take effect from Saturday morning).

[12] See *Minories Finance Ltd v Afribank Nigeria Ltd* [1995] 1 Lloyd's Rep 134, 140 ('The present case, however, is a case where the ordinary principles do not apply because both sides agree that, by the custom and practice of banking [as regards collections], a contract can and does come into existence by doing nothing, in other words without the necessity for the acceptance to be communicated. The present case is more analogous to an offer to sell goods which the offeror makes by sending the goods to the offeree with an implicit invitation to keep and pay for them. If a wine merchant offers me a case of claret and I accept the offer by drinking it, the resulting contract must be made in the place where I drink it.') See further 4.57ff.

[13] *Brinkibon Ltd v Stahag Stahl und Stahlwarenhandelsgesellschaft mbH* [1983] 2 AC 34, 41, 48. See also United Nations Convention on Contracts for the International Sale of Goods (1980), Art 18(2) and Unidroit Principles of International Commercial Contracts (2004), Art 2.1.6(2); Principles of European Contract Law, Art 2:205(1) and (2). See also Restatement (2d) Contracts §§ 56, 63, 64. See further 4.91.

Generally, unless the offeror has waived the need to communicate an acceptance,[14] or the postal acceptance rule applies,[15] this will be the place where acceptance is communicated.[16] For example, if an offer is accepted over the phone the place of formation will be where the offeror hears that acceptance.[17]

B. Objective Theory

The concept of acceptance is grounded in the objective theory of contract. In order to determine whether there has been an acceptance it is necessary to interpret the relevant communication from the position of a reasonable person in the position of the offeror.[18] **4.04**

As noted earlier, despite a reasonable person in the position of the offeror concluding that there was an acceptance, it is open to the offeree to prove that the offeror knew the offeree did not intend to accept. Such evidence generally must address the offeror's state of mind at the alleged moment of formation which means that a court generally will not take into account the statements or conduct of the offeree after the statement or act which is alleged to constitute acceptance.[19] The offeree cannot confuse the issue with its action after it has put forward an alleged acceptance.[20] However, in order to determine the offeror's state of mind it is legitimate and often necessary to consider the conduct of the offeror after the alleged point of formation.[21] It is at this point that the conduct of the offeree may **4.05**

---

[14] See 4.57ff.

[15] See 4.99.

[16] *Brinkibon Ltd v Stahag Stahl und Stahlwarenhandelsgesellschaft mbH* [1983] 2 AC 34, 41; *Tallerman & Co Pty Ltd v Nathan's Merchandise (Victoria) Pty Ltd* (1957) 98 CLR 93, 112; *Reese Bros Plastics Ltd v Hamon-Sobelco Australia Pty Ltd* (1988) 5 BPR 11, 106. See also *FCT v Sara Lee Household & Body Care (Australia) Pty Ltd* (2000) 201 CLR 520, 549.

[17] Cf Restatement (2d) Contracts § 64 comment c, where the relevant place is where the acceptor speaks. For authority in the United States holding that although the rule is that the validity of a contract is determined by the law of the state in which it was made, if an acceptance is communicated by telephone then that acceptance is effective and the 'contract is created at the place where the acceptor [offeree] speaks', see *Linn v Employers Reinsurance* Corp 392 Pa 58 (1958); *Lipshutz v Gordon Jewelry* Corp 373 F Supp 375, 385 (1974).

[18] See 1.07ff.

[19] *Felthouse v Bindley* (1862) 11 CBNS 869, 142 ER 1037. Cf *Howard Smith & Co Ltd v Varawa* (1907) 5 CLR 68, 78. Of course if the statement is not an acceptance but does not reject or otherwise kill the offer, then the offeree's later conduct may be evidence of an acceptance of the offer.

[20] It would be different under a reliance model of contract. It is also different if a party is attempting to prove a contract by conduct rather than whether a certain statement or act constituted an acceptance of an offer. In such a case recourse to the parties' conduct post an alleged point of formation is admissible, see *Integrated Computer Services Pty Ltd v Digital Equipment Corp (Aust) Pty Ltd* (1988) 5 BPR 11,110, 11, 117–18; *Brambles Holdings Ltd v Bathurst City Council* (2001) 53 NSWLR 153, 163; *Kriketos v Lipschitz* [2009] NSWCA 96.

[21] See *Compagnie de Commerce et Commission SARL v Parkinson Stove Co* [1953] 2 Lloyd's Rep 487, 492 (here Singleton LJ suggests that where there is a exclusive method of acceptance and the offeree does not follow that method but nevertheless clearly evidences an intention to accept, then the conduct of the offeror after that event can be taken into account to determine whether he or she elected to waive the strict requirements of acceptance or is otherwise prevented from relying on them; however, he also suggests that if the alleged acceptance would not be construed as an acceptance by a reasonable person in the position of the offeror, then the conduct of the offeror after communication of that alleged acceptance cannot be taken into account to prove that the offeror subjectively understood it to be an acceptance of his or her terms and waived strict compliance with its terms).

be relevant, not for the purpose of accepting evidence of the offeree's state of mind, but because the offeror's conduct must be interpreted within context. It follows that as a general statement the conduct of the parties may be used to evidence that no agreement was reached at an earlier point in time.[22] At the same time care must be exercised when considering such evidence, in some cases one view of the offeror's conduct might suggest he or she was not of the view that the offeree intended to accept while another view of that same conduct might be that the offeror did understand that the offeree intended to accept the offer but that the offeror then signalled that he or she wished to renegotiate the terms of the contract.[23]

4.06 As regards the relevance of the offeree's conduct after the alleged acceptance, one further scenario should be noted. If an offeree seeks to argue that it has accepted the offeror's offer in circumstances where a reasonable person in the position of the offeror might conclude there was an acceptance, then, if the offeror seeks to challenge the acceptance by arguing the offeree did not subjectively intend to accept, then resort may be had to the offeree's conduct before and after the alleged moment of acceptance to prove the transaction was still in the process of negotiation.[24]

4.07 In determining whether any conduct or statement is an acceptance of the terms of an offer, it is necessary to look at all the circumstances.[25] A court is not limited to merely construing the terms of any written document or the manner of communications between the parties. For example, a document on its face may appear to introduce a new term not mentioned in a written offer but when read in context may be referring to an issue that was discussed and agreed upon prior to that written offer and which the offer can then be said to impliedly adopt. Similarly an oral offer and acceptance when seen in context may include as part of the contract a written term introduced earlier.[26]

4.08 Finally, to the extent to which the determination of whether a document is an acceptance is an issue of construction, then, if it purports to be an unequivocal acceptance but is otherwise ambiguous as to its meaning and legal effect but is nevertheless capable of being construed as an acceptance then a court will construe it as an acceptance.[27] However, as has been noted earlier, the process should not be seen as a pure matter of construction. The search is not for the meaning and legal effect of the terms of any document in so far as they relate to issues of performance but whether the parties intended to enter into a contract.

---

[22] *Barrier Wharfs Ltd v W Scott Fell & Co Ltd* (1908) 5 CLR 647.

[23] See *Hussey v Horne-Payne* [1879] 4 App Cas 311; *Bellamy v Debenham* (1890) 45 Ch D 481, 493–4, (affirmed on other grounds [1891] 1 Ch 412). See generally *Brunner v Moore* [1904] 1 Ch 305; *Andrews v Calori* (1907) 38 SCR 588; *Perry v Suffields* [1916] 2 Ch 187; *Harvey v Perry* [1953] 1 SCR 233, [1953] 2 DLR 465; *Universal Guarantee Pty Ltd v Carlile* [1957] VR 68; *Integrated Lighting & Ceilings Pty Ltd v Philips Electrical Pty Ltd* (1969) 90 WN (Pt 1) (NSW) 693; *OTM Ltd v Hydranautics* [1981] 2 Lloyd's Rep 211; *Commonwealth of Australia v Crothhall Hospital Services (Aust) Ltd* (1981) 36 ALR 567; *Terrex Resources NL v Magnet Petroleum Pty Ltd* [1988] 1 WAR 144.

[24] *Harvey v Perry* [1953] 1 SCR 233, [1953] 2 DLR 465, 469; *Bristol, Cardiff and Swansea Aërated Bread Co v Maggs* (1890) 44 Ch D 616, 621.

[25] *Gissing v Gissing* [1971] AC 886, 925. See also *Hughes v NM Superannuation* (1993) 29 NSWLR 653, 670. See further 1.20.

[26] *Zambia Steel & Building Supplies Ltd v James Clark & Eaton Ltd* [1986] 2 Lloyd's Rep 225.

[27] *Cavallari v Premier Refrigeration Co Pty Ltd* (1952) 85 CLR 20, 25. See further 4.43.

The issue is essentially an issue of fact, to the extent it involves issues of 'construction' some have expressed it involving a question of mixed law and fact.[28]

C. Manner of Acceptance

Prescribed manner of acceptance

Generally an acceptance may occur by words or conduct.[29] The key is that the offeree must be seen to be assenting to the terms of the offer. It follows that if the acceptance is by conduct it will not be sufficient that the act is consistent with an intention to accept, it must be unequivocal and lead to no other conclusion than that of acceptance.[30] Ultimately whether or not an offer calls for a return promise or the performance of an act depends on the terms of the offer or what is reasonable in the circumstances.[31] If the terms of the offer are not clear and either method is possible then a court will usually allow acceptance by either method.[32] However, if the offer requires the parties to first agree the terms prior to performance then the offer cannot be immediately accepted by conduct, although such conduct may evidence a counter-offer which could be accepted.[33] More generally, the commencement of performance may amount to a promise to perform.[34]

4.09

As a general rule where an offeror prescribes a method of acceptance then the offeree must comply with the terms for acceptance.[35] There are two aspects to this power of the offeror. First, the offeror can prescribe the form an acceptance must take. Second the offeror may prescribe the manner of acceptance.

4.10

---

[28] *Covington Marine Corp v Xiamen Shipbuilding Industry Co Ltd* [2006] 1 Lloyd's Rep 745. See further 1.23.

[29] This is accepted and reflected in international instruments, eg United Nations Convention on Contracts for the International Sale of Goods (1980), Art 18(1); Unidroit Principles of International Commercial Contracts (2004), Art 2.1.6(1); Principles of European Contract Law, Art 2:204(1); Draft Common Frame of Reference II—4:204(1). Eg *Photolibrary Group Ltd v Burda Senator Verlag GmbH* [2008] 2 All ER (Comm) 881 (photographs sent together with lender's terms and conditions; this constituted an offer which was accepted by the offeree forwarding those photos on to its clients for review).

[30] *Kriketos v Livschitz* [2009] NSWCA 96.

[31] Restatement (2d) Contracts § 50, Comment *c*.

[32] See Restatement (2d) Contracts §§ 30(2) and 32; Uniform Commercial Code §2-206(1)(b) and see Farnsworth, *Farnsworth on Contracts* (3rd edn, Vol 1, Aspen Publishers, New York, 2004) § 3.12, p 267. Note also Uniform Commercial Code §2-206(1)(a) which states, 'Unless otherwise unambiguously indicated by the language or circumstances ... an offer to make a contract shall be construed as inviting acceptance in any manner and by any medium reasonable in the circumstances.' Farnsworth suggests that this section is not so much concerned with the distinction between acceptance by promise and acceptance by conduct, but is concerned with the different ways in which a promise can be made, for example, a nod of the head, see Farnsworth, § 3.12, p 271.

[33] Farnsworth, *Farnsworth on Contracts* (3rd edn, Vol 1, Aspen Publishers, New York, 2004) § 3.13, p 276.

[34] See Restatement (2d) Contracts §§ 32, 50(2), 62. See further n 3.82.

[35] See Restatement (2d) Contracts § 58. Although the offeror can prescribe a method of acceptance, he or she cannot dictate that the occurrence of a prescribed act or certain conduct of the offeree will amount to acceptance, see *McMahon's (Transport) Pty Ltd v Ebbage* [1999] 1 Qd R 185, 195–6. See 4.62ff. See further Miller, 'Felthouse v Bindley Re-Visited' (1972) 35 Mod LR 489, 490.

4.11   If an offeror prescribes a form or manner of acceptance and that form or manner is construed to be exclusive, then that method must be followed.[36] If some other form or manner is used then it will not be effective as an acceptance and will either carry no legal significance[37] or, in some cases, it may amount to a counter-offer. The capacity for it to be a counter-offer is helped by virtue of the intention to contract inherent in it being an attempted acceptance.[38] A doctrinal difficulty that has been raised in treating such acceptances as counter-offers is that they are given with the intention of finalizing a transaction rather than being a counter-offer. They are not informed by an intention that they can be accepted.[39] However, if they are put forward as purported acceptances it would generally appear to a reasonable person in the position of the original offeror that the other party intended to contract on those terms which would be sufficient to render it a counter-offer.[40] It is then akin to a document provided in the negotiation process which sets out alternative terms and evidences an intention to contract on those terms if the other party accepts. Such a document is a clear counter-offer if it follows an offer. Similarly if an 'acceptance' is put forward which contains additional or different terms with the intention that these must be agreed to before the 'acceptance' is effective, that will constitute a counter-offer.[41] An 'acceptance' that is actually a conditional acceptance such as where the acceptance is subject to the approval of some third party may operate as a counter-offer.[42] Moreover, where an offeree purports to accept an offer but has not carried out any prescribed conditions precedent to the offer then the acceptance will not be effective and may constitute

---

[36]   Eg *Baugham v Rampart Resources Ltd* (1995) 4 BCLR (3d) 146, [1995] 6 WWR 99, (1995) 124 DLR (4th) 252; *Brooke v Garrod* (1857) 3 Kay & J 608, 69 ER 1252 (affirmed (1857) 2 De G & J 62, 44 ER 911); *Gilbert J McCaul (Aust) Pty Ltd v Pitt Club Ltd* (1957) 59 SR (NSW) 122; *Rushton (SA) Pty Ltd v Holzberger* [2003] QCA 106. See also Restatement (2d) Contracts § 60 and cf § 67. Where an acceptance requires the offeror's cooperation which is not forthcoming then the offeree may be excused from strict compliance with its terms and in some cases excused from compliance completely if any attempt would be futile, see *Bragg v Alam* [1981] 1 NSWLR 668 (affirmed *Bragg v Alam* (1982) NSW Conv R ¶55-082) (here a notice of exercise of option was delivered out of time due to the offeror taking steps to evade service; there are comments (see 673–4) made by the court suggesting that in the right circumstances the offeree may be excused from all conditions precedent to acceptance). See also *Carmichael v Bank of Montreal* [1972] 3 WWR 175, (1972) 25 DLR (3d) 570 (terms of offer were that it was open for acceptance till 6 pm; it was held that where such terms are made the offeror must make it possible for the offeree to accept; here there is an implied term that there would be a person available to accept the offer up till that time). See further *Beneficial Finance Corp Ltd v Multiplex Constructions Pty Ltd* (1995) 36 NSWLR 510, 533–4. It is likely that the position here is strict as regards options but such evasive conduct may in some cases constitute a communication of a revocation of the offer.

[37]   Eg *Richards v Hill* [1920] NZLR 724 (in this case it was found that a memorandum of offer made and executed by a prospective purchaser required the signature of the vendor; the signature of the agent of the vendor was not sufficient even if that agent was authorized by the vendor to sell the property). In contracts for the sale of land it is customary that no contract comes into effect prior to both parties executing and exchanging copies of the contract, see *Eccles v Bryant* [1948] Ch 93; *Carruthers v Whitaker* [1975] 2 NZLR 667. This position can be rebutted, see *Storer v Manchester City Council* [1974] 1 WLR 1403.

[38]   That is, a counter-offer to enter into a contract on the terms of the original offer, see *Wettern Electric Ltd v Welsh Development Agency* [1983] QB 796, 802. See also Restatement (2d) Contracts § 60 comment *a*.

[39]   See *Kingsley & Keith v Glynn Brothers (Chemicals) Ltd* [1953] 1 Lloyd's Rep 211.

[40]   Alternatively such cases may be seen as instances of the offeror waiving the need for compliance.

[41]   See United Nations Convention on Contracts for the International Sale of Goods (1980), Art 19(1). See also Unidroit Principles of International Commercial Contracts 2004, Art 2.1.11(1); Principles of European Contract Law Article 2:208; Draft Common Frame of Reference II–4:208(1). It may be different if the differing terms of the acceptance are the result of a mistake, see 4.43.

[42]   *Frampton v McCully* [1976] 1 NZLR 270, 276.

a counter-offer.[43] Finally, where the manner of acceptance concerns the way in which acceptance is communicated or the place of communication, the courts are less likely to conclude that this is exclusive.[44]

It is often said that an offeror can waive its requirements for acceptance so long as that does **4.12** not adversely affect the offeree.[45] For example in *Manchester Diocesan Council for Education v Commercial and General Investments Ltd*,[46] the plaintiff and defendant had negotiated for the sale of the plaintiff's property through their respective surveyors. Those negotiations came to nothing and the plaintiff decided to call for tenders for the purchase of the property. The form of tender supplied provided that any acceptance by the plaintiff would be sent by letter to the address given in the tender. In due course the plaintiff decided to accept the defendant's offer. However, rather than send the acceptance to the address given in the tender, the plaintiff's surveyor addressed a letter of acceptance to the defendant's surveyor. Buckley J held that it nevertheless constituted an effective acceptance. Here, the condition was not an exclusive method of acceptance. More importantly for the purposes of this section, the form of tender was drafted by the plaintiff and the condition for acceptance was inserted for the benefit of the plaintiff and the plaintiff could waive it so long as that did not adversely affect the defendant. Here the plaintiff could have used the proposed method and acceptance would have occurred when it was sent but this did not stop the plaintiff adopting another method whereby acceptance would only take effect when it was communicated and this is what occurred here.

---

[43] See *Gilbert J McCaul (Aust) Pty Ltd v Pitt Club Ltd* (1957) 59 SR (NSW) 122, 123–4. See also *Weston v Collins* (1865) 34 LJ Ch 353, 354.

[44] Eg *Tinn v Hoffman & Co* (1873) 29 LT 271; *Manchester Diocesan Council for Education v Commercial & General Investments Ltd* [1970] 1 WLR 241. See also *FAI General Insurance Co Ltd v Parras* (2002) 55 NSWLR 498 (general provisions in contract for the service of notices were held not to apply to the 'notice in writing' requirement for the exercise of an option to renew lease), cf *Rushton (SA) Pty Ltd v Holzberger* [2003] QCA 106. Prescribed methods of performance are dealt with in the United States in § 60 of the Restatement (2d) Contracts which provides: 'If an offer prescribes the place, time or manner of acceptance its terms in this respect must be complied with in order to create a contract. If an offer merely suggests a permitted place, time or manner of acceptance, another method of acceptance is not precluded.' Examples are given in the comments which evidence how clear an offer must be framed to achieve a mandatory stipulation.

[45] *Manchester Diocesan Council for Education v Commercial & General Investments Ltd* [1970] 1 WLR 241. See also *Bowman v Durham Holdings Pty Ltd* (1973) 131 CLR 8 (here a notice to extend an option was given out of time but accepted by the other party which then conducted itself as if the extension was operational; doubt was expressed (18, 20) as to the use of the concept of 'waiver' here; the result was based on the conduct of the parties evidencing a consensus between the parties). See further *Williamson v Standard Insurance Co Ltd* [1935] NZLR 224; *Compagnie de Commerce et Commission SARL v Parkinson Stove Co* [1953] 2 Lloyd's Rep 487, 492 (n 21 above). As to the ability to rely on estoppel to overcome a failure to satisfy the requirements of an exclusive method of acceptance, see *Gilbert J McCaul (Aust) Pty Ltd v Pitt Club Ltd* (1957) 59 SR (NSW) 122, 129 ('An estoppel cannot create a contractual right or give rise to a cause of action. It operates only to prevent a person from asserting the existence or non-existence of a fact. It was essential for the plaintiff in the present case to prove that it had accepted the offer ... this it could do only by showing that it had performed the conditions for acceptance ... In fact it proved that it had not accepted the defendant's offer but instead had made a counter-offer, and we cannot agree that it is entitled to overcome this difficulty by relying upon the doctrine of estoppel. The argument seems to us to be based upon the fallacious notion that the fact that a defendant is estopped from denying the existence of a fact affords evidence that that fact exists'.) See also *Lundberg v Royal Exchange Assurance Corp* [1933] NZLR 605. Aspects of this statement in *Gilbert J McCaul* may need to be reviewed in light of later Australian authority, but would still carry weight in England, see 3.65ff.

[46] [1970] 1 WLR 241.

4.13   This case can be contrasted with that of *Financings Ltd v Stimson*,[47] where an acceptance clause made for the benefit of one party operated against them on the facts. Here a finance company's standard hire purchase form was handed to the defendant by a car dealer and the defendant signed it. The form, though drafted by the finance company, encapsulated an offer by the defendant to take a car on hire purchase and stated that the agreement would only become binding on the finance company when it had been signed by them. However, before any such signature, the defendant was permitted by the car dealer to take the car away. Later the defendant returned the car to the dealer stating that he did not wish to proceed with the purchase. The Court of Appeal held that there was no contract binding on the defendant as the defendant had revoked the offer to purchase prior to acceptance. Allowing the defendant to take the car did not constitute acceptance by the plaintiff because of the stipulation as to signature.[48] The majority held that the dealer had ostensible authority to accept the revocation on behalf of the finance company.[49] The case is interesting because at the time the defendant returned the car the hirer was of the belief that the finance company had signed the form and so the hirer's intention was to rescind the contract and forfeit the deposit. However, the majority was of the view that the intention to no longer proceed with the contract was sufficient to revoke the offer.

4.14   The difficulty with the concept of waiver here is that in doctrinal terms a party can only waive a 'right' to have a condition performed. In the case of contract formation the offeror would rarely have a right to the performance of a condition of acceptance.[50]

4.15   The offeror may prescribe a method of acceptance that is not exclusive.[51] Whether or not a prescribed method of acceptance is exclusive is determined by reference to the presumed intention of the offeror and is generally said to be an issue of construction where it is in writing.[52] This intention is determined from the perspective of a reasonable person in the

---

[47] [1962] 1 WLR 1184.

[48] In addition to this reason, after the car was returned it was damaged while in the possession of the dealer and this meant that the finance company was no longer in the position to accept the offer as the offer to purchase the car was conditional upon the car remaining in the condition it was in at the time of the offer up to the time of acceptance.

[49] Cf *Branwhite v Worcester Works Finance Ltd* [1969] 1 AC 552, 573 per Lord Morris, 575–9 per Lord Upjohn, cf 585–90 per Lord Wilberforce.

[50] See *Gilbert J McCaul (Aust) Pty Ltd v Pitt Club Ltd* (1957) 59 SR (NSW) 122, 124, 125 (here an option to renew a lease required as one of its conditions the punctual payment of rent; the rent was often paid late but accepted by the lessor; it was held that the even though the lessee may have satisfied the other conditions to exercise the option this condition for payment had to be met for acceptance and was not waived by the lessor, the lessor having no right to the performance of the conditions in the renewal clause).

[51] Note Malaysian Contracts Act 1950 § 7(b) which provides that: 'If the proposal prescribes a manner in which it is to be accepted, and the acceptance is not made in that manner, the proposer may, within a reasonable time after the acceptance is communicated to him, insist that his proposal shall be accepted in the prescribed manner, and not otherwise; but, if he fails to do so, he accepts the acceptance.'

[52] *Kennedy v Thomassen* [1929] 1 Ch 426, 433. See also *Tinn v Hoffman & Co* (1873) 29 LT 271 (offer requiring reply 'by letter by return of post' held not exclusive); *White Trucks Pty Ltd v Riley* (1948) 66 WN (NSW) 101 (offeree sent standard order form to be filled in by offeror and which contained a clause stating 'this instrument is not binding on you [the offeree] until the memorandum of acceptance hereunder is duly signed; this provision was held to be for the benefit of the offeree and was not an exclusive method of acceptance; cf *Financings Ltd v Stimson* [1962] 1 WLR 1184); *George Hudson Holdings Ltd v Rudder* (1973) 128 CLR 387 (the terms of an offer required certain documents to be placed in an enclosed envelope and

position of the offeree.[53] A prescribed method of acceptance may appear on its face to be exclusive but when read in context that apparent exclusivity is merely intended to achieve some purpose such as obtaining a prompt response or a reply that is in a form or delivered in a manner that is convenient to the offeror. Often these purposes can be achieved by using other methods. Where the method prescribed is not exclusive then the offeree may accept using a different method as long as it is as efficient in fact or as convenient to the offeror as the one prescribed.[54] In practice the issue that arises is more often that of communication of acceptance rather than the form of acceptance. The prescribed manner of acceptance is usually intended to achieve a response within a certain time. It necessarily follows that if the offeree used a faster method of communication that will suffice. For example in *Tinn v Hoffmann and Co*,[55] where the offeror was told to 'reply by return of post' it was held by the court that any reply which would reach its destination before a letter sent by post would constitute an effective acceptance. It is also the case that if the method chosen could be less efficient than that prescribed by the offeror but in fact does not operate less efficiently then it will be effective.[56]

The risk in adopting a different method is that if it does not achieve the purpose intended **4.16** by the offeror for any reason then it will not be effective.[57] In *Eliason v Henshaw*,[58] the appellants who were in Harper's Ferry offered in a letter delivered by a wagon to purchase flour from the respondent. The letter stated: 'Please write by return of wagon whether you accept our offer.' The wagon was at the time in the employ of the respondent and took flour from the respondent's mill at Mill Creek to Harper's Ferry. There was therefore a time frame

---

posted; it was held that the post was not an exclusive method of acceptance). See further *Manchester Diocesan Council for Education v Commercial & General Investments Ltd* [1970] 1 WLR 241.

[53] See further, Farnsworth, *Farnsworth on Contracts* (3rd edn, Vol 1, Aspen Publishers, New York, 2004) § 3.13, p 277.

[54] *Manchester Diocesan Council for Education v Commercial & General Investments Ltd* [1970] 1 WLR 241; *Yates Building Co Ltd v R J Pulleyn & Sons (York) Ltd* [1976] EG 123; *Nieckar v Sliwa* (1976) 67 DLR (3d) 378. See also Uniform Commercial Code §2-206; Restatement (2d) Contracts §§ 30, 65, 67.

[55] (1873) 29 LT 271.

[56] Eg *Spectra Pty Ltd v Pindari Pty Ltd* [1974] 2 NSWLR 617 (exercise of option required notice to be 'sent' by registered post; if the offeree used that method then he or she would be relieved of ensuring the notice reached the offeror; but this was construed to be a non-exclusive manner of acceptance and a method that relied on the actual receipt of notice could be used; the lessee sent the notice by ordinary post but it still arrived no later than it would have arrived had it been sent by registered post and was therefore effective). See also *George Hudson Holdings Ltd v Rudder* (1973) 128 CLR 387. See further *Re Gambrinus Lager Beer Brewery Co Ltd* (1886) 12 VLR 446; *Malthouse v Adelaide Milk Supply Co-operative Ltd* [1922] SASR 572; *Re Clifton Springs Hotel Ltd* [1939] VLR 27; *Farmers Mercantile Union & Chaff Mills Ltd v Coade* (1921) 30 CLR 113. Cf *Re F H Ring & Co Ltd* [1924] SASR 138; *DJE Constructions Pty Ltd v Maddocks* [1982] 1 NSWLR 5, 19.

[57] Note, however, the rules as to late acceptance in Unidroit Principles of International Commercial Contracts, Art 2.1.9(1), see 4.24n.

[58] 17 US 225 (1819). See also *Walker v Glass* [1979] NI 129 (the terms of an offer for the sale of land required an annexed acceptance to be signed and delivered to the vendor's solicitors together with a deposit; the purchaser signed the acceptance and communicated this to the vendor by telephone; it was held that this was not an acceptance; it did not follow the prescribed method and was less advantageous to the vendor than the prescribed method; under the prescribed method the vendor would have a signed acceptance in his possession as well as the deposit; in addition as the mode of acceptance also required payment of the deposit the communication that the acceptance had been signed was not a sufficient act of acceptance in any case; cf *Bowman v Durham Holdings Pty Ltd* (1973) 131 CLR 8, where the purchase price was to be paid 'upon the exercise of the option' did not mean simultaneously with exercise of the option).

for acceptance, it was the time it would take for a wagon to make the round trip; the appellants were put on notice by the wagoner who took the letter that he would probably not be returning. Instead of sending an acceptance by wagon, the respondent sent it by post to the plaintiff's offices in Georgetown and later commenced an action against the appellant for refusing to accept tender of the flour. The United States Supreme Court held that there was no contract. The principal point of the court's reasoning was that the offer required acceptance at a certain place, namely Harper's Ferry and this could not be unilaterally varied by the offeree. This was an improper departure from the terms of the offer which had not been waived.[59] However, the court did state:[60]

> The meaning of the writers was obvious. They could easily calculate, by the usual length of time which was employed by this wagon, in travelling from Harper's Ferry to Mill Creek, and back again with a load of flour, about what time they should receive the desired answer, and therefore, it was entirely unimportant, whether it was sent by that, or another wagon, or in any other manner, provided it was sent to Harper's Ferry, and was not delayed beyond the time which was ordinarily employed by wagons engaged in hauling flour from the defendant's mill to Harper's Ferry.

No prescribed manner of acceptance

4.17   An offeror may not prescribe any method of acceptance. In such a case, what constitutes a proper method of acceptance must be determined by reference to the presumed intention of the offeror. This will depend on a construction of the terms of the offer which will include a consideration of the circumstances surrounding the transaction. For example, the method by which the offer is communicated may imply an appropriate method of acceptance. Thus, it has been observed that an offer sent by telegram may indicate that the offeror requires a prompt reply which may discount acceptance by some postal methods.[61] Similarly, an offer sent by post may usually be accepted by post.[62] As a general rule where there is no prescribed manner of acceptance the offeree may use any method that is reasonable in the circumstances.

4.18   As to what is reasonable, section 65 of the Restatement (2d) Contracts states: 'Unless circumstances known to the offeree indicate otherwise, a medium of acceptance is reasonable if it is the one used by the offeror or one customary in similar transactions at the time and place the offer is received.'[63] The comments to this section make it clear that factors used in assessing reasonableness will also include the speed and reliability of the medium chosen and methods used in any prior course of dealing between the parties.[64] In the case of postal acceptance comment *c* states that 'Acceptance by mail is ordinarily reasonable where the parties are negotiating at a distance, unless there is some special reason for speed such as

---

[59] See above 4.12.
[60] 17 US 225, 228–9 (1819).
[61] *Quenerduaine v Cole* (1883) 32 WR 185.
[62] The subject matter of the contract may change this, for example, if the subject matter was of a wasting nature this might call for a rapid response.
[63] See also Uniform Commercial Code § 2-206(a).
[64] Comment *b*.

rapid price fluctuation' and 'Even though an offer is transmitted by telephone or telegraph, acceptance by mail may well be reasonable.'

Acceptance by conduct

It was noted above that acceptance can be by conduct. The ability to accept by conduct is **4.19** well recognized.[65] Usually this is not a controversial aspect of a transaction because the offer will call for some conduct which may or may not require communication of acceptance. A typical example is where an offer to buy goods is accepted by sending the goods to the buyer.[66]

In practice there are two issues that tend to arise in the context of acceptance by conduct. **4.20** The first concerns whether or not the acceptance is complete. This question in turn usually arises where the offeror has communicated a revocation of the offer while the offeree is attempting to carry out the act of acceptance. The rules governing the revocation of offers prior to or during performance of the act of acceptance are dealt with in Chapter 3. For the purposes of this chapter, it is important to note that as a general rule, if the offer calls for acceptance by conduct, then in order for there to be acceptance the offeree must fully carry out the act of acceptance.[67] What that act of acceptance involves will be determined by construing the terms of the offer. In most cases this is generally a straightforward issue. Interesting questions have arisen in the context of offers for rewards, particularly offers for information leading to the arrest and conviction of felons. Here there has been some acceptance that when a crime is committed, generally no one person will provide all the information needed to identify the felon or all the evidence needed for a conviction. Such information will usually be provided piecemeal by different people and the offer of reward will be construed as providing a reward to be shared amongst those people who substantially comply with the terms of the offer and are links in the chain of information with amounts being apportioned by reference to the value of information provided.[68] Of course

---

[65] See United Nations Convention on Contracts for the International Sale of Goods, Art 18(1). See also Unidroit Principles of International Commercial Contracts 2004, Art 2.1.6(1).

[66] Eg United Nations Convention on Contracts for the International Sale of Goods, Art 18(3); Uniform Commercial Code § 2-206(2). See also Unidroit Principles of International Commercial Contracts (2004), Art 2.1.6(3); Principles of European Contract Law, Article 2:205(1), (3); Draft Common Frame of Reference II–4:205(3). See further *Mooney v Williams* (1905) 3 CLR 1.

[67] As noted above, if the offer may be accepted by a counter-promise then the commencement of performance may evidence such a promise, see 4.09. Cf Restatement (2d) Contracts § 50(2). Under the Restatement where acceptance must be by performance and not promise, the commencement of performance creates an option contract preventing the offeror revoking the offer, § 45. If the commencement of performance also constitutes a promise to perform then generally the offeree is bound to perform, § 69. An exception to this exists in § 53. See also Uniform Commercial Code 2-206(1)(b).

[68] *Tobin v McComb* 156 SW 237, 239 (1913); *Smirnis v Toronto Sun Publishing Corp* (1997) 37 OR (3d) 440. Various statements have been made as to how important the information must be for it to qualify for a reward. In England, in *Tarner v Walker* (1866) LR 1 QB 641 (affirmed (1867) LR 2 QB 301) the issue was analysed in terms of chains of causation and the information not being too remote. Similarly in Canada in *Smirnis v Toronto Sun Publishing Corp* (1997) 37 OR (3d) 440 it was said that the information must at least lead, 'through one or more successive links in the chain of cause and effect to the ultimate arrest and conviction'. A high standard has been expressed in some decisions in the Unites States requiring the information to be the effective cause of an arrest. For example, in *Tobin v McComb* 156 SW 237, 239 (1913), it was said: 'Such a reward can only be claimed by a person who has substantially complied with the terms and

where the same information is given by different people then generally the reward must go to the person who first gave the information.[69]

4.21 The second issue is where one or both parties have carried out some acts of performance but at some point one of the parties claims there was no formal acceptance of an offer and therefore no contract. Here the fact the parties may have conducted themselves according to some agreed terms may evidence that a contract was entered into by conduct despite the fact that on its face the parties had not fully settled the terms of the agreement.[70] For example, in *Brogden v Metropolitan Railway Co*,[71] there was a long-standing relationship between the parties for the supply of coal and coke although there was no formal agreement. It was suggested by the appellant supplier that a contract should be put in place. The appellant drafted a proposal and sent it to the respondent railway company. The respondent, on the basis of that proposal, drew up a formal contract adding some material terms. This was sent to the appellant who made a few minor changes. The appellant also added the name of an arbitrator. The appellant then wrote 'approved' on the agreement and signed the document. Lord Cairns noted that because of the addition of the name of the arbitrator it was not possible to say there was a contract at this point as that term required the approval of the respondent.[72] The agreement was then sent back to the respondent who put it in a drawer and never formally executed it. Clearly the parties had embarked on a course of conduct with a view to entering into a contract.[73] Moreover, for the majority of the House of Lords the evidence showed that although the contract was never executed by the respondent, the parties conducted themselves on the basis of an agreement on those terms being in place by ordering, supplying and accepting deliveries according to the terms of the agreement.[74] The course of conduct engaged in by each party clearly made the other aware that a contract had come into existence between them.[75] Of course it is not possible to rely on some conduct as evidencing an acceptance if the offeree has expressly rejected the offer.[76] In such a case it is necessary to either prove a separate contract entered into by conduct or pursue restitutionary remedies.

---

conditions of the reward as it is offered, and who has been the moving cause of the accomplishment of the purposes for which the reward was offered ... As to whether a person who simply gives information concerning a crime, which is of assistance in the apprehension of the criminal, is entitled to participate in the reward the authorities are in conflict'. See also *Genesee County v Pailthorpe* 246 Mich 356, 224 NW 418, 418 (1929).

[69] *Thatcher v England* (1846) 3 Com Bench 254, 136 ER 102.

[70] *G Percy Trentham Ltd v Archital Luxfer Ltd* [1993] 1 Lloyd's Rep 25. Cf *Capital Finance Co Ltd v Bray* [1964] 1 WLR 323. See further *Fisher v Brooker* [2009] 1 WLR 1764, 1777 (suggesting that the question whether a contract can be implied is one inference rather than primary fact).

[71] (1877) 2 App Cas 666. Cf *Jayaar Impex Ltd v Toaken Group Ltd* [1996] 2 Lloyd's Rep 437.

[72] (1877) 2 App Cas 666, 675.

[73] (1877) 2 App Cas 666, 676.

[74] The majority were Lord Cairns LC, Lord Hatherley, Lord Selborne. Lord Gordon dissented and Lord Blackburn did not dissent from the view of the majority but was hesitant in coming to the same view on the evidence.

[75] (1877) 2 App Cas 666, 682.

[76] *Transpower New Zealand Ltd v Meridian Energy Ltd* [2001] 3 NZLR 700. See also *Airways Corp of New Zealand Ltd v Geyserland Airways Ltd* [1996] 1 NZLR 116.

Finally, it should be noted that unless negated by the terms of the offer or the nature of the **4.22**
contract,[77] the conduct must be communicated to the offeror.[78]

Time of acceptance

An acceptance must comply with any time set for acceptance in the terms of the offer.[79] **4.23**
Where no time is set then acceptance must be within a reasonable time as the offer will be
open for a reasonable time.[80] What constitutes a reasonable time depends on the facts of the
case.[81] Important factors will often be the manner in which the offer is communicated and
the circumstances of the case. Not only may the manner of communication impliedly
dictate the manner of acceptance but also the time frame for acceptance. Thus, as already
noted, an offer sent by a prompt means will often require a response by similar means and
that response may also need to be prompt.[82] An oral offer may need to be accepted immediately.[83] The subject matter of the contract may also dictate the speed of acceptance. For
example, if the subject is perishable goods or goods that are subject to sudden fluctuations
in price, this will generally dictate that what is a reasonable time is shorter than when the
dealing is in a more stable subject matter such as land.[84]

As a general rule an acceptance sent out of time is not effective.[85] On one view, the offeror **4.24**
could waive the time limitation,[86] however, at a doctrinal level if the offer has lapsed it
needs to be made again and a proper acceptance given. From a commercial standpoint the

---

[77] See 4.54ff.

[78] See also Uniform Commercial Code § 2-206(2): 'If the beginning of a requested performance is a
reasonable mode of acceptance, an offeror who is not notified of acceptance within a reasonable time may
treat the offer as having lapsed before acceptance.' See further § 2-206(1)(b).

[79] *Nyulasy v Rowan* (1891) 17 VLR 663. Where a date is not fixed but a time frame is given in the offer
then on general principles this time will run from the moment the offer takes effect, that is, upon receipt, see
further Principles of European Contract Law, Art 1: 304; Draft Common Frame of Reference I-1:104 Annex
2. Cf Unidroit Principles of International Commercial Contracts, Art 2.1.8 (this provision states that where a
period of acceptance is fixed, time runs from the when the offer is dispatched and goes on to state that a 'time
indicated in the offer is deemed to be the time of dispatch unless the circumstances indicate otherwise') and
see United Nations Convention on Contracts for the International Sale of Goods (1980), Art 20.

[80] *Manchester Diocesan Council for Education v Commercial & General Investments Ltd* [1970] 1 WLR 241,
247; *Clark v Barrick* [1951] SCR 177. See also *United Dominions Trust (Commercial) Ltd v Eagle Aircraft
Services Ltd* [1968] 1 WLR 74. See further Restatement (2d) Contracts § 41(1); United Nations Convention
for the International Sale of Goods (1980), Art 18(2). See further Restatement (2d) Contract § 41(3) 'Unless
otherwise indicated by the language or the circumstances, and subject to the rule in §49, an offer sent by mail
is seasonably accepted if an acceptance is mailed at any time before midnight on the day on which the offer is
received.'

[81] Restatement (2d) Contracts § 41(2). See also *Clark v Barrick* [1951] SCR 177.

[82] See above 4.15. See also United Nations Convention on Contracts for the International Sale of Goods,
Art 18(2); Unidroit Principles of International Commercial Contracts, Art 2.1.7; Principles of European
Contract Law, Art 2:206; Draft Common Frame of Reference II–4:206.

[83] United Nations Convention on Contracts for the International Sale of Goods, Art 18(2).

[84] *Clark v Barrick* [1951] SCR 177.

[85] Late delivery may be available if the offeror does not make it possible for the offeree to accept within
time, see *Carmichael v Bank of Montreal* [1972] 3 WWR 175, (1972) 25 DLR (3d) 570. There are also
situations where even though the acceptance is late the offeror will need to take positive steps if it does not
want the contract to take effect, see *The Farmers' Mercantile Union and Chaff Mills Ltd v Coade* (1921) 30 CLR
113 (offer to purchase shares, no acceptance sent but purchaser knew that its name had been registered as a
shareholder when it received calls). See n 36 above.

[86] See *Carello v Jordan* [1935] St R Qd 294, 321.

better result is probably that if the acceptance is late then although from the offeree's perspective it must be considered ineffective, the offeror should have the ability to recognize the acceptance.[87] Perhaps one way the common law could give effect to such commercial considerations is to consider the acceptance a counter-offer allowing the original offeror to accept it as offeree.

4.25 The doctrinal basis of the position that an offer must be accepted within a reasonable time when no time is expressed in the terms of the offer remains unresolved. However, depending on the view adopted, this may impact on the evidence available to determine what constitutes a reasonable time. The leading statement remains that of Buckley J in *Manchester Diocesan Council for Education v Commercial & General Investments Ltd* [88] where it is stated:[89]

> There appear to me to be two possible views on methods of approaching the problem. First, it may be said that by implication the offer is made upon terms that, if it is not accepted within a reasonable time, it must be treated as withdrawn. Alternatively, it may be said that, if the offeree does not accept the offer within a reasonable time, he must be treated as having refused it ... The first of these alternatives involves implying a term ... the second is based upon an inference to be drawn from the conduct of the offeree ... If in the first alternative the time which the offeror is to be treated as having set for acceptance is to be such a time as is reasonable at the date of the offer, what is reasonable must depend on circumstances then existing and reasonably likely to arise during the continuance of the offer ... [T]his approach clearly involves a certain degree of uncertainty about the precise terms of the offer. If, on the other hand, the time which the offeror is to be treated as having set for acceptance is to be such a time as turns out to be reasonable in the light of circumstances then existing and of circumstances arising thereafter during the continuance of the offer, whether foreseeable or not, an additional element of uncertainty is introduced. The second alternative, on the other hand, involves simply an objective assessment of facts and the determination of the question whether on the facts the offeree should, in fairness to both parties, be regarded as having refused the offer.
>
> ... Unless authority constrains me to do otherwise, I am strongly disposed to prefer the second alternative to the first.

4.26 As a general rule under offer and acceptance analysis a contract takes effect from the moment the acceptance is effective. However, it is necessary to emphasize a couple of points. First, the parties can execute a contract which is expressed to have an effective date

---

[87] See Unidroit Principles of International Commercial Contracts, Art 2.1.9(1) which states: 'A late acceptance is nevertheless effective as an acceptance if without undue delay the offeror so informs the offeree or gives notice to that effect.' Subsection (2) goes on to protect the offeree where the late acceptance is due to a delay in transmission. It states: 'If a communication containing a late acceptance shows that it has been sent in such circumstances that if its transmission had been normal it would have reached the offeror in due time, the late acceptance is effective as an acceptance unless, without undue delay, the offeror informs the offeree that it considers the offer having lapsed.' See further Vogenauere and Kleinheisterkamp (eds), *Commentary on the Unidroit Principles of International Commercial Contracts* (PICC) (OUP, Oxford, 2009), 272ff paras 1–14. See also United Nations Convention on Contracts for the International Sale of Goods, Art 21; Principles of European Contract Law, Art 2: 207; Draft Common Frame of Reference II–4:207. See 3.02.

[88] [1970] 1 WLR 241. This question and its answer is the same as determining why an offer lapses after a reasonable time, see 3.08.

[89] [1970] 1 WLR 241, 247–8. To the extent this relies on an implied term it may be better explained by reference to construction.

prior to the date of execution. This will be given effect to.[90] Even without such an express term it may be possible to imply a term to that effect. Moreover, an earlier effective date may be inferred where the parties conduct themselves on the understanding that if a contract is entered into in the future it will govern their initial relations or, more generally, if they conduct themselves according to some agreed terms and later execute a formal contract incorporating those terms; this is subject to any agreement expressing a different date.[91]

D. Who May Accept an Offer?

For an offer to be capable of acceptance it must be communicated to the offeree either by the offeror or someone authorized to make the communication.[92] Once communicated, an offer may be accepted only by the offeree[93] or an agent appointed by the offeree but no one else.[94] There are two interrelated reasons for this. First, offers are personal to the offeree as a matter of intention; they are not choses in action and cannot be assigned.[95] Second, the law requires the parties to a contract to be certain. **4.27**

In addition to being made to a particular person, an offer may be made to a group, and an offer can be made to the entire world.[96] Where an offer is made to a group of people it is necessary to determine whether it is made to them jointly or severally. If jointly, then it will be necessary for all to accept the offer.[97] When made to the whole world there may still be limits on acceptance. For example, offers of rewards can often only be accepted by the first person who provides the relevant information.[98] Offers made to the whole world to sell certain goods may be subject to an express or implied condition that the offer is only capable of acceptance 'while goods last'. **4.28**

---

[90] *Newlands v Argyll General Insurance Co Ltd* (1958) SR (NSW) 130, 135 per Sugerman J (dissenting).

[91] *Trollope & Colls Ltd v Atomic Power Constructions Ltd* [1963] 1 WLR 333; *City of Box Hill v EW Tauschke Pty Ltd* [1974] VR 39, 47–8. See also *Akron Tyre Co Pty Ltd v Kittson* (1951) 82 CLR 477, 488; *G Percy Trentham Ltd v Archital Luxfer Ltd* [1993] 1 Lloyd's Rep 25, 27. Cf *Newlands v Argyll General Insurance Co Ltd* (1958) SR (NSW) 130, *Hawkins v Clayton Utz & Co* (1986) 5 NSWLR 109, 130.

[92] *Cole v Cottingham* (1837) 8 Car & P 75, 173 ER 406; *Banks v Williams* (1912) 12 SR (NSW) 382; *First Energy (UK) Ltd v Hungarian International Bank Ltd* [1993] 2 Lloyd's Rep 194.

[93] *Reynolds v Atherton* (1922) 127 LT 189. See also Restatement (2d) Contracts § 52.

[94] Generally, unless the terms of the offer are to the contrary, an offeree cannot bring a contract into existence between the offeror and a third party by purporting to accept as the agent of the third party. Moreover, an offer made by A to B cannot be accepted by B and C nor B as agent for B and C; such actions may constitute a counter-offer, see *Lang v James Morrison and Co Ltd* (1912) 13 CLR 1, 6; *Boulton v Jones* (1857) 2 H & N 564, 157 ER 232. Where an offeree would be personally bound, such as by accepting on behalf of an undisclosed principal, a contract will exist, see *Wilson v Winton* [1969] Qd R 536. See further *Lee v Sayers* (1909) 28 NZLR 804. As to the operation of nominee clauses, such as where an offer is made to 'A and/or A's nominee', see Tolhurst, *The Assignment of Contractual Rights* (Hart, Oxford, 2006) para 3.07.

[95] *Meynell v Surtees* (1854) 3 Sm & G 101, 65 ER 581; (1854) 25 LJ Ch 257.

[96] *Carlill v Carbolic Smoke Ball Company* [1893] 1 QB 256, 266, 268–9 per Bowen LJ.

[97] *Meynell v Surtees* (1854) 3 Sm & G 101, 65 ER 581; (1854) 25 LJ Ch 257. See also *Plimmer v O'Neill* [1937] NZLR 950.

[98] Cf 4.20.

4.29 The identity of the offeree is determined by construing the offer, it is determined by reference to a reasonable person in the position of the offeree rather than the subjective state of
mind of the offeror. This is usually a simple matter. However, in any given case it may
involve difficult issues of construction and require a consideration of the subject matter of
the contract, the nature of the obligations that are to be performed under the contract and
the circumstances surrounding the making and purpose of the offer.[99] The offeree's subjective state of mind might also be relevant. For example, in *McMahon v Gilberd and Co
Ltd*,[100] a soft drink manufacturer retained title in its bottles taking a 'deposit' for the bottle
at the point of sale. It advertised to refund the deposit upon the return of the bottle. Some
of these advertisements made it clear that this offer was limited to 'customers' and some did
not. The plaintiff who was a bottle and scrap dealer claimed this reward. It was held that on
construction the offer was only made to 'customers' but in any case, even if the offer was to
the whole world, the facts were such that the plaintiff had actual knowledge that the offer
was not made to him.

E. Offeree Must Accept With Knowledge of the Offer

4.30 Generally, in order to accept an offer the offeree must have knowledge of the offer.[101]
However, it is not necessary that the offeree have knowledge of all the terms of the offer in
order to accept.[102] What the law of contract requires for there to be a bargain is that 'each
party manifest assent with reference to the manifestation of the other'.[103] It follows that in
the case of cross offers, such as where A writes to B offering to sell A's car to B for £5,000
and at the same time B writes to A offering to purchase A's car for £5,000 and the letters

---

[99] *Carter v Hyde* (1923) 33 CLR 115, 120, 123–4, 128 (option exercised by personal representatives of
offeree held to be valid). See also *Varley v Fotheringham* [1905] SALR 19.

[100] [1955] NZLR 1206.

[101] *R v Clarke* (1927) 40 CLR 227, 231–2, 240, 244. See also *Fitch v Snedaker* 38 NY 248, 249 (1868);
Tobin v McComb 156 SW 237 (1913); *Genesee County v Pailthorpe* 246 Mich 356, 224 NW 418 (1929);
Taylor v Allon [1966] 1 QB 304; *Dalgety Australia Ltd v Harris* [1977] 1 NSWLR 324, 328; *Port Jackson
Stevedoring Pty Ltd v Salmond & Spraggon (Aust) Pty Ltd (The New York Star)* (1978) 139 CLR 231, 271;
(reversed on other grounds *Port Jackson Stevedoring Pty Ltd v Salmond & Spraggon (Aust) Pty Ltd (The New York
Star)* (1980) 144 CLR 300; [1981] 1 WLR 138); *Gjergja v Cooper* [1987] VR 167, 206, 208–11. Cf *Gibbons
v Proctor* (1891) 64 LT 594 (and see the facts in *Neville v Kelly* (1862) 12 CBNS 740, 142 ER 1333 although
the issue was not decided), criticized in *R v Clarke* (1927) 40 CLR 227, 240 and *Bloom v American Swiss Watch
Co* [1915] App D 100, 103. The decision in *Gibbons v Proctor* has been explained away on the basis that the
'offeree' was aware of the offer by the time the information he had given to an agent to convey was given to
the offeror, see Peel, *Treitel, The Law of Contract* (12th edn, Thomson, Sweet & Maxwell, London, 2007) para
2-047. Contrast also Restatement (2d) Contracts § 51, comment *a*.

[102] One interesting issue is the protection that third parties, such as stevedores, can obtain by proving that a
contract exists between them and the consignor/consignee which contains an exclusion clause and which was
negotiated on their behalf by the carrier. The principles by which this is achieved are well known and discussed
in *New Zealand Shipping Co Ltd v AM Satterthwaite & Co Ltd (The Eurymedon)* [1975] AC 154; *Port Jackson
Stevedoring Pty Ltd v Salmond & Spraggon (Aust) Pty Ltd (The New York Star)* (1980) 144 CLR 300; [1981] 1
WLR 138. The facts may be that the stevedore has no knowledge of the offer. However, it may be sufficient for
the agent to have this knowledge, cf *Celthene Pty Ltd v WKJ Hauliers Pty Ltd* [1981] 1 NSWLR 606, 616.

[103] Restatement (2d) Contracts § 23. However it is generally only necessary that a manifestation of assent
be in evidence to a reasonable person in the position of the offeror, see Restatement (2d) Contracts § 23
comments *b* and *e*.

cross in the post, there is no contract until one of the parties formally accepts the other's offer.[104]

This is an issue that does not often arise in the context of a bilateral contracts—at least not **4.31** in those created by the exchange of express promises—but it has arisen in the context of unilateral contracts. For example, if an offer of a reward is made in return for a certain act, then if a person happens to carry out that act without knowledge of the offer then they cannot be said to have accepted the offer.[105]

The knowledge requirement is made out if a person learns of an offer whilst carrying out **4.32** the act of acceptance and then continues to complete the act of acceptance.[106] In such cases there is an assumption, rebuttable by evidence, that one reason for continuing the act was to accept the offer.[107] Difficulties arise where the offer contains a number of conditions such as where an offer of reward is given in return for information leading to the 'arrest *and* conviction' of a person and, without knowledge of the offer, a person gives information leading to arrest. Here arguably even if information is later given at trial leading to a conviction it would be too late for the offeree to collect the reward as one of the cumulative conditions of the offer was already made out by the time knowledge was gained, that is, the accused was already arrested and it is now impossible for the offeree to bring about that condition.[108]

F. Offeree Must Intend to Accept Offer

For there to be an acceptance, it is not enough for the offeree to signal that the offered terms **4.33** are acceptable.[109] For the requirement of consensus and an intention to contract to be made out an offeree must have an intention to accept, that is, the offeree must act in reliance on the offer.[110] This is an issue that rarely arises in the context of the formation of a bilateral

---

[104] *Tinn v Hoffmann & Co* (1873) 29 LT 271, 275 per Archibald J, 277 per Grove J, 278 per Brett J, 278 per Keating J, 279 per Blackburn J. See also Restatement (2d) Contracts § 23 comment *d*.

[105] The reason why that is not a sufficient manifestation of assent is explained in Restatement (2d) Contracts § 23 comment *c* in the following terms: 'Obligations arising from unintended manifestations of assent by an offeree are imposed in order to protect the offeror in justifiable reliance of the offeree's promise. If the offer clearly contemplates no commitment by the offeree, so that no binding return promise can be made and justifiable reliance by the offeror is impossible the reason disappears. Thus if a general offer of reward to anyone who does a certain act or achieves a certain result is treated as contemplating a bargain, the only expectations to be fulfilled are those of the offeree, and he may have none unless he knows of the offer.'

[106] Restatement (2d) Contracts § 51. See also *Gibbons v Proctor* (1891) 64 LT 594.

[107] Carter, *Carter on Contract* (Butterworths, Sydney), § 03-270 citing *Robinson v M'Ewan* (1865) 2 WW & A'B (L) 65. See also *Genesee County v Pailthorpe* 246 Mich 356, 224 NW 418 (1929).

[108] See *Fitch v Snedaker* 38 NY 248, 249 (1868).

[109] *OTM Ltd v Hydranautics* [1981] 2 Lloyd's Rep 211, 215. This is another reason why, as noted above, if both parties make the same offer to each other, although that might suggest the terms are acceptable to each party it does not evidence an agreement as neither has accepted the terms of the other, see *Tinn v Hoffmann & Co* (1873) 29 LT 271.

[110] *R v Clarke* (1927) 40 CLR 227, 235. See also *Genesee County v Pailthorpe* 246 Mich 356, 224 NW 418, 418 (1929); *Tobin v McComb* 156 SW 237 (1913); *Blair v Western Mutual Benefit Association* [1972] 4 WWR 284. Cf *Upton-on-Severn Rural District Council v Powell* [1942] 1 All ER 220. It is only necessary that one reason for the offeree's conduct is to act in reliance of the offer. It does not have to be the sole or main reason for acting. Thus, where a party is under a contractual obligation to carry out an act for a third party, the promise

contract created by an exchange of express promises but it can arise in the unilateral contract context especially where the terms of the offer are such that communication of acceptance is not required.

4.34 Whether the offeree intended to accept is an issue of fact. Generally, in terms proof, where an offeree, with knowledge of the offer, carries out the act of acceptance, the court will infer the intention.[111] Such facts have been said to give rise to a prima facie case.[112] It follows that generally it is for the offeror to prove that the offeree did not hold such an intention. Without an admission from the offeree this is a heavy burden.[113] However the inference or presumption is a product of the objective theory of contract focusing on an outward appearance of agreement which may be rebutted by reliable evidence of subjective intent or understanding.[114] Some limits to this inference were suggested by Glass JA (with whom Samuels agreed) in *Dalgety Australia Ltd v Harris*,[115] viz:[116]

> [T]there is only one legal principle, viz. that the conduct of the offeree relied upon both as acceptance and performance must be actuated by the offer at least in part ... Since knowledge of the offer standing alone is by definition insufficient, there can be no general proposition that it will always evidence, in a prima facie way, the acceptance of the offer by conduct. The situations in which acts are proffered as evidence of the acceptance of an offer can exhibit endless variety. They will require individual examination to determine whether there is a basis for holding that the requirements of principle have been fulfilled. An inference available in an evidentiary situation where offeree and offeror are the only parties involved may not be available where the offeree's conduct is explicable by reference to a contract with a third party. Where the evidence establishes a course of dealing between the offeree and a third party which precedes the offer and follows it without alteration, the basis for inferring a causal connection between the offer and subsequent dealing may be entirely lacking.

4.35 In *R v Clarke*[117] Starke J put the matter in the following terms:[118]

> In my opinion the true principle applicable to this type of case is that unless a person performs the conditions of the offer, acting upon its faith or in reliance upon it, he does not

---

to carry out that same act can operate as an acceptance of (and consideration for) a further promise from the offeror, see *Scotson v Pegg* (1861) 6 H & N 295, 158 ER 121.

[111] See 1.13. See also Mitchell and Phillips, 'The Contractual Nexus: Is Reliance Essential?' (2002) 22 OJLS 115, 123.

[112] *R v Clarke* (1927) 40 CLR 227, 244 per Starke J (see also 232 per Isaacs ACJ, 242 per Higgins J), approved *Jackson Stevedoring Pty Ltd v Salmond & Spraggon (Aust) Pty Ltd (The New York Star)* (1978) 139 CLR 231, 271 per Mason and Jacobs JJ (reversed without reference to the point *Port Jackson Stevedoring Pty Ltd v Salmond & Spraggon (Aust) Pty Ltd (The New York Star)* (1980) 144 CLR 300; [1981] 1 WLR 138). See also *Williams v Williams* [1867] LR 2 Ch 294, 305; *Re Commonwealth Homes and Investment Co Ltd* [1943] SASR 211, 224; *Veivers v Cordingley* [1989] 2 Qd R 278, 291–2, FC. As noted above (n 102), in the case of third parties such as stevedores taking the benefit of an exclusion clause, it is sufficient that its agent, the carrier, has knowledge of the offer and reliance will be inferred by the stevedore carrying out the act of taking the goods off the ship; moreover, in most cases the stevedore will act in reliance of that offer, it would not take on the risk if that were not the case. See further Mitchell and Phillips, 'The Contractual Nexus: Is Reliance Essential?' (2002) 22 OJLS 115, 122.

[113] Mitchell and Phillips, 'The Contractual Nexus: Is Reliance Essential?' (2002) 22 OJLS 115, 121.

[114] See 1.13.

[115] [1977] 1 NSWLR 324.

[116] [1977] 1 NSWLR 324, 328, cf 332 per Mahoney JA.

[117] (1927) 40 CLR 227.

[118] (1927) 40 CLR 227, 244.

accept the offer and the offeror is not bound to him. As a matter of proof any person knowing of the offer who performs its conditions establishes prima facie an acceptance of that offer ... From such facts an acceptance is probable but it is not, as was urged, 'an absolute proposition of law' that one, who, having the offer before him, acts as one would naturally be induced to act, is deemed to have acted on the faith of or in reliance upon that offer. It is an inference of fact and may be excluded by evidence ... The statements or conduct of the party himself uncommunicated to the other party, or the circumstances of the case, may supply that evidence. Ordinarily, it is true, the law judges of the intention of a person in making a contract by outward expression only by words or acts communicated between them ... But when the offeror, as in the anomalous case under consideration, has dispensed with any previous communication to himself of the acceptance of the offer the law is deprived of one of the means by which it judges of the intention of the parties, and the performance of the conditions of the offer is not in all cases conclusive for they may have been performed by one who never hears of the offer or who never intended to accept it. Hence the statements or conduct of the party himself uncommunicated to the other party are admissible to show the circumstances under which an act, seemingly within the terms of the offer, was done and the inducement which led to the act.

4.36 A further issue which rarely arises concerns the type of intention required. Generally, 'the mind of the acceptor must go, not merely to the doing of the act but, in the appropriate way, to the offer'.[119] Thus, in the case of an offer for reward the party seeking to collect the reward must provide the information with the intention that it be acted upon, it is not enough (even with knowledge of the offer) to simply mention it in conversation.[120] It is usually enough for the offeree to show that the act was done in reliance of the offer. But that of itself does not deal with the issue of mixed motives and the extent to which an intention to accept can exist when other motives are involved. Some courts have expressed the view that motive is irrelevant. For example, in *Smirnis v Toronto Sun Publishing Co*,[121] it was said:[122]

> The motive of the person who comes forward is not relevant. It may be greed, shame, or public-spiritedness. The character of the person who comes forward is not a factor. It would be expected that the persons more likely to have knowledge and information concerning the commission of a crime may well be unsavoury individuals. Who else would be expected to have a close connection with crimes and criminals?

4.37 The issue of mixed motives and intention was before the High Court of Australia in *R v Clarke*.[123] In this case the Western Australian government offered a reward for information leading to the arrest and conviction of persons involved in the murder of two police officers. Later Clarke was charged in connection with the murder of one of the police officers. Clarke had seen the offer of reward and he gave information and evidence which led to the arrest of one person and the conviction of two people for the murder of one of the officers.

---

[119] *Dalgety Australia Ltd v Harris* [1977] 1 NSWLR 324, 330 per Mahoney JA.
[120] *Lockhart v Barnard* (1845) 14 M & W 674, 153 ER 646.
[121] (1997) 37 OR (3d) 440. *Williams v Carwardine* (1933) 5 Car & P 566, 573, 172 ER 1101, 1104 per Parke J (Hereford Assizes), (1933) 5 Car & P 566, 574 per Littledale J, 574 per Patteson J, 172 ER 1101, 1104, 1005 (Court of King's Bench); (1933) 4 B & Ad 621, 623, 110 ER 590, 591 per Patteson J.
[122] (1997) 37 OR (3d) 440. See generally *Simmons v US* 308 F 2d 160 (1962).
[123] (1927) 40 CLR 227.

For the purposes of the appeal it was assumed this satisfied the terms of the offer.[124] However, Clarke admitted that he gave the evidence not for the purpose of accepting the offer but to avoid being charged with these crimes and to clear his name. There was also evidence that by the time he gave this information he had in fact forgotten about the offer. Higgins J held that Clarke had no right to the reward because he did not satisfy the knowledge requirement.[125] Others went further and said that Clarke was not entitled to the reward because his own evidence showed that he lacked the necessary intent, he had not acted in pursuance of the offer of reward.[126] On the evidence that too seems a reasonable conclusion given the admission that he did not give the evidence to accept the reward.

4.38 Clarke lost before the trial judge but that decision was reversed by a majority on appeal. The majority based their decision on *Williams v Carwardine*[127] which in their view had stood a long time and must therefore be regarded as accurate. When the matter came before the High Court of Australia it was therefore necessary to look at that decision. In investigating that decision it is the judgment of Isaacs ACJ that has sparked the most controversy because he concluded that on the evidence Clarke had neither a legal or moral claim to the reward.[128]

4.39 In *Williams v Carwardine,*[129] a woman with knowledge of an offer of reward for information 'as might lead' to the discovery of the murderer of Walter Carwardine, gave evidence so as to ease her guilty conscience. It was held that she was entitled to the reward. That is, with knowledge of the offer she carried out the act of acceptance. Isaacs J noted that the proceedings in the case had been reported in four different reports and they differed so that it was not certain as to what the exact facts were in the case. Certainly some reports suggest that it is sufficient if the offeree knows of the offer and carries out the required act.[130] Indeed the view is strongly held by some commentators that there is no legal requirement that the offeree act in reliance of the offer; the doing of the act with knowledge of the offer is sufficient and that *Williams v Carwadine* is authority for this.[131] Certainly this would be sufficient to raise the presumption or inference but if reliance is jettisoned at the level of contract theory it is difficult to see how the further requirement for contract formation, namely, the need for an intention to contract, could survive. In *R v Clarke*, Isaacs ACJ thought that the court in *Williams v Carwadine* had concluded that there was nothing in her motives for giving the information that was inconsistent with the prima facie inference

---

[124] (1927) 40 CLR 227, 237, 238 (the reasons for it not satisfying the terms of the offer are set out in the judgment of Higgins J at 242).
[125] (1927) 40 CLR 227, 241 per Higgins J.
[126] (1927) 40 CLR 227, 231 per Isaacs ACJ, 244–5 per Starke J.
[127] (1833) 5 Car & P 566, 172 ER 1101 contains the judgment of Parke J (Hereford Assizes) and the King's Bench decision; (1933) 4 B & Ad 621, 110 ER 590 contains a summary of the decision of Parke J and the decision of King's Bench. See also *Williams v Carwardine* (1833) 1 N & M 418 and *Williams v Cawardine* (1833) 2 LJ KB (NS) 101 which summarize both decisions.
[128] (1927) 40 CLR 227, 231.
[129] (1833) 5 Car & P 566, 172 ER 1101.
[130] See (1833) 5 Car & P 566, 573, 172 ER 1101, 1104; (1933) 4 B & Ad 621, 623, 110 ER 590, 590–1.
[131] See Mitchell and Phillips, 'The Contractual Nexus: Is Reliance Essential?' (2002) 22 OJLS 115.

that arose upon her carrying out the act with knowledge of the offer.[132] That is, there is a distinction between intention and motive, motive can indicate a state of mind but cannot usurp the 'legal place of intention'.[133] He thought that if that was the correct understanding of *Williams v Carwardine*, then it was in line with accepted doctrine, but if it went further then it was to be disregarded.[134] Higgins J too said that the reports of the case show that 'the informer knew of the offer when giving the information, and meant to accept the offer though she had also a motive in her guilty conscience'.[135] Thus, it is possible to have multiple motives for carrying out the act of acceptance. It is only necessary that one also has the intention to accept.[136] However, it would appear that Isaacs ACJ was of the view that some motives will be inconsistent with an intention to accept or, if they are held, are so all encompassing of thought that it is not possible to also entertain an intention to contract. In short an intention to contract cannot co-exist with certain motives and if such motives are admitted by the offeree or proven by the offeror then the presumption of reliance will be rebutted.

G. Correspondence with Offer[137]

For an acceptance to be effective it must correspond to the terms of the offer.[138] This is known as the 'mirror image rule'.[139] To a certain extent this rule is strict, for there to be a contract upon communication of an acceptance that acceptance must assent to the terms of the offer.[140] However, there is no rule that the acceptance must be in the form of 'I accept your offer' or that it exactly duplicate the terms of the offer. It may rephrase the terms. Therefore, ultimately whether or not an offeree accepts an offer depends on intention. There is therefore an aspect of the 'mirror image rule' that is a 'default rule' in that where an offeree sends a communication to the offeror that does not correspond to the terms of the offer then a reasonable person in the position of the offeror will usually conclude that the offeree does not intend to accept.[141] However, ultimately the result must depend on how the communication is to be interpreted by a reasonable person in the position of the

4.40

---

[132] (1927) 40 CLR 227, 232.

[133] (1927) 40 CLR 227, 232.

[134] (1927) 40 CLR 227, 233.

[135] (1927) 40 CLR 227, 240, (see also at 243 per Starke J).

[136] Contract law has had to deal with the distinction between motive and intention for a long time. Thus, in the case of a mistake, generally a mistake about an attribute of the subject matter of the contract will not negate an intention to contract so as to void the contract for mistake.

[137] As regards errors in the transmission of an acceptance, see 4.92.

[138] As to the effect on an offer of a purported acceptance that is not the 'mirror image' of the offer, see 3.18.

[139] This term was used by Hogan, 'The Highways and Some of the Byways in the Sales and Bulk Sales Articles of the Uniform Commercial Code' (1962) 48 Cornell Law Quarterly 1, 44. See also Davenport, 'How to Handle Sales of Goods: The Problem of Conflicting Purchase Orders and Acceptances and New Concepts in Contract Law' (1963) 19 Bus Lawyer 75; Baird and Weisberg, 'Rules, Standards, and the Battle of the Forms: A Reassessment of §2-207' (1982) 68 Va L Rev 1217, 1231–7.

[140] *Tonitto v Bassal* (1992) 28 NSWLR 564, 574.

[141] Although the reference to a 'default rule' is convenient, it is perhaps better expressed as a default position or 'interpretive standard', see Eisenburg, 'Expression Rules in Contract Law & Problems of Offer and Acceptance' (1994) 82 Cal L Rev 1127, 1128.

offeror[142] and a 'communication is sufficient which shows that the offeree is accepting the offer, and a communication of information showing that the offeree is treating the offer as accepted is sufficient'.[143]

4.41   One aspect of the requirement of correspondence is that the offeree must accept all the terms of the offer. It is not possible to accept an offer in part.[144] For example, if an offeror offers to sell 100 tons of grain for £100 pounds, the buyer cannot purport to accept 50 tons at £50.[145] However, an offer may propose alternatives. For example, to sell or lease land or sell or hire goods.[146] It is also common for a seller of goods to offer varying quantities of goods at varying prices. In each of these examples the offeree can accept one of the alternatives on offer.[147] But neither example would constitute a partial acceptance. Whether or not an offer includes such alternatives is a question of construction.[148] Where the benefit of an offer is taken by conduct and the offer is not divisible, it will usually be inferred that the offeree is assenting to all the terms of the offer and agreeing to take on the burden of the contract which results in a true acceptance.[149]

4.42   Another aspect of the correspondence requirement is that generally an acceptance must not add to, vary or seek to modify the terms of an offer.[150] Such a communication may amount to a counter-offer where it evidences an intention to contract and is certain and complete.[151] In determining whether an alleged acceptance adds to the terms of the offer all the circumstances must be looked at. Thus, the letter of acceptance must be looked at as a whole with each sentence read in context.[152] It is not possible to ignore sentences if they are not meaningless or made in error.[153] Nor can they be ignored if they are intended to have some effect and are not capable of severance from the terms of the acceptance. In some cases

---

[142]   *Carter v Hyde* (1923) 33 CLR 115, 126 per Isaacs J citing *Jones v Daniel* [1894] 2 Ch 332.

[143]   *Integrated Lighting & Ceilings Pty Ltd v Philips Electrical Pty Ltd* (1969) 90 WN (Pt 1) (NSW) 693, 697 per Hope J.

[144]   *Davies v Smith* (1938) 12 ALJR 258.

[145]   *Ocean Coal Co Ltd v Powell Duffryn Steam Coal Co Ltd* [1932] 1 Ch 654; *McClay v Seeligson* (1904) 7 WALR 87.

[146]   Eg *Morrison v Neill* (1875) 1 VLR (L) 287; *Georgoulis v Mandalinic* [1984] 1 NSWLR 612.

[147]   However, the offeree must accept one of the offers. An ambiguous acceptance which does not identify the alternative adopted is not effective, see *Peter Lind & Co Ltd v Mersey Docks & Harbour Board* [1972] 2 Lloyd's Rep 234.

[148]   *Georgoulis v Mandalinic* [1984] 1 NSWLR 612, 615.

[149]   *Brambles Holdings Ltd v Bathurst City Council* (2001) 53 NSWLR 153. Contrast an express acceptance of the benefit of an offer which may be ambiguous as to whether the offeree is accepting all the terms of the offer.

[150]   See Restatement (2d) Contracts § 59. See generally *Tucker v Godfrey* (1862) 1 SCR (NSW) 292; *Holland v Eyre* (1825) 2 Sim & St 194, 57 ER 319; *Turner Kempson & Co Pty Ltd v Camm* [1922] VLR 498; *Bastard v McCallum* [1924] VLR 9; *Davies v Smith* (1938) 12 ALJR 258; *Reporoa Stores Ltd v Treloar* [1958] NZLR 177; *Gulf Corporation Ltd v Gulf Harbour Investments Ltd* [2006] 1 NZLR 21. See further *Grainger v Vindin* [1865] 4 SCR (NSW) 32 (offer to purchase goods but requesting three months to pay but payment to be made before delivery; the seller 'accepted' forwarding an invoice and promissory note for signature which was payable in three months; held that the promissory note introduced a new term as it could be circulated with the result that the buyer might be forced to pay third persons).

[151]   Cf 4.11.

[152]   *Reporoa Stores Ltd v Treloar* [1958] NZLR 177. See also *Gulf Corporation Ltd v Gulf Harbour Investments Ltd* [2006] 1 NZLR 21, 25.

[153]   *Nicolene Ltd v Simmonds* [1953] 1 QB 543; *Universal Guarantee Pty Ltd v Carlile* [1957] VR 68.

it may be necessary to consider all the correspondence between the parties.[154] It may be that the acceptance refers to an issue agreed to by the parties prior to the issue of a formal offer and which does not appear in the offer expressly but is nevertheless implied by the circumstances.[155] It may be that what appears to be an additional term is no more than an intimation of the steps the offeree will take if there is a breach of a term of the agreement and so can be ignored.[156] It may be that what is additional is simply the provision of some information which does not seek to introduce a new term.[157] Similarly, it may be that an acceptance restates the terms of the offer imprecisely thereby adding a reference to a matter that has no real effect on the terms put forward in the offer or the meaning of the acceptance. Here too it may be possible to ignore certain words or sentences.[158] However, it is also possible that a series of communications on their face may objectively evidence an agreement which is then shown to be false according to the subjective understanding of the parties when other relevant communications are taken into account.[159] When investigating relevant post acceptance conduct it is important to determine whether that conduct evidences that the parties did not intend the apparent agreement to be effective or whether it evidences an attempt to renegotiate a contract.[160] Finally, the terms of an acceptance may not have to correspond to those of the offer if, in the acceptance, the offeree introduces a term that is for the sole benefit of the offeror.[161]

An acceptance that does not seek to vary or add to the terms of an offer but which does 'not **4.43** precisely match the words of the offer', will still be effective if it evidences an intention to accept determined by reference to a reasonable person in the position of the offeror.[162] Acceptances of that sort are often explicable on the basis of mistake,[163] they are not intended

---

[154] *Hussey v Horne-Payne* [1879] 4 App Cas 311, 316; *Costello v Loulakas* [1938] St R Qd 267. See also *Harmony Shipping Co SA v Saudi-Europe Line Ltd (The Good Helmsman)* [1981] 1 Lloyd's Rep 377, 409.

[155] Eg *Simpson v Hughes* (1897) 66 LJ Ch 334.

[156] *Re Imperial Land Co of Marseilles (Harris' Case)* (1872) 7 Ch App 587 QBD. See also *Reporoa Stores Ltd v Treloar* [1958] NZLR 177, 189, 204, 210.

[157] *In re Scottish Petroleum Co* (1883) LR 23 Ch D 413.

[158] *Carter v Hyde* (1923) 33 CLR 115 (option offered the 'lease, licence furniture and goodwill' of a business; the acceptance and exercise of the option stated, in a sentence that attempted to refer to and set out the terms of the option, 'as per inventory' after 'licence, goodwill and furniture'; however, the following sentence was a clear unequivocal statement of acceptance; the first statement was a mere misstatement of the terms).

[159] See *Hussey v Horne-Payne* [1879] 4 App Cas 311. See also *Howard Smith & Co Ltd v Varawa* (1907) 5 CLR 68.

[160] See *Perry v Suffields* [1916] 2 Ch 187; *Costello v Loulakas* [1938] St R Qd 267, 276; *Terrex Resources NL v Magnet Petroleum Pty Ltd* [1988] 1 WAR 144. See also *Albrecht Chem Co v Anderson Trading Corp* 298 NY 437, 84 NE 2d 625 (1949). See 4.05.

[161] Eg *Ex parte Fealey* (1897) 18 LR (NSW) 282 (request to place a half-inch advertisement in a newspaper; the proprietor published a one-inch advertisement, the charge for a one-inch advert being the same as a half-inch advert; held, being a variation in favour of the offeror it was not a variation the court would recognize). See also *Boreland v Docker* [2007] NSWCA 94, [76], [78], [86], CA.

[162] *Lark v Outhwaite* [1991] 2 Lloyd's Rep 132, 139.

[163] In a transaction where the parties exchange contracts it can happen that by error one contract is not the mirror image of the other, for example because there has been a failure to attach certain documents to one copy. Generally, if the error can be remedied by an order for rectification the 'mirror image' rule would be satisfied; it may be different if the documents contradict each other and raise a doubt as to whether there has been an agreement on terms; the issue is discussed in *Sindel v Georgiou* (1984) 154 CLR 661, 667–8. See further *Harrison v Battye* [1975] 1 WLR 58 (prior to the exchange of an agreement for the sale of land made subject to contract, the parties agreed to a reduction of the amount of the deposit; the purchasers made the

to introduce new terms but rephrase the terms of the offer.[164] In such cases the discrepancies can be ignored.[165] However, where a reasonable person in the position of the offeror would conclude that by reason of the discrepancy the offeree was not intending to accept the terms of the offer then the mistake cannot be ignored.[166] There is a difference between a mere misstatement of a term and a re-statement of the terms that would indicate to a reasonable person in the position of the offeror a misunderstanding of the construction or operation of the contract[167] such as would amount to the introduction of a different term or otherwise evidence a lack of assent to the terms of the offer.[168] An offeree communicating such a misunderstanding of the terms of the offer in its acceptance—and then seeking to adopt those terms as set out by the offeree in its acceptance—is not accepting the offeror's offer. However, where a reasonable person in the position of the offeror would conclude that the statement of the offeree is an acceptance then, if the offeree wishes to argue otherwise (in order to vitiate the offeree's own consent), the offeree would generally need to prove an operative

---

change to their copy, executed it and sent it to the vendor; the vendor's solicitor failed to make the change to their copy and the vendor signed this unchanged copy; then in error the solicitor returned the purchaser's copy with a covering letter that stated, 'We enclose part contract signed by our client to complete the exchange'; it was held that there was no contract because there was no exchange of contracts in the same terms; although the error of sending back the purchasers' copy might be overlooked the differences in terms could not; there was no evidence of the vendor agreeing to the alteration so rectification was not possible).

[164] *The Proprietors and c, of the English and Foreign Credit Company Ltd v Ludovico Arduin* (1871) LR 5 HL 64.
[165] See generally *Cavallari v Premier Refrigeration Co Pty Ltd* (1952) 85 CLR 20, 26–7; *Quadling v Robinson* (1976) 137 CLR 192, 201. See below 4.53. In such cases it will often not be possible to interpret the acceptance as a counter-offer as the offeree does not intend to be bound by the 'mistaken' terms and the offeror in such a case might otherwise be able to take advantage of the offeree, see *United States v Braunstein* 75 F Supp 137, 139 (1947).
[166] Eg *Redowood Pty Ltd v Mongoose Pty Ltd* [2005] NSWCA 32 (public offer to purchase rights in a publicly listed company; the offeree properly completed one rights acceptance form to sell 65,087,000 rights by referring to the security holder reference number (SRN) for those rights; however, when completing a second rights acceptance form to sell 55 million rights it, in error, put in the SRN for the 65,087,000 figure again; it was held there was no contract; the objective meaning of the second acceptance form was clear on its face, it attempted to sell rights the offeror already owned by virtue of the first acceptance; the manner of acceptance was strict and this acceptance did not comply; this was an offer to buy a massive number of rights from thousands of rights holders and the time frame was short; in those circumstances compliance with the manner of acceptance would be intended to be strict; in such circumstances the proper approach was to require strict compliance with the terms of the offer rather than consider the particular communications that passed between these particular parties; the latter approach would create too much uncertainty in such transactions).
[167] *Reporoa Stores Ltd v Treloar* [1958] NZLR 177, 190, per Gresson J ('I appreciate that if a person assents to an offer in an erroneous belief regarding the obligations imposed that may well have no effect. A written contract cannot be impeached simply because one of the parties to it put an erroneous construction on the words in which the contract is expressed: *Wilding v Sanderson* [1897] 2 Ch 534. But, when the acceptance is conveyed in such a form as to make it apparent that, what is accepted is not the offer as made but what the acceptor mistakenly thinks to be the offer, no consensus ad idem can arise. It is true that a contract will be concluded once the parties whatever their innermost state of mind may be, have to outward appearances, agreed with sufficient certainty in the same terms and on the same subject matter; but it will not be so when the tenor of an acceptance shows that the terms which purport to have been accepted have been misapprehended.') See also *United States v Braunstein* 75 F Supp 137, 139 (1947); *Evans Deakin Industries Ltd v The Queensland Electricity Generating Board* (1984) 1 BCL 334.
[168] *Cavallari v Premier Refrigeration Co Pty Ltd* (1952) 85 CLR 20; *Carter v Hyde* (1923) 33 CLR 115, 126, 133. There is a distinction between a dispute over the meaning and legal effect of the terms of a contract as regards the performance of an existing contract (where the contract must be taken to express the intention of both parties), and a statement made (either consciously or informed by a mistake) in the context of contract formation which evidences a lack of assent to the terms offered.

unilateral mistake.[169] Instances of operative unilateral mistake would be rare if the offeree has merely attempted to restate the terms of the offer so that they do not precisely match the words of the offer. Moreover, if the discrepancy is significant enough to be an operative unilateral mistake it would be most unlikely that it could be ignored under the objective test and so it would be a rare case that would ever need to resort to unilateral mistake.[170]

In addition the courts have generally been reluctant to rewrite the terms of an acceptance **4.44** even where there is a high probability of knowing what was intended. For example, in *United States v Braunstein*[171] a bid was made for a certain number of boxes of raisins for '10 cents per pound'. The acceptance read '10 cents per box'. It was held that there was no contract. In reply to a submission that the offeror knew in the circumstances what the offeree intended, it was said that the offeror knew that the offeree did not intend what was written in the 'acceptance' and that is sufficient to negate any alleged contract. It was not possible from this position to derive what the offeree might have intended and thereby create an agreement.[172] Medina J then said:[173]

> [T]he courts have refrained from reforming offers and acceptances. Thus, in the classic case of *Harvey v Facey* [1893] AC 552, PC, it would have taken but little interpretation to construe as an offer the defendant's telegram, 'Lowest price for Bumper Hall Pen £900,' which was a reply to plaintiff's telegram, 'Will you sell us Bumper Hall Pen? Telegraph lowest cash price.'

Where clear words of acceptance are used but there are other ambiguous provisions in the **4.45** 'acceptance' then, if possible, the court will lean towards a construction of the ambiguous provisions that is consistent with the clear words of acceptance.[174] There is a view that where an offeree uses very clear words of acceptance such that the offeror would reasonably believe there to be an acceptance, but also seeks to change the terms of the offer, then the offeree comes under a duty to bring that variation to the attention of the offeror and if they do not they should be bound by the terms of the offer.[175]

The express statement of a term in an acceptance that did not appear in the offer but which **4.46** would in any case be implied either in law or in fact does not vary or add to the terms.[176]

An acceptance that suggests a variation or additional terms will be effective if, on construc- **4.47** tion, the acceptance expresses an intention to be immediately bound and is not conditional

---

[169] See Furmston, *Cheshire, Fifoot and Furmston's, Law of Contract* (15th edn, OUP, Oxford, 2007) 304ff; Carter, Peden and Tolhurst, *Contract Law in Australia* (5th edn, Butterworths, Sydney), para 20-50.
[170] Similarly an offeree cannot accept ('snap up') an offer that the offeree knew or a reasonable person in the offeree's position would know was not intended to be made according to its terms, *Hartog v Colin & Shields* [1939] 3 All ER 566, 568; *Belle River Community Arena Inc v WJC Koffmann Co Ltd* (1978) 20 OR (2d) 447. Cf *Imperial Glass Ltd v Consolidated Supplies Ltd* (1960) 22 DLR (2d) 759. See further Nozick, (1982) 60 Can Bar Rev 345; Phang, 'Contract Formation and Mistake in Cyberspace' (2005) 21 JCL 197 discussing *Chwee Kin Keong v Digilandmall.com Pte Ltd* [2004] SLR 594 (affirmed [2005] 1 SLR 502).
[171] 75 F Supp 137 (1947).
[172] 75 F Supp 137, 138–9 (1947).
[173] 75 F Supp 137, 139 (1947).
[174] *The Proprietors and c, of the English and Foreign Credit Company Ltd v Ludovico Arduin* (1871) LR 5 HL 64, 79, see also at 81 dealing with replies to ambiguous offers. See above 4.08.
[175] *The Proprietors and c, of the English and Foreign Credit Company Ltd v Ludovico Arduin* (1871) LR 5 HL 64. See also *Braund v Mutual Life and Citizens' Assurance Co Ltd* [1926] NZLR 529.
[176] *Lark v Outhwaite* [1991] 2 Lloyd's Rep 132, 139.

upon that term being agreed to by the offeror.[177] Here the suggested term is akin to an enquiry.[178] Whether or not a suggested term is put forward as conditioning the acceptance or not will depend on the facts of each case.[179] This issue can often arise where the offer is silent on some point and the acceptance makes a suggestion to fill that gap but is not conditional upon the offeror agreeing to the suggestion. For example, if the offer is silent on a date for delivery of goods or for the handing over of possession in respect to land, an acceptance may suggest or request a time.[180] This idea is adopted in the Uniform Commercial Code. Section 2-206(3) provides:

> A definite and seasonable expression of acceptance in a record operates as an acceptance even if it contains terms additional to or different from the offer.

4.48 This is the primary rule of acceptance under Article 2 and is expressed in Official Comment 2 as a rejection of the mirror image rule. However, Official Comment 3 makes it clear that it is not far removed from the position at common law and relevantly provides:

> This rule applies, however, only to an expression of acceptance that is not only seasonable but also 'definite'. A purported expression of acceptance containing additional or different terms would not be a 'definite' acceptance when the offeree's expression clearly communicates to the offeror the offeree's unwillingness to do business unless the offeror assents to those additional or different terms ... In a situation in which the offer clearly indicates that the offeror is unwilling to do business on any terms other than those contained in the offer, and the offeree responds with an expression of acceptance that contains additional or different terms, a court could also conclude that the offeree's response does not constitute a definite expression of acceptance.[181]

4.49 The mirror image rule is a rule generally accepted within systems of contract law.[182] However, within the international arena there is softening of its strict approach. For example, Article 19(2) of the United Nations Convention on Contracts for the International Sale of Goods relevantly provides:[183]

> [A] reply to an offer which purports to be an acceptance but contains additional or different terms which do not materially alter the terms of the offer constitutes an acceptance, unless

---

[177] See *Universal Guarantee Pty Ltd v Carlile* [1957] VR 68; *Parbury Henty & Co Pty Ltd v General Engineering & Agencies Pty Ltd* (1973) 47 ALJR 336. This is to be distinguished from a reply that is not an acceptance but which seeks to keep the offer open while making a separate offer that does not operate as a counter-offer and kill the first offer, see 3.24. See Restatement (2d) Contracts § 61.

[178] *Costello v Loulakas* [1938] St R Qd 267, 273. See 3.22. Similarly if an additional term is not intended to form part of the acceptance it will not be considered to be an additional term, see *EJ Armstrong v The Wellington-Manawatu Railway Co Ltd* (1885) NZLR 3 SC 441.

[179] See *Costello v Loulakas* [1938] St R Qd 267. See further *Crossley v Maycock* [1874] LR 18 Eq 180; *Jones v Daniel* [1894] 2 Ch 332. See also Restatement (2d) Contracts § 59.

[180] *Dunlop v Higgins* (1848) 1 HLC 381, 9 ER 805; *Clive v Beaumont* (1848) 1 De G & SM 397, 63 ER 1121. See also *Simpson v Hughes* (1897) 66 LJ Ch 334; *Costello v Loulakas* [1938] St R Qd 267. See also *B Seppelt & Sons Ltd v Commissioner for Main Roads* (1975) 1 BPR 9147, 9149, 9153. Cf *Cross v Davidson* [1899] 17 NZLR 576.

[181] The terms of a contract formed within Article 2 are determined under § 2-207.

[182] Eg United Nations Convention on Contracts for the International Sale of Goods (1980), Art 19(1); Unidroit Principles of International Commercial Contracts 2004, Art 2.1.11(1); Principles of European Contract Law Art 2:208; Draft Common Frame of Reference II–4:208(1).

[183] See also Unidroit Principles of International Commercial Contracts 2004, Art 2.1.11(2). See further Principles of European Contract Law Art 2:208 (the Draft Common Frame of Reference II–4:208(2) and (3) are in similar terms).

the offeror, without undue delay, objects orally to the discrepancy or dispatches a notice to that effect.

If the offeror fails to object then the additional or different terms will be incorporated into **4.50** the contract.[184] In practice much will turn on whether or not any addition is 'material'.[185] Article 19(3) provides some guidance stating:

> Additional or different terms relating, among other things, to the price, payment, quality and quantity of the goods, place and time of delivery, extent of one party's liability to the other or the settlement of disputes are considered to alter the terms of the offer materially.

Arguably because the 'mirror image rule' is actually based on intention the factual situation **4.51** dealt with in these provisions could be accommodated within the common law. That is, being based on intention, it must be possible for a reply to an offer to contain a very clear expression of acceptance and yet add to the terms of the offer in a non-material way such as to not negate the clear intention to accept. If those terms are clearly brought to the notice of the offeror who then conducts him or herself as if there is a contract then arguably those terms will form the basis of the agreement between the parties. In the result it all depends on how a reasonable person in the position of the offeror would construe the communication. It should also be noted that despite what a reasonable person in the position of the offeror might conclude, if the offeror in fact knew the offeree did not intend to accept the offeror's terms, the alleged acceptance will not be effective.[186]

H. Acceptance Must Be Unequivocal

Overlapping to some extent with the mirror image rule is the requirement that the accep- **4.52** tance be unequivocal.[187] This goes to the language of the acceptance. It must be absolute and unconditional. However, the requirement that the language be unequivocal is merely a default rule.[188] Ultimately the issue is one of intention and generally, in order for an offeree to communicate an intention to accept and be bound by the terms of the offer, he or she must use unequivocal language.[189] If that language is in evidence the law then gives the communication the legal effect of an acceptance. For example, in *National Cash Register Co v McCann*[190] the defendant sent the plaintiff company an order which requested immediate shipment of a particular cash register. The plaintiff had sent the following reply: 'This is to

---

[184] See also Unidroit Principles of International Commercial Contracts 2004, Art 2.1.11(2); Principles of European Contract Law Art 2:208(2); Draft Common Frame of Reference II–4:208(2).

[185] For a discussion on what constitutes a 'material' modification, see Honnold, *Uniform Law For International Sales* (3rd edn, Kluwer Law International, The Netherlands, 1999) para 169. See also Unidroit Principles of International Commercial Contracts 2004, Art 2.1.11 Comment 2.

[186] *Reporoa Stores Ltd v Treloar* [1958] NZLR 177, 192, per Gresson J. See 1.10.

[187] *Lark v Outhwaite* [1991] 2 Lloyd's Rep 132, 139.

[188] As to the precision of this phrase, see n 141 above.

[189] See Restatement (2d) Contracts § 57, which provides: 'Where notification is essential to acceptance by promise, the offeror is not bound by an acceptance in equivocal terms unless he reasonably understands it as an acceptance.'

[190] 80 Misc Rep 165, 140 NYS 916 (1913). See also *Tucker v Godfrey* (1862) 1 SCR (NSW) 292; *Appleby v Johnson* (1874) LR 9 CP 158; *Spencer's Pictures Ltd v Cosens* (1918) 18 SR (NSW) 102; *Ballas v Theophilos (No 2)* (1957) 98 CLR 193, 196.

acknowledge receipt of your order dated 6-23-1911 for one of our No. 542 cash registers. We thank you for your order and assure you that it will have our best attention.' The defendant then wrote to cancel his order. The company contended that the reply amounted to an acceptance which had resulted in a binding contract. However, the court refused to recognize a contract on the basis that the words 'assure you that it will have our best attention' meant 'nothing more than the plaintiff will think about the offer—will consider it. It certainly [did] not mean that the plaintiff [had] thought about it, [had] considered it, and [agreed] to accept, abide by and comply with the terms of the offer.'[191]

4.53 Whether or not a statement is sufficiently unequivocal is determined by reference to a reasonable person in the position of the offeror and is generally referred to as being a question of construction.[192] However, as the issue is one of contract formation, as noted elsewhere, the evidence available to determine the issue is wider than that available to determine the meaning of a term of a valid contract.[193] Where a communication is given that corresponds to the terms of an offer it will generally be held to be an acceptance. Thus, a communication in the form of 'I accept your offer', assuming the offer is identifiable, will constitute an acceptance.[194] So too an acceptance that sets out exactly or otherwise precisely the terms of the offer and expressly agrees to those terms.[195] Moreover, if it is clear that the offeree intended to accept an offer according to its terms but simply misstated those terms, as opposed to expressing an erroneous understanding of those terms,[196] the acceptance will be sufficiently unequivocal and effective.[197] However, if a purported acceptance was given for some other purpose it will not constitute an unequivocal acceptance.[198] It also follows that generally words of acceptance will not operate as an acceptance if they suggest a further formal step needs to be taken before the offeree intends to assume any legal obligation.[199] Thus, where a buyer communicates an acceptance to buy goods but goes on to state that a

---

[191] 80 Misc Rep 165, 140 NYS 916, 918 (1913). See also Unidroit Principles of International Commercial Contracts Art 2.1.6(1) and the commentary to this article which expressly refers to the fact that acknowledging receipt and expressing interest will not in themselves indicate the necessary assent. Any assent must also be unconditional and not be dependent on any further approval or steps to be taken by either party. Article 2:204(1) and (2) of the Principles of European Contract Law and Book II, Art 4:204(1) and (2) of the Draft Common Frame of Reference, are in similar terms to that of Unidroit.

[192] See *Quadling v Robinson* (1976) 137 CLR 192, 196, 201; *Prudential Assurance Co Ltd v Health Minders Pty Ltd* (1987) 9 NSWLR 673, 677, 681, 683; *Lark v Outhwaite* [1991] 2 Lloyd's Rep 132, 139. See also the analysis in *Ballas v Theophilos (No 2)* (1957) 98 CLR 193, 204–6.

[193] See 1.21. See also *Collingridge v Niesmann* (1920) 37 WN (NSW) 224, 225.

[194] *Bigg v Boyd Gibbons Ltd* [1971] 1 WLR 913.

[195] See *Anangel Atlas Compania Naviera SA v Ishikawajima-Harima Heavy Industries Co Ltd (No 2)* [1990] 2 Lloyd's Rep 526, 541.

[196] See *Cavallari v Premier Refrigeration Co Pty Ltd* (1952) 85 CLR 20, 26–7; *Quadling v Robinson* (1976) 137 CLR 192, 201. See above 4.43.

[197] *Prudential Assurance Co Ltd v Health Minders Pty Ltd* (1987) 9 NSWLR 673; *Quadling v Robinson* (1976) 137 CLR 192, 201; *Ballas v Theophilos (No 2)* (1957) 98 CLR 193, 209. See also *Fightvision Pty Ltd v Onisforou* (1999) 47 NSWLR 473, 495 (an imprecise statement or misdescription would not negate an acceptance if it is immaterial so that it could not mislead and if in the result there is evidence of an absolute unqualified intention to accept).

[198] *Tonitto v Bassal* (1992) 28 NSWLR 564. In addition such an acceptance may fail for lack of an intention to accept.

[199] See *Crossley v Maycock* (1874) LR 18 Eq 180; *Davies v Smith* (1938) 12 ALJR 258; *Lewis Construction Co Pty Ltd v M Tichauer Societe Anonyme* [1966] VR 341, 345.

formal order and terms follow there would be no immediate acceptance.[200] Not only would the language in such a case not be unequivocal, the acceptance would be conditional.[201] Similarly if an acceptance is said to be contingent on the occurrence or non-occurrence of an event, it will not take immediate effect.[202] Nevertheless, the construction of any purported acceptance will depend on the facts of each case. Therefore, words that might suggest future conduct such as 'we intend to accept' or 'subject to contract' may evidence an immediate intention to accept on the facts of the case.[203]

I. Acceptance Must Be Communicated

Introduction

Generally, acceptance must be communicated for it to take effect.[204] A contract does not **4.54** come into effect merely because the offeree has subjectively decided to accept.[205] Nor will the acceptance be effective if the offeree accepts by conduct and the fact of that conduct is

---

[200] *EJ Armstrong v The Wellington-Manawatu Railway Co Ltd* (1885) NZLR 3 SC 441. Cf *Homeward Bound Extended Goldmining Co Ltd v Anderson* (1884) NZLR 3 SC 266 (an unequivocal acceptance followed by a document incorporating a new term would not invalidate the acceptance). See also *Lamont v Heron* (1970) 126 CLR 239 (here a telegram sent giving notice of the exercise of an option and stating 'Letter following' was held to be valid; the reference to a letter to follow did not indicate that the exercise was qualified). See further *Reese Bros Plastics Ltd v Hamon-Sobelco Australia Pty Ltd* (1988) 5 BPR 11,106.

[201] Farnsworth, *Farnsworth on Contracts* (3rd edn, Vol 1, Aspen Publishers, New York, 2004) § 3.13, p 273.

[202] Farnsworth, *Farnsworth on Contracts* (3rd edn, Vol 1, Aspen Publishers, New York, 2004) § 3.13, p 274.

[203] *Ballas v Theophilos (No 2)* (1957) 98 CLR 193, 205; *Prudential Assurance Co Ltd v Health Minders Pty Ltd* (1987) 9 NSWLR 673. See also *Mills v Haywood* (1877) 6 Ch D 196; *Collingridge v Niesmann* (1920) 37 WN (NSW) 224; *B Seppelt & Sons Ltd v Commissioner for Main Roads* (1975) 1 BPR 9147, 9149; *Traywinds Pty Ltd v Cooper* [1989] 1 Qd R 222.

[204] *Yona International Ltd v La Réunion Française Société Anonyme d'Assurances et de Réassurances* [1996] 2 Lloyd's Rep 84, 110; *DJE Constructions Pty Ltd v Maddocks* [1982] 1 NSWLR 5, 19; *Schiller v Fisher* [1981] 1 SCR 593, 124 DLR (3d) 577. For doctrinal arguments for the requirement of notice, see Farnsworth, *Farnsworth on Contracts* (3rd edn, Vol 1, Aspen Publishers, New York, 2004) § 3.15, p 302. See Restatement (2d) Contracts § 56, (cf §54) which is subject to § 69. See also United Nations Convention on Contracts for the International Sale of Goods (1980), Art 18(2); Unidroit Principles of International Commercial Contracts (2004), Art 2.1.6 (2); Principles of European Contract Law Art 2:205(1) and (2). The Draft Common Frame of Reference II–4:205(1) and (2) are in the same terms as the European Principles.

[205] *Felthouse v Bindley* (1862) 11 CBNS 869, 142 ER 1037 (offer made to purchase horse; offeree instructed auctioneer not to sell the horse as it had been sold; auctioneer mistakenly sold horse to third party; later offeree wrote to offeror acknowledging the sale to the offeror; the instruction to take the horse out of auction may have evidenced a subjective intention to accept but was not communicated to the offeror; the subsequent letter was not relevant in a claim by the offeror against the auctioneer for conversion). See also *Kingsley & Keith v Glynn Brothers (Chemicals) Ltd* [1953] 1 Lloyd's Rep 211. As to the resolution of corporate or statutory bodies to accept offers and whether a contract is formed prior to the communication of such resolutions, see *Connolly v United Shire of Beechworth* (1874) 5 AJR 50, 52; *Powell v Lee* (1908) 99 LT 284; *Blair v Western Mutual Benefit Association* [1972] 4 WWR 284. There are also numerous cases dealing with the allotment of shares, generally the allotment of shares in response to an offer to purchase shares will constitute the acceptance but there is still a requirement that the shareholder obtain knowledge of the allotment, see generally, *Re Scottish Petroleum Co* (1883) 23 Ch D 413, 430; *Commonwealth Homes and Investment Co Ltd v Smith* (1937) 59 CLR 443; *DJE Constructions Pty Ltd v Maddocks* [1982] 1 NSWLR 5, 19. The better view is that the postal acceptance rule applies to such acceptances, see *Re Imperial Land Company of Marseilles (Harris's Case)* (1872) LR 7 Ch 587 and cf *British and American Telegraph Co Ltd v Colson* (1871) LR 6 Ex Ch 108, 111–12.

not communicated to the offeror.[206] Even the execution of a written contract will generally not take effect unless communicated to the other party,[207] nor will a discussion over an aspect of the manner of performance necessarily communicate an acceptance.[208] It is therefore generally necessary for the offeree to notify the offeror of the conduct. However, despite the general rule that acceptance must be communicated to the offeror or an authorized person,[209] it is arguable that it should be sufficient if the fact of such conduct comes to the attention of the offeror or would come to the attention of the offeror in the normal course of events.[210]

4.55   The requirement of communication is related to the rule that silence is not acceptance which is discussed in more detail below.[211] In practice, the rule that silence is not acceptance tends to be referred to in situations where an offeror has sought to force a contract on an offeree. Any other position would inhibit the offeree's freedom not to contract. Both these rules are predicted by the objective theory of contract which requires some outward expression of acceptance. Moreover, as that theory is informed by a reasonable person in the position of the parties it can be seen that communication must generally be to the offeror. In addition, the basis of the communication rule has been said to be that of hardship in that it would cause hardship for an offeror to be bound without being on notice of this.[212] However, neither rule is necessarily dictated by the objective theory. An offeror cannot force a contract on the offeree by making silence acceptance but can, in theory, bind him or herself by making silence a method of acceptance.[213] Similarly, the offeror may allow for the offeree's assent to be by way of an act the occurrence of which does not have to be communicated to the offeror. In short, if the communication rule protects the offeror from hardship and operates for the benefit of the offeror then it is within the power of the offeror to waive it. Indeed there is no doctrinal impediment to the courts creating exceptions to this rule to give effect to some overriding concern such as fairness, convenience and practicality.[214] In the result, the requirement of communication is merely a default rule[215] that is applied unless a contrary intention is expressed in the terms of the offer, or by reason of the subject matter involved or the circumstances of the case.

---

[206] Cf Restatement (2d) Contracts § 54. See also Uniform Commercial Code 2-206(2).

[207] *Robophone Facilities Ltd v Blank* [1966] 1 WLR 1428, 1432; *Larking v Gardiner* (1895) 27 OR 125; *Schiller v Fisher* [1981] 1 SCR 593. As to whether an offeree could claim there is no contract where the offeree drafted the terms of the offer and those terms stated that the agreement was binding upon execution by the offeree without communication, see *Universal Guarantee Pty Ltd v Carlile* [1957] VR 68; *Latec Finance Pty Ltd v Knight* [1969] 2 NSWR 79 and see *Newlands v Argyll General Insurance Co Ltd* [1959] SR (NSW) 130.

[208] Eg *Soares v Simpson* [1931] NZLR 1079 (option to purchase share in motor vessel; communication of intention to exercise option had to be given within a certain time; a discussion about the method of payment and a later statement by the purchaser to the vendor that he was paying the money into vendor's bank account was not a communication of acceptance but rather a statement as to the mode of performance and not the method of concluding the agreement).

[209] See 4.56.

[210] See Restatement (2d) Contracts § 62 comment *b*. Cf Uniform Commercial Code §2-504(c). See further Farnsworth, *Farnsworth on Contracts* (3rd edn, Vol 1, Aspen Publishers, New York, 2004) § 3.15, p 301.

[211] See 4.62ff.

[212] Peel, *Treitel, The Law of Contract* (12th edn, Thomson, Sweet & Maxwell, London, 2007) para 2-023.

[213] See 4.85.

[214] See Coote, 'The Instantaneous Transmission of Acceptances' (1971) 4 NZULR 331, 332, 333.

[215] As to the precision of this phrase, see n 141 above.

As noted the acceptance must be communicated to the offeror or someone authorized to **4.56** receive it rather than merely having authority to relay it to the offeror.[216] Similarly the communication of acceptance must come from the offeree or someone authorized by the offeree to communicate the acceptance. The communication of an intention to accept by an unauthorized person, even if reflecting the subjective intention of the offeree, is not effective. The offeree retains the freedom to change his or her mind until there is an authorized communication.[217] In *Powell v Lee*,[218] the managers of a school had passed a resolution appointing the plaintiff to the position of headmaster but had not formally communicated this to the plaintiff. However, one of the managers, acting in his individual capacity and without authority, had informed the plaintiff of the resolution. Subsequently the resolution was rescinded and the plaintiff was not appointed to the post. Although the plaintiff argued that acceptance had been communicated to him, the court held that since the manager was not authorized to communicate the decision, there had been no communicated acceptance.[219] Despite this, there is an argument for the view that the offeror should be bound so long as he or she hears of the acceptance from some reliable source or otherwise in the normal course of events.[220]

Offeror waiving need for communication

It is possible for the offeror to dispense with the need for communication of acceptance.[221] In **4.57** some cases the nature of the transaction itself may dictate that communication is not required.[222] Similarly a course of dealing or trade practice may suggest this. However, generally

---

[216] See 4.54. See *Manchester Diocesan Council for Education v Commercial & General Investments Ltd* [1970] 1 WLR 241; *Felthouse v Bindley* (1862) 11 CBNS 869, 142 ER 1037 (affirmed on other grounds (1863) 7 LT 835); *Batt v Onslow* (1892) 13 LR (NSW) Eq 79; *Manufacturers' Mutual Insurance Ltd v John H Boardman Insurance Brokers Pty Ltd* (1994) 179 CLR 650; *Island Properties Ltd v Entertainment Enterprises Ltd* (1983) 146 DLR (3d) 505 (appeal allowed in part (1986) 26 DLR (4th) 347); *Powierza v Daley* [1985] 1 NZLR 558. See *Carmichael v Bank of Montreal* (1972) 25 DLR (3d) 570 (emphasizing the need to take into account trade practice in determining who is authorized to receive an acceptance). Once an acceptance is communicated to a person authorized to accept it, the offeror can no longer seek to revoke the offer even though the offeror may not yet know of the acceptance, see *Powierza v Daley* [1985] 1 NZLR 558. Interesting issues arise in reward cases where a person communicates the relevant information to a third party and it is the third party who then passes that onto the offeror or the agent of the offeror, see *Lockhart v Barnard* (1845) 14 M & W 674, 153 ER 646. Generally, the information must be given with the intention that it be acted upon, therefore merely mentioning it in conversation generally will not suffice.

[217] See 4.54.

[218] (1908) 99 LT 284. See also *Banks v Williams* (1912) 12 SR (NSW) 382. Similarly in the context of communications of offers see *Wilson v Belfast Corp* (1921) 55 ILT 205; *Blair v Western Mutual Benefit Association* [1972] 4 WWR 284.

[219] This assumes, of course, that the plaintiff offered to take the post and that the managers purported to accept that offer. This is not the usual practice in the employment context. In practical terms it would be preferable to interpret the offer of the post as being made by the managers so that the plaintiff, employee, would decide whether or not to accept.

[220] See Farnsworth, *Farnsworth on Contracts* (3rd edn, Vol 1, Aspen Publishers, New York, 2004) § 3.15, p 301 citing Restatement (2d) Contracts §§ 54(2)(b), 56.

[221] The ability of dispensing with the need for communication is of general recognition, eg United Nations Convention on Contracts for the International Sale of Goods, Art 18(3); Unidroit Principles of International Commercial Contracts 2004, Art 2.1.6(3). See further Principles of European Contract Law Art 2:205(3) and the Draft Common Frame of Reference II–4:205(3) and see Uniform Commercial Code § 2-206(1)(b).

[222] *Carlill v Carbolic Smoke Ball Company* [1893] 1 QB 256, 270 per Bowen LJ.

the issue is determined by reference to the terms of the offer and here very clear language or necessary implication is required to negate the requirement of communication.[223] It is possible for communication of acceptance to be dispensed with in a bilateral contract where the offer requires the doing of an act which implies a counter-promise of acceptance.[224] However, the typical scenario where the need for communication is negated is in those unilateral contracts which call for the performance of an act other than the communication of information to the offeror.[225] Some may include within this group offers which do not negate the need for communication but call for communication of acceptance to be dealt with in a particular manner and where the acceptance will be operable if that manner is complied with even if the communication is not actually received by the offeror, for example, where acceptance may be by post.[226]

4.58 The case that is usually cited as authority for the view that the need for communication of acceptance may be negated is *Carlill v Carbolic Smoke Ball Co.*[227] Here the Carbolic Smoke Ball Company promised to pay £100 to anyone who caught the flu after using the smoke ball as instructed. Mrs Carlill followed the instructions but nevertheless contracted the flu and brought an action to recover the reward. It was held that the advertisement constituted an offer and that she had accepted that offer by using the smoke as instructed.[228] One of the issues raised in the appeal was that of communication of acceptance. Mrs Carlill did not tell the Smoke Ball Company that she intended to carry out the act of acceptance or that she had carried out the act of acceptance. The first the Smoke Ball Company heard of her actions was when she claimed the reward which was refused by the Smoke Ball Company

---

[223] Eg *Latec Finance Pty Ltd v Knight* [1969] 2 NSWR 79 (terms of offer which the offeree sought to argue negated the need for communication and came into effect upon the offeree signing where drafted by the offeree finance company to be put to it by the hirer; those terms stated that the offer was irrevocable for a period of time but was not binding on the offeree until it signed; held the need for communication not negated). See also *Robophone Facilities Ltd v Blank* [1966] 1 WLR 1428, 1432; *Entores Ltd v Miles Far East Corporation* [1955] 2 QB 327, 336. See further *Newlands v Argyll General Insurance Co Ltd* [1959] SR (NSW) 130.

[224] Carter, *Carter on Contract* (Butterworths, Sydney), § 03-030. See also McCamus, *The Law of Contracts* (Irwin Law, Toronto, 2005), 70. An example might be where a buyer places an order for goods and states that if the offeree agrees to the terms then he or she may accept the offer by shipping the goods, see *Brogden v Metropolitan Railway Co* (1877) 2 App Cas 666, 691 per Lord Blackburn. See also *Menzies v Williams* (1893) 10 WN (NSW) 13; *Melbourne Chilled Butter Co Pty Ltd v Downes* (1900) 25 VLR 559; *Mayers & Co v Johnson & Co* [1905] QWN 39. See further Miller, 'Felthouse v Bindley Re-Visited' (1972) 35 Mod LR 489. Similarly, a vendor may send goods to a buyer and state that the opening of the packaging constitutes an acceptance, eg *Commerce Commission v Telecom Mobile Ltd* [2004] 3 NZLR 667 (the appeals to this decision dealt with other issues, see [2006] 1 NZLR 190, [2006] 3 NZLR 323). In many instances such as in the case of an option, upon the occurrence of the act of acceptance the unilateral contract gives rise to a bilateral contract, see *United Dominions Trust (Commercial) Ltd v Eagle Aircraft Services Ltd* [1968] 1 WLR 74, 83–4.

[225] Often in offers for reward the act will involve communication of information to a third party, such as the police, rather than communication to the offeror, see *Williams v Carwadine* (1833) 5 Car & P 566, 172 ER 1101; *R v Clarke* (1927) 40 CLR 227, discussed at 4.37.

[226] See *Manchester Diocesan Council for Education v Commercial & General Investments Ltd* [1970] 1 WLR 241, 245; *Latec Finance Pty Ltd v Knight* [1969] 2 NSWR 79, 81.

[227] [1893] 1 QB 256. See also *Brogden v Metropolitan Railway Company* (1877) 2 App Cas 666, 691; *Ward v Byham* [1956] 1 WLR 496, 498; *New Zealand Shipping Co Ltd v A M Satterthwaite & Co Ltd (The Eurymedon)* [1975] AC 154, 168; *Associated Midland Corp Ltd v Bank of NSW* (1984) 51 ALR 641; *First Sport Ltd v Barclays Bank Plc* [1993] 1 WLR 1229, 1234–5; *Minories Finance Ltd v Afribank Nigeria Ltd* [1995] 1 Lloyd's Rep 134, 140.

[228] See 2.35.

which then resulted in her commencing proceedings. Despite this lack of communication it was held that there was a contract. The clearest statement of the ability of the offeror to waive the need for communication was expressed by Bowen LJ. He said:[229]

> the person who makes the offer may dispense with notice to himself if he thinks it desirable to do so, and I suppose there can be no doubt that where a person in an offer made by him to another person, expressly or impliedly intimates a particular mode of acceptance as sufficient to make the bargain binding, it is only necessary for the other person to whom such offer is made to follow the indicated method of acceptance; and if the person making the offer, expressly or impliedly intimates in his offer that it will be sufficient to act on the proposal without communicating acceptance of it to himself, performance of the condition is a sufficient acceptance without notification ...

Similarly Lindley LJ said:[230]   **4.59**

> But then it is said, 'Supposing that the performance of the conditions is an acceptance of the offer, that acceptance ought to have been notified.' Unquestionably, as a general proposition, when an offer is made, it is necessary in order to make a binding contract, not only that it should be accepted, but that the acceptance should be notified. But is that so in cases of this kind? I apprehend that they are an exception to that rule, or, if not an exception, they are open to the observation that the notification of the acceptance need not precede the performance. This offer is a continuing offer. It was never revoked, and if notice of acceptance is required—which I doubt very much, for I rather think the true view is that which was expressed and explained by Lord Blackburn in the case of *Brogden v Metropolitan Ry Co* (1877) 2 App Cas 666, 691—if notice of acceptance is required, the person who makes the offer gets the notice of acceptance contemporaneously with his notice of the performance of the condition. If he gets notice of the acceptance before his offer is revoked, that in principle is all you want. I, however, think that the true view, in a case of this kind, is that the person who makes the offer shews by his language and from the nature of the transaction that he does not expect and does not require notice of the acceptance apart from notice of the performance.

Lindley LJ's reference to *Brogden v Metropolitan Railway Company* here clearly evidenced   **4.60**
that he was of the view that the offeror may do away with the need for communication of acceptance. Thus, in this case the contract was formed when the act of acceptance was performed. The Smoke Ball Company's performance was then contingent upon the user catching the flu. Much of what Lindley LJ said in respect of notice was concerned with performance rather than formation. Clearly if Mrs Carlill wanted to call on the Smoke Ball Company to perform then she would need to inform them of her performance and of the occurrence of the contingency.

The distinction between formation and performance is dealt with under the Restatement   **4.61**
(2d) Contracts in section 54. This provision recognizes that a contract may be formed by performance without communication of acceptance but then allows for the offeror's obligations to be discharged in certain circumstances where the offeror has no notice of the

---

[229] [1893] 1 QB 256, 269–70, see also 273 per AL Smith LJ.
[230] [1893] 1 QB 256, 262–3.

performance. The provision recognizes and gives effect to the reality that it is a rare case where the need for notification is completely negated by the offeror.[231] It provides:[232]

§ 54. Acceptance by Performance; Necessity of Notification to Offeror

(1) Where an offer invites an offeree to accept by rendering a performance, no notification is necessary to make such an acceptance effective unless the offer requests such a notification.

(2) If an offeree who accepts by rendering a performance has reason to know that the offeror has no adequate means of learning of the performance with reasonable promptness and certainty, the contractual duty of the offeror is discharged unless

(a) the offeree exercises reasonable diligence to notify the offeror of acceptance, or

(b) the offeror learns of the performance within a reasonable time, or

(c) the offer indicates that notification of acceptance is not required.

J. Silence and Acceptance

4.62   Generally, silence cannot constitute acceptance.[233] This rule is predicted by the objective theory of contract which requires an external manifestation of assent.[234] It is generally not possible to determine, from the position of a reasonable person in the position of the offeror, that there has been an assent to the terms of the offer when the offeree has remained silent throughout.[235] Silence is equivocal, it does not communicate a clear decision.[236]

---

[231] Comment *b*.

[232] Section 30 recognizes that an offer may invite acceptance by words or acts and except where otherwise indicated 'by the language or the circumstances, an offer invites acceptance in any manner and by any medium reasonable in the circumstances'. Section 32 then states: 'In case of doubt an offer is interpreted as inviting the offeree to accept either by promising to perform what the offer requests or by rendering the performance, as the offeree chooses.' See also Uniform Commercial Code § 2-206(1)(a). Section 2-206(1)(b) deals with the particular situation of an offer to buys goods requiring prompt shipment and provides, 'an order or other offer to buy goods for prompt or current shipment shall be construed as inviting acceptance either by a prompt promise to ship or by the prompt or current shipment of conforming or nonconforming goods, but the shipment of nonconforming goods is not an acceptance if the seller seasonably notifies the buyer that the shipment is offered only as an accommodation to the buyer.' Section 2-206(2) treats an offer as lapsing if the act of acceptance begins and the offeror is not notified within a reasonable time.

[233] This rule is reflected in international instruments, see United Nations Convention on Contracts for the International Sale of Goods (1980), Art 18(1); Unidroit Principles of International Commercial Contracts 2004, Art 2.1.6(1); Principles of European Contract Law, Art 2:204(2).

[234] *Empirnall Holdings Pty Ltd v Machon Paull Partners Pty Ltd* (1988) 14 NSWLR 523, 534. Although there may be instances in law where there is a legitimate expectation that a person will receive a reply or there might be a duty to reply, this would be rare in the context of contract formation, cf *Brooks Towers Corp v Hunkin-Conkey Construction Co* 454 F 2d 1203 (1972). The more usual situation is where the circumstances are such that a failure to speak gives rise to an estoppel preventing a person denying another's authority to make an offer or communicate an acceptance, see generally *Yona International Ltd v La Réunion Française Société Anonyme d'Assurances et de Réassurances* [1996] 2 Lloyd's Rep 84, 107; *Spiro v Lintern* [1973] 1 WLR 1002.

[235] *Allied Marine Transport Ltd v Vale do Rio Doce Navegacao SA (The Leonidas D)* [1985] 1 WLR 925, 936–7; *MSC Mediterranean Shipping Co SA v B R E-Metro Ltd* [1985] 2 Lloyd's Rep 239, 241–2; *Re Selectmove Ltd* [1995] 1 WLR 474, 478; *Yona International Ltd v La Réunion Française Société Anonyme d'Assurances et de Réassurances* [1996] 2 Lloyd's Rep 84, 110.

[236] *Allied Marine Transport Ltd v Vale do Rio Doce Navegacao SA (The Leonidas D)* [1985] 1 WLR 925, 937; *Yona International Ltd v La Réunion Française Société Anonyme d'Assurances et de Réassurances* [1996] 2 Lloyd's Rep 84, 110–11.

Usually where a reasonable period of time elapses without communication of acceptance it will be concluded that the offer is rejected.[237]

The classic decision on this point is *Felthouse v Bindley*.[238] In this case an uncle heard that **4.63** his nephew was intending to sell his farming stock at auction. The uncle had mistakenly thought that his nephew wanted £30 for a certain horse when in fact his nephew wanted 30 guineas. Upon learning that the parties were at cross purposes the uncle wrote to his nephew offering to 'split the difference' and stating 'if I hear no more about him, I consider the horse mine at £30 15s'. The nephew did not reply to this offer, however, upon receipt of the offer he did inform the auctioneer that the horse had been sold and that it was to be taken out of the auction. By mistake the auctioneer sold the horse at the auction to a third party. The uncle wished to sue the auctioneer in conversion and to do that had to show that a contract of sale had been entered into with his nephew prior to the auction. The uncle's action failed. Given the nephew's action, there can be no doubt as to his subjective state of mind.[239] Moreover, there was an outward expression of that state of mind to the auctioneer although the statement to the auctioneer was not of itself referable to any contract with the uncle. However, there had been no communication of acceptance to the uncle and to hold otherwise would have allowed the uncle to force a contract on his nephew by making his silence an acceptance. An offeree cannot be made to take active steps in order to avoid being held to have accepted an offer or being held to have assented to a variation of terms such as when one party forwards further terms by way of confirmation of an oral contract.[240]

The decision in *Felthouse v Bindley* seems a harsh one given the facts of the case even though **4.64** it has doctrinal force. Whether or not silence can ever amount to acceptance has received more detailed analysis in a number of cases that have dealt with the abandonment of a contract. The particular context was in relation to arbitration proceedings, however, the discussion in these cases is of wider import. The particular question that arose and which is of concern here was whether an offer to abandon a contractual obligation to arbitrate disputes (assuming such an offer can be proven) can be accepted by silence or inactivity? The answer to that question is yes, but the principles to be applied are not clear in the case law to be discussed.

It can often happen that processes for arbitration proceedings are begun but not followed **4.65** through. The court has no inherent power to dismiss such proceedings for delay.[241] Yet one

---

[237] *Empirnall Holdings Pty Ltd v Machon Paull Partners Pty Ltd* (1988) 14 NSWLR 523, 534.

[238] *Felthouse v Bindley* (1862) 11 CBNS 869, 142 ER 1037 (affirmed on other grounds (1863) 7 LT 835). See also *Albrecht Chem Co v Anderson Trading Corp* 298 NY 437, 84 NE 2d 625 (1949) where the offer stated that the 'order and the terms and conditions thereof shall be deemed accepted' if the offeree fails to inform the offeror within ten days that he does not wish to accept. See further *Boyd v Holmes* (1878) 4 VLR (E) 161; *Russell and Baird v Hoban* [1922] 2 IR 159; *Karlin v Avis* 457 F 2d 57 (1972); *Fairline Shipping Corporation v Adamson* [1975] QB 180, 189; *Empirnall Holdings Pty Ltd v Machon Paull Partners Pty Ltd* (1988) 14 NSWLR 523.

[239] After the auction the nephew wrote to his uncle explaining what had happened and admitted to having subjectively accepted the offer. However, this document was too late and only evidenced an acceptance at that time and not prior to the auction.

[240] *Jayaar Impex Ltd v Toaken Group Ltd* [1996] 2 Lloyd's Rep 437.

[241] See *Bremer Vulkan Schiffbau und Maschinenfabrik v South India Shipping Corp Ltd* [1981] AC 909. The court has an inherent power to dismiss an action before a court for delay, see *Allen v Sir Alfred McAlpine and Sons Ltd* [1968] 2 QB 229; *Birkett v James* [1978] AC 297.

of the parties might need to know where it stands. That issue has now been dealt with by statute.[242] Nevertheless, prior to the enactment of that legislation a number of arguments were put forward to suggest that in such circumstances proceedings could not go on. Several of these arguments were based on general principles of contract law. The reason for that approach was that an agreement to arbitrate is a contract and therefore subject to the same rules as any other contract. One argument was that the claimant had made a fundamental breach of the contract to arbitrate by failing to carry the arbitration forward. This argument was rejected on the ground that each of the parties to an arbitration has an obligation to keep the proceedings moving. Neither party could rely on the other's breach to terminate the agreement.[243]

4.66 Another argument was that the contract had been frustrated by the delay. The attraction of this argument was that the purpose of the arbitration agreement was to arrive at a fair resolution of the dispute and if the delay was sufficiently long then such a resolution may be impossible. This approach was rejected by the House of Lords in *Paal Wilson & Co A/S v Partenreederei Hannah Blumenthal*.[244] The reasoning of the House of Lords was that since the obligation to move the arbitration proceedings forward fell equally on both parties, then, if a delay resulted in there being no possibility of a just resolution, this must be because of the default of both parties and the doctrine of frustration only operates where there is no default. In short any frustration was self-induced.

4.67 However, in this case the House of Lords recognized that a third possibility (not available on the facts before them) was open, namely, that the parties may have entered into a contract to abandon the contract to arbitrate.[245] The principal speech was given by Lord Brandon. The speeches of Lords Diplock, Lord Roskill and Lord Brightman were to be read as 'supplementary to and in amplification of' Lord Brandon's speech.[246] It is necessary to set out parts of these speeches in some detail.

4.68 Lord Brandon stated that:[247]

> The concept of the implied abandonment of a contract as a result of the conduct of the parties to it is well established in law: see *Chitty on Contracts* 23rd ed. (1968) vol I, p 577, para 1231 and cases there cited. Where A seeks to prove that he and B have abandoned a contract in this way, there are two ways in which A can put his case. The first way is by showing that the conduct of each party, as evinced to the other party and acted on by him, leads necessarily

---

[242] See now Arbitration Act 1996, s 41(3).

[243] *Bremer Vulkan Schiffbau und Maschinenfabrik v South India Shipping Corp Ltd* [1981] AC 909.

[244] [1983] 1 AC 854.

[245] Distinctions may be drawn between abandoning the contract to arbitrate, abandoning the reference to arbitration and abandoning the claim or cause of action, see *Allied Marine Transport Ltd v Vale Do Rio Doce Navegacao SA, The Leonidas D* [1984] 1 WLR 1, 11 (overruled *Allied Marine Transport Ltd v Vale Do Rio Doce Navegacao SA, The Leonidas D* [1985] 1 WLR 925); *Gebr Van Weelde Scheepvaartkantor BV v Compania Naviera Sea Orient SA (The Agrabele)* [1985] 2 Lloyd's Rep 496, 508 (overruled [1987] 2 Lloyd's Rep 223).

[246] [1983] 1 AC 854, 900.

[247] [1983] 1 AC 854, 914. See also *Manco Ltd v Atlantic Forest Products Ltd* (1971) 24 DLR (3d) 194, 200 ('I take the applicable rule to be that failure to reject an offer does not of itself constitute evidence of its acceptance unless the offeree's silence would in the circumstances lead a reasonable person in the position of the offeror to believe that the offeree had accepted the terms offered, and unless the offeror did in fact believe the offeree had accepted them and proceeded under that belief.')

to the inference of an implied agreement between them to abandon the contract. The second method is by showing that the conduct of B, as evinced towards A, has been such as to lead A reasonably to believe that B has abandoned the contract, even though it has not in fact been B's intention to do so, and that A has significantly altered his position in reliance on that belief. The first method involves actual abandonment by both A and B. The second method involves the creation by B of a situation in which he is estopped from asserting, as against A, that he, B, has not abandoned the contract: *Pearl Mill Co Ltd v Ivy Tannery Co Ltd* [1919] 1 KB 78.

In the first method outlined in the above quote, Lord Brandon looks at the transaction **4.69** from both sides there being an offer and an acceptance. Both the offer and acceptance derive from conduct. The relevance of the subjective understanding of the parties lies in his reference to the importance of looking at how a party acts when confronted with the conduct of the other party. The conduct of one party must evidence to a reasonable person in the position of the other party that they intend to contract and the second party must believe that the first party so intends to contract. As noted earlier the latter requirement exists in contract law because of the requirements of consensus and intention to contract.[248] However, that knowledge is usually presumed. The onus is on the first party—if they wish to contest the contract—to prove the second party knew the first party did not intend to contract.

Lord Diplock after noting that the abandonment of a contract requires the formation of a **4.70** contract of abandonment stated:[249]

> To the formation of the contract of abandonment, the ordinary principles of English law of contract apply. To create a contract by exchange of promises between two parties where the promise of each party constitutes the consideration for the promise of the other, what is necessary is that the intention of each as it has been communicated to and understood by the other (even though that which has been communicated does not represent the actual state of mind of the communicator) should coincide ...

> Thus if A (the offeror) makes a communication to B (the offeree) whether in writing, orally or by conduct, which, in the circumstances at the time the communication was received, (1) B, if he were a reasonable man, would understand as stating A's intention to act or refrain from acting in some specified manner if B will promise on his part to act or refrain from acting in some manner also specified in the offer, and (2) B does in fact understand A's communication to mean this, and in his turn makes to A a communication conveying his willingness so to act or to refrain from acting which mutatis mutandis satisfies the same two conditions as respects A, the consensus ad idem essential to the formation of a contract in English law is complete.

> The rule that neither party can rely upon his own failure to communicate accurately to the other party his own real intention by what he wrote or said or did, as negativing the consensus ad idem, is an example of a general principle of English law that injurious reliance on what another person did may be a source of legal rights against him ...

> In the instant case, as in most cases where abandonment of a former contract is relied on, the contract of abandonment of the arbitration agreement is said by the sellers to have been created by the conduct of the parties, consisting of their common inaction, after the buyers'

---

[248] See 1.10.
[249] [1983] 1 AC 854, 915–16.

letter of 12 December 1979. Where the inference that a reasonable man would draw from the prolonged failure by the claimant in an arbitration procedure is that the claimant is willing to consent to the abandonment of the agreement to submit the dispute to arbitration and the respondent did in fact draw such inference and by his own inaction thereafter indicated by his own consent to its abandonment in similar fashion to the claimant and was so understood by the claimant, the court would be right in treating the arbitration agreement as having been terminated by abandonment. In *André & Cie SA v Marine Transocean Ltd, The Splendid Sun* [1981] 1 QB 694 all three members of the Court of Appeal drew such an inference from the conduct of both parties in the arbitration. That case was, in my view, rightly decided, though not for reasons other than those which were given by Eveleigh and Fox LJJ.

The facts in the instance case, however, are very different from those of *The Splendid Sun*… [T]hey are inconsistent with any actual belief on the part of the sellers that the buyers had agreed to abandon the arbitration.

4.71 Lord Diplock's speech has proven to be the most controversial and it is convenient to note a few points here before moving on.[250] First, it can be seen in the first and second paragraph that Lord Diplock acknowledges the concept of consensus in contract law discussed earlier.[251] As noted in the paragraph above, it is suggested that Lord Brandon made the same acknowledgement. However, Lord Diplock was very clear in his statement pointing out that for there to be an offer not only must a reasonable person in the position of the offeree be of the belief that the offeror is making an offer but the offeree must positively believe that an offer is being made.[252] He sets out the same requirements for a valid acceptance. Second, note that in this passage, when he deals with acceptance, he does not talk about any waiver of the need to communicate acceptance. The example he sets out involves a communication either by words or conduct; it is not silence itself that is acceptance but such conduct may communicate to the other party an offer or acceptance. Third, in his third paragraph he makes it clear that in interpreting a statement, the law is not concerned with the subjective beliefs of the party making the statement.[253]

4.72 Lord Brightman stated:[254]

The basis of 'tacit abandonment by both parties', to use the phraseology of the sellers' case, is that the primary facts are such that it ought to be inferred that the contract to arbitrate the particular dispute was rescinded by the mutual agreement of the parties. To entitle the sellers to rely on abandonment, they must show that the buyers so conducted themselves as to entitle the sellers to assume, *and that the sellers did assume,* that the contract was agreed to be abandoned sub silentio. The evidence which is relevant to that inquiry will consist of or include: (1) What the buyers did or omitted to do *to the knowledge of the sellers.* Excluded from consideration will be the acts of the buyers of which the sellers were ignorant, because those acts will have signalled nothing to the sellers and cannot have founded or fortified any assumption on the part of the sellers; (2) What the sellers did or omitted to do, *whether or not to the knowledge of the buyers.* These facts evidence the state of mind of the sellers, and therefore the validity of the assertion by the sellers that they assumed that the contract was agreed to be abandoned. The state of mind of the buyers is irrelevant to a consideration of what the

---

[250] Eg Beatson, 'Abandoning the Contract of Abandonment' (1986) 102 LQR 19.
[251] See 1.10.
[252] See 1.11.
[253] See 1.13.
[254] [1983] 1 AC 854, 924.

sellers were entitled to assume. The state of mind of the sellers is vital to what the sellers in fact assumed.

A couple of comments about this speech are warranted before the discussion that follows. **4.73** It can be seen from this passage that Lord Brightman, like Lord Diplock and Lord Brandon, thought it relevant to not only require a reasonable person in the position of the offeree to conclude that an offer was made, but that the offeree believe that an offer was made. Again this recognizes the requirements of consensus and intention to contract and is not a replacement of the objective theory of contract with a subjective theory. Where these speeches differ is that Lord Brightman only looks at the position of one party. So if we assume it is the buyer making the offer to abandon, Lord Brightman's test appears to result in an agreement to abandon if a reasonable person in the position of the seller believed an offer was being made and if the seller believed an offer was being made. He does not then consider the requirements for acceptance. One reason for this might be that he was thinking of a unilateral contract being an offer for an act where the act is silence and inaction on the part of the offeree. Another reason might be that he did not see it as necessary to break the situation down to one of offer and acceptance and that such an analysis was not appropriate here. A further reason may simply be that the necessity of looking at the issue from both sides was implied.

It follows from what has been said above that the possibility of deducing abandonment by **4.74** mutual inaction was clearly established. However, the cases that followed suggested some confusion as to what circumstances would allow a court to conclude that the inaction was of a kind which should be treated as constituting abandonment. There were numerous decisions. These cases included another visit to the House of Lords in *Food Corporation of India v Antclizo Shipping Corp (The Antclizo)*,[255] but the court did not think the case was appropriate for a review of the authorities.

A number of other cases should be discussed. The first is *Andre et Compagnie SA v Marine* **4.75** *Transocean Ltd, The Splendid Sun*.[256] As noted above, Lord Diplock approved this decision in *Paal Wilson & Co A/S v Partenreederei Hannah Blumenthal* in so far as the court found the contract there had been abandoned.[257] In this case a vessel under charter grounded as she was berthing at the point of discharge in Venezuela in May 1969. The owners claimed that the charterers had ordered the vessel to discharge at an unsafe berth. The charterers claimed that the Captain was at fault and the owners were liable. The dispute was referred to arbitration in London and in September and October 1969 each side appointed an arbitrator. Nothing further had happened when in 1973 the charterers closed their file on the claim. In February 1975 the arbitrator appointed by the charterers died and no appointment was made to replace him. In December 1977 the owners wrote to the charterers enclosing their points of claim. This letter was received on 3 January 1978. The Court of

---

[255] [1988] 1 WLR 603. See Lawson, 'Abandonment of Arbitration by Silence or Inactivity' [1988] LMCLQ 302.
[256] [1981] QB 694.
[257] So too did Lord Roskill and Lord Brightman, see the comments of Lord Roskill [1983] 1 AC 854, 922, agreeing with the reasoning of Fox LJ in *The Splendid Sun*, and see at 924 per Lord Brightman.

Appeal held that the owners could be restrained from proceeding with the arbitration on the basis of abandonment.[258] Lord Justice Fox said:[259]

> The reference to arbitration was contractual. The parties could put an end to that contract by agreement whenever they liked. The question in the present case is whether it can be inferred that, having regard to the very long period of total inactivity, the parties have impliedly agreed to put an end to the agreement. Thus in *Pearl Mill Co Ltd v Ivy Tannery Co Ltd* [1919] 1 KB 78, 82, Rowlatt J refers to a 'lapse of time allowed to pass by both sides so long as to induce the court to draw the inference that both parties thought that each of them had treated the contract as at an end.' and later Rowlatt J refers to the fact 'that the lapse of time had been so long on both sides that ... the proper inference to be drawn was that each party was justified in assuming that the matter was off altogether'.

> It seems to me that, by the end of 1973, the charterers regarded the whole matter as at an end. They closed their file and put it away. It may be that they were not justified in doing that in 1973. But I think that they were justified by, at the very latest, 1978, when the points of claim were delivered ... In these circumstances, I think that any person in the position of the charterers would reasonably have supposed that the matter was quite dead.

> The owners say that they never intended to put an end to the arbitration. I do not think that the owners can be heard to say that. It seems to me that they must be taken to intend what a reasonable person would conclude from their acts ... In my opinion the lapse of time in this case, unaccompanied by any activity from the parties, is so great that the reasonable inference in January 1978 is that the owners had decided not to proceed with the arbitration and that the charterers had accepted that and were agreeable to it.

4.76 Although each case is dependent on its own facts, given the approval of this decision by the House of Lords, it must stand as an example of the circumstances where a successful claim of abandonment may be made. In terms of principle, perhaps the most important point is the reaffirmation that when determining how a statement or act is to be construed you do not consider the subjective state of mind of the person who made the statement or engaged in the conduct.

4.77 An important case was the decision of the Court of Appeal in *Allied Marine Transport Ltd v Vale Do Rio Doce Navegacao SA, The Leonidas D.*[260] In this case a dispute arose between the parties in 1976 and a notice of arbitration was given by the charterers following which two arbitrators were appointed, one by each party. Thereafter nothing happened until August 1981 when the charterers wrote to the owners asking for admission of liability. In November 1981 the charterers served their points of claim. In this case the Court of Appeal

---

[258] Lord Denning MR thought that the agreement was discharged by frustration. However, in the light of the later decision of the House of Lords in *The Hannah Blumenthal* this ground cannot now be sustained.

[259] [1981] QB 694, 713–14. See also at 706 per Eveleigh LJ, the owners 'must be taken to intend that which any reasonable man would conclude that they intended, particularly when the other party has acted to his detriment in consequence. That the charterers did so act is quite apparent. They made no further preparations for their defence, they treated the matter as at an end, and as time went on evidence ceased to be available to them ... [I]t is not necessary to prove an actual intention to rescind or withdraw the claim'.

[260] [1985] 1 WLR 925. See further Atiyah, 'The Hannah Blumenthal and Classical Contract Law' (1986) 102 LQR 363.

held that the facts did not amount to a mutual abandonment of the agreement to arbitrate. Reversing the decision of Mustill J, Robert Goff LJ said:[261]

> We have all been brought up to believe it to be axiomatic that acceptance of an offer cannot be inferred from silence, save in the most exceptional circumstances … Yet it is here suggested that silence and inaction can give rise both to an offer and to an acceptance; and there do not appear to be any special circumstances, in the silent abandonment of this reference to arbitration, which could justify departure from general principle. In the absence of special circumstances, silence and inaction by a party to a reference are, objectively considered, just as consistent with his having inadvertently forgotten about the matter; or with his simply hoping that the matter will die a natural death if he does not stir up the other party; or with his office staff, or his agents, or his insurers, or his solicitors, being appallingly slow. If so, there should, on ordinary principles, be no basis for the inference of an offer. Exactly the same comment can be made of the silence and inaction of the other party, for the same reasons, there appears to be no basis for drawing the inference of an acceptance in response to the supposed offer, still less of the communication of that acceptance to the offeror.

There can be no doubting the correctness of this statement. Silence generally is equivocal   **4.78** and for it to give rise to either an offer or an acceptance there must be facts that make that silence unequivocal in the circumstances.[262] However, in reaching his conclusion, Robert Goff LJ referred to the three approaches to implied abandonment proffered by Lords Brandon, Diplock and Brightman in *Paal Wilson & Co A/S v Partenreederei Hannah Blumenthal*. He thought the three approaches were distinct. He singled out Lord Diplock as suggesting that there is a requirement that the actual intention of both parties coincide.[263] He expressed a preference for the reasoning of Lord Brightman concluding:[264]

> It is apparent that these three approaches are not identical. However, if we have to choose between them, we would respectfully prefer to follow the approach of Lord Brightman. In his speech Lord Brightman was, as we understand it, asserting that if one party, O, so acts that his conduct, objectively considered, constitutes an offer, and the other party, A, believing that the conduct of O represents his actual intention, accepts O's offer, then a contract will come into existence, and on those facts it will make no difference if O did not in fact intend to make an offer, or if he misunderstood A's acceptance, so that O's state of mind is, in such circumstances, irrelevant. With that proposition we very respectfully agree and so, if it is necessary for us to choose, we would prefer to follow the reasoning of Lord Brightman in so far as it differs from the reasoning of Lord Brandon and Lord Diplock.

It can been seen from this passage that the speech of Lord Diplock, in *Paal Wilson & Co A/S*   **4.79** *v Partenreederei Hannah Blumenthal* was seen as problematic with its emphasis on the subjective intention of both parties. Later, not only were further concerns about Lord Diplock's speech raised but there were also concerns about the decision in *The Leonidas D*. The particular concern with *The Leonidas D* was reconciling that decision with *The Splendid Sun*.

---

261 [1985] 1 WLR 925, 936–7.
262 See *Unisys International Services Ltd v Eastern Counties Newspapers Ltd* [1991] 1 Lloyd's Rep 538, 553.
263 [1985] 1 WLR 925, 936.
264 [1985] 1 WLR 925, 936.

Perhaps the most important decision was *Food Corp of India v Antclizo Shipping Corp (The Antclizo).*[265] Here Bingham LJ stated:[266]

> It is plain that this Court must apply the ratio of the most recent authority binding upon it, *The Leonidas D.* But some problems do remain, even if it is not for us to solve them. The Court's reasoning in *The Leonidas D* might prompt the conclusion that silence and inactivity could never lead to the inference that the claimant was offering to abandon. But that cannot be so, because the Court acknowledged the authority of *The Splendid Sun.* Lord Diplock's prefatory remarks in *The Hannah Blumenthal* might suggest that if there was any difference in their Lordships' formulations of principle, Lord Brandon's was to be preferred. But in *The Leonidas D* this Court preferred the approach of Lord Brightman. It is not entirely clear what subjective state of mind the respondent to the claim in the arbitration must be shown to have had, although the answer may well be that given by Mr Justice Staughton in *The Golden Bear* ([1987] 1 Lloyd's Rep 330 at p 341):
>
> > 'For my part I cannot see why it should in practice make any difference whether on the one hand the respondent in fact assumed that the claimant was offering to abandon the reference, or on the other hand, he would have made that assumption if he had thought about the case at all. Indeed the older a case is, the less likely it is that the respondent will give it consideration from time to time. When the case is so old that he has ceased to consider it at all, a fortiori the doctrine of abandonment should apply.'
>
> If, according to ordinary principles, it is necessary for the respondent's acceptance of the claimant's offer to be communicated to the claimant, it is not clear whether it is necessary for the claimant subjectively to understand the respondent's silence and inactivity as having that effect.
>
> …
>
> In accordance with the rule as emphasized by Lord Brightman in *The Hannah Blumenthal* (… *'and that the sellers did assume'*), which also formed part of Lord Diplock's formulation …, the learned Judge turned to consider the charterers' actual understanding of the effect of the owners' conduct. Mr Buckley submitted that it was not strictly necessary for him to do so and that (as Mr Justice Staughton held in *The Golden Bear*) those statements were concerned to exclude the case where although a claimant appeared to be offering to abandon the respondent knew or believed that in fact he was not doing so. I think this is probably right, and such a qualification would appear the more necessary where the conduct in question is silence and inactivity.

4.80 Lord Nicholls stated:[267]

> I agree that this appeal should be dismissed for the reasons given in the judgment of Lord Justice Bingham.

---

[265] [1987] 2 Lloyd's Rep 130 (affirmed on other grounds *Food Corp of India v Antclizo Shipping Corp (The Antclizo)* [1988] 1 WLR 603). See also *Gebr Van Weelde Scheepvaartkantor BV v Compania Naviera Sea Orient SA (The Agrabele)* [1985] 2 Lloyd's Rep 496, [1987] 2 Lloyd's Rep 223; *Cie Francaise d'Importation et de Distribution SA v Deutsche Continental Handelsgesellschaft* [1985] 2 Lloyd's Rep 592; *Excomm Ltd v Guan Guan Shipping (Pte) Ltd (The Golden Bear)* [1987] 1 Lloyd's Rep 320; *Tankrederei Ahrenkeil GMBH v Frahuil SA (The Multitank Holsatia)* [1988] 2 Lloyd's Rep 486. See further *Unisys International Services Ltd v Eastern Counties Newspapers Ltd* [1991] 1 Lloyd's Rep 538.
[266] [1987] 2 Lloyd's Rep 130, 138, 143.
[267] [1987] 2 Lloyd's Rep 130, 145–6.

I add some observations only on two matters. The first of these, on which at present the law is in a state of some uncertainty, concerns the relevance of the state of mind of the charterers and of the owners as parties to the alleged agreement to abandon the reference to arbitration. Varying views have been expressed on this. In *The Hannah Blumenthal* …, Lord Diplock appears to have said that one of the necessary ingredients of a contract of abandonment is that the respondents understood that the claimants were willing to consent to the abandonment of the agreement to submit the dispute to arbitration and that the claimants understood that the respondents had agreed to this. On this footing the state of mind of both charterers and owners would be relevant. In the same case Lord Brightman … regarded the state of mind of the respondents as material but not, it seems, that of the claimants.

…

In *The Hannah Blumenthal* Lord Diplock's formulation … was, expressly, of the ordinary principles of the English law of contract. But consider this example which was mentioned in the course of the argument. O makes to A an offer in terms which reflect his actual intention and which could not reasonably be understood by A as bearing any other meaning. A misunderstands the offer and communicates his acceptance to O. O does not know, nor ought he reasonably to have known, of A's mistake, nor did he cause or contribute to A's mistake. On principle I would have thought that a binding contract was created in that case…

It is a well-established principle of the English law of contract that an offer falls to be interpreted not subjectively by reference to what has actually passed through the mind of the offeror, but objectively, by reference to the interpretation which a reasonable man in the shoes of the offeree would place on the offer. It is an equally well-established principle that ordinarily an offer, when unequivocally accepted according to its precise terms, will give rise to a legally binding agreement as soon as acceptance is communicated to the offeror in the manner contemplated by the offer, and cannot thereafter be revoked without the consent of the other party.

…

However, Lord Diplock's formulation appears to lead to the conclusion that in my example there would not be a contract. An explanation may be that Lord Diplock's reference to each party's actual understanding of the other's intention as communicated was intended only to exclude the formation of a contract in cases where one party knows that the other's actual intention is not in accordance with his apparent intention. This possibility gains some support from Lord Diplock's statement … of the rule that neither party can rely upon his own failure to communicate accurately to the other party his own real intention by what he wrote or said or did.

4.81 With respect to these statements, there is nothing in Lord Diplock's speech that would suggest there is no contract in the example given. It is suggested that there is little difference between the speeches of Lords Brandon, Diplock and Brightman in *Paal Wilson & Co A/S v Partenreederei Hannah Blumenthal* and that Lord Diplock's merely sets out a fuller statement of the concept of consensus in the common law of contract.[268] Lord Diplock made it clear that he was not concerned with the subjective intention of the party making an offer

---

[268] See 1.10. Cf *Unisys International Services Ltd v Eastern Counties Newspapers Ltd* [1991] 1 Lloyd's Rep 538, 552.

or acceptance, a person's subjective state of mind is only relevant when determining the legal characterization of a statement or conduct directed to them.[269]

4.82 In the result, it is suggested that, accepting that an offeror cannot dictate that silence is acceptance, if a reasonable person in the position of the offeree would conclude that an offer to abandon was made by conduct and by its terms it could be accepted by silence, and if the offeree conducts itself in such a way that by its silence a reasonable person in the position of the offeror would conclude that there has been acceptance by silence, then a contract will result. Of course this would be a rare event as silence is usually equivocal.[270] Thus, when a party relies only on silence, the delay would have to be for a significant period of time so that the intention of the parties is unequivocal; when combined with other conduct the time period can be shortened.[271] There are two provisos. First, despite what a reasonable person would conclude, if there is evidence that the offeree knew that the offeror did not intend to make such an offer then no acceptance can occur as there is no offer to accept. Second, despite what conclusion a reasonable person in the position of the offeror would arrive at, if the offeror knew that the offeree did not intend to accept then no contract will come into being. As noted earlier it is not necessary for one party to prove they positively believed that the other party was making an offer or acceptance. However, in the rare case of A making a statement to B which a reasonable person in the position of B would not construe as an offer (or acceptance as the case may be) but which B knew A intended to be an offer (or acceptance), B can seek to prove that fact and the full statement of the consensus theory by Lords Brandon, Diplock and Brightman allows for that.

4.83 Silence will not prevent a contract coming into existence if there is conduct that amounts to an acceptance.[272] Generally that conduct would have to be communicated to the offeror.[273] Moreover, the conduct must be referable to the contract.[274] Whether or not there is such conduct is an issue of fact.[275] An important modern statement of where conduct will amount to acceptance, despite silence on the part of the offeree, is contained in the

---

[269] See further *Gebr Van Weelde Scheepvaartkantor BV v Compania Naviera Sea Orient SA (The Agrabele)* [1987] 2 Lloyd's Rep 223, 235.

[270] *Allied Marine Transport Ltd v Vale do Rio Doce Navegacao SA (The Leonidas D)* [1985] 1 WLR 925, 940 ('[I]t is not enough that O should appear to have given up pursuing his claim in the reference, and that A assumed that he had given up the pursuit of his claim, because there could be a number of reasons why O should not be pursuing it; for example, forgetfulness, or culpable delay by his solicitors. What has to be shown is that O appeared to be offering to agree that the reference should be abandoned and that A, having so understood O's offer, by his conduct accepted O's offer.')

[271] See *Gebr Van Weelde Scheepvaartkantor BV v Compania Naviera Sea Orient SA (The Agrabele)* [1985] 2 Lloyd's Rep 496, 509, (overruled [1987] 2 Lloyd's Rep 223).

[272] See *Way and Waller Ltd v Ryde* [1944] 1 All ER 9; *Minories Finance Ltd v Afribank Nigeria Ltd* [1995] 1 Lloyd's Rep 134, 139–40; *Yona International Ltd v La Réunion Française Société Anonyme d'Assurances et de Réassurances* [1996] 2 Lloyd's Rep 84, 110–11.

[273] Eg *Felthouse v Bindley* (1862) 11 CBNS 869, 142 ER 1037 (affirmed on other grounds (1863) 7 LT 835).

[274] *White v Corlies* 1 Sickels 467, 46 NY 467 (1871). See also *Re FH Ring & Co Ltd* [1924] SASR 138. Where the issue is not so much acceptance by conduct but rather the creation of a contract by conduct it is 'not enough that the conduct is consistent with what are alleged to be the terms of a binding agreement ... [the] ... evidence must positively indicate that both parties considered themselves bound by that agreement', *Adnunat Pty Ltd v ITW Construction Systems Australia Pty Ltd* [2009] FCA 499, [39]. See also as to implied contracts, *Fisher v Brooker* [2009] 1 WLR 1764, 1777.

[275] *Empirnall Holdings Pty Ltd v Machon Paull Partners Pty Ltd* (1988) 14 NSWLR 523, 535.

judgment of McHugh JA in *Empirnall Holdings Pty Ltd v Machon Paull Partners Pty Ltd*[276] where he said:[277]

> [W]here an offeree with a reasonable opportunity to reject the offer of goods or services takes the benefit of them under circumstances which indicate that they were to be paid for in accordance with the offer, it is open to the tribunal of fact to hold that the offer was accepted according to its terms. A useful analogy is to be found in the 'ticket cases' where an offeree, who has or ought to have knowledge of the terms of a contract of carriage or bailment, is generally bound unless he raises objection ...

> The ultimate issue is whether a reasonable bystander would regard the conduct of the offeree, including his silence, as signalling to the offeror that his offer has been accepted.

In this case the appellant, a property developer, asked the respondent, an architect, to undertake the role of project manager for a certain development. The architect had already done some of the planning work for this development as well as the design work. The respondent forwarded a contract to the appellant which was never executed by the appellant. Nevertheless, the appellant called on the respondent to carry out certain tasks which were done and accepted by the appellant. The respondent invoiced the appellant according to the terms of the written document. The appellant even made payments to the respondent in accordance with those terms. In the circumstances it was held that the despite the appellant's silence, it had accepted the offer by conduct. **4.84**

Despite the general need for conduct to be communicated there are examples which are at odds with *Felthouse v Bindley*[278] where conduct that has not been communicated to the offeror is acceptance. The classic example is where a seller sends goods together with a statement which says that the seller will assume that the buyer has agreed to take the goods if he or she does not send them back.[279] In such a case, although the offeree is not bound to do anything, if he or she does an act which evidences an agreement to purchase the goods they **4.85**

---

[276] (1988) 14 NSWLR 523. See also *St John Tug Boat Co v Irving Refinery Ltd* [1964] SCR 614, (1964) 46 DLR (2d) 1. See further *Wheeler v Klaholt* 178 Mass 141, 59 NE 756 (1901) (here goods were sent by the plaintiff to the defendant under the mistaken belief that an agreement existed between them; while in possession of the goods the defendants made an offer to purchase them for a certain price; the plaintiff replied that the purchaser could keep them at that price or otherwise return the goods; a failure to return the goods within a reasonable time evidenced an acceptance). Cf *Manco Ltd v Atlantic Forest Products Ltd* (1971) 4 NBR (2d) 100, 24 DLR (3d) 194.

[277] (1988) 14 NSWLR 523,535. See also *Way and Waller Ltd v Ryde* [1944] 1 All ER 9; *Alliance Manufacturing Co v Foti* 146 So (2d) 464 (1962); *Rust v Abbey Life Assurance Co Ltd* [1979] 2 Lloyd's Rep 334; *Integrated Computer Services Pty Ltd v Digital Equipment Corp (Aust) Pty Ltd* (1988) 5 BPR 11,110; *Custom Credit Corp Ltd v Gray* [1992] 1 VR 540; *Brambles Holdings Ltd v Bathurst City Council* (2001) 53 NSWLR 153; *Midlink Development Pte Ltd v The Stansfield Group Pte Ltd* [2004] 4 SLR 258; *Kriketos v Lipschitz* [2009] NSWCA 96.

[278] (1862) 11 CBNS 869, 142 ER 1037 (affirmed on other grounds (1863) 7 LT 835).

[279] Legislation now deals with this situation to prevent inertia selling, see Unsolicited Goods and Services Act 1971. Prior to the legislation the recipient by its conduct could evidence acceptance or the acceptance of the goods could result in an obligation to make restitution. The typical example would be where the recipient uses or consumes the goods, see *Weatherby v Banham* (1832) 5 Car & P 228, 172 ER 950 (a publisher not knowing of the death of a customer continued to send the publication to the deceased's address where it was taken by the successors of the deceased without ever offering to return them). See also *Minories Finance Ltd v Afribank Nigeria Ltd* [1995] 1 Lloyd's Rep 134 at 140. See further Carter, Peden and Tolhurst, *Contract Law in Australia* (5th edn, Butterworths, Sydney, 2007) para 3-29; McCamus, *The Law of Contracts* (Irwin Law, Toronto, 2005) at 71 note 133.

will be bound even though the offeror may not be aware of that conduct.[280] For example, on-selling the goods, consuming the goods or giving them as a gift to a third party.[281] This shows that although an offeror cannot force a contract on a person by making silence acceptance, they can make silence a method of acceptance which can then be adopted by the offeree. The uncle did just this in *Felthouse v Bindley* and so there has always been a question mark over that case as to whether the contract would have been upheld if it was the nephew seeking to uphold the contract against the uncle.[282] Admittedly it is rare for an offeror to make it a term of the offer that silence can constitute acceptance. The most likely way for this to occur is where the offeree drafts the terms of the offer and those terms state that the offeror can consider the offer accepted if it has not heard from the offeree by a certain date. A variation of those facts is provided by *Re Selectmove Ltd*[283] which concerned an offer by a company to an Inland Revenue Collector to pay arrears of tax in instalments, the collector told the company that he would get back to them if the proposal was not acceptable to his superiors. The company heard nothing further. Peter Gibson LJ suggested, without expressing a concluded view, that there was no reason in principle why there should not be an exceptional case where it is the offeree who indicates that the offer will be taken as accepted if there is no indication to the contrary. In such circumstances the offeree is clearly undertaking to speak if he or she does not want a concluded agreement and silence would then constitute acceptance. In this case he held the tax collector has no authority to bind the revenue to an acceptance by silence. In addition the course of dealings between the parties may be such that the offeror can reasonably believe that the silence of the offeree is acceptance.[284] In *Empirnall Holdings Pty Ltd v Machon Paull Partners Pty Ltd*[285] Kirby P emphasized that a relevant factor would be the history of the parties, whether they had entered into similar transactions in the past.[286]

4.86   Finally, turning to the position in the United States, the general principle that silence is not acceptance is adopted under the Restatement (2d) Contracts.[287] However, section 69(1) of the Restatement recognizes that a contract may result from silence: (a) where that silence is linked with conduct evidencing acceptance; (b) where the terms of the offer allow silence

---

[280] See further Farnsworth, *Farnsworth on Contracts* (3rd edn, Vol 1, Aspen Publishers, New York, 2004) § 3.13, p 278. If the conduct occurs inadvertently it may in some cases be excused, see *Magnum Photo Supplies Ltd v Viko New Zealand Ltd* [1999] 1 NZLR 395.

[281] See Carter, Peden and Tolhurst, *Contract Law in Australia* (5th edn, Butterworths, Sydney, 2007) para 3-29; Miller, 'Felthouse v Bindley Re-Visited' (1972) 35 Mod LR 489, 490. See further *Weatherby v Banham* (1832) 5 C & P 228, 172 ER 950.

[282] See 4.88.

[283] [1995] 1 WLR 474. See Phang, 'Acceptance by Silence and Consideration Reined In' [1994] LMCLQ 336.

[284] *Ammons v Wilson & Co* 176 Miss 645, 170 So 227 (1936). Cf *Boyd v Holmes* (1878) 4 VLR (E) 161. In *Empirnall Holdings Pty Ltd v Machon Paull Partners Pty Ltd* (1988) 14 NSWLR 523, 534, McHugh JA pointed out that in some cases where there is a course of dealing between the parties or a trade custom there may be a duty to reject an offer, citing *CMI Clothesmakers Inc v ASK Knits Inc* 85 Misc 2d 462, 380 NYS 2d 447 (1975); *Brooks Towers Corporation v Hunkin-Conkey Construction Co* 454 F 2d 1203 (1972); *Alliance Manufacturing Co Inc v Foti* 146 So 2d 464 (1962). See also *Albrecht Chem Co v Anderson Trading Corp* 298 NY 437, 440–1, 84 NE 2d 625, 626 (1949); *Brown v Brown* (1905) 5 SR (NSW) 146.

[285] (1988) 14 NSWLR 523.

[286] (1988) 14 NSWLR 523, 528, citing *Rust v Abbey Life Assurance Co Ltd* [1979] 2 Lloyd's Rep 334, 340.

[287] See generally Restatement (2d) Contracts §§ 53, 54, 56. See also Farnsworth, *Farnsworth on Contracts* (3rd edn, Vol 1, Aspen Publishers, New York, 2004) § 3.14.

to be a method of acceptance and the offeree intends to accept by such silence; and (c)[288] where the course of dealing between the parties is such that a reasonable offeree 'should notify the offeror if he does not intend to accept'.[289] In the Restatement itself it is said that the provision recognizes two classes of case where silence amounts to acceptance. First where an 'offeree silently takes offered benefits' and second, 'where one party relies on the other party's manifestation of intention that silence may operate as acceptance'.[290]

To fall within the exception in (a) there must be both a reasonable opportunity to reject the offered services and reason to know that the services were offered with the expectation of compensation.[291] Many such cases would give rise to a restitutionary claim based on acceptance, but there can be little doubt that in Anglo-Australian law if an offer is made then such conduct would amount to an acceptance giving rise to a contract.[292]   **4.87**

Exception (b) is not intended to protect the offeror, an offeror cannot force a contract on an offeree by stating that silence is acceptance. But if an offeror introduces such a term into the offer then he or she may be bound by that term and the uncertainty it may give rise to. Thus, exception (b) would cover the situation which might have arisen on the facts of *Felthouse v Bindley* had the nephew been suing his uncle for failure to accept the horse and the uncle had contended that acceptance had not been communicated.[293] Clearly the uncle had given the nephew reason to understand that silence would constitute assent, the nephew intended to accept but relied on the uncle's letter in not sending a response.[294] The offeree, nephew, is 'entitled to rely on such a statement if he chooses'.[295] Moreover, this provision would cover the abandonment cases discussed above.[296]   **4.88**

Exception (c) refers to the fact that 'usage of trade' or a 'course of dealing' between the parties may give the offeror reason to understand that silence will constitute acceptance.[297]   **4.89**

---

[288] *Ammons v Wilson & Co* 176 Miss 645, 170 So 227 (1936).

[289] See further Restatement (2d) Contracts § 69(2).

[290] Comment *a*.

[291] Eg Illustration 1 provides 'A gives several lessons on the violin to B's child, intending to give the child a course of 20 lessons, and to charge B the price. B never requested A to give this instruction but silently allows the lessons to be continued to their end, having reason to know A's intention. B is bound to pay the price of the course.'

[292] See 4.83.

[293] See further *Dominion Building Corp Ltd v The King* [1933] AC 533 and see McCamus, *The Law of Contracts* (Irwin Law, Toronto, 2005), 70.

[294] See further Miller, 'Felthouse v Bindley Re-Visited' (1972) 35 Mod LR 489, 493. Cf *Fairline Shipping Corp v Adamson* [1975] QB 180.

[295] Comment *c*.

[296] See 4.65ff.

[297] 'Usage of trade' is defined in § 222 of the Restatement (2d) Contracts and § 223 defines 'course of dealing'. This exception is illustrated as follows; 'A, through salesmen, has frequently solicited orders for goods from B, the orders to be subject to A's personal approval. In every case A has shipped the goods ordered within a week and without other notification to B than billing the goods to him on shipment. A's salesman solicits and receives another order from B. A receives the order and remains silent. B relies on the order and forbears to buy elsewhere for a week. A is bound to fill the order.'(Illustration 5). See also *Ammons v Wilson & Co* 176 Miss 645, 170 So 227 (1936). See further *Boyd v Holmes* (1878) 4 VLR (E) 161. Cf the South African case of *East Asiatic Co (SA) Ltd v Midlands Manufacturing Co (Pty) Ltd* [1954] (2) SA 387.

There is no reason to think an English court would not find that there is a contract is such circumstances.[298]

4.90 A similar set of exceptions exists under the Unidroit Principles of International Commercial Contracts 2004, Article 2.1.6(1). This provision states that silence or inactivity does not amount to acceptance. However, the aim of the provision is to prohibit an offeror forcing a contract on an offeree by stating, in the terms of the offer, that silence will constitute acceptance. The commentary explains this and states that '[t]he situation is different if the parties themselves agree that silence shall amount to acceptance, or if there exists a course of dealing or usage to that effect'.[299]

K. Instantaneous Communications and the Postal Acceptance Rule

Instantaneous communications[300]

4.91 The general position under English law is that an acceptance must be communicated to the offeror in order for it to be effective.[301] It is at that point in time that a contract is formed.[302] Moreover, generally a contract is formed at that place where the acceptance takes effect.[303] Thus, in the case of instantaneous modes of communication this is where acceptance is communicated or received.[304] Examples of instantaneous communications include face-to-face communications, telephone,[305] fax[306] and telex.[307] It is likely that email and text messaging will be categorized as instantaneous forms of communication.[308]

---

[298] See further Furmston, *Cheshire, Fifoot and Furmston's Law of Contract* (15th edn, OUP, Oxford, 2007), 62.

[299] Illustration 2 then provides an example: 'Under a long-term agreement for the supply of wine B regularly met A's orders without expressly confirming its acceptance. On 15 November A orders a large stock for New Year. B does not reply, nor does it deliver at the requested time. B is in breach since, in accordance with the practice established between the parties, B's silence in regard to A's order amounts to an acceptance.'

[300] See further Chapter 6.

[301] See 4.54.

[302] *Brinkibon Ltd v Stahag Stahl und Stahlwarenhandelsgesellschaft mbH* [1983] 2 AC 34, 41.

[303] See 4.03.

[304] *Brinkibon Ltd v Stahag Stahl und Stahlwarenhandelsgesellschaft mbH* [1983] 2 AC 34, 41, 42. See also *Mendelson-Zeller Co Inc v T & C Providores Pty Ltd* [1981] 1 NSWLR 366. Under the Restatement (2d) Contracts § 64, acceptance by way of instantaneous methods of communication are governed by the same principles as those applicable when the parties are face to face. More generally, in the United States, where a reasonable medium of acceptance is used, it is operative from the moment of dispatch; if for any reason it is not operable on dispatch it may become operable upon receipt, see Restatement (2d) Contracts § 67 comment *a*. As noted above (n 17) in the United States a contract formed over the phone is created at the place the acceptor speaks.

[305] *Firm Kanhaiyalal v Dineshchandra* All India Reporter (1959) Madhya Pradesh 234.

[306] *Reese Bros Plastics Ltd v Hamon-Sobelco Australia Pty Ltd* (1988) 5 BPR 11, 106; *Eastern Power Ltd v Azienda Comunale Energia & Ambiente* (1999) 178 DLR (4th) 409. See further Burrows, Finn and Todd, *Law of Contract in New Zealand* (3rd edn, LexisNexis NZ Ltd, Wellington, 2007) para 3.4.6.

[307] *Brinkibon Ltd v Stahag Stahl und Stahlwarenhandelsgesellschaft mbH* [1983] 2 AC 34; *Entores Ltd v Miles Far East Corporation* [1955] 2 QB 327.

[308] *Olivaylle Pty Ltd v Flottweg AG (No 4)* (2009) 255 ALR 632. Receipt will occur when the message is received in the offeror's server, see UNCITRAL Model Law on Electronic Commerce and see Carter, *Carter on Contract* (Butterworths, Sydney), § 03-430; Hill, 'Flogging a Dead Horse—the Postal Acceptance Rule and Email' (2001) 17 JCL 151. For reasons of fairness and convenience, communication should be taken to have occurred at this point. For the position in Canada, see McCamus, *The Law of Contracts* (Irwin Law, Toronto, 2005), 80–1 and in New Zealand see Burrows, Finn and Todd, *Law of Contract in New Zealand* (3rd

It is not difficult to envisage situations where the above position can become problematic.[309] **4.92** The use of an instantaneous method of communication is no guarantee that the message being sent will get through. Phone lines can be cut or interrupted preventing an acceptance by word of mouth or a fax getting through. People dial or fax the wrong number.[310] Similarly, although not used much today, a telex message may be interrupted. Moreover, many instantaneous communications in business are not in fact immediately received or communicated to the offeror but by some office intermediary who must then follow an internal procedure for sending that message on to the offeror. Even in a face-to-face conversation, a sudden noise may result in one party not hearing another.

Despite many statements to the effect that a contract is complete 'only' when acceptance is **4.93** 'received',[311] as it is only then that it can be said that there is a meeting of the minds,[312] as noted earlier, the objective theory of contract does not dictate that communication must occur.[313] The key to an enforceable contract lies in there being evidence of assent rather than there being a meeting of the minds. Therefore, exceptions to that general position can be made to bring about a fair and practical decision.[314] In *Brinkibon Ltd v Stahag Stahl und Stahlwarenhandelsgesellschaft mbH*[315] Lord Wilberforce said: 'No universal rule can cover all such cases: they must be resolved by reference to the intentions of the parties, by sound business practice and in some cases by a judgment where the risks should lie.'[316] The cases appear to have adopted the position that if the offeree uses a permissible method of acceptance and does all that he or she can do to ensure that the acceptance is communicated then the risk that it is not communicated lies with the offeror and there will be a contract.

In many cases the sender will be aware that the message has not been received. For example, **4.94** a fax machine will notify the sender that the fax was not sent. Similarly, if there is a problem with an email address the sender will be told. Even in the case of a telephone conversation the party in the position of the offeree will be aware as to whether his or her acceptance was heard by the offeror. Usually he or she would expect some reply will be given by the offeror[317] and if it is a case of the line going dead then the offeree will know this.

Where the fault lies at the other end, for example, the offeror did not read the communica- **4.95** tion or failed to check the paper in his or her fax machine and the message could not print, then the risk shifts to the offeror and he or she will be estopped from asserting that the message was not received.[318] A choice though must be made as to whether the reason for

---

edn, LexisNexis NZ Ltd, Wellington, 2007) para 3.4.7. Cf Fasciano, 'Internet Electronic Mail: A Last Bastion for the Mailbox Rule' (1996–7) 25 Hofstra L Rev 971.

[309] See the examples provided by Denning LJ in *Entores Ltd v Miles Far East Corporation* [1955] 2 QB 327, 332–3 and Lord Wilberforce in *Brinkibon Ltd v Stahag Stahl und Stahlwarenhandelsgesellschaft mbH* [1983] 2 AC 34, 42.

[310] *LJ Korbetis v Transgrain Shipping BV* [2005] EWHC 1345.

[311] Eg *Entores Ltd v Miles Far East Corporation* [1955] 2 QB 327, 334.

[312] Eg *Household Fire and Carriage Accident Insurance Co Ltd v Grant* (1879) 4 Ex D 216, 221.

[313] See 4.55.

[314] See Restatement (2d) Contracts §§ 20 and 64.

[315] [1983] 2 AC 34.

[316] [1983] 2 AC 34, 42.

[317] See Restatement (2d) Contracts § 64 comment *b* and Illustration 1.

[318] *Entores Ltd v Miles Far East Corporation* [1955] 2 QB 327, 332.

shifting the risk to the offeror is grounded in fault or whether the perspective should be from the position of the offeree. The better view, it is suggested, is that in such a case the acceptance is effective because the offeree had used 'a mode of transmission contemplated by the parties for the purpose [and] has done all he [or she] can to ensure communication to the offeror'.[319] If this is adopted as the rationale it can also be used to explain the postal acceptance rule discussed below. Finally, as noted earlier, if the method of acceptance is not exclusive and the offeree adopts a method of acceptance not contemplated by the offer, then any risk that the acceptance is not communicated or not communicated in time remains with the offeree.[320]

4.96 A common occurring situation is a communication sent outside office hours. On this the law would appear to be that the sender cannot reasonably assume that the message would be read until the following day.[321] What then of a communication sent within business hours but not read until later, perhaps the following day? This could be because the offeror has not got around to it, or the internal communications were such that the offeror was not given the message until the following day. It appears from *Tenax Steamship Co Ltd v The Brimnes (Owners) (The Brimnes)*,[322] that in the case of communications to businesses which are sent and received by telex machines within normal office hours but not read until the following day, they will nevertheless be taken to be communicated and therefore effective when they appear on the machine. It would seem that this result is based on the perspective of the sender, such a sender could reasonably be expected to assume that messages received within normal office hours would be read and the sender would have done all he or she reasonably could do to get the message through that day.[323] The legitimacy for the law focusing on receipt rather than actual communication in the sense of the message being read, lies in the fact that at that stage the offeree has done all he or she can reasonably do to communicate the acceptance.[324] Presumably this would also be the position with regard to communications by fax.

4.97 An interesting issue is the effect of an acceptance left on a telephone answering machine. Coote argues that the postal rule analogy should apply here, namely, that if the sender has no reason to believe that the recipient's answering machine is not working correctly, the message is communicated when it is recorded by the machine since the sender has then done all he or she can to ensure communication to the recipient.[325] The only problem is the

---

[319] Coote, 'The Instantaneous Transmission of Acceptances' (1971) 4 NZULR 331, 335, 339, see also 340. See further Carter, *Carter on Contract* (Butterworths, Sydney), § 03-420 (where 'the offeree reasonably believed that the acceptance was heard or received, and the offeror ought to have realised that this was the case, the offeror may in certain circumstances be estopped from denying that the acceptance was received').

[320] See 4.16.

[321] See *Brinkibon Ltd v Stahag Stahl und Stahlwarenhandelsgesellschaft mbH* [1983] 2 AC 34, 42; *Mondial Shipping and Chartering BV v Astarte Shipping Ltd* [1995] CLC 1011, 1015.

[322] [1975] QB 929. Cf 3.27 note 81.

[323] See *Brinkibon Ltd v Stahag Stahl und Stahlwarenhandelsgesellschaft mbH* [1983] 2 AC 34, 43 ('once the message has been received on the offeror's telex machine, it is not unreasonable to treat it as delivered to the principal offeror, because it is his responsibility to arrange for prompt handling of messages within his own office').

[324] Coote, 'The Instantaneous Transmission of Acceptances' (1971) 4 NZULR 331, 336.

[325] Coote, 'The Instantaneous Transmission of Acceptances' (1971) 4 NZULR 331, 335.

fact that the sender would know from the machine being in operation that the message had not been communicated, although equally it probably would not indicate when the recipient would be present to receive the message. A similar situation arises where a written communication is delivered to a large corporation just prior to the close of business hours where it is reasonably likely it will have to pass through a number of hands before it reaches its destination within the company. But as a number of these 'exceptions' indicate, it is not communication that counts so much as receipt. Nevertheless, in the case of an answering machine, it is suggested the result will depend on the circumstances. If a message is left with a business during business hours the views expressed by Coote may apply. But it may be different in a less commercial environment where a person accepts another's offer by leaving a message on their answering machine at home.

The focus on receipt is adopted by the Vienna Convention for the International Sale of **4.98** Goods[326] and the Unidroit Principles of International Commercial Contracts 2004.[327] Under the Unidroit Principles, this is expressed to occur either when given orally to the relevant person or 'delivered at that person's place of business or mailing address'.[328] This has been argued to be the most practical approach since it is not easy to prove when a communication actually comes to someone's attention.[329] However, it has also be noted that there may be difficulties of proof with this approach such as where delivery is made to a place of business when the business is shut down for a holiday period.[330]

The postal acceptance rule

Introduction

It is a general principle of English law that where the post may be used to accept an offer **4.99** then the acceptance is effective from the moment the acceptance is posted.[331] Since the

---

[326] Article 18(2). This is subject to the exception is subsection (3) which allows for acceptance by performance rather than notification in the circumstances described in the subsection.

[327] Article 2.1.6(2). This is subject to the exception in subsection (3) which allows for acceptance by performance rather than notification in the circumstances described in the subsection. See also Principles of European Contract Law Art 2:205(2) and (3) and the Draft Common Frame of Reference II–4:205(2) and (3).

[328] Article 1.10(3). The Vienna Convention contains a more complicated provision in Art 24 but is similar in effect. Under this Article an 'offer, declaration of acceptance or any other indication of intention "reaches" the addressee when it is made orally to him or delivered by any other means to him personally, to his place of business or mailing address or, if he does not have a place of business or mailing address, to his habitual residence.' See further Principles of European Contract Law Art 1:303(3) and the Draft Common Frame of Reference II–1:106(4).

[329] Farnsworth, in Bianca and Bonell (eds), *Commentary on the International Sales Law: The 1980 Vienna Sales Convention* (Giuffrè, Milan, 1987), 203.

[330] Farnsworth, in Bianca and Bonell (eds), *Commentary on the International Sales Law: The 1980 Vienna Sales Convention* (Giuffrè, Milan, 1987), 204.

[331] *Adams v Lindsell* (1818) 1 B & Ald 681, 106 ER 250; *Dunlop v Higgins* (1848) 1 HLC 381, 9 ER 805; *Re Imperial Land Co of Marseilles (Harris' Case)* (1872) 7 Ch App 587; *Household Fire and Carriage Accident Insurance Co Ltd v Grant* (1879) 4 Ex D 216. Australian authorities include *Tooth v Fleming* (1859) 2 Legge 1152, SC(NSW); *Pratten v Thompson* (1895) 11 WN (NSW) 162; *Remilton v City Mutual Life Assurance Society Ltd* (1908) 10 WALR 19; *Tallerman & Co Pty Ltd v Nathan's Merchandise (Victoria) Pty Ltd* (1957) 98 CLR 93; *Williams v The Society of Lloyd's* [1994] 1 VR 274, 316. The rule also applies in New Zealand (see Burrows, Finn and Todd, *Law of Contract in New Zealand* (3rd edn, LexisNexis, Wellington, 2007) para 3.4.6 and see *Sommerville v Rice* (1912) 31 NZLR 370), in Canada (see *Island Properties Ltd v Entertainment Enterprises Ltd* (1983) 146 DLR (3d) 505, (appeal allowed in part (1986) 26 DLR (4th) 347))

acceptance is effective at this point, the contract is taken to be formed at that time and made at that place where the acceptance is posted.[332] It necessarily follows that the acceptance is effective even if the mail is delayed or is never delivered.[333] It also follows that once the acceptance is posted, the offeror cannot revoke the offer.[334] Moreover, if the acceptance is operative upon posting then it would be too late for the offeree to revoke its acceptance once posted.[335]

4.100 The classic authority for the postal acceptance rule is *Adams v Lindsell*.[336] On 2 September the defendants had written to the plaintiffs offering to sell them wool and requiring an answer by post. However, the defendants had misdirected this letter of offer and it did not reach the plaintiffs until 5 September. The plaintiffs posted their acceptance on that date and it reached the defendants on 9 September. Since they might have expected a reply by 7 September had the offer letter not been misdirected, on 8 September the defendants sold the wool in question to third parties. The court held that the acceptance was effective on 5 September when it was posted. Consequently, the defendants were in breach of contract.

4.101 The rule developed in *Adams v Lindsell* is often referred to as an exception to the general rule requiring communication of acceptance.[337] A couple of points need to be made in this regard. First, at the time *Adams v Lindsell* was decided there was no general rule requiring the communication of acceptances, this was the first case dealing with the issue. Therefore the court may not have intended to make any 'exception'.[338] The court was also clearly influenced by the fact that the delay was attributable to the defendants and 'must be taken

---

and in Singapore (see Phang, *Cheshire, Fifoot and Furmston's Law of Contract* (2nd Singapore and Malaysian edn, Butterworths, Singapore, 1998), 120). In Malaysia, § 4(2)(a) of the Malaysian Contracts Act 1950 (based on the Indian Contract Act 1872, § 4) provides that an acceptance is complete as against the offeror 'when it is put in a course of transmission to him, so as to be put out of the power of the acceptor'. However, by § 4(2)(b) the acceptor (offeree) would not be bound until such acceptance 'comes to the knowledge of the proposer'. It follows that the acceptor would not be bound if the acceptance was lost in the post. See also Winfield, 'Some Aspects of Offer and Acceptance' (1939) 55 LQR 499, 505ff.

[332] *Brinkibon Ltd v Stahag Stahl und Stahlwarenhandelsgesellschaft mbH* [1983] 2 AC 34; *Tallerman & Co Pty Ltd v Nathan's Merchandise (Victoria) Pty Ltd* (1957) 98 CLR 93; *Imperial Life Assurance Co of Canada v Colmenares* [1967] SCR 443, 62 DLR (2d) 138; *Pratten v Thompson* (1895) 11 WN (NSW) 162; *Williams v The Society of Lloyd's* [1994] 1 VR 274.

[333] *Household Fire and Carriage Insurance Co Ltd v Grant* (1879) 4 Ex D 216. See also *Adams v Lindsell* (1818) 1 B & Ald 681, 106 ER 250; *Re London and Northern Bank; Ex parte Jones* [1900] 1 Ch 220; *Georgoulis v Mandalinic* [1984] 1 NSWLR 612; *Sibtac Corp Ltd v Sooj Lienster Investments Ltd* (1978) 18 OR (2d) 395, (1978) 83 DLR (3d) 116. Query the position with telegrams, see below 4.105. Query also whether this should be the position if the offeree is aware that there might be a delay.

[334] See further 4.113ff.

[335] See 4.113ff.

[336] (1818) 1 B & Ald 681, 106 ER 250.

[337] Eg *Brinkibon Ltd v Stahag Stahl und Stahlwarenhandelsgesellschaft mbH* [1983] 2 AC 34, 48; *Bressan v Squires* [1974] 2 NSWLR 460, 461; *Nunin Holdings Pty Ltd v Tullamarine Estates Pty Ltd* [1994] 1 VR 74, 80. See also Hill, 'Flogging a Dead Horse—The Postal Acceptance Rule and Email' (2001) 17 JCL 151, 154; Pannam, 'Postal Regulation 289 and Acceptance of an Offer by Post' (1960) 2 Melb Uni L Rev 388.

[338] Furmston, *Cheshire, Fifoot and Furmston's Law of Contract* (15th edn, OUP, Oxford, 2007), 68 'the exception is historically anterior to the rule'.

as against them'.[339] Second, as noted earlier, under the objective theory of contract there is no requirement for a rule that dictates that communication of acceptances is necessary.[340]

Justification for the rule

Many explanations have been put forward in an attempt to justify this rule.[341] Some expla- **4.102** nations have emphasized the practical need for such a rule. In *Adams v Lindsell*[342] itself it was suggested that if the acceptance took effect from the moment it was received then the offeree ought not to be bound until it received notification of that receipt from the offeror who in turn could then expect a notification from the offeree and 'so it might go on ad infinitum'.[343] Other explanations have attempted a more doctrinal explanation. The most well known is the argument that the postal service operates as the agent of both parties.[344] That view is now discredited.[345] Similarly, some have argued that it is based on control and the acceptance should take effect once the letter of acceptance is out of the effective control of the offeree.[346]

Clearly as a matter of commercial convenience and expediency it is necessary for the law to **4.103** take a position as to when such an acceptance is to operate. It is this convenience and expediency that is adopted in most authorities as the true basis for the rule.[347] The issue then is where should the risk lie? Should the offeree be in the position that the offer could be revoked after he or she has sent the acceptance or should the offeror carry the risk that for a period of time he or she will not know whether the offer has been accepted. The effect of

---

[339] (1818) 1 B & Ald 681, 683, 106 ER 250, 251.

[340] See further Coote, 'The Instantaneous Transmission of Acceptances' (1971) 4 NZULR 331, 337.

[341] See Evans, 'The Anglo-American Mailing Rule: Some Problems of Offer and Acceptance in Contracts by Correspondence ' (1966) 15 ICLQ 533, 558–61; Macneil, 'Time of Acceptance: Too Many Problems for a Single Rule' (1964) 112 U Pa L Rev 947. See also Hill, 'Flogging a Dead Horse—The Postal Acceptance Rule and Email' (2001) 17 JCL 151, 154–5; Samek, 'A Reassessment of the Present Rule Relating to Postal Acceptance' (1961) 35 ALJ 38. See further Gardner, 'Trashing with Trollope: A Deconstruction of the Postal Rules in Contract' (1992) 12 OJLS 170 (suggesting that the rule may have some basis in the reform of the mail system that was occurring at the time it was derived and the confidence the community had in that system). It might be added that the postal service of the nineteenth century was arguably more efficient than the postal service today. Back then you could expect same day delivery in some areas and more than one mail delivery a day. It is little wonder then why a rule would be derived that places a lot of confidence in the mail service.

[342] (1818) 1 B & Ald 681, 106 ER 250.

[343] (1818) 1 B & Ald 681, 683, 106 ER 250, 251.

[344] See *Re National Savings Bank Association (Hebb's Case)* (1867) LR 4 Eq 9, 12; *Household Fire and Carriage Accident Insurance Co Ltd v Grant* (1879) 4 Ex D 216, 221; *Byrne & Co v Van Tienhoven & Co* (1880) 5 CPD 344, 348; *Re London and Northern Bank; Ex parte Jones* [1900] 1 Ch 220, 222.

[345] See *Henthorn v Fraser* [1892] 2 Ch 27, 35–6.

[346] The strength of this basis is questioned in *Morrison v Thoelke* 155 So (2d) 889, 897, 899–902 (1963). In addition, this explanation is arguably weakened if the offeree has a legal right to recover a letter once it is placed in the post but not yet delivered, cf Pannam, 'Postal Regulation 289 and Acceptance of an Offer by Post' (1960) 2 Melb Uni L Rev 388, 395.

[347] See *Brinkibon Ltd v Stahag Stahl und Stahlwarenhandelsgesellschaft mbH* [1983] 2 AC 34, 41, 43, 48; *Bressan v Squires* [1974] 2 NSWLR 460, 461; *Entores Ltd v Miles Far East Corporation* [1955] 2 QB 327, 337; *Household Fire and Carriage Accident Insurance Co Ltd v Grant* (1879) 4 Ex D 216, 223–4. See further Carter, *Carter on Contract* (Butterworths, Sydney), § 03-400; Coote, 'The Instantaneous Transmission of Acceptances' (1971) 4 NZULR 331, 338–9.

the rule is to protect the offeree from the risk mentioned.[348] Thus, in English law, rather than protecting the offeree in all cases by making offers generally irrevocable, a discrete rule applies for acceptances sent by post. The reason given for allocating the risk in this discrete way, although it is perhaps not a full explanation, is that it is the offeror who controls the terms of the offer and the method of acceptance. If the offeror allows the post to be used for acceptances then he or she should carry the risk and this is the effect of the rule.[349] It is suggested that although that reasoning remains relevant, the preferred focus in terms of legal principle is to determine whether the offeree has done all that is necessary, according to the terms of the offer, to communicate the acceptance.[350] If the offer allows for an acceptance by post, then once the offeree has placed the acceptance in the post then he or she has done all they can in law to bring the acceptance to the notice of the offeror.[351]

When does the postal acceptance rule apply?

4.104   The postal acceptance rule will apply when 'the circumstances are such that it must have been within the contemplation of the parties that, according to the ordinary usages of mankind, the post might be used as a means of communicating the acceptance of an offer'.[352] This is determined by reference to a reasonable person in the position of the parties. Usually where an offer is sent by post, it will be possible to accept that offer by post.[353] Historically, it would also apply where the parties were dealing at a distance[354] except where the market is volatile which may call for a quick response.[355] Similarly, if the goods are of a wasting nature, the circumstances may be such that the offer cannot be accepted by mail, or, at least, the time frame for acceptance by mail would be short.[356] It is not necessary for the parties to have in their contemplation the postal acceptance rule.[357]

---

[348]   *Re Imperial Land Co of Marseilles (Harris' Case)* (1872) 7 Ch App 587, 594; *Brinkibon Ltd v Stahag Stahl und Stahlwarenhandelsgesellschaft mbH* [1983] 2 AC 34, 41. Some have questioned whether this preference given to the offeree should still be made available now that there is available various efficient instantaneous methods of communication, see Eisler, 'Default Rules for Contract Formation by Promise and the Need for Revision of the Mailbox Rule' (1990–91) 79 Kentucky LJ 557, 567ff.

[349]   *Household Fire and Carriage Accident Insurance Co Ltd v Grant* (1879) 4 Ex D 216, 223–4 per Thesiger LJ. See also Coote, 'The Instantaneous Transmission of Acceptances' (1971) 4 NZULR 331, 338.

[350]   See Coote, 'The Instantaneous Transmission of Acceptances' (1971) 4 NZULR 331, 338–340.

[351]   Although distinct, this basis is often linked to the explanation based on the idea that on posting the letter is no longer under the control of the offeree, see *Dunlop v Higgins* (1848) 1 HLC 381, 398, 9 ER 805, 812.

[352]   *Henthorn v Fraser* [1892] 2 Ch 27, 33 per Lord Herschell. See further *Holwell Securities Ltd v Hughes* [1974] 1 WLR 155, 157, 160–1; *White Cliffs Opal Mines Ltd v Miller* (1904) 4 SR (NSW) 150, 153; *Sibtac Corp Ltd v Sooj Lienster Investments Ltd* (1978) 18 OR (2d) 395, (1978) 83 DLR (3d) 116; *Nunin Holdings Pty Ltd v Tullamarine Estates Pty Ltd* [1994] 1 VR 74, 83.

[353]   *Dunlop v Higgins* (1848) 1 HLC 381, 9 ER 805; *Henthorn v Fraser* [1892] 2 Ch 27, 32. For an instance where this was not the case, see *Nunin Holdings Pty Ltd v Tullamarine Estates Pty Ltd* [1994] 1 VR 74.

[354]   *Henthorn v Fraser* [1892] 2 Ch 27, 33; *Bruner v Moore* [1904] 1 Ch 305. Cf *Re Imperial Land Co of Marseilles (Harris' Case)* (1872) 7 Ch App 587, 593.

[355]   See Restatement (2d) Contracts § 65 comment *c*.

[356]   *Shatford v BC Wine Growers Ltd* [1927] 2 DLR 759.

[357]   *Bressan v Squires* [1974] 2 NSWLR 460, 462. It should be noted that Lord Herschell in *Henthorn v Fraser* [1892] 2 Ch 27, 33, when formulating when the rule applied disagreed with a view expressed by both Thesiger LJ and Baggallay LJ in *Household Fire and Carriage Accident Insurance Co Ltd v Grant* (1879) 4 Ex D 216, 218, 228, that the rule applies where the offeror expressly or impliedly 'authorizes' the use of the post for acceptances. There is a suggestion in that formulation that the offeror must contemplate the effect of the rule.

The postal acceptance rule does not apply to instantaneous modes of communication and **4.105** will only apply to a form of communication that is analogous to mail. The only extension of the rule has been to telegrams.[358]

It is open to the offeror to exclude the application of the rule by the terms of the offer.[359] **4.106** Clearly the most obvious way to do this is to state that acceptance will be effective only upon 'receipt'.[360] In *Holwell Securities Ltd v Hughes*,[361] in order to exercise an option there had to be 'notice in writing to the intended vendor'. The Court of Appeal held that this form of wording required communication of the notice. Similarly, in the South African case of *SA Yster en Staal Industriële Korporasie BPK v Koschade*,[362] in order to exercise an option it was necessary to 'notify the owner to this effect in writing' and a particular post office box address was given. This was interpreted as requiring arrival at the post office box address so that posting, which had occurred within the option period, was not sufficient.[363] In addition, the nature of the transaction and the subject matter of the contract may

---

Arguably some support for the latter approach can be seen in *Tallerman & Co Pty Ltd v Nathan's Merchandise (Victoria) Pty Ltd* (1957) 98 CLR 93, 111–12, where Dixon CJ and Fullagar J said: 'The general rule is that a contract is not completed until acceptance of an offer is actually communicated to the offeror, and a finding that a contract is completed by the posting of a letter of acceptance cannot be justified unless it is to be inferred that the offeror contemplated and intended that his offer might be accepted by the doing of that act ...' This appears to be more in line with the 'authorization' requirement. Nevertheless, as was pointed out by Bowen CJ in *Bressan v Squires* [1974] 2 NSWLR 460, 462, Dixon CJ and Fullagar J cited *Henthorn v Fraser* for this statement and did not therefore mean to differ from it.

[358] *Cowan v O'Connor* (1888) 20 QBD 640. See also *Dehle v Denham* (1899) Tas LR (1 N & S) 128; *Lewis Construction Co Pty Ltd v M Tichauer Societe Anonyme* [1966] VR 341, 345; *Brinkibon Ltd v Stahag Stahl und Stahlwarenhandelsgesellschaft mbH* [1983] 2 AC 34, 43. Cf *Express Airways v Port Augusta Air Services* [1980] Qd R 543 (telegram sent through telex system effective when received). In Canada there is authority applying it to couriers, see *R v Commercial Credit Corp Ltd* (1983) 61 NSR (2d) 410, (1983) 4 DLR (4th) 314.

[359] The mere fact that an offer is irrevocable, such as in the case of an option, probably does not of itself abrogate the rule, see *Bressan v Squires* [1974] 2 NSWLR 460. See also *Holwell Securities Ltd v Hughes* [1974] 1 WLR 155.

[360] Eg *Nunin Holdings Pty Ltd v Tullamarine Estates Pty Ltd* [1994] 1 VR 74. The need for acceptance to be 'received' is not achieved solely by making the offer open for an express period of time, eg *Jacobsen, Sons & Co v Underwood & Sons Ltd* (1894) 1 SLT 578 ('this for reply by Monday'). See also *Bruner v Moore* [1904] 1 Ch 305; *Lewes Nominees Pty Ltd v Strang* (1983) 49 ALR 328.

[361] [1974] 1 WLR 155. See also *Bressan v Squires* [1974] 2 NSWLR 460 (an option which stated that it 'may be exercised by you by notice in writing addressed to me', was held to displace the postal acceptance rule). See further *Affiliated Realty Corp Ltd v Sam Berger Restaurant Ltd* (1973) 42 DLR (3d) 191.

[362] 1983 (4) SA 837.

[363] Any displacement of the rule will require a determination as to whether the acceptance is to be effective upon receipt or communication, see *Holwell Securities Ltd v Hughes* [1974] 1 WLR 155, 158 per Russell LJ dealing with facts that may result in receipt being sufficient. See *Bowman v Durham Holdings Pty Ltd* (1973) 131 CLR 8 (here notice for the exercise of an option was 'deemed duly given or made [if sent by post] at the time when such envelope would in the ordinary course of post be delivered'; here the notice was sent on a Friday afternoon and would ordinarily be delivered on the Saturday morning but the postman would not deliver the letter to a closed building; held that it took effect as if duly delivered on Saturday as the terms adopted the usual practices of the postal authority (see further on 'ordinary course of post, *Kemp v Wanklyn* [1894] 1 QB 583, 585) and not the practices of the offeror; it therefore did not matter that the recipient chose not to open its offices on that day). See also on deemed delivery and deemed receipt dates, *Lewes Nominees Pty Ltd v Strang* (1983) 49 ALR 328; *Kudeweh v T and J Kelleher Builders Pty Ltd* [1990] VR 701. For an example of a delivery date deemed by statute, see *WX Investments Ltd v Begg (Fraser, Part 20 defendant)* [2002] 1 WLR 2849.

prevent the rule from operating.[364] It should also be noted that a negation of the postal acceptance rule does not necessarily mean the post may not be used to send an acceptance.[365]

4.107 The postal acceptance rule will not apply if 'its application would produce manifest inconvenience, and absurdity'.[366] For example, in the context of a contract for the sale of land, if the buyer was the offeree and could accept by post then there would be a period of time where the vendor would be a trustee without knowledge.[367] Perhaps for this reason the rule also does not apply if there is no regular postal service such as where it might be interrupted by war.[368]

4.108 The rule will not apply if the offeree has not properly addressed the letter and affixed the proper stamp.[369] If, however, the reason for the incorrect address is that the offeror has supplied the wrong address, then the acceptance will take effect from the time it is posted. Where the fault is that of the offeree but the incorrectly addressed letter does end up being delivered to the offeror in due course, it is an open question as to whether it should take effect from the moment of receipt. It is possible on any given set of facts for that error to work in the offeree's favour.[370]

4.109 Errors in the transmission of telegrams or telemessages raise slightly different problems as they may be caused by third parties. *Henkel v Pape*[371] concerned an error in the transmission of a telegraph offer/counter-offer rather than an acceptance. The telegraph clerk telegraphed the word 'the' instead of 'three' so that instead of reading 'send three rifles' the telegram read 'send the rifles'. The plaintiffs sent 50 rifles which had been referred to in their earlier correspondence with the defendant. It was held that the defendant was not bound to accept more than three rifles since he was not responsible for the error in transmission. But what if the facts were that an offer is made to sell 50 rifles and the telemessage

---

[364] See further *Tallerman & Co Pty Ltd v Nathan's Merchandise (Victoria) Pty Ltd* (1957) 98 CLR 93, 112 ('where solicitors are conducting a highly contentious correspondence, one would have thought actual communication would be regarded as essential to the conclusion of agreement on anything').

[365] See *A to Z Bazaars (Pty) Ltd v Minister of Agriculture* 1975 (3) SA 468. See also *Holwell Securities Ltd v Hughes* [1974] 1 WLR 155, 158.

[366] *Bressan v Squires* [1974] 2 NSWLR 460, 462.

[367] *Bressan v Squires* [1974] 2 NSWLR 460, 462. See also *Nunin Holdings Pty Ltd v Tullamarine Estates Pty Ltd* [1994] 1 VR 74, 81–2; *Holwell Securities Ltd v Hughes* [1974] 1 WLR 155, 161. See further *British and American Telegraph Co Ltd v Colson* (1871) LR 6 Ex Ch 108, 111–12 (acceptance of offer for allotment of shares sent by post; held not to be effective until receipt on the basis that it would cause injustice if the position were otherwise), disapproved in *Re Imperial Land Company of Marseilles (Harris's Case)* (1872) LR 7 Ch App 587 and *Household Fire and Carriage Accident Insurance Co Ltd v Grant* (1879) LR 4 Ex D 216. See further Gardner, 'Trashing with Trollope: A Deconstruction of the Postal Rules in Contract' (1992) 12 OJLS 170, 172–3, 184–9.

[368] *Bal v Van Standen* [1902] TS 128.

[369] *Getreide-Import-Gesellschaft mbH v Contimar SA Compania Industrial Comercial y Maritima* [1953] 1 WLR 201 (affirmed [1953] 1 WLR 793). The rule may also be displaced if the acceptance is not properly placed in the post, eg *Re London and Northern Bank; Ex parte Jones* [1900] 1 Ch 220 (letter given directly to postman who was not authorized to take charge of letters was not equivalent to placing the letter with the postal authority).

[370] Peel, *Treitel, The Law of Contract* (12th edn, Thomson, Sweet & Maxwell, London, 2007) para 2-034.

[371] (1870) LR 6 Ex 7.

response which as dictated by the offeree should read 'send the rifles'—which would be an acceptance complying with the terms of the offer—is actually transmitted in error by a third party as 'send three rifles'? One considered view is that the offeror could not treat the response as a counter-offer and would be bound to treat it as an effective acceptance on the basis that the offeror should 'take the risk of errors in the transmission of a telegraphed message' and the offeree will not know of the error.[372]

The postal acceptance rule in the United States

In the United States the postal acceptance or 'mail box rule' is adopted in section 63(a) of **4.110** the Restatement (2d) Contracts.[373] Therefore, as is the position in England, the rule will apply if the post is a reasonable medium of acceptance.[374] A medium will be 'reasonable if it is the one used by the offeror or one customary in similar transactions at the time and place the offer is received'.[375] As in England the rule can be excluded by the terms of the offer.[376] Similarly, the rule can be excluded by implication, for example, if the receipt of a notice of acceptance is necessary to enable the offeror to perform.[377] Further, as in England, the rule will not apply unless the acceptance is properly addressed, prepaid and dispatched.[378] The rule will not therefore apply unless the offeree 'exercises reasonable diligence to notify the offeror'.[379]

The postal acceptance rules under the Convention for the International Sale of Goods (CISG) and Unidroit[380]

Under both the United Nations Convention for the International Sale of Goods (1980), **4.111** Article 18(2) and the Unidroit Principles of International Commercial Contracts (2004), Article 2.1.6(2), an acceptance is effective when it 'reaches' the offeror.[381] A notice 'reaches' a person for the purposes of CISG 'when it is made orally to him or delivered by any other means to him personally, to his place of business or mailing address or, if he does not have

---

[372] Peel, *Treitel, The Law of Contract* (12th edn, Thomson, Sweet & Maxwell, London, 2007) para 2-035.
[373] The rule does not apply to option contracts which are effective upon receipt of acceptance, see § 63(b). Option contracts are excluded from the operation of the general rule on the ground that the offeree is protected against revocation by the offeror so that the primary justification for the postal rule is not applicable.
[374] Restatement (2d) Contracts § 30(2).
[375] Restatement (2d) Contracts § 65.
[376] Eg Restatement (2d) Contracts § 63 illustration 3.
[377] Eg Restatement (2d) Contracts § 63 illustration 4.
[378] Restatement (2d) Contracts § 66. Cf Restatement (2d) Contracts § 67 deals with the receipt of an acceptance improperly dispatched and provides: 'Where an acceptance is seasonably dispatched but the offeree uses means of transmission not invited by the offer or fails to exercise reasonable diligence to insure safe transmission, it is treated as operative upon dispatch if received within the time in which a properly dispatched acceptance would normally have arrived.' An offeror may contract out of this provision, however, when the provision applies then as the acceptance is effective from dispatch any revocation overtaking the letter would not be operable, see Restatement (2d) Contracts § 67 comment *a*.
[379] Restatement (2d) Contracts § 66 comment *a*.
[380] See further on comparative aspects of the rule, Nussbaum, 'Comparative Aspects of the Anglo-American Offer—and—Acceptance Doctrine' (1936) 36 Columbia Law Rev 920.
[381] See also Principles of European Contract Law Art 2:205(1); Draft Common Frame of Reference II–4:205(1).

a place of business or mailing address, to his habitual residence'[382] and under Unidroit, 'when given to that person orally or delivered at that person's place of business or mailing address'.[383] Both the CISG and Unidroit Principles contain an exception to the receipt rule where acceptance can be by performance without communication.[384]

4.112　This position is adopted as opposed to the dispatch rule on the basis that it is the offeree who makes the choice of what mode of acceptance is adopted and is in the best position to determine the risks and chances of delay.[385] But is should also be noted under both the CISG and Unidroit the offeree is protected from having the offer revoked prior to acceptance because any revocation must arrive prior to the dispatch of acceptance.[386]

The postal acceptance rule and revocation of acceptance[387]

4.113　The postal acceptance rule does not apply to revocations. A revocation of an acceptance must be received and is only operative if it is received prior to any acceptance becoming operative.[388] Therefore, doctrinally, if an acceptance is effective from the moment it is put into the post so that a contract is formed at that point, then it is too late for the offeree to then forward, by any means, a revocation of that acceptance.[389]

4.114　There has been a long debate as to whether this should be the position or whether the law should allow the offeree to revoke the acceptance by delivering a revocation to the offeror prior to the offeror receiving the acceptance. However, the case support for allowing revocation is fairly thin. The Scottish case of *Dunmore v Alexander*[390] appears to support the view that such revocation is possible. Here the acceptance and revocation were communicated to the offeror at the same time and the court placed a lot of weight on that fact. However, the facts of this case may be interpreted differently and may have involved the revocation of an offer. The case may have involved an offer made by a servant through her employer as agent to a future potential employer which was accepted by that future employer by post to the agent followed by a revocation with both the acceptance and

---

[382] United Nations Convention for the International Sale of Goods (1980), Art 24. See also Principles of European Contract Law Art 1:303(3); Draft Common Frame of Reference II–1:106(4).

[383] Unidroit Principles of International Commercial Contracts (2004), Art 1.10(3).

[384] United Nations Convention for the International Sale of Goods (1980), Art 18(3); Unidroit Principles of International Commercial Contracts (2004), Art 2.1.6(3). See also Principles of European Contract Law Art 2:205(3); Draft Common Frame of Reference II–4:205(3).

[385] See Unidroit Principles of International Commercial Contracts (2004), Art 2.1.6 Comment 4.

[386] United Nations Convention for the International Sale of Goods (1980), Art 16(1); Unidroit Principles of International Commercial Contracts (2004), Art 2.1.4(1).

[387] As to the ability of consumers to cancel a 'distance contract' see Peel, *Treitel, The Law of Contract* (12th edn, Thomson, Sweet & Maxwell, London, 2007) para 2-037.

[388] See generally on revocation of offers and acceptances, Chapter 3.

[389] See *Wenkheim v Arndt* (1873) 1 JR 73; *Morrison v Thoelke* 155 So (2d) 889 (1963). See also *Kinch v Bullard* [1999] 1 WLR 423.

[390] (1830) 9 Shaw 190. See also *Dick v US* 82 F Supp 326 (1949); *Rhode Island Tool Co v US* 128 F Supp 417 (1955) (in both these cases postal regulations were in place allowing a sender to recover mail after posting but before delivery; this impacted on the reasoning in the cases; the view was taken that where such a right exists the sender retains control of the letter until it is delivered and so the rule does not apply). See Hudson, 'Retraction of Letters of Acceptance' (1966) 82 LQR 169; Pannam, 'Postal Regulation 289 and Acceptance of an Offer by Post' (1960) 2 Melb Uni L Rev 388, cf *Morrison v Thoelke* 155 So (2d) 889 (1963)). See further *Nunin Holdings Pty Ltd v Tullamarine Estates Pty Ltd* [1994] 1 VR 74, 80–1.

revocation being actually communicated to the servant at the same time. Alternatively, it might have involved some initial enquiries by the future employer as to the availability of the servant followed by an authorization by the future employer of the servant's employer to make an offer to the servant followed by a revocation of that authority and offer, which were both communicated to the servant at the same time prior to the servant communicating an acceptance.

At first instance in the South African case of *A to Z Bazaars (Pty) Ltd v Minister of* **4.115** *Agriculture*,[391] Van Heerden J was of the opinion that a letter of acceptance could not be overtaken by a revocation. In the Appellate Division,[392] it was held that on the facts that actual communication of acceptance was required so that the postal acceptance rule did not apply and therefore the telegram withdrawing acceptance was effective because it was received before the letter of acceptance. However, the court queried why a rule designed to protect the offeree should necessarily preclude the offeree from neutralizing the acceptance prior to its receipt.[393]

There is far more academic support for acknowledging the efficacy of a revocation. For **4.116** example, if the postal acceptance rule is justified on the basis of the offeror assuming the risk 'of delay and accident in the post, it would not seem to strain matters to say that he also assumes the risk of a letter being overtaken by a speedier means of communication'.[394] Note should also be taken of the point made in *A to Z Bazaars (Pty) Ltd v Minister of Agriculture* that the doctrinal result referred to above should not be applied if the postal acceptance rule itself is no more than a rule of convenience. The argument usually put up against this is that after mailing an acceptance, the offeree should not be 'permitted to speculate at the offeror's expense during the time required for the letter to arrive'.[395] More fundamentally, what these views fail to answer is that no matter what the basis for the rule, the rule itself results in a certain legal effect, namely that a contract is formed upon application of the rule. Any reason for allowing the offeree to revoke the acceptance after posting it must provide a basis for rescinding a contract.

Clearly the doctrinal result would not apply if the model of contract was a reliance model **4.117** as the offeror would not have acted in reliance on an acceptance put in the post which he or she does not yet know about. In addition, in any system that does not adopt the postal acceptance rule so that acceptances are only effective upon receipt, it would be possible to communicate a revocation prior to the acceptance being received and becoming effective.[396] It should be added that there are common law systems which adopt the postal

---

[391] 1974 (4) SA 392. See Turpin 'Postal Contracts: Attempted revocation of Acceptance' [1975] CLJ 25.
[392] 1975 (3) SA 468.
[393] 1975 (3) SA 468, 476.
[394] Hudson, 'Retraction of Letters of Acceptance' (1966) 82 LQR 169, 170.
[395] Restatement (2d) Contracts § 63 comment *c*. See also Peel, *Treitel, The Law of Contract* (12th edn, Thomson, Sweet & Maxwell, London, 2007) para 2-036.
[396] Eg United Nations Convention on Contracts for the International Sale of Goods (1980), Art 22; Unidroit Principles of International Commercial Contracts (2004), Art 2.1.10.

acceptance rule but which nevertheless allow for a revocation to neutralize any acceptance sent by post.[397]

4.118 The issue should also be considered from the point of view of the offeror. In the majority of cases, the offeror would not be prejudiced if a revocation of acceptance is received before an acceptance.[398] Indeed, to insist on the binding effect of the postal acceptance when a revocation has been received first may be prejudicial to the offeror as the offeror may have acted on the revocation. For example, the offeror may, in reliance on the revocation, sell the goods that were originally offered for sale to the offeree to a third party. If the postal rule were to be strictly applied, the offeree could change his or her mind again, rely on the postal rule and claim damages for breach of contract from the offeror. Two suggestions have been put forward to avoid this conclusion. It could either be argued that although a contract came into force it has been rescinded by mutual consent, namely the revocation of acceptance which the offeror acted upon,[399] or, the revocation could be regarded as a repudiatory breach of contract which the offeror accepted by his or her acts of reliance.[400]

4.119 These suggestions are reflected in the Restatement (2d) Contracts. As in England, the position in the United States is that an offeree cannot revoke its acceptance once it has been posted.[401] However, it is acknowledged that such a revocation may have some effect in that 'it may amount to an offer to rescind the contract or to a repudiation of it, or it may bar the offeree by estoppel from enforcing it'.[402]

4.120 Another scenario concerns the offeree first mailing a rejection (or counter-offer) to the offeror and then changing his or her mind and mailing an acceptance which is posted before the rejection is communicated to the offeror. As a general rule the rejection is not effective until it is communicated but the result of this conduct may be that the rejection is still nevertheless received prior to the letter of acceptance and the offeror may act on that rejection. In such circumstances the offeror should be protected from the effect of the postal acceptance rule. In the Restatement (2d) Contracts, the issue is dealt with in section 40. This provides that the offer remains open for acceptance prior to the communication of

---

[397] India allows for postal acceptances to be revoked. This is the effect of § 4 and § 5 of the Indian Contract Act 1872. Section 5 provides that 'an acceptance may be revoked at any time before the communication of the acceptance is complete as against the acceptor, bur nor afterwards'. The effect of § 4 is that an acceptance sent by post binds the offeror when posted but binds the offeree when received and a revocation binds the person sending it on dispatch and binds the person to whom it is sent when it comes to his or her knowledge. Therefore a postal acceptor may revoke that acceptance before, or at the moment when, the letter of acceptance reaches the offeror. See also § 4 and § 5 of the Malaysian Contracts Act 1950.

[398] Query whether the offeror is prejudiced by the fact that any change to the current position would allow the offeree to withdraw an acceptance after posting but would not allow the offeror to withdraw its offer after the posting of the acceptance.

[399] As has been noted though if 'the retraction did not refer to the letter of acceptance but read as a mere rejection and the offeror acted upon this before he knew of the prior letter of acceptance this construction would not be possible. Nevertheless, the retraction should still be effective to the extent that the retracting acceptor should be estopped from alleging that a contract existed', see Hudson, 'Retraction of Letters of Acceptance' (1966) 82 LQR 169, 169–70.

[400] Peel, *Treitel, The Law of Contract* (12th edn, Thomson, Sweet & Maxwell, London, 2007) para 2-036.

[401] Restatement (2d) Contracts § 63 comment *c*.

[402] Restatement (2d) Contracts § 63 comment *c*. Illustration 7 provides an example.

the rejection or counter-offer, however, an acceptance sent after the rejection or counter-offer operates as a counter-offer unless it is received by the offeror prior to the rejection.[403]

Finally, where an offeree attempts to overtake an acceptance in order to correct a mistake, **4.121** then since the contract will have become effective upon the posting of the acceptance then the offeree must rely on the doctrine of mistake to vitiate the contract or, if appropriate seek an order of rectification.[404]

L. Standard Form Contracting and the 'Battle of the Forms'

The 'battle of the forms' defined

It is common practice today for commercial entities to use standard form contracts. This **4.122** obviously saves time and costs in negotiating each and every term of an individualized contract. Such contracts usually leave only those terms which vary from transaction to transaction to be negotiated. For example, in a standard form contract for the sale of goods the face of the form will contain a number of blanks which are to be filled in with those essential terms which are negotiable, such as quality, quantity, price, payment and delivery. Usually on the back of such forms there will be pre-printed general terms and conditions commonly referred to as 'boilerplate clauses'. These clauses often favour the party who has drafted the document. This necessarily means that the standard terms drafted by, for example, a seller, will often conflict with those drafted by a buyer. Such conflicts can give rise to what has become known as a 'battle of the forms'. This typically occurs when one party, for example, a seller, makes an offer based on the terms included in its own standard form, whilst the buyer purports to accept the offer on a document incorporating its own differing standard terms.[405] The battle may not end there as the seller might send the goods accompanied by its standard conditions and there is nothing to stop the buyer acknowledging receipt on its standard form while at the same time keeping the goods.[406] Similarly, such a battle can occur where both parties send written confirmations of an earlier oral contract and which contain differing conditions. The various permutations that can arise when dealing with such standard forms are limitless. For example, in the case of a buyer purporting to accept the seller's offer but doing so subject to its own standard terms, would it matter if the purported acceptance was not in fact on the buyer's standard form such as where the purported unequivocal acceptance is contained in a covering letter with the buyer's

---

[403] See Farnsworth, *Farnsworth on Contracts* (3rd edn, Vol 1, Aspen Publishers, New York, 2004) § 3.22, p 341.

[404] See Restatement (2d) Contracts, comment *c* and illustration 8 and see §§ 153 and 154.

[405] In such a case where there is no acknowledgement of the other's terms much less an acceptance of them, it is arguably difficult to conclude that there is an agreement. However, on another view it may be possible to conclude there is an agreement to buy and sell but difficult to determine the terms of sale. Much may depend on the view one takes as to whether or not the existence of an agreement in contract law is dependent on it being certain and complete or whether these are contract law requirements that are additional to the existence of an agreement, see 11.02.

[406] McCamus, *The Law of Contracts* (Irwin Law, Toronto, 2005), 59. If a buyer has notice of the seller's terms and retains possession of the goods without acknowledging receipt of the goods on its own terms then usually the buyer will be taken to have accepted the seller's terms.

standard terms being sent in the same envelope as the covering letter but now less likely to be read by the seller. Would it matter if the seller's offer stated that it only intended to contract on its terms and that those terms are to prevail over the buyer's terms?[407] Would it constitute an acceptance of the buyer's terms if the seller sends the goods after receipt of the buyer's acceptance on the buyer's standard form but with a covering letter again reinforcing the sellers' standard terms.[408] Can the buyer accept the goods but reject the seller's terms? What if the goods and letter were sent separately and the goods were received by the buyer first?[409] In all these situations, the law must determine whether a concluded agreement has resulted between the parties, and, if so, on what terms. The two issues are intertwined.

The application of contract law principles to a battle of the forms[410]

4.123 There is no distinct set of rules governing standard form contracting in English law. The general principles of contract formation apply. It is possible then to make some general observations.

4.124 First, the rules of offer and acceptance may be applied where appropriate. This was done by a majority of the Court of Appeal in the most famous 'battle of forms' case in English law, *Butler Machine Tool Co Ltd v Ex-Cell-O Corporation (England) Ltd.*[411] The case concerned an offer to sell a machine at a stated price with delivery in ten months time. The offer was made on 23 May 1969 and was on the seller's standard terms. The buyer then ordered one of these machines using a purchase note incorporating the buyer's standard terms and which made some changes to the seller's quotation including changing the delivery date from 10 months to 10–11 months. The seller's sales note contained a price variation clause allowing for an increase in price if there was an increase in costs at the time of delivery. In addition, the seller's note contained a term stating that the seller's terms were to prevail over

---

[407] It is perhaps such clauses that are the basis of the expression, 'Battle of the Forms', see Hondius and Mahé, 'The Battle of the Forms: Towards a Uniform Solution' (1998) 12 JCL 268.

[408] Usually, on a traditional analysis, the act of sending the goods would constitute an acceptance of the buyer's terms under the last shot analysis, see eg United Nations Convention on Contracts for the International Sale of Goods (1980), Art 18(3). See further Moccia, 'The United Nations Convention on Contracts for the International Sale of Goods and the "Battle of the Forms"' (1990) 13 Fordham Int'l LJ 649, 657–9.

[409] See Waddams, *The Law of Contracts* (5th edn, Canada Law Book, Toronto, 2005), paras 72–74. Where one of the parties has carried out an act that would otherwise be in performance of the contract there is no doubt some pressure on the court to find that a contract exists. But there is no distinct set of contract law rules to deal with such a case.

[410] As to the relevance of the law of restitution in this area, see McKendrick, 'The Battle of the Forms and the Law of Restitution' (1988) 8 OJLS 197. See also Ball, 'Work Carried Out in Pursuance of Letters of Intent—Contract or Restitution' (1983) 99 LQR 572.

[411] [1979] 1 WLR 401. See also *British Road Services Ltd v Arthur V Crutchley & Co Ltd* [1968] 1 Lloyd's Rep 271, 282 (here there was a long established delivery practice whereby the plaintiff's driver handed his delivery note to the defendants and requested permission to bring his load into the defendants' warehouse for storage; if agreed, the defendants would stamp the delivery note with the words 'Received under [the defendant's] conditions'; the plaintiffs' driver would then bring his load into the warehouse; the Court of Appeal in agreeing with the trial judge on this point, held that the defendants' stamp constituted an offer (or counter-offer) which was accepted by the plaintiffs when they deposited the goods in the warehouse; therefore, the contract terms included the defendants' conditions; some emphasis was placed on the fact that this had occurred a number of times so that the driver could be considered the plaintiff's agent to accept the terms). See further *Sauter Automation Ltd v Goodman (Mechanical Services) Ltd* [1986] 34 BLR 81; *Cubitt Building and Interiors Ltd v Richardson Roofing (Industrial) Ltd* [2008] EWHC 1020 (TCC).

any terms of the buyer's order. The purchase note sent by the buyer made no provision for price variation. There was a tear-off acknowledgement slip at the foot of the buyer's purchase note which stated: 'We accept your order on the Terms and Conditions stated thereon.' The sellers signed and returned this slip with a covering letter which stated that delivery was to be 'in accordance with our revised quotation of May 23 for delivery in 10/11 months, ie, March/April …'.

The machine was not ready for delivery until September 1970. Because of this lateness, the **4.125** buyers had to rearrange their schedule and were not able to accept delivery until November 1970. The sellers sought to rely on the price variation clause to increase the price between May 1969 and April 1970 when the machine should have been available for delivery. The buyer refused to pay any increase in the price which led to the sellers commencing an action against the buyers.

The Court of Appeal held that a contract had been concluded on the buyer's terms which **4.126** did not include a price variation clause.[412] Both Lawton and Bridge LJJ adopted the traditional analysis and held that the buyer's order amounted to a counter-offer which had been expressly accepted by the sellers when they signed and returned the acknowledgement slip.[413] In their view[414] the terms of the covering letter were not sufficient to incorporate the seller's terms and conditions and merely referred to the price as quoted and identified the machinery to be sold.[415] This approach has become known as the last shot approach, meaning that the battle will be won by the party firing the last shot. For example, if a seller made an offer on its standard form which is accepted by the buyer on its standard form and the goods are then sent by the seller then the battle is won by the buyer as the seller's action of sending the goods is an acceptance of the buyer's terms. However, if the seller in this example sent the goods with a further set of its terms and, unlike the position in the *Butler Machine Tool Co Ltd v Ex-Cell-O Corporation (England) Ltd* case, it was clear the seller intended to contract only on those terms, then the acceptance of the goods by the buyer may be interpreted as an acceptance of the seller's term. There can be no doubt that this 'last shot' approach may be appropriate on the facts of a particular case. However, it is important that it not lead to the taking of a superficial view of what constitutes an offer or an acceptance. As noted earlier, it is often necessary to look at all communications to determine whether there is an offer and an acceptance.[416] Moreover, to say that the party firing the last shot wins focuses too much on formation and not enough on the incorporation of terms. As noted

---

[412] Whether or not there would have been a contract, and if there was, what were its terms, would have been different if the buyers had not drawn the seller's attention to its terms and without the sellers' acknowledgement of the buyers' terms, see eg, *Twywood Industries Ltd v St Anne-Nackawic Pulp & Paper Co Ltd* (1979) 100 DLR (3d) 374.

[413] For a sustained defence of the offer and acceptance approach to a battle of the forms, see Baird and Weisberg, 'Rules, Standards, and the Battle of the Forms: A Reassessment of §2-207' (1982) 68 Va L Rev 1217, 1251ff; Vaver, '"Battle of the forms", A Comment on Professor Shanker's Views' (1979–80) 4 Can Bus LJ 277.

[414] Lord Denning MR came to the same conclusion using a different route which is discussed later, see 4.134ff.

[415] See also *OTM Ltd v Hydranautics* [1981] 2 Lloyd's Rep 211.

[416] See 4.05.

above, the two here are intertwined and to say that the party firing the last shot wins could only apply to those terms of which it can be said there has been sufficient notice.

4.127   Second, if the scenario is one where an oral contract is entered into with a later exchange of written confirmations, then, assuming the oral terms are sufficiently certain, then the parties would have already reached agreement on the essential terms and any additional terms on the written confirmation would be a request to renegotiate the contract.[417] As such, these other terms are of no effect unless they are expressly or impliedly agreed to by words or conduct and supported by consideration.[418] The written terms only replace the oral terms if according to the intention of the parties they are taken to represent the contract rather than merely evidence the contract.

4.128   To this point of principle it is necessary to keep in mind the technique of incorporating terms by a course of dealing. The basis of this technique is that where parties enter into a series of contracts over a period of time on the same terms then they are taken to have assented to those terms in future transactions unless expressly varied.[419] There is no need for the parties to have actual knowledge of the terms.[420] The terms in question may be the standard terms of one of the parties. In a transaction where it was the sellers who consistently introduced their standard terms to the transaction without any objection by the buyer, Lord Pearce expressed the operation of the principle in these terms:[421]

> The question, therefore, is not what [the buyer itself] … thought or knew about the matter but what they should be taken as representing to [the seller] about it or leading [the seller] to believe. The only reasonable inference from the regular course of dealing over so long a period is that [the buyer was] … evincing an acceptance of, and a readiness to be bound by, the printed conditions of whose existence they were well aware although they had not troubled to read them. Thus the general conditions became part of the oral contract.

4.129   A typical situation where this issue arises is where a buyer and seller agree a standard set of terms, say the seller's terms, and use them over a period of time, then an occasion arises where the seller breaches the contract and on that particular occasion the parties did not expressly agree to the seller's terms. The seller may wish to rely on an exclusion clause in those terms and the buyer will deny that those terms were incorporated on that occasion.

4.130   This technique can also be used to resolve confirmation issues where a deal is made over the phone and after that call the seller sends a confirmation notice to the buyer which contains

---

[417] The position would be different if the oral agreement is made subject to written confirmation in the sense that the 'subject to' provision prevents the formation of a contract, see 9.16.

[418] *Jayaar Impex Ltd v Toaken Group Ltd* [1996] 2 Lloyd's Rep 437. On the relevance of estoppel here when the facts are such that a contract is not made out, see Hoggett, 'Changing a Bargain By Confirming it' (1970) 33 MLR 518. See also Uniform Commercial Code § 2-209.

[419] Whether or not there is a sufficient course of dealing is a question of fact. There has been some debate as to whether it is necessary to have a course of dealing given that after the first transaction the offeree will usually know the terms upon which the offeror does business, see Waddams, *The Law of Contracts* (5th edn, Canada Law Book, Toronto, 2005) para 70.

[420] *Henry Kendall & Sons v William Lillico & Sons* [1969] 2 AC 31.

[421] *Henry Kendall & Sons v William Lillico & Sons* [1969] 2 AC 31, 113.

the seller's standard terms and conditions. [422] Usually in such a case it would be held that the terms contained in the confirmation came too late as they were introduced after formation. The fact that the other party did not object to the terms would not help as silence is not acceptance. However, the result may be different if there is a course of dealing.[423] In *Henry Kendall & Sons v William Lillico & Sons*,[424] the terms on a written confirmation note were held to be incorporated into a contract by means of a course of dealing. An oral contract for the sale of feeding stuff for poultry was followed by the sellers issuing a confirmation note prior to the delivery of the goods. This confirmation note had additional terms on the reverse, including a clause which stated that 'the buyer takes responsibility for any latent defects'. One of the issues before the court was whether the terms of this sale note were incorporated into the contract. There was evidence that this procedure represented the normal course of dealing between the parties. They had made three or four such contracts a month over the preceding three-year period without objection to this term. The House of Lords held that the terms on the confirmation note were incorporated into the oral contract since, in the light of this course of dealing, the buyer would expect to receive such a confirmation note and contracted on the basis that the sale agreement would be on the terms and conditions set out in the confirmation note. In Australia it has been held that the confirmation must be provided prior to the discharge of obligations by performance. Thus, in the case of a contract for the carriage of goods, the document cannot be handed over at the same time as the goods are delivered.[425] With respect this seems to be at odds with the principle upon which incorporation by course of dealing is based, namely that by virtue of the course of dealing the parties are taken to have assented to the terms. This does not introduce terms after formation because that assent existed at the time of formation due to the course of dealing existing prior to that point in time. It would therefore follow

---

[422] In such a scenario, one commentator has raised the point that it may be relevant to ask whether the document in question was one that was usually signed by the parties during the course of dealing. If it is and it is not signed for the transaction in question this might suggest that it was not incorporated, see Waddams, *The Law of Contracts* (5th edn, Canada Law Book, Toronto, 2005) para 70. There is also a view that a term cannot be incorporated by a course of dealing if the facts are that the document usually handed over was not in fact handed over in the subject case because the course of dealing has not been followed, see Hoggett, 'Changing a Bargain by Confirming it' (1970) 33 MLR 518 at 520. See also *McCutcheon v David MacBrayne Ltd* [1964] 1 WLR 125, 129 per Lord Hodson, 132 per Lord Guest, 134 per Lord Devlin, 138 per Lord Pearce, cf, 128 per Lord Reid and cf *AR Kitson Trucking Ltd v Rivtow Straits Ltd* [1975] 4 WWR 1, (1975) 55 DLR (3d) 462. Query whether reliance on such a technicality defeats the purpose of this doctrine whereby incorporation is based on assent informed by consistency of dealing over a period of time, see Furmston (ed), *The Law of Contract* (3rd edn, LexisNexis, Butterworths, London, 2007), para 3.18; Peel, *Treitel, The Law of Contract* (12th edn, Thomson, Sweet & Maxwell, London, 2007) para 7-011.

[423] *Fairline Shipping Corporation v Adamson* [1975] QB 180, 189.

[424] [1969] 2 AC 31. See also *Transmotors Ltd v Robinson, Buckley and Co Ltd* [1970] 1 Lloyd's Rep 224; *Photolibrary Group Ltd v Burda Senator Verlag GmbH* [2008] 2 All ER (Comm) 881.

[425] *DJ Hill & Co Pty Ltd v Walter H Wright Pty Ltd* [1971] VR 749 (the court also held that the document containing the terms must be contractual in nature and a document handed over at discharge was not contractual, see also *Transmotors Ltd v Robinson, Buckley and Co Ltd* [1970] 1 Lloyd's Rep 224, 234; *McCutcheon v David MacBrayne Ltd* [1964] 1 WLR 125; query whether this requirement of a contractual document is at odds with the decision in *Henry Kendall* and maintains the now rejected knowledge requirement; the transactions that tend to give rise to arguments concerning the incorporation of terms by course of dealing are generally oral contracts, so it makes little sense to insist that the document that is produced and which is said to contain the terms must be contractual in nature).

that the written terms can be communicated after formation[426] and conceivably at the point of discharge.

4.131　It should also be noted that although terms may be produced after formation they may still form part of the contract if there is an assumption by the parties that they are to apply. This may occur when the parties operate in the same trade and the terms in question are standard in the trade. In *British Crane Hire Corporation Ltd v Ipswich Plant Hire Ltd*,[427] an oral contract was entered into over the phone for the urgent delivery of a crane. On delivery the defendants were sent a set of written conditions of hire which included a clause stating that the defendants were liable to indemnify the plaintiffs against all expense in connection with the use of the crane hired. The plaintiffs claimed that these conditions had been incorporated into the contract on the basis of the common understanding of the parties who were both operating in the same hire business. The court assumed that the defendants therefore knew that similar printed terms were in common use in the business.[428]

4.132　Third, as already discussed, the mirror image rule applies to acceptances.[429] All the terms of the offer must be unconditionally accepted if a contract is to result. If the buyer alters or adds terms as was done in the *Butler Machine Tool Co Ltd v Ex-Cell-O Corporation (England) Ltd* case, then the buyer would have made a counter-offer which in turn must be accepted by the seller to result in a contract.[430] Even an 'acknowledgement' sent in reply to an order (offer) may constitute a counter-offer if it is given with the requisite intention.[431]

4.133　Fourth, since the issue before the court is one of contract formation, the court can generally take into account evidence of the conduct of the parties after the point of alleged formation.[432] That conduct may not only evidence that the parties considered themselves in agreement but also on what terms.[433] This may resolve a battle of the forms.[434] Of course the parties' conduct may be inconsistent with there being an agreement or, more generally, their conduct may be explicable on grounds other than there being a concluded contract. For example, in *British Steel Corporation v Cleveland Bridge & Engineering Co Ltd (1981)*,[435] after a number of discussions, the defendant sent a letter of intent to the plaintiff proposing to enter into a contract with the plaintiff under which the plaintiff would construct certain steel nodes. The letter of intent stated that the terms were to be on the defendant's standard

---

[426] *J Spurling Ltd v Bradshaw* [1956] 1 WLR 461; *AR Kitson Trucking Ltd v Rivtow Straits Ltd* (1975) 55 DLR (3d) 462.

[427] [1975] QB 303. Cf *Western Processing & Cold Storage Ltd v Hamilton Construction Co Ltd* (1965) 51 DLR (2d) 245, 250 ('The agreement ... was oral. It would be grossly unjust to saddle [the other party] with a responsibility which it never entered into or agreed to accept, unless it can be said that through the course of well-established prior business conduct [that other] knew that it was to be bound by an acknowledgement of order form ... which would contain such a specially onerous term.').

[428] Lord Denning MR also suggested that because of the urgent request, the circumstances were such as to entitle the plaintiffs to conclude that the defendants were agreeing to their terms [1975] QB 303, 311.

[429] See 4.40.

[430] Eg *Jones v Daniel* [1894] 2 Ch 332.

[431] *Chichester Joinery v John Mowlem* (1987) 42 Build LR 100.

[432] See 4.05.

[433] *Re Production Sheet Metals Pty Ltd* [1971] QWN 16.

[434] Eg *Chichester Joinery Ltd v John Mowlem & Co plc* (1987) 42 Build LR 100. See also *Sauter Automation Ltd v Goodman (Mechanical Services) Ltd* [1986] 34 BLR 81.

[435] [1984] 1 All ER 504.

form and that the plaintiff should commence work immediately pending preparation of the formal agreement. As a consequence the plaintiff carried out substantially all the work. However, during that period, negotiations continued between the parties on various essential terms. The plaintiff did not agree to the defendant's standard terms and the defendant did not agree to the plaintiff's quotation. In these circumstances Robert Goff J held that no contract existed between the parties. The plaintiff's commencement of production was not held to constitute an acceptance of the defendant's standard terms since it was quite clearly carried out pending a formal contract.

A different approach?

There has long been a concern among commentators that the 'last shot' approach referred to above simply encourages the parties to try and fire the last shot, frustrates the expectation of commercial parties because, in many cases, they clearly want a contract albeit on their own terms,[436] or allows one party to unjustifiably take advantage of the other.[437] For example, in the case of a discrepancy between the terms of a seller's note—which purports to accept a buyer's order—and the terms of that buyer's purchase note, if the market price of the goods increases, the seller could refuse to supply the goods at the agreed price on the grounds that no contract existed. Similarly, if the market price fell, the buyer could use the same argument in an action for non-acceptance despite the fact that there had been agreement as to price. Thus, it has been suggested that a strict application of contract law principles will result in businessmen enjoying 'an unjustifiable locus poenitentiae' in being able to use the 'no contract' argument at any stage, even where the other party has already substantially performed in the belief that there was a contract.[438] One commentator concludes 'where the reason for non-performance relates to terms on which the parties had agreed, the mirror image rule ... may thus allow one party to take advantage of the other'.[439]   **4.134**

In *Butler Machine Tool Co Ltd v Ex-Cell-O Corporation (England) Ltd*,[440] the facts of which are discussed above,[441] Lord Denning MR suggested what he considered to be a different approach. In fact he envisaged two additional approaches. He thought the traditional approach did not reflect commercial reality and the increasing use of standard forms. He made it very clear that he thought the issue before him was one of determining the terms of the contract as it was quite clear that the parties had reached a concluded contract.[442] His approach to such a case was then directed to trying to work out the terms of the bargain. This approach has been termed the 'knock out' approach. Such an approach is likely to   **4.135**

---

[436] Cf Waddams, *The Law of Contracts* (5th edn, Canada Law Book, Toronto, 2005) paras 76–7.

[437] Von Mehren, 'The "Battle of the Forms": A Comparative View' (1990) 38 Am J Comp Law 265, 270.

[438] Rawlings, 'The Battle of Forms' (1979) 42 Mod LR 715, 717.

[439] Von Mehren, 'The "Battle of the Forms": A Comparative View' (1990) 38 Am J Comp Law 265, 270.

[440] [1979] 1 WLR 401.

[441] See 4.124ff.

[442] [1979] 1 WLR 401, 403, 404. See also *Transmotors Ltd v Robinson, Buckley and Co Ltd* [1970] 1 Lloyd's Rep 224, 234 per Mocatta J ('I do not know of any case that has previously arisen in which, there having been conflicting sets of printed terms relied upon by the two parties, the Court has reached the conclusion not that there was no contract between the parties on the grounds that they were not *ad idem*, but that the two sets of terms cancelled each other out and the matter must accordingly be considered as governed only by the provisions of the common law'.)

arrive at a result which upholds the agreement as it is less likely that an agreement today will fall for want to certainty or completeness.[443] He explained his approach and the basis for it in the following terms: [444]

> [t]he better way is to look at all the documents passing between the parties—and glean from them, or from the conduct of the parties, whether they have reached agreement on all material points—even though there may be differences between the forms and conditions printed on the back of them ... Applying this guide, it will be found that in most cases when there is a 'battle of forms' there is a contract as soon as the last of the forms is sent and received without objection being taken to it ... The difficulty is to decide which form, or which part of which form, is term or condition of the contract. In some cases the battle is won by the man who fires the last shot. He is the man who puts forward the latest terms and conditions: and, if they are not objected to by the other party, he may be taken to have agreed to them ... In some cases the battle is won by the man who gets the blow in first. If he offers to sell at a named price on the terms and conditions stated on the back: and the buyer orders the goods purporting to accept the offer—on an order form with his own different terms and conditions on the back—then if the difference is so material that it would affect the price, the buyer ought not to be allowed to take advantage of the difference unless he draws it specifically to the attention of the seller. There are yet other cases where the battle depends on the shots fired on both sides. There is a concluded contract but the forms vary. The terms and conditions of both parties are to be construed together. If they can be reconciled so as to give a harmonious result, all well and good. If differences are irreconcilable—so that they are mutually contradictory—then the conflicting terms may have to be scrapped and replaced by a reasonable implication.

4.136 It can be seen in this paragraph that in addition to the 'knock out' approach, Lord Denning MR also envisaged that in some cases the battle could be won by the party firing the first shot. He envisaged that could apply when a party purports to accept but attempts to incorporate its own terms and those terms are so materially different that they would impact on the price. Perhaps his reference to those terms being 'on the back' of the acceptance alludes to a requirement of notice whereby if one party leads the other party to reasonably believe he or she is accepting but nevertheless includes additional terms in the acceptance which are presented in such a way that the offeror would not ordinarily take notice of them given the style and tenor of the purported acceptance then a court may simply give effect to the 'acceptance' and ignore the additional terms.[445] This has become known as the 'first blow' approach.[446] This approach is related to the concept of incorporation by notice requiring reasonable steps to be taken to bring terms to the attention of the other party if they are to be incorporated and what is reasonable requires more steps to be taken if the document purports to be an acceptance on its face.

---

[443] Beale and Dugdale, 'Contracts between Businessmen: Planning and the Use of Contractual Remedies' (1975) 2 British Journal of Law & Society 45, 50–1.

[444] [1979] 1 WLR 401, 404–5.

[445] See further *Cubitt Building and Interiors Ltd v Richardson Roofing (Industrial) Ltd* [2008] EWHC 1020 (TCC).

[446] Hondius and Mahé, 'The Battle of the Forms: Towards a Uniform Solution' (1998) 12 JCL 268.

In the result Lord Denning MR considered that in this case the crucial document was the **4.137** acknowledgement slip sent by the seller to the buyer. Thus, he came to the same conclusion as the rest of the court and the buyer's terms prevailed.

Conclusions

There have been a number of criticisms of Lord Denning MR's approach. One alleged dif- **4.138** ficulty often attributed to his approach is that the parties cannot be sure of their position unless they go to court and receive a ruling. It has thus been criticized as 'essentially arbitrary and liable to produce much litigation' and inevitably would not stop attempts to fire the last shot.[447]

It is also important to note that Lord Denning MR applied his approach to formation in **4.139** *Gibson v Manchester City Council* which was not a battle of the forms case.[448] Later, in an appeal to the House of Lords, Lord Denning MR's approach was rejected.[449] Lord Diplock said:[450]

> The corporation's appeal against this judgment was dismissed by a majority of the Court of Appeal (Lord Denning MR and Ormrod LJ); Geoffrey Lane LJ dissented. Lord Denning MR rejected what I have described as the conventional approach of looking to see whether upon the true construction of the documents relied upon there can be discerned an offer and acceptance. One ought, he said ... to 'look at the correspondence as a whole and at the conduct of the parties and see therefrom whether the parties have come to an agreement on everything that was material' ...
>
> Geoffrey Lane LJ in a dissenting judgment, which for my part I find convincing, adopted the conventional approach. He found that upon the true construction of the documents relied upon as constituting the contract, there never was an offer by the corporation acceptance of which by Mr Gibson was capable in law of constituting a legally enforceable contract. It was but a step in the negotiations for a contract which, owing to the change in the political complexion of the council, never reached fruition.
>
> My Lords, there may be certain types of contract, though I think they are exceptional, which do not fit easily into the normal analysis of a contract as being constituted by offer and acceptance; but a contract alleged to have been made by an exchange of correspondence between the parties in which the successive communications other than the first are in reply to one another, is not one of these. I can see no reason in the instant case for departing from the conventional approach of looking at the handful of documents relied upon as constituting the contract sued upon and seeing whether upon their true construction there is to be found in them a contractual offer ... and an acceptance of that offer ...

The criticism of Lord Denning MR's judgment by Lord Diplock overlaps with another **4.140** criticism that has been made and which directly calls into question the 'knock out' approach, namely that Lord Denning MR improperly separated the question of contract formation from the identification of terms seeing the issue as solely about the latter.[451] It is true that

---

[447] Rawlings, 'The Battle of Forms' (1979) 42 Mod LR 715 at 718–19.
[448] [1978] 1 WLR 520.
[449] [1979] 1 WLR 294.
[450] [1979] 1 WLR 294, 296–7.
[451] Jacobs, 'The Battle of the Forms: Standard Terms Contracts in Comparative Perspective' (1985) 34 ICLQ 297, 303. At the same time Lord Denning MR has been accused of confusing 'the distinct concepts

the offer and acceptance approach is intimately tied to the identification of terms as an offer must contain all the express and implied terms of the contract and those terms must be accepted by the offeree. You cannot conclude there is an agreement if you cannot determine the terms. The error in Lord Denning MR's approach as identified by Lord Diplock is his willingness to consider all the communications between the parties and try to glean from them whether there was an agreement and what were the terms of any agreement. To that extent the criticism is justified at least on a traditional analysis of agreement. There must be a process whereby each communication is considered on its own merits as that is how the transaction progressed. But it is also true that each communication must be read in context which requires the court to consider what went before it in order to discover the intention behind each communication and there is therefore a cumulative building up of correspondence to consider at each stage.[452] However, the pooling of information under Lord Denning MR's approach suggests that a communication might be construed in light of what went after it. But that is not necessarily heresy as a contract can be formed through conduct outside of an offer and acceptance analysis.[453] The importance of the conduct of the parties to a communication has already been noted.[454] Such conduct may evidence how a communication was interpreted by the parties. For example, if one party seeks an acknowledgement from the other side which is not forthcoming and never chased up it should be difficult to then argue that the term forms part of the contract.[455] Moreover, in practice, the process of considering the cumulative correspondence between the parties often results in a search for terms. Perhaps this was the point that Lord Denning MR was trying to get across and if that is the case then some of the criticism of this aspect of his judgment is misplaced as the search for terms is itself often a search for agreement. Therefore, he was not improperly separating the two issues. By first stating that the parties had reached an agreement he may have no more than suggested there was an intention to contract. It must be said that for many contract terms the 'knock out' approach reflects commercial reality. For example, if the parties' standard terms are not in conflict then both may be able to stand together.[456] Moreover, often only one set of terms will contain the technical specifications of the subject matter of the contract and it would be expected that these would form part of the contract.

4.141 However, there is also legitimacy in an approach that determines agreement first and terms second. Approaches to the battle of the forms problem elsewhere, which are discussed

---

of the very existence of the contract on the one hand and the effect of a discrepancy between offer and acceptance on the other', see Vergne, 'The "Battle of the Forms" under the 1980 United Nations Convention on Contracts for the International Sale of Goods' (1985) 33 Am J Comp Law 233, 243.

[452] See *Hussey v Horne-Payne* [1879] 4 App Cas 311; *Howard Smith & Co Ltd v Varawa* (1907) 5 CLR 68; *Perry v Suffields* [1916] 2 Ch 187; *Boulder Consolidated Ltd v Tangaere* [1980] 1 NZLR 560.

[453] See 4.05.

[454] See 4.05

[455] See *Tywood Industries Ltd v St Anne-Nackawic Pulp & paper Co Ltd* (1979) 100 DLR (3d) 374. It has been suggested that the judgment in this case used an approach similar to that of Lord Denning MR in the *Butler Machine Tool Co* case. However, generally that approach has not been adopted in Canada, see McCamus, *The Law of Contracts* (Irwin Law, Toronto, 2005), 62.

[456] See *Ralph McKay Ltd v International Harvester Australia Ltd* [1999] 3 VR 675. Cf *Albrecht Chem Co v Anderson Trading Corp* 298 NY 437, 84 NE 2d 625 (1949).

below, emphasize the legitimacy of establishing an agreement by reference to the overall conduct of the parties with a consequent settling of terms. Indeed, it is a legitimate tool of investigation to look at the conduct of the parties to see if an agreement has been reached if it is not possible to make a clear finding from the communications that flowed between the parties. The clearest example is often the commencement of performance by one of the parties when that is not accompanied by some other contradictory act such as where a seller sends the goods, but includes a covering letter that suggests the seller is not agreeing to the buyer's terms.[457] A very clear example of where it can be said that an agreement has been reached but where there may be argument as to the terms of the contract is where a seller makes an offer which is expressed to incorporate its standard terms but those terms are not provided but will be provided upon request. In such a case if the buyer communicates an acceptance there will be a contract and it will be on the seller's standard terms but there may still be argument over whether or not this method of incorporation constituted the taking of reasonable steps to bring to the attention of the buyer some terms that might be particularly onerous.[458]

Usually where the parties have not intended to assume legal obligations, this will be clear from the facts. The facts in *British Steel Corporation v Cleveland Bridge & Engineering Co Ltd* discussed above are an example of this. More often the parties will have expected their arrangements to give rise to some legal obligations,[459] but are debating the actual terms of that arrangement.[460] Perhaps in many cases they might see the issue as a potential problem in the future but based on their experience believe it is one that is unlikely to arise or one **4.142**

---

[457] See further Unidroit Principles of International Commercial Contracts 2004, Arts 2.1.1 and 2.1.6(1) and see Vogenauere and Kleinheisterkamp (eds), *Commentary on the Unidroit Principles of International Commercial Contracts* (PICC) (OUP, Oxford, 2009), 279 paras 4, 5.

[458] Eg *Maxitherm Boilers Pty Ltd v Pacific Dunlop Ltd* [1998] 4 VR 559. Cf *Cubitt Building and Interiors Ltd v Richardson Roofing (Industrial) Ltd* [2008] EWHC 1020 (TCC) (acceptance attempting to incorporate offeree's standard terms but did not attach them). Of course any terms in those standard terms would not be incorporated if they are inconsistent with any terms that may have been actually produced to the purchaser in a short form document at the point of sale, *Commonwealth Homes and Investment Co Ltd v Smith* (1937) 59 CLR 443, 459. Moreover, if the circumstances of the transaction are such that the term incorporating the detailed terms by reference is not itself part of the contract then those detailed terms will not be incorporated. This may occur where, for example, the term incorporating the detailed terms by reference is in a written document which is usually signed by a buyer and on the particular occasion the parties entered into an oral contract which did not include that incorporating provision, see *McCutcheon v David MacBrayne Ltd* [1964] 1 WLR 125.

[459] Cf Beale and Dugdale, 'Contracts between Businessmen: Planning and the Use of Contractual Remedies' (1975) 2 British Journal of Law & Society 45, 50.

[460] See Beale and Dugdale, 'Contracts between Businessmen: Planning and the Use of Contractual Remedies' (1975) 2 British Journal of Law & Society 45, 50. This might be the case in many relatively simple sale contracts where the parties put forward their own standard terms such as occurred in *Butler Machine Tool Co Ltd v Ex-Cell-O Corporation (England) Ltd* [1979] 1 WLR 401 and see Beale and Dugdale, 'Contracts between Businessmen: Planning and the Use of Contractual Remedies' (1975) 2 British Journal of Law & Society 45, 49.

that is otherwise manageable.[461] They therefore take a calculated risk.[462] It is also for this reason that many try to have procedures that ensure that they fire the last shot in the flow of standard terms between the parties, that is, to sure up the terms and not the existence of the contract.[463]

4.143   Finally, much of this criticism of Lord Denning MR's approach is informed by the offer and acceptance method of formation. That methodology is just a tool that aids analysis and which must not be used if it clearly contradicts the transaction process in question. Once jettisoned then on any given facts it might be correct to determine that an agreement exists and then go onto to determine its terms. In an important passage, McHugh JA in *Integrated Computer Services Pty Ltd Digital Equipment Corp (Aust) Pty Ltd*[464] said of the dynamic commercial relationship:[465]

> It is often difficult to fit a commercial arrangement into the common lawyers' analysis of a contractual arrangement. Commercial discussions are often too unrefined to fit easily into the slots of 'offer', 'acceptance', 'consideration' and 'intention to create a legal relationship' which are the benchmarks of the contract of classical theory. In classical theory, the typical contract is a bilateral one and consists of an exchange of promises by means of an offer and its acceptance together with an intention to create a binding legal relationship ...
>
> Moreover, in an ongoing relationship, it is not always easy to point to the precise moment when the legal criteria of a contract have been fulfilled. Agreements concerning terms and conditions which might be too uncertain or too illusory to enforce at a particular time in the relationship may by reason of the parties' subsequent conduct become sufficiently specific to give rise to legal rights and duties. In a dynamic commercial relationship new terms will be added or will supersede older terms. It is necessary therefore to look at the whole relationship and not only at what was said and done when the relationship was first formed.

4.144   It follows from what has been said that a battle of the forms may be resolved in a number of different ways involving all the general contract law techniques referred to above together with the three approaches derived from the *Butler Machine Tool Co* case. Much depends on the circumstances and what approach best reflects the presumed intention of the parties on any given set of facts. For example *Ralph McKay Ltd v International Harvester Australia Ltd*,[466] may be seen as involving aspects of the 'knock out' approach together with incorporation by course of dealing. Here an agricultural machinery components supplier had a long course of dealing with a buyer who either used the goods itself or on-sold them. The practice of the parties was that the buyer would give the seller a purchase order which in general terms set out the buyer's requirements over a certain period. It set down some

---

[461] As Beale and Dugdale point out, 'provided the two sets of conditions contained terms commonly found in the trade a sufficient basis would exist to enable any dispute to be settled without difficulty', Beale and Dugdale, 'Contracts between Businessmen: Planning and the Use of Contractual Remedies' (1975) 2 British Journal of Law & Society 45, 50.

[462] See Murray, 'A Corporate Counsel's Perspective of The "Battle of the Forms" (1980) 4 Canadian Business Law Journal 290, 293, 295.

[463] See Murray, 'A Corporate Counsel's Perspective of The "Battle of the Forms" (1980) 4 Canadian Business Law Journal 290, 293.

[464] (1988) 5 BPR 11,110.

[465] (1988) 5 BPR 11, 110, 11,117–18.

[466] [1999] 3 VR 675.

general conditions for the goods and incorporated certain standard terms and conditions. It included a modification clause that attempted to prevent any modification to these terms. A copy of this was signed by the seller and sent back. During the currency of that purchase order the purchaser would periodically call for the shipping of certain goods. A document would detail the exact goods required. This document included a price which was based on the seller's pricing schedule which the seller had provided to the purchaser and which contained the seller's terms and conditions. The seller would then deliver the goods and produce a delivery docket containing its standard terms and conditions; these dockets did not state a price. A few days later the seller would follow this up with an invoice which contained a price and its standard terms and conditions. The dispute in question concerned whether a Romalpa clause in the seller's terms and conditions was part of the contract between the parties. It was held that it was. In this case Tadgell J thought that the terms and conditions of each party were not conflicting as they were in the *Butler Machine Tool Co* case and could be read together. To the extent there was any conflict then the course of dealing between the parties resulted in the buyer having accepted or not dissented from the seller's terms and conditions.

The American approach

The relevant section of the Uniform Commercial Code is §2-207 which provides:[467]   **4.145**

§ 2-207. Terms of Contract; Effect of Confirmation.

Subject to Section 2-202, if (i) conduct by both parties recognizes the existence of a contract although their records do not otherwise establish a contract, (ii) a contract is formed by an offer and acceptance, or (iii) a contract formed in any manner is confirmed by a record that contains terms additional to or different from those in the contract being confirmed, the terms of the contract are:

    (a) terms that appear in the records of both parties;

    (b) terms, whether in a record or not, to which both parties agree; and

    (c) terms supplied or incorporated under any provision of this Act.

This section does not deal with contract formation. The formation provisions of the Code   **4.146** are contained in sections 2-204 and 2-206.[468] The concern of 2-207 is with identifying the

---

[467] This is a recently amended provision. The provision as originally drafted became infamous for being one of the most difficult provisions of the Code. It was strongly criticized by judges and academics alike. Given the amendment there is now little point in discussing the original provision in any detail in this book. For detailed comments and critique of the original provision, see Furmston, Norisada and Poole, *Contract Formation and Letters of Intent* (John Wiley & Sons, Chichester, 1977) paras 4.5–4.8; Waddams, *The Law of Contracts* (5th edn, Canada Law Book, Toronto, 2005) paras 79–88; Farnsworth, *Farnsworth on Contracts* (3rd edn, Vol 1, Aspen Publishers, New York, 2004) § 3.21, pp 319ff. See further, Davenport, 'How to Handle Sales of Goods: The Problem of Conflicting Purchase Orders and Acceptances and New Concepts in Contract Law' (1963) 19 Bus Law 75; Kove, '"The Battle of the Forms": A Proposal to Revise Section 2-207' (1970) 13 UCCLJ 7; Duesenberg, 'Contract Creation: The Continuing Struggle with Additional and Different Terms Under Uniform Commercial Code Section 2-207 (1979) 34 Bus Law 1477; Baird and Weisberg, 'Rules, Standards, and the Battle of the Forms: A Reassessment of §2-207' (1982) 68 Va L Rev 1217; Jacobs, 'The Battle of the Forms: Standard Terms Contracts in Comparative Perspective' (1985) 34 ICLQ 297; Von Mehren, 'The "Battle of the Forms": A Comparative View' (1990) 38 Am J Comp Law 265, 279ff.

[468] As noted above 2-206 rejects the mirror image rule in the United States, see 4.47.

terms of the contract.[469] It is also not solely concerned with resolving any battle of the forms but applies to all sale of goods contracts. As regards the battle of the forms, if the parties conduct themselves so as to recognize an agreement, then if they have exchanged conflicting or inconsistent records, subsection (a) results in the terms of the contract being those terms that appear in the records of both parties. There is no automatic recognition of a term in an acceptance that does not materially alter the terms of the offer. But there is still allowance for there to be agreement on a term or terms that might appear in the records of only one of the parties.[470]

4.147   A few other points about this section are worth noting here. First, the section does not give a preference to any document produced before or during performance. Thus, in a battle of the forms, no preference is given to either the first or last shot. Second, the provision does not give any operation to terms that insist on one party's terms governing the agreement. It follows that the normal common law position will prevail. If one party insists on such a term as a condition of formation and the other party does not agree to it, there will be no contract under the formation provisions.[471]

CISG and Unidroit

4.148   Article 19 of the United Nations Convention on Contracts for the International Sale of Goods, (1980) is not solely aimed at determining a battle of the forms but will in some cases have an impact on such a dispute.[472] Although Article 19(1) states the general mirror-image rule, this is then qualified by Article 19(2) and (3). These provisions provide:[473]

(1) A reply to an offer which purports to be an acceptance but contains additions, limitations or other modifications is a rejection of the offer and constitutes a counter-offer.

(2) However, a reply to an offer which purports to be an acceptance but contains additional or different terms which do not materially alter the terms of the offer constitutes an acceptance, unless the offeror, without undue delay, objects orally to the discrepancy or dispatches a notice to that effect. If he does not so object, the terms of the

---

[469] Official Comment 2.

[470] Official Comment 3. This Comment also goes on to state: 'In a rare case the terms in the records of both parties might not become part of the contract. This could be the case, for example, when the parties contemplated an agreement to a single negotiated record, and each party submitted to the other party similar proposals and then commenced performance, but the parties never reached a negotiated agreement because of the differences over crucial terms. There is a variety of verbal and nonverbal behaviour that may [sic] suggest agreement to another's record. This section leaves the interpretation of that behaviour to the discretion of the courts.' Farnsworth states, 'by asking a court to determine under (b) whether a party "agrees" to the other party's terms, the revised section gives the courts discretion in including or excluding terms in a manner different from the more mechanical rules or the original section. A court might, for example, find that parties agreed to arbitration even though the arbitration provisions in their forms differed in minor respects', Farnsworth, *Farnsworth on Contracts* (3rd edn, Vol 1, Aspen Publishers, New York, 2004) § 3.21, p 333.

[471] Farnsworth, *Farnsworth on Contracts* (3rd edn, Vol 1, Aspen Publishers, New York, 2004) § 3.21a, p 335, this paragraph also provides a discussion of 'winning the battle of the forms' under the UCC provisions.

[472] See generally Wildner, 'Art 19 CISG: The German Approach to the Battle of the Forms in International Contract Law: The Decision of the Federal Supreme Court of Germany of 9 January 2002' (2008) 20 Pace Int'l L rev 1. As to the extent to which the Convention can and should be used to resolve a battle of the forms both as to questions of formation and terms, see Moccia, 'The United Nations Convention on Contracts for the International Sale of Goods and the "Battle of the Forms"' (1990) 13 Fordham Int'l LJ 649, 666–78.

[473] The article does not deal with confirmations, see Farnsworth in Bianca and Bonell, *Commentary on the International Sales Law* (Giuffrè, Milan, 1987), 177.

contract are the terms of the offer with the modifications contained in the acceptance.

(3) Additional or different terms relating, among other things, to the price, payment, quality and quantity of the goods, place and time of delivery, extent of one party's liability to the other or the settlement of disputes are considered to alter the terms of the offer materially.

A detailed discussion of this provision is beyond this text but a few points may be noted.[474]   **4.149**
It will be clear that subsection (1) is concerned with the formation of the contract and subsection (2) with both formation and the terms of the contract. As noted above, subsection (1) adopts the traditional mirror-image rule. It classifies as counter-offers only those replies that purport to be acceptances. A mere enquiry would not fall within that notion. Where there is a purported acceptance that does not materially alter the terms of the offer then that will constitute an acceptance under subsection (2) and any dispute about terms will be resolved under subsection (2).[475] This is a modified version of the last shot rule.[476] The party firing the last shot will have its terms govern the relationship so long as they do not materially alter the terms of the offer (thus being a counter-offer under subsection (1)) and so long as the offeror did not object to these terms without undue delay. Usually, if the contract has been performed then no such objection would have been lodged. Subsection (3) provides a non-exhaustive list of matters that constitute a material alteration. This provision is perhaps the most problematic aspect of the article. Since it is not exhaustive, questions arise as to what else might fall within the concept of a 'material alteration'. In addition, within the subsection itself concepts are used that could give rise to argument, for example, what clauses could be said to deal with the 'extent of one party's liability' and what clauses could be said to deal with the 'settlement of disputes'.[477]

The Unidroit Principles of International Commercial Contracts (2004) have, in Article   **4.150**
2.1.11, a provision that is in the same terms as Article 19(1) and (2) of the United Nations Convention on Contracts for the International Sale of Goods (1980). However, there is no description of what might constitute a 'material' alteration.[478] The Unidroit Principles also

---

[474] For a discussion of these provisions, see Honnold, *Uniform Law for International Sales* (3rd edn, Kluwer Law International, The Netherlands, 1999), paras 165–70.4. See also Farnsworth in Bianca and Bonell, *Commentary on the International Sales Law* (Giuffrè, Milan, 1987), 177–84; Vergne, 'The "Battle of the Forms" under the 1980 United Nations Convention on Contracts for the International Sale of Goods' (1985) 33 Am J Comp Law 233; Moccia, 'The United Nations Convention on Contracts for the International Sale of Goods and the "Battle of the Forms"' (1990) 13 Fordham Int'l LJ 649; Nicholas, 'The Vienna Convention on International Sales Law' (1989) 105 LQR 201, 217–18.

[475] Farnsworth in Bianca and Bonell, *Commentary on the International Sales Law* (Giuffrè, Milan, 1987), 179.

[476] Farnsworth in Bianca and Bonell, *Commentary on the International Sales Law* (Giuffrè, Milan, 1987), 179–80.

[477] Farnsworth in Bianca & Bonell, *Commentary on the International Sales Law* (Giuffrè, Milan, 1987), 182–4.

[478] For discussion, see Vogenauere and Kleinheisterkamp (eds), *Commentary on the Unidroit Principles of International Commercial Contracts* (PICC) (OUP, Oxford, 2009), 281–4, paras 10–17. Article 2:208 (Modified Acceptance) of the Principles of European Contract Law distinguishes more clearly between terms which materially alter and those which do not. If the terms materially alter the terms of the offer the reply is a 'rejection and a new offer'; Art 2:208(1). Non-material alterations will not prevent the reply operating as an acceptance and the 'additional or different terms then become part of the contract'; Art 2:208(2). Article 2:208(3) then goes on to provide: 'However, such a reply will be treated as a rejection of the offer if: (a) the offer expressly limits acceptance to the terms of the offer; or (b) the offeror objects to the additional or

attempt to deal with confirmations in Article 2.1.12. This provision seeks to deal with confirmations that are sent after a contract has been formed which contain all the essential terms.[479] It therefore differs from Article 2.1.11 which deals with formation and where terms modifying an offer are contained in an acceptance. However, because in practice it is often difficult to distinguish these situations the terms of Article 2.1.12 are the same as those contained in Article 2.1.11(1). That is, the solution to any issue involving confirmations is the same as acceptances which contain additional or different terms to the offer.[480]

4.151 More importantly, in addition to these provisions Unidroit has specific provisions to deal with parties transacting on standard terms. In such cases the general rules on formation apply subject to the rules contained in Articles 2.1.20–2.1.22.[481] 'Standard terms' are defined as 'provisions which are prepared in advance for general and repeated use by one party and which are actually used without negotiation with the other party'.[482] The relevant provision dealing with a battle of the forms is Article 2.1.22 which provides:[483]

> Where both parties use standard terms and reach agreement except on those terms, a contract is concluded on the basis of the agreed terms and any standard terms which are common in substance unless one party clearly indicates in advance, or later and without undue delay informs the other party, that it does not intend to be bound by such a contract.

4.152 Usually in the situation envisaged by the Article, namely where both parties are putting forward their standard terms then no contract would eventuate as there is no offer and acceptance.[484] The exception would be if they commenced performance and then the terms would often be those of the party who fired the last shot. However, this article adopts the 'knock out' approach calling for there first to be a conclusion that the parties have reached an agreement and then setting in place a rule to settle the terms of the agreement. If the parties have reached an agreement then notwithstanding the rules of offer and acceptance, a contract will come into effect and the terms of the contract will be those agreed and any

---

different terms without delay; or (c) the offeree makes its acceptance conditional upon the offeror's assent to the additional or different terms, and the assent does not reach the offeree within a reasonable time'. Article 1:301(5) contains a definition of a material matter as 'one which a reasonable person in the same situation as one party ought to have known would influence the other party in its decision as to whether to contract on the terms or to contract at all'. See also Draft Common Frame of Reference II–4:208.

[479] There is an equivalent provision in the Principles of European Contract Law Art 2:210. However this article applies only to contracts concluded by 'professionals' where one of these professionals subsequently (and without delay) sends what purports to be a written confirmation.

[480] See Article 2.1.12 Comment 1.

[481] Article 2.1.19(1). Article 2.1.20 deals with 'surprising terms' and relevantly provides in subsection (1): 'No term contain in standard terms which is of such a character that the other party could not reasonably have expected it, is effective unless it has been expressly accepted by that party'. Article 2.1.21 deals with conflicts between standard terms and non-standard terms resolving that conflict in favour of the non-standard term. See also Principles of European Contract Law Arts 2:104, 5:104.

[482] Article 2.1.19(2).

[483] See also Principles of European Contract Law Art 2:209. For commentary see Hondius and Mahé, 'The Battle of the Forms: Towards a Uniform Solution' (1998) 12 JCL 268.

[484] Article 2.1.22, Comment 2. See also Comment 3 suggesting that the '"last shot" doctrine may be appropriate if the parties clearly indicate that the adoption of their standard terms is an essential condition for the conclusion of the contract'.

standard terms that are common in substance. The reason for this approach is explained as follows:[485]

> Where … the parties, as is very often the case in practice, refer to their standard terms more or less automatically, for example by exchanging printed order and acknowledgment of order forms with the respective terms on the reverse side, they will normally not even be aware of the conflict between their respective standard terms. There is in such cases no reason to allow the parties subsequently to question the very existence of the contract or, if performance has commenced, to insist on the application of the terms last sent or referred to.

---

[485] Article 2.1.22, Comment 3.

5

AUCTIONS AND TENDERS

This Chapter considers the process of making contracts by auction and by tender. Although these processes are different they have important features in common both in fact and in law. Reasoning from one transaction has been carried over to the other. **5.01**

Both auctions and tenders are an attempt to achieve the best price by competition without entering into negotiations. Auctions are typically used to sell valuable chattels such as paintings or houses or other buildings. The assumption is that if the sale by auction is effectively advertised, a number of potential buyers will attend and that the process of bidding is likely to drive the price up to an acceptable level. The most obvious danger is that potential bidders may agree in advance not to bid against each other. Such collusive 'rings' are believed to be quite common in some areas and in some jurisdictions are criminal but the law of contract ignores them.[1] **5.02**

Competitive tendering can also be used for selling but is more commonly used for the procurement of services, particularly in the construction industry. Here the assumption is that those who desire the work will bid the lowest price they can afford, thus ensuring a low price for the person procuring the service. There is a major difference between auctions and tenders. Attending the auction imposes very little cost except the cost of going to the auction and the opportunity cost of one's time. Tendering however is itself an expensive business. Take the case of a contractor invited to tender for the building of a major sports stadium. He will need to spend substantial sums on investigation of the ground conditions, deciding what subcontractors he needs and discovering their prices. This is likely itself to cost a substantial sum of money. For instance in *Harmon CFEM Facades (UK) Ltd v House of Commons Corporate Officer*,[2] the claimant tendered for the fenestration work on the new **5.03**

---

[1] See *Harrop v Thompson* [1975] 1 WLR 545 where Templeman J held that an agreement between potential bidders that one of them should not bid would not invalidate the contract between the other and the auctioneer

[2] (1998) 67 ConLR 1; (2000) 72 ConLR 21.

House of Commons Building. Its tender was slightly over £40 million and the tendering costs were estimated to be more than £200,000.

5.04 It is clear that in normal circumstances an unsuccessful tenderer will bear the costs of tendering. This is likely to mean that tenderers will be reluctant to bear these costs unless there is a reasonable chance of success. Practice reflects this. Work of this kind is not commonly let on open tenders where anyone can bid. It is much more common to invite tenders from a select list. A reasonably confident tenderer may think that if he is usually competing against three other tenderers he will win a quarter of his bids and price accordingly.

5.05 Another consequence of this system is that someone invited to tender will be reluctant to refuse even though he does not want the job, because he will not want to lose his place on the list of invited tenderers. In such cases it is said to be common to put in a bid which is clearly too high. However such high bids may also be the result of collusion, which will be anti-competitive. The Office of Fair Trading in England has recently imposed very substantial fines on firms in the construction industry which were agreeing to put in high bids so that someone else would be awarded the contract.

A. Auctions

5.06 Auctioneers usually are not the owners of what is being sold but act as agents of the seller. In some but not all cases the identity of the seller will be revealed. There are often printed conditions of auction but these do not usually appear to change significantly the basic law.

5.07 The analysis of auction sales was one of the first acts of the analysis by way of offer and acceptance. It was held in *Payne v Cave*[3] that in modern terminology the advertisement of the auction was an invitation to treat; the successive bids were offers, each bid replacing the previous bid and that the contract came into existence when the auctioneer signified acceptance for instance by dropping his hammer. In *Payne v Cave* itself the defendant was clearly the highest bidder but he had withdrawn his offer before the auctioneer had accepted it. The Court of Kings Bench were clear that there was no contract.

5.08 This analysis was given statutory form in 1893 by section 57 of the Sale of Goods Act which provided:

  (2) A sale by auction is complete when the auctioneer announces its completion by the fall of the hammer, or in other customary manner; and until the announcement is made any bidder may retract his bid.
  (3) A sale by auction may be notified to be subject to a reserve or upset price, and a right to bid may also be reserved expressly by or on behalf of the seller.
  (4) Where a sale by auction is not notified in the conditions of sale to be subject to a right to bid by or on behalf of the seller, it is not lawful for the seller to bid himself or to employ any person to bid at the sale, or for the auctioneer knowingly to take any bid from the seller or any such person.
  (5) A sale contravening subsection (4) may be treated as fraudulent by the buyer.

---

[3] (1789) 3 TR 148.

Provisions in this form are widespread and in the UK now form section 57 of the 1979 Act.

It was deduced from this analysis that the auctioneer did not by advertising the auction **5.09** make any binding promise actually to hold the auction. This was the point of the decision in *Harris v Nickerson*.[4] In this case the defendant auctioneer had advertised a three-day auction in Bury St Edmunds. The plaintiff had attended on the third day intending to bid for office furniture which was advertised for sale on that day. The furniture was withdrawn and the plaintiff claimed the wasted expenditure of going to Bury St Edmunds. The Court of Queen's Bench rejected the claim. Blackburn J thought the claim 'startling' and 'excessively inconvenient if carried out'. Clearly if the plaintiff could recover, all or nearly all those who attended the third day could do likewise. The plaintiff's claim was in effect an early attempt at a second contract theory which has become very important in later cases. The Court did not say so but if the advertisement had been treated as a promise there would have been problems finding consideration for it.

B. Reserve Prices

The auction particulars may state that the auction is 'without reserve' or 'with reserve' or **5.10** may say nothing. The English practice seems to be to assume that if nothing is said there is a reserve[5] but an explicit statement may make a difference. In *McManus v Fortescue*[6] the auction was explicitly said to be with reserve but the auctioneer, in a fit of absence of mind, knocked the article down to a bidder who had bid less than the reserve price. The Court of Appeal held that the bidder had no remedy. As far as the seller was concerned, he had clearly and expressly limited the auctioneer's authority. The bidder also argued that the auctioneer had warranted his authority but this view also was rejected.

Fletcher Moulton LJ said

> The public is informed by the fact that the sale is subject to a reserve that the auctioneer has agreed to sell for the amount which the highest bidder is prepared to give only in case that amount is equal to or higher than the reserve. There was therefore no false representation of authority.

Where the auction is said to be without reserve it is clear that the seller cannot bid or **5.11** employ someone to do so but can the auctioneer refuse to drop the hammer on the highest bid? Clearly the traditional offer and acceptance analysis means that there is not a contract of sale until he does so but the statement that the auction is without reserve looks like a promise to sell to the highest bidder. In 2009 this looks like a second and separate contract, particularly because of developments in the law relating to tenders which are discussed later in this Chapter but this was not so clear in the nineteenth century.

For a long time the leading case was the decision of the Court of Exchequer Chamber in **5.12** *Warlow v Harrison*.[7]

---

[4] (1873) LR8 QB 286.
[5] Other jurisdictions may have different presumptions.
[6] [1907] 2 KB 1.
[7] (1859) 1 EL&EL 309. See also *Johnston v Boyes* [1899] 2 Ch 73; *Tully v Irish Land Commission* (1961) 97 ILT 174.

Here the facts were that the defendant auctioneer had advertised a sale by auction of horses. One of the items was a horse called Janet Pride which was for sale without reserve. The plaintiff bid 60 guineas and another person immediately bid 61 guineas. This bidder was apparently the owner, a Mr Henderson, and the auctioneer knocked the horse down to him, the evidence being that he knew he was the owner.

The Court of Queen's Bench held that as the case was pleaded the defendant should win. The Court of Exchequer Chamber agreed but thought that the plaintiff should have leave to amend and that his claim as amended would win.

Martin B speaking for himself, Byles J and Watson B said:

> It seems to us that the highest bona fide bidder at an auction may sue the auctioneer as upon a contract that the sale shall be without reserve. We think the auctioneer who puts the property up for sale upon such a condition pledges himself that the sale shall be without reserve; or, in other words, contracts that it shall be so; and that this contract is made with the highest bona fide bidder; and, in case of a breach of it that he has a right of action against the auctioneer.

Willes J said:

> My brother Bramwell and myself do not dissent from the judgment which has been pronounced. But we prefer to rest our decision, as to the amendment, upon the ground that the defendant undertook to have, and yet there was evidence that he had not authority to sell without reserve. The result is the same.

5.13 The decision is perhaps technically *obiter* since all that the Court was strictly doing was to approve an amendment but the defendant could hardly have been told more clearly not to come back. The Court, which included some great common lawyers, clearly thought that on such facts the auctioneer should be liable. Nevertheless succeeding generations have continue to agonize over the decision.

5.14 The case was the subject of a famous exchange of views between the future Lord Justice Slade and Professor LCB Gower in the *Law Quarterly Review*.[8] The arguments can perhaps not unfairly be characterized as technical. No one suggests that someone who gets to an auction and bids in the belief that it is without reserve will not have a legitimate sense of grievance if they discover that this promise is not to be kept. The question is how to fit this perception into the rest of the law. This is significantly easier if we treat the promise about without reserve as a separate, second obligation. It is not difficult to treat this promise as being made to all who attend the auction and accepted by all who make bids in reliance on the promise. Only the highest bona fide bidder will suffer substantial damages.

5.15 On this approach the most difficult case is *Harris v Nickerson* but in his judgment in this case Blackburn J was careful to underline that *Warlow v Harrison* was different. The policy in favour of holding those who advertise auctions without reserve to their word is much stronger.

---

[8] Slade (1952) 68 LQR 238; Gower (1952) 68 LQR 457; Slade (1953) 49 LQR 21.

The question is resolved for English law at least by the decision of the Court of Appeal in **5.16** *Barry v Davies*.[9] The plaintiff attended an auction at the third defendant's auction house and bid for two machines which were entered as without reserve. He bid £200 each but the auctioneer thought the price too low, refused to accept the bid and withdrew the machines from the sale. The Court of Appeal held that there was a collateral contract between the auctioneer and the highest bidder and that there was consideration both in the form of detriment to the bidder whose bid could be accepted and of benefit to the auctioneer in the possibility of increased attendance and more bids.[10]

The Australian position seems not wholly clear. *Warlow v Harrison* was followed by the **5.17** Supreme Court of Victoria in *Ulbrick v Laidlaw*[11] but in the later Victorian case of *Horden House Pty Ltd v Arnold*[12] both these cases where treated as turning on the principal being undisclosed. In *AGC (Advances) Ltd v Mcwhirter*[13] Holland J thought *Warlow v Harrison* anomalous.

The leading Canadian texts think that *Warlow v Harrison* is law in Canada.[14] The same rule **5.18** appears to be stated in the Uniform Commercial code section 2-328(3) and the Restatement (2d) Contracts, section 28(1)(b) though not without some complexities in application.[15]

C. Tenders

The basic rule for tenders is the same as for auctions. The invitation to tender is an invita- **5.19** tion to treat; the tender is an offer and the contract comes into existence, if at all, when a tender is accepted.[16] There is however an important difference. In an auction each succes- sive bid knocks out earlier bids so that only the highest bid can be accepted. This is not the case with tenders. Absent a promise to accept the best bid or the application of public pro- curement law the inviter can accept any tender. It is also common to negotiate details with the successful tenderer before completing the contract.

There have been important developments in the case law in both England and Canada. **5.20** Though there are similarities it appears that different rules may have been developed and we shall consider the developments separately as a first step.

The starting point is the decision of the House of Lords in *Harvela Investment Ltd v Royal* **5.21** *Trust Company of Canada (CI) Ltd*.[17] In this case the first defendant, a Jersey Trust com- pany, were owners of shares in a company. The plaintiff and the second defendants were

---

[9] [2000] 1 WLR 1962; Carter (2001) 17 J Contract law 69; Meisel (2001) 64 MLR 468.
[10] The Court approved the trial Judge's award of damages of some £27,600 based on a new value of £14,000 per machine.
[11] [1924] VLR 274.
[12] [1989] VR 402.
[13] (1977) 1 BPR 9454.
[14] Swan, *Markham on Canadian Contract Law* (Lexis Nexis Butterworths, 2006), 210; Waddams, *Law of Contracts* (5th edn, Canada Law Book, Toronto, 2007) 25. See *McManus v Nova Scotia* (1995) 144 NSR (2d) 182.
[15] For a full and helpful statement of the North American position see Hickling (1970) 5 UBCl Rev 187.
[16] *Spencer v Harding* (1870) LR 5 CP 561.
[17] [1986] 1 AC 207.

also owners of shares in the same company and if either bought the shares owned by the first defendant, they would gain control of the company. The first defendant decided to sell the shares by competitive tender. They invited the plaintiff and the second defendant to make sealed bids by 3 p.m. on 16 September 1981. They promised to accept the highest tender received by them. Both parties made offers in time. The plaintiffs offered C '$2,175,000' and the second defendants offered C '$2,100,000 or C $101,000 in excess of any other offer ... expressed as a fixed monetary amount, whichever is the higher'.

5.22 The first defendant thought that the second defendant had made the highest bid and that they were bound to accept it. The plaintiffs disagreed. The House of Lords, reversing the Court of Appeal, held that a referential bid of the kind adopted by the second defendant was not permitted on the proper construction of the offer and that therefore the plaintiffs had made the highest bid.[18]

5.23 The important point for present purposes is the analysis of the contractual situation. This is clearly explained by Lord Diplock in his judgment with which all the other Law Lords agreed. There were three contracts: a unilateral contract with each of the bidders in which the first defendant undertook to sell to the highest bidder and a bilateral or synallagmatic contract for the sale of the shares with the highest bidder.

Lord Diplock said:

> The construction question turns upon the wording of the telex of 15 September 1981 referred to by Lord Templeman as 'the invitation' and addressed to both Harvela and Sir Leonard. It was not a mere invitation to negotiate for the sale of the shares in Harvey & Co. Ltd. of which the vendors were the registered owners in the capacity of trustees. Its legal nature was that of a unilateral or 'if' contract, or rather of two unilateral contracts in identical terms to one of which the vendors and Harvela were the parties as promisor and promisee respectively, while to the other the vendors were promisor and Sir Leonard was promisee, such unilateral contracts were made at the time when the invitation was received by the promisee to whom it was addressed by the vendors; under neither of them did the promisee, Harvela and Sir Leonard respectively, assume any legal obligation to anyone to do or refrain from doing anything.

> The vendors, on the other hand, did assume a legal obligation to the promisee under each contract. That obligation was conditional upon the happening, after the unilateral contract had been made, of an event which was specified in the invitation; the obligation was to enter into a synallagmatic contract to sell the shares to the promisee, the terms of such synallagmatic contract being also set out in the invitation. The event upon the happening of which the vendor's obligation to sell the shares to the promisee arose was the doing by the promisee of an act which was of such a nature that it might be done by either promisee or neither promisee but could not be done by both. The vendors thus did not by entering into the two unilateral contracts run any risk of assuming legal obligations to enter into conflicting synallagmatic contracts to sell the shares to each promisee.

> The two unilateral contracts were of short duration; for the condition subsequent to which each was subject was the receipt by the vendors' solicitors on or before 3 p.m. on the following day, 16 September 1981, of a sealed tender or confidential telex containing an offer by

---

[18] On this analysis the first defendant had clearly committed a repudiatory breach by purporting to accept the second defendants' bid but the plaintiffs had elected to continue to hold them to the contract.

the promisee to buy the shares for a single sum of money in Canadian dollars. If such an offer was received from each of the promisees under their respective contracts, the obligation of the promisor, the vendors, was to sell the shares to the promisee whose offer was the higher; and any obligation which the promisor had assumed to the promisee under the other unilateral contract came to an end, because the event the happening of which was the condition subsequent to which the vendors' obligation to sell the shares to that promisee was subject had not happened before the unilateral contract with that promisee expired.

Since the invitation in addition to containing the terms of the unilateral contract also embodied the terms of the synallagmatic contract into which the vendors undertook to enter upon the happening of the specified event, the consequence of the happening of that event would be to convert the invitation into a synallagmatic contract between the vendors and whichever promisee had offered.

This is an analysis of fundamental importance. It recognizes that the contract-making **5.24** process may involve two stages and that the first stage may itself involve contractual liability. This has led to further developments which we shall consider but it also reflects back light on the auction problems which we have just considered.

In *Harvela* the first defendants had explicitly promised to accept the highest tender. The **5.25** decision of the House of Lords is important primarily for the contractual analysis of how this promise is binding. In *Blackpool & Fylde Aero Club Ltd v Blackpool Borough Council*[19] the Court of Appeal went significantly further in discovering and enforcing an implicit promise about the conduct of the tendering process.

In this case the defendants owned and managed the local airport. They had been accus- **5.26** tomed to lease a concession to operate pleasure flights from the airport. In 1983 they were minded to renew the concession and decided to do so by sealed competitive tender. They wrote to the plaintiff and six others inviting them to tender. They expressly said that they did not bind themselves to 'accept all or any part of any tender'. They also said that any tender submitted late would not be considered. The plaintiffs' tender was submitted on time and complied in all respects with the requirements but was excluded from consideration by the defendants because their staff had wrongly marked it as submitted late. The concession was awarded to another tenderer.

When the plaintiffs discovered that they had been unsuccessful they asked why and were **5.27** told that they had applied late. When they pointed out that this was wrong the council's first reaction was to start the process again but the successful tenderer pointed out that they had a valid contract and were in no way to blame. The council then elected to let the process stand. The Court of Appeal held that the council had implicitly promised to consider all tenders which were formally valid and submitted in time. Bingham LJ said:

A tendering procedure of this kind is, in many respects, heavily weighted in favour of the invitor. He can invite tenders from as many or as few parties as he chooses. He need not tell any of them who else or how many others, he has invited. The invitee may often, although not here, be put to considerable labour and expense in preparing a tender, ordinarily without recompense if he is unsuccessful. The invitation to tender may itself, in a complex case,

---

[19] [1990] 1 WLR 1195.

although again not here, involve time and expense to prepare, but the invitor does not commit himself to proceed with the project, whatever it is; he need not accept the highest tender; he need not accept any tender; he need not give reasons to justify his acceptance or rejection of any tender received. The risk to which the tenderer is exposed does not end with the risk that his tender may not be the highest or, as the case may be, lowest. But where, as here, tenders are solicited from selected parties all of them known to the invitor, and where a local authority's invitation prescribes a clear, orderly and familiar procedure—draft contract conditions available for inspection and plainly not open to negotiation, a prescribed common form of tender, the supply of envelopes designed to preserve the absolute anonymity of tenderers and clearly to identify the tender in question, and an absolute deadline—the invitee is in my judgment protected at least to this extent: if he submits a conforming tender before the deadline he is entitled, not as a matter of mere expectation but of contractual right, to be sure that his tender will after the deadline be opened and considered in conjunction with all other conforming tenders or at least that his tender will be considered if others are. Had the club, before tendering, inquired of the council whether it could rely on any timely and conforming tender being considered along with others, I feel quite sure that the answer would have been 'of course'. The law would, I think, be defective if it did not give effect to that.

5.28 This decision attracted considerable comment both favourable[20] and critical.[21] Because a split trial had been ordered the Court of Appeal did not have to consider the question of damages. It would seem clear that the plaintiff could recover the wasted costs of tendering (on the facts not great) and at least damages reflecting the loss of the chance of being considered.[22]

5.29 These possibilities were explored much more fully in *Harmon CFEM facades (UK) Ltd v Corporate Officer Of the House of Commons*[23] this case arose out of the construction of a new parliamentary building in Bridge Street, Westminster to provide offices for some 210 MPs and their staff.[24] The plaintiff was asked to tender for the fenestration[25] contract. The tendering process was complex, involving retendering. The plaintiff was at all stages the lowest tenderer but it was not awarded the contract, principally because of the desire of those controlling the process to award the contract to a British company. Judge Humphrey Lloyd QC held that the defendant had impliedly agreed to conduct the process fairly and had failed to do so. He analysed the tendering process in meticulous and elaborate detail to show that it was unfair. Post tender negotiations took place with the preferred tenderer which meant that the parties were not tendering on the same basis.

5.30 The judge held that Harmon could recover the costs of tendering and the profit it would have made on the contract. Of course if Harmon had been awarded the contract, as it

---

[20] Davenport 'Safe hands' (1991) 107 LQR 201; Adams and Brownsword (1991) 54 MLR 881.

[21] Phang (1991) 4 J Contract Law 46.

[22] It seems on the facts suggested in the report that they were very likely the best tenderers. The council had not bound itself to accept the best tender but the most likely event was that they would do so.

[23] (1999) 67 ConLR 1, (2000) 72 ConLR 21. See also *Fairclough Building v Port Talbot Borough Council* [1992] 62 BLR 82.

[24] This was an extremely expensive building, already planned to cost £250 million before it started.

[25] This was 'probably the most expensive fenestration system ever built'.

should have been, its gross profit on the contract would have covered the tender cost. This would be relevant to the process of quantification.[26]

The leading New Zealand decision is *Pratt Contractors Ltd v Palmerston North City Council.*[27] **5.31**
In this case the invitation to tender stated the form in which tenders should be submitted, set out criteria by which they would be assessed and indicated that the lowest confirming tender would be accepted. The plaintiff submitted the lowest conforming tender but the contract was awarded to another, non-conforming, tender. It was held that this was a breach of contract.[28]

The leading Australian case is the important decision of Finn J sitting in the Federal Court **5.32**
in *Hughes Aircraft Systems International v Air Services Australia.*[29] In this case it was desired to let the Australian advanced air traffic system (TAAATS). This was a very high profile project which had already been the subject of an abortive process (TAAATSI). It was essential to procure the participation of at least two plausible candidates in TAAATS II. The invitation to tender addressed to *Hughes and Thomson* set out the criteria for evaluating the tender in great detail with priority listing for the four major criteria. It stated that an independent auditor had been appointed 'to verify that the evaluation procedures' were followed: Finn J said:

> Authority makes it clear that the starting point is that a simple uncomplicated request for bids will generally be no more than an invitation to treat, not giving rise to contractual obligations, although it may give rise to obligations to act fairly. On the other hand, it is obviously open to persons to enter into a preliminary contract with the expectation that it will lead in defined circumstances to a second or principal contract ... *whether or not the particular case falls into one category or the other will depend upon a consideration of the circumstances and the obligations expressly or impliedly accepted.*

> For the reasons I have given, I have concluded that in the distinctive circumstances that obtained in this case—and I here agree with Hughes' submission as to the strength of the 'factual matrix'—contractual obligations were accepted. (emphasis added)

In due course after the careful examination of the history of the tendering process he held that that defendant had failed to evaluate the tenders fairly.

All of the cases discussed above adopt a two contract analysis. If all goes well there will be a **5.33**
conventional bilateral contract formed by the tender and its acceptance. In addition there is a contract in which the party inviting tenders makes a promise about the tendering process. Thus is treated as, in Lord Diplock's analysis, creating a unilateral contract in which the invitor makes a promise in return for the tenderer submitting a tender. In this analysis the tenderer makes no promise. The leading Canadian case *R v Ron Engineering and*

---

[26] It is understood that at this stage the parties settled. The figures discussed in the judgment would suggest an award in the region of £4 million. In view of the sum involved it is striking that the defendants did not appeal.
[27] [1995] 1 NZLR 469.
[28] In the later Privy Council case of *Pratt Contractors v Transit New Zealand* [2005] 2 NZLR 433, [2003] UKPC 83, [2004] BLR 143, it was assumed by all parties that the tendering process imposed a duty to act fairly and in good faith.
[29] (1997) 146 ALR 1.

Construction (Eastern) Ltd[30] also adopts a two contract analysis but one in which a promise is made by the tenderer.

5.34 In this case the appellant (Ron Engineering) submitted a tender for work under conditions of tender which provided for the payment of a tender deposit of $150,000 and that the tender was not revocable for 60 days after being opened. Ron Engineering's tender was for $2,748,000 which was $632,000 lower than the next lowest tender. Immediately after the opening of the tenders Ron Engineering said that it had made an error of $750,058.[31] Ron Engineering did not purport to revoke its offer but said that in view of the mistake it was not open to the Crown to accept it and that its deposit should be returned. The Crown delivered a contract for signature which Ron Engineering refused to sign.

5.35 The Supreme Court of Canada in a judgment delivered by Estey J held that by virtue of the conditions of tender the tenderer had entered into a contract which made the tender irrevocable for 60 days after the opening of the tender. This was a contract separate from the contract which would come into existence on acceptance of the tender. He did not refer to *Harvela* and any of the other cases discussed above, which had not yet been decided. The contract is several times described by Estey J as a unilateral contract but he went on to say:

> The principal term of Contract A is the irrevocability of the bid, and the corollary term is the obligation in both parties to enter into a contract (Contract B) upon the acceptance of the tender. Other terms include the qualified obligations of the owner to accept the lowest tender, and the degree of this obligation is controlled by the terms and conditions established in the call for tenders.

This would surely mean that the contract is bilateral. Of course no question of the Crown being under any obligation to accept the tender arose in the case.

5.36 In this case the Crown had counter-claimed for damages. This counter-claim had been dismissed by the Ontario Court of Appeal and there appears to have been no appeal against that part of the decision.[32] Logically once it is held that the tender cannot be withdrawn there seems no reason why damages for loss of a contract at the tendered price cannot be recovered.[33]

5.37 The decision in the *Ron Engineering* case has given rise to extensive litigation in the Canadian Courts. Two further cases call for further discussion. In *MJB Enterprises Ltd v Defence Construction (1951) Ltd*[34] the defendant invited tenders for the demolition of a water tank and construction of a pump house at a Canadian Forces base. The invitation to tender contained a 'privilege clause' which stated that the lowest or any tender would not necessarily be accepted. The plaintiff submitted a tender but another tender was accepted.

---

[30] [1981] 1 SCR 111, (1981) 119 DLR (3d) 267. See above n 14.

[31] It was not alleged that there was anything on the face of the tender which revealed a mistake. It is not uncommon for there to be arithmetical mistakes in tenders which can be detected by someone who adds up the figures but this was not such a case. Further the Crown had been advised by consulting engineers before the tenders were opened that a likely figure was $2,744,700.

[32] See para 23 of the judgment.

[33] See Waddams, *Law of Contracts* (5th Edn 2007) 26–8; Swan, *Canadian Contract of Law* 212–16; *Toronto Transit Commission v Gottardo Construction Ltd* (2005) 77 OR (3d) 269.

[34] [1999] 1 SCR 619, Waddams (1999) 32 CBLJ 308.

It appeared that the tender included a handwritten note which amounted to a qualification which was held to make that tender invalid. The Supreme Court of Canada held that although the privilege clause meant that the defendant was not obliged to accept the lowest bid it had undertaken only to accept a compliant bid and it had broken that promise and that the plaintiff could recover for breach of that promise the profit it would have made if it had been awarded the contract. The Supreme Court treated the obligation created by the tendering process as bilateral.

In *Double N Earthmovers Ltd v Edmonton (City)*[35] the defendant invited tenders. The invitation specified that equipment used had to have been manufactured in 1980 or later.[36] S Ltd submitted the lowest bid. The plaintiff told the City that S Ltd equipment was not compliant but the contract was awarded to S Ltd. The Supreme Court of Canada held 5-4 that the plaintiff's action failed. The majority view appears to treat the use by the tenderer of old equipment as not making the tender non-compliant. They thought that the tender was compliant because the successful tenderer had undertaken to use compliant equipment even though it in fact intended to use old equipment and was in fact allowed to do so. **5.38**

In a number of the cases discussed above the conditions of the tender are expressly stated. In such cases it does not seem to matter whether the body inviting tenders is public or private. What is decisive is the fair construction of what has been expressly stated. However in some of the cases much turns on what is to be implied and in most of these cases the body inviting tenders is a public body. It is easier to imply an obligation on a public body to behave in a fair, rational and transparent way but it is thought that the identity of the invitor is only one of the factors to be considered in determining what has been expressly or impliedly agreed. **5.39**

In this respect it should be noted that public bodies within the European Union are nowadays under increasingly important rules about public procurement. No attempt has been made to state these rules here or to consider the UNCITRAL model law on procurement of goods, construction and services.

---

[35] [2007] 1 SCR 416, (2007) 275 DLR (4th) 577.
[36] The contract appears to have been made in 1986 and has taken a long time to reach the Supreme Court.

6

FORMATION ONLINE*

A. Introduction

Future editions of this book may not contain a chapter on 'electronic' or 'online' contract **6.01** formation. The Internet and all Internet-based methods of communication will no longer be referred to as 'modern' or 'novel', the fascination with everything 'e-' will have died down. It can be expected that some of the issues discussed in this chapter will be slowly assimilated by legal doctrine and case law. After all, contract law has always displayed an inherent ability to adapt to new situations—without the need for major revisions of its underlying principles. For the time being, however, this assimilation has not taken place. There is a genuine need to address certain problems brought about by the change in how people conduct business—or manifest intention in general. Contract law lies at the heart of e-commerce, ie the 'use of digital systems to create/perform commercial transactions'.[1] Irrespective of the business model and the type of contractual subject matter, all e-commerce transactions rely on the same contract formation principles. Ultimately, '[a]lmost every question posed by business dealings in cyberspace can be reduced to a question involving contract law'.[2] Although both the Internet and e-commerce have been

---

* This chapter was written by Eliza Mik.

[1] Nimmer and Towle, *Law of Electronic Commercial Transactions* (Arlington, 2003), para 1.01; see also: *Guide to Measuring the Information Society*, OECD Working Party on Indicators for the Information Society, DSTI/ICCP/IIS (2005) 6/Final, p 41, which introduces a distinction depending on whether the sale and purchase of goods and services is conducted over computer-mediated networks or over the Internet; for different definitions and a discussion of basic business models see: Rayport and Jaworski, *Introduction to E-commerce* (New York, 2002), 4, 5; Laudon and Traver, *E-commerce: Business, Technology, Society* (Sydney, 2001), 57; the Australian Report of the Electronic Commerce Expert Group to the Attorney General (1998) para 1.2, defines e-commerce as including facsimile and telephone.

[2] Cavazos and Morin, *Cyberspace and the Law: Your Rights and Duties in the On-line World* (Cambridge, 1994), 34.

mainstream phenomena for over 15 years,[3] a thorough analysis of their implications for contract law remains outstanding. Many basic questions remain unanswered, many problems have passed unnoticed.

6.02 Legal literature abounds with statements about the challenges created by the Internet. Some of those challenges are real, some imaginary. Not every challenge needs to result in change. The fact that this book contains a separate chapter does not mean that a separate set of rules for online contracts is required. Readers expecting a revisionist or revolutionist approach will be disappointed. New methods of communicating do not imply a need to create new principles or a parallel regime to accommodate online contracting. The revolution in how people communicate need not result in a revision of contract law. The general assumption made in this chapter is that contract law can absorb technological change. This process, however, must be based on a sound understanding of technology and on an acknowledgement of the differences between the 'old' and the 'new' transacting environments.[4] Legal arguments must be based on correct technical assumptions.[5] The process of 'absorbing' technology into contract law must also be based on a recognition of which problems are truly 'Internet-specific', ie which questions are in fact created by the new communication technologies. Care must be taken not to mistake some pre-existing problems for new ones—just because they become more visible or resurface in the online environment. The approach taken must be one of subtle adaptation, not one of revisionist creativity.

6.03 Judges and academics alike seem to shun technology.[6] This has two implications. First, instead of analysing the actual functioning and characteristics of a specific method of communication, they tend to revert to metaphors or analogies. Metaphors, however, can only stretch so far. Analogies may lead to absurd results. At some stage, all comparisons fail. An endless repetition of analogies or the creation of elaborate metaphors often results in the application of the incorrect principle, or 'the creation of bad law'.[7] The second implication of a techno-phobic approach is that the impact of certain technologies is being overstated

---

[3] The start of the commercial, widely accessible Internet can be associated with the privatization of the Internet backbone by the NSF in 1995, see Laudon and Traver, *E-Commerce: Business, Technology, Society* (Sydney, 2001), 113, 114.

[4] Lessig, *Code and other Laws of Cyberspace* (New York, 1999), 78, 79; Benkler, 'Net Regulation: Taking Stock and Looking Forward' (2000) 71 U Colo L Rev 1203; Kidd and Daughtrey, 'Adapting Contract Law to Accommodate Electronic Contracts: Overview and Suggestions' (2000) 26 Rutgers Computer & Tech L J 215 at 240.

[5] See Easterbrook, 'Cyberspace and the Law of the Horse' (1996) U Chi Legal F 207: 'Beliefs lawyers hold about computers and predictions they make about new technology are highly likely to be false.'

[6] Only on few occasions have courts presented a detailed and correct understanding of 'how things work;' see: *American Civil Liberties Union v Reno* 929 F Supp 824 (ED Pa 1996); *Dow Jones & Company v Gutnick* (2002) 194 ALR 433; *Godfrey v Demon Internet Ltd* [2001] QB 201; *Yahoo! Inc v La Ligue Contre le Racisme et L'Antisemitisme* 145 F Supp 2d 1168 (ND Cal 2001).

[7] Lee, 'Rules and Standards for Cyberspace' (2002) 77 Notre Dame L Rev 1275 at 1292; see also Blavin and Cohen, 'Gore, Gibson and Goldsmith: The Evolution of Internet Metaphors in Law and Commentary' (2002) 16 Harv J L & Tech 265; see also Salbu, 'Who Should Govern the Internet?: Monitoring and Supporting a New Frontier' (1998) 11 Harv J L & Tech 429 at 462, 463; Lemley, 'Place and Cyberspace' (2003) 91 Cal L Rev 521 who speaks of 'the logical steps that courts seem to miss as they move from metaphor to decision' at 522; Madison, 'Rights of Access and the Shape of the Internet' (2003) 44 B C L Rev 433 for a discussion of the implications of the 'Internet-as-a-place' metaphor.

while the importance of others is being played down or ignored. Much legal analysis is devoted to so-called 'digital signatures' and their role in fulfilling formal requirements. Little attention is directed to the contractual implications of hypertext or how differences between network environments impact the ability to communicate intention. No attention is paid to how the client-server model affects the time of contract formation and to the fact that messages are often processed by the system of the addressee. Examples abound.

The basic rule remains the same: everything is a question of intention—both online and in the real world. Intention is based on an objective assessment of what the parties said or did.[8] In the real world, manifestations of intention take the form of words, spoken or written, and conduct. Online, intention is manifested through electronic messages, websites and interactions with graphical user interfaces. It is also assumed that the offer and acceptance model is the best analytical tool available. Moreover, this model remains unchanged irrespective of whether intention takes the form of an instant message, an email, a website or a click. It must be admitted, however, that a number of factors affect its application depending on the method used to manifest, that is communicate, intention. To fully appreciate the impact of technology, the term 'communication' must be divided into 'presentation' and 'transmission'. After all, if intention is not communicated, it is irrelevant. A statement is presented (assumes a particular form, an arrangement of text or graphic material) and transmitted (conveyed from one party to the other). While the manner of presenting content (apart from the content itself) bears on the differentiation between offers and invitations to treat, the establishment of contractual contents and the incorporation of terms, the manner of transmission relates to the determination of the time of contract formation. In other words, intention can be examined either with regards to how the online environment changes the manner intention is presented or transmitted. Each communication method creates a different set of problems and each stage in the contract formation process faces different technological challenges. The point made is simple: technology—while not changing contract law—adds complexity to the traditional analysis. The question is not 'do traditional principles apply?' but 'how do they apply?'[9] This chapter illustrates how each step in the traditional legal analysis encounters a technological hurdle. **6.04**

Many readers would expect a chapter called 'Contract Formation on the Internet'. The latter term has been omitted intentionally and is generally used with some reluctance. Although 'Internet' has a number of technical definitions,[10] it means different things to different people.[11] Most importantly, the term represents a wholesale approach, which fails to appreciate the variety of activities enabled by the Internet and the diversity of technologies **6.05**

---

[8] See Perillo, 'The Origins of the Objective Theory of Contract Formation and Interpretation' (2000) 69 Fordham L Rev 427.

[9] *Chwee Kin Keong v Digilandmall.com Pte Ltd* [2004] SGHC 71 at 91 per V K Rajah JC.

[10] The Internet is a network of networks, a combination of internets, an amalgam of multiple technologies, relying on the TCP/IP protocol stack. Hall, *Internet Core Protocols: The Definitive Guide* (Cambridge, 2000), Ch 1, 'An Introduction to TCP/IP', para 1.1.3; RFC 1594, Answers to Commonly Asked 'New Internet User' Questions, A Marine et al (1994); for other general descriptions of the Internet see: Fitzgerald et al, *Going Digital 2000, Legal Issues for E-commerce, Software and the Internet* (2nd edn, Sydney, 2000), 4; Perrit, *Law and the Information Superhighway* (New York, 1996), 13.

[11] For a discussion of the historical approaches to the Internet see: Geist, 'The Reality of Bytes: Regulating Economic Activity in the Age of the Internet' (1998) 73 Wash L Rev 521 at 531–54.

comprising it.[12] To speak of 'Internet communications' in general over-simplifies the matter. Parties communicate via email, instant messengers and websites, to name a few methods. All those communication methods rely on the Internet. The Internet itself, however, is not a method of communication but an infrastructure supporting various methods of information exchange. Each of those methods serves different communication needs. Each method differs with regards to its intrusiveness, immediacy of communication and the ability to reach the other party in real time.

6.06   The term 'online' appeared more suitable as it reflects the pervasive and uninterrupted connectivity and the networked character of practically all modern means of communication. 'Online' also presupposes that the Internet is involved in the communication process. It must be borne in mind that the Internet is no longer limited to a fixed connection at a physical address. People have grown accustomed to being connected to their services all the time, whatever their device type and wherever their location. Computers are no longer office or household devices but personal devices with a built-in mobile broadband connection.

6.07   When analysing the online contract formation process, the dichotomy between email and instant messengers on one side and web-based interactions on the other must be emphasized. People exchange emails and instant messages. People do not 'exchange' websites but interact with them. Communications via email or instant messengers can be compared to traditional correspondence.[13] Problems of identifying an offer and an acceptance are similar—irrespective of whether one analyses letters or electronic messages. The sequence and content of each message must be examined to discern an offer and an acceptance.[14] The most likely scenario for mass-market e-commerce, however, are transactions occurring on websites, where goods or services are presented for purchase by a 'web-merchant' and where users, having browsed through a series of web pages, fill out online forms to provide shipping and payment information. A typical example is amazon.com.

6.08   The structure of this chapter has been chosen with some difficulty. The point of departure is always the legal principle in its most basic formulation, then it is examined how various technological factors affect its application. One could examine the table of contents in a textbook on contract law and ask: which elements in the contract formation process are affected by the novel transacting environment? An intuitive, common-sense analysis reveals that very few are. The basic building blocks of agreement remain the same: intention and consideration. Offers are binding and can be revoked before acceptance. They are terminated by rejection, the death of the offeror or by the occurrence of a condition subsequent. Acceptances must be communicated within the timeframe prescribed by the offer. The same principles apply online. The intention of the parties remains decisive, the offer-acceptance analysis aims at determining such intention by construing the statements made or conduct engaged in during the contracting process. Not every aspect of 'offer and

---

[12] In the words of one author: 'the whole Internet is rarely an appropriate level on which to generalize'; see Wu, 'Application-Centered Internet Analysis' (1999) 85 Va L Rev 1163 at 1164.

[13] *Butler Machine Tool Co Ltd v Ex-Cell-O Corporation (England) Ltd* [1979] 1 WLR 401 at 404.

[14] *Gibson v Manchester City Council* [1979] 1 WLR 294.

acceptance' needs to be discussed because not every aspect is affected by the novel communication possibilities. Parts of the discussion may be accused of some artificiality. Some aspects of the contract formation process are isolated, some problems with modern communication technologies are exaggerated to illustrate a point. Due to spatial constraints, it is impossible to paint the whole picture. This chapter only sketches certain issues and points to further challenges. It does not attempt to present ready-made solutions and all-encompassing rules. This chapter asks some seemingly simple questions: is there an offer? If so, what are its contents? Is there acceptance? If so, when is it effective?

The discussion of online contracts would not be complete without mentioning the harmo- **6.09**
nization efforts in this area. The recently enacted United Nations Convention on the Use of Electronic Communications in International Contracts (CUECIC)[15] attempts to regulate certain aspects of transactions concluded over the Internet. The CUECIC is based on the 1996 Model Law on Electronic Commerce (MLEC).[16] The latter provides a template for national legislatures and serves as a guide for drafting contracts in the area of e-commerce. Its solutions exemplify early attempts to resolve legal uncertainties pertaining to electronic transactions. The CUECIC combines most of the MLEC's wording with some of the approaches adopted by the Vienna Convention, especially in terms of scope of application, principles of statutory interpretation and declarations of variations by the ratifying countries.[17] Both the MLEC and the CUECIC aim to facilitate online commerce and remove 'obstacles' to the validity and enforceability of online contracts. Both regulations state that electronic contracts are equally valid as 'traditional' contracts, and establish criteria for the fulfillment of the requirements of 'writing', 'signatures' and 'originals' in electronic form.[18] Their guiding principle is that any discrimination on the sole basis that a contract originated in electronic form is prohibited.[19] It could be claimed that some of the problems they are trying to address are non-existent[20] and that provisions that contracts can be formed electronically merely state the obvious.[21] After all, the electronic form does not pose an obstacle to valid and enforceable online transactions as the substantive rules of contract law permit intention to be manifested in any manner.[22] There being no general requirement for contracts to be in writing or to be signed, formal requirements are an exception not the rule.[23] The more so, that most transactions that are accompanied by formalities are specifically excluded from the scope of the regulations.[24] A simple prohibition to

---

[15] Convention on the use of Electronic Communications in International Contracting, adopted on 23 November 2005.

[16] UNCITRAL Model Law on Electronic Commerce with Guide to Enactment (1996) with additional Art 5 *bis* as adopted in 1998, developed by the UN Commission on International Trade Law.

[17] For a detailed description of the procedural and international aspects of CUECIC see: Martin, 'The UNCITRAL Electronic Contracts Convention: Will it be Used or Avoided?' (2005) 17 Pace Int'l L Rev 261.

[18] The objectives and scope of the MLEC are described in detail in the 'Introduction' to the Guide to Enactment, paras 2–21.

[19] MLEC, Art 5; CUECIC, Art 8.

[20] Braucher, 'Rent-Seeking in the New Statutory Law of Electronic Commerce: Difficulties in Moving Consumer Protection Online' (2001) Wis L Rev 527 at 527.

[21] DeZilva, 'Electronic Transactions Legislation: An Australian Perspective' (2003) 37 Int'l Law 1009 at 1012.

[22] *Carter on Contract* (Butterworths, Sydney), § 02-060.

[23] *Carter on Contract* § 01-001.

[24] CUECIC Explanatory Note, para [7] p 14.

discriminate on the basis of the 'electronic' form would have sufficed to appease those uncomfortable with transactions concluded by electronic means. Anything beyond that seems an unnecessary repetition of the obvious. The aim of this chapter, however, is not to discuss contract formalities but contract formation.

B. A Challenge to Objectivity

6.10   The first 'technological hurdle' encountered by contract law relates to the basic principle that intention is evaluated objectively from the perspective of the addressee. This principle implicitly assumes that what the maker of the statement says or writes is what the addressee hears or reads. Generally, authors control the layout and contents of their documents, shop owners control the display of their goods, speakers tailor the language and tone of their voice to the needs of the addressee. This 'control' may, however, be absent when intention is manifested by means of a web page. In this instance, the contents of a web page viewed by the user may be presented differently than originally expressed. To explain the point: setting up a website consists in placing an HTML file on a web server.[25] HTML files contain text that represents the content and instructions that specify how this content is displayed.[26] The manner the content is presented (and sometimes whether it is presented at all) depends on how a specific browser processes these instructions. Each browser displays HTML files differently.[27] A website viewed on Internet Explorer will not look the same as viewed on Firefox. While the HTML file hosted on the web server remains unchanged, every user accessing such file may see something different. As a result, web merchants generally cannot control how websites, or individual web pages, are displayed to their end-users.[28]

6.11   To date, HTML has not been the subject of much academic debate from a contract law perspective. It has been discussed mainly with regards to copyright, trademark infringement and unfair competition.[29] The implications of HTML for contract law are, however, surprising and affect more than just the principle that intention is evaluated from the side of the addressee. When a party attempts to incorporate terms into a contract, the effectiveness of their incorporation often hinges on the reasonableness of the notice that terms exist. This 'reasonableness' generally translates into visibility or conspicuousness, such as placing the notice in proximity to the contractual subject matter and/or accentuating it by prominent colours or fonts. Colours and fonts, however, may not survive a specific browser type.[30] The conspicuousness of a notice, the visibility or positioning of a hyperlink providing the terms depend on the specific browser. A notice may not be displayed because the

---

[25] Additional requirements are the registration of a domain name, which serves as an address pointing to the specific HTML file(s).

[26] Deitel, Deitel and Goldberg, *Internet & World Wide Web, How to Program* (3rd edn, Prentice Hall, New Jersey, 2004) 83.

[27] Lynch and Horton, *Web Style Guide* (2nd edn, available at www.webstyleguide.com, Ch 3, 16; see generally: Zeldman, *Designing with Web Standards* (Indianapolis, 2003), 24, 26, 27.

[28] Niederst, *Web Design in a Nutshell* (2nd edn, safari online version), part 1, p 1.

[29] See, eg Nimmer and Towle, para 9.03.

[30] Nimmer and Towle, para 5.05[5].

addressee's browser cannot process the relevant instruction from the HTML file, terms may not be available because the relevant link is not visible. This problem is even more prominent whenever a web merchant is required to make product-specific disclosures, such as in the case of financial or insurance products or in consumer-oriented transactions. Again, the 'success' of a particular disclosure may depend on the browser used to view the website. Have the terms been incorporated if the notice was not displayed because the addressee's browser did not support the required technology? Who should bear the risk of such 'invisible notices'?

Assumedly, in accordance with the objective theory of contract the addressee's side must **6.12** prevail: the intention of a person setting up a website is evaluated on the basis of what the addressee sees on his computer screen. It is not the original expression but its processed version that are taken into account. Accordingly, if a particular notice or link are not displayed, it is the web merchant who bears the risk of his terms not being incorporated or the required disclosure not being made. While only this approach reflects the traditional principle, its limitations must be recognized. It is an oversimplification to state that web merchants bear all risks resulting from the users' browser version or type. The problem illustrates how additional, technological factors must be included in an otherwise, classic legal analysis.

From the side of the web merchant, the question is: which browser should websites be **6.13** designed for? It appears reasonable to code websites in accordance with applicable standards, the web development specifications published by the World Wide Web Consortium (W3C).[31] It is also reasonable to develop websites for the browser with the largest market share. It is common knowledge, however, that the most popular browser, Microsoft's Internet Explorer (IE), does not adhere to W3C standards. Web merchants face a difficult choice: design websites for display on IE or follow the standards? From the perspective of the addressee, is it reasonable to use a browser other than IE? IE is the most popular browser, not the best browser. An important factor is security. As IE is notorious for being prone to security breaches, it may be reasonable to use a different browser—especially if a user stores sensitive data on his computer. Persons who are sufficiently computer literate to use a browser other than IE will most likely be able to explain such choice by technical considerations. Designing for IE can be considered reasonable for the web merchant, avoiding IE may be reasonable for the user. For the web merchant, the only practical solution is to design multiple versions of the same website for different browsers or, as is often the practice, specifically indicate which browser type and version the website is designed for.

It must also be borne in mind that each browser exists in multiple, newer and older ver- **6.14** sions. Users may fall so far behind in upgrading their browser that their use of an older version cannot be regarded as reasonable. On one hand, browser software is available for free and therefore each user could, theoretically, upgrade his browser to view the website the way it was designed to be viewed. On the other hand, users may be limited in their ability to instal new browser versions in shared environments, such as within corporate or

---

[31] See www.w3c.org.

academic networks. While web merchants cannot bear the risks of outdated browsers, users cannot be expected to immediately upgrade their browsers whenever a new version becomes available.

6.15 An additional factor is that browsers can be customized. User settings override default settings. It is an oversimplification to state that users customize their browsers at their own risk because they change the manner a website was intended to display. Security considerations may enter the discussion again. It may be reasonable to deploy high security settings and permit only content from trusted sites. This operation may, however, prevent the display of certain elements of a website, including notices. These problems will not disappear anytime soon. A general trend in browser design is endowing the user with more choice regarding the display of contents. Consequently, the risk of invisible notices will remain difficult to apportion. Courts will therefore face increasingly difficult decisions involving not just a legal analysis of the reasonableness of notice, but a technical analysis of the reasonableness of browser choice and settings—both from the side of the merchant and from the side of the addressee.

6.16 Leaving aside problems created by different browser choices, an additional complication results from the fact that the 'amount' of content presented on a web page depends on the size of the computer display. The whole webpage may not fit onto the screen—even when the browser window is maximized. Users may be required to scroll horizontally or vertically to see all of its text and graphical elements. Only a small amount of a web page is visible by default, generally the upper left area. The displayed content is even more limited when websites are viewed on mobile devices, such as smart-phones. In a prominent case on online contracting, *Specht v Netscape Communications*,[32] the visibility of the hyperlink, which constituted the notice of the legal terms, depended exclusively on the size of the display and on the necessity to scroll down to the bottom of the page. The court emphasized that scrolling reduces the likelihood of noticing the relevant link.[33] In another case, however, the court did not perceive the necessity of scrolling through the terms as a factor preventing their incorporation.[34]

6.17 Finally, it must be remembered that it is the user who decides on the sequence in which to view the statements made on a website. As HTML 'destroys' the linearity of print,[35] pages may be viewed non-sequentially,[36] there being no logical order determined by the physical constraints of a book or real-world shop. As each web page has multiple points of access,[37] users may bypass the homepage and 'enter' the transactional part of the website directly.[38] This has little precedent in the real world, where shops have one entry point and a number

---

[32] *Specht v Netscape Communications* 306 F 3d 17 at 23.
[33] *Specht v Netscape Communications* 306 F 3d 17 at 24, 32.
[34] *Novak v Overture Services Inc* 309 F Supp 2d 446 (EDNY 2004) at 452.
[35] Delapenna, 'Law in a Shrinking World: The Interaction of Science and Technology with International Law' (1999–2000) 88 Ky J 809 at 872.
[36] Lynch and Horton, n 27 above, 2.
[37] Effross, 'The Legal Architecture of Virtual Stores: World Wide Web Sites and the Uniform Commercial Code' (1997) 34 San Diego L Rev 1263 at 1290, 1291.
[38] The problem is commonly referred to as 'deep-linking'.

of fixed or unavoidable elements, such as doors and counters. Again, this very problem arose in *Specht v Netscape Communications*[39] where one of the plaintiffs accessed the page presenting the product for download not from the homepage but through a shareware site that deep-linked straight into the transactional part. Accordingly, he was not able to see the hyperlink indicating the existence of terms. The latter did not become incorporated.

Is there an offer?

The first question in the traditional line of analysing contract formation concerns the existence of an offer, ie a binding expression of intention, which can be accepted by a simple 'yes'. Textbooks proceed with a discussion of the differences between offers and invitations to treat. Assuming that intention expressed by modern methods of communication is evaluated just like any other expression, it would seem that any debate of the distinctions between offers and invitations online is redundant. Some recent statements suggest otherwise.[40] It is a common pitfall in legal analyses to imply that the basic principles of analysing contract formation do not apply or that online transactions must be treated differently due to the mere fact that they are formed by novel methods of communication. Surprisingly, this very mistake is made by the CUECIC—an instrument allegedly affirming the principles of media and technology neutrality, ie that legal principles apply irrespective of the technology used.[41]

    6.18

CUECIC, Article 11, establishes a presumption that websites are invitations and are therefore not binding.[42] During the preparatory works, it was explained that websites should be regarded as invitations because they are 'like advertisements' and they are addressed to the world at large.[43] It was also observed that: '[i]nternet transactions may not easily fit into the established distinctions between what might constitute an "offer" and what should be interpreted as an "invitation to treat"'.[44] These statements illustrate some common misunderstandings.

    6.19

First, to claim that Internet transactions do not fit the traditional analytical model implies that real-world transactions do. This is obviously not the case. Most difficulties in transposing the offer and acceptance analysis to novel transacting scenarios result from the fact that it is a model. Applying models against real-life situations is inherently difficult. The difficulties are more pronounced in the case of online contracts because manifestations of intention often take an unusual form.

Second, the 'distinctions' between offers and invitations are by no means 'established'. The treatment of certain stereotyped situations as indications of final intention is inconsistent

---

[39] *Specht v Netscape Communications* 306 F 3d 17 at 24.
[40] Treitel, *The Law of Contract* (Sweet & Maxwell, London, 2007), 14.
[41] See, eg CUECIC Explanatory Note [47], p. 26.
[42] Squires, 'Some Contract Issues Arising from Online Business-Consumer Agreements' (2000) 5 Deakin LR 95 at 104; see also Treitel, 12, who states that where a supplier indicates the availability of goods or services on a website, 'the offer would seem to come from the customer (e.g. when he clicks the appropriate "button") and it is open to the supplier to accept or reject that offer'. Chissick and Kelmann, *Electronic Commerce: Law and Practice* (Sweet & Maxwell, London, 2000) 75.
[43] See A/CN.9/WB.IV/ WP.91, paras 47, 48; A/CN.9/484, para 125.
[44] A/CN.9/WG.IV/WP.95, para 53.

and does not provide universal rules. Although the interpretation of certain kinds of expressions appears standardized,[45] care must be taken not to generalize.

Most importantly, why should a statement made on a website be interpreted differently than the same statement made in a newspaper or verbally? It is the content of a statement, not the method of its expression that determines its legal effect. The fact that a statement is posted on a website must not automatically prejudice the outcome of the analysis. A website must be approached like any other manifestation of intention.[46] It is incorrect to mechanically subsume all websites under either category on the mere ground that they are websites.

6.20   The CUECIC approach may be explained by the fact that invitations shield the maker of the statement from overexposure, ie the inability to perform when the number of acceptances exceeds the number of items in stock.[47] This 'protective' function of invitations was highlighted in the explanatory notes to the CUECIC.[48] It can be assumed that this emphasis derives from a number of cases where a website displayed incorrect pricing information and the vendor was obliged to sell its goods at the incorrect, heavily discounted price.[49] In this sense, the provision seems to be a protective mechanism against computer errors, which are a side effect of automation. Protecting a person from overexposure or computer errors does not, however, require a manipulation of the basic rule that the effect of a statement depends on the intention of its maker—not on its form. Moreover, the protective function of invitations is not necessarily required in e-commerce transactions as the risk of over-exposure can be prevented by technological means. Applications can be programmed not to accept orders of goods low on stock and dynamically change product information to reflect the number of items available. With digital products, such as music downloads and information, the risk of over-acceptance is absent altogether. The web merchant can also protect himself by explicitly stating that the website does not constitute an offer. A simple disclaimer is as effective as technological measures.

6.21   The CUECIC also proposes criteria to determine whether a website is an invitation or an offer: interactivity and number of addressees.[50] From a theoretical perspective, however, neither criterion is admissible. The binding character of a website cannot depend on the degree of interactivity,[51] ie whether the user interface accepts input which can be processed in real time. The presence of an interactive interface does not imply that the terms are

[45] Eisenberg, 'Expression Rules in Contract Law and Problems of Offer and Acceptance' (1994) 82 Cal L Rev 1127 at 1129.

[46] Wilmot, Christensen and Butler, *Contract Law* (2nd edn, Melbourne, 2005) [3.4], [3.130].

[47] *Grainger & Son v Gough (Surveyor of Taxes)* [1896] AC 325 at 334; *Partridge v Crittenden* [1968] 2 All ER 421; proposal likely to be considered an invitation, if it does not limit quantity, see: *Kelly v Caledonian Coal Co* (1898) 19 LR (NSW) 1.

[48] CUECIC explanatory note, [204], p 67.

[49] Rees and Calleja 'News Update—E-commerce—Offers You Can't Refuse' (2002) 3 IJECL & P Ecom 1.4 at 1; Thompson, 'Contracting over the Internet—Argos's Failure to Honour Internet Orders' (2000) 53 IJECL & P Ecom 1.1 at 1; *Chwee Kin Keong v Digilandmall.com Pte Ltd* [2004] SGHC 71; Chissick and Kelmann, n 42 above, 75.

[50] A/CN.9/WG.IV/WP.91, para 47.

[51] The 'non-interactive'/'interactive' division is also mentioned in the CUECIC preparatory works. See A/CN.9/WG.IV/WP.95, para 54. It was stated that websites containing interactive applications enable the

certain and complete. While websites, which do not have interactive capabilities and may require additional steps to contact the merchant, they may still be construed as offers if a contract can be formed exclusively on the basis of their contents. Similarly, the legal character of a website cannot depend on the number of addressees. If an offer is made to the public at large the offeror becomes liable to the person who accepts, not to everyone.[52] It is trite law that the unlimited number of addressees does not preclude a statement from being binding.[53]

Care must also be taken when drawing comparisons. Websites can be likened to virtual **6.22** shop displays, mail-order catalogues and to traditional advertising in mass media, which are routinely regarded as invitations.[54] Both advertisements and shop displays may, however, constitute offers if they are sufficiently certain to allow the inference of intention.[55] The fact that a website resembles an advertisement does not automatically preclude it from being binding. Moreover, websites can also be compared to vending machines, which are generally regarded as offers.[56] The resemblance to vending machines is particularly strong, whenever the delivery of a digital 'product' or service occurs directly on the website.[57] Whoever submits payment information or 'clicks' the appropriate button is provided with the service. If the transaction can be executed online in its entirety and the final choice whether to contract rests with the user, websites display more similarity to vending machines than to shopping displays. Provided the contents are certain and complete, the intention to be bound derives from the immediate ability to execute the transaction.[58]

In sum, the introduction of a presumption unnecessarily prejudices the analysis and con- **6.23** stitutes an alteration of well-established rules. The question is not whether websites are binding or whether they resemble other forms of expression. The question is whether the maker of a statement intended it to be binding. If the contents of a website are sufficiently certain and complete to evince an intention to be bound, the website constitutes an offer.

What are the contents of the offer?

Establishing the contents of an offer is part of two interrelated analyses: determining the **6.24** presence of a final intention to be bound and determining the contents of the future contract. As the promises of the parties must be certain and complete, the problem lies in establishing whether there is sufficient content to make a contract, ie whether the offer

---

immediate conclusion of a contract and may therefore be regarded as offers. It was not explained why the possibility to conclude a contract should predetermine the legal character of websites.

[52] *Carter on Contract,* § 03-020; *Carlill v Carbolic Smoke Ball Co* [1893] 1 QB 256 at 268.

[53] Carter, Peden and Tolhurst, *Contract Law in Australia* (5th edn, LexisNexis Butterworths, Sydney, 2007) 3-08, p 42.

[54] Furmston (ed), *The Law of Contract* (London, 1999) para 2.196.

[55] *Carlill v Carbolic Smoke Ball Co* [1893] 1 QB 256 at 262, see also *Lefkowitz v Great Minneapolis Surplus Store* 86 NW 2d 689 (Minn 1957); *Lexmead (Basingstoke) Ltd v Lewis* [1982] AC 225; see also Eisenberg, n 45 above, 1167, 1168, who criticizes the counter-intuitive nature of the construction rule that shop displays are invitations, as such rule cannot be based on the understanding of the reasonable addressee.

[56] *The Law of Contract,* para 2.199; *Thornton v Shoe Lane Parking Ltd* [1971] 2 QB 163; Atiyah, *An Introduction to the Law of Contract* (Oxford, 1995) 58.

[57] Endeshaw, 'Web Services and the Law: A Sketch of the Potential Issues' (2003) 11 IJT & IT 251.

[58] *The Law of Contract,* para 2.198.

itself or the exchanged communications are detailed enough to describe the obligations of the parties. In the event of transactions concluded on websites, the problem can be quite different: the interconnected nature of websites may create an overabundance of raw material from which the terms of the contract must be 'pieced together'. HTML enters the stage again, albeit this time a different technical aspect comes into play. Earlier, the problem was one of balancing objectivity with the fact that each manifestation of intention is processed on the addressee's side. The problem was one of potential discrepancies between the original expression on the server and its processed version on the client side. This time the focus is on another characteristic of the web environment: the distributed and interlinked nature of HTML files.

6.25   Logically, the first step in ascertaining the contents of an offer consists in identifying the relevant statements made by the alleged offeror. Both in the real world and online it must be determined, how much of what [the parties] have said or written has been caught up into the contract?[59] In online transactions, this question takes the form: which of the elements displayed on-screen during the formation process should become part of the traditional analysis? A contract emerges from the statements made during the contract formation process. A 'statement' can take the form of text, audio or graphical elements capable of conveying meaning. For all practical purposes, 'statement' is synonymous with 'manifestation of intention'. 'Statement' must be, however, distinguished from 'contents of the statement'. If the website is regarded as a 'statement', then it is logical to inquire about its contents. If the website is regarded as containing multiple statements from different sources (as is often the case), it is preferable to ask what statements were made on the website and examine the contents of each respective statement. The choice between the two questions depends on what is regarded as the basic unit of analysis: the website, the webpage, the screen, the browser window or the HTML file hosted on the web server. The problem is less prominent in the case of email or instant messengers, where information takes the form of discernible messages coming from one source. With this terminological (or technical?) difficulty in mind, one might ask the rhetorical question: should the discussion centre on websites or web pages?

6.26   Websites owe their interconnected nature to so-called hyperlinks (or 'links'). The latter are a mechanism of connecting two files or two parts of the same file. Any file placed on the web can be linked to without the need to request permission.[60] Hyperlinks are embedded within the text of the HTML file and consist of an address of another file, usually in the form of a uniform resource locator.[61] Upon activation, the hyperlink displays the contents

[59] Allan, 'The Scope of the Contract, Affirmations and Promises Made in the Course of Contract Negotiations' (1967) 41 ALJ 275.
[60] Berners-Lee, *Links and Law: Myths*, in *Axioms of Web Architecture*, p 1 of Internet version, available at www.ws.org/designissues/linkmyths.html; see also: Pope, 'Missing Link(s): Protecting Public Image and Corporate Profits in Cyberspace' (2001) 38 Hous L Rev 651 at 652; Gasparek, 'Applying the Fair Use Defense in Traditional Trademark Infringement and Dilution Cases to Internet Meta Tagging or Linking Cases' (1999) 7 Geo Mason L Rev 794; Sableman, 'Business on the Internet, Part II: Liability Issues' (1997) 53 J Mo B 223 at 224, 225.
[61] Schafer, *Web Standards Programmer's Reference: HTML, CSS, JavaScript, Perl, Python and PHP* (Wiley, Indianapolis, 2005) 4.

of the file, enabling a seamless transition from one page to another.[62] The new page may be displayed in the same window and replace the original web page, or open in a separate window, retaining the original page. Accordingly, hyperlinks may create confusion as to the scope and the source of a given statement. Not everything printed in a mail-order catalogue or prospectus becomes part of the contract. It is clear, however, where the document begins and where it ends. It is also clear who makes the statement. In web-based transactions, it may be difficult to establish which contents should be analysed in the first place. Although the concept of 'referencing' is not new, its application to interconnected HTML files encounters difficulties due to the manner of referencing, the sheer amount of material being referenced and the speed of transition between the cross-referenced material.[63] A real world analogy would be the process of discerning contractual contents from various documents, where all the documents cross-refer or are physically attached to each other.[64] The problem can be summarized in one question: when file A contains a hyperlink to file B, should they be read together?

A number of cases deal with the implications of hypertext for copyright, trademark infringe-   **6.27**
ment and unfair competition. Their common thread is the difficulty in determining the relationship between two or more hyperlinked web pages. 'When should A and B be read together?' is analysed from two perspectives: the maker of a statement and its addressee. In the first scenario, the question often takes the form of 'when is the person who linked from A to B liable for the contents of B'; in the second, 'when can a person be confused whether A and B come from the same source'.[65]

While web merchants cannot be held responsible for all content they link to[66] and while   **6.28**
hyperlinks only identify the location of specific content and are not the content themselves,[67] it is suggested that there may be little difference between directly posting content on a website and linking to such content.[68] Technically, the content linked to does not become part of the HTML file containing the link and does not involve its inclusion into the web page containing the link.[69] At the same time, although a hyperlink is only an address of the information, it 'has the functional capacity to bring the content of the linked web page to

---

[62] Sableman, 'Link Law Revisited: Internet Linking Law at Five Years' (2001) 16 Berkeley Tech LJ 1273 at 1276, 1277.

[63] Balloon, 'From Wax Seals to Hypertext: Electronic Signatures, Contract Formation, and a New Model for Consumer Protection in Internet Transactions' (2001) 50 Emory L J 905 at 915, 932.

[64] For an illustration of the difficulties of construing references see: *Riverwood International Australia Pty Ltd v McCormick* [2000] FCA 889, Treitel, 176, 191.

[65] See, eg, the first and most famous case regarding hyperlinking, *Shetland Times v Shetland News* 1997 S L T 669 (Sess Cas 1996), where the court recognized the potential for confusion as to the source of the statement.

[66] *DVD Copy Control Ass'n v McLaughlin* No 786804, 2000 WL 48512 (Cal Super Ct Santa Clara Cty 2000); see also *Bernstein v JC Penny Inc* 1998 US Dist Lexis 19048 (CD Cal Sept 29, 1998).

[67] Cavazos and Miles, 'Copyright on the WWW: Linking and Liability' (1997) 4 Rich J L & Tech 3.

[68] *Intellectual Reserve, Inc v Utah Lighthouse Ministry Inc* 75 F Supp 2d 1290 (D Utah 1999); *Universal Studios Inc v Reimerdes* 111 F Supp 2d 294 (SDNY 2000). See also MLEC, Art 5 *bis* ('Incorporation by Reference') and Comment 46-1, which imply that hyperlinking to information may have the same legal effect as providing the text in full in the data message.

[69] *Ticketmaster Corp v Tickets.com* 2000 WL 525390 (CD Cal).

the user's computer screen'.[70] A famous case stated that hyperlinks serve as a tool of transferring users from one webpage to another, analogous to a library card index but faster and more efficient.[71] This comparison, however, failed to appreciate the cognitive difficulties of differentiating between interconnected files given that hyperlinks often defy the very purpose of referencing—to convey the distinct origins of the referenced work.[72] It must be appreciated that hyperlinks may navigate the visitor to a completely different website, giving little or no warning that he has exited the first website. Users may view a picture of 'an item available for sale by clicking on a graphic image of the item. That item may be for sale at the current site or at another site.'[73] It may be unclear that a product is no longer displayed by the original site. The transfer can be imperceptible. The ease of transition between different websites may create confusion as to whose statements are displayed on-screen or what is the scope of a given statement. From the perspective of the addressee, the contents present on the computer screen appear as one unit or one statement made by the web merchant.

6.29 Although this characteristic of web-based transaction has passed under the radar of contract lawyers, the associated problems have been noticed by US and Australian regulators. The North American Securities and Exchange Commission stated that issuers may be liable for statements made by third parties on the basis of the design of their websites.[74] Hyperlinks may imply an association or adoption of the other document, so that two websites are regarded as forming part of the same document or that one incorporates the other by reference. In line with one theory, documents in close proximity on the same website menu or linked to each other are considered delivered together, as if they were in the same paper envelope.[75] Accordingly when a prospectus is posted on the website the envelope theory causes everything on the site to become part of that prospectus. Hyperlinks embedded within documents to be delivered under federal securities laws, cause the linked information to be part of a document.[76] Issuers must assume responsibility for the linked information 'as if it were part of the document'.[77]

6.30 Similarly, the Office of the Comptroller of the Currency introduced a rule designed to reduce the risk of customer confusion as to who is providing a particular product or service in those instances where banks share co-branded websites with third parties.[78] As 'access to the third party is through the bank's website, customers are likely to associate the bank with the third party'.[79] Banks are therefore required to take reasonable steps to clearly and conspicuously

---

[70] *Universal City Studios Inc v Corley*, 272 F 3d 429 (2nd Cir 2001); see also Lemley, 'Place and Cyberspace' (2003) 91 Cal L Rev 521 at 525.

[71] *Ticketmaster Corp v Tickets.com* 2000 WL 525390 1344 (CD Cal) at 1346.

[72] Burk, 'Proprietary Right in Hypertext Linkages' (1998) 2 JILT at 10.

[73] Nimmer and Towle, para 9.02.

[74] SEC Interpretation, *Use of Electronic Media*, SEC Release No 7856, 65 Fed. Reg 25843, available at www.sec.gov/rules/interp/34-42728.htm, 8 (Internet version).

[75] SEC Interpretation, 7.

[76] SEC Interpretation, 4.

[77] SEC Interpretation, 24.

[78] Office of the Comptroller of the Currency, OCC Bulletin 2001-31 on Weblinking, 12 CFR para 7.5002.

[79] OCC Bulletin 2001-31, 7.

distinguish between products and services offered by the bank and those offered by a third-party. 'Reasonable steps' depend upon the specific product and context, and include page formatting, the 'look and feel' of the website and other audio or visual clues.

Last but not least, the Australian Securities and Investment Commission's Policy Statement 107,[80] which deals with the preparation and distribution of electronic prospectuses, permits links from the prospectus to external documents only if no reasonable person is likely to confuse the linked document with the electronic prospectus. In the electronic environment, there is greater risk of confusion as to whether the information is of promotional character or part of the prospectus.[81] Issuers should not link from the electronic prospectus directly to promotional material. The latter must be published in a way that a reasonable person would be unlikely to confuse it with the prospectus,[82] eg by using separate files and including prominent statements in both documents indicating whether the information constitutes part of the prospectus. **6.31**

In light of the above examples it becomes apparent that there may be a difference between the questions: 'what statements were made?' and 'which of those statements are attributable to the other party?'. When a notice is displayed at the point of sale, legal analysis normally concerns its sufficiency or reasonableness for incorporation purposes. If its existence and sufficiency are not in question, no one will ask the question whether it was actually made by the other party. In the case of web-based transactions it may not be obvious who placed the notice as there may be confusion as to the source of the displayed information. An analogy would be a billboard advertising extended warranty periods in Marks & Spencer. Customers would logically assume that all announcements are made by Marks & Spencer and would not suspect that the billboards were secretly placed in the store by its competitor. Any analogy appears stretched and unlikely to occur, whereas problems of discerning the source of a statement online are quite common. Logically, a party should only be liable for its own statements made during the formation process. It appears, however, that a party can be held liable for statements made by others on the basis of a visual association created by a hyperlink. Accordingly, the analysis of ascertaining the contents of online contracts must be enriched with some additional steps. The traditional inquiry 'which statements become terms?' must be preceded with 'what statements were made' or, depending on the unit of analysis adopted, 'what were the contents of these statements?' as well as 'which statements are attributable to the other party?'. **6.32**

Is there acceptance?

Having established the existence of an offer, the next step is determining whether the offer has been accepted in accordance with its terms. Again, if a transaction is concluded online, the traditional analysis must include some novel, technology-related factors. This time, the focus is not on one, specific method of communication, but on the very fact that the contracting parties can choose between an unprecedented number of **6.33**

---

[80] ASIC Policy Statement 107 (PS 107) issued 18/9/1996, updated 10/2/2000.
[81] PS 107.85.
[82] PS 107.86.

communication channels. The basic rule remains the same: an offer may stipulate that acceptance be communicated by a particular method.[83] Absent explicit instructions, the circumstances of the offer may indicate what method should be used.[84] Situations where acceptance is communicated via the prescribed method and where both offer and acceptance are communicated in the same manner lend themselves to straightforward analyses. Complications arise where: (a) the offeree accepts via a method that is different from that requested by the offeror ('alternative acceptance'); and (b) the offer is silent and acceptance is communicated via a different method than the offer. Two questions arise: (i) are alternative acceptances legally effective; and (ii) when can acceptance be communicated by electronic means?

6.34 The above questions acquire additional complexity in the changed communication landscape. When the leading cases were decided the methods of communication were few: addresses and numbers were tied to specific devices or locations; letters, telegrams or telexes were delivered to an office or home address. Nowadays, contracting parties are exposed to many different channels and methods of communication. The average person has several communication terminals, such as mobile phones, fax machines, desktop and laptop computers, as well as several addresses, both physical and electronic. Electronic addresses are not tied to specific devices or locations. Emails may be received on mobile phones, voice calls can be terminated on computers. It must be remembered that the legal effect of an act done in response to an offer depends on the construction of the offer. The Internet does not change anything in this regard, but introduces new elements into the discussion. The offeree's convenience must be weighed against transactional security and any potential prejudice to the offeror. It can be assumed that the latter chooses the method of acceptance based on the required immediacy of response and the preferred format. Two situations must be analysed: first, the offer prescribes the method of acceptance; second, the offer is silent.

Offer prescribes the method of acceptance

6.35 The offeror may request any method of acceptance and demand compliance.[85] If the offeror insisted on a particular method, 'a purported acceptance in any other manner is not an acceptance'.[86] A popular view, however, is that where an alternative method is as timely and not less disadvantageous to the offeror, that method will suffice.[87] Accordingly, even when the method is prescribed, the offeree may use a different method, which is 'just as good'.[88] It is claimed that in order to preclude other methods, the requested method must be indicated as exclusive.[89] Only in the latter instance can alternative acceptances be regarded as

---

[83] *Manchester Diocesan Council for Education v Commercial and General Investments Ltd* [1970] 1 WLR 241 at 245.

[84] *The Law of Contract*, para 2.226.

[85] *Manchester Diocesan Council for Education v Commercial and General Investments Ltd* [1970] 1 WLR 241 at 245.

[86] Carter, Peden & Tolhurst, 3-28.

[87] Christensen, 'Formation of Contracts by Email—Is it Just the Same as the Post?' (2001) QUT LJJ at 29; Willmot, Christensen and Butler, *Contract Law* (2nd edn, Melbourne, 2005), 3.435, see n 46 above; *Tinn v Hoffman & Co* (1873) 29 LT 271.

[88] *The Law of Contract*, para 2.226.

[89] Carter, Peden & Tolhurst, 3-28.

ineffective.[90] The problem is discussed mainly in relation to option contracts, where the exercise of the option did not comply with the prescribed method.[91] The question is: how should the offer be interpreted? Is a precise observance of the method of acceptance necessary? Is an indication of exclusivity required to preclude the effectiveness of alternative acceptances?[92] When dealing with these issues it must be remembered that the effectiveness of alternative acceptances concerns the very existence of a contract. Accordingly, the admissibility of alternative acceptances is more than a theoretical exercise. The problem can be analysed from two angles.

From a practical perspective, account must be taken of the multiplicity of electronic **6.36** addresses, accounts, telephone numbers and devices by which a person can be reached. The speed of a given communication method is, by itself, not determinative. Convenience, cost and accessibility must also be taken into account. If it were speed alone, the offeror would request acceptance by phone. Arguments to the effect that offerees can protect themselves against revocation by reverting to faster methods of communication are therefore inherently flawed.[93] It is also proposed that a request for a reply 'by return' post should be interpreted as indicating the need for a 'prompt reply rather than as stipulating that acceptance must be by letter and no other means'.[94] This argument holds true if the acceptance arrives no later than a letter would normally reach its destination. It does not hold true if the acceptance is sent via a method that is equally fast but arrives at a device or location which are not easily accessible by the addressee.[95]

Regarding 'more advantageous' methods, the prescribed method is the most advantageous. **6.37** There can be nothing more advantageous than what the offeror requested. The offeror prescribes a particular method of acceptance in order to monitor only one communication channel, address or device.[96] The liberal view disregards the fact, that the offeror's request may be based on a willingness to accept the risks inherent in a given method.[97] Even if electronic methods are fast they are often less reliable. Certain methods also imply the use of a particular format and may be stipulated for evidentiary purposes.[98] Taking into account that the offeror knows his communication status at the stipulated time of acceptance, prescribing a specific method may be the only means of ensuring actual communication.

---

[90] *The Law of Contract*, para 2.226.

[91] *White Trucks Pty Ltd v Riley* (1948) 66 WN (NSW) 101; *Yates Building Co Ltd v R J Pulleyn & Sons (York) Ltd* (1975) 119 Sol Jo 370; *Mobil Australia Ltd v Kosta* (1969) 14 FLR 343; *Spectra Pty Ltd v Pindari Pty Ltd* [1974] 2 NSWLR 617 *Mannai Investment Co Ltd v Eagle Star Life Assurance Co Ltd* [1997] AC 749.

[92] Cheshire, Fifoot and Furmston, 134.

[93] Eisler, 'Default Rules For Contract Formation by Promise and the Need for Revision of the Mailbox Rule' (1990/1991) 79 Ky LJ 557 at 567.

[94] Carter, Peden and Tolhurst, para 3-28.

[95] *Eliason v Henshaw* (1819) 4 Wheaton 225, offeror requested acceptance by wagon, which brought the offer. Offeree thinking the post would be speedier, accepted by mail. He was wrong. No contract was formed. See also: *Frank v Knight* (1937) OQPD 113.

[96] See Treitel, 31, who states that the offeror prescribes the method of acceptance with a particular object in view.

[97] Evans, 'The Anglo-American Mailing Rule: Some Problems of Offer and Acceptance in Contracts by Correspondence' (1966) 15 ICLQ 553 at 560, see also *Financings Ltd v Stimson* [1962] 1 WLR 1184 at 1186, offeror not bound by oral acceptance if acceptance in writing was requested.

[98] *The Law of Contract*, para 2.226, citing *Walker v Glass* [1979] NI 129.

To illustrate the point: anticipating that his mobile phone will be out of range, the offeror requests acceptance by fax, which guarantees delivery to the office and immediate attention. Ultimately, the motives for the request are irrelevant. A liberal approach was easy to maintain in cases like *George Hudson Holdings Ltd v Rudder*,[99] where the personal delivery of the letter occurred to the same address as indicated in the request for a mailed acceptance. The effectiveness of the acceptance would have been questionable had it been delivered to a branch office or broadcast on the radio.

6.38   From a theoretical perspective, two arguments can be raised against the permissibility of alternative acceptances. First, the offeror is entitled to insist that he is not bound unless acceptance is communicated in the requested manner.[100] It is argued that as the instruction is for the offeror's benefit, he may waive it and recognize another method by making no objection to a non-complying acceptance.[101] Unquestionably, the offeror may waive the right to insist on the stipulated method. The offeror may also decide not to. The existence of the contract is left to his discretion: the legal effect of the act purporting to be 'acceptance' is conditional on its (explicit or implied) recognition by the offeror. Second, if acceptance occurs otherwise than by prescribed method, the offer is 'never accepted in accordance with its terms'.[102] The method can be regarded as part of the offer and acceptance should mirror the offer unconditionally.[103] An 'alternative acceptance' can therefore be regarded as a counter-offer, which is then accepted by the original offeror.[104] Again, acceptance of the counter-offer is left to the discretion of the original offeror. Offerors may be estopped from denying formation or their insistence on the prescribed method may be regarded as unreasonable. Both the 'waiver' and the 'counter-offer' approach encourage speculation at the expense of the offeree. If offerors can prescribe any sign to constitute acceptance or request acceptance within a specified time, it must be assumed that they can also request— and insist on—a specific method of acceptance. Prescribing the method can be regarded as a way of stipulating the time and the sign. The request for the offer to be accepted within a specified time is interpreted strictly. The prescribed method should be treated identically. Acceptance must be expressed in accordance with the offeror's request: a notice delivered on pink paper is not effective if it was to be delivered on blue paper.[105] After all, the offeror may have trouble reading text from specific background colours.

6.39   In light of the above, it appears that a liberal approach provides no transactional security to either the offeree or the offeror. Instead of leaving effectiveness to the offeror's discretion, be it in the form of waiver, acceptance of counter-offer or making acceptance conditional

---

[99] (1973) 128 CLR 387 at 392, 395.

[100] *Manchester Diocesan Council for Education v Commercial and General Investments Ltd* [1970] 1 WLR 241 at 246.

[101] Cheshire and Fifoot, para 3.42; Treitel, 31.

[102] *Manchester Diocesan Council for Education v Commercial and General Investments Ltd* [1970] 1 WLR 241 at 245; see also: *United Dominion Trust (Commercial) Ltd v Eagle Aircraft Services* [1968] 1 All ER 104 per Lord Denning at 107; *Phillips Fox (A Firm) v Westgold Resources NL & Ors* [2000] WASCA 85.

[103] *Carter on Contract*, § 03-220.

[104] *Gilbert J McCaul (Aust) Pty Ltd v Pitt Club Ltd* [1959] SR (NSW) 122; *Duncan Properties Pty Ltd v Hunter* [1991] 1 Qd R 101.

[105] *Mannai Investment Co Ltd v Eagle Star Life Assurance Co Ltd* [1997] AC 749 at 329–30.

upon coming to his actual attention, alternative acceptances should be regarded as ineffective from the outset. Otherwise, one is left to a post factum evaluation whether the offeror's insistence on a particular method or the exercise of his discretion were reasonable and whether the chosen method caused prejudice to the offeror. A liberal approach also forces the offeror to monitor all communication devices and addresses—even those which are not held out for contracting purposes. Given the multiplicity of novel methods of communication, alternative acceptances should be ineffective.[106] The offeror is entitled to recognize solely those acceptances which are communicated via the requested method.

Offer does not prescribe method of acceptance

Where the method is not prescribed, 'acceptance can be given by the same or an equally expedient method'[107] as adopted for the offer. Acceptance sent by ordinary post was held ineffective where the offer was made by telegram, as the use of telegram was an indication that a prompt reply was expected.[108] Absent instructions, the method must be 'reasonable'.[109] It is safest to accept via the same method as used by the offeror.[110] The practical questions are: How far can the offeree depart from the offer? When is it reasonable to accept by electronic means? Where an offer is made electronically and no form of acceptance is specified, acceptance must generally be by electronic means.[111] If, however, the offer is not made electronically, it can be doubted whether email or an instant message can be regarded as reasonable.[112] The issue is part of a larger problem: when can it be assumed that the other party agreed to communicate by electronic means?[113] Absent prior dealings, responding to an offer made by traditional means with an electronic 'acceptance' raises objections. Everything depends on the terms of the offer and the communication information (such as address, telephone number) provided by the offeror. If the offeror desires actual communication then any method requiring additional steps, such as retrieval from a mailbox or mail-server, is undesirable. Unless specifically instructed or where prior communications originated in electronic form, the choice of an electronic method of communication cannot be regarded as reasonable. If the method of acceptance is prescribed, alternative acceptances should be ineffective. If the method of acceptance is not prescribed, the use of electronic methods of communication may not always be perceived as reasonable, especially if the offer was expressed by traditional means. The increasing complexity of the communication landscape dictates a strict approach to the manner chosen to communicate acceptance.

6.40

---

[106] Willmot, Christensen and Butler, para 3.435.

[107] Christensen, n 88 above, 29.

[108] *Quenerduaine v Cole* (1883) 32 WR 185.

[109] See also Restatement (2d) Contracts § 65; *Polhamus v Roberts* 175 P 2d 196 (NM 1946), holding that authorized methods of acceptance are determined by what can reasonably be expected by the contracting parties; *Farley v Champs Fine Foods Inc* 404 NW 2d 493 (ND 1987), holding that any 'reasonable and usual' mode of acceptance may be used where the mode of acceptance is not specified by the offeror.

[110] *Hayne v Cook* 109 NW 2d 188 (Iowa 1961); Williston, *A Treatise on the Law of Contracts* (4th edn, New York, 1991), para 6.35.

[111] D Campbell (ed), *Law of International On-Line Business, A Global Perspective* (London, 1998), 78.

[112] Fasciano, 'Internet Electronic Mail: A Last Bastion for the Mailbox Rule' (1997) 25 Hofstra L Rev 971 at 995.

[113] The problem is particularly prominent in the UETA, which does not apply unless the parties have agreed to transact by electronic means; see UETA, § 5.

The time of contract formation

6.41 Establishing the time of formation in online contracts must be split into two independent analyses. First, it must be determined whether an acceptance communicated via one of the Internet-based methods of communication becomes effective upon dispatch or upon receipt. Second, it must be established when exactly dispatch and receipt are deemed to occur. At first glance, such division may appear surprising as problems of contract formation are rarely, if ever, examined at this level of detail. As will be explained below, the separation of effectiveness from dispatch and receipt is dictated by the unprecedented complexity of the communication infrastructure on the one hand, and the vague formulation of the existing principles on the other. In other words, the traditional rules—which developed around letters and telexes—are difficult to transpose onto emails and instant messengers.

Effectiveness of acceptance

6.42 A contract is formed when an acceptance becomes effective.[114] In principle, effectiveness is tied to receipt. In exceptional circumstances, effectiveness is associated with the moment of dispatch. The exception is commonly referred to as the postal acceptance or mailbox rule. The moment of effectiveness depends on the intention of the parties. Absent a clear and definite indication of such intention, it may be unclear what factors should be taken into account when choosing between the principle and the exception. While this 'dormant' uncertainty hardly causes any problems in scenarios where parties communicate by traditional means, once contracts are formed online, the problem re-emerges: should acceptances communicated online be governed by the principle or by the exception? To date, legal literature persistently focused on the alleged 'instantaneousness' of modern means of communication, devoting little, if any, attention to other factors that might be taken into account. Once a given method is considered instantaneous, the application of the principle is taken for granted. Moreover, the focus seems to be mainly on email, the problem usually being formulated as 'does the postal acceptance rule apply to email?'.[115] Moreover, despite their aspirations to introduce certainty into the electronic contracting process, neither the MLEC nor the CUECIC contain substantive rules governing the time of formation. Instead they focus on defining 'dispatch' and 'receipt'—not on whether acceptances become effective on dispatch or receipt.

6.43 When the existing rules were conceptualized, the methods of communicating at a distance were few. Apart from personal delivery or the use of agents, the post was the only viable means of conveying acceptance. Distance always implied a delay between dispatch and receipt of the letter. At present, distance is no longer synonymous with delay. Novel methods of communication can reduce the interval between dispatch and receipt to the point of

---

[114] Carter, Peden and Tolhurst, para 3-26, p 58.

[115] Eg Samek, 'A Reassessment of the Present Rule Relating to Postal Acceptance' (1961) 35 ALJ 38 at 40; Watnick, 'The Electronic Formation of Contracts and the Common Law "Mailbox Rule"' (2004) 56 Baylor L; Davies, 'Contract Formation on the Internet, Shattering a Few Myths', in Edwards and Waelde (eds), *Law and the Internet* (Oxford, 2000), 106; Hill, 'Flogging A Dead Horse—The Postal Acceptance Rule and Email' (2001) 17 JCL 2 at 14 Rev 175 at 200.

non-existence. This lack, or brevity, of delay is often accompanied by a high risk of non-delivery. Neither the principle, nor the exception, address such scenario. The judges in the leading cases, *Entores Ltd v Miles Far East Corporation*[116] (*'Entores'*) and *Brinkibon v Stahag und Stahlwarenhandelsgesellschaft mbH*[117] (*'Brinkibon'*) did not anticipate that their reasoning would form the basis for evaluating the potential expansion of the exception to email, instant messengers and web-applications. Although these cases are cited in practically all discussions relating to the time of formation, it is often forgotten that they do not establish an absolute rule.[118] In his famous speech, Lord Wilberforce stated that cases must be resolved 'by reference to the intention of the parties, by sound business practice and ... by a judgment where the risks should lie'.[119]

Before proceeding, two general observations come to mind. First, the principle of receipt **6.44** derives from face-to-face dealings. A principle that originated from a perfect communication scenario cannot be automatically applied to govern scenarios, which are 'less perfect'. Second, one might expect that in light of the novel communication possibilities, the postal acceptance rule should be facing its demise. If the exception developed specifically around the post,[120] why even consider its application online? Upon closer examination, it turns out that the exception may be facing its revival in relation to some novel methods of communication. It cannot be discarded solely on the ground that everything on the Internet 'happens fast'. The simplistic (yet predominant) view that the postal acceptance rule relates to non-instantaneous methods of communication disregards the historical background of the rule and provides no guidance as to its potential application. The following discussion identifies some common mistakes in existing approaches while at the same time attempting to find the criteria for applying the principle or the exception.

One would intuitively assume that the choice between the principle and the exception **6.45** depends on the devices used by the parties. Upon closer examination, however, it becomes clear that devices cannot form a decisive criterion. This is so despite the traditional equation between conversations over the telephone and face-to-face dealings and the multiple references to telex in both *Entores* and *Brinkibon*. First, one communication process can combine multiple devices: a message may originate on the phone and terminate on a fax machine. The originating device may differ from the terminating device.[121] Given a wide range of possible combinations, it would always be debatable whether it is the originating or the terminating device that is decisive. Second, due to a growing trend for convergence, a single device can combine multiple functionalities, blurring the distinctions between

---

[116] [1955] 2 QB 327.

[117] [1983] 2 AC 34.

[118] *Brinkibon v Stahag und Stahlwarenhandelsgesellschaft mbH* [1983] 2 AC 34 at 42; see also Coote, 'The Instantaneous Transmission of Acceptances' (1971) 4 NZULR 331.

[119] *Brinkibon v Stahag und Stahlwarenhandelsgesellschaft mbH* [1983] 2 AC 34 at 42.

[120] Goodrich, 'The Posthumous Life of the Postal Acceptance Rule' (2005) Benjamin N Cardozo School of Law, WP No 127, p 8.

[121] See *Express Airways v Port Augusta Air Services* [1980] QdR 543, where the acceptance was sent by telegram to the Post Office and then via telex to the offeror; Douglas J held, without a detailed explanation, that acceptance was effective on receipt; see also *Leach Nominees Pty Ltd v Walter Wright Pty Ltd* [1986] WAR 244 at 431 for explanation of possible combinations of telex, telegram and telephone.

individual devices. Given that most mobile phones carry the computing power of early computers it may be unclear whether a particular device should be classified as a phone or a computer. Furthermore, telephone calls can originate on computers and terminate on fixed or mobile phones, email and instant messengers can be sent and received from mobile phones. The choice between the exception of the principle cannot be based on the device as in many instances one would not be able to clearly define the device itself. Alternatively, one would have to prescribe technical criteria when a device is to be treated like a phone and when it is to be regarded as a computer. This argument can also be extended to specific methods of communication, such as emails or short message services. If an email is sent via a mobile phone, are we dealing with communication via email or communication by telephone? If an SMS is send from a web-interface to a mobile phone, are we dealing with communications via SMS, telephone or on the web?

6.46 The most prominent criterion for the application of the principle is 'instantaneousness'. The term is used with little precision.[122] 'Instantaneous' means 'occurring with no delay'[123] or 'done or completed in an instant'.[124] 'Delay' and 'instantaneousness' are different sides of the same coin: if something is instantaneous there is, logically, no delay. Qualifiers like 'virtually', 'almost' or 'more or less' permit the existence of some delay. How much delay is tolerable for something to remain instantaneous? Premising the exception exclusively on the length of delay necessitates a gradation: if the delay is longer than 'x' (seconds/minutes?) acceptance is effective on dispatch, otherwise acceptance is effective on receipt. Arguments built around 'instantaneousness' lead into a blind alley as they tie the time of contract formation to a factor that is difficult to quantify and often unpredictable. Despite its saliency, it is also unclear what instantaneousness refers to—the method of communication or the communication process itself. This confusion is also reflected in *Brinkibon* and *Entores*, where the term is used alternatively in reference to the communication process and to the devices used by the parties.[125]

6.47 A popular example used in legal analyses of the postal acceptance rule is email. It is claimed that because email is instantaneous it must be subsumed under the principle. The email example is particularly useful in illustrating the difficulty of using the method of communication and/or the speed of transmission as decisive criteria in choosing between the principle and the exception. Technically, email is an asynchronous, non-real-time, delayed access, store-and-forward method of communication.[126] Email systems comprise

---

[122] Norman, The ASB Home Page: *Alabama Lawyers Go On-Line for a Wealth of Information* (1996) 57 Ala Law 328; *Entores Ltd v Miles Far East Corporation* [1955] 2 QB 327 at 337; Burnstein, 'Note, Conflicts on the Net: Choice of Law in Transnational Cyberspace' (1996) 29 Vand J Transnat'l L 79; *Entores Ltd v Miles Far East Corporation* [1955] 2 QB 327 at 328; Counts and Martin, 'Libel in Cyberspace: A Framework for Addressing Liability and Jurisdictional Issues in This New Frontier' (1996) 59 Alb L Rev 1083 at 1086; *Carter on Contract*, §§ 03-360 and 03-390.

[123] WordNet ® 2.0 (Princeton University, 2003).

[124] Macquarie Online Dictionary (2003).

[125] See: *Entores Ltd v Miles Far East Corporation* [1955] 2 QB 327 at 327 per Lord Denning; *Brinkibon v Stahag und Stahlwarenhandelsgesellschaft mbH* [1983] 2 AC 34 at 41, 42 per Lord Wilberforce.

[126] See also Wright and Winn, *The Law of Electronic Commerce* (Gaithersburg, 1999), para 2.02; Terret and Monaghan, 'The Internet—An Introduction For Lawyers', in Edwards and Waelde (eds), *Law and the Internet* (Oxford, 2000) 25; Crocker, RFC 5598, *Internet Mail Architecture* (2009) 34: 'Basic email transfer

mail-clients, which are the originators and final destinations for messages, and mail-servers, which relay messages along the transmission path. The protocol underlying email, SMTP, is characterized by intermediate storage, message queuing, delays, retransmission and delivery attempts.[127] The transmission between intermediating mail-servers may be very fast or 'almost instantaneous'. There is, however, no instantaneous transmission between the originating and the destination mail-clients: messages do not travel instantaneously from the computer of the sender to the computer of the addressee.[128] Instantaneity can only refer to the speed of transmission between some of the relaying mail-servers. Moreover, incoming messages must be requested and retrieved by mail-clients from mail-servers.[129] This last step resembles the interval between placing the letter in the addressee's mailbox and its subsequent retrieval.[130] Even with always-on broadband connections, retrieval occurs periodically: there is no permanent, open session between the mail-client and the incoming mail-server resulting in the immediate display of new messages.[131] In light of the above, it appears technically incorrect to call email instantaneous—at least with regards to communication.

If email is not instantaneous, one is tempted to subsume it under the exception. Before set- **6.48** tling on this conclusion, however, it must be determined whether email sufficiently resembles the post.[132] After all, it is the characteristics of postal communications that gave rise to the exception. At first glance, email and postal communications are structurally similar in the sequence of events: dispatch, transmission, intermediate storage and retrieval. Both are characterized by delayed access: an interval between the receipt of the message (end of transmission), and its retrieval (notification).[133] Both require the performance of an additional step to read the message or letter. The difference between them, however, lies not in the transmission speed but in their reliability. The latter is a function of the risks inherent in the communication method and the ability to manage those risks. In postal communications, the risk of receipt is placed on the addressee as the risk is minimal.[134] Does this allocation

---

is accomplished with an asynchronous store-and-forward communication infrastructure, in a sequence of independent transmission through some number of MTSs.'

[127] J Klensin (ed), RFC 2821, *Simple Mail Transfer Protocol* (2001) 5, 10, 57.

[128] Messages can travel from the sender's mail-server to the addressee's mail-server if they are in the same transport service environment, which is not the case if the parties communicate over an open electronic network; see RFC 2821, 6.

[129] The purpose of this discussion is not establishing *when* receipt occurred but *whether* email is instantaneous.

[130] See Kiat, *Paperless International Trade: The Law of Telematic Data Exchange* (Butterworths Asia, Singapore, 1992) 51.

[131] Commentators claiming that email is instantaneous may have been misled by the speed of intra-company communications, when messages are transmitted within the same LAN. See Fasciano, n 63 above, 1001. Technologies like blackberry or so-called push-email, enable the 'pushing' of messages to the terminating device. They rely on the classic architecture but interpose an additional server between the incoming mail-server and the end-user. The message is pushed to the terminating device because the addressee previously configured a server or device to do so.

[132] Cheshire and Fifoot, para 3.44, who state that electronic communications have some parallels with old-fashioned letters: 'perhaps the postal rule will have a renaissance'; see also: Christensen, n 88 above, who describes email as an 'electronic version of the postal system'.

[133] Hill, n 45 above, at 21.

[134] As was said by Lord Esher MR in *Kemp v Wanklyn* (1894) 1 QB 583, at p 585: 'The Post Office is the authority which, under its statutory powers, determines the ordinary course of the post—that is to say, how

remain justified if the risk increases? The number of reasons precluding an email from reaching the intended mail-server by far exceeds the number of reasons that might preclude a letter from reaching its destination mailbox.[135] While transmission speeds are on the increase, the reliability of email is decreasing.[136] Whereas the principle of receipt is not designed to allocate risks, the exception was conceived to deal with situations where due to the reliability of the post those risks were minimal. Effectiveness on dispatch is fair to the offeror (addressee) if the method is reliable. It seems less fair to the offeror if the likelihood of receipt decreases. Effectiveness on receipt combined with unreliability is not fair to the offeree (sender). The only way to protect the latter is to require offerors to acknowledge receipt or notify of communication failures. This, however, leads to the very situation the exception was designed to avoid: circular communications.[137] Subsuming email under the postal acceptance rule may lead to disastrous results.

6.49 The principle of receipt can only be debated when the communication process displays the same characteristics as face-to-face dealings. The latter ensure instantaneous communication: the manifestation of acceptance by the offeree is concurrent with its notification to the offeror. There is no delay between 'dispatch and receipt' and between 'receipt and notification'. The communication process is interactive: bi-directional, synchronous, imparting not only immediate knowledge of receipt but also ensuring a communication process without the dependencies inherent in dealings at a distance.[138] Are email communications sufficiently similar to face-to-face dealings to apply the principle? After all, if both parties attend their computers and regularly poll their mail-servers for new messages, they can exchange messages 'as if' they were having a conversation.

6.50 To answer the above question, the difference between 'transmission' and 'communication' as well as the two-way nature of face-to-face dealings must be included in the discussion. It must be remembered that 'communication' can be tied to a number of events. The term, by itself, does not indicate the specific moment that concludes the formation process.[139] Its definition depends on how far one departs from the classic 'meeting of minds' and how

---

the letters shall be carried, and at what time they shall, as a general rule, be delivered within any particular district to the persons taken as a body who reside in that district.' See also *Bowman v Durham Holdings Pty Ltd* (1973) 131 CLR 8 at 13.

[135] For a detailed description of what can go wrong see: RFC 3463, G Vaudreuil, 'Enhanced Mail System Status Codes' (2003).

[136] Moors, *Email Dependability* (School of Electrical Engineering and Telecom, University of New South Wales, Australia, available at www.mm-tools.be/MASTER/agents/ego/cox/images/upload/emw_moors. pdf); Martin, 'The Time Has Come to Ditch Email', *The Register*, SecurityFocus Published 1 June 2006: '[E]mail is a terrible mess. It's dangerous, insecure, unreliable, mostly unwanted and out-of-control' available at www.theregister.co.uk/2006/06/01/ditch_email/print.html; Dunn, 'Yahoo accused of poor email service Tests find half its servers are shut down', *Techworld* 13 April 2006, available at www.techworld.com.

[137] Christensen, n 88 above, 30.

[138] 'In a two-way communication, one party can determine readily whether the other party is aware of the first party's communication, through immediate verbal response or, when the communication is face-to-face, there are nonverbal cues. When the communication is not instantaneous and is not face-to-face, there is much greater uncertainty as to whether the other party is aware of a particular transaction.' Baum and Perritt, *Electronic Contracting, Publishing and EDI Law* (New York, 1991) 321.

[139] See Winfield, 'Some Aspects of Offer and Acceptance' (1939) 55 LQR 499 at 506 for a review of different systems of determining the moment of formation.

much focus is placed on the objective theory of contract. On the one hand, agreement is reached when the offeror knows that the offer has been accepted.[140] On the other, acceptance must be tied to an objectively ascertainable event.[141] Given that 'communication' refers to the process of conveying information as well as to the act of transmitting information by telephone, radio, etc[142] the term can denote both notification and transmission. The term 'receipt' can be regarded as equally ambiguous—it can imply knowledge (bringing the fact of acceptance to the offeror's mind)[143] or the end of transmission (arrival at a machine).[144]

Interactions over the phone are treated like face-to-face dealings,[145] but only when both parties simultaneously use the device. When messages are left on answering machines, the communication process no longer approximates the quality of face-to-face dealings.[146] Communication is delayed due to the very fact that the other party is not present and accesses the message later.[147] According to Coote, the mere use of an instantaneous mode of transmission is never decisive by itself. It must be established whether the parties are also placed in instantaneous communication with each other.[148] Devices, which provide instantaneous transmission may not necessarily provide instantaneous communication. It must be remembered that each communication device can be used in multiple ways. Devices that operate automatically (like telex) can be attended by both parties and render the communication process similar to face-to-face dealings. Devices like the telephone, which—by definition—presuppose the simultaneous presence of both parties, may also be used in a way that delays communication, eg when messages are left on the answering machine. Leaving aside the difference between transmission and communication, the above discussion also highlights the difficulties in deciding what 'instantaneousness' should relate to: the method (or device?) of communication or the communication process itself. Coote's argument implies that various devices can bring about instantaneous communication but the device itself should not be regarded as the premise of instantaneousness. It is the actual communication that must be instantaneous. Everything depends on how a device is used in a given scenario.

6.51

---

[140] *Carter on Contract*, § 03-310; Goodrich, 'Habermas and the Postal Rule' (1996) 17 Cardozo L Rev 1457 at 1463.

[141] *Brinkibon v Stahag und Stahlwarenhandelsgesellschaft mbH* [1983] 2 AC 34 at 42; *Entores Ltd v Miles Far East Corporation* [1955] 2 QB 327 at 331; *Schelde Delta Shipping BV v Astarte Shipping Ltd (The Pamela)* [1995] 2 Lloyd's Rep 249; *Tenax Steamship Co Ltd v The Brimnes (Owners)* [1975] QB 929; *Anson v Trump* [1998] 1 WLR 1404; *Carter on Contract*, § 03-310; it is unclear whether 'actual communication' requires that acceptance is brought to the offeror's mind, see *Bressan v Squires* [1974] 2 NSWLR 460, at 461.

[142] Macquarie Online Dictionary (2003).

[143] *Holwell Securities Ltd v Hughes* [1974] 1 All ER 161 at 164; *Carlill v Carbolic Smoke Ball Co* [1893] 1 QB 256, at 256, 269; *Tallerman & Co Pty Ltd v Nathan's Merchandise (Victoria) Pty Ltd* (1957) 98 CLR 93; *Tenax Steamship Co Ltd v The Brimnes (Owners)* [1975] QB 929 at 970.

[144] *Schelde Delta Shipping BV v Astarte Shipping Ltd (The Pamela)* [1995] 2 Lloyd's Rep 249; *Tenax Steamship Co Ltd v The Brimnes (Owners)* [1975] QB 929.

[145] *Aviet v Smith & Searle Pty Ltd* (1956) 73 WN (NSW) 274; *Express Airways v Port Augusta Air Services* [1980] Qd R 543; *W A Dewhurst & Co Pty Ltd v Cawrse* [1960] VR 278.

[146] Thomsen and Wheble, *Trading with EDI, The Legal Issues* (IBC Financial Books, London, 1989), 133.

[147] Nimmer, 'Electronic Contracting: Legal Issues' (1996) 14 J Marshall J Computer & Info L 211 at 223, who implies that delayed access prevents the application of the face-to-face analogy.

[148] Coote, n 119 above, 342.

6.52 Face-to-face dealings are also characterized by their two-way nature. This is reflected in the Restatement (2d) Contracts: '[a]cceptance given by telephone or other medium of substantially instantaneous two-way communication is governed by the principles applicable to acceptances where the parties are in the presence of each other'.[149] 'Substantial instantaneousness' requires transmission without any substantial lapse of time,[150] 'two-way', an interaction among the parties, so that 'ambiguities and misunderstandings, if perceived, can be cleared up on the spot'.[151] Instantaneity is therefore only one of two essential characteristics of face-to-face dealings. The Restatement applies the receipt rule whenever the medium of communication is instantaneous and bi-directional, the postal exception— where communication is time-delayed and unidirectional.[152]

6.53 Technically, email is a one-way method of communication. The two-way characteristic can be 're-created' only if both parties attend their computers, regularly poll their mail-servers and automatically and immediately generate confirmations of receipt. The generation of such notifications, however, presupposes certain technical capabilities of the addressee's system. The re-creation of the two-way quality may therefore not be possible. The difficulty in treating email communications at par with face-to-face dealings becomes even more apparent when email is compared to interactions via instant messengers (IMs). In principle, dealings via IM occur in real time as both parties must be online to exchange messages. Messages are typed and immediately appear on the screen, becoming visible to both parties at the same time.[153] Dispatch and receipt are simultaneous, communication is instantaneous. Both parties monitor the communication process in real time: if a message cannot be delivered, there is an immediate notification to that effect or the message does not appear on the screen. The communication process is interactive, instantaneous and two-way.[154] Moreover, virtually all IM applications display so-called presence indicators, which show whether a person is online, offline, does not want to be disturbed etc.[155] Despite the technical differences between email and IM, either method can be used in ways resembling the other: email can be used to exchange messages in real time, when both parties attend their computers, IM can be used for delayed communications when senders type messages for later delivery. As a general rule, instant messaging applications provide instantaneous two-way communication, whereas email is one-way and its instantaneous

---

[149] Restatement (2d) Contracts § 64.

[150] Restatement (2d) Contracts § 64 comment *a*; see also Nimmer, n 149 above, 222.

[151] Restatement (2d) Contracts § 64 comment *b*.

[152] Waddams, *The Law of Contracts* (3rd edn, 1993) 73, 74; Macchione, 'Overview of the Law of Commercial Transactions and Information Exchanges in Cyberspace—Canadian Common Law and Civil Law Perspectives' (1996) 13 CIPR 129 at 133,134; see also *Vocabulary of Terms for Broadband Aspects of ISDN*, ITU-T Recommendation I.113 (06/97) which distinguishes between conversational services and messaging services. The former are characterized by a bi-directional exchange by means of real-time (no store-and-forward) information transfer, whereas the latter offer communication via storage units with store-and-forward message handling.

[153] Differences of micro-seconds are disregarded.

[154] Morrison, 'Instant Messaging for Business: Legal Complications in Communication' (2004) 24 J L & Com 141 at 142, 143; see also Nimmer, n 149 above, 222.

[155] See generally: RFC 2778, Day, Rosenberg and Sugano, *A Model for Presence and Instant Messaging* (2000).

character depends on a number of variables, including the actual presence of both parties and the configuration of their mail-servers.

In light of the above, it becomes clear that arguments built around 'instantaneousness' **6.54** doom the outcome of any analysis and lead the argument into a blind alley. Email is 'nothing by itself', it can only enable a certain type of interaction. The 'instantaneousness' of email is a logical shortcut that derives from an undisciplined and vague formulation of the principle. It must be admitted, however, that before the emergence of the current, more complex communication landscape, such logical shortcut was excusable. At present, the focus must be shifted from the communication devices or methods to the characteristics of the communication process. The latter resembles either dealings face-to-face or dealings at a distance. This simple division should constitute the starting point for all analyses. Whenever the communication process is interactive and real-time, the application of the principle is unquestionable. The exception can only be debated in those instances where the exchange between the parties does not resemble face-to-face dealings. An additional factor that should be included in legal analyses is 'reliability'. The choice between the principle and the exception may be crucial not because of the length of delay between dispatch and receipt but because the increased risks of communication failure. Accordingly, the inquiry 'when was the contract formed' turns into 'who should bear the risk of failed receipt'?[156]

Defining 'dispatch' and 'receipt'

The second part of the analysis of the time of formation consists in establishing what is **6.55** meant by 'dispatch' and 'receipt'. In traditional communications, dispatch is generally associated with 'posting': placing a letter in a letterbox of the postal service or handing it to a postal employee.[157] Postal communications involve at least two post offices and two mailboxes, the sender's and the addressee's. These 'components' form one system, no distinction is made between the delivery of a letter to the post office or its placement in a mailbox in the street.[158] As a result, when an acceptance is effective on dispatch, addressees bear the risk of all accidents during the time letters remain in the sender's mailbox, as well as during their subsequent transfer to the sender's post office. Even if a letter is lost during these initial stages, acceptance is effective.

In the case of telegrams, dispatch occurs at the telegraph office where the machine is **6.56** located.[159] It is not clear whether the message must leave the machine or whether typing the message 'into' the machine suffices. Unlike telegrams, telexes can be received directly in the office.[160] In the landmark cases of *Entores*[161] and *Brinkibon*[162] the contracting parties

---

[156] The risk factor was explicitly mentioned by Lord Wilberforce in *Brinkibon v Stahag und Stahlwarenhandelsgesellschaft mbH* [1983] 2 AC 34 at 42.

[157] *Carter on Contract*, § 03-350.

[158] *Corbin on Contracts*, vol 1 (West Pub Co, St Paul, 1993) para 3.2.

[159] *Henkel v Pape* (1870) LR 6 Exch 7; *Bruner v Moore* [1904] 1 Ch 305; *Cowan v O'Conner* (1888) 20 QBD 640 at 642; *Brinkibon v Stahag und Stahlwarenhandelsgesellschaft mbH* [1983] 2 AC 34 at 38.

[160] Gregory, 'Receiving Electronic Messages: *Eastern Power v Azienda Communale Energia & Ambiente*' (1999–2000) 15 BFLR 473 at 480.

[161] [1955] 2 QB 327.

[162] [1983] 2 AC 34.

operated their own telex machines.[163] No additional steps to send or access messages were necessary and there was no dependence on intermediaries. In *Leach Nominees Pty Ltd v Walter Wright Pty Ltd*,[164] however, the telex machine used by the sender was operated by third parties. Acceptance was considered dispatched when the sender committed the message to a public telex operator, not when the message was sent from the telex machine.

6.57 Receipt is generally associated with the arrival of a message at the addressee's machine.[165] After business hours, it may be deemed to take place only once the office is re-opened on the following business day.[166] The law deems certain occurrences as constituting receipt, presumably because they enable communication in the normal course of events. If the terminating device malfunctions due to the addressee's fault, the latter is deemed to have received the message or is estopped from denying receipt.[167] If, however, a communication failure is not the fault of the addressee, there is no receipt and therefore no contract.[168]

6.58 The above principles are straightforward and attracted relatively little legal analysis over the years. Once transactions are taken online, however, the existing rules of establishing dispatch and receipt become difficult to apply due to a number of complicating factors.

6.59 The first of those factors relates to the fact that when communicating over the phone, fax or telex there is only one machine on each side of the communication channel. Only the originating and the terminating devices are taken into account, not the underlying communications infrastructure. Most online communications, however, rely on the client-server architecture.[169] In the case of email, there are at least two originating devices (the sender's mail-client and the outgoing mail-server) and two terminating devices (the addressee's incoming mail-server and the mail-client). Is it the mail-client or the mail-server that should be taken into account? The decision has important implications for the time of contract formation, as there may be substantial delays between the moment a message arrives at the server and the moment it is transferred to the client—despite the fact that

---

[163] In both instances, the interactions were taking place between principals who operated their own telex machines, *Brinkibon v Stahag und Stahlwarenhandelsgesellschaft mbH* [1983] 2 AC 34 at 42.

[164] (1986) 85 FLR 427 at 434.

[165] *Tenax Steamship Co Ltd v Owners of the Motor Vessel 'Brinmes' (The Brinmes)* (1974) 3 All ER 88 at 93.

[166] *Tenax Steamship Co Ltd v Owners of the Motor Vessel 'Brinmes' (The Brinmes)* (1974) 3 All ER 88; *Schelde Delta Shipping BV v Astarte Shipping Ltd (The 'Pamela')* [1995] 2 Lloyd's Rep 249.

[167] *Carter on Contract*, § 03-410.

[168] *Entores Ltd v Miles Far East Corporation* [1955] 2 QB 327 at 333.

[169] The Internet provides a general-purpose infrastructure that permits applications on an arbitrary pair of computers to exchange information. One application must initiate this process, whereas the other must accept it. This is the so-called 'client-server paradigm' of interaction. The application that actively initiates contact and requests a particular service or resource is called *client*, the application passively awaiting such requests and providing services or resources on demand is called *server*. In general, clients reside locally on the user's computer and are directly invoked by such user, whereas servers run on more powerful remote computers. Information may pass in either or both directions. The terms 'client' and 'server' refer to applications or processes but are often used in relation to the computers that run those processes. For a detailed description see Comer, *Computer Networks and Internets with Internet Applications* (4th edn, New Jersey, 2004), 422.

the transmission itself might be regarded as instantaneous. The exact time of formation depends on whether it is the server or the client that is selected as the relevant device.[170]

The second complicating factor is that online communications are characterized by a num- **6.60**
ber of novel risks. The Internet is not like the post or the telephone. Despite its ubiquity, it does not (yet) have the uniformity of one global system. The Internet is heterogeneous—each of its component networks retains some individual characteristics.[171] Routing from one network to another may involve a conversion between the 'idiosyncrasies of the two original networks'[172] and require the trans-coding, translation or reformatting of messages. Each of these operations aims to adapt the message to the requirements of the next step in the transmission. Such conversions are, however, not always successful. As a result, there are many reasons an email may not be delivered or be delivered in unreadable form.[173] Some risks can be compared to technical failures or bad maintenance. Others are novel. It is difficult, for example, to find paper-based counterparts for 'wrong protocol version' or 'failure in trans-coding'. Each of the risks must be allocated to one of the contracting parties, ie the sender or the addressee. Intuitively, risks relating to dispatch should be borne by the sender, risks relating to receipt by the addressee. Furthermore, it can be assumed that each party should be responsible for the risks it can control.

The general transmission risks are roughly apportioned by the principle of receipt and the **6.61**
postal exception. The risks inherent in the operation of the originating and terminating information systems are allocated by defining 'dispatch' and 'receipt'. The moment of contract formation must be established with the full realization of its implications for the distribution of risks between the contracting parties. It must also be remembered that the earlier the risk is transferred from the sender, the more risk is borne by the addressee. It is possible to allocate each risk to one of the parties or to one of the intermediaries. If receipt fails due to the fault of an intermediary, the question arises which of the parties should bear the risk? The intermediary at fault may not be in a contractual relationship with or under the control of either contracting party. It may also be difficult to regard it as part of the general transmission infrastructure. Even those risks, however, that cannot be prevented or mitigated by either party must be placed on one of them.

Suggested approaches under the MLEC and the CUECIC

The MLEC and the CUECIC attempt to transpose the existing principles onto a novel **6.62**
communication infrastructure and to electronically replicate the tests used for dispatch and

---

[170] Both the Internet and the client-server architecture are networking concepts that may not readily translate into physically separable pieces of hardware. Determining the network element a message must pass through or arrive at for dispatch or receipt to occur, is therefore ridden with difficulties. Even the terminology used in this chapter would raise the eyebrows of some computer scientists: is it correct to speak of 'devices', 'servers', 'networks' and 'information systems'? Technically, servers and clients are *processes*, not discrete pieces of machinery. The current discussion often treats those processes as if they were spatially separable network elements, whereas in many instances their separation is only logical.

[171] RFC 1122, Braden (ed), *Requirements for Internet Hosts—Communication Layers* (1989).

[172] Brookshear, *Computer Science, An Overview* (Boston, 2004) 138.

[173] For a detailed description see: RFC 3463, Vaudreuil, *Enhanced Mail System Status Codes* (2003).

receipt in paper-based communications.[174] This 'transposition', however, is done without factoring in the aforementioned complicating factors.

6.63   The MLEC associates 'dispatch' with the message entering an information system beyond the control of the sender.[175] In other words, dispatch occurs when the sender loses control of the message. Given that it is unclear whether 'information system' refers to clients, servers or the whole network,[176] it is difficult to ascertain when loss of control occurs. This moment depends on which part of the communication infrastructure is regarded as being under the sender's control. The mail-client is on the sender's computer and therefore under his control.[177] Mail-servers, however, are generally operated by Internet Service Providers (ISPs). 'Loss of control' could be associated with the dispatch of the message from the mail-client whenever senders use an ISP to provide the mail-server. Accordingly, the moment of dispatch would depend on who controls the mail-server. This raises a broader question about the role of ISPs and intermediaries.[178] It must be remembered that in the case of traditional communications, the telecommunication carriers and the post are regarded as independent third parties, which constitute part of the communications infrastructure. Are ISPs like the post and mail-servers like mailboxes? It must also be recalled that when the postal acceptance rule applies, 'transmission' commences when letters are placed in the mailbox, which in turn constitutes part of the postal system. The latter is not considered as an agent of either the sender or the addressee but an independent third party.[179] This approach is, however, difficult to transpose onto online communication scenarios. Mail-servers cannot be equated with mailboxes and ISPs cannot be regarded as independent third parties. ISPs are chosen by and remain in contractual relationships with senders, providing their part of the communication infrastructure. Although senders may have no technical control over mail-servers, they must be taken to assume the risks of their operation. After all, if the outgoing ISP was not regarded as acting on the sender's behalf, the risks of operation of the sender's mail-server would be borne by the addressee. This in turn, would render the latter liable for any shortcomings in the sender's choice of ISP. Technically, the ISP is only providing a service that the sender could be undertaking himself. Only if Internet connectivity and mail-servers were provided exclusively by a single, universal telecommunications provider, such 'ISP' would bear more similarity to the post and the mail-server could be regarded as part of the general transmission infrastructure. Leaving the mail-client would be synonymous with loss of control, similar to placing a letter into a mailbox. The CUECIC replaces 'entry' with 'leave'.[180] As the definition of

---

[174] A/CN.9/528, para 149.

[175] MLEC, Art. 10.

[176] See Knight, 'The Electronic Transactions Bill 1999' (2000) 6 CTLR 105 at 110.

[177] For the sake of simplicity we disregard whether the sender uses a shared computer, eg in an Internet cafe. It is also irrelevant whether the mail-client takes the form of a browser, as in the case of web-mail, or a dedicated email application, such as Outlook.

[178] Neither the CUECIC nor the MLEC deal with the role of intermediaries, see CUECIC, Art 4(d), (e); EN 99, 39.

[179] Fasciano, 'Internet Electronic Mail: A Last Bastion for the Mailbox Rule' (1997) 25 Hofstra Law Rev 971 at 995; see also Williston, *A Treatise on the Law of Contracts* (4th edn, Vol 2, 1991) para 6:37.

[180] CUECIC, Art 10.1.

'information system' is identical to the one in the MLEC,[181] it remains unclear whether messages must leave the mail-client or the mail-server.[182]

The MLEC defines receipt as entry into a designated information system.[183] Again, it is not **6.64** clear whether a message should enter the addressee's mail-server or mail-client. Given the breadth of the definition of 'information system', entry could relate to a whole network or to one machine. A broad meaning implies an early cessation of the risks borne by the sender. To illustrate the point: if 'information system' means 'network', entry occurs when a message enters any first point considered as belonging to the network.[184] Once inside, the sender would not bear the risks of any occurrences within the network, including protective measures placed before the mail-server (eg spam filters). A narrower meaning, exposes the sender to the risks occurring within the network—until a specific machine or point in the network is reached. The CUECIC replaces 'information system' with 'electronic address', which points to a specific part of an information system: the storage area on a mail-server.[185] The CUECIC also replaces the term 'entry' with 'becoming retrievable'. This replacement supports the view that the relevant terminating device is the mail-server.

The moment of receipt also depends on whether a message is sent to a designated or non- **6.65** designated address or information system. If a message was sent to a non-designated system, receipt only occurs when the message is retrieved.[186] The practical implications of designating an address are far-reaching. There may be a significant delay between a message entering and the moment a message is retrieved. Despite its significance, 'designation' remains undefined.[187] The MLEC guide to enactment explicitly states that the mere indication of an email or telecopy address on a letterhead does not constitute designation.[188] One must ask: what does? 'Designation' obligates senders to investigate the correct address without imposing an equivalent obligation on addressees to clearly designate their systems. If a system is held out to receive communications, its designation should be implied. This would mirror the traditional rules of receipt. Under the regime created by the MLEC and the CUECIC receipt may not occur even if an information system is held out—as long as it is not expressly designated. If addresses of particular information systems or accounts are

---

[181] CUECIC, Art 4(g) compared to the Electronic Transactions Act (Commonwealth) 1999 (ETA), § 5.

[182] A/CN.9/528, para 149: The preparatory works elaborate that information systems must be distinguished from 'information service providers or telecommunication carriers that might offer intermediary services or technical support infrastructure for the exchange of data messages'.

[183] MLEC, Art 15(2).

[184] The choice of computer network device would also depend on which layer of the TCP/IP protocol is examined.

[185] Electronic addresses generally refer to accounts on mail-servers. One mail-server can host multiple accounts. Multiple mail-servers may be part of the same information system. This can be explained by looking at the structure of an email address. The latter consists of a character string identifying the individual account, the symbol @ and the name of the mail-server that should receive the message. The name of the mail-server is specific to the domain in which it is located, ie the network to which the server belongs. The second part of an email address could be regarded as pointing to an information system, whereas the first part as indicting an individual account. See Brookshear, n 100 above, 141–2.

[186] MLEC, Art 15(2)(a)(ii).

[187] It was stated that difficulties in applying § 15 cannot be overcome by defining 'designated information system'. A/CN.9/528, para 148, see also EN 187, p 63.

[188] MLEC, Guide to Enactment, para 103.

disseminated or made public, addressees should not be permitted to claim that such systems or accounts are not designated. [189]

6.66   According to CUECIC, Article 10.2, receipt occurs when messages become 'capable of being retrieved by the addressee at an electronic address designated by the addressee'. Receipt at a non-designated address occurs when messages become 'capable of being retrieved by the addressee at that address and the addressee becomes aware that the message has been sent to that address'. As a result, the objective component (capability of being retrieved) is supplemented by a subjective element (awareness). Although 'awareness' raises problems of proof,[190] it was considered more 'equitable than holding the addressee bound by a message sent to an information system that the addressee could not reasonably expect would be used in the context of its dealings with the originator or for the purpose for which the data message had been sent'.[191] Considering the vagueness of 'designation', in many instances receipt could exclusively depend on 'awareness'. This would constitute a significant alteration of the traditional principles which regard 'receipt' as an objective event, unrelated to any subjective occurrences on the addressee's side.

6.67   To complicate matters, messages are presumed to be capable of being retrieved when they reach the addressee's electronic address.[192] Technically, however, the 'capability of being retrieved' points to a later stage in the transmission process than the original term used in the MLEC, 'entry'. Messages must first 'enter' an information system, or electronic address, before becoming 'retrievable'. CUECIC, however, associates 'retrievability' with an event that precedes 'entry'. After all, messages may reach an electronic address or particular network but be rejected by a protective measure, fail to enter and never become retrievable. Spam filters, firewalls and anti-virus software, operate on various points in the network.[193] Depending on the circumstances, messages may be precluded from entering the mailserver, the mail-client or the network. According to the presumption, 'receipt' would occur despite such rejection—as long as the message reached an address or information system.[194] A literal reading of Article 10, however, suggests that 'receipt' does not occur as the message does not become retrievable. In other words, the 'capability of being retrieved' may not necessarily result from the message reaching an electronic address.

---

[189] See Giles, 'You've Got Mail….or Have You?' (2000) 3 Internet Law Bulletin 12 at 14, who suggests that to avoid the consequences of designation people may use disclosures like 'nothing in this email constitutes designation for the purposes of …' See also *Carter on Contract*, § 03-430, where it is assumed that the designation of an information system is synonymous with the provision of an email address.

[190] A/60/17, para 82. During the preparatory works it was admitted that the provision created legal uncertainty as 'awareness' is a subjective circumstance not easily proven by the sender. It was held, however, that awareness 'could be proven by other objective evidence'.

[191] A/CN.9/528, para 143.

[192] CUECIC, Art 10, see also UNCITRAL Convention on Contracts for the International Sale of Goods (CISG), Art 18.

[193] Hunt, *TCP/IP Network Administration* (2nd edn, Sebastopol, 1997), Ch 12.

[194] A/CN.9/528, para 80, concerns were expressed over technologies restricting receipt. For general discussion see Martin, 'The UNCITRAL Electronic Contracts Convention: Will it be Used or Avoided?' (2005) 17 Pace Int'l L Rev 261 at 294.

Additional considerations

Before closing the discussion of the time of contract formation in online transactions, two
additional considerations must be pointed out. Illegible acceptances and the right to preclude receipt. Both can be characterized by an absence of a suitable analogy in traditional
communications. Both can be considered as a potential source of complications in legal
analyses. Last but not least, both illustrate the level of technical detail that legal analysis
might be forced to include.
6.68

In principle, for receipt to occur addressees need not attend or maintain their devices. It is,
however, assumed that they do so at their own risk and that receipt implies the ability to
learn about the contents of the message. While actual knowledge of acceptance is not
required, the ability to gain such knowledge by reading the message is presumed.[195] In
Internet-based communications, successful 'receipt' (in the sense of arrival at the addressee's mail-client or server) does not necessarily imply that the message can be read. The
reason for this unusual situation is that the addressee's mail-client may not be able to process and display a message composed on the sender's mail-client. Addressees may not be
able to read messages in certain formats or from certain sources.[196] Senders, in turn, cannot
always anticipate the addressees' client application. The characteristics of the latter may not
be apparent from the email address. The problem differs from the failure to maintain a
terminating device. In the current situation, both the originating and the terminating
device function correctly. The addressee's mail-client, however, is unable to trans-code or
translate a message, resulting in its illegibility.[197] Neither party is at fault or unreasonable,
both the sender's and the addressee's client applications are widely used. Senders cannot be
'blamed' for composing and dispatching messages from Microsoft Outlook, addressees are
not at fault when receiving messages on hotmail.com. Yet, one mail application may not be
able to display a message composed on the other.
6.69

In paper-based communications the 'format' of a letter is not problematic. What is placed
in an envelope is identical to what is delivered to the addressee. Letters can be lost or damaged, but are not rewritten by postal employees or by the addressee's mailbox.[198] Letters
may be written in foreign languages and necessitate a translation or encrypted and require
decryption. In both instances the addressee obtains 'unreadable' content. In both instances,
however, it is the sender who intentionally dispatched the letter in an 'unreadable' form,
most likely to preserve the confidentiality of its contents. With online communications,
illegibility may be the result of processing by one of the intermediating systems, most probably the addressee's client. It can no longer be assumed that proper dispatch and successful
transmission result in receipt enabling communication.
6.70

---

[195] *Carter on Contract*, § 03-310.

[196] The problem is practically non-existent in instant messengers, as both parties must use the same system.

[197] For a detailed explanation regarding the compatibility problems between email clients see *Avoiding and Surmounting E-Mail Incompatibility Problems*, available at www.gustavus.lib.ak.us/computer/training/readable-email.htm. See also Chacker, 'E-Effectuating Notice: *Rio Properties v Rio International Interlink*' (2003) 48 Vill L Rev 597 for a discussion of the limitations of email as a means of giving notice.

[198] Chissick and Kelmann, n 42 above, 76, 81.

6.71   The problem of illegible acceptances must be acknowledged but not over-exaggerated. Garbled, altered or incomplete email messages occur frequently enough to warrant legal attention[199] and are statistically more likely to occur than in the case of traditional communications. The mere fact that there is no single case on 'garbled acceptances' speaks for itself.[200]

6.72   The addressee's inability to process messages originating from the sender's system raises two questions: is there receipt if a message cannot be read and are senders obligated to ensure that messages are readable (ie do they bear the risk of illegibility)? There are two possible approaches.

6.73   First, it is commonly understood that if receipt fails without the fault of the addressee, there is no contract. As in the case of traditional communications, senders must not bear the risk of the correct functioning of the addressee's terminating devices, in this case the mail-server and/or mail-client. The 'ability to process' cannot, however, be subsumed under the category of 'proper functioning' as there is nothing improper about the addressee's system and the inability to read a message is most likely the result of differences between client software—not bad maintenance. If both parties use popular email systems, neither party is at fault. As it is impossible to fairly allocate the risk of illegibility, it is safest to assume that there is no receipt and therefore no contract. As long as there are differences in email applications, online transactions can be characterized by a large number of instances where no contract was formed due to the fact that the addressee was not at fault. At the same time, recipients of illegible messages should be obliged to immediately notify the sender about such occurrence to enable them to re-send the message.

6.74   Second, it is possible to regard receipt as more than a mechanical fact, such as arrival at a specific machine. Consequently, it could be claimed that senders must ensure that messages are readable. While this approach is consistent with the classic theory of the meeting of minds and the requirement of communication, it also implies that the sender's risk extends to the moment the recipient can read the message. As a result, senders should bear the risks of the message's retrieval from the addressee's mail-server, the risk of intermediary storage as well as the risks inherent in the processing and reproduction on the addressee's mail-client. Senders would bear the risks of occurrences over which they do not have any control. To mitigate those risks, they would be forced to provide messages in multiple formats or inquire about the characteristics of the addressee's system prior to the dispatch of the email containing acceptance. This would, however, require a relatively high level of IT literacy on both sides of the transaction and possibly the need to install additional email applications. Alternatively, all emails could be sent in plain text. Although only the latter possibility guarantees universal legibility, it seems unrealistic as email relies on the enhanced formatting capabilities of HTML. It is just as unrealistic to require that everybody exchanged email in plain text, as it is to require that everybody used the latest versions of an email application, which supports multiple formats and message content encodings.

---

[199] Mozzila-based browsers do not display any graphics in gmail, both Mozzilla and gmail are considered more advanced applications than Internet Explorer and hotmail.com respectively.

[200] In *Henkel v Pape* [1870] 23 LT 419, the offeror sent the offeree a telegraphic message offering to buy three rifles, the word 'three' was transcripted as 'the'. The offeror was held liable to purchase 50 rifles.

Requiring that senders ensure legibility would not only extend their risk beyond those encountered in traditional communications but have far-reaching implications for the general usage of email in online contracting. The risk of illegibility becomes easier to apportion when either party uses an outdated, proprietary or uncommon email application. While it remains difficult to speak of fault, at least the problem becomes attributable to one of the parties. In practice, courts will face difficult situations, with the legal recognition of receipt hinging on a technicality.

The previous section described the difficulties of recognizing receipt in the event the message is illegible due to processing on the addressee's side. The following section discusses another problem relating to establishing receipt, namely, the addressee's right to reject a message and preclude receipt—a situation rather uncommon in traditional communications.   **6.75**

As indicated earlier, if failed receipt is not the addressee's fault there is no contract.[201] If, on the other hand, failed receipt is attributable to the addressee the addressee is estopped from denying receipt.[202] In online communications, there may be situations where receipt fails due to reasons attributable to the addressee but the latter cannot be estopped from denying receipt. The addressee may reject a message, such rejection may, however, be justified or reasonable. Justified restrictions placed on incoming communications must be distinguished from bad maintenance, such as failure to empty one's mailbox or update the email application.   **6.76**

While a 'right to reject' a message may appear incomprehensible at first, its existence can be explained on the basis of the growing security concerns created by viruses, Trojan horses, worms and unsolicited commercial email, otherwise known as spam.[203] Individually and collectively, these phenomena pose a threat to any resource or application hosted on mail-servers and mail-clients. It must be assumed that any person connected to the Internet has the right—and sometimes a legal obligation—to protect his network resources from the above threats by appropriate technical measures. Protective measures, such as spam filters, firewalls and anti-virus software, operate on various points in the network.[204] For example, anti-virus software and spam filters may be implemented on servers or on client machines. The individual settings of these methods depend on the security policy of the addressee.[205] Depending on the type and configuration of a given measure, messages may be precluded from entering (ie rejected by) the mail-server, the mail-client or the network. There is always a risk of so-called false positives—the rejection of messages that carry legitimate content. Security measures are justified but create the risk that they will occasionally 'filter out' a legitimate message containing an acceptance.   **6.77**

---

[201] *Entores Ltd v Miles Far East Corporation* [1955] 2 QB 327 at 333 by Denning LJ.

[202] *Tenax Steamship Co Ltd v Owners of the Motor Vessel 'Brinmes' (The Brinmes)* (1974) 3 All ER 88 at 113 per Megaw LJ; *Car and Universal Finance Co Ltd v Caldwell* (1965) 1 QB 525, see also Hill, 'Flogging A Dead Horse—The Postal Acceptance Rule and Email' (2001) 17 JCL 157.

[203] Zwicky and Cooper, *Building Internet Firewalls* (2nd edn, O'Reilly Media, Sebastopol, 2000), paras 16.1.2.1, 16.1.2.2.

[204] Hunt, *TCP/IP Network Administration* (2nd edn, Sebastopo, 1997), Ch 12.

[205] Ford and Baum, *Secure Electronic Commerce, Building the Infrastructure for Digital Signatures and Encryption* (2nd edn, Prentice Hall, New Jersey, 2001) 144.

6.78   In deciding whether the rejection of a particular message is permitted, it must be considered whether the security measures are reasonable in light of the resources being protected. If the rejection of a message is unjustified or unreasonable, the default situation is reverted to—deemed receipt and the formation of a contract. This places the risk of unreasonable security measures on the addressee. The latter must regularly monitor so-called 'quarantined' messages, ie emails that have not been permitted inside his network or mail-server but kept in an external repository for inspection before final deletion. The addressee's protective measures must, however, also be taken into account by senders. The latter must make certain assumptions regarding the addressee's ability to receive messages. Care must be taken not only with regards to the correct address, but also regarding the format of messages, the address the message is sent from, the size of messages and the text in the subject line. Sending a 300 MB file to an email account, which is generally known to provide little storage, is as unreasonable as putting the words 'sex' or '$$$' in the subject line or sending corporate communications from a hotmail account. In both instances, the sender faces a high likelihood of failed receipt—even the least conservative security software will reject messages containing the said words, many corporate networks reject messages dispatched from hotmail and similar services.

6.79   Where the rejection is justified or reasonable in light of the prevailing security practices, addressees cannot be estopped from denying receipt and no contract is formed. As any evaluation of a rejection occurs post factum, in many instances there will be uncertainty as to whether receipt occurred and a contract exists. Legitimate messages carrying acceptances may fall victim to conservative filter settings and firewalls. There will be no receipt unless the rejection of the message was unreasonable, such as in the case of misconfigured filter software.[206] Determining whether the addressee is 'at fault' will require a consideration of multiple additional factors. As in the case of problems relating to legibility, a more nuanced approach must be developed.

---

[206] Greenstein and Feinman, *Electronic Commerce: Security, Risk Management and Control* (Irwin/McGraw-Hill, Boston, 2000) 276.

7

LETTERS OF INTENT[1]

Many contracts arise without any negotiation between the parties. The supermarket shop- **7.01** per arrives at the checkout with her trolley and empties the goods onto the space in front of the cashier. The cashier enters them into the till and states the price. Little if anything will be said. Whether we characterize the arrival at the till as the offer or an acceptance,[2] it is clear that the transaction has moved very quickly from no contract to contract.

In most countries it would be a surprise if the shopper arrived at the checkout and said to **7.02** the cashier 'I will give you $100 for these'. But this is a matter of culture and not of law. Even in England we would not be surprised if a potential buyer of a second-hand car offered the dealer less than the marked price. In England if one was in a shoe shop looking at shoes one would be unlikely to ask the assistant for a discount; in Singapore in a physi- cally very similar shop with identical shoes one would not be at all surprised if the assistant offered 10 per cent off if one looked likely to leave the shop without making a purchase.[3]

In some of these cases there will be no negotiation at all. In others there will be brief nego- **7.03** tiations about the price but the parties will still move quickly from no contract to contract. This is largely the situation which classical contract law deals with but it is by no means the whole range of transactions for which contract law has to provide rules. Many contracts are the product of months or years of negotiations, often involving consideration of many side

---

[1] Lake and Draetta, *Letters of Intent and other Pre-contractual Documents* (2nd edn, Butterworths, 1994) (hereafter Lake and Draetta); Farnsworth, 'Pre-contractual Liability and Preliminary Agreements: Fair Dealing and Failed Negotiations'(1987) 87 Columbia LR 217; Ball, 'Work Carried Out in Pursuance of Letters of Intent—Contract or Restitution' (1983) 99 LQR 572.
[2] See Chapter 2.
[3] I once asked a Singapore shopkeeper why he marked the price of goods if he offered me a discount as I entered the store and he replied 'those prices are for Japanese'.

issues and involving teams of experts and advisers. Such situations give rise to a whole set of extra problems.

7.04   One relatively simply possibility is that the parties will make a deal but postpone its coming into legal effect until some further event. A well known example is the standard method of English house purchase. Here the most common scenario is that the parties negotiate about the price, often with the assistance of estate agents but usually without that of lawyers. Once the price is agreed there is said to be an agreement 'subject to contract' and things are handed over to the parties' lawyers, who do the things that lawyers normally do in this situation, including the preparation of the contract. It is accepted that neither side is bound until copies of the contract are prepared, signed and exchanged.

7.05   It is important to understand that this practice is in most circumstances for the benefit of the buyer. The buyer usually needs to borrow money to complete the purchase and binding offers cannot usually be obtained from lenders until a specific property and an agreed price can be proposed. Further the buyer's lawyer needs to make sure that the seller actually owns the property and that there is not a plan to build a motorway through the back garden. Nevertheless neither party is legally bound and from time to time on rising markets, sellers decide at the last minute to refuse to sign the contract unless the price is increased. This practice known as 'gazumping', not surprisingly causes fury among buyers but the English Law Commission advised that the problem was not sufficiently serious to be attacked by legislation.[4] In falling markets the reverse practice by which buyers refuse at the last minute to sign unless the price is reduced is not unknown but does not seem to have attracted so much publicity or a pejorative name (perhaps gazundering). The legal problems arising from agreements 'subject to ...' are discussed below.[5]

7.06   In many cases the parties make written statement of provisional agreement during the negotiation. Such cases are the subject matter of this chapter and the next. The names given to such provisional statements are many and various: Letters of Intent; Heads of Agreement; Memorandum of Understanding; Agreement in Principle; and so on. In these chapters we will for convenience usually call them Letters of Intent. In this Chapter we shall consider the possible legal effect of such documents and in the next chapter what useful advice may be given about their drafting.

7.07   The problem appears to occur across all legal systems but the results are not necessarily exactly the same. An invaluable survey was carried out by a group led by Professor Marcel Fontaine.[6] Their report was for many years available only in French but since 2006 it is also available in English.[7] A major factor is whether the governing law is one which imposes a duty to negotiate in good faith or which permits the parties to make a binding agreement to negotiate in good faith.[8]

---

[4]   See Law Com 65 (1975).
[5]   See Chapter 9.
[6]   The working group on international contracts.
[7]   Marcel Fontaine and Filip De LY, *Drafting International Contracts* (Transnational Publishers Inc, 2006) (hereafter Fontaine and De LY).
[8]   This is discussed in Chapter 12.

Perhaps the only general rule is that there is no general rule, that is one cannot say in advance that a Letter of Intent has or has not legal effect and if it does what the effect would be. Everything must depend on an objective analysis of what the parties have said and done.[9]   **7.08**

In their consideration the working group on International Contracts looked at 26 examples. These examples fall however into a rather smaller number of groups. We may consider first cases where the Letter of Intent does not give rise to a contract; then these where on the contrary it gives rise to a full contract and then consider situations which fall in between. As we shall see this third group falls into a number of subgroups.   **7.09**

Before we come onto this analysis it is worth saying a little about the practical problems which give rise to the difficulties. One is that in many business situations there are many parties and contracts involved. So if a hotel chain wishes to build a new hotel it will typically enter into a contract with someone who is usually called a main contractor but the hotel will not be built by the main contractor or its employees. Nearly all the work, the building of the foundations; the erection of the framework of the building, the windows; the roof, the electrical appliances, the plumbing, the lifts and so on will be done by specialists. Most of these will be subcontractors to the main contractor or sub-subcontractors to the subcontractors. It is inconceivable that all the contracts could come into existence at the same time. Typically the main contractor will quote a price to the customer (usually called the employer) based on quotations obtained from subcontractors but he will usually not want to bind himself to the subcontractors until he has a binding contract with the employer. In practice there is often pressure to start work before the contracts are all in place. As we shall see many problems arise from this pressure.   **7.10**

In other cases the contract will depend on some governmental permission or on obtaining finance and it is not possible to obtain such finance or permission without having carried the contract-making process forward.   **7.11**

Even where the contract is being negotiated simply between the parties, the negotiation may be long and complex running over weeks or months. In such cases it is common to divide the negotiation up into stages. In such cases what has been agreed at each stage may well be treated as binding but there may be serious practical problems in giving effect to such an assumption.   **7.12**

It is also important to bear in mind that the underlying assumptions of lawyers and businessmen in these circumstances are by no means the same   **7.13**

The following quotations, representing respectively the attitude in the United States and England, can be used to illustrate this proposition:

> Often businessmen do not feel they have 'a contract'—rather they have 'an order'. They speak of 'cancelling the order' rather than 'breaching our contract'. When I began practice I referred to order cancellations as breaches of contract, but my clients objected since they do

---

[9] The United States Court of Appeals for the Ninth circuit come quite close in *Rennick v O.P.T.I.O.N. carl Inc* (1996) 77F 3d 309 to saying that there is a presumption that a letter of intent is not legally binding but reading the opinion as a whole supports rather the proposition in the text.

not think of cancellation as wrong. Most clients, in heavy industry at least, believe that there is a right to cancel as part of the buyer-seller relationship. *There is a widespread attitude that one can back out of any deal within some very vague limits.* Lawyers are often surprised by this attitude.[10] (emphasis added)

Not every businessman necessarily 'uses' contract law even in the planning sense when making an agreement. *So little may be planned that the agreement is unenforceable for uncertainty, and if an enforceable contract is created the parties may not adhere to it thereafter. It [sic] some contingency arises which threatens to disrupt the agreement, the parties may not use the remedies provided by the law or by the agreement itself.* If they do appear to adhere to the contract or to use contractual remedies, this may be unconscious.[11] (emphasis added)

Therefore, the distinction in attitude to contracts is between businessmen, and lawyers. For lawyers a contract is a mixture of rights, obligations and remedies for breach. For businessmen, however, it is 'primarily a facilitative device within an economic cycle which turns on such processes as the acquisition of materials, the production of finished goods, marketing and sales, finance and payment'.[12] Thus, businessmen believe that they need not insist on the rights associated with the contractual relationship if some other device or method can achieve their goals. They can begin their performance relying on '"a man's word" in a brief letter, a handshake, or "a common honesty and decency"'.[13] They keep their promises because they fear business sanctions rather than legal sanctions.

7.14   Therefore, we might conclude that businessmen insist on receiving letters of intent which deny any legally binding effect because they expect that, regardless of legal force, such a document obliges the other party to abide by what he has promised.

7.15   Letters of intent can be binding ethically, if not legally. Indeed, it seems that businessmen frequently do not take the legal effect of a document into consideration and are rarely conscious of the legal position when they insert provisions which deny legal effect. This explains why such documents are often so vague and ambiguous in terms of their legal effect.

7.16   This vagueness in expressing the legal effect of a document can also be attributed to the fact that a letter of intent may be an 'un-gentlemen's agreement' which is intended to bind one party while giving the other a free hand. In many instances businessmen wish to obtain the other party's acceptance before binding themselves to conclude the contract. They seek to achieve this by inserting a clause such as, 'This offer is subject to formal approval by our Board of Directors' into the offer. Letters of intent can therefore seek to bind one party whilst leaving the other free. For example, some drafters of letters of intent do not allow the other party a right to negotiate in parallel with a third party, but expressly reserve their own right to do so. As an example, main contractors often bind subcontractors but remain uncommitted themselves.[14] Main contractors calculate their figures based upon particular subcontractors' estimates and expect the subcontractor to abide by his assurance that he

---

[10] Macaulay, 'Non-contractual Relations in Business: A Preliminary Study' (1963) 28 Am Soc Rev 55, 61.

[11] Beale and Dugdale, 'Contracts between Businessmen: Planning and the Use of Contractual Remedies' (1975) 2 British Journal of Law and Society 45.

[12] Tillotson, *Contract Law in Perspective* (4th edn, Cavendish, 2004), 3.

[13] Macaulay (n 10 above), 58.

[14] See Chapters 8 and 11 for a discussion of this issue.

will not withdraw that estimate. However, since the award of the main contract is not guaranteed, the main contractor does not wish to give any assurance that a contract will be concluded with the subcontractor. Therefore in letters of intent any commitment on the part of the main contractor is skillfully avoided, yet a promise not to withdraw the estimate is demanded from the subcontractor.

A. Cases Where the Letters of Intent Do Not Create a Contract

This must in practice be the most common case. Many letters of intent are no more than measures of goodwill and encouragement. To a lawyer this might not seem worth much but this is too simple a view. If a contractor or subcontractor who is competing for a job receives a letter of intent, he knows (unless the sender is a complete crook) that he is now the only person being effectively considered. His chances of getting the job have gone up from say 20 per cent to 80 per cent. If he has a boss, he can send it to his boss and hope to be popular for a day or two.   **7.17**

Examples 14 to 19 of the Fontaine working group appear to be of this kind. Example 14   **7.18**
assesses the use of the phrase 'subject to contract' which in English law has the effect of denying a legally binding agreement[15] and example 15 includes an express statement that the document is not to be contractual. This also appears to be clear from the remaining content of the letter in example 15, which indicates that this is early in the negotiation process with many uncertainties still to be resolved: 'We shall of course need to discuss the details of all these documents …; but if our proposal seems to you to be a starting point for negotiations, we should be glad if you would return to us the enclosed copy of this letter with your signature, which should be preceded by the remark, "valid as a letter of intent only, without being contractual".'

The commentary assesses this as thoughtful drafting and compares it to example 8 ('We hereby inform you of our intention to award you in due course the order …').

Examples 16 and 17 illustrate further methods of achieving a denial of legal effect. Example   **7.19**
16 indicates that there is not agreement on terms but in any event includes the following: 'In case no agreement is reached on all terms and no contract is signed before … we reserve the right to cancel this award, without any right for indemnification from your part.'

Example 17 denies any obligation and for good measure excludes any liability (other than for fraudulent conduct) in the event that the matter does not proceed: 'It is clearly understood that so far as concerns our company, no decision has been taken about this acquisition, any such decision being subject to various considerations about the prospects … It is further understood that in the event that we should not proceed with these proposals … we would be free of any obligation to you …'

---

[15] Fontaine and De Ly, 20.

7.20 Finally, an individual negotiator may indicate that he does not have authority to bind his organization by including a form of wording such as 'subject to the approval of the Board of Directors of Company A'.[16]

7.21 An important English case illustrating this is *British Steel Corp v Cleveland Bridge Engineering Co.*[17] In this case Cleveland Bridge and Engineering Co Ltd (CBE) entered into negotiations with British Steel Corp (BSC) for the manufacture of a variety of cast-steel nodes for a project in Saudi Arabia. BSC prepared an estimated price and telexed production and delivery information to CBE. After further discussions on technical aspects and specifications, CBE sent the following letter of intent to BSC:

> We are pleased to advise you it is the intention of Cleveland Bridge Engineering Co. Ltd to enter into a Sub-contract with your company, for the supply and delivery of the steel castings which form the roof nodes on this project. The price will be as quoted in your telex dated 9th February '79... The form of Sub-contract to be entered into will be our standard form of sub-contract for use in conjunction with the ICE General Conditions of contract, a copy of which is enclosed for your consideration ... We understand that you are already in possession of a complete set of our node detail drawings and we request that you proceed immediately with the works pending the preparation and issuing to you of the official form of sub-contract.

The ICE Conditions provided for unlimited liability for consequential loss due to late delivery by BSC.

7.22 BSC would not have agreed to unlimited liability for late delivery and intended to submit a formal quotation for individual prices once they had the full set of drawings from which they could make calculations.

Anticipating that a formal order would follow shortly, BSC went ahead with the request to commence manufacture.

CBE then indicated for the first time that they required the nodes to be delivered in a particular sequence. There were further discussions and negotiations between the parties over the specifications but no final agreement was reached. BSC sent CBE a formal quotation on their standard form, quoting an increased price and stating that delivery dates were to be agreed. CBE rejected this. Meanwhile BSC went ahead with the casting and delivery of nodes in stages in an effort to comply with requirements for delivery.

7.23 Although agreement was eventually reached on price, there was no agreement on liability for consequential loss or on progress payments. By 28 December 1979 BSC had delivered all but one of the nodes, the last node being held back by BSC to ensure that payment would be made by CBE. Due to a steelworkers' strike, the last node was not delivered to CBE until April 1980. CBE claimed damages from BSC for late delivery and refused to make any payment for the nodes. BSC claimed the value of the nodes on a quantum meruit basis, contending that no binding contract had been entered into. CBE claimed that a

---

[16] Fontaine and De LY, 24.
[17] [1984] 1 All ER 504.

binding contract could be found in the various documents including the letter of intent, and by conduct in proceeding with the manufacture of the nodes.

On the general effect of a letter of intent Robert Goff J stated that: 'There can be no hard and fast answer to the question whether a letter of intent will give rise to a binding agreement: everything must depend on the circumstances of the particular case.' He continued by analysing the particular letter of intent: 'In that letter, the request to BSC to proceed immediately with the work was stated to be "pending the preparation and issuing to you of the official form of sub-contract", being a sub-contract which was plainly in a state of negotiation, not least on the issues of price, delivery dates, and the applicable terms and it was "impossible to say with any degree of certainty what the material terms of [the formal] contract would be"'. Accordingly he rejected the submission that BSC, by starting work, were contractually bound.   **7.24**

Although, because of Robert Goff J's distinction, this case is commonly treated as the leading English case on letters of intent, it is important to see that the facts are very special. Normally where the transaction has in fact been completed, the temptation to hold that there was a contract would be difficult to resist but in the present case the question on which the parties had not reached agreement—the timetable—was the very matter on which they were clearly in dispute. If there had been instead a dispute about the quality of the nodes, the problem would have been much more difficult.[18]   **7.25**

It is not at all easy to believe that if the building in Saudi Arabia had collapsed because the nodes were defective Cleveland Bridge would have been liable to their main contractor but would have had no claim against BSC.

B. Cases Where Letters of Intent Do Create a Contract

The English case of *Damon Cia SA v Hapag-Lloyd International SA, The Blankenstien*[19] is a good example of a situation where, despite the reference to a formal contract, it was evident that agreement had already been reached between the parties.   **7.26**

Negotiations had taken place between the sellers and the Raftopoulos brothers for the sale of three ships to a prospective purchaser whose identity was not disclosed. The principal terms of the sale had been agreed with the exception of the name of the purchasing company. The purchase price was to be US$2,364,000 with a 10 per cent deposit. The sellers sent a memorandum of agreement incorporating the agreed terms and stating that the 10 per cent deposit was payable on signing the contract. A Panamanian company was then nominated as the purchaser and the sellers were requested to prepare a new memorandum of agreement on that basis which they sent to the buyer's broker. Telexes were sent to the sellers indicating the company's intention to go ahead with the purchase but the memorandum was not executed.   **7.27**

---

[18] The restitutionary relief is discussed more fully in Chapter 13.
[19] [1985] 1 All ER 475.

7.28   A few days later the sellers gave the buyers notice to sign the agreement and pay the deposit and stated that if this was not done, the contract would be rescinded. The buyers did not respond and the sellers claimed to be entitled to the deposit on the grounds that the buyers had rescinded.

7.29   The question for the court to determine was whether there was any concluded contract between the parties. The purchaser company claimed that there was no contract because they had not signed the memorandum or paid the deposit and since clause 2 of the memorandum only required the deposit to be paid 'on signing' the contract, the sellers could not recover the deposit amount.

7.30   However, the Court of Appeal held that all the terms of the sale had been agreed before the memorandum was sent and there was no indication that this agreement was to be subject to the execution of a memorandum. As a result, the fact that the memorandum was not signed did not prevent a binding contract existing. The deposit requirement was a term of the agreement itself so that it could not be argued that it was a condition precedent to the existence of the contract. There was also evidence that the shipping market would regard such an agreement as a binding contract without the necessity for a signed memorandum.

7.31   Fox LJ explained the position of the memorandum as follows:[20]

> That they contemplated and indeed agreed on the execution of a written memorandum I accept. But that, of itself, is not conclusive. It is open to parties to agree to execute a formal document incorporating terms which they have previously agreed. That is a binding contract. In the present case, on 8 July all the terms of the sale were agreed. And it seems to me that all the indications are that they were not intended to be subject to the execution of the memorandum.

Significantly, therefore, the Court of Appeal denied that the agreement between the parties was in any way conditional.

7.32   In *AC Controls v British Broadcasting Corp*[21] the BBC wished to install a centrally controlled software access system to 57 of its properties. ACC submitted a tender for £3,118,074.14. Under BBC internal controls it was not permissible to incur an obligation to make payments until a contract had been entered into. No formal contract was ever entered into though the BBC indicated its preferred form of contract.

7.33   On 4 June 1999 authorized representatives of both parties signed what was referred to (though not in the document itself) as a letter of intent. By this time some £400,000 of work had been done. The BBC did not want to enter into a formal contract until the program of work had been devised. This could not be done without significant survey work which ACC would not do without either payment or binding assurances of payment. Matters were made more difficult because the BBC wished to adhere to a strict and ambitious timetable. There was provision for payments against certifications by an independent consultant.

---

[20]   [1985] 1 All ER 475 at 481.
[21]   (2002) 89 ConLR 52.

On 7 July 1999 a second letter was sent authorizing further works up to an additional value **7.34**
of £500,000. His Honour Judge Anthony Thornton QC held that there was a contract for
ACC to do the work subject to the BBC's right to stop work once the existing cap had been
exceeded. The provision for payment based on the independent consultant's assessment
must involve an obligation to pay a reasonable sum for work done.

A Canadian example is *Canada Square Corp Ltd v Versa Food Services Ltd*.[22] The case was **7.35**
concerned with the question of whether there was a contract between Canada Square
Corporation (CS) and Versafood Services (VS) whereby VS had agreed to lease the restaurant on the top floor of a building being constructed by CS. Specifically at issue was the
status of a letter of October 1969 which, following negotiations, had been drafted by VS
and signed by both parties. The letter stated that it was 'to confirm our verbal understanding' and set out a list of respective responsibilities in some detail. It stated that the term of
the lease 'will be for a period of thirty years from the date of substantial completion of the
building' and finished with a statement that these constituted 'the general principles of our
agreement with you'. The agreement was accepted by CS 'subject to the approval of the
Occidental Life Insurance Company'. In May 1971 VS notified CS that it would not be
proceeding and denied the existence of any contract.

The Ontario Court of Appeal was heavily influenced by the fact that this agreement **7.36**
appeared to have been acted on by the parties for one and a half years on the basis that it was
contractually binding. Therefore the court concluded that in such circumstances a court
'should not be astute to strike down agreements'. After referring to 'the genesis and aim of
the transaction', the court concluded that it was in the interests of both parties to finalize
their agreement as quickly as possible since neither party could commence this level of
expenditure without first obtaining a commitment from the other.

After the execution of the letter, design changes were made to the building to accommodate
the rooftop restaurant and both parties spent considerable sums of money. Morden JA
stated:

> ... the parties by their words and actions following October 14, 1969, conducted themselves
> in a way which showed that it was more probable than not that from that date forward they
> regarded their relationship as being of a binding nature rather than one of two parties still
> engaged in negotiation.

VS had argued that the acceptance was conditional in that the agreement was accepted **7.37**
'subject to the approval of the Occidental Life Insurance Company' and constituted nothing more than a counter-proposal which had not been accepted by VS. However, the court
held that this had to be read in the context of the document as a whole which indicated that
the parties had in fact reached an agreement. Since the document itself had been drafted by
the President of VS, it was clear that VS were assenting to the condition in the acceptance
and it was a condition for the benefit of CS.

The second contention was that the condition had never been satisfied. CS had written to **7.38**
Occidental requesting their approval and had received a reply which, although it stated that

---

[22] (1981) 130 DLR (2d) 205; 34 OR (2d) 250.

Occidental had not had an opportunity as yet to review all aspects of the agreement in detail but approved 'the general aspects of the agreement', then went on to question and seek clarification on some points. However, the Court of Appeal considered the whole context and concluded that Occidental intended its letter to be a sufficient approval for these purposes.

7.39 The final contention was that there was no concluded contract because the parties were negotiating subject to contract and, in any event, the terms of the letter were so uncertain and impossible to perform that they were necessarily unenforceable. The court acknowledged that even if the parties did consider themselves bound, if the essential terms of the alleged contract lacked certainty there could not be a binding contract. In particular, it was alleged that the language used when detailing some responsibilities tended to indicate that they were only 'the basis' for future agreement, 'the rental arrangements will be the basis of a condominium type agreement' and 'the basis of the lease will be on a minimum annual net lease ...'. Nevertheless, the court held that these paragraphs did not look forward to the making of a formal contract but were complete in themselves because the meanings of 'basis of a condominium type agreement' and 'minimum annual net lease' were defined in the letter.

7.40 Although language such as 'is to confirm our verbal understandings' and 'constitutes the general principles of our agreement with you' might be taken as supporting the contention that there was no concluded contract, the document referred in two places to the fact that it was an 'agreement' and did not refer at any point to any further formal documentation. The description of the premises to be leased was sufficiently certain, taking the entire document into consideration and drawing certain inferences from some clauses. It referred to the whole of the top floor of the building. Extrinsic evidence was admissible to show what was meant by the 'top' of the building. The commencement date of the lease was also sufficiently certain since the parties had agreed that it was to commence on a future specified contingency.

7.41 In dismissing all of the contentions of VS, the Ontario Court of Appeal considered that it was clear that as an agreement to lease, the letter was 'crudely expressed' and contained 'some very loose language'. Nonetheless, Morden JA concluded that:

> ... accepting that the parties intended to create a binding relationship and were represented by experienced businessmen who had full authority to represent their respective companies, a Court should not be too astute to hold that there is not that degree of certainty in any of its essential terms which is the requirement of a binding contract.

It was therefore held that the letter which had been acted on by the parties, constituted a binding lease agreement.

7.42 A famous American case is *Texaco Inc v Pennzoil*[23] Negotiations had taken place between Pennzoil, a company which had sought to acquire the stock of Getty Oil, and the two main

---

[23] 729 S.W. 2d 768 (1987) cf *Murray v ABT Associates* 18 F. 3d 1376 (1994), a Decision of 7th Circuit Court of Appeals (Posner CJ, Easterbrook and Ripple JJ).

shareholders of Getty Oil, Gordon Getty and the Getty Museum. The purpose was to persuade Pennzoil to withdraw their bid for Getty Oil. Following negotiations, a document, referred to as a 'Memorandum of Agreement', was signed on 2 January, the outcome of which was that there would be only two shareholders of Getty Oil, namely Pennzoil and Gordon Getty. The 'Memorandum' detailed various steps and commitments with the object of achieving joint restructuring of the company.

The Memorandum of Agreement provided 2 January 1984:　　　　　　　　　　　　　**7.43**

> The following plan (the 'Plan') has been developed and approved by (i) Gordon P. Getty, as Trustee (the 'Trustee') of the Sarah C. Getty Trust dated December 31, 1934 (the 'Trust'), which Trustee owns 31,805,800 shares (40.2% of the total outstanding shares) of Common Stock, without par value, of Getty Oil Company (the 'Company'), which shares as well as all other outstanding shares of such Common Stock are hereinafter referred to as the 'Shares', (ii) The J. Paul Getty Museum (the 'Museum'), *which Museum owns 9,320,340 Shares (11.8% of the total outstanding Shares) and (iii) Pennzoil Company ('Pennzoil'), which owns 593,900 Shares through a subsidiary,* Holdings Incorporated, a Delaware corporation (the 'Purchaser'). The Plan is intended to assure that the public shareholders of the Company and the Museum will receive $110 per Share for all their Shares, a price which is approximately 40% above the price at which the Company's Shares were trading before Pennzoil's subsidiary announced its Offer (hereinafter described) and 10% more than the price which Pennzoil's subsidiary offered in its Offer for 20% of the Shares. The Trustee recommends that the Board of Directors of the Company approve the Plan. The Museum desires that the Plan be considered by the Board of Directors and has executed the Plan for that purpose.
>
> (1) *Pennzoil agreement.* Subject to the approval of the Plan by the Board of Directors of the Company as provided in paragraph 6 hereof, Pennzoil agrees to cause the Purchaser promptly to amend its Offer to Purchase dated December 28, 1983 (the 'Offer') for up to 16,000,000 Shares so as:
>   (a) to increase the Offer price to $110 per Share, net to the Seller in cash and
>   (b) to increase the number of Shares subject to the Offer to 23,406,100 (being 24,000,000 Shares less 593,900 Shares now owned by the Purchaser).
> (2) *Company agreement.* Subject to approval of the Plan by the Board of Directors of the Company as provided in paragraph 6 hereof, the Company agrees:
>   (a) to purchase forthwith all 9,320,340 Shares owned by the Museum at a purchase price of $110 per Share (subject to adjustment before or after closing in the event of any increase in the Offer price or in the event any higher price is paid by any person other than the Company who hereafter acquires 10 percent or more of the outstanding Shares) payable either (at the election of the Company) in cash or by means of a promissory note of the Company, dated as of the closing date, payable to the order of the Museum, due on or before thirty days from the date of issuance, bearing interest at a rate equivalent to the prime rate as in effect at Citibank, N.A. (the 'Company Note' and backed by an irrevocable letter of credit (the 'Company Note').
>   (b) to proceed promptly upon completion of the Offer by the Purchaser with a cash merger transaction whereby all remaining holders of Shares (other than the Trustee and Pennzoil and its subsidiaries) will receive $110 per Share in cash, and
>   (c) in consideration of Pennzoil's agreement provided for in paragraph 1 hereof and in order to provide additional assurance that the Plan will be consummated in accordance with its terms, to grant to Pennzoil hereby the option, exercisable at Pennzoil's election at any time on or before the later of consummation of the Offer referred to in paragraph 1 and the purchase referred to in (a) of this

paragraph 2, to purchase from the Company up to 8,000,000 Shares of Common Stock of the Company held in the treasury of the Company at a purchase price of $110 per share in cash.

(3) *Museum agreement.* Subject to the approval of the Plan by the Board of Directors of the Company as provided in paragraph 6 hereof, the Museum agrees to sell to the Company forthwith all 9,320,340 Shares owned by the Museum at a purchase price of $110 per Share (subject to adjustment before or after closing in the event of any increase in the Offer price) as provided in paragraph 2(a)) payable either (at the election of the Company) in cash or by means of the Company Note referred to in paragraph 2(c).

(4) *Trustee and Pennzoil agreement.* The Trustee and Pennzoil hereby agree with each other as follows:

    (a) *Ratio of Ownership of Shares.* The Trustee may increase its holdings to up to 32,000,000 Shares and Pennzoil may increase its holdings to up to 24,000,000 Shares of the approximately 79,132,000 outstanding Shares. Neither the Trustee nor Pennzoil will acquire in excess of such respective amounts without the prior written agreement of the other, it being the agreement between the Trustee and Pennzoil to maintain a relative Share ratio of 4 (for the Trustee) to 3 (for Pennzoil). In connection with the Offer in the event that more than 23,406,100 Shares are duly tendered to the Purchaser, the Purchaser may (if it chooses) purchase any excess over 23406,000; *provided, however,* (i) the Purchaser agrees to sell any such excess Shares to the Company (and the Company shall agree to purchase) forthwith at $110 per Share and (ii) pending consummation of such sale to the Company the Purchaser shall grant to the Trustee the irrevocable proxy to vote such excess Shares.

    (b) *Restructuring plan.* Upon completion of the transactions provided for in paragraphs 1, 2 and 3 hereof, the Trustee and Pennzoil shall endeavor in good faith to agree upon a plan for the restructuring of the Company. In the event that for any reason the Trustee and Pennzoil are unable to agree upon a mutually acceptable plan on or before December 31, 1984, then the Trustee and Pennzoil hereby agree to cause the Company to adopt a plan of complete liquidation of the Company pursuant to which (i) any assets which are mutually agreed to be sold shall be sold and the net proceeds there from shall be used to reduce liabilities of the company and (ii) individual interests in all remaining assets and liabilities shall be distributed to the shareholders pro rata in accordance with their actual ownership interest in the Company. In connection with the plan of distribution, Pennzoil agrees (if requested by the Trustee) that it will enter into customary joint operating agreements to operate any properties so distributed and otherwise to agree to provide operating management for any business and operations requested by the Trustee on customary terms and conditions.

    (c) *Board of Directors and Management.* Upon completion of the transactions provided for in paragraphs 1, 2 and 3 hereof, the Trustee and Pennzoil agree that the Board of Directors of the Company shall be mutually agreeable to the Trustee and Pennzoil (which Directors may include certain present Directors) and who shall be nominated by the Trustee and Pennzoil, respectively, in the ratio of 4 to 3. The Trustee and Pennzoil agree that the senior management of the Company shall include Gordon P. Getty as Chairman of the Board, J. Hugh Liedtke as President and Chief Executive Officer and Baine P. Kerr as Chairman of the Executive Committee.

    (d) *Access to information.* Pennzoil, the Trustee and their representatives will have access to all information concerning the Company necessary or pertinent to accomplish the transactions contemplated by the Plan.

- (e) *Press releases.* The Trustee and Pennzoil (and the Company upon approval of the Plan) will coordinate any press releases or public announcements concerning the Plan and any transactions contemplated hereby.
- (5) *Compliance with regulatory requirements.* The Plan shall be implemented in compliance with applicable regulatory requirements.
- (6) *Approval by the Board of Directors.* This Plan is subject to approval by the Board of Directors of the Company at the meeting of the Board being held on January 2, 1984 and will expire if not approved by the Board. Upon such approval, the Company shall execute three or more counterparts of the 'Joinder by the Company' attached to the Plan and deliver one such counterpart to each of the Trustee, the Museum and Pennzoil.

Note that it refers to all matters being 'subject to the approval of the Plan by the Board of   **7.44**
Directors of the Company (Getty Oil)'. This approval was secured on 3 January. On 4
January a press release was issued.

The Press release stated:

Press Release

FOR IMMEDIATE RELEASE

JANUARY 4, 1984

LOS ANGELES—Getty Oil Company, the J. Paul Getty Museum and Gordon P. Getty, as Trustee of the Sarah C. Getty Trust, announced today that they have agreed in principle with Pennzoil Company to a merger of Getty Oil and a newly formed entity owned by Pennzoil and the Trustees.

In connection with the transaction, the shareholders of Getty Oil other than Pennzoil and the Trustee will receive $110 per share cash plus the right to receive a deferred cash consideration in a formula amount. The deferred consideration will be equal to a pro rata share of the net after-tax proceeds, in excess of $1 billion, from the disposition of ETC Corporation, the Getty Oil reinsurance subsidiary, and will be paid upon the disposition. In any event, under the formula, each shareholder will receive at least $5 per share within five years.

Prior to the merger, Pennzoil will contribute approximately $2.6 billion in cash and the Trustee and Pennzoil will contribute the Getty Oil shares owned by them to the new entity. Upon execution of a definitive merger agreement, the December 28, 1983, tender offer by a Pennzoil subsidiary for shares of Getty Oil stock will be withdrawn.

The agreement in principle also provides that Getty Oil will grant to Pennzoil an option to purchase eight million treasury shares for $110 per share.

The transaction is subject to execution of a definitive merger agreement, approval by the stockholders of Getty Oil and completion of various governmental filing and waiting period requirements.

Following consummation of the merger, the Trust will own 4/7ths of the outstanding common stock of Getty Oil and Pennzoil will own 3/7ths. The Trust and Pennzoil have also agreed in principle that following consummation of the merger they will endeavor in good faith to agree upon a plan for restructuring Getty Oil on or before December 31, 1984, and that if they are unable to reach such an agreement then they will cause a division of assets of the company.

On 5 January secret negotiations were commenced by the two shareholders with Texaco   **7.45**
and on 6 January it was announced that Texaco had signed an agreement to take over the
company. Texaco were offering $125 a share. Pennzoil brought an action against Texaco

alleging that Texaco had intentionally interfered with its existing contract and had induced the breach of contract. It was therefore necessary for Pennzoil to establish that there was a valid contract contained in the 'Memorandum of Agreement'.

7.46   The jury found that 'from a preponderance of the evidence' there was an intention to be bound by an agreement containing the terms of this 'Memorandum'. Pennzoil were awarded the considerable figure of $7.53 billion in damages, plus punitive damages of $3 billion. On appeal the Texas Court of Appeal upheld the $7.53 billion actual damages award but reduced the punitive damages to $1 billion. It held that the jury had been correctly instructed and that the verdict was open to the jury on the evidence.

7.47   Whether there was an intention to be bound was a question of fact to be determined by the jury in the light of all the circumstances of the case. The court concluded that 'the release as a whole is worded in indicative terms, not in subjective or hypothetical ones'. In particular, the court found that the words 'after the execution and delivery of this Agreement' was simply a phrase used before a statement of each party's obligations to indicate the timing of acts that were to occur and 'did not impose any express precondition to the formation of a contract'.

The division of function between judge and jury which no longer exists in other common law systems is clearly of great significance in this case. Since there are plausible arguments either way as to the correct result it is hard to see that either side was entitled to a directed verdict. Pennzoil were not suing the Getty interests for breach of contract but Texaco for inducing breach but clearly the existence of a binding contract was an essential part of their case. There was a possible second line of defence for Texaco that they did not know there was a contract. Texaco led evidence that they had been told that there was no contract but clearly this evidence was not accepted. Indeed the size of the punitive damage award shows that the jury formed a very hostile view of the behaviour of Texaco.

7.48   Texaco argued that the addition of the words 'in principle' after the word 'Agreement' meant that the transaction was not intended to be legally binding and led evidence that on Wall Street everybody knew that 'agreement in principle' meant not binding but it seems dangerously simplistic to rely on such a formula in such a case. As can be seen the memorandum of agreement was very detailed and expressly provided that it was subject to the approval of the board. Once the board approved it is perhaps not surprising that the jury thought that it had become binding.

7.49   It is not surprising that about a case involving such vast sums there has been much discussion[24] including it is said, at least three books, one by one of the jurors. It is perhaps unlikely that the case will inspire any common law jurisdiction to restore jury trials in such matters[25] but the situation could occur in any jurisdiction. It would be bold to assert that in a case tried by a judge alone, the result would be certain. The most striking feature of the facts is

---

[24] See Lake and Draetta, 130–44; Ansaldi (1990) 27 Houston LR 733; Weintraub (1990) 9 Review of Litigation 371; Gergen (1990) 9 Review of Litigation 441.

[25] It is hard to believe that an English judge would have taken such a wide view of the jury's function at any time in history. For this purpose the legal effect of the memorandum of agreement would surely have been treated as a question of law.

that in the key meeting between Pennzoil and the representatives of the various Getty interests which went on for many hours and was deeply populated by lawyers, no one took adequate steps to make the legal status of the agreement clear.[26]

C. Cases Where the Letters of Intent Have Some Legal Effect

Letters of intent followed by performance

As explained above, there will be many cases where there are commercial pressures to start performance before negotiations are complete. If performance confers benefits on the other party there will usually be at least a restitution remedy as in *British Steel v Cleveland Bridge*[27] but quite often instruction to proceed will be treated as promises to pay for the work done. In *Emcor Drake & Scull v Sir Robert McAlpine*[28] the claimant was the M&E subcontractor on a major hospital contract on which the defendant was the main contractor. The defendant indicated from an early stage that the claimant was its preferred subcontractor and a price of £34.25 million was soon agreed but there were long and complex negotiations over the terms. The parties never signed a formal contract. The defendants sent a number of letters which the claimant was invited to sign but it did not sign any of them. The defendant issued a letter instructing the claimant to start work and promising to pay up to £1 million. There was no dispute about the scope of work. The claimant started work and there were successive letters raising the authorized payments up to £14 million before the parties fell out. The Court of Appeal held that no contract for the whole work had ever been concluded. There were a string of contracts under which the claimant was entitled to a reasonable sum for work of a good and workmanlike quality up to a maximum. This is a classic example. There was never a final contract but there were a series of interim contracts in which there was identifiable work to be done and an agreed price for the work. **7.50**

Where there is an instruction to start work and the work is of a kind for which, objectively speaking, payment is reasonably expected there will be a contract of this kind. If a price is not stated it will still usually be possible to hold that there is a promise to pay a reasonable price. **7.51**

D. Letters of Comfort

Suppose an English company is dealing in England with the English subsidiary of a large American company. Discreet searches reveal that the English subsidiary does not itself have much money. Caution suggests that it would be wise to check whether the American company will stand behind its English subsidiary. The foolproof way to do this is to request a parent company guarantee but there may be resistance to doing this and instead the American company may offer a letter of comfort. What is that effect of such a letter? **7.52**

The orthodox answer must be that it all depends on an objective construction of what the letter says but something may turn on the approach. The leading English case is **7.53**

---

[26] For further discussion see Chapter 3.
[27] See above and for further discussion see Chapter 13.
[28] (2004) 98 Con LR 1.

Kleinwort Benson Ltd v Malaysia Mining Corp Bhd[29] where the defendant parent company had issued a 'Letter of Comfort' which stated 'it is our policy to ensure that the business of [the subsidiary company] is at all times in a position to meet its liabilities to you [under the loan agreement]'. When the subsidiary became insolvent the plaintiff bank claimed that the defendant should cover the subsidiary's indebtedness to them in accordance with the comfort letter.

7.54 Hirst J, at first instance,[30] treated the question of the enforceability of the comfort letter as resting on whether there was any intention to create legal relations. This was a commercial agreement where it was difficult to rebut the presumption of an intention to create legal relations and Hirst J held that the presumption had not been rebutted. However, the Court of Appeal considered this approach to be incorrect and preferred a test involving an examination of the words used in the comfort letter to determine if a promise was being made. The Court of Appeal held the words in question to be only a statement of current policy and intention and that the words used did not amount to a promise to abide by this statement of policy. In their view the presumption of an intention to create legal relations in commercial agreements could only arise if the words used were clearly promissory.

7.55 In the decision of the Commercial Division of the Supreme Court of New South Wales in Australia in *Banque Brussels Lambert v Australian National Industries Ltd*[31] this approach was forcefully criticized by Rogers CJ as leading to uncertainty in commercial contracts and as placing the enforceability of bargained for comfort letters in the realms of clauses binding in honour only without there being any express statement to this effect.

7.56 In *Bank of New Zealand v Ginivan*[32] the New Zealand Court of Appeal considered the Kleinwort Benson decision but rejected an argument to apply it to the mixed wording of the comfort letter in that case. The comfort letter stated that: 'Our policy is that this company will conduct its affairs in a responsible manner, maintain a sound financial condition and meet its obligations promptly and will use our "best endeavours" to see that the company continues to do so.' The New Zealand Court of Appeal appeared to suggest that despite the reference to the future in the last sentence, ie 'will use', the existence of a best endeavours clause indicated a legally binding obligation.

7.57 The distinction between guarantees and letters of comfort occurs equally in French practice.[33] The President of the Association of Banks (in France) issued an opinion stating that a letter of comfort should be 'considered as providing in practical terms security comparable to a guarantee'.

---

[29] [1989] 1 All ER 785. See also *Chemco Leasing SPA v Rediffusion* [1987] 1 FTLR 201, *Monk Construction v Norwich Union Life Insurance Society* (1992) 62 BLR 107, Reynolds (1988) 104 LQR 353; Davenport [1988] LMC LQ 290; Prentice (1989) 105 LQR 346; Ayres and Moore [1989] LMCLQ 281; Tyree (1988–1990) 2 JCL 279; Brown [1990] JBL 281.
[30] [1988] 1 All ER 714.
[31] (1989) 21 NSWLR 502.
[32] [1991] 1 NZLR 178.
[33] Fontaine and De LY, 6–8.

E. Agreements Imposing Obligations as to the Course of the Negotiations

In long and complex negotiations the parties may very well make binding agreements **7.58** which are separate from the main negotiations.[34] So they may agree that the details of the negotiation are to be confidential. There are good reasons why such an agreement should be binding at once. Similarly they might enter into binding obligations not during the negotiation to enter into negotiations about the same subject matter with anyone else.

The process of negotiation is often itself expensive. The general rule is no doubt that usually **7.59** each party bears its own costs but there is no reason why in exceptional circumstances the parties cannot make another agreement. So a letter of intent may produce this effect. Similarly it may impose on one party specific duties, such as obtaining the consent of third parties.

---

[34] Fontaine and De LY, examples 20–25.

8

PRACTICAL ASPECTS OF LETTERS OF INTENT

A. Letters of Intent—Some Practical Considerations

It is possible to read at least some of the cases discussed in Chapter 7 and conclude that the parties would have avoided trouble if they had behaved in a more business-like fashion or employed (better) lawyers. Although this is not wholly untrue and indeed much of this Chapter will be devoted to considering what might be done differently it is undoubtedly an over simplification. Many of the difficulties arise out of the fact that negotiation is often a tricky business and that the interests of the parties often diverge. **8.01**

A good example is *Texaco Inc v Pennzoil*,[1] the facts and decision of which we have already discussed. The one thing we can say for certain about this case is that we do not know all the facts but only those which the parties chose or were forced to reveal. Nevertheless it is clear that the interests of the two sides were not the same. There was one principle area of negotiation—the price to be paid for the shares. Pennzoil had started by offering $100 for 20 per cent of Getty oil stock which had been refused. They had increased the offer to $110. During the negotiation which followed this offer was increased by a 'stub'—an offer relating to the proceeds of the future liquidation of a Pennzoil subsidiary. This 'stub' was said to be worth about another $5 a share. At this stage Pennzoil's clear interest was not to have to make a further, larger offer—in other words to have a binding contract. The interests of the Getty team were different and fragmented. **8.02**

There were in fact three sub-teams on the Getty side; Gordon Getty who was the trustee of the Sarah Getty trust which controlled 40.2 per cent of Getty oil stock; the museum trustees who controlled 11.8 per cent and the other members of the board. It appears that, subject to their fiduciary duties, Gordon Getty and the museum trustees had complete **8.03**

---

[1] 729 S.W. 2d 768 (1987) Sections 7.42–7.49

de facto control of their shares and the consequent voting rights. This was not true of the other members of the board who must have been aware that as Gordon Getty and the museum trustees controlled 52 per cent of the shares they could reconstitute the board. They must have also been aware that the 48 per cent of the shareholders whom they in a sense represented but did not control might complain of the result of the negotiations. If the Pennzoil offer fell through they risked complaints from shareholders that they had missed the chance of a good sale. If they believed that the shares were worth more than $115 they would be praying for a white knight to appear. The interest of Gordon Getty in the value of the shares would be different. The effect of the Pennzoil deal would be to increase the trust holding from 40.2 per cent to four-sevenths—in other words the trust would be a net purchaser of shares.

8.04   At the time the memorandum of agreement was signed Pennzoil had a clear interest to enter into a binding agreement. The position of the Getty team is much less clear. They clearly did not want to reject the Pennzoil proposals and lead Pennzoil to go away. Some parts of the team may have been happy to enter into a binding agreement. The amount of detail outstanding was not great. Making the Memorandum of Agreement subject to board approval and then quickly giving board approval do not seem the ideal way to keep the question in the air. At the trial it was argued by the Texaco lawyers that the key words were the statement that there was 'Agreement in principle' since everybody on Wall Street knew that meant that there was no binding contract. This evidence was clearly not persuasive to a Texas jury but it is puzzling that anyone should have relied on it if the whole of the Getty team were agreed at this stage that they did not want to be bound. If they had been clear amongst themselves as to this it would surely not have been impossibly difficult to find some reason not to have the confirmatory board meeting for a day or two.

8.05   It is clear in this case that the parties had ample access to normally competent lawyers. We do not know what instructions were given to the lawyers nor what the lawyers said to each other. It is however unlikely that the Getty lawyers sought to make it completely clear that the deal was not yet binding. This would have invited an ultimatum from Pennzoil—make up your mind by breakfast or the offer will be withdrawn.

8.06   This was a classic letter of intent situation. One party does not want to enter into a binding legal relationship but does not want to say so in clear terms. The case emphasized in clear terms the dangers posed by the resultant ambiguities. We will consider some possible solutions.

B. Possible Ways of Delaying Legal Effect of Letters of Intent

8.07   Making the agreement subject to board approval may well be a good way of processing. Ideally the transaction needs to be one which the requirement of board approval is commercially plausible and the board needs to be restricted from giving approval too quickly.[2]

---

[2] There have been a substantial number of US cases involving the question whether the transaction is binding once the board has approved. See Farnsworth 'Pre-contractual Liability and Preliminary Agreements:

In the same way apparent agreements may be made subject to conditions which are within the control of the party imposing conditions such as 'subject to satisfactory finance'. If the condition is regarded as valid, there will be a contract if it is satisfied. Such conditional contracts are discussed more fully in Chapter 9. **8.08**

Main contractors might write to potential subcontractors to say that they will be appointed if the main contractor secures the main contract. This would seem to be a binding conditional contract but main contractors appear not to do this on the basis that if the subcontractor falls out it will be possible to get another subcontractor at much the same price.[3] This will usually be true but not in the critical case where the subcontractor has made a mistake and quoted too low a price.[4] **8.09**

Of course there will be cases where neither party wants to be legally bound at this stage. It will usually be best to say so by putting a clause in the letter of intent saying: 'This letter of intent is not intended to have legal effect.' This will save a lot of trouble if one party subsequently seeks to argue that the letter does have legal effect. **8.10**

C. Letters of Intent and Partially Completed Negotiations

This is a completely different situation. The parties are engaged in long and complex negotiation which will extend over months or even years. In such negotiations there will often be agreements at an early stage which colour all the future negotiations. **8.11**

An excellent example, though not in a commercial or legal context, is the negotiation conducted during the Second World War between the United States, led by President Roosevelt and General George Marshall and the British led by Winston Churchill and General Sir Alan Brooke. We know a great deal about those negotiations because not only are there official records but many of the participants kept (although forbidden to do so) diaries. **8.12**

The discussion started immediately after the Japanese attack on Pearl Harbour on 8 December 1941. The British team left for the first conference in the United States in the battleship *Duke of York* on Saturday 13 December 1941. There were 15 conferences before the end of the war in 1945. Fortunately we have a magisterial account of the process by Andrew Roberts in *Masters and Commanders*.[5] From the first meeting it was agreed to operate on the principle of 'Germany First' that is to concentrate the greater part of the joint resources on the defeat of Germany. This was because 'the defeat of Germany would make the defeat of Japan a matter of time, whereas the defeat of Japan would not materially weaken Germany'.[6] This principle was adhered to for the rest of the war though not without some anxious reconsideration. **8.13**

Fair Dealing and Failed Negotiations' (1987) 87 Columbia L Rev 217 and cases cited therein at footnotes 121–125.

[3] Lewis, 'Contracts between Businessmen: Reform of the Law of Firm Offers and an Empirical Study of Tendering Practices in the Building Industry' (1982) 9 Journal of Law and Society 153.
[4] This has been the factual basis of a number of the leading cases on tenders discussed in Chapter 5.
[5] Allen Lane, 2008.
[6] *Masters and Commanders*, 69.

8.14 It is clear that much the same may happen in commercial negotiations. If it does it seems sensible to record this in writing. The American case law recognizes the possibility of an agreement with open terms. Farnsworth states that 'an agreement with open terms has two consequences. First it implies an obligation to carry out the deal even if the parties are unable to agree upon the open terms. Second, it imposes a general obligation of fair dealing in the negotiation of the open terms'.[7]

8.15 A good example is *Borg-Warner Corp v Anchor Coupling Co*.[8] There had been negotiation over Borg-Warner's possible acquisition of Anchor. Borg-Warner wrote a letter suggesting that they be given an option to buy Anchor on stated terms. Conroy and Fritsch, the chief officers of Anchor wrote a reply indicating that they did not want to grant an option but might be willing instead to agree a sale on the same terms but with four exceptions, two of which would have to be negotiated. These were that Borg-Warner would give 'suitable assurances ... for the retention of the lower level executive personnel' and that it would make 'mutually satisfactory arrangements ... for the continued employment' of Conroy. Conroy and Fritsch assured Borg-Warner that this was an offer; that the open terms were minor details and that the 'parties would be obligated to work out in good faith in a reasonable manner'. Borg-Warner agreed but in due course Anchor argued that there was no contract. The Supreme Court of Illinois held that there was a binding contract capable of specific performance.

D. Agreements to Negotiate in Good Faith

8.16 It is clear that this decision turns in part on the willingness of the Illinois Court to hold that there was a duty to negotiate in good faith. An English Court might reach the same conclusion but not for the same explicit reasons. It is important to bear in mind however that it is easier for a common law court to give effect to an express promise to negotiate in good faith than to impose a duty to do so and that it is far from clear that even English law will not come to give effect to express undertakings to negotiate in good faith.[9]

8.17 Some have argued, echoing Lord Ackner, that an agreement to negotiate in good faith has no content beyond abstaining from conduct, like fraud, which is prohibited anyway. In this view negotiation is like the gun fight in *Butch Cassidy and the Sundance Kid*, an activity free from rules. This is surely too bleak a view. It is possible to identify a number of examples of bad faith negotiation.

E. Refusal to Negotiate

8.18 If one has agreed to negotiate, it is bad faith to refuse to negotiate or to say we will only negotiate if you change your team or to negotiate in a deliberately dilatory manner.

---

[7] (1987) 87 Columbia LR 217. See particularly footnotes 148–155.
[8] 16 Ill 2d 234 156 N.E 2d 513 (1958) Knapp, 'Enforcing the Contract to Bargain' (1969) 44 NYULR 673.
[9] For fuller discussion see Chapter 12.

A key question is whether it is acceptable to negotiate with someone else. If it is sought to exclude this possibility it is safest to do so explicitly. **8.19**

A more difficult question is to what extent it is bad faith to go back on things that have already been agreed. In a developed system one might expect a recognition that this was usually but not always bad faith. There could be cases where it was an imaginative way of putting the negotiations on a new track.

F. Starting Work

A letter of intent may be issued where the issuer wants work to start but is not yet ready to **8.20** enter into a complete contract. Undoubtedly this makes lawyers with tidy minds nervous but there are business situations where it is difficult or impossible to avoid. The classic example is the building of a stadium for a major sporting event such as the Olympic Games or the World Cup. The opening ceremony cannot be postponed for a month because the stadium is not complete. The pressure to get started cannot therefore be resisted. Even in less pressured situations the cases in Chapter 7 show that millions of pounds worth of work may be done on a contract that is not yet complete. What should be done to reduce the dangers?

The first step is to define carefully what is to be done. It is not sensible simply to tell the **8.21** contractor or subcontractor to start. It is essential to define precisely how far he is to go. The instruction should also make it clear how much the contractor is to be paid. By itself an instruction to start would normally carry an implied promise to pay a reasonable sum but it will usually be safer to state precisely a sum or at least to state a rate or rates by which the sum can be calculated. The contractor needs also to be sure that he knows how much he will be paid and that this is an acceptable amount.

9

CONDITIONAL CONTRACTS

A. Introduction

The word 'condition' has many meanings in contract law.[1] It can be used to describe a term **9.01** of a contract. As regards legal effect, it can be used to refer to a term any breach of which gives rise not only to a right to damages but to a right to terminate a contract.[2] It may also be used in the sense of a 'condition precedent' or 'condition subsequent'.[3] These terms have been used to describe the order of performance[4] and are relevant to questions of enforcement. They are sometimes used alongside the terms 'dependent obligation' and

---

[1] See Stoljar, 'The Contractual Concept of Condition' (1953) 69 LQR 485, 486–8.

[2] The non-fulfilment of the condition excuses the innocent party from performing if it elects to do so and the breach of the promise that the condition would be fulfilled gives the innocent party a right to damages. A warranty on the other hand is a term any breach of which gives rise only to a right to damages.

[3] Traditionally, even when 'condition' is used in the sense of a term any breach of which gives rise to a right to terminate, it was expressed as a 'condition precedent', see *Bayerische Vereinsbank Aktiengesellschaft v National Bank of Pakistan* [1997] 1 Lloyd's Rep 59, 65 and see Carter, 'Intermediate Terms Arrive in Australia and Singapore' (2008) 24 JCL 226, 227.

[4] For example an obligation to pay wages may be dependent on the employee first carrying out the work, see *Automatic Fire Sprinklers Pty Ltd v Watson* (1946) 72 CLR 435. See also *Michaels v Harley House (Marylebone) Ltd* [2000] Ch 104, 115–16. See further Furmston (ed), *The Law of Contract* (3rd ed, LexisNexis Butterworths, London, 2007) para 3.33.

'independent obligation'.[5] Traditionally the term 'condition precedent' refers to the situation where a contingency must occur to bring a contract into existence, that is, it impacts on contract formation.[6] Alternatively, a contingency may condition the performance of a contract. These may or may not be promissory in nature. Many describe such 'conditions' as 'conditions subsequent' in order to emphasize that the contract exists.[7] More traditionally the term 'condition subsequent' is used to describe an event after formation which would either discharge the contract if it did or did not occur or 'will extinguish a duty after performance has become due'.[8] The concept of a condition subsequent is well established outside of the law of contract, a typical example might occur under a will where an annuity is promised to someone until a certain event occurs such as upon their marriage. Conditions subsequent are not much litigated in modern contract law although in practice they do exist.

9.02   The typical 'conditional contract' is the agreement that is expressed to be 'subject to' the performance or occurrence of some event that is not certain to occur.[9] The event itself is termed a 'contingency' and it is the contract or its performance that is termed 'conditional'. The contingency may be one requiring some conduct or decision to be made by one of the parties, or a third party, or it may refer to some other event that is out of the control of

---

[5] These too have other meanings. Traditionally whether a debt was recoverable was analysed in terms of dependent and independent obligations. In time a dependent obligation was aligned with a condition while an independent obligation was aligned with a warranty, see Carter and Tolhurst, 'Recovery of Contract Debts Following Termination for Breach' (2009) 25 JCL 191 and see Stoljar, 'Dependent and Independent Promises' (1957) 2 Syd LR 217.

[6] See *Wickman Machine Tool Sales Ltd v L Schuler AG* [1972] 1 WLR 840, 850, 854, 859. See also Carter, 'Conditions and Conditions Precedent' (1991) 4 JCL 90, 91. Cf Harnett and Thornton, 'The Insurance Condition Subsequent: A Needle in a Semantic Haystack' (1948) 17 Fordham L Rev 220, 221, 223.

[7] See *Perri v Coolangatta Investments Pty Ltd* (1982) 149 CLR 537, 543. Another categorization is between events which the parties have no control over (conditions precedent) and events the parties do have control over (conditions subsequent), see Robinson, 'Waiver of Benefit of Conditional Clauses' (1975) 39 The Conveyancer 251. For others 'conditions subsequent' refer to non-promisory contingencies in an existing contract, see Proksch, 'In Praise of Conditions Subsequent' (1982) 14 UWALR 333.

[8] Where a cheque is given in payment of a debt it is a conditional payment, that is, conditional on the cheque being honoured when deposited, thus it is said that '[s]ubject to non-fulfilment of the condition subsequent, the payment is complete at the time when the cheque is accepted by the creditor', *National Australia Bank Ltd v KDS Construction Services Pty Ltd* (1987) 163 CLR 668, 676. See Restatement (2d) Contracts § 224, comment *e* and illustrations 8 and 9 and see § 230. See also Swanton, '"Subject to Finance" Clauses in Contracts for the Sale of Land' Part II (1984) 58 ALJ 690, ('a condition precedent is a condition attached to the creation of an obligation while a condition subsequent is a condition attached to the destruction of an obligation') and see *Head v Tattersall* (1871) Lr 7 Ex 7; *Hunt v Wilson* [1978] 2 NZLR 261, 267–8; *Perri v Coolangatta Investments Pty Ltd* (1982) 149 CLR 537, 556; *Thompson v ASDA-MFI plc* [1988] Ch 241. It follows that many conditions precedent to performance may be conditions subsequent in this sense as the non-fulfilment of the condition may entitle a party to terminate the contract, see *Perri v Coolangatta Investments Pty Ltd* (1982) 149 CLR 537, 551 per Mason J, 565 per Brennan J. More generally whether a condition is considered precedent or subsequent is entirely dependent on what is chosen as the reference point, see Harnett & Thornton, 'The Insurance Condition Subsequent: A Needle in a Semantic Haystack' (1948) 17 Fordham L Rev 220, 224ff and see Holmes, *The Common Law* (Little Brown & Co, Boston, 1882) at 315–24. See further Perillo (ed), *Corbin on Contracts* (Revised edn, Vol 8, Lexis Law Publishing, Virginia, 1999) § 30.7, pp 11ff and §§ 39.1ff, pp 473ff.

[9] See Restatement (2d) Contracts § 224. Where the performance of an obligation is merely subject to the expiration of a time period this would not usually be described as a conditional obligation, see Restatement (2d) Contracts § 224 comment *b*.

anyone such as an act of nature.[10] It has become commonplace to refer to the event as either a condition or a contingency and both 'condition' and 'contingency' are used here interchangeably.

The concern of this chapter is with those conditions that impact on the formation of a contract. The classic example is the unilateral contract.[11] The study of such conditions necessarily involves distinguishing conditions that merely impact on performance but no detailed discussion of performance obligations is entered into. Indeed, the performance of all contracts can to some extent be described as conditional. For example, many contracts would be conditional upon the continued existence of the subject matter of the contract and most performance obligations could be described as conditional upon the other party not repudiating the contract or on the other party being ready, willing and able to accept performance. These are broader topics of contract law and fall outside this book.   **9.03**

The distinction between conditions that impact on formation and performance was explained by Denning LJ in *Trans Trust SPRL v Danubian Trading Co Ltd*.[12] The case concerned a contract for the sale of goods which contained a stipulation requiring the defendant buyer to open a letter of credit in favour of the plaintiff seller. The credit was never opened and the plaintiff claimed damages for breach of contract. Denning LJ in assessing the legal position of such a stipulation stated:[13]   **9.04**

> Sometimes it is a condition precedent to the formation of a contract, that is, it is a condition which must be fulfilled before any contract is concluded at all. In those cases the stipulation 'subject to the opening of a credit' is rather like a stipulation 'subject to contract'. If no credit is provided, there is no contract between the parties. In other cases a contract is concluded and the stipulation for a credit is a condition which is an essential term of the contract. In those cases the provision of the credit is a condition precedent, not to the formation of a contract, but to the obligation of the seller to deliver the goods. If the buyer fails to provide the credit, the seller can treat himself as discharged from any further performance of the contract and can sue the buyer for damages for not providing the credit.

Here the buyers had agreed that 'a credit will be opened forthwith' and Denning LJ concluded that in the circumstances of the case this constituted 'a firm promise by the buyers pursuant to which they gave their personal assurance that a credit would be opened forthwith'.[14] It therefore was a term of an existing contract and, moreover, an essential term.   **9.05**

Today the courts are more likely to construe a condition as conditioning performance rather than formation. It follows that in practice the usual legal issues arising are issues of performance, waiver of conditions and avoidance. Despite this, ultimately whether or not   **9.06**

---

[10] Examples of such conditions commonly found in contracts include where performance is conditional upon execution of a contract; where the obligations of a purchaser are subject to the purchaser finding satisfactory finance; where a payment obligation under a building contract is subject to work being signed off by an architect; where the right to draw down on a loan is subject to provision of adequate security; where a sale is subject to a satisfactory survey.

[11] See *United Dominion Trust (Commercial) Ltd v Eagle Aircraft Services Ltd* [1968] 1 WLR 74.

[12] [1952] 2 QB 297.

[13] [1952] 2 QB 297, 304.

[14] [1952] 2 QB 297, 304.

a condition impacts on formation or performance is dependent on the intention of the parties and therefore, in order to distinguish them, it is necessary to discuss many cases that deal with conditions precedent to performance. The concern is with the decision-making process by which a court determines whether a condition impacts on formation or performance. The main focus of the chapter will be agreements made 'subject to contract' and this is the principal area where issues of contract formation arise. The other principal 'subject to' provision is the 'subject to finance' clause and this too is discussed in detail in this chapter.

B. The 'Construction' of 'Subject to' Clauses

9.07   Where an agreement does not use the words 'subject to contract' then whether or not the agreement is conditional upon the execution of a formal contract will be determined by construction.[15] However, it is often said that the determination of the meaning of the expression 'subject to contract' is an issue of construction.[16] The same applies to other forms of 'subject to' clauses.[17] In *Von Hatzfeldt-Wildenburg v Alexander*,[18] Parker J explained the general position by stating that:[19]

> It appears to be well settled by the authorities that if the documents or letters relied on as constituting a contract contemplate the execution of a further contract between the parties, it is a question of construction whether the execution of the further contract is a condition or term of the bargain or whether it is a mere expression of the desire of the parties as to the manner in which the transaction already agreed to will in fact go through. In the former case there is no enforceable contract either because the condition is unfulfilled or because the law does not recognize a contract to enter into a contract. In the latter case there is a binding contract and the reference to the more formal document may be ignored.

9.08   The word 'construction' is capable of wide import and it is true that the search is for the presumed intention of the parties and so a reference to 'construction' is not entirely misplaced.[20] Thus, in *Australian Broadcasting Corporation v XIVth Commonwealth Games Ltd*,[21] an issue of formation was said to be determined by construction if the alleged

---

[15] *Elias v George Sahely & Co (Barbados) Ltd* [1983] 1 AC 646, 653.

[16] *Winn v Bull* (1877) 7 Ch D 29, 32; *Rossiter v Miller* (1878) 3 App Cas 1124, 1152; *Commonwealth Homes and Investment Co Ltd v Mackellar* (1939) 63 CLR 351; *Masters v Cameron* (1954) 91 CLR 353, 362. For an extensive discussion of the cases on this point, see *Air Great Lakes Pty Ltd v KS Easter (Holdings) Pty Ltd* (1985) 2 NSWLR 309, 313ff, per Hope JA.

[17] Eg *Aberfoyle Plantations Ltd v Cheng* [1960] AC 115, 124.

[18] [1912] 1 Ch 284. Cf *Godecke v Kirwan* (1973) 129 CLR 629, 638 per Walsh J (who makes the point that this is not a complete statement of the legal effects such a provision may have as it leaves out the second category referred to in *Masters v Cameron* (1954) 91 CLR 353 (see 9.16 and 9.55)).

[19] [1912] 1 Ch 284, 288–9.

[20] *Barrier Wharfs Ltd v W Scott Fell & Co Ltd* (1908) 5 CLR 647, 661 per Higgins J (affirmed (1908) 5 CLR 647); *GR Securities Pty Ltd v Baulkham Hills Private Hospital Pty Ltd* (1986) 40 NSWLR 631, 634. See also *Mississippi & Dominion Steamship Co Ltd v Swift* 86 Me 248, 29 A 1063, 1066 (1894).

[21] (1988) 18 NSWLR 540. See also *Brambles Holdings Ltd v Bathurst City Council* (2001) 53 NSWLR 153, [26]; *GEC Marconi Systems Pty Ltd v BHP Information Technology Pty Ltd* (2003) 128 FCR 1, 229; *Sagacious Procurement Pty Ltd v Symbion Health Ltd* [2008] NSWCA 149, [67]–[69], [99]–[105], note also [106] dealing with admissions and subsequent conduct.

agreement was in writing.[22] However, in carrying out that process the court held that it was legitimate to have regard to the surrounding circumstances and conduct of the parties after the alleged date of formation. This emphasizes the difference between finding an intention to contract and finding the meaning of a term of a contract. It is the latter that is referred to as an issue of construction in a technical sense and the evidence that is available to find the intention of the parties in such an exercise will depend on those principles that govern the construction of contracts.[23] The formal or informal nature of the agreement that has been reached by the parties will be relevant to that investigation.[24]

However, it needs to be kept in mind that generally the evidence available to determine **9.09** whether a contract has been formed is wider than the evidence available to construe and determine the meaning and legal effect of the terms of a contract. Nevertheless, determining whether or not a condition impacts on the formation of a contract may involve questions of law or questions of fact.[25] Where a party seeks to argue that the phrase 'subject to contract' evidences a lack of an intention to contract that party can resort to extrinsic evidence as it involves a question of fact.[26] If that argument fails then the exact implications of the phrase will be determined by the rules of construction including the parole evidence rule.[27] That construction process may result in a finding that, despite the existence of an intention to contract, the parties did not intend to immediately assume legal obligations until execution of an agreement. Thus the construction exercise is not limited to determining issues of performance but also formation. It follows that depending on the question being asked of the court, the interpretation of a 'subject to contract' clause may be an issue of law or an issue of fact.[28] Often statements to the effect that the issue is one of construction are made in cases where the only issue before the court was whether or not certain documents constituted a contract.[29] Counsel have not sought to argue that it is necessary to look at statements made outside those documents. In such cases one can understand why a court would generally see such an issue as one of 'construction'.

At a practical level it may be difficult to maintain these distinctions. It is perhaps easier to **9.10** maintain the distinction in those cases where a party makes an offer 'subject to contract' and there is a purported acceptance of that offer.[30] However, often the parties execute a

---

[22] See also *Woodside Offshore Petroleum Pty Ltd v Atwood Oceanics Inc* [1986] WAR 253, 258 per Burt CJ.

[23] See further 1.20ff.

[24] *Allen v Carbone* (1975) 132 CLR 528, 532 ('To ascertain [the parties] relevant intention it is often necessary to resort to inference, a process for which there is little or no scope when the parties have taken care to comprehensively record the terms of their agreement in written form.').

[25] Perillo (ed), *Corbin on Contracts* (Revised edn, Vol 1, St Paul, Minn, West Publishing Co, 1993) § 2.9, p 144. See further 1.20ff.

[26] *Air Great Lakes Pty Ltd v KS Easter (Holdings) Pty Ltd* (1985) 2 NSWLR 309, 334, 336, 337 per McHugh JA, cf 319 per Hope JA. See also *Howard Smith & Co Ltd v Varawa* (1907) 5 CLR 68; *Fong v Cilli* (1968) 11 FLR 495, 500. See further *Pym v Campbell* (1856) 6 E & B 370, 119 ER 903.

[27] *Perry v Suffields* [1916] 2 Ch 187.

[28] *Terracom Development Group Inc v Coleman Cable & Wire Co* 50 Ill App 3d 739, 365 NE 2d 1028, 1031 (1977). Cf *Air Great Lakes Pty Ltd v KS Easter (Holdings) Pty Ltd* (1985) 2 NSWLR 309, 315, per Hope JA. See further *Fitzwood Pty Ltd v Unique Coal Pty Ltd (in liq)* (2001) 188 ALR 566, 591.

[29] See *Air Great Lakes Pty Ltd v KS Easter (Holdings) Pty Ltd* (1985) 2 NSWLR 309, 337, per McHugh JA.

[30] *Howard Smith & Co Ltd v Varawa* (1907) 5 CLR 68, 73, 79.

memorandum of agreement that is 'subject to contract' and where that is the case that memorandum must be taken to encapsulate the understanding of *both* parties. In such a case, where one party argues that the phrase was intended to prevent a contract coming into existence, that may raise factual issues of intention to contract or it may be directed to whether or not there was an intention to immediately assume legal obligations. The latter is a matter of construction. In *Air Great Lakes Pty Ltd v KS Easter (Holdings) Pty Ltd*,[31] Hope JA suggested the following approach to the issues being discussed here:[32]

> All these decisions are not necessarily inconsistent with the application in appropriate cases of the ordinary principles of construction in resolving whether a binding contract has been entered into, or of having regard, again in appropriate cases, to presumed as opposed to actual intention. They are however consistent with a view that there are circumstances in which, in this area of the law of contract, it is appropriate to have regard to actual intention to resolve the question whether a binding contract has been concluded. Amongst the many approaches appearing in the cases, two might be noticed for present purposes. One is that, where intention to contract is a live issue and evidence is available as to mutual actual intention, that evidence may be adduced to establish that intention. If a finding of intention to contract results, but not otherwise, the document or documents which have been signed should be construed and dealt with in the light of that conclusion of fact. The other approach is that the document or documents which have been signed are first construed in the same way as if they were contracts. Apart from cases falling within recognized exceptions, extrinsic evidence may be looked at only in those cases where it would be permittible to do so in construing an admitted contract, and then, as regards intention, only for the purpose of ascertaining a presumed intention. On this approach it is only in cases falling within one of the recognized exceptions that evidence as to actual intention is admissible.

9.11 Finally, there is a also a difference between the case where the parties agree all the terms of a bargain but make that bargain 'subject to contract' (the dispute being about the meaning of that clause) and where there is a true formation dispute between the parties and where one of the factors to be taken into account to determine whether the negotiations have reached the point where a contract was formed is whether they contemplated further documentation.[33] The former is a technical construction exercise.[34] Moreover, as regards 'subject to contract' clauses it is the former case that typically comes before a court although the latter often arises in practice typically where the parties have agreed on nothing more than the price and made the agreement 'subject to contract'.[35] However, a dispute as to the

---

[31] (1985) 2 NSWLR 309.

[32] (1985) 2 NSWLR 309, 319. Cf 337 (and 338) per McHugh JA ('The intention to create a legally binding contract although a matter to be proved objectively, may, nevertheless, in my opinion, be proved by what the parties said and did as well as by what they wrote. The intention may be proved in that way even in a case where the document is intended to comprise all the terms of their bargain. This is because the intention to be bound is a jural act separate and distinct from the *terms* of their bargain.'). See also *Perry v Suffields* [1916] 2 Ch 187. See further *Interway Inc v Alagna* 85 Ill App 3d 1094, 407 NE 2d 615, 618–19, (1980) (suggesting that the issue of intention will be one of law if the language used is unambiguous and one of fact if it is ambiguous).

[33] *Toyota Motor Corp Australia Ltd v Ken Morgan Motors Pty Ltd* [1994] 2 VR 106, 204.

[34] See *Air Great Lakes Pty Ltd v KS Easter (Holdings) Pty Ltd* (1985) 2 NSWLR 309, 313ff, per Hope JA. See also *Woodside Offshore Petroleum Pty Ltd v Atwood Oceanics Inc* [1986] WAR 253, 258.

[35] Where an offer is made subject to such a condition, this will often evidence an intention that the offer is only capable of acceptance upon the fulfilment of the contingency, see eg *Buhrer v Tweedie* [1973] 1 NZLR 517, 520 (drawing a distinction between conditional contracts and conditional offers).

meaning of a 'subject to contract' clause can arise in either situation. Typically, other 'subject to' clauses such as 'subject to finance clauses' or 'subject to survey' or 'subject to the issuing of a licence', arise where all the terms are otherwise agreed.

In any case it is generally accepted that the meaning and effect of such provisions are determined by the intention of the parties. In *Mississippi & Dominion Steamship Co Ltd v Swift*,[36] Emery J expressed this point in the following way:[37] **9.12**

> If the party sought to be charged intended to close a contract prior to the formal signing of a written draft, or if signified such an intention to the other party, he will be bound by the contract actually made, though the signing of the written draft be omitted. If, on the other hand, such party neither had nor signified such an intention to close the contract until it was fully expressed in a written instrument, attested by signatures, then he will not be bound until the signatures are affixed. The expression of the idea may be attempted in other words: If the written draft is viewed by the parties merely as a convenient memorial or record of their previous contract, its absence does not affect the binding force of the contract. If, however, it is viewed as the consummation of the negotiation, there is no contract until the written draft is finally signed.

Section 27 of the Restatement (2d) Contracts similarly accepts that the issue is ultimately is one of intention. It provides: **9.13**

> Manifestations of assent that are in themselves sufficient to conclude a contract will not be prevented from so operating by the fact that the parties also manifest an intention to prepare and adopt a written memorial thereof; but the circumstances may show that the agreements are preliminary negotiations.[38]

Before moving on, it may be noted that if a 'subject to' clause is, in the circumstances, meaningless, then it may be ignored.[39] **9.14**

C. 'Subject to Contract'

Introduction

The 'subject to contract' clause, or words of similar effect, are well known in conveyancing transactions.[40] Moreover, as a growing body of case law indicates, it is not peculiar to that area and is often used in commercial transactions, particularly in preliminary agreements. Nevertheless, the issue in such cases is always the same, namely, what was the intention of the parties? The parties may agree nothing but the price and make the agreement 'subject to contract'. Such cases rarely come before the courts and except where all the other terms **9.15**

---

[36] 86 Me 248, 29 A 1063 (1894).

[37] 86 Me 248, 29 A 1093, 29 A 1063, 1066–7 (1894).

[38] Comment *b* emphasizes the relevance of subjective knowledge and states, 'if either party knows or has reason to know that the other party regards the agreement as incomplete and intends that no obligation shall exist until other terms are assented to or until the whole has been reduced to another written form, the preliminary negotiations and agreements do not constitute a contract'. See further 1.09ff.

[39] Eg *Michael Richards Properties Ltd v Corporation of Wardens of St Saviour's Parish, Southwark* [1975] 3 All ER 416.

[40] See the Law Commission, *Transfer of Land, Report on 'Subject to Contract' Agreements* (Law Com 65, 1975).

could be implied in law or fact, neither party would usually contest that the arrangement was to have immediate effect.[41] Alternatively the parties may agree to all the essential terms of a contract, those terms may be sufficient to give rise to a contract, but by incorporating terms such as 'subject to contract' they may evidence an intention not to be bound until a formal contract is executed and, in some cases, exchanged.[42] Indeed, even if negotiations are at an end, without an intention to be bound there can be no contract.[43] This section discusses the possible legal effects of such provisions.

The legal effect of a 'subject to contract' provision

9.16 Since the meaning of such a provision depends on the intention of the parties there is in theory an infinite amount of possibilities as to the literal meaning of the expression 'subject to contract'. However, the High Court of Australia in *Masters v Cameron*,[44] held that there can be only three possible legal effects. The court stated:[45]

> Where parties who have been in negotiation reach agreement upon terms of a contractual nature and also agree that the matter of their negotiation shall be dealt with by a formal contract, the case may belong to any of three classes. It may be one in which the parties have reached finality in arranging all the terms of their bargain and intend to be immediately bound to the performance of those terms, but at the same time propose to have the terms restated in a form which will be fuller or more precise but not different in effect. Or, secondly, it may be a case in which the parties have completely agreed upon all the terms of their bargain and intend no departure from or addition to that which their agreed terms express or imply, but nevertheless have made performance of one or more of the terms conditional upon the execution of a formal document. Or, thirdly, the case may be one in which the intention of the parties is not to make a concluded bargain at all, unless and until they execute a formal contract.
>
> In each of the first two cases there is a binding contract: in the first case a contract binding the parties at once to perform the agreed terms whether the contemplated formal document comes into existence or not, and to join (if they have so agreed) in settling and executing the formal document; and in the second case a contract binding the parties to join in bringing the formal contract into existence and then to carry it into execution. Of these two cases the first is the more common.
>
> Cases of the third class are fundamentally different. They are cases in which the terms of agreement are not intended to have, and therefore do not have, any binding effect of their own ... The parties may have so provided either because they have dealt only with major matters and contemplate that others will or may be regulated by provisions to be introduced into the formal document ... or simply because they wish to reserve to themselves a right to withdraw at any time until the formal document is signed. These possibilities were both referred to in *Rossiter v Miller* [(1878) 3 App Cas 1124]. Lord O'Hagan said [(1878) 3 App Cas 1124

---

[41] Similarly an offer made subject to contract will usually not take immediate effect upon acceptance, see *Buhrer v Tweedie* [1973] 1 NZLR 517, and see below nn 67, 68.

[42] On the requirement of an exchange of contract in sale of land transactions under English law, see Peel, *Treitel, The Law of Contract* (12th edn, Sweet & Maxwell, London, 2007), 2-091–2-093.

[43] *Barrier Wharfs Ltd v W Scott Fell & Co Ltd* (1908) 5 CLR 647, 650 per Higgins J (affirmed (1908) 5 CLR 647), see also, 666 per Griffith CJ, 671 per Isaacs J; *Marek v Australasian Conference Association Pty Ltd* [1994] 2 Qd R 521, 529.

[44] (1954) 91 CLR 353.

[45] (1954) 91 CLR 353, 360–2.

at 1149]: 'Undoubtedly, if any prospective contract, involving the possibility of new terms, or the modification of those already discussed, remains to be adopted, matters must be taken to be still in a train of negotiation, and a dissatisfied party may refuse to proceed. But when an agreement embracing all the particulars essential for finality and completeness, even though it may be desired to reduce it to shape by a solicitor, is such that those particulars must remain unchanged, it is not, in my mind, less coercive because of the technical formality which remains to be made'. And Lord Blackburn said [(1878) 3 App Cas 1124 at 1152]: 'parties often do enter into a negotiation meaning that, when they have (or think they have) come to one mind, the result shall be put into formal shape, and then (if on seeing the result in that shape they find they are agreed) signed and made binding; but that each party is to reserve to himself the right to retire from the contract, if, on looking at the formal contract, he finds that though it may represent what he said, it does not represent what he meant to say. Whenever, on the true construction of the evidence, this appears to be the intention, I think that the parties ought not to be held bound till they have executed the formal agreement'. So, as Parker J said in *Von Hatzfeldt-Wildenburg v Alexander* [[1912] 1 Ch 284 at 289] in such a case there is no enforceable contract, either because the condition is unfulfilled or because the law does not recognise a contract to enter into a contract.

In summary, in the first category the agreement is a binding contract and must be per- **9.17** formed when the time for performance accrues. In the second category there is a binding contract but the parties are not required to perform until a formal contract is executed.[46] When expressing the existence of the first two categories, the court emphasized that the words 'subject to contract' do not in all cases mean that the parties are still in negotiation.[47] They said:[48]

Throughout the decisions on this branch of the law the proposition is insisted upon which Lord Blackburn expressed in *Rossiter v. Miller* [(1878) 3 App Cas 1124] when he said that the mere fact that the parties have expressly stipulated that there shall afterwards be a formal agreement prepared, embodying the terms, which shall be signed by the parties does not, by itself, show that they continue merely in negotiation. His Lordship proceeded: '... as soon as the fact is established of the final mutual assent of the parties so that those who draw up the formal agreement have not the power to vary the terms already settled, I think the contract is completed' [(1878) 3 App Cas 1124, 1151].

In the third category there is no binding contract until a formal contract is executed. Often **9.18** such an agreement is characterized as an unenforceable agreement to agree.[49]

In terms of legal effect, these three categories represent three points on a continuum of all **9.19** possible legal effects.[50] The parties may express an intention that falls between category 3 and category 2 but if that intention does not fall within category 2 it remains category 3

---

[46] The High Court said that the first category is more common than the second category, see (1954) 91 CLR 353, 360. This is perhaps still true in transactions dealing with interests in land but may not be true outside of that area.

[47] See also 9.35, 9.36.

[48] (1954) 91 CLR 353, 361.

[49] *Chillingworth v Esche* [1924] 1 Ch 97, 105; *Summergreene v Parker* (1950) 80 CLR 304. Cf *Von Hatzfeldt-Wildenburg v Alexander* [1912] 1 Ch 284, 289.

[50] See Peden, Carter and Tolhurst, 'When Three Just Isn't Enough: the Fourth Category of the "Subject to Contract" Cases' (2004) 20 JCL 156, 161. See further David McLauchlan, 'In Defence of the Fourth Category of Preliminary Agreements: Or Are There Only Two?' (2005) 21 JCL 286; Walker, 'The Fourth Category of Masters v Cameron' (2009) 25 JCL 108.

even though there may be some aspects of the case that put it above the most obvious of category 3 cases.

9.20 Recently in Australia a fourth category has emerged. The fourth category has its genesis in the judgment of McLelland J in *Baulkham Hills Private Hospital Pty Ltd v GR Securities Pty Ltd*.[51] In turn McLelland J relied on an earlier decision of the High Court of Australia in *Sinclair, Scott & Co Ltd v Naughton*,[52] where reference was made to a transaction 'in which the parties were content to be bound immediately and exclusively by the terms which they had agreed upon whilst expecting to make a further contract in substitution for the first contract, containing, by consent, additional terms'.[53] McLelland J identified this as a separate category whereby: 'In the absence of agreement as to further terms to be inserted in the formal contract, the obligation of each party would be to execute a formal contract in accordance with the terms of the agreement appearing from the ... [evidence of an informal contract]'.[54] The efficacy of this category will be discussed later, it is only important to note at this point that although the High Court has not yet expressed an opinion on the efficacy of this fourth category, it has been adopted in many decisions of lower courts.[55]

9.21 There is no magic in the categorisation set out in *Masters v Cameron*.[56] In practice the only issue is to determine the intention of the parties and then give that intention its desired

---

[51] (1986) 40 NSWLR 622 (affirmed (1986) 40 NSWLR 631).

[52] (1929) 43 CLR 310.

[53] (1929) 43 CLR 310, 317–18 per Knox CJ, Rich and Dixon JJ referring to a passage of Lord Loreburn in *Love & Stewart Ltd v S Instone & Co* (1917) 33 TLR 475, 476, which they thought mentioned such a case. There Lord Loreburn said: 'It was quite lawful to make a bargain containing certain terms which one was content with, dealing with what one regarded as essentials, and at the same time to say that one would have a formal document drawn up with the full expectation that one would by consent insert in it a number of further terms. If that were the intention of the parties, then a bargain had been made, none the less that both parties felt quite sure that the formal document could comprise more than was contained in the preliminary bargain.' The report of the case in the *Times Law Report* is descriptive and it is not clear whether this quote is verbatim. The case concerned an alleged contract for the sale of coal, Lord Loreburn thought the parties had agreed all the essential terms and did not think the contract was intended to be conditional upon execution of a formal contract but the parties also agreed that the contract was to contain a strike clause the form of which had not yet been agreed and on this basis he thought there was no contract, he said (at 476): 'They were *ad idem* that there should be such a clause, but they were not *ad idem* as to what it should be. The law would not come in and say that they must agree on what was reasonable. It would say that there was no bargain.' See also, 476 per Lord Parker (with whom Lord Shaw agreed), 477 per Lord Sumner, 478 per Lord Parmoor.

[54] (1986) 40 NSWLR 622, 629.

[55] A sample includes, *Baulkham Hills Private Hospital Pty Ltd v GR Securities Pty Ltd* (1986) 40 NSWLR 622; *Tern Minerals NL v Kalbara Mining NL* (1990) 3 WAR 486; *Telstra Corporation Ltd v Australis Media Holdings* (1997) 24 ACSR 55; *Summertime Holdings Pty Ltd v Environmental Defender's Office Ltd* (1998) 45 NSWLR 291, 294–5; *Brunninghausen v Glavanics* (1999) 46 NSWLR 538; *Cleary v Masterton* [1999] NSWSC 207; *Anaconda Nickel Ltd v Tarmoola Australia Pty Ltd* (2000) 22 WAR 101; *Concrete Construction Group Ltd v Litevale Pty Ltd* [2002] NSWSC 670; *Randwick City Council v Nancor Trading Co Pty Ltd* [2002] NSWCA 108; (2002) 120 LGERA 261; *Rural Insurance (Aust) Pty Ltd v Reinsurance Australia Corp Ltd* (2002) 41 ACSR 30; *GEC Marconi Systems Pty Ltd v BHP Information Technology Pty Ltd* (2003) 128 FCR 1; *ABB Engineering Construction Pty Ltd v Abigroup Contractors Pty Ltd* [2003] NSWSC 665; *Westpoint Constructions Pty Ltd v Lord* [2004] WASC 86; *Capitol Theatre Management v Council of the City of Sydney* [2005] NSWSC 5; *Tasman Capital Pty Ltd v Sinclair* [2008] NSWCA 248; *Donald Financial Enterprises Pty Ltd v APIR Systems Ltd* [2008] FCA 1112; *Iacullo v Remly Pty Ltd* [2008] NSWSC 1176; *Ciavarella v Polimeni* [2008] NSWSC 234; *Laidlaw v Hillier Elsley Pty Ltd* [2009] NSWCA 44.

[56] Commenting on the position in the United States, Corbin also identifies four categories of case where a formal contract is contemplated, see Perillo, *Corbin on Contracts* (Revised edn, Vol 1, St Paul Minn, West

legal effect, the possibilities of which are set out in *Masters v Cameron*. The following sections deal with the categorization of cases in terms of legal effect. It is convenient to begin with category three, then move to category one and finally consider category two.

No intention to be bound

The phrase 'subject to contract' is often found in conveyancing transactions. Here there is **9.22** a presumption that these words evidence an intention that no contract is to arise until formal contracts are executed and exchanged.[57] In *Chillingworth v Esche*[58] Sargant LJ stated that, in the context of real estate contracts, these words have 'acquired a definite ascertained legal meaning—not quite so definite a meaning perhaps as such expressions as fob or cif in mercantile transactions, but approaching that degree of definiteness'.[59] Despite this, the presumption can be rebutted with clear evidence and there are examples of this occurring.[60] As noted above,[61] in certain circumstances the inclusion of such a provision will be meaningless and can be ignored.[62] However, generally, where negotiations have commenced 'subject to contract', all subsequent negotiations continue 'subject to contract' unless that

---

Publishing 1993) § 2.9, pp 157–8. Corbin's first and fourth categories are akin to categories three and one of *Masters v Cameron*. In his second category the parties point out one or more specific matters on which they must agree before negotiations are concluded. In the third category, although the parties have expressed definite agreement on the necessary terms, they have not dealt with other matters which are not essential but are usually included in similar contracts. Corbin suggests that cases falling within his categories 2 and 4 give rise to a valid contract.

[57] *Masters v Cameron* (1954) 91 CLR 353, 363 ('such words prima facie create an overriding condition so that what has been agreed upon must be regarded as the intended basis for a future contract and not as constituting a contract'). See further *Winn v Bull* (1877) 7 Ch D 29; *Thompson & Son Ltd v The King* [1920] 2 IR 365; *Farmer v Honan* (1919) 26 CLR 183, 192; *Coope v Ridout* [1921] 1 Ch 291; *Sinclair Scott & Co Ltd v Naughton* (1929) 43 CLR 310; *Raingold v Bromley* [1931] 2 Ch 307; *Eccles v Bryant* [1948] Ch 93; *Zimin v Wentworth Properties Pty Ltd* (1958) 59 SR (NSW) 101; *D'Silva v Lister Development Ltd* [1971] Ch 17; *Allen v Carbone* (1975) 132 CLR 528; *Carruthers v Whitaker* [1975] 2 NZLR 667, 671; *Bridle Estates Pty Ltd v Myer Realty Ltd* (1977) 15 ALR 415; *Derby & Co Ltd v ITC Pension Trust Ltd* [1977] 2 All ER 890; *Shell Oil New Zealand Ltd v Wordcom Investments Ltd* [1992] 1 NZLR 129; *Marek v Australasian Conference Association Pty Ltd* [1994] 2 Qd R 521; *New Selangor Plantations SDN BHD v Talam Management Services SDN BHD* [1996] 4 CLJ 94; *Fitzwood Pty Ltd v Unique Coal Pty Ltd (in liq)* (2001) 188 ALR 566, 591.

[58] [1924] 1 Ch 97. See also *Tiverton Estates Ltd v Wearwell Ltd* [1975] Ch 146.

[59] [1924] 1 Ch 97, 114 (see also, 109 per Warrington LJ).

[60] See *Rossiter v Miller* (1878) 3 App Cas 1124. See also *Bonnewell v Jenkins* (1878) 8 Ch D 70; *Filby v Hounsell* [1896] 2 Ch 737; *North v Percival* [1898] 2 Ch 128; *Hall v Gilmore* [1968] Qd R 406; *Fauzi Elias v George Sahely & Co (Barbados) Ltd* [1983] 1 AC 646; *Alpenstow Ltd v Regalian Properties plc* [1985] 1 WLR 721; *Moffatt Property Development Group Pty Ltd v Hebron Park Pty Ltd* [2009] QCA 60, and see the discussions in *Rossdale v Denny* [1921] 1 Ch 57, 64ff and *Storer v Manchester City Council* [1974] 1 WLR 1403, 1407–8, 1409–10. Note that *North v Percival* was doubted in *Von Hatzfeldt-Wildenburg v Alexander* [1912] 1 Ch 284. See further *Darter Pty Ltd v Malloy* [1993] 2 Qd R 615, 619 (here the words, 'if the terms are acceptable to you could you please arrange for a revised contract to be submitted' were held not to be equivalent to 'subject to contract' but 'more closely resemble the expression "please forward contract", which in *Lennon v Scarlett & Co* (1921) 29 CLR 499, 509 were held to mean "please forward a document embodying the terms on which we have agreed"').

[61] See 9.14.

[62] Eg, *Michael Richards Properties Ltd v Corporation of Wardens of St Saviour's Parish, Southwark* [1975] 3 All ER 416 (all the terms appeared in a tender document which was accepted and in error the words 'subject to contract' were included in the acceptance; nothing remained to be negotiated and no further document was contemplated).

term is excluded by the parties[63] or they conduct themselves in a manner to show that they consider themselves bound before signature.[64]

9.23 Very often, particularly in the context of transactions dealing with interests in land, the 'subject to' clause will be drafted so as to require approval by one or both of the party's solicitors.[65] Such provisions do not mean that the contract is necessarily formed merely upon approval and prior to exchange.[66] Moreover, where the 'subject to' provision refers to 'approval' or 'review' by a solicitor, as opposed to suggesting that the agreement reached is final and will be merely documented by a solicitor[67]—the solicitor not being empowered to add to or vary the terms agreed—then in many cases the document will suggest that terms are still in the process of negotiation and no concluded contract is intended.[68]

---

[63] See *Cohen v Nessdale Ltd* [1982] 2 All ER 97, 103ff. Cf *Alpenstow Ltd v Regalian Properties plc* [1985] 1 WLR 721, 730; *Vroon BV v Foster's Brewing Group Ltd* [1994] 2 VR 32.

[64] See *Sociedade Portuguesa de Navios Tanques Limitada v Hvalfangerselskapet Polaris AIS* [1952] 1 Lloyd's Rep 407, 417. See also *Laidlaw v Hillier Hewitt Elsley Pty Ltd* [2009] NSWCA 44. Similarly, although a subject to contract condition will usually require documentation of the transaction and execution, the requirement of signature can be later negated by the intention of the parties objectively ascertained, *Grant v Bragg* [2009] 1 All ER (Comm) 674.

[65] Examples of such clauses include *Winn v Bull* (1877) 7 Ch D 29 ('subject to the preparation and approval of a formal contract'); *Lloyd v Nowell* [1895] 2 Ch 744 ('subject to the preparation by my solicitor and completion of a formal contract'); *Santa Fé Land Co Ltd v Forestal Land, Timber, and Railways Ltd* (1910) 26 TLR 534 ('subject to a formal contract to be approved by your solicitors and ourselves on acceptance of the offer, when any minor details can be settled'); *Rossdale v Denny* [1921] 1 Ch 57 ('subject to a formal contract to embody such reasonable provisions as my solicitors may approve'); *Chillingworth v Esche* [1924] 1 Ch 97 ('subject to a proper contract to be prepared by the vendor's solicitors'); *Lockett v Norman-Wright* [1925] Ch 56 ('subject to suitable agreements being arranged between your solicitors and mine'); *Masters v Cameron* (1954) 91 CLR 353 ('subject to the preparation of a formal contract of sale which shall be acceptable to my solicitors').

[66] See *Von Hatzfeldt-Wildenburg v Alexander* [1912] 1 Ch 284, 288 where Parker J suggested that where a document is expressed to require the approval of a solicitor, 'it was no doubt also contemplated that it would be executed'. See also *Spottiswoode Ballantyne & Co Ltd v Doreen Appliances Ltd* [1942] 2 KB 32, 34.

[67] See *Rossiter v Miller* (1878) 3 App Cas 1124, 1143; *Oxford v Provand* (1868) LR 2 PC 135; *Farmer v Honan* (1919) 26 CLR 183, 192; *Lamont v Heron* (1970) 126 CLR 239; *Moffatt Property Development Group Pty Ltd v Hebron Park Pty Ltd* [2009] QCA 60. See also *Bonnewell v Jenkins* (1878) 8 Ch D 70, 74 (here an offer was made to purchase a leasehold property 'subject to the conditions of the lease being modified to my solicitor's satisfaction'; this was accepted by the other party; it was held there was a contract and the 'subject to' provision on its proper construction was only intended to result in the arrangement being reduced into writing). Even in this case the intention of the parties may be that no contract is to come into existence until the parties have signed a formal contract, see generally *Ridgway v Wharton* (1857) 6 HLC 238, 263–4ff, 10 ER 1287, 1297ff. Note that even when words used in a document refer only to the solicitor documenting the transaction agreed, it may be clear that the parties still intend to negotiate more terms before they would have committed themselves to a contract, see eg *Zimin v Wentworth Properties Pty Ltd* (1958) 59 SR (NSW) 101.

[68] See *Crossley v Maycock* (1874) LR 18 Eq 180, 181–2; *Winn v Bull* (1877) 7 Ch D 29, 30; *Rossdale v Denny* [1921] 1 Ch 57, 61; *Caney v Leith* [1937] 2 All ER 532; *Carruthers v Whitaker* [1975] 2 NZLR 667, 671; *Terracom Development Group Inc v Coleman Cable & Wire Co* 50 Ill App 3d 739, 365 NE 2d 1028 (1977); *Marek v Australasian Conference Association Pty Ltd* [1994] 2 Qd R 521; *New Selangor Plantations SDN BHD v Talam Management Services SDN BHD* [1996] 4 CLJ 94; *Verissimo v Walker* [2006] 1 NZLR 760. Cf *North v Percival* [1898] 2 Ch 128; the correctness of this decision was doubted in *Von Hatzfeldt-Wildenburg v Alexander* [1912] 1 Ch 284. A distinction can be drawn between a fully negotiated transaction made subject to approval by the parties' solicitors and an 'offer' made subject to approval by the offeror's solicitors. In the latter case it is more likely to be intended that the 'offer' is not effective as an offer until that approval is given, see eg *Buhrer v Tweedie* [1973] 1 NZLR 517, 520 (drawing a distinction between conditional contracts and conditional offers), see also *Frampton v McCully* [1976] 1 NZLR 270.

On one view, where a 'subject to' clause requires the formal contract to be approved by the parties or their solicitors or some other third party, this is a strong indicator that any legal obligations are only to arise in the future.[69] However, every case depends on its facts. It is equally arguable that an approval or satisfaction provision is merely intended to suspend performance or is a mere formality and is not intended to impact on performance or formation;[70] the case for such arguments arises where the transaction requires no further agreement by the parties.[71] In *Marten v Whale*,[72] there were to be simultaneous exchanges whereby Marten (the plaintiff) agreed to buy land from Thacker 'subject to purchaser's solicitor's approval of title and restrictions' and, in consideration, the plaintiff was to sell a car to Thacker. However, Thacker obtained possession of the car prior to this occurring and sold it to an innocent third party purchaser. The plaintiff's solicitor did not approve certain restrictions so that both sales could not be completed. The innocent purchaser of the car could only acquire good title to it by relying on the buyer in possession exception to the *nemo-dat* rule which required Thacker to have 'agreed to buy' the car. It was argued that both sales were dependent and the transaction in relation to the land, due to the condition, was no more than an option which was not an agreement for sale and therefore there was no agreement for sale in respect to the car.

9.24

The Court of Appeal held that even assuming the two parts of the transaction were dependent upon one another, there was still an agreement for sale as the condition for approval did not prevent the contract from coming into existence. Scrutton LJ emphasized that the plaintiff was under an implied obligation to 'appoint a solicitor and ... consult him in good faith, and that the solicitor shall give his honest opinion'.[73] He continued: 'That is not an option; it is a conditional contract.'[74]

9.25

Similarly in *Godecke v Kirwan*,[75] the vendor and purchaser signed a document that contained all the terms necessary for a sale of land; it contained detailed execution provisions referring to offer and acceptance, it required immediate payment of a considerable sum of money, it referred to a present purchase rather than a future event and expressed a clear intention to be bound. In those circumstances a further clause that stated that the purchaser would, if required by the vendor, execute a 'further agreement' prepared by the vendor's solicitors containing the terms agreed and any other terms the solicitors 'may reasonably require' did not prevent the agreement reached having immediate effect.

9.26

---

[69] Eg *Barrier Wharfs Ltd v W Scott Fell & Co Ltd* (1908) 5 CLR 647.

[70] Eg *Oxford v Provand* (1868) LR 2 PC 135.

[71] See *Provost Developments Ltd v Collingwood Towers Ltd* [1980] 2 NZLR 205. See also Burrows, Finn and Todd, *Burrows, Finn and Todd, Law of Contract in New Zealand*, (3rd edn, LexisNexis NZ Ltd, Wellington, 2007), para 8.2.3.

[72] [1917] 2 KB 480. See also *Chipperfield v Carter* (1895) 72 LT 487 (a term stating 'such lease to be approved in the customary way by my solicitor' was held to be a condition of a concluded contract and not a 'subject to approval' clause).

[73] [1917] 2 KB 480, 486–7. On the duties of a solicitor in such a case, see *Provost Developments Ltd v Collingwood Towers Ltd* [1980] 2 NZLR 205.

[74] [1917] 2 KB 480, 487.

[75] (1973) 129 CLR 629. See also *Rossiter v Miller* (1878) 3 App Cas 1124.

The 'subject to' provision impacted on performance not formation.[76] Indeed, if all the essential terms have been agreed and the transaction is stated to be subject to the approval of only one of the party's solicitors, then even if that solicitor has the capacity to add to the terms this may not prevent an immediate contract coming into existence because the contract does not require further agreement by the parties.[77]

9.27 The position is the same in America and some of the cases there are instructive. For example, in *Southern Bell Telephone & Telegraph Co v John Hancock Mutual Life Insurance Co*,[78] the central question was whether there was a contract whereby Hancock, the defendant corporation, was to issue the plaintiff corporation, Southern Bell, with a GIC (a type of investment with a guaranteed return). The relevant facts were that the defendant had offered to Southern Bell a contract with the guaranteed gross rate of 15.5 per cent on the basis that a deposit be paid. On Monday 14 April Southern Bell had responded in the following terms: 'It is our intent, subject to review of the contract by our Legal Counsel, to deposit $20 million in good funds on Friday, April 18, 1980, in Boston for the purchase of a guaranteed return contract ...' This letter was received by the defendant on 15 April. However, interest rates had begun to fall late on 14 April and at a meeting on 16 April the defendant had decided only to honour obligations at the 15.5 per cent interest rate where they were already bound. The defendant took the view that the plaintiff's letter contained conditional language which did not commit the plaintiff to purchase and that these conditions had not been fulfilled because no monies had been deposited at the time of the 16 April meeting. Accordingly, the defendant informed the plaintiff that the offer was withdrawn.

9.28 Forrester J held that there was no legally binding contract, the acceptance was an acceptance in escrow, it was to take effect in the future and upon the occurrence of a contingency. He stated:[79]

> the facts suggest that prior to [the withdrawal of the] offer on April 16, Southern Bell did not demonstratively assent to enter into an immediate bargain. The language 'subject to the review of the contract by our legal counsel' in ... [the] ... letter of April 14 cannot be said to encompass a context of the parties' settled expectations, especially in light of the fact that prior to the writing of this letter, no one at Southern Bell had ever seen or reviewed a copy of the GIC. Whether ... the 'subject to review' clause [was] tantamount to a rigorous examination or a cursory evaluation by Southern Bell's counsel of the specimen contract, future actions by Southern Bell were anticipated.

9.29 By comparison, and again showing that each case is dependent on its own facts, in *Arnold Palmer Golf Co v Fuqua Industries Inc*,[80] an approval clause was not considered fatal on the

---

[76] Similarly a clause that stated 'Possession shall be given and taken on settlement upon signing and execution of a formal contract of sale within 28 days of acceptance of this offer' did not prevent an immediate contract coming into effect but suspended performance; there being an implied obligation that the parties would sign the subject document within the time set down by the contract.

[77] Eg *Powell v Jones* [1968] SASR 394.

[78] 579 F Supp 1065 (1982).

[79] 579 F Supp 1065, 1071 (1982).

[80] 541 F 2d 584 (1976). See also *F & W Grand Five-Ten-Twenty-Five Cent Stores Inc v Eisman* 160 Ga 321, 127 SE 872 (1925), where counsel was only required to prepare a lease document on terms that were already

basis that the language used indicated that the parties were already in agreement so that counsel were merely being asked to approve documents.

The issue in the case concerned a six page 'Memorandum of Intent' and the question of whether both parties intended to enter into a binding agreement when they signed it. Palmer (the plaintiff corporation) had been negotiating with Fuqua with a view to a possible business relationship between the two in order to give Palmer its own manufacturing base for its golf equipment. A general understanding was reached towards the end of 1969 and embodied in the 'Memorandum of Intent'. This provided that agreement had been reached regarding the acquisition of 25 per cent of the Palmer stock by Fuqua in exchange for all the stock in Fernquest and Johnson Golf Co Inc (a wholly owned subsidiary of Fuqua), a payment of $700,000 and an agreement that Fuqua were to provide management services. **9.30**

The Memorandum also contained further details of the relationship between the parties and the manner in which the business would be conducted. Before it had been signed, Fuqua had issued a press release stating that the parties had agreed to cooperate in golfing enterprises. **9.31**

Fuqua later withdrew from the arrangement and Palmer claimed that there had been a breach of contract. In assessing whether the Memorandum constituted a binding contract, the interpretation of paragraphs (10) and (11) was crucial. These paragraphs were in the following terms: **9.32**

> (10) *Preparation of Definitive Agreement.* Counsel for Palmer and counsel for Fuqua will proceed as promptly as possible to prepare an agreement acceptable to Palmer and Fuqua for the proposed combination of businesses. Such agreement will contain the representations, warranties, covenants and conditions, as generally outlined in the example submitted by Fuqua to Palmer ...
> (11) *Conditions.* The obligations of Palmer and Fuqua shall be subject to fulfilment of the following conditions:
> > (i) preparation of the definitive agreement for the proposed combination in form and content satisfactory to both parties and their respective counsel;
> > (ii) approval of such definitive agreement by the Board of Directors of Fuqua;
> > (iii) approval of such definitive agreement by the Board of Directors of Palmer;
> > (iv) approval by the stockholders of Palmer of certain amendments to the Articles & Regulations of Palmer which are necessary in order to consummate said agreement;
> > (v) approval by the respective counsel of Palmer and Fuqua of all legal matters ...

---

agreed between the parties. The relevant document stated: '... we have secured ... acceptance and approval to the lease, the terms and conditions of which are outlined in your letter of April 9, 1924. We suggest that to expedite the matter you have your counsel get in touch with ... the owners' attorneys for the preparation and consummation of the lease'; this statement did not qualify the acceptance. See further *Zelazny v Pilgrim Funding Corp* 41 Misc 2d 176, 244 NYS 2d 810 (1963) where the relevant contingency stated 'subject to compliance with law, rules, regulations and/or directives of government body and/or agency controlling and/ or affecting this transaction and approval by our attorneys of all closing papers'. Gibbons J (817) refused to accept the argument that there was no binding contract and specifically stated that 'closing papers' referred to 'those papers necessary to effectuate the transfer of title to the plaintiff as provided by the contract of sale. It does not mean subject to approval of credit by the attorneys. If it was the defendant's intention to so provide the defendant could have done so.'

9.33   Although the district court determined that the parties were not subject to any obligations until a definitive agreement satisfactory to the parties and their counsel had been prepared, the United States Court of Appeals reversed this as there was evidence suggesting that the Memorandum of Intent could not be considered as non-contractual as a matter of law and the issue was remanded for trial to be determined as a matter of fact. Two factors appear to have been particularly significant in reaching this conclusion. First, all the essential terms concerning the transfer of the stock were agreed and stated in unqualified language and in an extensive document. Second, the press release given by Fuqua evidenced an intention to be bound.

9.34   McCree CJ also felt that although there was a referral to counsel of both parties in paragraph (10) this could be read 'merely to impose an obligation upon the parties to memorialize their agreement'.[81]

9.35   Many cases can be cited that characterize facts as falling within this category as being cases where the parties are still in negotiation so no concluded contract exists.[82] It is no doubt true that if the parties are in the process of negotiation they may not have formed an intention to be immediately bound.[83] But that does not necessarily follow in all cases. The parties may agree to enter into a binding preliminary agreement and then continue negotiating the remaining terms;[84] such a preliminary agreement may fail for uncertainty or incompleteness in some cases but the mere fact it is made 'subject to' the more detailed contract to follow does not of itself dictate that it has no contractual effect. In short, the fact that the formal contract will contain terms in addition to that which have been agreed does not mean the parties have not completed their negotiations for the agreement that has been reached and intend to be bound immediately by that which has been agreed. This was the point addressed by the High Court in *Sinclair Scott & Co Ltd v Naughton*,[85] where it was said of the facts in that case that it was 'not one in which the parties were content to be bound immediately and exclusively by the terms which they had agreed upon whilst expecting to make a further contract in substitution for the first contract, containing, by consent, additional terms'.[86] As noted above, in Australia, this sentence has given birth to a fourth

---

[81] 541 F 2d 584, 589 (1976).

[82] See *Rossiter v Miller* (1878) 3 App Cas 1124, 1149, per Lord O'Hagan: '[U]ndoubtedly, if any prospective contract, involving the possibility of new terms, or the modification of those already discussed, remains to be adopted, matters must be taken to be still in a train of negotiation'; see also, 1151 per Lord Blackburn. Similarly in *Eccles v Bryant* [1948] Ch 93, 101, Lord Greene MR said, 'it has been well settled that the result of an offer "subject to contract" means that the matter remains in negotiation'. See also *Bridle Estates Pty Ltd v Myer Realty Ltd* (1977) 15 ALR 415, 421; *Hoffinghouse & Co Ltd v C-Trade SA (The Intra Transporter)* [1986] 2 Lloyd's Rep 132. There can be an overlap on the facts of any case between conditional contract principles, uncertainty in the context of agreements to agree and illusory consideration, see, *Loftus v Roberts* (1902) 18 TLR 532.

[83] Eg *Barrier Wharfs Ltd v W Scott Fell & Co Ltd* (1908) 5 CLR 647 (affirmed (1908) 5 CLR 647); *Ratto v Trifid Pty Ltd* [1987] WAR 237; *Manatee Towing Co v Oceanbulk Maritime SA* [1999] 2 Lloyd's Rep 227. In such cases the transaction can often be characterized as an agreement to agree, see *Foxtel Management Pty Ltd v Seven Cable Television Pty Ltd* (2000) 175 ALR 433, 479. This possibility was recognized by the High Court of Australia in *Masters v Cameron* (1954) 91 CLR 353, 361–2.

[84] *Pagnan SpA v Feed Products Ltd* [1987] 2 Lloyd's Rep 601, 619.

[85] (1929) 43 CLR 310. See also *Godecke v Kirwan* (1973) 129 CLR 629.

[86] (1929) 43 CLR 310, 317.

category of case which is discussed further below.[87] However, with respect to those views, the High Court in *Masters v Cameron* clearly envisaged such a case as falling within its first category.

In addition, it is not possible to classify all cases falling within this category as cases where **9.36** the parties are still negotiating a contract because it is possible for the parties to have agreed on all terms and still not intend to immediately assume legal obligations and a 'subject to contract' clause may be used to communicate that intention; that is, a reservation of a right to withdraw from the transaction at any time prior to execution.[88] In *Smissaert v Chiodo*,[89] Smissaert made an offer to purchase real estate owned by Chiodo by issuing a form of a standard deposit receipt together with a deposit of $2,500. Before acceptance, Chiodo attached the following addendum to the offer: 'It is further mutually understood and agreed by and between the parties to this agreement that the validity of said proposed agreement is subject and conditioned upon the parties agreeing upon and reducing to writing all terms and conditions necessary and incidental to the validity of said proposed agreement; and that seller shall pay total real estate commission of 5% upon completion of said sale.' This addendum was signed by Smissaert. The parties then continued to negotiate about the price and the security for the lease back to Chiodo. The negotiations broke down and Chiodo took the property off the market. Smissaert sought specific performance of the alleged contract of sale.

Bray J in the District Court of Appeal of California stated that the meaning of this clause **9.37** depended on the intention of the parties which was to be determined objectively.[90] He then went on to say: 'Where all of the essential terms of an agreement are definitely agreed upon in the writing there is a binding contract even though there is an intention that a formal writing will be executed later.'[91] On its face this overstates the position because in all cases there must be an intention to assume legal obligations. Indeed Bray J picks up this point in his conclusion where he held that although the receipt probably represented an assent to all the essential elements necessary for a valid contract, the addendum containing the 'subject to' clause evidenced an intention not to be bound until a formal written contract was executed. He said: 'Even though the informal agreement might have contained all the essential elements of a contract, the addendum conditioned validity on a formal document which would contain all the incidental terms.'[92]

---

[87] See 9.20, 9.61.

[88] See above 9.17. See also *Pagnan SpA v Feed Products Ltd* [1987] 2 Lloyd's Rep 601, 619. Statements can be found that appear to deny this by suggesting that if all the terms are agreed upon and are in writing then there is a contract and any further intended writing or execution is a mere formality, see *Rossiter v Miller* (1877) 5 Ch Div 648, 658 per Coleridge CJ (overruled (1878) 3 App Cas 1124) who was here summarizing the effect of previous authority, in particular *Chinnock v Marchioness of Ely* (1865) 4 DJ & S 638, 645–6, 46 ER 1066, 1069 per Lord Westbury, but concluded that in the case before him there was no final agreement on terms so the parties were not bound.

[89] 163 Cal App 2d 827, 330 P 2d 98 (1958). See also *Terracom Development Group Inc v Coleman Cable & Wire Co* 50 Ill App 3d 739, 365 NE 2d 1028 (1977).

[90] 163 Cal App 2d 827, 330 P 2d 98, 100 (1958).

[91] 163 Cal App 2d 827, 330 P 2d 98, 100 (1958).

[92] 163 Cal App 2d 827, 330 P 2d 98, 101 (1958).

9.38 There will be other cases outside dealings in land where the intention of the parties is that the effect of a 'subject to' contract provision is that no contract is to come into existence prior to the execution of a written contract.[93] In addition, there may be customs and practices of a particular industry where the phrase 'subject to contract' or some equivalent gives rise to a presumption that no legal obligations arise until a formal contract is executed.[94] There have also been decisions that appear to adopt the position that the presumption or prima facie meaning, which applies in the case of transfers of interests in land, is of general application.[95] This probably results from courts being alive to the need for parties to be able to introduce a condition upon which the contract depends and the words 'subject to contract' have been adopted into that role. This was recognized by Sargant LJ in *Chillingworth v Esche*,[96] where he said that the words 'subject to contract', 'are words appropriate for introducing a condition, and it would require a very strong and exceptional case for this clear prima facie meaning to be displaced'.[97] Similarly in *Von Hatzfeldt-Wildenburg v Alexander*[98] Parker J said: 'The fact that the reference to the more formal document is in words which according to their natural construction import a condition is generally if not invariably conclusive against the reference being treated as the expression of a mere desire' as 'to the manner in which the transaction already agreed to will in fact go through.'[99]

9.39 There is no doubt a commercial need for such an intention to be capable of being made clear where the negotiations might otherwise appear complete. However, there are clearly many ways such an intention can be made manifest in unequivocal terms.[100] Generally, it

---

[93] See *Regalian Properties Plc v London Docklands Development Corp* [1995] 1 WLR 212. See also *Howard Smith & Co Ltd v Varawa* (1907) 5 CLR 68; *GH Lindekugel & Sons Inc v The Brezina Construction Co Inc* 83 SD 404, 160 NW (2d) 121 (1968); *Chromalloy American Corp v Universal Housing Systems of America Inc* 495 F Supp 544 (1980); *RG Group Inc v The Horn & Hardart Co* 751 F 2d 69 (1984); *Blanton Enterprises Inc v Burger King Corp* 680 F Supp 753 (1988); *Ignazio Messina & Co v Polskie Linie Oceaniczne* [1995] 2 Lloyd's Rep 566; *Glatzer v Bradston Ltd (The Ocean Enterprise)* [1997] 1 Lloyd's Rep 449; *Russell and Baird Ltd v Hoban* [1922] 2 IR 159.

[94] Eg *Samos Shipping Enterprises Ltd v Eckhardt & Co KG (The Nissos Samos)* [1985] 1 Lloyd's Rep 378, 385 per Leggatt J (who, in the context of a ship sale, said, '"subject to detail" is a well-known expression in broking practice which is intended to entitle either party to resile from the contract if in good faith either party is not satisfied with any details as discussed between them'). The same applies to ship charters, see *Star Steamship Society v Beogradska Plovidba (The Junior K)* [1988] 2 Lloyd's Rep 583, 586, 588 and see *Atlantic Marine Transport Corp v Coscol Petroleum Corp (The Pina)* [1992] 2 Lloyd's Rep 103. See also *Thoresen & Co (Bangkok) Ltd v Fathom Marine Co Ltd* [2004] 1 Lloyd's Rep 622, 626; *CPC Consolidated Pool Carriers GmbH v CTM Cia Transmediterranea SA (The CPC Gallia)* [1994] 1 Lloyd's Rep 68; *Granit SA v Benship International Inc* [1994] 1 Lloyd's Rep 526; *Ignazio Messina & Co v Polskie Linie Oceaniczne* [1995] 2 Lloyd's Rep 566. See further *Henderson v Amadio Pty Ltd (No 1)* (1995) 140 ALR 391, 557 (partnership).

[95] See *Concorde Enterprises Ltd v Anthony Motors (Hutt) Ltd* [1981] 2 NZLR 385, 388 (suggesting that where negotiations are conducted at least in part by the parties' solicitors and the matter is complex and the aim of negotiations is to produce an agreement for execution then the usual inference is that there is no binding agreement until the final document is produced and executed). See also *Bunker-Smith v Freeza Meats Ltd* [1987] BTLC 20. Cf *May v Thomson* (1882) 20 Ch D 705, 723 per Lindley LJ.

[96] [1924] 1 Ch 97.

[97] [1924] 1 Ch 97, 114.

[98] [1912] 1 Ch 284. See also *Ridgway v Wharton* (1857) 6 HLC 238, 268, 10 ER 1287, 1299.

[99] [1912] 1 Ch 284, 289.

[100] Eg, see the clause in *Terracom Development Group Inc v Coleman Cable & Wire Co* 50 Ill App 3d 739, 365 NE 2d 1028, 1029–30 (1977).

is only if some common practice exists that dictates that parties do not intend to contract unless that practice is carried out that a presumption can apply, there is no inherent magic in the words, 'subject to contract'.[101]

In the result whether or not an agreement falls within this class is dependent on the **9.40** intention of the parties. As that determination is dependent on the facts of each individual case little can be gained by citing endless examples. Nevertheless, a number of factors have been enunciated in the cases which make it more likely that the agreement will fall within this class. They include, whether the contract is of a type that would normally be made in writing; whether the contract requires agreement on many detailed terms that have not been agreed; whether any documentation evidences that some terms are still to be agreed; whether there is absent terms one would normally expect in the type of agreement in question; whether there has been reference made to a formal contract being drafted for 'approval' and 'signature' either throughout or at some stage of the negotiation practice.[102]

In more recent times, the courts have become reluctant to allow a party to escape a contract **9.41** on the basis that it is void by reason of a condition precedent.[103] This reflects that the courts are aware of how commercial parties transact and expect obligations to arise out of transactions that in the past would be held void for uncertainty and incompleteness. Indeed the whole process of entering into preliminary agreements reflects such methods of transacting. It is therefore not surprising that today many more cases are being held to fall within the second category of *Masters v Cameron*. In addition, outside of land transactions and other transactions where the phrase has traditionally been accepted as evidencing that no contract exists, it could be argued that there is a growing acceptance of a presumption in favour of characterizing transactions as falling within category two.[104] We consider these cases after the next section which deals with category one of *Masters v Cameron*.

---

[101] *Sheehan v Zaszlos* [1995] 2 Qd R 210, 213.

[102] See *Mississippi & Dominion Steamship Co Ltd v Swift* 86 Me 248, 29 A 1063 (1894); *Barrier Wharfs Ltd v W Scott Fell & Co Ltd* (1908) 5 CLR 647 (affirmed (1908) 5 CLR 647); *Farmer v Honan* (1919) 26 CLR 183, 192; *May v Thomson* (1882) 20 Ch D 705, 722ff per Lindley LJ. See also Restatement (2d) Contracts § 27, comment *c*. See further Perillo (ed), *Corbin on Contracts* (Revised edn, Vol 1, St Paul, Minn, West Publishing Co, 1993) § 2.9, pp 152ff; Farnsworth, *Farnsworth on Contracts* (3rd edn, Aspen Publishers, New York, 2004) § 3.8, pp 223–30.

[103] The High Court of Australia in *McRae v Commonwealth Disposals Commission* (1951) 84 CLR 377 stands at the forefront of this approach.

[104] Carter, *Carter on Contract* (Butterworths, Sydney) § 05-020. Perhaps this assumption can be seen in the drafting of Restatement (2d) Contracts § 27, see above 9.13.

**Intention to be immediately bound and to perform when
the time for performance accrues**

9.42   This category has long been recognized and a number of cases falling within this category
have already been noted.[105] In *Masters v Cameron*,[106] the High Court of Australia said of
this category:[107]

> Throughout the decisions on this branch of the law the proposition is insisted upon which
> Lord Blackburn expressed in *Rossiter v Miller* [(1878) 3 App Cas 1124] when he said that the
> mere fact that the parties have expressly stipulated that there shall afterwards be a formal
> agreement prepared, embodying the terms, which shall be signed by the parties does not, by
> itself, show that they continue merely in negotiation. His Lordship proceeded: '... as soon as
> the fact is established of the final mutual assent of the parties so that those who draw up the
> formal agreement have not the power to vary the terms already settled, I think the contract is
> completed' [(1878) 3 App Cas 1124, 1151]: see also *Sinclair, Scott & Co Ltd v Naughton*
> [(1929) 43 CLR 310, 317].

9.43   The passage from *Rossiter v Miller* cited here by the High Court of Australia provides the
general key to determining whether a case falls within this category or not. In order for a
party to prove the existence of an immediately binding contract in the face of a 'subject to'
contract provision they must establish 'the final mutual assent of the parties so that those
who draw up the formal agreement have not the power to vary the terms already settled'.[108]
This approach is applied where the presumption, applicable in dealings with land, does not
apply.[109] Where the presumption applies then generally it is necessary to show that there is
on the facts some ambiguity as to the meaning of the phrase 'subject to contract' and then
go on to show the stronger case is that the parties intended to contract.[110]

9.44   It is doubtful that when Lord Blackburn wrote these words in *Rossiter v Miller* that his reference to 'mutual assent' was intended to refer merely to the fact that the parties have agreed
on the terms of the bargain. Rather it is necessary that they have agreed to be bound by the
terms.[111] As noted earlier,[112] even where there is agreement on all the terms, this does not
of itself necessarily rob the 'subject to' contract clause of effect as it may in the circumstances evidence a lack of intention to assume legal obligations.

---

[105] Eg *Rossiter v Miller* (1878) 3 App Cas 1124, 1143; *Bonnewell v Jenkins* (1878) 8 Ch D 70; *Lamont
v Heron* (1970) 126 CLR 239; *Sheehan v Zaszlos* [1995] 2 Qd R 210, 213. See also *Elmslie v FCT* (1993)
118 ALR 357; *GR Securities Pty Ltd v Baulkham Hills Private Hospital Pty Ltd* (1986) 40 NSWLR 631. In
addition, an industry practice or custom may treat the execution of a formal contract as a mere formality, eg
in the context of insurance, see *General Reinsurance Corp v Forsakringsaktiebolaget* [1983] QB 856. See also
Ionides v The Pacific Fire and Marine Insurance Company (1871) LR 6 QB 674, 685; *Cory v Patton* (1872) LR
7 QB 304, 308; *Royal Botanic Gardens and Domain Trust v South Sydney City Council* (2002) 186 ALR 289,
298. See further Peel, *Treitel, The Law of Contract* (12th edn, Sweet & Maxwell, London, 2007) 2-095.
[106] (1954) 91 CLR 353.
[107] (1954) 91 CLR 353, 360–1.
[108] *Rossiter v Miller* (1878) 3 App Cas 1124, 1151.
[109] See 9.22.
[110] See the approach in *Interway Inc v Alagna* 85 Ill App 3d 1094, 407 NE 2d 615 (1980).
[111] Cf *Rossiter v Miller* (1878) 3 App Cas 1124, 1143–4 per Lord Hatherley, 1149 per Lord O'Hagan.
[112] See 9.35.

Despite the above warning, as a practical matter, outside of contracts dealing with interests **9.45** in land, if the parties have agreed all the terms that they regard as essential, and the contract contains provisions that the law may require (if any), then the reference to the execution of a formal contract is less likely to prevent the formation of the contract without a clear expression of an intention not to contract.[113] If there is also evidence that a document is in existence which is detailed, evidences careful drafting or is signed, then these would be further factors strongly suggesting that it was intended to have immediate effect as a contract.[114] This may apply even if the formal contract is expected to contain additional and consistent terms.[115] For example, *Field v Golden Triangle Broadcasting Inc,*[116] concerned an alleged sale of two radio stations owned by Golden Triangle Broadcasting, Inc. On 14 August 1968, the seller's agent prepared a typed letter of agreement prior to a meeting between Jones, the president and chief executive officer of the seller, Triangle, and Field, one of the various possible purchasers. Various changes were made to this document which was initialled by both Jones and Field, who then signed the letter the following day. They also resolved the question of which of their attorneys should proceed with the preparation of a formal contract containing the terms and provisions of the letter of agreement accepted by them.

On 19 August, Field sent a cheque for $10,000 as a deposit pursuant to the terms of the **9.46** letter of agreement. However, a disagreement arose concerning the formation of a new corporation to complete the purchase; Jones wanted security safeguards if this was to occur. Finally, on 1 November, Jones wrote to Field, stating that since his minimum security safeguard had not been fulfilled, he would not enter into a formal binding contract. Field sought specific performance claiming that the letter of agreement constituted an enforceable contract. Triangle contended that it was not a complete agreement but merely contemplated a formal contract. Triangle pointed to the conditional language used in the letter of agreement and the numerous references to the signing of a formal contract to argue that this was a necessary future requirement. The letter also contained a clause which stated that it was: 'subject to agreement on a formal contract containing the provisions hereinafter set forth ...'.

The Supreme Court of Pennsylvania considered that the letter of agreement 'embodied the **9.47** essential terms to constitute a binding contract'.[117] The court concluded that the letter, 'by

---

[113] Eg *Tooth & Co Ltd v Bryen (No 2)* (1922) 22 SR (NSW) 541 (this case involved an offer and acceptance for the lease of a hotel the acceptance being 'subject to the usual conditions'; as these conditions were all those that would be implied in law in any case it was held that the parties had come to a final unconditional agreement). See also *MacDonald v Australian Wool Innovation Ltd* [2005] FCA 105.

[114] *Elmslie v FCT* (1993) 118 ALR 357, 368–9. See also *Garner v Boyd* 330 F Supp 22 (1970).

[115] See *Commercial Bank of Australia Ltd v G H Dean & Co Pty Ltd* [1983] 2 Qd R 204, 209.

[116] 451 Pa 410, 305 A 2d 689 (1973), certiorari denied, 414 US 1158, 94 SCT 916 (1974). See also *Dohrman v Sullivan* 310 Ky 463, 220 SW 2d 973 (1949); *City of Box Hill v E W Tauschke Pty Ltd* [1974] VR 39; *Tooth & Co Ltd v Bryen [No 2]* (1922) 22 SR (NSW) 541.

[117] 451 Pa 410, 305 A 2d 689, 692 (1973) ('It covers the purchase price, the down payment to be made, the security to be given, a description of the assets to be sold, and numerous other details usually contained in contracts.').

its terms, formality and the extraordinary care in its execution, [indicated] that the signatories intended to bind themselves to an enforceable contract'.[118]

9.48 A further example is provided by the facts in *Branca v Cobarro*.[119] Here in a document for the sale of a lease, it was stated: 'This is a provisional agreement until a fully legalized agreement, drawn up by a solicitor and embodying all the conditions herewith stated, is signed.' In a dispute as to whether the parties had entered into a contract, the court held that the word 'provisional' meant that the parties had intended the document to be a binding agreement, albeit that it would subsequently be replaced by a formal contract. The input by the solicitor was not to vary the terms already agreed.[120]

9.49 Similarly in *Alpenstow Ltd v Regalian Properties plc*,[121] the plaintiffs, the owners of particular property, entered into negotiations with the defendant, a property development company. By a letter of 12 July 1983, the plaintiffs agreed that if they wished to sell the property they would give notice to this effect specifying that they would sell a 51 per cent stake to the defendants for a consideration of £1,530,000. The letter also laid out a precise timetable for events thereafter including the fact that the defendants had 28 days in which to inform the plaintiffs of their acceptance of the notice, 'subject to contract', that the plaintiffs would then submit a draft contract for approval within seven days and, within 28 days of receipt of the draft contract, the defendants would approve it and exchange within seven days thereafter. The defendants accepted this agreement. It was admitted that these documents replaced an earlier binding pre-emptive right agreement.

9.50 Subsequently the plaintiffs gave notice of their intention to sell and the defendants accepted this. When the defendants requested the draft contract in accordance with the agreement, the plaintiffs claimed that, since it was 'subject to contract', the letter of 12 July was not a binding agreement.

9.51 In his judgment, Nourse J concluded that the facts here were sufficient to depart from the normal meaning given to these words in conveyancing practice. In particular, the duty imposed on the parties to exchange contracts within seven days after approval of the draft contract, was not compatible with the normal meaning of 'subject to contract' whereby the parties could withdraw at any time before exchange of contracts.[122]

9.52 Nourse J also listed some other important features of the letter in question. He considered that in general a 'subject to contract' clause would be expected at the preliminary stage of a negotiation, and not, as here, some four or five months on.[123] In addition, the clause would not be expected to condition formation in 'a detailed and conscientiously drawn

---

[118] 451 Pa 410, 305 A 2d 689, 693 (1973).
[119] [1947] KB 854.
[120] Many preliminary agreements are intended to have immediate effect, particularly those requiring performance prior to the execution of the formal contract and many of these might fall within this category even though not all use the expression 'subject to contract'. The facts of this case also show that there is no need for a fourth category (see 9.61ff).
[121] [1985] 1 WLR 721.
[122] [1985] 1 WLR 721, 732.
[123] [1985] 1 WLR 721, 730. Cf above 9.22.

document' which cancelled and replaced a previous binding agreement.[124] Nourse J justified his conclusion by finding support for it from the fact that the agreements were professionally drawn and the draftsman would not have gone into so much detail if the document was to have only the limited effect of recognizing that, until the formal exchange of contracts, the parties could freely withdraw. They were not 'preliminary nor primitive documents'.[125] The obvious comment to be made in response to these findings is that if the documents are professionally drawn up then the use of the phrase 'subject to contract' is generally used in its usual sense.[126] This decision shows that that will not always be the case. More importantly the case is a clear example of how the parties may reach agreement on some issues and intend to be bound by that agreement even though negotiations are still required on other issues.[127]

Although not conclusive,[128] an important indicator as to whether the parties intend to be immediately bound will be the manner in which they conduct themselves after the alleged point of formation.[129] For example, a letter of intent issued in *Frank Horton & Co v Cook Electric Co*[130] stated that it was 'issued in anticipation of the execution of a definitive construction contract for cable placements and materials' and contemplated execution of the formal contract within 60 days. The letter acknowledged that some work needed to be undertaken immediately, it used words of acceptance and expressed that the offeree was bound upon execution of the letter. Although no formal contract was executed, performance in accordance with the agreed terms had begun. It was later alleged that a breach of contract had occurred and the issue of whether there was in fact a contract between the parties was raised. It was contended for 'the party in breach' that all the negotiations were preliminary to a later formal execution of an agreement. This was rejected on the basis that the letter of intent included all the terms essential to the contract and that performance had commenced. The language used and the surrounding circumstances indicated that agreement had already occurred and that this was more than a step in the preliminary negotiation process. Swygert CJ giving judgment for the court stated that '[i]t is true that the parties may have contemplated the execution of a formal agreement at a later date. But such fact does not render the earlier agreements mere negotiations where it is clear that the ultimate contract will be substantially based upon the terms then stated'.[131]

9.53

---

[124] [1985] 1 WLR 721, 730.

[125] [1985] 1 WLR 721, 731.

[126] This point was put by counsel, [1985] 1 WLR 721, 729.

[127] The fact one party conducts itself as if there is a contract does not of itself evidence that they believed there was a contract, they may have been taking a commercial risk, see *Star Steamship Society v Beogradska Plovidba (The Junior K)* [1988] 2 Lloyd's Rep 583. See also Peel, *Treitel, The Law of Contract* (12th edn, Sweet & Maxwell, London, 2007) para 2-092.

[128] See *Australian Securities and Investments Commission v Edwards* (2005) 220 ALR 148, 167. See also *Perry v Suffields* [1916] 2 Ch 187.

[129] Of course such conduct may evidence a later agreement whereby the parties have changed their minds as to the need for execution of a contract, see Perillo (ed), *Corbin on Contracts* (Revised edn, Vol 1, St Paul, Minn, West Publishing Co, 1993) § 2.9, p 155.

[130] 356 F 2d 485 (1966), certiorari denied, 384 US 952, 86 S Ct 1572 (1966). See also *Borg-Warner Corp v Anchor Coupling Co* 16 Ill 2d 234, 156 NE 2d 513 (1958); *Elmslie v FCT* (1993) 118 ALR 357, 369.

[131] 356 F 2d 485, 490 (1966). Swygert CJ (490) went on to cite the following passage of the district judge in this case: 'The language of the letters, and the surrounding circumstances which were considered

9.54   Similarly in *City of Box Hill v E W Tauschke Pty Ltd*[132] the plaintiff council called for tenders for the construction of a road. The tender documents prepared by the plaintiff contained all the detailed terms of the transaction and required parties answering the tender to fill in the blank spaces with the particular job they were tendering for and their asking price. The conditions of the tender contained terms requiring the successful tenderer to indemnify the council against certain claims and to execute a contract after acceptance of the tender by the council. The council accepted the defendant's tender and work commenced with some progress payments being made prior to the tenderer signing. By the time the tenderer signed the contract a worker had been injured. The council required the tenderer to indemnify it against that claim. It was held that the detailed agreed terms and the conduct of the parties evidenced that the execution of a formal contract was a 'mere formality' and the omission to execute the contract was not of 'any moment'.[133]

Intention to be immediately bound but performance is suspended until a formal contract is executed

9.55   As already noted,[134] courts today are more likely to find an intention to assume legal obligations despite the existence of a 'subject to contract' provision; this is particularly the case where there have been formal negotiations and agreement on all the essential terms.[135] However, a 'subject to contract' clause is intended to achieve some purpose and that purpose will often be that the performance of the contract or a particular obligation of the contract is to be suspended until the formal contract is executed.[136]

9.56   The High Court of Australia, in *Masters v Cameron*[137] when identifying this category of case cited as an example the decision in *Niesmann v Collingridge*.[138] Here the vendor granted the purchaser an option to purchase certain land. The price was payable in instalments the first being payable 'on the signing' of the contract and others payable within fixed times from that date. The buyer verbally communicated his wish to exercise the option and the issue before the court was whether a contract for the sale of land came into being upon this

---

in interpreting the language, clearly indicate that these things did not constitute mere inoperative steps in preliminary negotiation. The acceptance of the letter of intent evidenced a meeting of the minds as to all the substantive and essential terms of the relationship between the parties. The fact that defendant demanded the immediate commencement of performance is a strong indication that A.C.E. expected the letter of intent and acceptance thereof to become binding and effective immediately. Defendant certainly did not expect Horton to commence performance only upon a "hope" of obtaining a contract. Furthermore, the words "it is nice to get going" has an air of conclusiveness about it.'

[132] [1974] VR 39.
[133] [1974] VR 39, 43.
[134] See 9.06. Cf *Compaq Computer Asia Pte Ltd v Computer Interface (S) Pte Ltd* [2004] 3 SLR 316, [35].
[135] Cf Tarrant, 'Preliminary Agreements' (2006) 3 UNELJ 151, 161.
[136] Carter, *Carter on Contract* (Butterworths, Sydney) § 05-001. The effect of the condition not occurring will depend upon such matters as whether the failure is due to the fault of one of the parties and the construction of the contract, see further 9.96ff.
[137] (1954) 91 CLR 353, 361.
[138] (1921) 29 CLR 177. See also *O'Brien v Dawson* (1942) 66 CLR 18, 31 per Starke J, and cf 36 per Williams J; *Godecke v Kirwan* (1973) 129 CLR 629; *Meredith v Anthony* [1980] 2 NSWLR 784; *Freedom v AHR Constructions Pty Ltd* [1987] 1 Qd R 59. See further, *Air Great Lakes Pty Ltd v KS Easter (Holdings) Pty Ltd* [1985] 2 NSWLR 309, 321; *South Coast Oils (Qld and NSW) Pty Ltd v Look Enterprises Pty Ltd* [1988] 1 Qd R 680, 701.

acceptance or whether the reference to the need for a signing of a contract prevented the contract from coming into existence. The court held this 'subject to' provision merely fixed the dates for payment and that there was an implied obligation on the parties to execute a document that embodied the terms of the agreement reached between them.[139] Thus, the offer itself was not 'subject to contract'.

The decision in *Damon Compania Naviera SA v Hapag-Lloyd International SA (The* **9.57** *Blankenstein)*[140] is another example. Here negotiations had taken place between the seller and the Raftopoulos brothers for the sale of three ships. The principal terms of the sale were agreed and documented, however, no purchaser was named as it was the intention of the brothers to purchase the ships through a company the details of which they had not yet supplied. The purchase price was to be US$2,364,000 with a 10 per cent deposit. The seller sent a memorandum of agreement incorporating the agreed terms and stating that the deposit was payable on signing the contract; the memorandum named the brothers as agents for the purchaser to be nominated. A Panamanian company was then nominated as the purchaser and the seller was requested to prepare a new memorandum of agreement on that basis. This was done and the seller sent that memorandum to the buyer's broker. Telexes were then sent to the seller indicating the company's intention to go ahead with the purchase but the memorandum itself was not executed.

A few days later the seller gave the buyer notice to sign the agreement and pay the deposit **9.58** and stated that if this was not done, the contract would be rescinded. The buyer did not respond and the seller terminated the agreement based on the repudiation of the buyer and claimed to be entitled to the deposit.

The question for the court to determine was whether there was any concluded contract **9.59** between the parties. The purchaser claimed that there was no contract because it had not signed the memorandum or paid the deposit and, since clause 2 of the memorandum only required the deposit to be paid 'on signing' the contract, the seller could not recover the deposit amount.

The Court of Appeal held that all the terms of the sale had been agreed before the memo- **9.60** randum was sent and there was no indication that the agreement was to be subject to the execution of a memorandum.[141] As a result, the fact that the memorandum was not signed did not prevent there being a binding contract. The obligation to pay the deposit was a term of the agreement and not a condition precedent to the existence of the contract. There was also evidence that the shipping market would regard such an agreement as a binding contract without the necessity for a signed memorandum.

---

[139] As to the power to award specific performance, see *Bahr v Nicolay (No 2)* (1988) 164 CLR 604, 611–12 per Mason CJ and Dawson J, 645–6 per Brennan J.

[140] [1985] 1 WLR 435. See also *Randwick City Council v Nancor Trading Co Pty Ltd* [2002] NSWCA 108; (2002) 120 LGERA 261.

[141] See especially [1985] 1 WLR 435, 443 per Fox LJ.

Intention to be immediately bound but contract to be replaced with a more formal document

9.61   As already noted there is now a considerable body of case law in Australia recognizing this category.[142] It has come to be known as the fourth category to distinguish it from the three categories recognized in *Masters v Cameron*. There are a number of difficulties accepting the category both in terms of precedent and doctrine.[143] First, the legal efficacy of a 'subject to contract' clause was directly before the High Court of Australia in *Masters v Cameron*. In that case, as noted above,[144] the High Court ruled that there are three categories. It is difficult to see how a court in Australia below the High Court can then conclude there are four.

9.62   Second, the fourth category was first recognized by McLelland J in *Baulkham Hills Private Hospital Pty Ltd v GR Securities Pty Ltd*.[145] McLelland J found authority for the fourth category in a statement made by the High Court of Australia in *Sinclair Scott & Co Ltd v Naughton*,[146] where the High Court referred to a transaction '*in which the parties were content to be bound immediately and exclusively* by the terms which they had agreed upon whilst expecting to make a further contract in substitution for the first contract, containing, by consent, additional terms'.[147] McLelland said of such a transaction: 'In the absence of agreement as to further terms to be inserted in the formal contract, the obligation of each party would be to execute a formal contract in accordance with the terms of the agreement appearing from the ... [informal contract].'[148] There are two immediate problems with this analysis. First, the words highlighted show that such an agreement falls within the first category of *Masters v Cameron* and the High Court so held in *Masters v Cameron*. Second, Dixon J was one of the judges responsible for this statement and he also was part of the court in *Masters v Cameron*. If he had thought there was a fourth category he would have said so in *Masters v Cameron* and he did not, he said there were three.

9.63   Third, any contract can be the subject of variation and re-negotiation.[149] It is difficult to see why that possibility, even if expressly envisaged and referred to on the face of a document, must create a fourth category. This category carries no independent legal effect and is therefore not required.[150] The preliminary agreement must stand on its own two feet. Thus,

---

[142] See 9.20.

[143] Some doubt as to the efficacy of this category was noted by Gray J in *Australian & International Pilots Association v Qantas Airways Ltd* [2008] FCA 1972, [75].

[144] See 9.16.

[145] (1986) 40 NSWLR 622 (affirmed without reference (1986) 40 NSWLR 631).

[146] (1929) 43 CLR 310, 317. He also relied on *Love v Stewart* (1917) 33 TLR 475.

[147] (1929) 43 CLR 310, 317 (emphasis added).

[148] He cited *Niesmann v Collingridge* (1921) 29 CLR 177 and *Godecke v Kirwan* (1973) 129 CLR 629. But *Niesmann v Collingridge* was recognized by the High Court in *Masters v Cameron* (1954) 91 CLR 353, 361 as a second category case. Similarly, *Godecke v Kirwan* is a second category case, see Peden, Carter and Tolhurst, 'When Three Just Isn't Enough: The Fourth Category of the "Subject to Contract" Cases' (2004) 20 JCL 156, 162.

[149] It should be noted that if the replacement agreement contains further promises given by one party but not the other then those extra promises will not be supported by consideration, see further Perillo (ed), *Corbin on Contracts* (Revised edn, Vol 1, St Paul, Minn, West Publishing Co, 1993) § 2.9, p 156.

[150] See *Terrex Resources NL v Magnet Petroleum Pty Ltd* [1988] 1 WAR 144, 159.

where the parties reach an agreement 'in principle', this could fall within the fourth category as it implies that there will be a further agreement. But that categorization carries no legal force and the efficacy of any in principle agreement will depend on its own facts.[151] That means that not only must there be an intention to contract but the terms must be sufficiently complete and certain to be given effect to. If not, then that agreement cannot be saved by reference to the intention to enter into a later more formal agreement; the possibility of such a future agreement does not, in the meantime, complete or add certainty to the preliminary agreement.

Perhaps the fourth category has grown out of a need to give effect to a transaction despite **9.64** the fact that further terms are still to be negotiated. In many instances the parties do intend or expect such legal obligations to arise, particularly where obligations must be performed under the preliminary agreement.[152] This could be a response to statements made in numerous cases that the preliminary agreement cannot be given effect to if the formal contract may contain further terms as that would suggest the parties are still in negotiation.[153] But such an arrangement has, in many cases, been dealt with under the other categories and the possibility of such an agreement being effective has been recognized in many modern decisions.[154] So long as such an agreement is sufficiently certain and complete and does not fall foul of the view courts take of agreements to agree at the time, then it can be enforced if there is an intention to contract.

D. 'Subject to Finance'

Introduction

A transaction, particularly a conveyancing transaction, may be made 'subject to finance'.[155] **9.65** Such clauses have raised a number of issues. Do they render the contract void for uncertainty? Are they intended to be a condition precedent to the formation of the contract or are they intended to condition performance? Do they operate as a condition subsequent. Are the clauses for the sole benefit of the buyer or for both parties? It is generally accepted that they benefit the buyer[156] and are often drafted in terms of the offers of finance being

---

[151] See *Yeoman's Row Management Ltd v Cobbe* [2008] UKHL 55; *Stephenson v Dwyer* [2008] NSWCA 123.

[152] See Burrows, Finn and Todd, *Burrows, Finn and Todd, Law of Contract in New Zealand*, (3rd edn, LexisNexis NZ Ltd, Wellington, 2007), para 8.2.2 discussing *Reid Motors v Wood* [1978] 1 NZLR 319. See also McCamus, *The Law of Contracts* (Irwin Law, Toronto, 2005), 128.

[153] Eg *Rossiter v Miller* (1878) 3 App Cas 1124, 1149 per Lord O'Hagan.

[154] See *Godecke v Kirwan* (1973) 129 CLR 629, 648 per Gibbs J; *Ermogenous v Greek Orthodox Community of SA Inc* (2002) 209 CLR 95, 102. Indeed the possibility of the formal contract containing 'fuller and more precise' terms was recognized by the High Court of Australia in *Masters v Cameron* (1954) 91 CLR 353, 360, see also *Foxtel Management Pty Ltd v Seven Cable Television Pty Ltd* (2000) 175 ALR 433, 502.

[155] These are contingent conditions because the required event is not certain to occur. However, as will be discussed below (at 9.78ff) in each case the party who has the benefit of such a provision comes under an obligation to act honestly (and perhaps reasonably) in finding finance and assessing offers of finance. That obligation, albeit an implied obligation, is arguably promissory in nature giving rise to a right to damages if breached. Such damages would usually only be substantial if the vendor elects to terminate the contract for the purchaser's failure to perform to the required standard.

[156] Eg see *Barber v Crickett* [1958] NZLR 1057, 1061; *Scott v Rania* [1966] NZLR 527, 532.

satisfactory to the buyer. From the purchaser's perspective, such clauses are intended to cement the transaction while also protecting the purchaser should it not be able to obtain finance. Being for the benefit of the buyer a further issue concerns the ability of the buyer to waive such a condition. In addition, if the buyer has the benefit of such a provision must it actively seek out finance and then assess offers of finance?

9.66   Such clauses can be viewed as protecting the vendor by preventing the purchaser from backing out from the transaction for any reason other than the availability of finance.[157] Nevertheless, they also pose a risk to the vendor as he or she cannot transact with other potential buyers. It follows that another issue concerns 'avoidance', if it becomes clear that the buyer cannot find finance, should the vendor be allowed to 'avoid' the 'contract' or must the vendor wait until any express or implied time period in which to find finance has elapsed before it can adopt the position that the contract is 'void'? More generally, what are the rights of the parties if it is the fault of the buyer that he or she has not been able to find finance? Much will depend on whether the provision forms part of an existing contract which would attract the normal rules governing discharge for breach or repudiation or whether the clause conditions the formation of the contract. Given the subject matter of this book, this section is principally concerned with the extent to which such provisions condition contract formation.

The efficacy of 'subject to finance' clauses

9.67   In modern English and Australian law there is tendency to construe such clauses as intended to impact on performance rather than formation.[158] This is usually what the parties would expect.[159] Therefore, if the intention is to prevent the contract coming into effect that intention must be clearly evidenced. It also follows that today such provisions will not be held to be void for uncertainty.[160]

---

[157]   See also *Meehan v Jones* (1982) 149 CLR 571, 592 per Mason J (suggesting the clause benefits each party because, 'although the primary object of the condition is to protect the purchaser, it is perhaps difficult to assert that the clause is for his benefit exclusively when it states that the result of non-performance is that the contract shall be null and void, rather than null and void at the option of the purchaser'. He continued, 'I see no justification for implying a right of avoidance on the part of the purchaser alone. In other circumstances to make this implication would be to reach a one-sided interpretation, allowing the purchaser to keep the contract on foot, despite non-performance of the condition, but denying the vendor the right to avoid. Here the vendors were protected by the fixing of the date for completion and the making of time of the essence. Even so, there is no adequate basis for concluding that the special condition authorized the purchaser alone to terminate.'). See also *Perri v Coolangatta Investments Pty Ltd* (1982) 149 CLR 537, 565 per Brennan J. See further Furmston, 'Subject to finance' (1983) 3 OJLS 438, 441; Carter, Peden and Tolhurst, *Contract Law in Australia* (5th edn, Butterworths, Sydney, 2007) para 5.07; Coote 'Agreements "Subject to Finance"' (1976) 40 Conveyancer 37, 44.

[158]   Prior to this the general position was that such conditions prevented a contract coming into existence and they were, in any case, void for uncertainty, see *Lee-Parker v Izzet (No 2)* [1972] 1 WLR 775. See also *Re Rich's Will Trusts* (1962) 106 SJ 75; *Meehan v Jones* (1982) 149 CLR 571, 579–80 per Gibbs CJ. See further Swanton, '"Subject to Finance" Clauses in Contracts for the Sale of Land' Part I (1984) 58 ALJ 633, 635ff. The position in Canada is not settled, see McCamus, *The Law of Contracts* (Irwin Law, Toronto, 2005), 107–9. These English cases can be explained on the basis that the transactions would have been void for uncertainty in any case, see Coote, 'Agreements "Subject to Finance"' (1976) 40 Conveyancer 37, 38.

[159]   Coote, 'Agreements "Subject to Finance"' (1976) 40 Conveyancer 37, 46–7.

[160]   If such a provision was held to be void for uncertainty, the agreement could not be upheld by severing the clause because of its importance to the entire transaction, see Swanton, '"Subject to Finance" Clauses in Contracts for the Sale of Land' Part I (1984) 58 ALJ 633, 635.

In England the leading modern decision is the decision of the Privy Council in *Graham v* **9.68**
Pitkin.[161] Here it was a condition of a contract for the sale of residential property that
completion was 'subject to the purchaser obtaining a mortgage from the Victoria Mutual
Building Society of $19,000 for 10 years'. Although the building society initially offered an
advance subject to a survey, it later revoked that offer before it was accepted. Therefore, the
condition was never fulfilled. The vendor later sought to rescind the contract for the purchaser's alleged repudiation in failing to complete. The purchaser sought specific performance. One of the vendor's arguments was that there was no contract until finance satisfying
the clause had been found. However, the Privy Council treated the condition as going to
performance rather than to the formation of the contract and held that, since the condition
was solely for the benefit of the purchaser, the purchaser could waive it.

In Australia the leading decision is *Meehan v Jones*.[162] This involved an agreement to sell **9.69**
certain land.[163] The relevant term stated:

> This contract is executed by the parties subject to ...
>
> (b) The Purchaser or his nominee receiving approval for finance on satisfactory terms and
>   conditions in an amount sufficient to complete the purchase hereunder;
> and should either of the above conditions not be satisfied on or before the Thirty-first day of
> July, 1979 (or such extended time as the parties may agree upon) then this Contract (other
> than for the provisions of this Clause) shall be null and void and at an end and all monies paid
> hereunder by the Purchaser shall be refunded in full.

On 30 July the purchaser informed the vendor that finance had been found. However, **9.70**
prior to this, on 23 July, the vendor had contracted to sell the land to a third party. The
vendor claimed, inter alia, that the contract was rendered void for uncertainty by reason of
the subject to finance clause. The High Court held that the clause was not uncertain.
Mason J (with whom Wilson J agreed in a separate judgment) said:[164]

> To say that clauses of this kind are void for uncertainty is to ignore the traditional doctrine
> that courts should be astute to adopt a construction which will preserve the validity of the
> contract. Moreover, it is a draconian solution—one which is best calculated to frustrate the
> expectations of the parties, because in an increasing number of cases purchasers depend on
> the provisions of finance in order to complete.

As to whether the words 'finance on satisfactory terms and conditions' created any uncer- **9.71**
tainty, he said:[165]

> [I]n the context of a contract for the sale and purchase of real estate which contains a condi-
> tion that the purchaser or his nominee receives approval for such finance so that the deposit
> is to be refunded to the purchaser if the condition is not satisfied, there can be no doubt that
> 'satisfactory' ordinarily means 'satisfactory to the purchaser or his nominee'.

---

[161] [1992] 1 WLR 403.
[162] (1982) 149 CLR 571. See also *Zieme v Gregory* [1963] VR 214.
[163] The subject matter of this contract was an oil refinery and not a suburban piece of land. It has been
suggested that this fact must be kept in mind because it suggests that all such clauses will now be upheld—at
least where the purchaser's standard of duty is subjectively determined—as this was not a standard form
contract with a history that would allow a court to more readily deal with any uncertainty, see Swanton,
'"Subject to Finance" Clauses in Contracts for the Sale of Land' Part I (1984) 58 ALJ 633, 641.
[164] (1982) 149 CLR 571, 589.
[165] (1982) 149 CLR 571, 587.

9.72 Whether or not the clause is uncertain may be tied to the duty to assess offers of finance. If there is no such obligation then the promise to purchase is arguably illusory.[166] If there is such a duty, a standard of performance must still be identified. If the standard of that duty is subjective then the clause cannot be void for uncertainty.[167] If the standard is objective, then to prevent the clause being void for uncertainty, there must be some objective criteria upon which the purchaser's performance can be tested to determine if the purchaser has acted reasonably.[168] However, the courts are used to using a standard of reasonableness to overcome uncertainty and there should be no such difficulty in finding relevant objective criteria in assessing suitable finance.[169] At the same time it has been noted that there would be some unfairness if a vendor could seek to avoid the contract on the basis of uncertainty arising from a lack of objective criteria when the purchaser had in fact found finance.[170]

9.73 In *Meehan v Jones*, Mason J went on to say that such a provision allows for the 'determination of a valid and binding contract in the event that the purchaser ... is unable to obtain approval for satisfactory finance on or before the appointed date'.[171] He rejected a submission that the purchaser had a discretion to elect not to perform so that the purchaser's consideration was illusory. He said:[172]

> The limitation that the purchaser must act honestly, or honestly and reasonably, takes the case out of the principle that: '... where words which by themselves constitute a promise are accompanied by words which show that the promisor is to have a discretion or option as to whether he will carry out that which purports to be the promise, the result is that there is no contract on which an action can be brought.' ... The judgment of the purchaser as to what constitutes finance on satisfactory terms is not an unfettered discretion—it must be reached honestly, or honestly and reasonably.[173]

---

[166] See Perillo and Bender (eds), *Corbin on Contracts* (Revised edn, Vol 2, West Publishing, St Paul, Minn, 1995) § 5.28, p 149.

[167] There is also a view that subsequent conduct can cure any uncertainty. Thus, if the clause would otherwise be found uncertain but the purchaser nevertheless finds finance then the contract will be effective, for a critique of the cases adopting this view, see Jane P Swanton, '"Subject to Finance" Clauses in Contracts for the Sale of Land' Part I (1984) 58 ALJ 633, 638ff, 641. See further 11.101ff.

[168] See *Lee-Parker v Izzet* [1971] 3 All ER 1099, 1105; *Janmohamed v Hassam, The Times*, 10 June 1976, (1976) 126 NLJ 696. Cf *Lee-Parker v Izzet (No 2)* [1972] 1 WLR 775, 779.

[169] Cf *Moran v Umback* [1966] 1 NSWR 437. See generally Coote, 'Agreements "Subject to Finance"' (1976) 40 Conveyancer 37, 38–9 setting out the difference between certainty concerning the obligations undertaken by the parties and certainty in relation to the condition upon which the obligations depend. In the latter he says the court is only concerned with 'whether the events which have occurred fall within or outside the condition. See further Swanton, '"Subject to Finance" Clauses in Contracts for the Sale of Land' (1984) 58 ALJ 633, 643. In *Meehan v Jones* (1982) 149 CLR 571, 581–2 Gibbs CJ used this distinction to overcome any argument that such agreement involved illusory consideration.

[170] Swanton, '"Subject to Finance" Clauses in Contracts for the Sale of Land' Part I (1984) 58 ALJ 633, 642.

[171] (1982) 149 CLR 571, 592, see also, 589 ('With some justification the vendor can claim that the agreement made by the parties is not an option but a binding contract which relieves the purchaser from performance only in the event that, acting honestly, or honestly and reasonably, he is unable to obtain suitable finance.').

[172] (1982) 149 CLR 571, 589–90 (footnotes omitted). See also Swanton, '"Subject to Finance" Clauses in Contracts for the Sale of Land' Part I (1984) 58 ALJ 633, 645.

[173] Up to this time there was a view that if the standard was purely subjective this would raise an issue of illusory consideration, see Swanton, '"Subject to Finance" Clauses in Contracts for the Sale of Land' Part I (1984) 58 ALJ 633, 645. Mason J rejected this view so that even if the purchaser must assess offers of finance on to his or her (honest) satisfaction that is sufficient.

Gibbs CJ commenced his judgment by noting that the issue is generally one of construc-   **9.74**
tion and each case is dependent on the drafting of the particular clause.[174] Here the clause
was 'directed to the question whether the terms and conditions of finance supplied are
satisfactory from the point of view of the purchaser'.[175] He also held that the 'subject to
finance' clause was not a condition precedent to formation.[176] He resolved the issue of
uncertainty by reference to the existence of a standard of performance. He said:[177]

> If the words of the condition are understood to import a subjective test—if the condition is
> fulfilled if the purchaser honestly thinks that the finance is satisfactory—it is impossible in
> my opinion to regard the condition as uncertain. The question whether the purchaser does
> think the finance satisfactory is a simple question of fact. In most cases it will be a question
> easily answered; if the purchaser thinks the finance satisfactory, he will normally seek to
> complete the contract, whereas if he does not think it satisfactory, usually he will not attempt
> to complete.

He also rejected arguments that the contract was void because it left the performance of a   **9.75**
promise at the discretion of one of the parties.[178] In overcoming this argument he did not
rely in the existence of a subjective or objective duty on the purchaser to assess offers of
finance. He said:[179]

> The submission on behalf of the respondents in the present case was that the condition left a
> discretion or option to the purchaser to decide whether he would carry out the contract and
> that the purported contract was therefore illusory. In my opinion that principle does not
> apply where the discretion or option of the contracting party relates, not to the performance
> of the contractual obligations themselves, but only to the fulfilment of a condition upon
> which the contract depends. That this is so is illustrated by the case of an option to purchase
> which is, in many cases at least, a contract to sell the land upon condition that the grantee
> gives the notice and does the other things stipulated in the option … Such an option gives
> the grantee a right, if he performs the stipulated conditions, to become the purchaser.
> However the fact that the grantee has a discretion as to whether or not he performs those
> conditions does not render the option illusory. The case of a conditional agreement is analo-
> gous. The fact that the condition is one whose performance lies wholly or partly within the
> power of one of the parties to the contract does not mean that there is no binding contract
> once the condition is fulfilled. There is a concluded agreement as to the terms of the contract
> which, if the condition is satisfied, leaves no discretion in either party as to whether he shall
> carry them out. Once the condition is fulfilled, within the time allowed by the contract for
> its fulfilment, the contract becomes completely binding.

---

[174] (1982) 149 CLR 571, 578.
[175] (1982) 149 CLR 571, 577 (see also 580).
[176] (1982) 149 CLR 571, 582.
[177] (1982) 149 CLR 571, 578 per Gibbs CJ.
[178] See *Loftus v Roberts* (1902) 18 TLR 532, 534 per Vaughan Williams LJ ('wherever words which by
themselves constituted a promise were accompanied by words which showed that the promisor was to have a
discretion or option as to whether he would carry out that which purported to be the promise, the result was
that there was no contract on which an action could be brought at all.') See also *Placer Developments Ltd v The
Commonwealth* (1969) 121 CLR 353.
[179] (1982) 149 CLR 571, 581–2. For a critical assessment of this aspect of Gibbs CJ's reasoning, see
Swanton, '"Subject to Finance" Clauses in Contracts for the Sale of Land' Part I (1984) 58 ALJ 633, 646–7.

9.76   In New Zealand, there is no history of holding such clauses void on the basis of uncertainty.[180] In *Martin v Macarthur*[181] where the agreement was made conditional on satisfactory finance being available to the purchaser by a specified date, Richmond J relying on *Barber v Crickett*,[182] treated this condition as a 'condition subsequent', the non-fulfilment of which would render the agreement voidable. If the purchaser wished to resile from the contract he or she carried the onus of proving that no such finance was available.[183] However, in the later decision of *Scott v Rania*,[184] the Court of Appeal, adopting the view that the meaning given to the term depends on the intention of the parties, it not being a phrase carrying an immutable legal meaning, held that an offer to purchase subject to the purchaser arranging mortgage finance on the property within a set period of 14 days, was on the facts before them a condition precedent to the formation of a binding contract rather than a condition subsequent. In the majority, McCarthy J drew a distinction between this clause which was expressed as: 'This offer' is subject to finance and the clause in *Barber v Crickett* which said that, 'in the event of [the buyer] being unable to secure the finance this agreement will become null and void'.[185] Hardie Boys J (dissenting) also dealing with the issue as one of intention considered the better construction was that it was a condition precedent not to formation but to the performance of one party's obligations under the agreement. In his view the clause did not condition the entire agreement to buy as there was an acceptance by the parties of a contract to buy and sell with the purchaser alone having the ability to avoid his obligation if he was unable to raise finance.[186] Then in a powerful passage that appears to accept a presumptive approach to the construction of such clauses he said:[187]

> [H]ere, there was acceptance of a contract to buy, subject to the right of the purchaser alone to avoid his obligation if unable to raise the mortgage; the conditional event being one which the purchaser, by his own acts, must bring about, one of three consequences could therefore follow: (a) He could fulfil it; (b) he could waive it if it were for his benefit and bind himself to the contract notwithstanding non-fulfillment ... or (c) he could invoke the non-fulfillment as discharging his obligation, but at the risk of losing at least his deposit if he had not taken reasonable steps to fulfil the condition. That last consideration is of great significance, for one must ask why it is (if through non-fulfillment of a condition within the stipulated time no contract has ever come into being) that one of the parties to it has obligations to the other which could only exist by virtue of a contractual relationship. If it is simply a case of no contract at all, the test of reasonableness of effort would not seem to arise and the purchaser could recover his deposit as money had and received by the vendor without consideration or upon a consideration which had failed. But our New Zealand reports alone are full of cases of similar 'subject to finance' clauses where, on a claim for a refund of the deposit on non-fulfillment of the condition, the question has always been whether reasonable steps have been taken by the purchaser to fulfil the condition and this has been so whether the conditional clause has

---

[180]   Coote, 'Agreements "Subject to Finance"' (1976) 40 Conveyancer 37, 38.

[181]   [1963] NZLR 403. See further Burrows, Finn and Todd, *Burrows, Finn and Todd, Law of Contract in New Zealand* (3rd edn, LexisNexis NZ Ltd, Wellington, 2007), para 8.2.3.

[182]   [1958] NZLR 1057.

[183]   See further 9.78ff.

[184]   [1966] NZLR 527.

[185]   [1966] NZLR 527, 533.

[186]   [1966] NZLR 527, 539 (distinguishing the decision in *Aberfoyle Plantations v Cheng* [1960] AC 115).

[187]   [1966] NZLR 527, 539–40.

been treated as precedent or subsequent. When, however, one comes to examine the authorities upon which such decisions are based, it is seen at once that the basic principle is that a man cannot take advantage of the existence of a state of things which he himself has produced, and that he is in a contractual relationship with the other party and owing duties thereunder. This, it seems to me, in turn stems from the fact that there can be conditions precedent not to the very formation of a contract, but merely to the obligations of one party under it, with the other party fully bound.

In the United States there have been numerous cases where the illusory consideration argument has been raised in a conditional contract context where the condition requires some event to occur to the satisfaction of one of the parties.[188] The modern decisions reflect the same trend noted above as regards English, Australian and New Zealand law, namely, that these conditions are generally intended to condition performance not formation and are not void for uncertainty or for the promise of illusory consideration.[189] For example, in *Brack v Brownlee*,[190] there was a clause in a contract for the sale of land which provided that 'this contract is contingent upon purchaser being able to secure [adequate] financing' and one of the questions before the court was whether, as argued on behalf of the sellers, the agreement was illusory because it allowed the purchasers 'to escape from the contract at any time without liability'. It was held that there was no lack of mutuality here because the purchaser had in fact paid a deposit. However, Nichols J went on to say that a purchaser could not avoid its obligations as there is an implied duty to diligently seek finance, therefore there could be no lack of mutuality in any case. On the issue of whether such a condition impacts on performance or formation, he said:[191] **9.77**

> If a vendor could successfully utilize this contract term (which is unquestionably for the buyer's protection) to rescind the contract at any time prior to the occurrence of the condition (presumably whenever the vendor received a better offer), a purchaser would never be able to rely on the contract while he sought financing. Any vendor could rescind such a contract with impunity. This result would be intolerable and would destroy the good faith reliance among individuals which permits them to act in accordance with their agreements.

The obligations of the buyer

As noted above, 'subject to finance' clauses are principally incorporated for the benefit of the buyer and are often drafted in terms of the finance being 'satisfactory to the buyer'.[192] What then is the buyer's obligation? Clearly the buyer can waive the clause if, for example, it decides to use its own funds.[193] But if that is not the case, can the buyer, should it change its mind and wish to get out of the contract, simply do nothing? The answer is 'no'. But it is not clear from the cases whether the standard to be applied is subjective or objective. This is important because if the purchaser wishes to resile from the contract and the contract **9.78**

---

[188] See 9.73.
[189] See the discussion in Perillo and Bender (eds), *Corbin on Contracts* (Revised edn, Vol 2, St Paul, Minn, West Publishing, 1995) § 5.32, p 179, noting the distinction drawn by some courts between a promise to buy conditional upon an ability to find finance and a condition of obtaining finance. See generally, Brook, 'Conditions of Personal Satisfaction in the Law of Contracts' (1981–82) 27 NYL Sch L Rev 103.
[190] 246 Ga 818, 273 SE 2d 390 (1980).
[191] 246 Ga 818, 273 SE 2d 390, 392 (1980).
[192] See 9.65.
[193] See 9.121.

contains a satisfaction clause such as a subject to finance clause or a clause requiring the issuing of a building certificate satisfactory to the purchaser, then the purchaser will carry the evidential burden of proving that the condition was not satisfied by reference to the subjective or objective standard required.[194]

9.79   The most detailed discussion in recent times is contained in *Meehan v Jones*.[195] Here, the court was of the view that the buyer must seek out finance and assess offers of finance but differed on the standard to be applied in determining whether the buyer has complied with these obligations. In this case the buyer had in fact found finance so the court did not have to rule on the issue.

9.80   Gibbs CJ was of the view that the appropriate test to assessing offers of finance was a subjective one. The standard was one of honesty.[196] Therefore, the purchaser was not bound by an offer of finance that he or she ought reasonably to regard as satisfactory. He did not think it was 'necessary, in order to give business efficacy to a contract, that a condition should be implied that the purchaser will make reasonable efforts to obtain finance'.[197] In giving his reasons for these conclusions he said:[198]

> A cautious purchaser might be satisfied only with finance which was repayable over a long term and at comparatively low rates of interest, whereas a more adventurous purchaser might wish to proceed with the sale even though the term of the loan was short and the rate of interest high. It would be strange if an adventurous purchaser, having obtained finance on terms which were satisfactory to him, but at which a reasonable man might cavil, could be told by the vendor that the sale would not proceed, although the vendor was to be paid out in full and would have no interest in the purchaser's financial situation thereafter. Equally it would hardly seem likely that the parties would intend that a purchaser should be bound to complete if he honestly regarded the terms and conditions on which finance was available as unsatisfactory, notwithstanding that a court might take a different view. The intention of such a clause in my opinion is to leave it to the purchaser himself to decide whether the terms and conditions on which finance is available are satisfactory. The condition prevents a purchaser from being obliged to go through with a sale when he does not believe that he can raise the necessary funds. Such a condition is generally entirely for the protection of the purchaser, and it is the satisfaction of the purchaser, not that of some hypothetical reasonable man, that will satisfy the condition. No doubt it may be implied that the purchaser will act honestly in deciding whether or not he is satisfied. However, it does not seem to me necessary, in order to give business efficacy to a contract, that a condition should be implied that the purchaser will make reasonable efforts to obtain finance. The parties may expect that he will, but he does not contract to so do.

9.81   Mason J concluded that the clause was incorporated to protect the purchaser so that finance had to be satisfactory to the purchaser. In the early part of his judgment he said that there was an implied obligation to 'act honestly, or honestly and reasonably, in endeavouring to obtain finance and in deciding whether to accept or reject proposals for finance'.[199] It has

---

[194] *Lerner v Schiehallion Nominees Ltd* [2003] 2 NZLR 671, 677.
[195] (1982) 149 CLR 571.
[196] (1982) 149 CLR 571, 581.
[197] (1982) 149 CLR 571, 581.
[198] (1982) 149 CLR 571, 580–1. See also *Katz v Jones* [1967] NZLR 861.
[199] (1982) 149 CLR 571, 588.

been noted that this objective criterion is in line with the general duty to take reasonable steps to bring about a condition.[200] Later in his judgment he concluded by saying:[201]

> In this case it is not necessary to decide whether the purchaser, in deciding whether finance is on satisfactory terms, is bound to act honestly or whether he is also bound to act reasonably. The cases already mentioned appear to support the first rather than the second alternative. And there is some ground for thinking that the parties contemplated that the question was to be left to the honest judgment of the purchaser rather than to the judgment of a court as to whether the purchaser acted reasonably in the circumstances.

> On the other hand, it has been said that a condition of this type imports an obligation or promise on the part of the purchaser to act honestly and reasonably ... The reasoning which underlies the decisions of this Court upholding the implication of an obligation on the part of a party to a contract to do all that was reasonable on his part to obtain a statutory consent applies with equal force here ...

> Here the expressed intention of the parties was that the purchaser would obtain finance; his obtaining of finance on satisfactory terms was necessary to give the transaction its intended efficacy. The consequence would be that he had an obligation to do all that was reasonable on his part to obtain that finance. It would make for greater consistency to say that, if the purchaser is bound to act reasonably in seeking to obtain finance, he is bound to act reasonably as well as honestly in deciding whether the finance was satisfactory. So understood the special condition would preserve an even balance between the vendors and the purchaser. However, I have no need to decide the question. Here it makes no difference whether the purchaser was under an obligation to act honestly or honestly and reasonably in deciding whether the terms of an offer of finance were satisfactory.

Murphy J suggested that the word 'honest' as a qualification to 'satisfaction' added nothing.[202] He was also of the view that no requirement of reasonableness should be implied.[203] Wilson J thought the issue was ultimately one of construction but that the weight of authority favoured a view that a purchaser must act honestly in deciding 'whether the available finance is satisfactory'.[204] He thought there was force in this view but expressed no concluded opinion. However, he did think a purchaser must make reasonable efforts to find finance.[205] **9.82**

The decision of the High Court leaves the situation in Australia unclear. The weight of authority that Wilson J was referring to was not so much cases dealing with 'subject to finance' clauses but other conditional contract cases where the subject matter of the contract was received 'subject to' approval by the buyer.[206] In the context of 'subject to finance' clauses, there are numerous cases that have adopted an objective test. Perhaps the most well-known English case is *Lee-Parker v Izzet*.[207] Here Goff J suggested that finance had to **9.83**

---

[200] Swanton, '"Subject to Finance" Clauses in Contracts for the Sale of Land' Part I (1984) 58 ALJ 633, 647.
[201] (1982) 149 CLR 571, 590–1.
[202] (1982) 149 CLR 571, 597.
[203] (1982) 149 CLR 571, 597.
[204] (1982) 149 CLR 571, 597.
[205] (1982) 149 CLR 571, 598.
[206] The cases are discussed by Mason J, see (1982) 149 CLR 571, 590.
[207] [1971] 3 All ER 1099. See further *Progress and Properties (Strathfield) Pty Ltd v Crumblin* (1984) 3 BPR 9496 (adopting an objective test).

be to the satisfaction of the purchaser acting reasonably.[208] A similar view was taken by Slade J in *Janmohamed v Hassam*.[209] This case concerned a sale of a house subject to the condition that if the purchaser did not obtain an offer of a mortgage on terms satisfactory to himself within one month, the contract should be rescinded. Slade J held that there was an implied term that this satisfaction should not be unreasonably withheld.[210] It would seem that Slade J was requiring the purchaser's dissatisfaction to be both honest and reasonable. In New Zealand there are a number of decisions which have taken the view that the purchaser must act reasonably.[211] Thus, in *Martin v Macarthur*,[212] Richmond J held that the words 'satisfactory finance' had to be given an objective meaning and it was for the purchaser to establish that, notwithstanding reasonable efforts, he or she failed to obtain mortgage finance of a kind a reasonable person acting fairly would consider to be satisfactory in the circumstances.

9.84   In the result it is difficult to state what the law is in any of these jurisdictions. In *Freedom v AHR Constructions Pty Ltd*,[213] McPherson J suggested a resolution in the following terms:[214]

> It may be possible to resolve the conflict of opinion in the case of a [subject to finance on satisfactory terms and conditions] clause ... by adopting honesty as the test, while adding that the failure of a purchaser to take such steps as are reasonably open to him to obtain finance is evidence, and may be strong evidence, that he has failed to act honestly in electing to terminate the contract.

9.85   It is suggested that in the end there is much force in the subjective standard. As Furmston noted in commenting on the decision in *Meehan v Jones*: 'Since the commercial purpose of the "subject to satisfactory finance" provision was to give the purchaser an opportunity to raise finance, the natural inference was that the finance must be satisfactory to him and not to some hypothetical reasonable purchaser.'[215] At the same time it would be consistent with the approach to other 'subject to' clauses to apply a standard of reasonableness to the

---

[208] [1971] 3 All ER 1099, 1105. The point is only summarized in this report and does not appear in the Weekly Law Report, see [1971] 1 WLR 1688.

[209] *The Times*, 10 June 1976, (1976) 126 NLJ 696.

[210] Slade J was of the view that by implication of this standard of reasonableness, the clause could not be said to be void for uncertainty, see 11.85ff. Of course the implication of such a promissory term only makes sense if the condition forms part of an existing contract. If the condition is a condition precedent to the formation of the contract this term would need to form part of a collateral contract, see further Coote, 'Agreements "Subject to Finance"' (1976) 40 Conveyancer 37, 48.

[211] See *Barber v Crickett* [1958] NZLR 1057, 1060 per Cleary J; *Scott v Rania* [1966] NZLR 527, 534 per McCarthy J; *Gardner v Gould* [1974] 1 NZLR 426, 428, per McCarthy P. See also the discussion and collection of the relevant cases in *Lerner v Schiehallion Nominees Ltd* [2003] 2 NZLR 671, 676–8. In *Meehan v Jones* (1982) 149 CLR 571, 591 Mason J, noted that McCarthy J, in *Scott v Rania* (1966) NZLR 527, 534, 'preferred to base his reasoning on the principle that a party to a contract cannot be permitted to rely on his own wrong, later in *Gardner v Gould* (1974) 1 NZLR 426, 428, he adopted the implied promise theory'.

[212] [1963] NZLR 403 discussed above.

[213] [1986] 1 Qd R 59. Cf *Meehan v Jones* (1982) 149 CLR 571, 578 per Gibbs CJ.

[214] [1986] 1 Qd R 59, 67. See also Swanton, '"Subject to Finance" Clauses in Contracts for the Sale of Land' Part I (1984) 58 ALJ 633, 642; Perillo (ed), *Corbin on Contracts* (Revised edn, Vol 8, Lexis Law Publishing, Virginia, 1999) § 31.7, p 76.

[215] Furmston, 'Subject to Finance' (1983) 3 OJLS 438, 440.

obligation to find finance. Of course what would be reasonable would depend on the facts of the case, in particular the subject matter of the contract.

In the United States, there are cases that have held that an objective test applies to all forms **9.86** of 'satisfaction' clause.[216] In other instances it has been said that a 'satisfaction' clause is only subject to the obligation to perform in good faith.[217] In *Brack v Brownlee*,[218] in the particular context of a 'subject to finance' clause it was said that the purchaser has a duty to diligently seek out finance and that duty must be exercised in good faith.[219] However, the reference to good faith is problematic because views as to the meaning of the phrase differ.[220] For example, in Australia some judges have taken the view that it means honesty and for others it includes a standard of reasonableness.[221] The debate on the meaning of the phrase is not limited to jurisdictions where it is a developing doctrine but also to jurisdictions like the United States where it has been established for a long time.[222]

Although not a 'subject to finance' case, the decision in *Mattei v Hopper*,[223] perhaps best **9.87** sums up the position in the United States where the satisfaction provision referred to the satisfaction of one of the parties and not a third party.[224] In discussing this case it should be noted that in addition to good faith dictating a standard to determine whether the duty has been complied with, courts have suggested that this obligation also ensures that the discretion is not unchecked and the promise not illusory.[225] This is the context of *Mattei v Hopper*.

---

[216] Eg *Lyon v Giannoni* 168 Cal App 2d 336, 335 P 2d 690 (1959). See further below 9.89. See also Perillo and Bender (eds), *Corbin on Contracts* (Revised edn, Vol 2, West Publishing, St Paul, Minn, 1995) § 5.32, p 178, § 5.33, pp 189–90. See generally, DiMatteo, *Equitable Law of Contracts* (Transnational Publishers, New York, 2001) ch 5; Brook, 'Conditions of Personal Satisfaction in the Law of Contracts' (1981–82) 27 NYL Sch L Rev 103; DiMatteo, 'The Norms of Contract: The Fairness Inquiry and the "Law of Satisfaction"— A Nonunified Theory' (1995–96) 24 Hofstra L Rev 349.

[217] See generally Farnsworth, *Farnsworth on Contracts* (3rd edn, Vol 2, Aspen Publishers, New York, 2004) § 8.6, p 456 who suggests it is more accurately described as a duty to use 'best efforts'. See also Perillo (ed), *Corbin on Contracts* (Revised edn, Vol 8, Lexis Law Publishing, Virginia, 1999) § 31.6, pp 67ff; Brook, 'Conditions of Personal Satisfaction in the Law of Contracts' (1981–82) 27 NYL Sch L Rev 103; DiMatteo, 'The Norms of Contract: The Fairness Inquiry and the "Law of Satisfaction"—A Nonunified Theory' (1995–96) 24 Hofstra L Rev 349.

[218] 246 Ga 818, 273 SE 2d 390 (1980).

[219] 246 Ga 818, 273 SE 2d 390, 391 (1980).

[220] In *Rodriguez v Barnett* 52 Cal 2d 154, 338 P 2d 907, 911 (1959), there is a very clear statement that an objective criterion is to be applied and that criterion is 'good faith'. See also *Vanadium Corp of America v Fidelity & Deposit Co of Maryland* 159 F2d 105, 108 (1947).

[221] Carter and Peden, 'Good Faith in Australian Contract Law' (2003) 19 JCL 155; Peden, *Good Faith in the Performance of Contracts* (LexisNexis, Sydney, 2003).

[222] Hunter, 'The Growing Uncertainty about Good Faith in American Contract Law' (2004) 20 JCL 50. See also Perillo (ed), *Corbin on Contracts* (Revised edn, Vol 8, Lexis Law Publishing, Virginia, 1999) § 31.6, pp 72, 75 referring to 'good faith' as a subjective standard. See further Brook, 'Conditions of Personal Satisfaction in the Law of Contracts' (1981–82) 27 NYL Sch L Rev 103, 109ff.

[223] *Mattei v Hopper* 51 Cal 2d 119, 330 P 2d 625 (1958). See further Goldberg, *Framing Contract Law* (Harvard University Press, 2006) ch 4.

[224] On third parties, see n 276 below.

[225] *Mattei v Hopper* 51 Cal 2d 119, 330 P 2d 625, 626–7 (1958). There have been a number of decisions in the United States that have approached these cases on the basis of illusory consideration. In *Stone Mountain Properties Ltd v Helmer* 229 139 Ga App 865, SE 2d 779 (1976) the court determined that on construction the satisfaction clause in issue left the purchaser to be the sole judge of whether the condition was fulfilled— that is, a subjective approach—and the contract was void for lack of mutuality. Cf *Meehan v Jones* (1982) 149 CLR 571, 579, 581 per Gibbs CJ.

The case concerned negotiations relating to the purchase of property adjacent to land upon which the plaintiff, the potential purchaser, was building a shopping centre. At issue was a clause in the parties' agreement stating that it was 'subject to [the purchaser] obtaining leases satisfactory to the purchaser'.[226] It was argued by the purchaser that no contract existed between the parties. It was held that the 'subject to' provision merely conditioned performance and not formation. In giving judgment Spence J went on to say:[227]

> While contracts making the duty of performance of one of the parties conditional upon his satisfaction would seem to give him wide latitude in avoiding any obligation and thus present serious consideration problems, such 'satisfaction' clauses have been given effect. They have been divided into two primary categories and have been accorded different treatment on that basis. First, in those contracts where the condition calls for satisfaction as to commercial value or quality, operative fitness, or mechanical utility, dissatisfaction cannot be claimed arbitrarily, unreasonably, or capriciously ... and the standard of a reasonable person is used in determining whether satisfaction has been received ... However, it would seem that the factors involved in determining whether a lease is satisfactory to the lessor are too numerous and varied to permit the application of a reasonable man standard ...
>
> The multiplicity of factors which must be considered in evaluating a lease shows that this case more appropriately falls within the second line of authorities dealing with 'satisfaction' clauses, being those involving fancy, taste or judgment. Where the question is one of judgment, the promisor's determination that he is not satisfied, when made in good faith, has been held to be a defense to an action on the contract ... Although these decisions do not expressly discuss the issues of mutuality of obligation or illusory promises, they necessarily imply that the promisor's duty to exercise his judgment in good faith is an adequate consideration to support the contract.

9.88 It is clear from these comments and from the passages that follow that the second category adopts a subjective approach.[228] The reference to good faith in the second category of case is a reference to a criterion that sets a standard upon which it is possible the judge the buyer's subjective view.[229]

9.89 The categorization set forth in *Mattei v Hopper* has been used in numerous decisions.[230] It is a categorization that is subject to the overriding intention of the parties[231] but it is also a categorization that would usually reflect the intention of the parties. For example, an objective criterion would not represent the intention of the parties where the condition depends on the personal idiosyncrasies of the buyer. Nor in such a case would it be practical to apply such a criterion. The test of practicality to determine when an objective standard applies is adopted in section 228 of Restatement (2d) Contracts requiring the objective approach to be applied if practical to do so. The provision is consistent with the categorization in

---

[226] The purchaser wanted to ensure leases were in place over the shopping centre before being committed to buying the defendant's property.
[227] 51 Cal 2d 119, 330 P 2d 625, 626–7 (1958). See further Brook, 'Conditions of Personal Satisfaction in the Law of Contracts' (1981–82) 27 NYL Sch L Rev 103, 145ff.
[228] See also *Action Engineering v Martin Marietta Aluminum* 670 F 2d 456, 461 (1982).
[229] 51 Cal 2d 119, 330 P 2d 625, 627–8 (1958) (citing Williston and Corbin).
[230] Eg *Lyon v Giannoni* 168 Cal App 2d 336, 335 P 2d 690 (1959); *Action Engineering v Martin Marietta Aluminum* 670 F 2d 456 (1982); *Misano di Navigazione v United States of America* 968 F 2d 273 (1992).
[231] *Misano di Navigazione v United States of America* 968 F 2d 273, (1992).

Mattei v Hopper and both would usually provide the same result.[232] However, the provision evidences a preference for the objective test.[233] Clear evidence of intention or necessity is required to attract a subjective standard.[234] The provision states:[235]

§228. Satisfaction of the Obligor as a Condition

When it is a condition of an obligor's duty that he be satisfied with respect to the obligee's performance or with respect to something else, and it is practicable to determine whether a reasonable person in the position of the obligor would be satisfied, an interpretation is preferred under which the condition occurs if such a reasonable person in the position of the obligor would be satisfied.

It is clear from this provision and the comments that the preference for the objective standard only applies if it is not contrary to the intentions of the parties.[236] If it is clear that the intention is that the contract only requires the purchaser to be honestly satisfied then that standard will applied.[237] But if the provision is ambiguous then the objective standard is applied if it is practical to do so.[238] The comments also make it clear that in all cases the purchaser is subject to the obligation of good faith and fair dealing.[239]   **9.90**

E. Other 'Subject to' Clauses

The 'subject to finance' clause is one form of a broader category of 'satisfaction' clauses.   **9.91**
That is, a clause that introduces a contingency that the contract or some performance obligation is 'subject to' and which must be fulfilled to the satisfaction of one or both of the parties to the contract or to the satisfaction of a third party. Most such clauses are incorporated for the protection of one party only.[240] Examples include, where the obligation to accept the subject matter of a contract is conditional upon inspection or testing or measuring by one of the parties or a third party;[241] where a contract is subject to the approval of the parties' legal advisers;[242] where an obligation, typically an obligation to pay, is subject to some work under the contract being approved by a third party such as an architect or

---

[232] Eg *Action Engineering v Martin Marietta Aluminum* 670 F 2d 456 (1982).

[233] See *Misano di Navigazione v United States of America* 968 F 2d 273, 274 (1992) ('Where a contract conditions performance upon the satisfaction of one party and is ambiguous as to the applicable standard of satisfaction, courts generally require performance to the satisfaction of a reasonable man, particularly when a definite objective test of satisfaction is available' (citing Restatement (2d) Contracts § 228)).

[234] See Perillo (ed), *Corbin on Contracts* (Revised edn, Vol 8, Lexis Law Publishing, Virginia, 1999) §§ 31.6–31.8, pp 69–93.

[235] See *Action Engineering v Martin Marietta Aluminum* 670 F 2d 456 (1982). See further Brook, 'Conditions of Personal Satisfaction in the Law of Contracts' (1981–82) 27 NYL Sch L Rev 103, 150.

[236] See *Action Engineering v Martin Marietta Aluminum* 670 F 2d 456 (1982).

[237] See comments *a* and *b*.

[238] *Misano di Navigazione v United States of America* 968 F 2d 273, 275 (1992).

[239] See comment *a*. See also *Misano di Navigazione v United States of America* 968 F 2d 273, 275 (1992).

[240] *Perri v Coolangatta Investments Pty Ltd* (1982) 149 CLR 537, 552.

[241] See *Mackay v Dick* (1881) 6 App Cas 251. See also *Pym v Campbell* (1856) 6 E & B 370, 119 ER 903 (contract for an interest in an invention was conditional upon approval by an engineer); *Albion Sugar Co Ltd v William Tankers Ltd (The John S Darbyshire)* [1977] 2 Lloyd's Rep 457 (here an offer was accepted for the carriage of goods subject to the 'satisfactory completion of two trial voyages'); *Marks v Board* (1930) 46 TLR 424 (sale 'subject to surveyor's report').

[242] This is discussed above at 9.23ff.

engineer; where a sale is made conditional upon approval of a public official;[243] where a transaction is subject to the issuing of a licence by a public body; where a sale is conditional upon the subject matter being valued by a third party.[244] Another example would be where directors make a transaction subject to shareholder approval. Not all contingencies fall into the category of 'satisfaction' clauses. A contract may be made subject to some event which is not dependent on the satisfaction of either a party or a third party.[245] Moreover, whether some of the examples already mentioned, particularly those involving third parties, fall into that category may depend on what the third party is required to do. Examples of 'subject to' clauses that would not be classified as satisfaction clauses would include where a contract is made subject to the discharge or the entering into of some other contract such as where a sale, typically a sale of land, is subject to the purchaser selling its property;[246] and where the contingency requires the maintenance of some status quo.[247]

9.92   It is not necessary or possible to review every possible type of conditional contract in this text. In terms of the subject matter of this text, the important point to make is that the parties can make any condition qualify the initial formation of a contract as a condition precedent or its continued existence as a condition subsequent.[248] In some instances such a contingency might be implied.[249] Today when all essential terms of the contract have been agreed, the tendency of the courts, unless there is a clear intention to the contrary, is to treat such conditions as impacting on performance rather than formation. The decision of the High Court of Australia in *Perri v Coolangatta Investments Proprietary Ltd*[250] clearly evidences this trend. The case concerned a contract for the sale of land which was conditional on the purchasers completing the sale of another property. No time was set for completion. After four months had elapsed and after giving a notice to complete, the vendor sought to terminate the contract. Ten months later the purchaser finally sold the other property and claimed specific performance of the contract. It was held that the condition was not a

---

[243] *Suttor v Gundowda Pty Ltd* (1950) 81 CLR 418.

[244] *George v Roach* (1942) 67 CLR 253.

[245] A statute may prevent the creation of a contract prior to the occurrence of some contingency, eg *Roach v Bickle* (1915) 20 CLR 663.

[246] *Maynard v Goode* [1926] 37 CLR 529. See also *Paul v Rosen* 3 Ill App 2d 423, 122 NE 2d 603 (1954) (agreement to buy and sell business conditional 'upon the Buyer obtaining a new lease' from the owner of the premises).

[247] *Thompson v ASDA-MFI plc* [1988] Ch 241 (right of employee to participate in share option scheme was conditional on subsidiary remaining part of the relevant company group).

[248] There are many examples of courts holding the condition to be one that prevents the formation of a contract, eg *Pym v Campbell* (1856) 6 E & B 370, 119 ER 903; *Weston v Collins* (1865) 12 LT (NS) 4; *Marks v Board* (1930) 46 TLR 424; *George v Roach* (1942) 67 CLR 253; *Paul v Rosen* 3 Ill App 2d 423, 122 NE 2d 603 (1954); *Albion Sugar Co Ltd v William Tankers Ltd (The John S Darbyshire)* [1977] 2 Lloyd's Rep 457; *Anictomatis v NTA* [2008] NTSC 28. See also *IOC Australia Pty Ltd v Mobil Oil Australia Ltd* (1975) 11 ALR 417, 424–5 (agreement subject to the 'filling of the blanks in the form in a manner satisfactory to both parties').

[249] Eg *Bentworth Finance Ltd v Lubert* [1968] 1 QB 680. See Carnegie, 'An Implied Condition in Motor-Car Hire-Purchase' (1968) 31 MLR 78.

[250] (1982) 149 CLR 537. See also the comments of Isaacs J in *Maynard v Goode* [1926] 37 CLR 529, 540 and see *Gregory v MAB Pty Ltd* (1989) 1 WAR 1, 9–10 per Malcolm CJ, 21 per Brinsden J. In *Scott v Rania*, [1966] NZLR 527, 540, Hardie Boys J suggested that 'where the non-fulfillment of a conditional clause … lay within the ability of one of the parties rather than a third party to fulfil and accomplish', it would be held to condition performance and not formation.

condition precedent to the formation of a binding contract; the contract was formed upon execution and from that moment the parties were subject to certain obligations such as the buyer's obligation to pay the deposit. However, it was also necessary for the purchaser to complete within a reasonable time[251] and the majority of the court were of the view that a reasonable time had expired by the time the vendor elected to terminate the contract and that the vendor could then terminate without first giving a notice to complete.[252] As regards the nature of the condition, Mason J gave the following reasons for preferring a construction that upholds the contract:[253]

> Generally speaking the court will tend to favour that construction which leads to the conclusion that a particular stipulation is a condition precedent to performance as against that which leads to the conclusion that the stipulation is a condition precedent to the formation or existence of a contract. In most cases it is artificial to say, in the face of the details settled upon by the parties, that there is no binding contract unless the event in question happens. Instead, it is appropriate in conformity with the mutual intention of the parties to say that there is a binding contract which makes the stipulated event a condition precedent to the duty of one party, or perhaps of both parties, to perform. Furthermore, it gives the courts greater scope in determining and adjusting the rights of the parties. For these reasons the condition will not be construed as a condition precedent to the formation of a contract unless the contract read as a whole plainly compels this conclusion.[254]

---

[251] See also *Aberfoyle Plantations Ltd v Cheng* [1960] AC 115, 124.

[252] Gibbs CJ after acknowledging that the authorities permit a party to terminate without notice if a non-promissory condition is not fulfilled within an express time period, thought that the same rule should apply where no time is fixed and a reasonable period of time has elapsed and where the condition is not one that is within the power of one of the parties to bring about. In such a case he thought that the notice to complete procedure was inappropriate as the purchaser had not promised to fulfil the condition but to take reasonable steps to try to find a buyer, see (1982) 149 CLR 537, 545–6 and see 569 per Brennan J, cf 554–6 per Mason J, 560, 563 per Wilson J. Where a party is under an obligation to take reasonable steps to bring about a condition and does so without success, they too can terminate the contract without giving such a notice, see *Steele v Serepisos* [2007] 1 NZLR 1.

[253] (1982) 149 CLR 537, 552. Gibbs CJ ((1982) 149 CLR 537, 541–2, 545) supported this approach by reference to the argument that if there was no existing contract it would be inconsistent to accept (as the courts have done) that there was any implied promise to the effect that the purchaser would take all reasonable steps or use their best endeavours to find a buyer for their property and to complete that sale. See also 9.97.

[254] Other examples include *Powell v Lee* (1908) 99 LT 284, 285 (requirement that employee get married as a condition of employment did not prevent formation of contract of employment); *Smith v Butler* [1900] 1 QB 694 (sale of purchase of leasehold subject to seller obtaining consent of mortgagee); *Commonwealth Homes and Investment Co Ltd v Mackellar* (1939) 63 CLR 351 (the respondent applied for 1,000 shares in a company in order to qualify as a director; he agreed to be a director on the condition that he was to be the only architect appointed to the board; held the condition was not a condition precedent to the respondent becoming a shareholder; the contract for the allotment of shares was effective subject to the condition; no other 'construction' was reasonable; it could not be that the offer to take up shares could not be accepted until his period of directorship had expired with no other architect being appointed in that time); *Suttor v Gundowda Pty Ltd* (1950) 81 CLR 418 (agreement for sale of land subject to the consent of the Treasurer being obtained); *Property and Bloodstock Ltd v Emerton* [1968] Ch 94, 117, 122, 125 (sale of leasehold subject to landlord's consent); *Smallman v Smallman* [1972] Fam 25; (property settlement 'subject to the approval of the court'; held that this did not prevent a binding agreement coming into effect); *Brien v Dwyer* (1978) 141 CLR 378, 393, 397–8 (payment of deposit held not to be a condition precedent to the coming into existence of a contract; the failure to pay the deposit was a breach of contract—see also *Damon Compania Naviera SA v Hapag-Lloyd International SA (The Blankenstein)* [1985] 1 WLR 435); *Alan Estates Ltd v WG Stores Ltd* [1982] Ch 511 (lease executed and exchanged but not dated, expressed to be subject to certain conditions contained in tenants' solicitors covering letter); *Roadworks (1952) Ltd v Charman* [1994] 2 Lloyd's Rep 99 (underwriter's quote subject to London Salvage Association approval). See further *Mackay v Dick* (1881) 6 App Cas 251;

9.93 Ultimately, whether or not a provision qualifies formation or performance is determined by reference to the intention of the parties and this is a matter upon which opinions may differ. Being relevant to contract formation the issue will involve issues of fact to the extent it raises intention to contract.[255] However, aspects of construction are involved and much will depend on the wording of the particular clause, the meaning of that clause when read in light of the contract as a whole and its meaning when taking into account any relevant surrounding circumstances. It is therefore difficult, and arguably incorrect, to seek to classify them into groups by reference to the nature of the contingency. For example, in England there have been differences of opinion expressed over agreements which are made subject to a surveyor's report with some cases taking the view that the condition qualifies formation[256] and others that it qualifies performance.[257] However, to the extent the issue is determined by construction and is seen as one of determining the legal effect of a provision, then precedent will have a role to play.[258] Moreover, commercial parties need to know with some certainty what the legal effect of a particular commonly used phrase will be. On this view there is nothing wrong in seeking to classify such phrases and on this view the different results in the above cases could be explained on the basis of a change in the approach of the courts to certain conditions which in turn reflects developments in contracting and the expectation of the parties.

9.94 Indeed, the modern view with its starting point of preferring an approach that will uphold the contract is the opposite of that which went before it and can lead to different results. It is therefore dangerous to rely on old cases not only because this is an issue that depends on the facts of each case but because even with a close factual analogy, the facts are likely to be interpreted differently today. That this is so is seen in many older authorities being departed from in more recent cases.[259] For example,[260] the correctness of the decision in *Aberfoyle Plantations Ltd v Cheng*,[261] where a contract for the sale of land conditional on the vendor obtaining the renewal of certain leases was held to qualify the formation of the contract was doubted by the High Court of Australia in *Perri v Coolangatta Investments Proprietary*

Marten v Whale [1917] 2 KB 480; *Haslemere Estates Ltd v Baker* [1982] 1 WLR 1109; *ANM Trading Pty Ltd v Commissioner of Business Franchises* [1996] 2 VR 312; *North Sea Energy Holdings NV v Petroleum Authority of Thailand* [1997] 2 Lloyd's Rep 418; *Lerner v Schiehallion Nominees Ltd* [2003] 2 NZLR 671, 677.

[255] 1.20ff.
[256] Eg *Marks v Board* (1930) 46 TLR 424; *Astra Trust Ltd v Adams and Williams* [1969] 1 Lloyd's Rep 81; *Graham and Scott (Southgate) LD v Oxlade* [1950] 2 KB 257 and see *John Howard & Co (Northern) Ltd v JP Knight Ltd* [1969] 1 Lloyd's Rep 364 (sale of ship 'subject to satisfactory running trials').
[257] Eg *Ee v Kakar* (1979) 40 P & CR 223 and see *Varverakis v Compagnie Navegacion Artico SA (The Merak)* [1976] 2 Lloyd's Rep 250, 254 (agreement for sale of ship 'subject to inspection by buyers'; per Lord Denning MR, doubting the correctness of the decisions in *Marks v Board* and *Astra Trust Ltd v Adams and Williams*).
[258] Carter, 'Commercial Construction and Contract Doctrine' (2009) 25 JCL 83, 84.
[259] See Carter, *Carter on Contract*, § 05-040.
[260] See also *Lee-Parker v Izzet (No 2)* [1972] 1 WLR 775 (sale subject to purchaser obtaining satisfactory mortgage), doubted in *Graham v Pitkin* [1993] 1 WLR 403 (sale subject to purchaser obtaining mortgage). See further *Myton Ltd v Schwab-Morris* [1974] 1 WLR 331 doubted in *Damon Compania Naviera SA v Hapag-Lloyd International SA (The Blankenstein)* [1985] 1 WLR 435, 446, 453–4.
[261] [1960] AC 115.

Ltd.[262] It was also doubted in *Property & Bloodstock Ltd v Emmerton.*[263] Similarly, *Astra Trust Ltd v Adams,*[264] in which a condition for a satisfactory survey in respect of the sale of a yacht was held to qualify formation, was doubted in *Ee v Kakar,*[265] and in *Varverakis v Compagnia de Navegacion Artico SA (The Merak).*[266]

In the result, where the parties have agreed all the essential terms, then any contingency is likely to be construed as impacting on some performance obligations rather than contract formation.[267] However, where the condition relates to the formulation—as opposed to the performance—of an essential term, such as where a valuer is required to fix the price of the contract,[268] then generally the condition will qualify formation because the failure of the condition will result in an incomplete or uncertain agreement. **9.95**

The obligations of the parties

What event is required to satisfy the contingency is determined by construing the contract.[269] In addition, there is a separate issue as to what, if anything, is required of the parties to bring about the contingency. **9.96**

Where a contingency qualifies contract formation, then neither party can be under a duty to take steps to ensure the contingency occurs.[270] For there to be such a duty it must form part of a contract or, in this case, part of a collateral contract.[271] **9.97**

Where the condition qualifies performance, then as a general proposition the parties are bound and cannot resile from the contract prior to the time set for the occurrence of the condition lapsing unless there is clear evidence that the condition will not occur within the time set under the contract.[272] In the case of non-promissory conditions, if the condition is not met there will be a point in time, determined by construction, upon which the **9.98**

---

[262] (1982) 149 CLR 537, 542 per Gibbs CJ, 550–1 per Mason J, 557 per Wilson J.
[263] [1968] 1 Ch 95, 116 per Danckwerts LJ. See also *Gregory v MAB Pty Ltd* (1989) 1 WAR 1, 9–10 per Malcolm CJ, 21 per Brinsden J.
[264] [1969] 1 Lloyd's Rep 81.
[265] (1979) 40 P & CR 223, 230.
[266] [1976] 2 Lloyd's Rep 250, 254 per Denning MR.
[267] Eg *Felixstowe Dock and Railway Co v British Transport Docks Board* [1976] 2 Lloyd's Rep 656, 660.
[268] Eg *George v Roach* (1942) 67 CLR 253.
[269] See *Yoshimoto v Canterbury Golf International Ltd* [2004] 1 NZLR 1.
[270] Eg *Paul v Rosen* 3 Ill App 2d 423, 122 NE 2d 603 (1954) (buyer agreed to buy a business conditional 'upon the Buyer obtaining a new lease' from the owner of the business premises; held (604) that the buyer's conditional promise left him 'free to get the lease or not as he willed'; the consideration was illusory); *Reinert v Lawson* 113 SW 2d 293 (1938) (contract terms for the sale of a gin plant expressly provided that there was no obligation unless the deal between the purchasers and a named bank was closed. Gallagher CJ (295) concluded that: 'Making the closing thereof a condition precedent to liability on said contract did not imply any promise on the part of appellee or impose any duty on him to close such deal if he could.').
[271] However, there are numerous cases that have held there to be an implied obligation to take reasonable steps even though the contingency was a condition precedent to formation, see eg *Marks v Board* (1930) 46 TLR 424 (cf *Ee v Kakar* (1979) 40 P & CR 223); *Caney v Leith* [1937] 2 All ER 532; *Mulvena v Kulman* [1965] NZLR 656, 661 (cf *Scott v Rania* [1966] NZLR 527, 539–40 per Hardie Boys J extracted above at 9.76).
[272] See *Smith v Butler* [1900] 1 QB 694; *Smallman v Smallman* [1972] Fam 25, 31; *Alan Estates Ltd v WG Stores Ltd* [1982] Ch 511; *Total Gas Marketing Ltd v Arco British Ltd* [1998] 2 Lloyd's Rep 209. See further Peel, *Treitel, The Law of Contract* (12th edn, Sweet & Maxwell, London, 2007) para 2-113.

contract is discharged.[273] It may be that if the condition is not met for a period then performance is merely suspended, but that cannot go on forever and at some point the agreement
will be discharged.[274]

9.99   Where the contingency conditions performance, then as in the case of a subject to finance
provision,[275] there may be issues as to what standard is to be applied where the contingency
must be fulfilled to the satisfaction of one party.[276] As already noted, if the contingency is
met to the standard required by the contract then a party cannot resile from the contract
merely because they have changed their mind.[277] Nor can they raise some further issue falling outside the expressed contingency to resile from the contract.[278] Here the debate discussed above in the context of 'subject to finance' clauses arises again;[279] the authorities are
not clear whether (without express or implied terms dealing with the issue)[280] the party for
whose benefit the clauses exists must act honestly or honestly and reasonably.[281] However,

---

[273] As to any requirement of notice of intention to elect to terminate the contract, see 9.92.

[274] *Total Gas Marketing Ltd v Arco British Ltd* [1998] 2 Lloyd's Rep 209.

[275] See 9.78ff. A separate and related question arises when the transaction is conditional upon a third party,
such as a solicitor, preparing a report or approving the transaction. Here there is the issue of the standard to
be applied in preparing that report or giving that approval, see *Caney v Leith* [1937] 2 All ER 532, 538 (lease
requiring 'such lease to be approved in the customary way by my solicitor'; it was held that the solicitor must
not act unreasonably and that 'unreasonableness' here meant a lack of good faith). See also *Hudson v Buck*
(1877) LR 7 Ch D 683. For a review of New Zealand authorities, see McMorland, 'A New Approach to
Precedent and Subsequent Conditions' (1980) 4 Otago L Rev 469, 477–8.

[276] Whether or not a condition must be met to the satisfaction of a party is an issue of construction, eg,
Stabilad Ltd v Stephens & Carter (No 2) [1999] 2 All ER (Comm) 651 (here a heads of agreement for the use
by a manufacturer of an invention for stabilizing ladders and the payment of a royalty for its use was expressed
to be 'subject to detailed evaluation of production and marketing feasibility'; it was conceded, and the court
agreed, that the manufacturer did not have to act reasonably or in good faith; there was no reason to read
into the provision the word 'satisfactory' to the manufacturer and such a term was void for uncertainty in
any case; the intention of the parties was that although the manufacturer was under an express duty to use
its best endeavours to complete the study, it was for the manufacturer alone to decide whether to go on with
the transaction and it could decide not to go on even if the study was satisfactory; the clause was an 'opt out'
provision allowing the relevant party to withdraw for any commercial reasons), cf *Ee v Kakar* (1979) 40 P &
CR 223, 230.

[277] *Felixstowe Dock and Railway Co v British Transport Docks Board* [1976] 2 Lloyd's Rep 656.

[278] *Richard West and Partners (Inverness) Ltd v Dick* [1969] 2 Ch 424.

[279] In addition, where right or obligation is conditional upon an event and the event is within the control
in whole or in part of one of the parties, there will always be an issue as to what that party must do to bring
about the contingency or, in some cases what he must not do or take into account, eg *El Awadi v Bank of
Credit and Commerce International SA Ltd* [1990] 1 QB 606 (a refund for lost or stolen traveller's cheques
was 'subject to the approval by the issuer'; the question before the court was whether the issuer could refuse a
refund if the customer had been grossly negligent with the cheques).

[280] Eg *Hargreaves Transport Ltd v Lynch* [1969] 1 WLR 215 (sale subject to approval of planning permission
which was not to be deemed received if it was subject to a condition that the purchaser reasonably considered
unacceptable); *Magnacrete Ltd v Douglas-Hill* (1988) 48 SASR 565, 595, 600 (share sale to be 'upon such
terms and conditions satisfactory to the PURCHASER upon reasonable grounds'). See also *Deemcope Pty Ltd
v Cantown Pty Ltd* [1995] 2 VR 44.

[281] It is likely that any principle of law here will follow developments in legal principle dealing with
exercising of discretion generally, such as where consent must be obtained in order to assign an interest;
must the party exercising its discretion to grant or refuse consent act reasonably or in good faith, see
further *Lymington Marina Ltd v Bingham Macnamara* [2006] 2 All ER (Comm) 200, 219–23. See also *Abu
Dhabi National Tanker Co v Product Star Shipping Ltd (The Product Star) (No 2)* [1993] 1 Lloyd's Rep 397
(shipowner's discretion to disregard charterer's order if it considered the nominated port was dangerous was
to be exercised honestly and in good faith and not arbitrarily, capriciously or unreasonably). For the position

as noted in relation to 'subject to finance' clauses,[282] even if a subjective standard applies, a failure to act reasonably may evidence a lack of honesty.[283]

Where a party promises to bring about the contingency, then that promissory obligation **9.100** will give rise to an action for breach of contract if it is not fulfilled.[284] More often, the contingency is one that is not within the control of the parties, this is particularly the case where the contingency requires a third party to take some action.[285] However, where relevant, a party will come under an implied (and often express) obligation to take reasonable steps to bring about the contingency. For example, if performance is conditional upon the issuing of a licence or other form of permission then reasonable steps will need to be taken in order to apply for the licence.[286] Many other examples could be given.[287] In *Booker Industries Pty Ltd v Wilson Parking (Qld) Pty Ltd*,[288] the rent to be paid upon a renewal of lease was to be determined by an arbitrator failing agreement by the parties. It was held that there was an implied term requiring the parties to do all that was reasonably necessary to appoint an arbitrator.[289] Similarly in *Perri v Coolangatta Investments Proprietary Ltd*,[290] where the completion of a purchase of land was conditional upon the purchaser selling its

---

in New Zealand, see Burrows, Finn and Todd, *Burrows, Finn and Todd, Law of Contract in New Zealand* (3rd edn, LexisNexis NZ Ltd, Wellington, 2007), para 8.2.3.

[282] See 9.84.

[283] *Ee v Kakar* (1979) 40 P & CR 223, 230.

[284] Eg *Peter Cassidy Seed Co Ltd v Osuustukkukauppa IL* [1957] 1 WLR 273 (sale of goods contract; delivery to be 'as soon as export licence granted'; obligation on sellers to apply for licence (see also *C Czarnikow Ltd v Centrala Handlu Zagranicznego Rolimpex* [1979] AC 351; cf *HO Brandt & Co v HN Morris & Co Ltd* [1917] 2 KB 784); contract not expressed to be subject to the grant of a licence and so the obligation on the seller was absolute rather than one of taking reasonable steps). See also Peel, *Treitel, The Law of Contract* (12th edn, Thomson, Sweet & Maxwell, 2007) para 2-115. See further *Wood Preservation Ltd v Prior* [1969] 1 WLR 1077, 1090.

[285] See Restatement (2d) Contracts § 228 comment *b*. See also Burrows, Finn and Todd, *Burrows, Finn and Todd, Law of Contract in New Zealand* (3rd edn, LexisNexis NZ Ltd, Wellington, 2007), para 8.2.5.

[286] Eg *Re Anglo-Russian Merchant Traders Ltd and John Batt & Co (London) Ltd* [1917] 2 KB 679; *HO Brandt & Co v HN Morris & Co* [1917] 2 KB 784; *AV Pound & Co v MW Hardy & Co Inc* [1956] AC 588; *Richard West & Partners (Inverness) Ltd v Dick* [1969] 2 Ch 424; *Overseas Buyers Ltd v Granadex SA* [1980] 2 Lloyd's Rep 608, 613.

[287] Eg *Hargreaves Transport Ltd v Lynch* [1969] 1 WLR 215 (sale subject to planning permission being granted; purchaser required to take reasonable steps to obtain planning permission); *Kennedy v Vercoe* (1960) 105 CLR 521, 526, 529 (agreement for the sale of dry-cleaning business subject to purchaser being accepted by the landlord as a tenant; the vendor had to obtain that consent; there was an obligation on the purchaser to do what was reasonably necessary to enable the vendor to obtain that consent); *Smallman v Smallman* [1972] Fam 25 (property settlement agreement subject to court approval; parties must take reasonable steps to obtain that approval); *Re Anglo Russian Merchant Traders Ltd and John Batt & Co (London) Ltd* [1917] 2 KB 679 (sale of goods; obligation to take reasonable steps to obtain export/import licence). See also *Re An Arbitration between the Anglo-Russian Merchant Traders Ltd, and John Batt & Co (London) Ltd* [1917] 2 KB 679; *Charles H Windschuegl Ltd v Alexander Pickering & Co Ltd* (1950) 84 Ll L Rep 89. Cf *Peter Cassidy Seed Co Ltd v Osuustukkukauppa IL* [1957] 1 WLR 273; *Waldron v Tsimiklis* (1975) 12 SASR 481; *Gyllenhammar & Partners International Ltd v Sour Brodogradevna Industrija* [1989] 2 Lloyd's Rep 403; *Gregory v MAB Pty Ltd* (1989) 1 WAR 1, 15.

[288] (1982) 149 CLR 600, 605.

[289] See also *Butts v O'Dwyer* (1952) 87 CLR 267, 279–80 (lease subject to minister's consent; obligation implied on the transferor to do all things reasonable to obtain consent).

[290] (1982) 149 CLR 537.

property, the purchaser came under an obligation to 'do all that was reasonable to find a buyer'.[291]

9.101 Even where a condition is one that must be met to the satisfaction of one party the condition may require acts of third parties to be carried out to provide the relevant information to make a decision and the party may be required to take steps to gain the information by appointing the third party. For example, if a contract of sale is subject to survey, the relevant party must take reasonable steps to appoint a surveyor.[292]

9.102 There is no need to take steps that would be futile.[293] The standard is one of reasonableness and so only a failure to take reasonable steps will amount to a breach of contract giving rise to an obligation to pay damages.[294] The failure to take a step does not of itself result in a breach of this obligation if that failure was not material to any lack of success.[295] It may be possible to obtain an order for specific performance if the relevant party refuses the act.[296]

9.103 What constitutes 'reasonable steps' will depend on the facts of each case.[297] A detailed discussion of this issue of performance falls outside this text, although a couple of examples may be given. In *Brauer & Co (Great Britain) Ltd v James Clark (Brush Materials) Ltd*,[298] a contract for the sale and purchase of goods from Brazil was entered into and expressed to be 'subject to any Brazilian export licence'. The sellers later informed the buyers that they could not ship the goods because the Bank of Brazil had stipulated that a licence could only be issued if certain minimum prices were paid by the sellers to their suppliers and these prices were higher than the prices the buyer had to pay the seller under the re-sale contract which was the subject of the litigation.

9.104 The English Court of Appeal held that the sellers could not be relieved from their liability under the contract on that ground. Although this condition would excuse the seller from performance if they could not obtain the necessary export licence this was not the case here. Denning LJ said that the sellers were under a duty 'to apply for an export licence and to use

[291] (1982) 149 CLR 537, 541 per Gibbs CJ ('there was implied a promise by the appellants that they would do all that was reasonable to find a buyer'), 553 per Mason J ('implied obligation on the purchasers to make all reasonable efforts to sell'; he did not agree with this obligation being described as 'promissory' but thought it was incorporated as an implied term and was associated with the condition of the sale), see also 557 per Wilson J ('make all reasonable efforts to bring about a sale'), 566 per Brennan J (the condition, 'imported an obligation upon [the purchaser] to do all that was reasonable on their part in order that a sale of that property might be completed).
[292] *Ee v Kakar* (1979) 40 P & CR 223; *Astra Trust Ltd v Adams* [1969] 1 Lloyd's Rep 81.
[293] *Parland Pty Ltd v Mariposa Pty Ltd* (1995) 5 Tas R 121, 133; *29 Equities Ltd v Bank Leumi (UK) Ltd* [1986] 1 WLR 1490, 1496; *Lipmans Wallpaper Ltd v Mason & Hodghton Ltd* [1969] 1 Ch 20, 34; *Brauer & Co (Great Britain) Ltd v James Clark (Brush Materials) Ltd* [1952] 2 All ER 497, 501. See also *Benjamin's Sale of Goods* (7th edn, Sweet & Maxwell, London, 2008), para 18-328.
[294] *Malik Co v Central European Trading Agency Ltd* [1974] 2 Lloyd's Rep 279.
[295] *Parland Pty Ltd v Mariposa Pty Ltd* (1995) 5 Tas R 121, 133.
[296] *Perri v Coolangatta Investments Proprietary Ltd* (1982) 149 CLR 537, 566.
[297] Where the parties expressly adopt a different standard, such as a more absolute obligation to ensure the contingency occurs, then whether or not that standard has been met must be judged by reference to the facts of the case, see *Innes v Mars* [1982] 2 NZLR 68.
[298] [1952] 2 All ER 497. See also *Charles H Windschuegl Ltd v Alexander Pickering & Co Ltd* (1950) 84 Ll L Rep 89.

due diligence and take all reasonable steps to get it'.[299] The sellers carried the onus of proving either that all such steps were taken or that it was pointless taking such steps as a licence would not be issued in any case. It was held on the facts that the sellers could reasonably have been expected to pay the higher prices which were the condition of obtaining a licence and therefore they had not taken all reasonable steps to obtain a licence. Here the price that would have had to be paid to the suppliers was accepted as the market price and 'any person who sells goods forward must be ready himself to bear any increase in the market price'.[300] The case would have been different if the seller was required to pay its suppliers a price that was one hundred times the re-sale contract price or the licence would only issue on other prohibitive terms that fell outside of the contemplation of the parties.[301]

This decision can be compared with *Hargreaves Transport Ltd v Lynch*.[302] Here the plaintiffs had agreed to purchase a piece of land subject to a condition that the plaintiffs were to receive planning permission (which the defendant, vendor, had already applied for) to use the site as a transport depot and to erect buildings. When the local council refused to approve the plans, the plaintiffs sought to rescind the contract and claimed the return of their deposit relying on this condition in the contract. The defendant refused to return the deposit contending that the plaintiffs still had the right to appeal to the Minister and should exercise it.   **9.105**

The Court of Appeal held that since the plaintiffs were a commercial firm where time was of the essence and such an appeal would take a further six to 12 months, they had done all that they could reasonably be expected to do in order to obtain the permission. Therefore the plaintiffs were entitled to rescind and to have their deposit returned.   **9.106**

In addition to the duty to take reasonable steps to bring about the condition, the parties may be under a duty not to take action which prevents the condition from being fulfilled[303] or not to engage in conduct that would bring about the occurrence of a condition subsequent.[304] For example, *Atlas Trading Corporation v SH Grossman Inc*[305] concerned an agreement for the purchase of some trucks. During the Second World War the War Production Board had forbidden the transfer of any new commercial motor vehicle unless that person held a permit. The defendant wrote to the plaintiff 'offering' to sell certain trucks to the plaintiff. The terms of that offer reminded the plaintiff that a permit was required in order to release the trucks. The plaintiff then sent the defendant an order for the trucks which was stated to be 'subject only to receipt of the necessary releases from the US Government'. The defendant seller was asked to sign the duplicate and did so.   **9.107**

---

[299] [1952] 2 All ER 497, 501.
[300] [1952] 2 All ER 497, 501. In the same way the seller would get the advantage if the price it had to buy the goods from its suppliers fell.
[301] [1952] 2 All ER 487, 500 per Singleton LJ, 501 per Denning LJ.
[302] [1969] 1 WLR 215.
[303] *Varverakis v Compagnia de Navegacion Artico SA (The Merak)* [1976] 2 Lloyd's Rep 250 (sale of ship subject to inspection; sellers failed in their duty to provide facilities for inspection by the buyer).
[304] *Thompson v Asda-MFI Group plc* [1988] Ch 241, 251.
[305] 169 F 2d 240 (1948).

9.108   The evidence was that the defendant had been made aware of the ultimate destination of the trucks (the Free French Delegation) and knew that a proposal from the United States Treasury Procurement Division would be issued inviting bids to supply these trucks. There was also evidence that the trucks which the plaintiff had ordered exactly met the specification in this proposal. The terms of the proposal provided that the successful bidder would be issued permits. The plaintiff had submitted a bid. The defendant submitted a lower bid to supply the trucks and was awarded the contract by the Treasury.[306] The plaintiff wrote to the defendant notifying the defendant that it expected it to honour the contract. The defendant attempted to get the Treasury to agree to cancel its acceptance of the defendant's bid. This was refused and the defendant then signed a confirmation of its contract with the Treasury and then wrote to the plaintiff withdrawing all previous 'quotations' on the basis that the plaintiff had failed to furnish the defendant with the necessary permits. The plaintiff sued the defendant for breach of contract.

9.109   The court held that there was a binding contract to supply these trucks to the plaintiff conditional on the necessary permits being obtained. However, O'Connell CJ stated that 'just as plaintiff could avoid its obligation only by a bona fide failure to secure the Permits within the time contemplated by the agreement, defendant had the duty of taking no action which would prevent plaintiff from obtaining the permits'.[307] On the evidence the 'defendant deliberately submitted a bid which the defendant knew, or should have known, was likely to prevent plaintiff from obtaining the Permits'[308] and by selling the goods to a third party had 'disabled itself from performing'[309] and thus had breached the contract.

9.110   The basis of the obligation to take reasonable steps to bring about the condition has been said to be an implied term.[310] However, it could also be said to flow from a construction of the contract.[311] In either case, as the duty flows from the intention of the parties, the contract may evidence an intention to negative any such duty.[312]

9.111   English courts have also emphasized that any duty not to act in a way that would prevent the contingency occurring must flow from a term of the contract. There is no 'independent principle of law that a party will not prevent fulfilment of a condition precedent'[313] and such an obligation does not flow from any broad notion that a party cannot take advantage of its own wrong to defeat the rights of the other party.[314] The principal cases have discussed

---

[306] The only trucks which the defendant had which met the specification were those covered by the order from the plaintiff.

[307] 169 F 2d 240, 244 (1948).

[308] 169 F 2d 240, 245 (1948).

[309] 169 F 2d 240, 245 (1948).

[310] See *Booker Industries Pty Ltd v Wilson Parking (Qld) Pty Ltd* (1982) 149 CLR 600, 605. See also *Wood Preservation Ltd v Prior* [1969] 1 WLR 1077, 1090. See further *Butts v O'Dwyer* (1952) 87 CLR 267, 279–80 (suggesting that the obligation is implied as an implication in fact necessary for the business efficacy of the contract).

[311] See 9.113.

[312] See *Gyllenhammar & Partners International Ltd v Sour Brodogradevna Industrija* [1989] 2 Lloyd's Rep 403.

[313] *Thompson v Asda-MFI Group Plc* [1988] Ch 241, 261.

[314] *Cheall v Association of Professional Executive, Clerical and Computer Staff* [1983] 2 AC 180, 188–9; *Thompson v Asda-MFI Group Plc* [1988] Ch 241; *Gyllenhammar & Partners International Ltd v Sour*

the issue by reference to a term implied in fact.[315] That is, because this is an issue not dealt with by an express term, for the duty to arise there must be a term implied to that effect. On this approach, outside of areas where there are clear obligations to cooperate such an implication will be rare as it is not usually necessary for the business efficacy of the contract.[316] Moreover, as is discussed below, the duty of cooperation flows from construction.

More generally, as the above paragraph suggests the duty to take steps to bring about the   **9.112**
condition or not doing anything to prevent it occurring may form part of the general duty of cooperation in the performance of contracts. This duty is wider in its import and may require positive acts from one of the parties to help the other bring about or perform the condition. The duty to cooperate generally arises where a party is bound to do some act under the contract rather than having a discretion to do it or not.[317] Here the other party may come under a duty to be cooperative in having that act carried out or not do anything that would prevent it being carried out. But such a duty flows from the construction of the contract and where that is the case there is no need to imply such a term. Moreover, a duty to cooperate does not mean that a party may not act in self interest. The classic example of the duty to cooperate is *Mackay v Dick*.[318] This case involved an agreement to sell an excavating machine on condition that it should be capable of excavating a given quantity of clay in a fixed time on a properly opened-up face at the defendant's cutting. It was agreed that it was to be tested to ensure it could carry out the work. This testing was to be conclusive so that if the machine passed the test the agreed price was to be paid, but if it failed then it was to be removed by the seller. The machine was made and some initial testing was done and the machine kept breaking down. The plaintiff made some adjustments and asked to be allowed to come back to the site to test it again. The defendant agreed but the plaintiff complained that the cutting face provided was inappropriate. The defendant refused to provide another site for testing and refused to pay for the machine.

The House of Lords held that there had been a breach by the buyer in that the buyer alone   **9.113**
had it in his power to provide a properly opened-up face in the railway cutting for the purposes of the test and had not provided one. Accordingly, the seller was entitled to the price.[319] The obligation to cooperate was said to be inherent in the contract and the

---

Brodogradevna Industrija [1989] 2 Lloyd's Rep 403. Cf *New Zealand Shipping Co Ltd v Société des Ateliers et Chantiers de France* [1919] AC 1. See also *Inchbald v The Western Neilgherry Coffee, Tea & Cinchona Plantation Co Ltd* (1864) 17 CBNS 733, 144 ER 293.

[315] The most detailed discussion of the cases is in *Thompson v Asda-MFI Group Plc* [1988] Ch 241, 251ff.

[316] Eg *Luxor (Eastbourne) Ltd v Cooper* [1941] AC 108, 118, 120, 128, 148, 153; *Mona Oil Equipment and Supply Co Ltd v Rhodesia Railways Ltd* [1949] 2 All ER 1014, 1016–17; *Cheall v Association of Professional Executive, Clerical and Computer Staff* [1983] 2 AC 180; *Thompson v Asda-MFI Group Plc* [1988] Ch 241.

[317] Where a jurisdiction recognizes a duty to perform a contract in good faith this may impact on such a discretion.

[318] (1881) 6 App Cas 251. See generally Peden, *Good Faith in the Performance of Contracts* (Butterworths, Sydney, 2003) paras 6.2–6.20.

[319] There has been debate over whether that was the appropriate remedy, see Peden, *Good Faith in the Performance of Contracts* (Butterworths, Sydney, 2003) para 6.3; Peel, *Treitel, The Law of Contract* (12th edn, Thomson, Sweet & Maxwell, London, 2007) para 2.116. The difficulty that the remedy granted creates is that it appears as if the law takes the position that if the party fails in its obligation, then the law should

contract was then construed to give effect to the obligation.[320] So although there was no express term requiring the buyer to provide the site for testing this was implied by construction, the machine had to be tested and had to work on the defendant's site, therefore the defendant had to provide the appropriate cutting face for testing.[321]

F. Time for the Occurrence of Contingency

9.114 Although it is ultimately a matter of construction,[322] as a general rule time is of the essence in these situations.[323] Where no time is fixed then the contingency must occur within a reasonable time.[324]

9.115 Where a party is under an obligation to take reasonable steps to bring about a contingency, that obligation cannot continue forever. Where no time is fixed under the contract for the fulfilment of the condition, or a time cannot be fixed by reference to the facts of the case, then the relevant party must attempt to satisfy the condition for a reasonable period of time.[325] It follows that there will come a point in time when the party will be discharged from that obligation.[326]

---

assume the contingency is made out. This is a fiction and will not be applied in all cases, see *Newmont Pty Ltd v Laverton Nickel NL* [1983] 1 NSWLR 181, 188.

[320] (1881) 6 App Cas 251, 263 per Lord Blackburn. See Peden, *Good Faith in the Performance of Contracts* (Butterworths, Sydney, 2003) paras 6.2–6.20.

[321] Although it is suggested this duty is properly seen as one that flows from construction, it is often held to be incorporated by way of an implied term, eg *Bournemouth & Boscombe Athletic Football Club Ltd v Manchester United Football Club Ltd* The Times, 22 May 1980 (here a footballer was sold by Bournemouth to Manchester United; part of the transaction involved a promise by Manchester to pay Bournemouth an extra sum of money when the footballer scored 20 goals for Manchester United; by virtue of a change in management at Manchester, the footballer was dropped after playing only 13 games; this did not give him a reasonable opportunity to score the required 20 goals; Lord Denning MR and Lord Justice Donaldson held that there was an term implied in fact into the contract that Manchester would give the footballer a reasonable opportunity to score; Lord Denning MR suggested that the result could flow from an implied term or simply a condition that Manchester do nothing to prevent the footballer earning the sum; Lord Justice Brightman dissented); for a critique of the decision, see Peel, *Treitel, The Law of Contract* (12th edn, Thomson, Sweet & Maxwell, London, 2007) para 2-114.

[322] *Clarke v Refeld* (1980) 25 SASR 246, 266 per Wells J (affirmed (1980) 25 SASR 246).

[323] *Aberfoyle Plantations Ltd v Cheng* [1960] AC 115, 124–5. See also *Neylon v Dickens* [1977] 1 NZLR 595. See generally Swanton, '"Subject to Finance" Clauses in Contracts for the Sale of Land' Part II (1984) 58 ALJ 690, 700ff.

[324] *Aberfoyle Plantations Ltd v Cheng* [1960] AC 115, 124–5; *Re Sandwell Park Colliery Co* [1929] 1 Ch 277; *Waldron v Tsimiklis* (1975) 12 SASR 481; *Ee v Kakar* (1979) 40 P & CR 223, 228. See Swanton, '"Subject to Finance" Clauses in Contracts for the Sale of Land' Part II (1984) 58 ALJ 690, 701. Once that reasonable period of time has elapsed the contract can be terminated without the issuing of a notice, see *Perri v Coolangatta Investments Pty Ltd* (1982) 149 CLR 537. See also *Steele v Serepisos* [2007] 1 NZLR 1.

[325] *Re Longlands Farm, Long Common, Botley, Hants Alford v Superior Developments Ltd* (1969) 20 P & CR 25.

[326] *Total Gas Marketing Ltd v Arco British Ltd* [1998] 2 Lloyd's Rep 209.

G. Waiver

Where a contingency is a condition precedent to the formation of a contract and the con-   **9.116**
tingency occurs, then subject to any notice requirements, an unconditional contract will
come into existence. Logically, since no party is under any contractual obligation in such a
case, there can be no issue of waiver, even when the condition is for the sole benefit of one
party.[327] Subject to any requirement of notice, each party is free to walk away from the
transaction.[328] In such circumstances any time provision for the occurrence of the contingency would not prevent a party walking away from the transaction beforehand. At the
same time, most time provisions are construed as being of the essence so that if the contingency did not occur in time, it would be too late for the contingency to be made out after
that period. Since the contingency conditions formation there is no need for one party to
elect to terminate at the end of that time period; whatever arrangements exist between the
parties will simply lapse.[329]

A true issue of waiver is capable of arising where the contingency conditions performance   **9.117**
rather than formation. Here, any waiver must be made within the time set for the occurrence of the contingency. The sense in which the word 'waiver' is used here is that of estoppel. Importantly this means that, unlike an election, in certain circumstances a party could
resile from a representation. For example, a party might waive the condition that a sale be
subject to a satisfactory survey and later, when the survey arrives, seek to rely on the survey
if it is not satisfactory. In order to do this it would be necessary that there either be no detrimental reliance on the initial waiver or, if there is, it is an estoppel that will cease upon the
issuing of an adequate notice. Once the time period for the occurrence of the condition
elapses the issue becomes one of election which can be made by words or conduct.[330] Here
the normal rules of election apply. Principally this requires an unequivocal act and communication of that act to the other party. A party does not necessarily lose a right to rescind
a contract just because a condition has been fulfilled, such as where it is fulfilled outside of
the time set for it under the contract, unless there is evidence that the person has waived
(elected) to affirm the contract. [331]

As a general rule, where a contingency conditions performance and is severable,[332] and is   **9.118**
for the benefit of one party, then that party can waive the condition prior to the time set for

---

[327] See Robinson, 'Waiver of Benefit of Conditional Clauses' (1975) 39 The Conveyancer 251; Swanton,
'"Subject to Finance" Clauses in Contracts for the Sale of Land' Part II (1984) 58 ALJ 690, 699; Coote
'Agreements "Subject to Finance"' (1976) 40 Conveyancer 37, 44. See also *Michael Richards Properties Ltd v
Corporation of Wardens of St Saviour's Parish, Southwark* [1975] 3 All ER 416, 421. Cf *George v Roach* (1942)
67 CLR 253, 261 per Rich J. See also 9.76 and n 250 above noting that a duty to take reasonable steps to bring
about the contingency has been recognized in cases where the contingency conditions formation. If correct
these cases would appear to prevent a party under such an obligation from resiling from the transaction at will.
See further *Samos Shipping Enterprises Ltd v Eckhardt & Co KG (The Nissos Samos)* [1985] 1 Lloyd's Rep 378,
385 (suggesting the parties can only resile from the transaction in good faith).
[328] *Astra Trust Ltd v Adams and Williams* [1969] 1 Lloyd's Rep 81, 88.
[329] *Aberfoyle Plantations Ltd v Cheng* [1960] AC 115.
[330] See *Neylon v Dickens* [1977] 1 NZLR 595.
[331] *Gilbert v Healey Investment Pty Ltd* [1975] 1 NSWLR 650.
[332] See *Globe Holdings Ltd v Floratos* [1998] 3 NZLR 331, 335ff.

its occurrence.[333] For example in *Ee v Kakar*[334] an agreement was entered into for the sale of certain property 'subject to survey'. No survey was obtained by the purchaser and the vendor sought to terminate the contract for repudiation. The purchaser sought an order for specific performance and was successful on the basis that the contingency was for the benefit of the purchaser and could therefore be waived by the purchaser.

9.119 It can be difficult to determine whether a condition is exclusively for the benefit of only one party.[335] Where a condition benefits both parties, neither can unilaterally waive it.[336] For example, in *Heron Garage Properties Ltd v Moss*,[337] the plaintiffs and defendants entered into a signed agreement on 16 August 1982 whereby the plaintiffs agreed to buy part of a site owned by the defendants. It had been clear throughout the negotiations that the plaintiffs wished to use the site to set up a new petrol filling station and the defendants had the intention of using the remaining part of the site for the sale of motor vehicles and so judged the sale to be advantageous to them. Clause 7 of this agreement provided that: 'This Agreement is expressly conditional upon [the plaintiffs] obtaining detailed town planning consent for the redevelopment of the property as a petrol filling and service station together with a car-wash in accordance with plans and drawings to be submitted to the local town planning authority by [the plaintiffs] ...' The agreement also provided that if the planning consent had not been granted within six months then either party could give notice in writing to determine the agreement. Clause 8 provided inter alia that completion was to occur on the expiry of one calendar month from the grant of unconditional planning consent. No planning consent was ever granted. On 27 February 1983 the plaintiffs wrote purporting to waive 'the benefit of clause 7' so that the contract was unconditional. The plaintiffs

---

[333] See *Perri v Coolangatta Investments Pty Ltd* (1982) 149 CLR 537, 543, per Gibbs CJ, 552 per Mason J, 560 per Wilson J, 565 per Brennan J. See also *Maynard v Goode* (1926) 37 CLR 529, 536, 538; *Gange v Sullivan* (1966) 116 CLR 418, 430, 443; *Waldron v Tsimiklis* (1975) 12 SASR 481; *Sandra Investments Pty Ltd v Booth* (1983) 153 CLR 153. There can be situations where the party with a right to waive the contingency acts in a way to estop it from exercising that right, for example, where it represents the contingency is made out and that is relied upon by the other party, see Swanton, '"Subject to Finance" Clauses in Contracts for the Sale of Land' Part II (1984) 58 ALJ 690, 698 and see *Connor v Pukerau Store Ltd* [1981] 1 NZLR 384. As to the relevance of an estoppel arising from reliance on representations made by one party in the face of a 'subject to' clause, see *A-G (Hong Kong) v Humphreys Estate (Queen's Gardens) Ltd* [1987] AC 114; *Star Steamship Society v Beogradska Plovidba (The Junior K)* [1988] 2 Lloyd's Rep 583, 589.
[334] (1979) 40 P & CR 223; *Cobbe v Yeoman's Row Management Ltd* [2008] 1 WLR 1752, 1767, 1784. See also *Wood Preservation Ltd v Prior* [1969] 1 WLR 1077, 1094; *Maynard v Goode* (1926) 37 CLR 529. See further Robinson, 'Waiver of Benefit of Conditional Clauses' (1975) 39 The Conveyancer 251, 252–4 and the cases discussed there.
[335] In *Ee v Kakar* (1979) 40 P & CR 223, the argument that the vendor was also interested in the condition of the property was rejected on the basis that there was no obligation on the purchaser to disclose the results of the survey. The survey could have shown that the property was dilapidated but that there were plans to build a nearby pool facility making the sale a bargain for the purchaser; on construction there was no obligation to disclose this to the vendor. See further Swanton, '"Subject to Finance" Clauses in Contracts for the Sale of Land' Part II (1984) 58 ALJ 690, 697.
[336] *George v Roach* (1942) 67 CLR 253 (sale of business at value and value to be determined by a named valuer; clause was for the benefit of both parties and could not be waived by one party alone). See also *Lloyd v Nowell* [1895] 2 Ch 744; *Smallman v Smallman* [1972] Fam 25, 31; *Newmont Pty Ltd v Laverton Nickel NL* [1983] 1 NSWLR 181.
[337] [1974] 1 WLR 148. See Robinson, 'Waiver of Benefit of Conditional Clauses' (1975) 39 The Conveyancer 251. Cf *Sandra Investments Pty Ltd v Booth* (1983) 153 CLR 153, 159ff. See further *Moreton v Montrose Ltd* [1986] 2 NZLR 496.

therefore requested that the defendants complete within one month. However, on 6 March the six-month period in clause 7 expired and the defendants then gave notice in writing determining the agreement.

At issue was whether the plaintiffs had the power to unilaterally waive the condition imposed by clause 7. Brightman J held that they had no such power because the condition was not for the plaintiffs' benefit alone. It did not merely affect the liability of the purchaser but was 'fundamental to the enforceability of the sale agreement as a whole'.[338] The terms in which it was expressed indicated that it conferred rights on both parties and, in any event, the defendants might be vitally affected by the grant of planning consent, since the redevelopment of the site as a petrol filling station would attract motorists to the vicinity of the land on which the defendants proposed to establish their showroom for the sale of cars. It was therefore not a condition which was precedent only to the liability of the plaintiffs as purchasers. Brightman J concluded:[339]   **9.120**

> Without seeking to define the precise limits within which a contracting party seeking specific performance may waive a stipulation on the ground that it is intended only for his benefit, it seems to me that in general the proposition only applies where the stipulation is in terms for the exclusive benefit of the plaintiff because it is a power or right vested by the contract in him alone ... or where the stipulation is by inevitable implication for the benefit of him alone ... If it is not obvious on the face of the contract that the stipulation is for the exclusive benefit of the party seeking to eliminate it, then in my opinion it cannot be struck out unilaterally.

The 'subject to finance' cases suggest that the fact the vendor might have a right to termi-   **9.121**
nate the contract for the failure of the condition is not a sufficient benefit to prevent the purchaser from waiving the condition. If the purchaser's right to waive the condition is limited to being exercised prior to the time for its occurrence elapsing then the vendor is arguably only being deprived of a potential right to terminate.[340] However, as noted above, there are circumstances where the vendor will not be allowed to terminate for the failure of the condition, such as where the purchaser has decided to use its own funds.

H. The Consequences of the Failure of a Condition

As this text is concerned with contract formation the consequences of a failure of condition   **9.122**
can be dealt with very shortly. As already noted, subject to any notice requirements, where the condition qualifies the formation of the contract the parties are under no obligation and are generally free to walk away from the transaction at any time.[341] There is no obligation to perform the contract.[342] Moreover, if the contingency does not occur within any

---

[338] [1974] 1 WLR 148, 153.
[339] [1974] 1 WLR 148, 153.
[340] Swanton, '"Subject to Finance" Clauses in Contracts for the Sale of Land' Part II (1984) 58 ALJ 690, 697–8. See also Tolhurst, 'Assignment of Contractual Rights: Some Reflections on Pacific Brands Sport and Leisure Pty Ltd v Underworks Pty Ltd' in Tolhurst and Peden (eds) *Commercial Issues in Contract Law* (Ross Parsons centre of Commercial, Corporate and Taxation Law, University of Sydney, Sydney, 2008) Ch 4, 61.
[341] See 9.97.
[342] Cf 9.76 and see Swanton, '"Subject to Finance" Clauses in Contracts for the Sale of Land' Part II (1984) 58 ALJ 690, 691–4.

express time period or within a reasonable time if no time period is set, then there will be no contract and it is too late if the contingency were to occur later.[343] There is no need for either party to elect to 'terminate' the transaction at the end of such a time period, the 'discharge' occurs automatically.[344]

9.123   No attempt is made to deal comprehensively with the situations that arise where the condition qualifies performance.[345] However, a few general comments may be made. First, generally where neither party is in default, such as where the condition is not a promissory condition, then each can elect to terminate the contract where the time set for the condition to occur has lapsed.[346] In this sense the condition is a condition subsequent because its non-fulfilment allows the parties to resile from the contract.[347] The courts generally prefer a construction that does not render the contract automatically discharged if the event does not occur, rather both parties (if neither is in default) or one party (if the other is in default) can elect to terminate the contract.[348] If the contingency requires a party to take some steps to bring about the contingency and they fail to do so, then generally they may not rely on the failure of the contingency to terminate the contract.

9.124   It is necessary to qualify some of the statements made in the above paragraph. First, everything depends on construction. A contract may allow a party who has failed in its obligation to take steps to bring about the contingency to nevertheless rely on a contractual right

---

[343] For rights to restitution for benefits provided in contracts that fail to materialize, see Jones, *Goff & Jones, The Law of Restitution* (7th edn, Sweet & Maxwell, London, 2007) Ch 26; Mason, Carter, Tolhurst, *Mason and Carter's, Restitution Law in Australia* (2nd edn, Butterworths, Sydney, 2008) Ch 10.

[344] *Aberfoyle Plantations Ltd v Cheng* [1960] AC 115.

[345] See generally, Peel, *Treitel, The Law of Contract* (12th edn, Thomson, Sweet & Maxwell, London, 2007) para 2.116; *Carter on Contract* (Butterworths, Sydney), § 31-020; Seddon and Ellinghaus, *Cheshire and Fifoot's Law of Contract* (9th Australian edn, Butterworths, Sydney, 2008) Ch 20.

[346] *Perri v Coolangatta Investments Pty Ltd* (1982) 149 CLR 537, 546 (and the cases there cited) per Gibbs CJ, 553 per Mason J. The vesting of a right to terminate does not appear to be based on the contingency being for the benefit of a particular party. If that were the case then the right to terminate would vest in the party for whose benefit the contingency exists, see Swanton, '"Subject to Finance" Clauses in Contracts for the Sale of Land' Part II (1984) 58 ALJ 690, 695–6.

[347] *Perri v Coolangatta Investments Pty Ltd* (1982) 149 CLR 537, 542.

[348] Courts require strong evidence to construe a clause as resulting in an automatic termination upon the non-fulfilment of the condition, see *Perri v Coolangatta Investments Pty Ltd* (1982) 149 CLR 537, 553–4. Cf *New Zealand Shipping Co Ltd v Société des Ateliers et Chantiers de France* [1919] AC 1. See also *Suttor v Gundowda Pty Ltd* (1950) 81 CLR 418, 441; *Gange v Sullivan* (1966) 116 CLR 418; *JAG Investments Pty Ltd v Strati* [1973] 2 NSWLR 450, 465; *Varverakis v Compagnia de Navegacion Artico SA (The Merak)* [1976] 2 Lloyd's Rep 250; *Booker Industries Pty Ltd v Wilson Parking (Qld) Pty Ltd* (1982) 149 CLR 600; *Gregory v MAB Pty Ltd* (1989) 1 WAR 1; *ANM Trading Pty Ltd v Commr of Business Franchises* [1996] 2 VR 312; *Total Gas Marketing Ltd v Arco British Ltd* [1998] 2 Lloyd's Rep 209. See further *Commonwealth Homes and Investment Co Ltd v McKellar* (1939) 63 CLR 351; *Progress and Properties (Strathfield) Pty Ltd v Crumblin* (1984) 3 BPR 9496; *Sandra Investments Pty Ltd v Booth* (1983) 153 CLR 153. Cf Louis Proksch, 'In Praise of Conditions Subsequent' (1982) 14 UWALR 333, 347–9. A distinction has been drawn between cases where the contingency is beyond the control of either party which leads to automatic termination if it does not occur and one where the contingency is capable of being affected by the act of the parties rendering the contract voidable, see, Swanton, '"Subject to Finance" Clauses in Contracts for the Sale of Land' Part II (1984) 58 ALJ 690, 694; Proksch, 'In Praise of Conditions Subsequent' (1982) 14 UWALR 333, 347. Ultimately the issue is one of construction and it is within the power of the parties to agree to automatic discharge, see *Neylon v Dickens* [1977] 1 NZLR 595; *Moreton v Montrose Ltd* [1986] 2 NZLR 496.

to rescind.[349] Second, the view that either party can terminate if the time elapses without default assumes that where the condition is for the benefit of one party, then that party has not waived the condition prior to this time for its occurrence. A waiver by such a party will prevent that party relying on the contingency if it gives rise to an estoppel and if it is not possible to resile from the representation upon giving notice. It also prevents the other party electing to terminate for the failure of the contingency where such a right would otherwise arise.[350] Moreover, it should be noted that it is not absolutely clear that in the case of a clause like a 'subject to finance' clause both parties do in fact have a right to terminate the contract once the time for the occurrence of the contingency elapses.[351]

Third, the courts do not assume that a party has elected to affirm the contract (waive the contingency) merely because the time period for it has elapsed. For example, in the case of a subject to finance clause, if the purchaser attempts to find and assess offers of finance at the standard required by the contract and is unable to do so, then he or she may elect to discharge the contract, but if that purchaser carries out those obligations and being unable to find finance fails to waive the condition before the time for performance lapses then the vendor may, on the principle stated above, elect to discharge the contract. At the same time, if the purchaser finds finance outside of the time frame set by the contract, then the purchaser, assuming he or she has not elected to affirm the contract, can still avoid the contract and not be held to the contract by the vendor.[352] However, much depends on the facts, for example, if a purchaser is given an express right to avoid a contract if a contingency does not occur and the time for its occurrence lapses without any exercise of that right, there may, in the circumstances be held to be an election to waive the contingency; in any case the vendor cannot assert simply by reason of the lapse of time that the purchaser has elected to avoid.[353] **9.125**

Fourth, arguably if termination is not automatic and if neither party is in default and neither elects to terminate then each may enforce the contract.[354] This proposition is problematic. There are situations where the law appears to take the view that where there is a failure to bring about a condition the law adopts the position that the condition is fulfilled. But these, if correct, are limited to where there is fault by way of a party failing to cooperate.[355] Generally, where a party breaches its obligation to take steps to bring about the **9.126**

---

[349] See *Gyllenhammar & Partners International Ltd v Sour Brodogradevna Industrija* [1989] 2 Lloyd's Rep 403.

[350] The fact a condition may be for the benefit of one party does not stop a right to terminate vesting in both parties if it is not made out.

[351] See Coote 'Agreements "Subject to Finance"' (1976) 40 Conveyancer 37, 44–6 (suggesting that if both parties can terminate, then arguably it cannot be said the clause is for the sole benefit of the purchaser; also the purchaser may only be able to waive those conditions where the purchaser has the sole right to terminate; if both parties cannot terminate then the purchaser may be able to waive the condition even after the time set for its occurrence). Of course the vendor may be given an express right to rescind, eg *Downham v McCallum* [2008] TASSC 81.

[352] Swanton, '"Subject to Finance" Clauses in Contracts for the Sale of Land' Part II (1984) 58 ALJ 690, 705.

[353] *Sandra Investments Pty Ltd v Booth* (1983) 153 CLR 153, 158.

[354] *Suttor v Gundowda Pty Ltd* (1950) 81 CLR 418, 441–2. See also *Scott v Rania* [1966] NZLR 527, 541 per Hardie Boys J (in dissent).

[355] See 9.112.

contingency, then, in addition to that party not being able to rely on the contingency to resile from the contract, the other party's right to terminate will be lost if he or she elects to affirm the contract.[356] But if a contract is dependent on a condition and the relevant party has done all they can to bring it about and has not been able to do so and are not in breach of contract, then arguably at some point the contract should be discharged.[357] But generally unless there are express words to the contrary this would not be automatic if the condition impacted on performance and not formation. Perhaps a practical example would be where a purchaser under a subject to finance clause only finds finance after the time limit for finding finance has elapsed. If upon the lapse of time the vendor has not terminated the contract then the contract remains on foot and on this view the vendor is then bound. However, the vendor is not necessarily required to make an election at the moment the time elapses and so long as the vendor has not affirmed the contract then arguably they would still have a right to terminate despite the purchaser finding finance.[358]

9.127   Fifth, there are some limitations on the right of a party to terminate when the contingency is not for his or her benefit. For example, assume a subject to finance clause which is for the benefit of the purchaser. The clause may say no more than that the contract is 'subject to finance' or it may be more detailed and state the source of the expected finance by, for example, naming a bank. Next assume that the purchaser does not obtain an offer of finance from that stated bank but does obtain an offer from another bank.[359] Alternatively, in a simple subject to finance clause, the purchaser may change its mind and decide to use its own funds. In either case the contingency is not strictly made out. But in either case, it is clear the vendor cannot terminate for the failure of the contingency.[360]

---

[356] See *Scott v Rania* [1966] NZLR 527, 536 per McCarthy J.

[357] See 9.115.

[358] See Proksch, 'In Praise of Conditions Subsequent' (1982) 14 UWALR 333, 348–9.

[359] It has been suggested that even though the contract would become unconditional once the contingency is fulfilled, the purchaser, in a subject to finance case, should give notice of the contingency being fulfilled because this will act as a waiver of the contingency if it turns out that the finance is not in accordance with the contract, see Swanton, '"Subject to Finance" Clauses in Contracts for the Sale of Land' Part II (1984) 58 ALJ 690, 703. See also the discussion in Burrows, Finn and Todd, *Burrows, Finn and Todd, Law of Contract in New Zealand* (3rd edn, LexisNexis NZ Ltd, Wellington, 2007), 8.2.4, usually notice of the fulfilment of the condition will be a requirement of the condition, eg *Downham v McCallum* [2008] TASSC 81.

[360] *Clarke v Refeld* (1980) 25 SASR 246.

10

DENIAL OF LEGALLY BINDING EFFECT

A. Intention to Contract

Introduction

For an agreement to be legally enforceable it must be supported by valuable consideration **10.01** and there must be an intention to contract. This chapter is concerned with this require- ment of an intention to contract which must exist in all the parties.[1] As this book is princi- pally concerned with commercial contracts and has an emphasis on preliminary agreements, no detailed treatment of such matters as collective agreements, government schemes or voluntary and non-profit associations is provided. These are dealt with in standard works on contract law.[2] However, family and social situations are discussed for three reasons. First, along with commercial transactions they are the other area where presumptions are applied. Second, the approach to family and social situations provides a contrast with the approach to commercial settings. Third, it is in family and social situations that the modern requirement of an intention to contract was first adopted.

The use of presumptions

The courts have made use of presumptions in this area. Generally, in a family or social set- **10.02** ting there is a presumption that the parties do not intend to contract.[3] In a commercial

---

[1] *Rose & Frank Co v J R Crompton & Bros Ltd* [1923] 2 KB 261, 293 per Atkin LJ; *Todd v Nicol* [1957] SASR 72, 78; *Riches v Hogben* [1986] 1 Qd R 315, 316.

[2] See Furmston (ed), *The Law of Contract* (3rd edn, LexisNexis Butterworths, London, 2007) paras 2.173– 2.177, 2.183; Peel, *Treitel, The Law of Contract* (12th edn, Sweet & Maxwell, London, 2007) paras 4-014-4- 017; Carter, *Carter on Contract* (Butterworths, Sydney) paras 08-080, 08-090; Burrows, Finn & Todd, *Law of Contract in New Zealand* (3rd edn, LexisNexis NZ Ltd, Wellington, 2007) paras 5.4.3, 5.4.4; Waddams, *The Law of Contracts* (5th edn, Canada Law Book, Toronto, 2005) paras 152–3, 155. See also Lücke, 'The Intention to Create Legal Relations' (1970) 3 Adel LR 419.

[3] *Jones v Padavatton* [1969] 1 WLR 328.

setting there is a strong presumption that the parties intend to contract.[4] When the presumptions apply, the onus of proof shifts and the party who wishes to challenge the legal efficacy of the agreement must bring into evidence facts that rebut the presumption.

10.03 Recently the High Court of Australia in *Ermogenous v Greek Orthodox Community of SA Inc*,[5] made some important remarks about the extent to which use can be made of presumptions in this area and the dangers which can follow if they become too entrenched. The issue in that case concerned whether a contract of employment existed between an archbishop and the respondent, an incorporated association. In coming to its conclusions, the court reviewed many of the cases that had dealt with the nature of relations between a member of the clergy and the church or an unincorporated association of church members.[6] The court was of the view that aspects of that relationship may be contractual. In an important passage Gaudron, McHugh, Hayne and Callinan JJ made the following comments about the use of presumptions:[7]

> In [the] context of intention to create legal relations there is frequent reference to 'presumptions'. It is said that it may be presumed that there are some 'family arrangements' which are not intended to give rise to legal obligations and it was said in this case that it should not be presumed that there was an intention to create legal relations because it was a matter concerning the engagement of a minister of religion. For our part, we doubt the utility of using the language of presumptions in this context. At best, the use of that language does no more than invite attention to identifying the party who bears the onus of proof. In this case, where issue was joined about the existence of a legally binding contract between the parties, there could be no doubt that it was for the appellant to demonstrate that there was such a contract. Reference to presumptions may serve only to distract attention from that more basic and important proposition.
>
> More importantly, the use of the language of presumptions may lead, as it did in this case, to treating one proposition (that an intention to create legal relations is not to be presumed) as equivalent to another, different proposition (that generally, or usually, or it is to be presumed that, an arrangement about remuneration of a minister of religion will not give rise to legally enforceable obligations). References to 'the usual non-contractual status of a priest or minister' and factors which 'generally militate against' a finding of intention to create legal relations illustrate the point. The latter proposition may then be understood as suggesting, in some way, that proof to the contrary is to be seen as particularly difficult and yet offer no guidance at all about how it may be done. Especially is that so when the chief factor said to justify the proposition that an intention to create legal relations must be proved (the essentially spiritual role of a minister of religion) is then put forward as the principal reason not to find that intention in a particular case, and any other matters suggesting that there may be an intention to create legal relations are treated as dealing only with 'collateral' or 'peripheral' aspects of the relationship between the parties. In practice, the latter proposition may rapidly ossify into a rule of law, that there cannot be a contract of employment of a minister of religion, distorting the proper application of basic principles of the law of contract.

---

[4] *Kleinwort Benson Ltd v Malaysia Mining Corp Berhad* [1989] 1 WLR 379, 383.

[5] (2002) 209 CLR 95.

[6] See further Peel, *Treitel, The Law of Contract* (12th edn, Sweet & Maxwell, London, 2007) para 4-017; Burrows, Finn & Todd, *Law of Contract in New Zealand* (3rd edn, LexisNexis NZ Ltd, Wellington, 2007) para 5.3.4.

[7] (2002) 209 CLR 95, 106–7 (footnotes omitted).

It is equally important to notice that the second form of proposition that we have identified may hide the making of some unwarranted assumptions that certain principles and practices of church governance are 'usual' or 'general', or that a particular kind of relationship between clergy and the church or community in which they work is the norm. No such assumptions can be made.

The High Court did not rule out the use of presumption in those areas where they have **10.04** been used for a long time.[8] The imputed intention that the presumptions give effect to deal with the legal effect of the words and conduct of the parties. Although the determination of this intention is an issue of fact, the legal effect of the words or conduct of the parties is a matter that they rarely turn their minds to and the presumptions help deal with what might otherwise be a black hole in contract formation.[9] As has been noted, 'businessmen may adopt language of deliberate equivocation in the hope that all will go well. It may, therefore, be artificial to try to ascertain the common intention of the parties as to the legal effect of … a claim if in fact their common intention was that the claim should have such effect as a judge or arbitrator should decide'.[10]

If the law always required a positive intention to contract then there would be many cases **10.05** where that would not be made out.[11] In *Air Great Lakes Pty Ltd v KS Easter (Holdings) Pty Ltd*,[12] Mahoney JA explained this point in the following terms:[13]

> The proper view is, in my opinion, that the existence of a contract is a consequence which the law imposes upon, or sees as a result of, what the parties have said and done. Actual subjective intention to contract is a factor which the law takes into account in determining whether a contract exists but it is not, or not always, the determining factor.

> The matter may be tested by an example: A says, 'I promise to sell Black Acre to B for $100'; and B says, 'I promise to buy Black Acre from A for that price', the promises being made orally. In such a case, a binding contract will be held to exist. And this will be so even though neither A nor B subjectively adverted to (and therefore had no actual subjective intention as to) whether, by the exchange of those promises, a binding contract would be made. The law will hold a binding contract to have been made even though neither had any actual subjective intention that there be a contract, in the sense that neither party gave any thought to the matter.

The legitimacy of Mahoney JA's conclusion and the legitimacy of the presumptions lies in **10.06** the objective theory of contract. Under this theory, intention is imputed by reference to a

---

[8] *Shahid v Australasian College of Dermatologists* (2008) 248 ALR 267, 330.

[9] *Pettit v Pettit* [1970] AC 777, 823. The law often has to impute a legal effect to the parties' words or conduct, this is part of the process of contract construction. Similarly, the law does not require the parties to contemplate that the postal acceptance rule applies to their agreement, only that the post may be used for acceptances.

[10] *Kleinwort Benson Ltd v Malaysia Mining Corp Berhad* [1989] 1 WLR 379, 383. See also Lücke, 'The Intention to Create Legal Relations' (1970) 3 Adel LR 419, 421 (suggesting that the purpose of the presumptions is to give effect to the 'familiar function of the law of contract to render legally articulate matters which the parties have expressed imperfectly or even considered insufficiently').

[11] Cf *Restatement* (2d) Contracts § 21, comment *a*.

[12] (1985) 2 NSWLR 309.

[13] (1985) 2 NSWLR 309, 330. See also Perillo (ed), *Corbin on Contracts* (Revised edn, Vol 1, St Paul, Minn, West Publishing Co, 1993) § 2.12, p 187.

reasonable person in the position of the parties.[14] That is, in determining whether an intention to contract exists, the correct perspective is with how a reasonable person in the position of the promisee would interpret the statement of the promisor. It follows that it is not necessary to prove a positive subjective intention to contract.[15] The intention is inferred as a matter of fact.[16] Of course evidence to rebut the presumption is allowed and this may take into account evidence of one party's subjective state of mind. For example, if the party arguing that a contract exists admits that they did not intend the term that they now allege to have been breached was to have legal effect then the presumption will be rebutted.[17] However, generally the promisor's subjective state of mind is irrelevant unless the promisee is aware of the promisor's state of mind.[18] Moreover, if an alleged agreement does not contain a promise then clearly there can be no intention to contract as one of the basal requirements for the presumption to operate, and for a contract, is missing.[19] This is an obvious statement of principle and where it tends to arise is where one party has a complete discretion as to whether or not they will perform. Often such cases are reasoned on the basis of an absence of consideration or uncertainty.[20] But in addition, there is a lack of an intention to contract.

---

[14] *Pettit v Pettit* [1970] AC 777, 823. See also *Jones v Padavatton* [1969] 1 WLR 328, 332; *Gould v Gould* [1970] 1 QB 275, 279; *Merritt v Merritt* [1970] 1 WLR 1211, 1213; *Air Great Lakes Pty Ltd v K S Easter (Holdings) Pty Ltd* (1985) 2 NSWLR 309, 336; *Ermogenous v Greek Orthodox Community of SA Inc* (2002) 209 CLR 95, 105. See further *Reid v Zoanetti* [1943] SASR 92, 98.

[15] See also Restatement (2d) Contracts § 21 ('Neither real nor apparent intention that a promise be legally binding is essential to the formation of a contract, but a manifestation of intention that a promise shall not affect legal relations may prevent the formation of a contract.') Cf United Nations Convention for the International Sale of Goods, Art 14(1).

[16] *Jones v Padavatton* [1969] 1 WLR 328, 332. See generally *Orion Insurance Co Plc v Sphere Drake Insurance Plc* [1992] 1 Lloyd's Rep 239.

[17] *Reid v Zoanetti* [1943] SASR 92, 98. See also *Air Great Lakes Pty Ltd v K S Easter (Holdings) Pty Ltd* (1985) 2 NSWLR 309, 336. Similarly, if a transaction gives the impression of the parties being in agreement but that outward appearance can be shown to be a 'sham' so that in reality there was no common intention to contract then there will be no contract, see *Glatzer and Warrick Shipping Ltd v Bradston Ltd (The Ocean Enterprise)* [1997] 1 Lloyd's Rep 449; *ICT Pty Ltd v Sea Containers Ltd* (1995) 39 NSWLR 640, 656. See also *Harmony Shipping Co SA v Saudi-Europe Line Ltd (The Good Helmsman)* [1981] 1 Lloyd's Rep 377. See generally, *Circuit Systems Ltd (in liq) v Zuken-Redac (UK) Ltd* [1997] 1 WLR 721, 727–8 (affirmed *Norglen Ltd v Reeds Rains Prudential Ltd* [1999] 2 AC 1); *Equuscorp Pty Ltd v Glengallan Investments Pty Ltd* (2004) 218 CLR 472, 486; *Official Trustee in Bankruptcy v Alvaro* (1996) 66 FCR 372, 430; *Raftland Pty Ltd as Trustee of the Raftland Trust v Commissioner of Taxation* [2008] HCA 21. See further Conaglen, 'Sham Trusts' [2008] CLJ 176.

[18] See 1.09. Cf *Upton-on-Severn Rural District Council v Powell* [1942] 1 All ER 220 (the appellant was in Upton police district and called the police when a fire broke out on his property asking them to send the fire brigade; the police called the Upton fire brigade who came and put out the fire; neither the appellant or the Upton fire brigade were aware that the land in fact came under the control of the Pershore fire brigade; if the appellant had called the Pershore fire brigade it would have had to provide its services for free; the Upton fire brigade could enter into a contract to charge for its services provided outside its area; it was held that there was a contract to provide for the services even though subjectively both parties were of the belief that the fire fell within the area of control of the Upton fire brigade; the reasoning of Lord Greene was that the appellant called Upton for services and received Upton services and therefore had to pay for them; that is, there was an offer and acceptance; this appears to be an application of detached objectivity and the facts are probably better dealt with under the law of restitution). See further Waddams, *The Law of Contracts* (5th edn, Canada Law Book, Toronto, 2005) para 145.

[19] *Bowerman v Association of British Travel Agents Ltd* [1996] CLC 451. See further 10.67.

[20] See generally *Placer Development Ltd v The Commonwealth* (1969) 121 CLR 353. See also Peel, *Treitel, The Law of Contract* (12th edn, Sweet & Maxwell, London, 2007) para 4-012. See further 11.20.

The concern of this chapter is with the presumption operating in commercial contracts. **10.07** The use of the presumption might suggest that the issue of intention is rarely litigated or, if it is, the issue before the court is one of rebutting the presumption. However, as noted elsewhere, issues surrounding the formation of contracts, particularly uncertainty, incompleteness and conditional contracts, are some of the most litigated areas of contract law.[21] Often where these issues arise a court will conclude there is no intention to contract because of some uncertainty or incompleteness or because the contract is made 'subject to contract'.[22] In these cases there is usually no discussion of the presumption or its rebuttal.[23] The intention must be proved using the objective standard.[24] It is necessary then to attempt to identify the field of operation of the presumptions.

Perhaps those cases of uncertainty and incompleteness referred to suggest that the pre- **10.08** sumption only applies where there is agreement on all the essential terms.[25] Where that is not the case then intention must be proved. If this were the only explanation, it would follow that a complete agreement made 'subject to contract' would usually attract the presumption.[26] Perhaps there is some support for this proposition to be found in the cases where, today, outside of contracts for the sale of land, an agreement made 'subject to contract' usually suspends performance and not formation. It would follow that in cases of uncertainty and incompleteness, intention must be positively proven. The difficulty with this explanation is that the usual starting point for a court is to assume a contract is complete and certain and leave it to the party who wishes to argue otherwise to prove their case. That approach would necessarily attract the presumption to such cases.[27]

Another way to look at the issue is to recognize a subtle difference between determining **10.09** whether or not the parties voluntarily assumed legal obligations in any given case and

---

[21] See 1.01.

[22] *Anaconda Nickel Ltd v Tarmoola Australia Pty Ltd* (2000) 22 WAR 101, [23].

[23] Cf *Stephenson v Dwyer* [2008] NSWCA 123, [102].

[24] *Maple Leaf Macro Volatility Master Fund v Rouvroy* [2009] 1 Lloyd's Rep 475, 512. See further Tarrant, 'Preliminary Agreements' (2006) 3 UNELJ 151, 162ff. Generally, the courts will look at the language of the agreement, the nature of the agreement, whether it is of a type that is usually in written form, whether there are acts of part performance and other surrounding circumstances including the negotiations, see *Arcadian Phosphates Inc v Arcadian Corp* 884 F 2d 69, 72 (1989).

[25] *Rose and Frank Co v JR Crompton and Bros Ltd* [1923] 2 KB 261, 293 per Atkin LJ (the presumption will apply, 'when parties enter into an agreement which is other respects conforms to the rules of law as to the formation of contracts'). But query how one can get to that point if the requirement of an intention to contract is inherent in the concept of an offer, see 11.02. See further Lücke, 'The Intention to Create Legal Relations' (1970) 3 Adel LR 419, 421–2, suggesting that the presumption only solves the most obvious cases.

[26] *Stephenson v Dwyer* [2008] NSWCA 123, [102] (applying the presumption to a 'subject to contract' situation).

[27] Hedley draws a distinction 'between "intent to create legal relations" and "contractual intent"'. He goes on to state: 'When the courts ask whether "contractual intent" is present in a particular case, they mean "Does what the parties intended qualify as a contract?" Thus by implication they refer to *all* the requirements of the law of contract and ask whether the intentions of the parties comply with them', see Hedley, 'Keeping Contract in its Place—*Balfour v Balfour* and the Enforceability of Informal Agreements' (1985) 5 OJLS 391.

whether they intended to contract.[28] The distinction appears to have been recognized by Windeyer J in *The State of South Australia v The Commonwealth*,[29] where he said:[30]

> An agreement deliberately entered into and by which both parties intend themselves to be bound may yet not be an agreement that the courts will enforce. The circumstances may show that they did not intend, or cannot be regarded as having intended, to subject their agreement to the adjudication of the courts. The status of the parties, their relationship to one another, the topics with which the agreement deals, the extent to which it is expressed to be finally definitive of their concurrence, the way in which it came into existence, these, or any one or more of them taken in the circumstances, may put the matter outside the realm of contract law.

10.10 For there to be an offer, it must be informed by an intention to contract, so too any acceptance. It follows that the existence of an intention to contract may exist throughout the negotiation process. The presumption can then attach to that expectation of a contract. In most commercial negotiations a reasonable person in the position of the parties will conclude that the parties were negotiating with the expectation of entering into a contract; why else negotiate in the first place? Even where a head contractor is negotiating with several subcontractors and all the parties know that only one contract with one subcontractor will eventuate, it is possible to presume that all *intend to contract* and are negotiating with the expectation that they will be awarded the contract. Arguably this is all the 'intention' that the presumption assumes and applies.[31] But this is a different issue from whether or not the parties intended to assume legal obligations at any point in time.

10.11 As already noted, often the parties have the point at which legal obligations are to be assumed at the forefront of their minds. A 'subject to contract' clause may evidence this. That is, the parties express a clear intention as to whether they intend their agreement to be subject to 'the adjudication of the courts'.[32] Thus, every time an agreement is made 'subject to contract', it is necessary to positively determine the intention of the parties as to whether they intended the agreement to have immediate effect. As noted, very often in these cases the courts will use the language of intention and may conclude the parties did not intend to contract and this may be so. But whether the parties can be said to have voluntarily assumed legal obligations at any point in time, such as at a particular stage of negotiations

---

[28] Cf *Reid v Zoanetti* [1943] SASR 92, 98. See also *Kleinwort Benson Ltd v Malaysia Mining Corp Berhad* [1989] 1 WLR 379, 383 (suggesting the latter is concerned with an intention to create legal relations).

[29] (1962) 108 CLR 130; *Australian Broadcasting Corp v XIVTH Commonwealth Games Ltd* (1988) 18 NSWLR 540, 548. See further *Ermogenous v Greek Orthodox Community of SA Inc* (2002) 209 CLR 95, 105; *Sagacious Procurement Pty Ltd v Symbion Health Ltd* [2008] NSWCA 149, [66].

[30] (1962) 108 CLR 130, 154. See also *Harvela Investments Ltd v Royal Trust Co of Canada (CI) Ltd* [1986] AC 207, 226. See further de Moor, 'Intention in the Law of Contract: Elusive or Illusory' (1990) 106 LWR 632, 636.

[31] Cf *Australian Broadcasting Corp v XIVTH Commonwealth Games Ltd* (1988) 18 NSWLR 540, 542. Unless the requirement of an intention to contract can be made out by reference to the anticipation of a contract, it is difficult to see how, in doctrinal terms, it is possible for the parties to enter into a contract that has retrospective effect, see *Trollope & Colls Ltd v Atomic Power Constructions Ltd* [1963] 1 WLR 333.

[32] *South Australia v The Commonwealth* (1962) 108 CLR 130, 154 (as noted here Windeyer J distinguishes intention to contract and the voluntary assumption of obligations and suggests that whether or not the parties intended their arrangement to be subject to adjudication by the courts goes to the latter). The investigation as to whether the parties envisaged legal proceedings to enforce their agreement is problematic, see 10.26.

or on any particular terms or upon the execution of a document, is arguably a different question. Perhaps there are many cases where a contract has failed for a lack of a voluntary assumption of legal obligation which commentators have interpreted as failing for lack of an intention to contract.[33] The latter finding may flow from the former. For example, take the case where the parties agree all the terms of a contract and make the contract 'subject to contract' in the sense that no enforceable contract is to come into being until execution of a formal contract.[34] If the negotiations were always carried out 'subject to contract' then there would be an argument that the parties would have evidenced that they do not intend to contract and have no intention to voluntarily assume any legal obligations until execution.[35] However, if the 'subject to contract' clause was introduced at the end of negotiations it may be that during negotiations the expectation of a contract would have been sufficient to attract the presumption but the introduction of the clause at the end of negotiations showed a lack of willingness to voluntarily assume legal obligations and this rebutted the presumption.

The presumptions and threshold intention

There are other situations where the presumptions are not applied. Indeed as evidenced by the decision *Ermogenous v Greek Orthodox Community of SA Inc*,[36] it can be difficult to determine when a presumption applies. That case also highlighted the problem of categorization for the purposes of the presumptions. That is, what constitutes a family or social agreement for the purposes of the presumptions? No list of appropriate settings exists and it can be difficult to determine when a family or social setting transcends into a commercial setting.[37]   **10.12**

Even within a commercial setting there will cases where the presumption does not apply because the statements made were not intended to be taken seriously. That is, unless there can be a reasonably held expectation of a contract, the presumption does not apply.[38] In such cases there is no need to rebut the presumption. In short there is a threshold which must be met in order for the presumption to apply. This is an issue that is more likely to arise where the transaction involves a consumer. Typical situations involve conditional gifts and here an intention to contract as well as the bargain theory of consideration help distinguish contracts from such gifts. The standard example is a promise of an outrageous sum of money in return for a mundane act. In a social setting this may take the form of, 'I promise   **10.13**

---

[33] See *Australian Woollen Mills Pty Ltd v Commonwealth* (1954) 92 CLR 424, 457; *Ermogenous v Greek Orthodox Community of SA Inc* (2002) 209 CLR 95, 105, and Lücke, 'The Intention to Create Legal Relations' (1970) 3 Adel LR 419, 420. See also *The Administration of the Territory of Papua and New Guinea v Leahy* (1961) 105 CLR 6, 13–14.

[34] See 9.22.

[35] *Rose and Frank Co v JR Crompton and Bros Ltd* [1923] 2 KB 261, 294 per Atkin LJ.

[36] (2002) 209 CLR 95.

[37] Eg see *Jones v Padavatton* [1969] 1 WLR 328, and compare *Roufos v Brewster* (1971) 2 SASR 218. See also *Gore v Van Der Lann* [1967] 2 QB 21 (here the provision of a free bus ticket to pensioners subject to certain conditions was proven to be based on an intention to contract between the ticket holder and the ticket supplier).

[38] See 10.10.

to pay you £1,000 if you change the television channel'.[39] One can put such a statement into a more commercial type arrangement. A practical example is the promotional puff. It is a general principle of contract law that a puff is not to be taken seriously and does not become a term of the contract.[40] This applies even in a commercial context. Thus, the advertising 'speak' of a car sales person who says 'the fuel consumption on this car is so efficient, if you fill it up once you will never have to fill it up again', is not intended to be taken seriously and does not of itself attract the presumption of an intention to contract nor would it be understood that the maker of the statement was voluntarily undertaking legal obligations in respect of such a statement.

10.14 However, whether or not a statement is intended to operate as a puff or not is a question that opinions can differ on.[41] Perhaps the most famous example is the decision of the House of Lords in *Esso Petroleum Co Ltd v Customs and Excise Commissioners*.[42] In this case Esso, which was in the business of supplying petrol, commissioned the production of certain 'World Cup coins'. Each coin bore the image of one member of the English football team. The coins were sold to their garage proprietors and were then advertised as free gifts to be given by Esso service station proprietors to consumers with every four gallons of petrol purchased. The question that went to the House of Lords was whether these coins were produced for sale. If they were then they attracted a purchase tax. The Court of Appeal held that no tax was payable. The House of Lords dismissed the appeal. Some members of the House of Lords concluded there was a contract taking effect as a collateral contract, the consideration for the coins was entry into the contract to buy petrol. They found an intention to contract between the consumers and proprietors for the supply of the coins. The basis for that conclusion was the commercial advantage Esso was seeking under the promotion; namely to sell more fuel than they might otherwise have by tempting customers to buy sufficient fuel to obtain a full set of coins. The whole promotion was set up to tempt customers in this way.[43] The transaction was said to take place in a business setting, despite involving a consumer sale, that is, it was seeking a commercial advantage.[44] The view was expressed that commercial promoters should not be allowed to argue that the statements made were mere puffs, that is, the presumption should apply.[45] Other members (Viscount

---

[39] It can be difficult to draw a line between a conditional gift and a contract and it would be possible to vary the facts of this example slightly so that it is more likely that a court would find such a promise as giving rise to a contract. For example if the facts were that of a scene in a crowded bar where the patrons are divided over which sporting event should be viewed and one group offers the other a sum of money if they agree to change the channel. If that statement is accepted then the requirement of a bargain would probably be held to be made out.

[40] Eg *Lexmead (Basingstoke) Ltd v Lewis* [1982] AC 225, 262–3 (here the Court of Appeal held that references to the subject goods as being 'foolproof' and 'required no maintenance' were not terms of the contract; the House of Lords did not discuss this issue). The classic example of where an advertisement crossed the line from promotional puff to a term of the contract is *Carlill v Carbolic Smoke Ball Co* [1893] 1 QB 256. See also *Dimmock v Hallett* (1866) LR 2 Ch App 21, 27, 30; *Thake v Maurice* [1986] QB 644, 685; *Leonard v Pepsico* 88 F Supp 2d (1999) (affirmed 210 F 3d 88 (2000)).

[41] Cf 10.15.

[42] [1976] 1 WLR 1. See also Waddams, *The Law of Contracts* (5th edn, Canada Law Book, Toronto, 2005) para 154.

[43] The details of the promotion are set out in the speech of Viscount Dilhorne [1976] 1 WLR 1, 3.

[44] [1976] 1 WLR 1, 5 per Lord Simon (with whom Lord Wilberforce agreed).

[45] [1976] 1 WLR 1, 5 per Lord Simon.

Dilhorne and Lord Russell) focused on the language of the advertisement which expressed the coin as a free gift; the lack of value in the coins and the fact that no legal proceedings were ever likely to be taken for refusal to supply a coin and held that no contract was intended between the customer and the individual garage proprietors in respect of the coins. Viscount Dilhorne expressed the view that on the facts of this case the onus did not lie on the person who was asserting that no contractual intention existed, that is, the presumption did not apply to the transaction. This appears to flow from his view that it was not a sufficient 'business' transaction to attract the presumption due to it being a consumer sale.[46] Although deciding there was no intention to contract both Viscount Dilhorne and Lord Russell expressed the view that if there was a contract in respect of the coins it was a collateral contract and not a contract by way of sale for a cash consideration.[47] Lord Fraser dissented, he was of the view that there was only one transaction and it was by way of sale. In the result a majority held Esso and the dealers were under a binding obligation to deliver coins to purchasers but this majority was divided on whether there was one or two contracts. A further majority held that to the extent there was a contract it was collateral to the contract for the sale of petrol and was therefore not caught by the legislation as it was not a contract by way of sale for a cash consideration.

Although opinions may always differ in determining an issue of fact, it is always necessary **10.15** to make such decisions by reference to contract doctrine. Where that doctrine intrudes here is in the application of the objective theory which may dictate what evidence is and is not relevant in making a decision. It is here that the case has been criticized on the basis that it is a finding as to the intention of Esso rather than that of the parties to the contract and that on a proper application of the objective test, 'the more realistic view is that contractual intention was negatived by the language of the advertisements (in which the coins were said to be "going free"), and by the minimal value of the coins'.[48] Despite this, it is suggested that if a football fan purchased petrol in the circumstances of this case and was told there were no coins, he or she would have a legitimate grievance based on the expectation of a reasonable person in their position.

A further example of where the courts appear to require some threshold level of intention **10.16** to exist before the presumption can apply is with letters of comfort. Given the importance of these documents, they are given separate treatment below.[49]

Consideration and intention to contract

There is a relationship between the presence of valuable consideration and intention to contract in that both issues go to the legal enforceability of an agreement. Moreover, they overlap **10.17** as the presence of consideration tends 'to suggest the presence of' an intention to contract.[50]

---

[46] [1976] 1 WLR 1, 4–5.
[47] [1976] 1 WLR 1, 5, 11.
[48] Peel, *Treitel, The Law of Contract* (12th edn, Sweet & Maxwell, London, 2007) para 4-023. See also at para 4-024, the author's discussion and critique of *J Evans & Son (Portsmouth) Ltd v Andrea Merzario Ltd* [1976] 1 WLR 1078.
[49] See 10.58ff.
[50] Carter, *Carter on Contract* (Butterworths, Sydney), § 08-010.

Williston went further taking the view that the provision of valuable consideration necessarily proved an intention to contract.[51] The basis of this view is that under the bargain theory of consideration, once the presence of valuable consideration is made out, then the parties have put a price on each other's promise and that is sufficient to prove intention. Thus, it is argued that many of the cases that fail for lack of intention, such as those between family members, should be seen as failing because neither party has given a promise as the price for a counter-promise; in short there is no bargain.[52] However, before one adopts Williston's view, it is necessary to take a position on whether the concept of a 'price' for a promise and hence a bargain, is determined by reference to intention or whether it is a legal determination based on whether the transaction is one that the courts believe should be given effect to in the marketplace. If it is the former then Williston's view carries much weight as there would be circularity in assessing intention twice. Indeed one can reasonably argue that many exchanges of promises given in family situations are not given in order to purchase some other promise as they are given gratuitously as 'gratuitous services' and would be given in any case.[53] They are therefore not referable to some counter-promise. But at the same time one cannot simply adopt the view that when one promise is given in return for another promise or act there is a bargain. Indeed it has been in such circumstances that the courts have used a legal concept of a bargain in addition to intention in order to distinguish a contract from a conditional gift.[54] The example given above is typical.[55] If A and B are sitting at home one night and A promises to pay B £1,000 if B changes the television channel, then if B does change the channel and the only reason B did that was because of A's promise then that act is referable to the promise and given in exchange for the promise. However, a court will not enforce that 'agreement' on the basis that it was not a bargain and there was no intention to contract. Here the notion of a 'price' is determined as a matter of law. Much of course will depend on the relations between the parties and the setting they are in.

10.18 None of this results in there being no need for an intention to contract and if this legal concept of a bargain is rejected then the only way to prevent enforcement of the type of exchange referred to above is by reference to intention. Moreover, the fact remains that members of a family may contract with one another and depending on the context the exact same exchange of promises in one instance may give rise to a contract and in another instance it may be held that there is no contract. What distinguishes them is intention.

---

[51] Lord (ed), *Williston on Contracts* (4th edn, Vol 1, Lawyers Cooperative Publishing, 1990) § 3:5. This view has received some support, for example, see Hamson, 'The Reform of Consideration' (1938) 54 LQR 233, 253ff; Tuck, 'Intent to Contract and Mutuality of Assent' (1943) 21 Can Bar Rev 123; Shatwell, 'The Doctrine of Consideration in the Modern Law' (1954) 1 Syd L Rev 289, 314–15; Unger, 'Intention to Create Legal Relations, Mutuality and Consideration' (1956) 10 MLR 96; Hepple, 'Intention to Create Legal Relations' [1970] CLJ 122; Cf Lücke, 'The Intention to Create Legal Relations' (1970) 3 Adel LR 419.

[52] See Hepple, 'Intention to Create Legal Relations' [1970] CLJ 122, 128.

[53] Unger, 'Intention to Create Legal Relations, Mutuality and Consideration' (1956) 10 MLR 96, 98.

[54] *Beaton v McDivitt* (1987) 13 NSWLR 162, 169–70. See also Carter, Peden and Tolhurst, *Contract Law in Australia* (5th edn, LexisNexis Butterworths, Sydney, 2007) para 6.16.

[55] See 10.13. Note also how a slight variation of the facts may bring about a different result, see above n 41.

Finally, the legal position is that under English law an intention to contract and consideration are separate legal requirements for a contract.[56]

Family and social agreements

In family and social situations there is a presumption that the parties do not intend to contract.[57] This is a presumption of fact.[58] It follows that an intention to contract must be proved. It has been suggested that this requirement of an intention to contract is no more than a policy position adopted by the courts to give effect to what agreements the courts think ought and ought not to be enforced.[59] Whether or not that view properly captures the initial reason for the adoption of this requirement, there can be little doubt that today the requirement of an intention to contract is a necessary aspect of contract formation and that it is said to be grounded in the presumed intention of the parties.[60] Thus, the presumption as regards family and social agreements is said to be based on 'experience of life and human nature which shows that in such circumstances men and women usually do not intend to create legal rights and obligations'.[61] What life experience dictates will depend on the relationship in question. It is also important to keep in mind that people in close relationships use 'unguarded speech' that might suggest an intention to contract in another context.[62] The social customs of the parties involved may also be important.[63] In the typical case of a marriage, many arrangements made between a husband and wife are made out of the natural love and affection that underpins the relationship and it is this that experience dictates means that the parties did not intend the arrangement to give rise to legal relations.[64] Finally, although human nature may not change (at least not in

10.19

---

[56] Numerous commentators argue that the requirements of consideration and intention should be kept distinct, see Furmston, *Cheshire, Fifoot and Furmston's, Law of Contract* (15th edn, OUP, Oxford, 2007) 143; Peel, *Treitel, The Law of Contract* (12th edn, Sweet & Maxwell, London, 2007) para 4-025–4-028; McCamus, *The Law of Contracts* (Irwin Law, Toronto, 2005), 112; Lücke, 'The Intention to Create Legal Relations' (1970) 3 Adel LR 419. See also *Cohen v Cohen* (1929) 42 CLR 91, 96 per Dixon J. See further *Jones v Padavatton* [1969] 1 WLR 328, 336 per Fenton Atkinson LJ.

[57] Cf Perillo (ed), *Corbin on Contracts* (Revised edn, Vol 1, St Paul, Minn, West Publishing Co, 1993) § 2.13, pp 189ff.

[58] *Jones v Padavatton* [1969] 1 WLR 328, 332 per Salmon LJ.

[59] Hedley, 'Keeping Contract in its Place—*Balfour v Balfour* and the Enforceability of Informal Agreements' (1985) 5 OJLS 391, 393 (on the same page, Hedley also makes the point that this requirement of intention only appeared in the English law of contract when the court was faced for the first time with an argument that a maintenance agreement between married couples was enforceable as a contract in *Balfour v Balfour* [1919] 2 KB 571; prior to that, intention was only considered when the parties 'deliberately excluded' it; the requirement of an intention to contract may then be seen as a quick, but perhaps not well thought out, solution to keeping such 'agreements' out of the law of contract). Cf Chloros, 'Comparative Aspects of the Intention to Create Legal Relations in Contract' (1959) 33 Tul L Rev 607.

[60] See also Peel, *Treitel, The Law of Contract* (12th edn, Sweet & Maxwell, London, 2007) para 4-028.

[61] *Jones v Padavatton* [1969] 1 WLR 328, 332 per Salmon LJ.

[62] *McBride v Sandland* (1918) 25 CLR 69, 94 (arrangement whereby a son-in-law would not bid against his father-in-law at an auction for a certain property so that the father could bid for that property and others in one lot in return for arranging for his daughter to rent the subject property and have a right to purchase it on her father's death; held that in the circumstances of this case there was no intention to contract, the conversation when taken in context evidenced a 'benefaction and not a bargain').

[63] See *Turner v Turner* (1918) 25 CLR 569, 570; *Taverner v Swanbury* [1944] SASR 194. In a commercial context, see *County Ltd v Girozentrale Securities* [1996] 3 All ER 834, 837.

[64] *Merritt v Merritt* [1970] 1 WLR 1211, 1214 per Widgery LJ.

the short term), life experience, community attitudes and expectations do vary with the times. This is important because many of the leading cases in this area are now quite dated and some may not necessarily be acceptable to a modern court if re-argued.

10.20 Perhaps the leading case dealing with arrangements between husbands and wives is still *Balfour v Balfour*.[65] In this case a husband, stationed in Ceylon, took leave and returned to England with his wife. When it came time for him to return to Ceylon she was not able to accompany him because of her poor health. The husband promised to pay his wife £30 a month as maintenance during this period. The wife later sued for breach of this agreement. The Court of Appeal held that no legal relations had been contemplated. The plaintiff carried the onus of proving the transaction was intended to operate as a contract.[66] Atkin LJ focused on the fact that this was an arrangement between a husband and wife and reasoned that although it was in the nature of such a relationship to make arrangements on many matters there is no intention to contract in respect of those arrangements.[67] Atkin LJ gave two further reasons for not enforcing such contracts,[68] first because it would multiply suits and second, because the consideration for most promises is that of natural love and affection which counts for little in the courts.[69] Warrington LJ emphasized some practical points saying:[70]

> If we were to imply such a contract in this case we should be implying on the part of the wife that whatever happened and whatever might be the change of circumstances while the husband was away she should be content with this £30 a month, and bind herself by an obligation in law not to require him to pay anything more; and on the other hand we should be implying on the part of the husband a bargain to pay £30 a month for some indefinite period whatever might be his circumstances.

10.21 A similar sentiment can be found in the leading Australian decision of the time, *Cohen v Cohen*.[71] Here a husband reneged on his promise to provide his wife with a dress allowance.

---

[65] [1919] 2 KB 571. For those arguing that there is no need for a separate requirement of intention in addition to that of consideration, the case is criticized on the basis that the action should have failed for lack of consideration moving from the wife as the price for the husband's promise, see Tuck, 'Intent to Contract and Mutuality of Assent' (1943) 21 Can Bar Rev 123; Unger, 'Intention to Create Legal Relations, Mutuality and Consideration' (1956) 10 MLR 96. A lack of consideration flowing from the wife was one of the reasons Atkin LJ relied on, see n 72. For an extended critique of this case and the law which it gave rise to, see Hedley, 'Keeping Contract in its Place—*Balfour v Balfour* and the Enforceability of Informal Agreements' (1985) 5 OJLS 391.

[66] [1919] 2 KB 571, 580.

[67] [1919] 2 KB 571, 578–9.

[68] Arguably these practical points were the principal reasons for the decision and the introduction of a requirement of an intention to contract was a doctrinal method of giving effect to these concerns even if not directly linked to those concerns, see n 62.

[69] [1919] 2 KB 571, 579. Cf *Dunton v Dunton* (1892) 18 VLR 114. Atkin LJ suggested that these arrangements were akin to arrangements to meet and go for a walk. This analogy has been criticized, see Stoljar, 'Enforcing Benevolent Promises' (1989) 12 Syd LR 17, 19–20, suggesting there is an important difference between a purely social promise—the arrangement for a walk—which is not intended to be enforceable, from a 'benevolent' promise which encourages action or reliance of a serious or injurious kind and which is exemplified by arrangements between family members.

[70] [1919] 2 KB 571, 575 (see also at 579 per Atkin LJ). For a critique of these reasons, see Stoljar, 'Enforcing Benevolent Promises' (1989) 12 Syd LR 17, 23.

[71] (1929) 42 CLR 91.

These cases suggest that the presumption, at least in the early 1900s, was quite strong in respect of arrangements between a husband and wife.

Perhaps the presumption may still be strong in situations like *Cohen v Cohen* to the extent **10.22** that the promise is directed to towards enjoyment rather than maintenance or subsistence and is thus more a gift promise. However, one could imagine where such an arrangement may be important to some affluent or influential members of society in the social, professional or political settings which they inhabit. However, it is difficult to see the present influence of *Balfour v Balfour* and, assuming the presence of valuable consideration, today one would expect that arrangement, on those facts, to be upheld insofar as intention is concerned.[72] It is relevant to note that as far back as 1970 the House of Lords suggested that *Balfour v Balfour* 'stretched [the] doctrine to its limits'.[73]

The presumption is most easily rebutted in respect of arrangements made upon the break- **10.23** down of a marriage.[74] In the view of some judges the presumption does not apply in such a case. For example, in *Merritt v Merritt*,[75] following the breakdown of their marriage, the husband signed a written note agreeing that he would transfer title to the former matrimonial home, then in their joint names, into his wife's sole name. This was given in return for her paying all charges connected with the house until the mortgage was repaid. The wife abided by these terms and paid off the mortgage partly out of the £40 a month her husband paid her as maintenance following the breakdown of their marriage and partly out of her own earnings. However, the husband refused to transfer the house to her although he did reduce the maintenance payment to £25 once the mortgage had been paid off. The Court of Appeal held that the parties had intended to create legal relations. In coming to this conclusion the court was heavily influenced by the fact that the husband and wife were no

---

[72] See Stoljar, 'Enforcing Benevolent Promises' (1989) 12 Syd LR 17, 31ff (suggesting that although such benevolent promises may not fit within the 'bargain-mould' they should be enforceable if they create reliable expectations and are acted on). The decision may be overtaken by legislation recognizing cohabitation agreements in addition to those agreed upon at the breakdown of a marriage, see McCamus, *The Law of Contracts* (Irwin Law, Toronto, 2005) 133; Burrows, Finn and Todd, *Law of Contract in New Zealand* (3rd edn, LexisNexis NZ Ltd, Wellington, 2007) para 5.3.1.

[73] *Pettit v Pettit* [1970] AC 777, 816 per Lord Upjohn, see also, 796 per Lord Reid, 806 per Lord Hodson, and see 822 per Lord Diplock ('It would, in my view, be erroneous, to extend the presumption accepted in *Balfour v Balfour* that mutual promises between man and wife in relation to their domestic arrangements are prima facie not intended by either to be legally enforceable to a presumption of a common intention of both spouses that *no* legal consequences should flow from acts done by them in performance of mutual promises with respect to the acquisition, improvement or addition to real or personal property—for this would be to intend what is impossible in law.')

[74] Similarly arrangements for the welfare of children are likely to be upheld, see *Tanner v Tanner* [1975] 1 WLR 1346 (arrangement between a man and woman for him to buy a house and let her live in it with the children of their relationship; this was held to be a contractual licence). See further as to promises made to induce marriage, *Synge v Synge* [1894] 1 QB 466. For a discussion contrasting the post-nuptial agreement with the efficacy of pre-nuptial agreements, see *Macleod v MacLeod* [2009] 3 WLR 437.

[75] [1970] 1 WLR 1211. See also *Eastland v Burchell* (1878) 3 QBD 432, 436; *McGregor v McGregor* (1888) 21 QBD 424, CA; *Milliner v Milliner* (1908) 8 SR (NSW) 471; *Peters (Executors) v Commissioners of Inland Revenue* [1941] 2 All ER 620; *Soulsbury v Soulsbury* [2008] Fam 1, CA. Cf *Gould v Gould* [1970] 1 QB 275 (upon the break up of a marriage, a husband promised his wife a weekly sum in maintenance to be paid as long as his 'business is OK' or 'so long as [he could] manage it'; it was held that this agreement was void for uncertainty and that uncertainty evidenced a lack of intention to contract attracting *Balfour v Balfour*, see further *Merritt v Merritt* [1970] 1 WLR 1211, 1213, per Lord Denning MR); *Popiw v Popiw* [1959] VR 197.

longer living together when they made this arrangement. It was on this basis that the court distinguished this case for the *Balfour v Balfour* line of cases. The presumption is rebutted because the natural love and affection that underpins the marriage also underpins the presumption and is gone when the marriage breaks up.[76] Widgery LJ said that it was 'unnecessary to go so far as to say that there is a presumption in favour of the creation of legal relationships when the marriage is breaking up, but certainly there is no presumption against the creation of such legal relations as there is when the parties are living happily together'.[77]

10.24 The leading decision dealing with family arrangements outside of husband and wife arrangements is *Jones v Padavatton*.[78] In this case, a mother invited her daughter to come to England and read for the bar for the purpose of practising law in Trinidad where the mother lived. The mother promised to pay her a certain sum of money (being $200 per month) by way of maintenance. There was confusion from the start as the mother intended by this to mean West Indian dollars and daughter took it to mean US dollars. Nevertheless, in reliance on this promise, the daughter, who was in her mid-thirties at the time and lived and worked in Washington, came to England with her son and commenced reading for the bar. In order to do this the daughter had to take her son out of school and give up both a good job and her flat. The mother initially paid her daughter's fees and provided a sum by way of maintenance. That sum was £42 per month and the daughter made no complaint that it did not equate to $200 US. However, it did equate to $200 West Indian. Later the mother purchased a large home and allowed her daughter to live there and sub-let the other rooms and keep the moneys obtained to pay outgoings and maintenance and remit the remainder to her mother; during the entire period no sum was ever remitted back to the mother. A couple of years later the mother indicated that she wanted to retake possession of the property. However, on her initial arrival from Trinidad, the daughter refused to let her into the property. The daughter claimed she was entitled to a sum to compensate her for the money she had spent on the property. At the time of the dispute the daughter had been studying for the bar for six years and had yet to pass Part I of the Bar examination.

10.25 The question for the court was whether there was a contractual arrangement made between the parties in respect of the property. For Danckwerts LJ the arrangement in respect of the property replaced the earlier maintenance arrangement and so depended on the enforcement of that earlier arrangement. He held that there was no intention to contract in respect of the early maintenance arrangement. There was, in his view, no evidence to rebut the presumption the mother was merely acting in a way she hoped would further her daughter's career.

10.26 Salmon LJ said it was up to the daughter to prove a variation of the original agreement which she had not done and so the two arrangements had to be evaluated separately.

---

[76] [1970] 1 WLR 1211, 1214 per Widgery LJ.
[77] [1920] 1 WLR 1211, 1214.
[78] [1969] 1 WLR 328. See also Phang, *Cheshire, Fifoot and Furmston's Law of Contract* (2nd Singapore and Malaysian edn, Butterworths, Asia, Singapore, 1998), 225 discussing *Choo Tiong Hin v Choo Hock Swee* [1959] MLJ 67. See further *Williamson v Suncorp Metway Insurance Ltd* [2008] QSC 244; *McMahon v McMahon* [2008] VSC 386.

The daughter carried the onus of rebutting the presumption and proving an intention to contract. He thought that in the special circumstances of this case the initial arrangement would give rise to contractual relations if the daughter came to England and stayed for a minimum period of six months.[79] This reasoning may suggest he was of the view that the contract formed over a period of time with no distinct point of acceptance of an offer. It may suggest that reliance plays an important factor in rebutting the presumption. It also suggests that estoppel may be relevant on the facts of any given case.[80] Salmon LJ was not impressed with the submission that it was unthinkable that the daughter would sue her mother if her mother fell on hard times and could not pay. He thought that the fact the daughter was unlikely to sue in such a situation did not shed any light on the issue of whether or not there was an intention to contract.[81] This is an important point because occasionally this factor is raised in order to help determine whether there was an intention to contract.[82] However, many commercial parties enter into contracts with the view that they will not involve the courts or any third parties in any dispute resolution process.[83] This is often based on firm commercial beliefs that it is better to deal with such issues between the parties; this belief might be based on concerns about market reputation or because the sums involved are too large to be left to chance. Moreover, it is suggested that the place for this consideration is when the voluntary assumption of legal obligations is a matter in the mind of the parties and this is distinct from that of an intention to contract.[84]

Salmon LJ also did not think there was an uncertainty about the arrangements that would render the agreement void. In particular, in dealing with the term of the arrangement which was not expressed, he said that it would exist for a reasonable period of time which he thought would be five years from the commencement of studies. That time had lapsed and so the daughter could make no further claim under the agreement. As regards the property, he thought there was no evidence to suggest that the mother had given up any of her proprietary rights in the property. The daughter was a mere licensee and could be evicted by her mother. In his view this arrangement was not made with any contractual intent, the mother was simply trying to help her daughter. He was clearly of the view that the daughter was trying to take advantage of her mother and her mother's patience with her daughter was at an end. **10.27**

Fenton Atkinson LJ thought the presumption applied to a case like this and then looked to see if there was any evidence to rebut it. He recognized that the daughter had given up a great deal but thought the subsequent conduct of the parties was the 'best guide' to their intentions. It is well accepted that such evidence may be resorted to in order to determine **10.28**

---

[79] The special circumstances he referred to was all that the daughter was giving up in America, the fact that this involved great inconvenience to the daughter in going to another country to study and taking her son out of his school in the United States and that the outcome was to practise law in Trinidad which the mother wished for so that she could see more of her daughter and grandson, see [1969] 1 WLR 328, 333.

[80] See also *Riches v Hogben* [1985] 2 Qd R 292 (affirmed *Riches v Hogben* [1986] 1 Qd R 315, 316).

[81] [1969] 1 WLR 328, 334. See also *Todd v Nicol* [1957] SASR 72, 77.

[82] See also Stoljar, 'Enforcing Benevolent Promises' (1989) 12 Syd LR 17, 19.

[83] See further Hedley, 'Keeping Contract in its Place—*Balfour v Balfour* and the Enforceability of Informal Agreements' (1985) 5 OJLS 391, 396.

[84] *The State of South Australia v The Commonwealth* (1962) 108 CLR 130, 154. See also 10.10.

whether a contract was formed.[85] However, in any given case such conduct may not evidence an intention to contract at the alleged point of formation but rather, as Salmon LJ appeared to suggest, an intention that evolved over time with the contract being formed by conduct.[86] Nevertheless, Fenton Atkinson LJ focused on three points. First, the daughter made no protest that she only received the equivalent of $200 West Indian. She never suggested to her mother that she was legally obliged to pay more. Second, many material matters in relation to dealing with the property were left open so that the arrangement was too vague to give rise to a contract.[87] There was no discussion by the daughter about how her alleged legal right to £42 per month was affected by this new arrangement. Third, and in conclusion, he said:[88]

> It is perhaps not without relevance to look at the daughter's evidence in cross-examination. She was asked about the occasion when her mother visited the house, and she, knowing perfectly well that her mother was there, refused for some hours to open the door. She said: 'I didn't open the door because a normal mother doesn't sue her daughter in court. Anybody with normal feelings would feel upset by what was happening.' Those answers and the daughter's conduct on that occasion provide a strong indication that she had never for a moment contemplated the possibility of her mother or herself going to court to enforce legal obligations, and that she felt it quite intolerable that a purely family arrangement should become the subject of proceedings in a court of law.

> At the time when the first arrangement was made, mother and daughter were, and always had been, to use the daughter's own words, 'very close'. I am satisfied that neither party at that time intended to enter into a legally binding contract, either then or later when the house was bought. The daughter was prepared to trust her mother to honour her promise of support, just as the mother no doubt trusted her daughter to study for the Bar with diligence, and to get through her examinations as early as she could.

> It follows that in my view the mother's claim for possession succeeds.

10.29 Today it may be that the judgment of Salmon LJ better reflects the times. This of course includes his conclusion that the contract period had lapsed. The case can be contrasted with the Australian case of *Raffaele v Raffaele*.[89] Here parents wishing that their son would

---

[85] *Todd v Nicol* [1957] SASR 72, 75, 77; *Riches v Hogben* [1985] 2 Qd R 292, 296 (affirmed *Riches v Hogben* [1986] 1 Qd R 315, 316, 329). See further 1.20ff.

[86] See further, Stoljar, 'Enforcing Benevolent Promises' (1989) 12 Syd LR 17, 30, making the point that if what is originally promised is a conditional gift, the later performance of the condition merely evidences the condition has been made out, it does not impact on the original intention and turn it into an intention to contract.

[87] For example, if the rents were below expectation, was the mother to make up the difference; how much was the daughter to get out of the rents; for how long was the arrangement to continue?

[88] [1969] 1 WLR 328, 337.

[89] [1962] WAR 29. See also *Errington v Errington* [1952] 1 KB 290 (promise by father to his son and daughter-in-law that if they paid the father's mortgage instalments on the father's property, which they were living in, then upon payment of the final instalment he would transfer the property to them; held that they had a contractual licence so long as they paid the instalments); *Roufos v Brewster* (1971) 2 SASR 218 (here an arrangement between members of a family whereby, in return for one member picking up another's truck from the repair workshop, he could use it to transport back a load of his goods; this was held to constitute a contract); *Schaefer v Schuhmann* [1972] AC 572 (here after a promise by an employer to his employee carer to leave property to the carer in the employer's will, the employer ceased paying the carer wages for the continued provision of care; the arrangement was held to be a contract; see Gilbert, 'The Return of Elizabeth Maddison's Ghost' (1972) 46 ALJ 522). See further *Fleming v Beevers* [1994] 1 NZLR 385; *Hardwick v Johnson* [1978] 1 WLR 683. Cf *Horton v Jones* (1935) 53 CLR 475 (here Horton sued the personal representatives of Jones

live closer to them promised to subdivide certain land they owned and transfer to him an interest in one of the subdivided blocks if he built a house on the land. The land in question was adjacent to where the parents lived. In reliance on that promise the son ceased construction of a home on a piece of land he owned and sold that land. He then built a house on the subject property and lived there until his death. The parents never transferred an interest in the property to him and his widow, as his administratrix, commenced an action against them. The court held that there was an intention to contract.

In addition to the above case, there have been a number of agreements between family **10.30** members involving promises of rewards if a family member took care of another family member—usually an older or unwell family member—and which have been upheld as contracts. Many of these have involved significant detriment to the promisee including having to cross international borders in order to tend to the promisor.[90] One important factor in determining the intention of the parties as inferred by the language of the agreement is how serious the consequences are for the promisee in taking any steps required under the contract.[91] In these cases, the fact the acceptance of the offer involved such a move was important in evidencing how serious the promise was to be taken.[92]

In the result, today, to the extent the presumption exists in family situations, it is a weak **10.31** presumption. Clearly the presumption will be rebutted where the family members are

---

on the basis of a promise made by Jones that he would make a will leaving a fortune to Horton in return for Horton looking after Jones and making a home for him for the rest of his life; the agreement failed for uncertainty and for not being evidenced in writing—part of the fortune included an interest in land—there is no suggestion that the contract failed for a want of an intention to contract but here the plaintiff and defendant appear to have been mere acquaintances when the offer was made). See further *Palmer v Bank of NSW* (1975) 133 CLR 150, 156.

[90] See *Parker v Clark* [1960] 1 WLR 286 (aunty with her husband and the niece with her husband); *Wakeling v Ripley* (1951) 51 SR (NSW) 183 (brother and sister); *Todd v Nichol* [1957] SASR 72 (mother-in-law and sister-in-law with niece of mother-in-law); *Riches v Hogben* [1985] 2 Qd R 292 (affirmed *Riches v Hogben* [1986] 1 Qd R 315) (agreement between mother and son). See also *Shadwell v Shadwell* (1860) 9 CBNS 159, 142 ER 62. Cf *Re Gonin (dec'd)* [1979] Ch 16 (parents and daughter). See further McCamus, *The Law of Contracts* (Irwin Law, Toronto, 2005) p 131. It can be the case that such an agreement fails for lack of certainty, the promised reward being too vague, see *Shiels v Drysdale* (1880) 6 VLR (E) 126; *Stinchcombe v Thomas* [1957] VR 509; *Reynolds v McGregor* [1973] 1 QL 314 and see also on uncertainty, *Gould v Gould* [1970] 1 QB 275; *Horton v Jones* (1935) 53 CLR 475. See further n 92 above.

[91] *Riches v Hogben* [1985] 2 Qd R 292, 297 (affirmed *Riches v Hogben* [1986] 1 Qd R 315, 326, 329); *Wakeling v Ripley* (1951) 51 SR (NSW) 183, 187. See further Stoljar, 'Enforcing Benevolent Promises' (1989) 12 Syd LR 17, 26–7.

[92] These cases may evidence that the courts are more prepared to uphold the argument that there is a contract if there has been some substantial reliance, see Peel, *Treitel, The Law of Contract* (12th edn, Sweet & Maxwell, London, 2007) para 4-011; Hedley, 'Keeping Contract in its Place—*Balfour v Balfour* and the Enforceability of Informal Agreements' (1985) 5 OJLS 391, 406ff. See also *Williams v Williams* [1867] LR 2 Ch 294. Of course such acts are necessary if the contract is unilateral in nature but not if it is a bilateral contract. However, the commencement of performance may in some cases evidence a promise and constitute an acceptance of an offer. Clearly acts of reliance may in some cases attract a remedy pursuant to principles of estoppel or the law of property (see *Pettitt v Pettitt* [1970] AC 777, 822; *Cobbe v Yeoman's Row Management Ltd* [2008] 1 WLR 1752), but English law does not adopt a reliance theory of contract and so unless it evidences an intention to contract, it cannot of itself prove there is a contract. If such acts of reliance do evidence an intention to contract then, there may still be an issue as to the point in time when the contract is created.

involved in commercial dealings with each other.[93] Moreover, like arrangements made in the context of a marriage breakdown, agreements entered into between members of a family when relations are strained or non-existent are likely to be intended to have legal effect.[94]

10.32 Litigation involving agreements derived from more social settings are not often litigated and usually are not intended to be legally binding nor attract legal consequences. The reason for this is that in most such cases the alleged promisor merely expresses an intention to do something and this falls short of a promise or undertaking.[95] The typical example is of an agreement to meet to have a meal at a restaurant and see a show.[96] It is assumed by the parties that these arrangements may be varied by either party without suffering any legal consequences. Similarly, if such an agreement went ahead and the friends agree to divide up responsibilities for the evening, such as one drives, one buys the tickets to the show and one pays for a meal, no legal responsibility is likely to be intended to follow if one party reneges on this arrangement although it might cause some friction between the friends as there would have been a contravention of social custom.[97] There have been a number of cases dealing with the sharing of prizes. If the parties pool funds to buy a lottery ticket, then any prize would have to be shared between the parties despite only one party having possession of the ticket. The result would be the same if they individually took responsibility each week to use their own funds to buy a ticket for the group.[98]

Commercial agreements

10.33 In commercial or business agreements the intention to create legal relations is presumed and must be rebutted by the party seeking to deny it.[99] The onus of rebutting the presumption is a heavy one.[100] The clearest way to rebut the presumption is by reference to an express provision.[101] But it is necessary that the words be clear.[102] In *Rose & Frank Co v J R Crompton & Bros Ltd*,[103] Scrutton LJ refers to the necessity of the parties 'expressing themselves

---

[93] *Snelling v John G Snelling Ltd* [1973] QB 87.
[94] *Snelling v John G Snelling Ltd* [1973] QB 87.
[95] *Public Trustee v Bussell* (1993) 30 NSWLR 111, 115.
[96] See Peel, *Treitel, The Law of Contract* (12th edn, Sweet & Maxwell, London, 2007) para 4-008.
[97] Cf Hedley, 'Keeping Contract in its Place—*Balfour v Balfour* and the Enforceability of Informal Agreements' (1985) 5 OJLS 391, 408 (suggesting the result here is not obvious if there has been reliance by one of the parties carrying out the obligation which they agreed to undertake).
[98] *Simpkins v Pays* [1955] 1 WLR 975 (noted Unger, 'Intention to Create Legal Relations, Mutuality and Consideration' (1956) 10 MLR 96). See also McCamus, *The Law of Contracts* (Irwin Law, Toronto, 2005) 134–5, discussing a line of Canadian cases dealing with sharing seasons tickets to sporting events. See further Burrows, Finn and Todd, *Law of Contract in New Zealand* (3rd edn, LexisNexis NZ Ltd, Wellington, 2007) para 5.3.3. and see the discussion in Peel, *Treitel, The Law of Contract* (12th edn, Sweet & Maxwell, London, 2007) para 4-20 (dealing with free travel passes).
[99] The presumption does not apply where the entire agreement is implied. Here the intention must be proved, see *Blackpool and Fylde Aero Club v Blackpool BC* [1990] 1 WLR 1195, 1202.
[100] *Orion Insurance Co Plc v Sphere Drake Insurance Plc* [1992] 1 Lloyd's Rep 239, 263.
[101] See generally Holmes, 'The Freedom Not to Contract' (1985–86) 60 Tul L Rev 751.
[102] Similarly if the presumption applies and is said to be rebutted by conduct, that conduct would need to be clear.
[103] [1923] 2 KB 261, 288.

so precisely that outsiders may have no difficulty in understanding what they mean'.[104] However, even where such words are missing, because the issue is one of determining whether a contract exists, it is possible to have regard to extrinsic evidence, including where relevant, subjective knowledge, to prove that what on its face looks like a contract was not in fact intended to operate as a contract.[105]

One technique used to prevent an agreement taking effect as a contract is the honour clause **10.34** which states that the agreement is to be binding in honour only.[106] At times an argument has been put to the court that there is a commercial expectation that such agreements should attract some legal support.[107] So far the courts have not accepted that in between there being a contract and there being no contract, there can exist in law the agreement that is binding in honour only.[108] It necessarily follows that there is no magic in these words and where a contract is expressed to be binding in honour, the court must still determine the intention of the parties and not every agreement expressed to be binding in honour will be held to be ineffective. For example, in *Home Insurance Co v Administratia Asigurarilor de Stat*,[109] a contract was upheld which contained an arbitration clause that stated:

> This treaty shall be interpreted as an honourable engagement rather than as a legal obligation and the award shall be made with a view to effecting the general purpose of this treaty rather than in accordance with a literal interpretation of its language. The Arbitrators and the Umpire may abstain from judicial formality and from following strictly the rules of law.

It was held that this did not evince an intention not to contract when read in context. In **10.35** particular, the clause required disputes to go to arbitration and the award was expressed to be final and binding. The intention behind the clause was simply to excuse the arbitrators from the strict rules of construction.[110]

---

[104] [1923] 2 KB 261, 288.

[105] See *Kind v Clark* 161 F 2d 36, 46 (1947) ('No sale results where one party to an outwardly seeming sale knows that the other does not mean his words or acts to be taken seriously'); *Kilpatrick Bros Inc v International Business Machines Corp* 464 F 2d 1080, 1082 (1972) ('there is an exception to the parol evidence rule under which it is possible to show that the parties' written contract was not intended to be carried out'). See generally 1.10.

[106] Eg, see the discussion of *Rose & Frank Co v J R Crompton & Bros Ltd* [1923] 2 KB 261 below at 10.36. See also Waddams, *The Law of Contracts* (5th edn, Canada Law Book, Toronto, 2005) para 148. References to an 'in principle' agreement or a 'heads of agreement' are not conclusive of an intention not to contract but may suggest that the agreement is not intended to have immediate effect and do, by their terms, at the very least envisage a later agreement, see *Stephenson v Dwyer* [2008] NSWCA 123; *Dib v Taylor* [2008] NSWSC 493; *Cobbe v Yeoman's Row Management Ltd* [2008] 1 WLR 1752. Cf *Texaco Inc v Pennzoil Co* 729 SW 2d 768 (1987).

[107] Eg, *Banque Brussels Lambert SA v Australian National Industries Ltd* (1989) 21 NSWLR 502.

[108] *Banque Brussels Lambert SA v Australian National Industries Ltd* (1989) 21 NSWLR 502, 523 per Rogers CJ Comm D ('There should be no room in the proper flow of commerce for some purgatory where statements made by businessmen, after hard bargaining and made to induce another business person to enter in a business transaction would, without any express statement to that effect, reside in a twilight zone of merely honourable engagement'). See also *Orion Insurance Co Plc v Sphere Drake Insurance Plc* [1992] 1 Lloyd's Rep 239. See further Bernstein and Zekoll, 'The Gentleman's Agreement in Legal Theory and Modern Practice' (1998) 46 Am Jnl Comp Law, 87, 97.

[109] [1983] 2 Lloyd's Rep 674.

[110] See also *Eagle Star Insurance Co Ltd v Yuval Insurance Co Ltd* [1978] 1 Lloyd's Rep 357.

10.36 Perhaps the most well known case where an express provision was used to rebut the presumption is *Rose & Frank Co v J R Crompton & Bros Ltd*.[111] Here a written agreement was entered into whereby the plaintiffs were appointed as sole US agents for the English defendants. Later the defendants terminated this agreement without giving the required notice and refused to deal with orders which had been received and accepted before termination. The plaintiffs claimed that the defendants had breached the contract. The action failed because the Court of Appeal held that the agreement was not legally binding or enforceable since it contained the following clause:

> This arrangement is not entered into, nor is this memorandum written, as a formal or legal agreement, and shall not be subject to legal jurisdiction in the Law Courts either of the United States or England, but it is only a definite expression and record of the purpose and intention of the ... parties concerned to which they each honourably pledge themselves with the fullest confidence, based on past business with each other, that it will be carried through by each of the ... parties with mutual loyalty and friendly cooperation.

10.37 Bankes LJ, having pointed out that the opening clause of the document was worded 'to avoid the usual appearance of a contract', said that the language adopted 'at times is strongly suggestive of a contract, and at times indicates something other than a contract'.[112] He concluded that the honourable pledge clause was 'a genuine attempt by some one not a skilled draftsman to go much further than merely providing a means for ousting the jurisdiction of the Courts of law ... [and] it appears ... to admit of but one construction, which applies to and dominates the entire agreement'.[113]

10.38 Scrutton LJ described the whole agreement as being 'of great vagueness'.[114] In particular, he stated that an agreement that the defendants 'will, subject to unforeseen circumstances and contingencies do their best, as in the past, to respond efficiently and satisfactorily to the calls of Messrs Rose & Frank Co for deliveries both in quantity and quality' is 'not very helpful or precise'.[115] He disagreed with the reasoning of the trial judge who rejected the clause on the basis that it was repugnant to the rest of the agreement and to the extent that it excluded recourse to the courts was contrary to public policy. He concluded:[116]

> In my view the learned judge adopts a wrong canon of construction. He should not seek the intention of the parties as shown by the language they use in part of that language only, but in the whole of that language. It is true that in deeds and wills where it is impossible from the whole of the contradictory language used to ascertain the true intention of the framers, resort

---

[111] [1923] 2 KB 261. The House of Lords agreed with the reasoning of the Court of Appeal on this point (particularly the reasoning of Scrutton LJ) but reversed the decision of the majority on another point, see [1925] AC 445. See also *Boord v Boord* (1866) SALR 58.

[112] [1923] 2 KB 261, 283.

[113] [1923] 2 KB 261, 283.

[114] [1923] 2 KB 261, 286.

[115] [1923] 2 KB 261, 286–7.

[116] [1923] 2 KB 261, 287–9. See also [1925] AC 445, 454 ('I think the right answer was made by Scrutton LJ. It is true that when the tribunal has before it for construction an instrument which unquestionably creates a legal interest, and the dispute is only as to the quality and extent of that interest, then later repugnant clauses in the instrument cutting down that interest which the earlier part of it has given are to be rejected, but this doctrine does not apply when the question is whether it is intended to create any legal interest at all. Here, I think, the overriding clause in the document is that which provides that it is to be a contract of honour only and unenforceable at law.')

may be had … [to] … rejecting clauses as repugnant according to their place in the document … But before this heroic method is adopted of finding out what the parties meant by assuming that they did not mean part of what they have said, it must be clearly impossible to harmonize the whole of the language they have used …

… I can see no reason why, even in business matters, the parties should not intend to rely on each other's good faith and honour, and to exclude all idea of settling disputes by any outside intervention, with the accompanying necessity of expressing themselves so precisely that outsiders may have no difficulty in understanding what they mean. If they clearly express such an intention I can see no reason in public policy why effect should not be given to their intention …

… I come to the same conclusion as the learned judge, that the particular clause in question shows a clear intention by the parties that the rest of their arrangement or agreement shall not affect their legal relations, or be enforceable in a Court of law, but in the words of the clause, shall be 'only a definite expression and record of the purpose and intention of the three parties concerned to which they each honourably pledge themselves', 'and shall not be subject to legal jurisdiction'. If the clause stood first in the document, the intention of the parties would be exceedingly plain …

… I think the parties, in expressing their vague and loosely worded agreement or arrangement, have expressly stated their intention that it shall not give rise to legal relations, but shall depend only on mutual honourable trust.

Atkin LJ agreed concluding:[117]   **10.39**

In this document, construed as a whole, I find myself driven to the conclusion that the clause in question expresses in clear terms the mutual intention of the parties not to enter into legal obligations in respect to the matters upon which they are recording their agreement. I have never seen such a clause before, but I see nothing necessarily absurd in business men seeking to regulate their business relations by mutual promises which fall short of legal obligations, and rest on obligations of either honour or self-interest, or perhaps both. In this agreement I consider the clause a dominant clause, and not to be rejected, as the learned judge thought, on the ground of repugnancy.

I might add that a common instance of effect being given in law to the express intention of the parties not to be bound in law is to be found in cases where parties agree to all the necessary terms of an agreement for purchase and sale, but subject to a contract being drawn up. The words of the preliminary agreement in other respects may be apt and sufficient to constitute an open contract, but if the parties in so agreeing make it plain that they do not intend to be bound except by some subsequent document, they remain unbound though no further negotiation be contemplated. Either side is free to abandon the agreement and to refuse to assent to any legal obligation; when the parties are bound they are bound by virtue only of the subsequent document.

Another example is the American case of *Dunhill Securities Corporation v Microthermal*   **10.40**
Applications Inc.[118] Here the parties had come together in relation to a public offering of stock of the defendant. The plaintiff underwriter was attempting to recover for his services under the terms of a letter of intent which had been executed by the parties and which provided in paragraph 11:

Since this instrument consists only of an expression of our mutual intent, it is expressly understood that no liability or obligation of any nature whatsoever is intended to be created

---

[117] [1923] 2 KB 261, 293–4.
[118] 308 F Supp 195 (1969).

as between any of the parties hereto. This letter is not intended to constitute a binding agreement to consummate the financing outlined herein, nor an agreement to enter into an Underwriting Agreement. The parties propose to proceed promptly and in good faith to conclude the arrangements with respect to the proposed public offering and any legal obligations between the parties shall be only those set forth in the executed Underwriting Agreement. In the event that the Underwriting Agreement is not executed and/or the purchase of the securities is not consummated, we shall not be obligated for any expenses of the Company or for any charges or claims whatsoever arising out of this letter of intent or the proposed financing or otherwise and, similarly, the Company shall not be, in any way, obligated to us.

10.41   The plaintiff contended that the letter either constituted a binding agreement upon its execution, or was transformed into one by the subsequent action of the parties. In the alternative, the plaintiff sought recovery on a quantum meruit basis for services actually performed and expenses sustained pursuant to the letter. Lasker J held that the terms of the letter prevented the plaintiff from succeeding on either argument. The letter clearly expressed an intention that no legal obligation was to arise from its execution but only when an underwriting agreement was executed. One difficulty with the above reasoning is that if the letter of intent gave rise to no contractual rights and obligations, then how did it operate against the plaintiff as a contracting out of his restitutionary rights? Presumably it evidenced an intention that each party accepted the risk that a contract would not eventuate and they would not be remunerated. The reliance on this representation may then raise an estoppel preventing the plaintiff from pursuing a restitutionary claim.

10.42   A final example is *I H Rubenstein & Son Inc v The Sperry & Hutchinson Company*.[119] Here the plaintiffs alleged that the subject instrument contained the complete terms and conditions for the sale to the plaintiffs of a division of the defendants' company. Nevertheless, the court concluded that the document was no more than a letter of intent. This conclusion flowed from the final paragraph of the document which stated:

> It is expressly understood that this is a Letter of Intent and that no liability or obligation of any nature whatsoever is intended to be created between the parties hereto. This letter is not intended to constitute a binding agreement to consummate the transaction outlined herein, nor an agreement to enter into a final agreement. The parties propose to proceed promptly and in good faith to prepare a final agreement providing for the transaction contemplated herein. In the event that such final agreement is not executed, neither party shall have any obligation to the other for expenses or otherwise.

10.43   If the intention to exclude legal relations is not clearly expressed, the courts are likely to interpret any ambiguous drafting as not operating to have this effect. This simply reflects that the onus of rebutting the presumption is a heavy one. This is illustrated by the decision *Edwards v Skyways Ltd*.[120] In this case the defendant company, which employed the plaintiff as a pilot, gave the plaintiff three months' notice to terminate his employment. Under the terms of the company's pension fund the plaintiff was entitled to choose either to withdraw his personal total contributions to the fund or to take the right to a paid-up pension payable at the age of 50. The plaintiff chose the first option because of the company's

---

[119] 222 So 2d 329 (1969).
[120] [1964] 1 WLR 349. See also *Hanjin Shipping Co Ltd v Zenith Chartering Corporation (The Mercedes Envoy)* [1995] 2 Lloyd's Rep 559. Cf *Moir v JP Porter Co Ltd* (1979) 103 DLR (3d) 22.

promise to make him an 'ex gratia' payment equivalent to (or approximating to) the company's contributions to the fund. However, the company later refused to make the payment and argued that the words 'ex gratia' showed that there was no intention to create legal relations. Megaw J said that in a commercial or business agreement there was a heavy burden on the party seeking to rebut the presumption of an intention to create legal relations and that the company had not discharged this burden by using such words as 'ex gratia' payment.[121] He said that the words do not 'carry a necessary, or even a probable, implication that the agreement is to be without legal effect'.[122] He drew an analogy with a compromise of litigation which is often done on an 'ex gratia' or 'without admission' basis but which is intended to be binding.[123]

Other factors may also be relevant, such as whether steps must be taken to bring the existence of the clause to the notice of the other party, whether there is an industry practice, whether there have been acts of reliance and performance of the contract and whether there are conflicting provisions.[124] **10.44**

The requirement of notice may form part of the more general requirement to be clear. In **10.45** *Rose & Frank Co v JR Crompton & Bros Ltd*, Bankes LJ, in judging the legal effect of the agreement, took into consideration the position of the honourable pledge clause. He said: 'It would no doubt have simplified matters if the clause in question had been inserted at the head of the document, or even at the end, rather than in the position it occupies. I attribute its position to the want of that skill in drafting of which the document affords plenty of evidence, rather than to any want of bona fides in the language used.'[125] This suggests that if a document is drafted by one party and contains an honourable pledge clause, then that clause should appear in a position which will attract the other party's attention. More generally, there is a link between the requirement of an intention to contract and the need for communication of offers and acceptances. It is difficult to evidence an intention to contract if a resolution to make an offer is never communicated to the offeree.[126]

In *Jones v Vernon's Pools Ltd*,[127] a football pools coupon drafted by the football pools com- **10.46** pany contained an honourable pledge clause and Atkinson J held that this prevented the plaintiff from bringing any action relating to his coupon. The fact that the plaintiff admitted that the conditions on the coupon were well known to him appears to have been significant. Atkinson J stated that the plaintiff 'makes no suggestion that there is anything in those rules which misled him in any way, or that he could not understand them, or that there was anything ambiguous about them, or that he thought they meant anything

---

[121] [1964] 1 WLR 349, 355.
[122] [1964] 1 WLR 349, 356.
[123] The defendant sought to rely on extrinsic evidence to show that there was a common understanding between the parties that this was to be a true non-contractual ex gratia payment so as to avoid it being taxable. This too was rejected as there was no evidence this alleged common intention was important in the minds of all parties so as to rebut the presumption.
[124] See further Lücke, 'The Intention to Create Legal Relations' (1970) 3 Adel LR 419, 422.
[125] [1923] 2 KB 261, 283.
[126] Eg *Blair v Western Mutual* [1972] 4 WWR 284.
[127] [1938] 2 All ER 626. See further *Appleson v H Littlewood Ltd* [1939] 1 All ER 464; *Guest v Empire Pools Ltd* (1964) 108 SJ 98; *Ferguson v Littlewoods Pools* 1997 SLT 309.

different from what in fact they do'.[128] In addition, this clause appeared at the beginning of the document.

10.47   Lawyers are well versed in the requirement that to incorporate a term, where no signature exists, there must be reasonable notice of the term. It may be that where the presumption applies there must be reasonable notice of any provision expressly negating that presumption and what is reasonable may equate to the steps required to bring a clause, such as an exclusion clause, to the notice of the other party.[129] Indeed one commentator draws a direct analogy between these clauses and exclusion clauses.[130] What then follows if there is a signature? Generally, a party is bound by the terms in a document that he or she executes if the document is contractual in nature; in terms of notice all the person signing can expect is to have notice of the 'existence' of terms which will be made out if a document is contractual in nature so long as there has been no misrepresentation as to the nature of the document being signed.[131] This is not an issue that usually arises with executed documents but we can see this idea in the ticket cases where the taking of a ticket is akin to the signing of a document where the contract is in writing.[132] If a person takes a ticket knowing it has writing on it but not knowing that writing refers to terms then they are still bound if a reasonable person in their position would know of the *existence* of terms in the document. Note there need not be reasonable notice of the terms, only their existence.[133] This goes to the very nature of the document, a reasonable person taking a ticket can legitimately expect to at least be on notice of the contractual nature of the document before they are bound. In the matter at hand that is exactly the issue albeit its mirror image, the presence of terms clearly evidences its otherwise contractual nature but the incorporation of such a clause seeks to negate what would otherwise be its nature and the party who is not responsible for its drafting may expect any such clause would be brought to their attention.

10.48   As noted above, in construing such expressions, the customs and practices of a particular industry must not be overlooked as part of the matrix of facts taken into account in construing the document. Lasker J in *Dunhill Securities Corporation v Microthermal Applications Inc*,[134] made this point in the following manner: 'A letter of intent is a customary device used within the financial community, and it is clear that the financial community does not regard such a document as a binding agreement, but rather, an expression of tentative intentions of the parties.'[135]

---

[128] [1938] 2 All ER 626, 629.

[129] See further Uniform Commercial Code 2-316(2) and 1-201(10).

[130] Smith, *Atiyah's Introduction to the Law of Contract*, (6th edn, OUP, Oxford, 2005) 99–100.

[131] See *Webster v Higgin* [1948] 2 All ER 127, 128.

[132] Alternatively the ticket case rules merely restate what generally constitutes reasonable notice in such circumstances.

[133] There is now an overriding requirement of reasonable notice of terms where the terms sought to be incorporated are particularly harsh, see *Thornton v Shoe Lane Parking Ltd* [1971] 2 QB 163; *Interfoto Picture Library Ltd v Stiletto Visual Programmes Ltd* [1989] QB 433.

[134] 308 F Supp 195 (1969). See also *County Ltd v Girozentrale Securities* [1996] 3 All ER 834, 837.

[135] 308 F Supp 195, 198 (1969). See further Holmes, 'The Freedom Not to Contract' (1986) 60 Tulane L Rev 751, 779.

It has also been emphasized in a number of cases that the court can take into account the **10.49** conduct of the parties to determine whether a contract was in fact contemplated.[136] Where a party acts in performance of an alleged contract it will be more difficult for the party relying on the provision ousting an intention to contract. Indeed, the presumption that the parties did intend to contract is perhaps at its highest when the contract is executed. It follows that if the terms agreed upon have been performed the courts are likely to find that a contract has been formed. For example, in *Garner v Boyd*,[137] negotiations were entered into between the defendant, Boyd, and the executive vice-president of the United American Industries Inc of Tucson, Arizona. These negotiations were formalized by a letter of intent, whereby it was agreed to exchange the absolute ownership of United's American Milling & Manufacturing Co for 1,733,333 shares of the capital stock of United American Industries Inc. Although the parties subsequently entered into a letter of rescission cancelling the letter of intent, the stock of the Arizona Corporation was actually delivered to Boyd.

Woodward J held as follows:[138]   **10.50**

> A true letter of intent is customarily employed to reduce to writing a preliminary understanding of the parties ... In this instance, the minds of the parties had met upon all the essential elements of a contract, and the acts to be performed were clear and unambiguous. So clear were they that all the contemplated acts were indeed performed.

It is interesting to note that whilst the House of Lords in *Rose & Frank Co v JR Crompton &* **10.51** *Bros Ltd*[139] agreed with the Court of Appeal concerning the effect of the honour clause on the agency agreement, the House of Lords considered that the orders which had been accepted had to be fulfilled since when each order was accepted it constituted a new separate contract. Clearly there is a concern to hold parties to their obligations under an executed agreement even though in this case there was no contractual obligation to order or to accept orders.[140]

As regards ambiguous provisions, Lücke, in noting that resort may be made to extrinsic **10.52** evidence, points out that 'the Courts have felt free to ignore such clauses when their meaning is hidden or obscure'.[141] He gives the example of *Ellison v Bignold*.[142] In this case a clause in a deed stated that the parties, 'resolved and agreed and did by way of declaration and not of covenant, spontaneously and fully consent and agree'. Lord Eldon construed the

---

[136] *Kleinwort Benson Ltd v Malaysia Mining Corp Berhad* [1989] 1 WLR 379, 383.

[137] 330 F Supp 22 (1970) (affirmed 447 F 2d 1373 (1971)). Cf *British Steel Corporation v Cleveland Bridge & Engineering Co Ltd* [1984] 1 All ER 504.

[138] 330 F Supp 22, 25–6 (1970) (affirmed 447 F 2d 1373 (1971)). See further, Holmes, 'The Freedom Not to Contract' (1986) 60 Tulane L Rev 751, 781–2, pointing out that the court does not reproduce the language of the letter of intent in this case and therefore it is not clear whether there was an honour clause. However, Holmes believes that in any event this would not have affected the outcome on the basis that such provisions are only significant while the agreement remains executory.

[139] [1925] AC 445.

[140] The fact of performance may also give rise to restitutionary remedies, see eg *British Steel Corporation v Cleveland Bridge & Engineering Co Ltd* [1984] 1 All ER 504 (commercial context) and *Stinchcombe v Thomas* [1957] VR 509 (social context). See further Mason, Carter and Tolhurst, *Restitution Law in Australia* (2nd edn, Butterworths, Sydney, 2007) Ch 10.

[141] Lücke, 'The Intention to Create Legal Relations' (1970) 3 Adel LR 419, 421.

[142] (1821) 2 Jac & W 503, 37 ER 720.

document 'laying aside the nonsense about agreeing and declaring without covenanting'.[143] Although this case involved a deed, it is necessary for each clause to be read in context and generally, where most of the agreement suggests an intention to contract and the parties have conducted themselves as if there is a contract, then an ambiguous clause which may on one reading suggest otherwise can be ignored. Either the parties intended to immediately contract all along despite the clause or have otherwise entered into a contract by conduct on those agreed terms. As the cases discussed earlier show, where the meaning of the clause is clear then despite the rest of the transaction appearing like a fully negotiated contract, effect will be given to the clause if it is construed to represent the true intention of the parties.

10.53   Perhaps underlying many decisions on such clauses, and implicit in decisions requiring notice of such provisions and the taking into account of trade custom as well as acts in performance and reliance are a number of policy-based considerations. These may work for or against either party depending on the facts. In *Jones v Vernon's Pools Ltd*[144] Atkinson J upheld a provision negating legal intent and emphasized the practical effect of him coming to a different conclusion. He said: 'Just imagine what it would mean if half the people in the country could come forward and suddenly claim that they had posted and sent in a coupon which they never had, bring actions against the pool alleging that, and calling evidence to prove they had sent in a coupon containing the list of winning teams. The business could not be carried on a day on terms of that kind.'[145] Holmes[146] in his discussion of the decision in the *Dunhill* case suggests that the expressed intent was only one of the factors influencing the decision. The other factors were, first, that there had been little performance so that the relationship was executory and consequently there was not the inducement to create a contractual intent that can be said to exist in executed cases. In addition, it was clear from the use of such documents within the industry that the underwriter could not reasonably have believed there to be a binding commitment. He concluded that, given these factors, 'the court might have reached the same result even absent the no-binding-effect clause' because reliance on the document would be unreasonable.[147]

10.54   More often policy will work against the party relying on such a clause, particularly when the document is a standard form contract drafted by one party. That this is so is reflected in the requirement that the clause be conspicuous, which was discussed above.[148] Waddams has suggested some doubt as to the effect of such a clause in a case where it is 'unexpectedly lurking in the fine print of a standard form contractual document'.[149] Some commentators

143 (1821) 2 Jac & W 503, 510, 510, 37 ER 720, 723. See also *Trustees Executors & Agency Co Ltd v Peters* (1959) 102 CLR 537, 545.
144 [1938] 2 All ER 626.
145 [1938] 2 All ER 626, 630.
146 Holmes, 'The Freedom Not to Contract' (1986) 60 Tulane L Rev 751, 779.
147 Holmes, 'The Freedom Not to Contract' (1986) 60 Tulane L Rev 751, 779.
148 See 10.45.
149 Waddams, *The Law of Contracts* (5th edn, Canada Law Book, Toronto, 2005) para 148. Waddams suggests that in such a case the court might take account of the promisor's conduct as well as the oral and written expressions in order to find a promise on which the promisee might reasonably rely. Alternatively, in his opinion, the court might attack the clause on the basis of unconscionability. See also McCamus, *The Law of Contracts* (Irwin Law, Toronto, 2005), 115.

believe that at least where the parties are not of equal bargaining power, such a provision should be dealt with in the same manner that exclusion clauses are construed.[150] Holmes has identified a number of American cases in the employment context involving promises of pensions and death benefits with clauses much clearer than that in *Edwards v Skyways Ltd* negating contractual intent, where the courts have nevertheless found reasons for restricting the operation of the clause or otherwise ignoring it.[151] The latter *contra proferentem* technique being used if the contract is drawn up by the party relying on the clause to avoid contractual obligations and if the court can find conflicting clauses, some expressing an intention to contract and others negating that intention. Acceptance of that technique appears in section 21 of the Restatement (2d) Contracts. As noted earlier,[152] that section provides:

> Neither real nor apparent intention that a promise be legally binding is essential to the formation of a contract, but a manifestation of intention that a promise shall not affect legal relations may prevent the formation of a contract.[153]

Comment *b* to this section recognizes that such provisions may give rise to difficult questions of construction. The comment refers specifically to the fact that such a manifestation 'may mean that no bargain has been reached, or that a particular manifestation of intention is not a promise', 'it may reserve a power to revoke or terminate a promise under certain circumstances but not others'. The comment then goes on to state: 'In a written document prepared by one party it may raise a question of misrepresentation or mistake or overreaching; to avoid such questions it may be read against the party who prepared it'. Lasker J also made this point in *Dunhill Securities Corporation v Microthermal Applications Inc*[154] where he stated: 'In passing, it may be noted that the letter of intent ... was drafted by the plaintiff, and if any ambiguity arises—although none does—it is to be construed against the plaintiff.'[155]   **10.55**

Perhaps the use of this technique in this context may be seen in England in the decision in *J H Milner & Son v Percy Bilton Ltd*.[156] Here negotiations were in progress between the defendants and the Bombergs, for whom the plaintiff solicitors had acted for many years, concerning a joint venture between the defendants and the Bombergs involving the development and leasing of certain property. On 11 March 1959, the plaintiffs wrote a letter to the defendants confirming the basis of agreement between the defendants and the Bombergs. The letter included the following paragraph: 'May we please take this opportunity of placing on record the understanding that all the legal work of and incidental to the completion of the development and the grant of the leases shall be carried out by us.' The defendants' reply included the following: 'I see that you have tied up the legal work and, of   **10.56**

---

[150] Smith, Atiyah's, *Introduction to the Law of Contract* (6th edn, 2005) at 99–100.
[151] Holmes, 'The Freedom Not to Contract' (1986) 60 Tulane L Rev 751, 757–70. Cf *Moir v JP Porter Co Ltd* (1979) 103 DLR (3d) 22.
[152] See n 16.
[153] See Klass, 'Intent to Contract' (2009) 95 Virginia Law Rev 1437.
[154] 308 F Supp 195 (1969).
[155] 308 F Supp 195, 197 (1969).
[156] [1966] 1 WLR 1582.

course, it has never been agreed and I do not like tying it up unless it has been agreed. I am quite prepared, however, to accept it in relation to this particular property.'

10.57 Three years later, the defendants wrote to the plaintiffs saying that they had established their own legal department and would not be instructing the plaintiffs. The question was whether the letters of March 1959 amounted to a binding legal contract to employ the plaintiffs. Fenton Atkinson J held that they did not and construed the document against the drafter:[157]

> This [the plaintiffs' letter of 11 March] is a letter being written by a solicitor to a layman, a prospective client, at a time when there is no existing agreement between them whatever for employment in legal business nor any understanding whatever between them to that effect; but the solicitor is clearly seeing the chance of some very profitable legal business for his firm and is anxious to obtain it ... If he had said in that letter:
>
> > 'We offer to enter into a binding legal contract and do all the legal work of and incidental to the completion of the development and the grant of the leases and furthermore you will appreciate that it will be a term of that contract that you cannot thereafter dispense with our services until all the work is completed, however long that may take.'
>
> I should have thought that it was quite plain that the defendants would not have agreed and equally plain that Mr Lyon [Milner & Son] knew this, or at least had a very shrewd suspicion to that effect, and it appears to me that he quite deliberately used this somewhat vague and equivocal language in his letter and that he did so on this basis: that if that was accepted ... he, Mr Lyon, reckoned that he would then have an agreement in his pocket ... If, instead of using the vague word 'understanding', he had said, 'We understand it is your present intention to instruct us as and when matters arise', and Mr Bilton had accepted that, clearly there would have been no legal claim arising when the defendants decided to make other arrangements, and in my judgment that was in truth the result of these letters.

B. Letter of Comfort[158]

10.58 Often when a bank is approached for finance by a subsidiary of a large company, any initial offer of finance will be subject to security being provided by the parent company. Where the parent company is not prepared to provide security, it may provide the bank with a letter of comfort.[159] Very often these letters are relied upon by banks to then finance the subsidiary.[160]

10.59 There would appear to be three principal forms such letters may take. The first type acknowledges the subsidiary's loan application and states that it is the policy of the parent company to ensure that its subsidiaries meet their loan obligations. The second type

---

[157] [1966] 1 WLR 1582, 1586.

[158] See also 7.52ff.

[159] This is not the only relationship in which comfort letters may be given, eg *Lasalle Bank National Association v Citicorp Real Estate Inc* US Dist LEXIS 15069 (2003) (comfort letter given by franchisor to secure finance to franchisee).

[160] For an outline of the reasons why a company would give such a letter and why a bank would lend on the basis of such a letter, see Thai, 'Comfort Letters—A Fresh Look?' (2006) 17 Journal of Banking Finance Law and Practice 15, 16–17. See also Szathmary, 'Letters of Responsibility' (1978) 6(3) International Business Lawyer 288, 289.

acknowledges the subsidiary's loan application and states that it intends to maintain its shareholding in the subsidiary. The third type simply acknowledges the loan application.[161] Often a letter of comfort will contain more than one of these elements and in many cases all; today they might best be described as the three usual components of a letter of comfort.

If a bank lends on the basis of a such a letter, then if the borrower defaults on the loan, the **10.60** bank may wish to enforce the comfort letter against the parent company if it contains an undertaking and if that undertaking has not been complied with.[162] In some cases it may be the borrower who seeks to enforce the letter against the parent.[163] In either case, the ability to enforce the letter will depend on whether it has contractual force.[164]

The leading English authority is the decision of the Court of Appeal in *Kleinwort Benson* **10.61** *Ltd v Malaysia Mining Corp Bhd*.[165] In this case, the defendant parent company had issued a 'Letter of Comfort' which stated 'it is our policy to ensure that the business of [the subsidiary company] is at all times in a position to meet its liabilities to you [under the loan agreement]'. The letter included a statement by the parent company that stated, 'We confirm that we will not reduce our current financial interest [in the subsidiary]'. It was accepted that this latter statement was contractual in effect. Moreover, the letter contained a statement acknowledging the application for finance and approved that application. When the subsidiary became insolvent the plaintiff bank claimed that the defendant should cover the subsidiary's indebtedness to them in accordance with the statement of 'policy' in the comfort letter.

---

[161] See Tyree, 'Southern Comfort' (1990) 2 JCL 279. See also Thai, 'Comfort Letters—A Fresh Look?' (2006) 17 Journal of Banking Finance Law and Practice 15, 16 adding a fourth category in which the letter provider undertakes to notify the financier if the borrower breaches any agreement it has with the letter provider. See further Szathmary, 'Letters of Responsibility' (1978) 6(3) International Business Lawyer 288, 290 setting out five categories and see DiMatteo and Sacasas, 'Credit and Value Comfort Instruments: Crossing the Line from Assurance to Legally Significant Reliance and Toward and Theory of Enforceability' (1994) 47 Baylor Law Review 357, 361–4.

[162] If the letter does not have contractual force the law in a particular jurisdiction may still allow for some other action such as one based on misrepresentation. Recourse may in some jurisdictions be had to statute, eg Trade Practices Act 1974 (Cth), s 52 (prohibition against misleading and deceptive conduct).

[163] See *Gate Gourmet Australia Pty Ltd v Gate Gourmet Holding AG* [2004] NSWSC 149.

[164] In the United States there appears to be a general presumption against enforceability but legal liability may arise under reliance principles, see DiMatteo and Sacasas, 'Credit and Value Comfort Instruments: Crossing the Line from Assurance to Legally Significant Reliance and Toward and Theory of Enforceability' (1994) 47 Baylor Law Review 357. For accounts of approaches taken to such instruments in various jurisdictions, see Szathmary, 'Letters of Responsibility' (1978) 6(3) International Business Lawyer 288; Franken, 'The Force of Comfort Letters Under German Law' (1985) 6(4) International Financial Law Review 14; Davidson, Wohl and Daniel, 'Comfort Letters Under French, English and American Law' (1992) 3 Journal of Banking Finance Law and Practice 3; DiMatteo and Sacasas, 'Credit and Value Comfort Instruments: Crossing the Line from Assurance to Legally Significant Reliance and Toward and Theory of Enforceability' (1994) 47 Baylor Law Review 357; Bernstein and Zekoll, 'The Gentleman's Agreement in Legal Theory and Modern Practice' (1998) 46 Am Jnl Comp Law, 87, 97; Thai, 'Comfort Letters—A Fresh Look?' (2006) 17 Journal of Banking Finance Law and Practice 15; Lipton, 'Good faith and Letters of Comfort' (1999) 28 UWALR 138.

[165] [1989] 1 WLR 379.

10.62   Hirst J, at first instance,[166] was of the view that it was crystal clear that the letter encapsulated an undertaking to ensure the debtor was able to meet its liabilities.[167] As regards intention to contract, in his view, this was a commercial transaction which attracted the presumption that the parties intend to contract and that the party wishing to rebut that presumption carried a heavy onus. He held that the presumption had not been rebutted. He noted in his reasons the reliance by the financier on the letter and the fact that the letter was authorized by a resolution of the board of the defendant.

10.63   The Court of Appeal reversed Hirst J's decision and held that the presumption did not apply because the relevant part of the letter did not contain a promise. In their view it is necessary for an agreement to first contain a promise before the presumption is attracted. Here the letter merely stated a present fact, it did not contain a promise of future conduct. That is, the words in question were a statement of current policy and did not amount to a promise to abide by this statement of policy. In reaching the decision that the letter did not contain a promise, the court did not merely rely on the words in the document but took into account the relevant factual matrix. In this case that included statements by the parent company to the bank that it would not accept joint and several liability for the loan to its subsidiary and that it did not wish to provide a guarantee but could provide a letter of comfort. Therefore, the bank was on notice that the parent did not wish to accept liability and in response the bank said that the letter of comfort would not be a problem but the bank would charge a higher commission rate to cover for the fact that it was not receiving a guarantee; thus, the bank had taken into account the risk.[168] In addition, the court engaged in a very detailed contextual analysis of the subject clause concluding that if it was interpreted as a promise then that would rob the other clauses which approved the application for finance and confirmed the parent's continued shareholding in the subsidiary of any purpose. The court also envisaged the use of the *contra proferentem* rule here on the basis that if the bank wanted a promise from the parent then as experienced bankers they should have drafted the clause in such terms. It should be noted that the bank drafted the letter of comfort and although the parent made some changes to it, neither the original version nor the later version ever contained the promise the bank was now arguing for.

10.64   There can be little doubt that if a document alleged to be a contract does not contain a promise, either express or implied, then it cannot be a contract and there are numerous cases concerning letters of comfort which, following *Kleinwort Benson*, have concluded that the letter fails because it does not contain a promise.[169] The leading Australian case,

---

[166] [1988] 1 WLR 799. See also *Chemco Leasing SpA v Rediffusion plc* [1987] 1 FTLR 201. See further Brown, 'The Letter of Comfort: Placebo or Promise?' [1990] JBL 281.

[167] [1988] 1 WLR 799, 811.

[168] Cf Brown, 'The Letter of Comfort: Placebo or Promise?' [1990] JBL 281, 284 ('The extra commission is, however, concomitant with the greater risk of a contractual claim as opposed to a claim under a guarantee for a liquidated sum.').

[169] Eg *Toronto-Dominion Bank v Leigh Instruments Ltd* (1988) 40 BLR (2d) 1 (affirmed 178 DLR (4th) 634); *Re Atlantic Computers plc* [1995] BCC 696; *Commonwealth Bank of Australia v TLI Management Pty Ltd* [1990] VR 510; *Australian European Finance Corp Ltd v Sheahan* (1993) 60 SASR 187. Cf *Bank of New Zealand v Ginivan* [1991] 1 NZLR 178 (here the court distinguished the letter of comfort before the court from that in *Kleinwort Benson* on the basis that it did not merely declare a position of policy, there was an

Banque Brussels Lambert v Australian National Industries Ltd,[170] while not calling that doctrinal point into question, did criticize the manner in which the English Court of Appeal went about determining whether the letter contained a promise. In this case, the financier required reassurance from the debtor's principal shareholder before it would make a line of credit available. The final form of the letter of comfort provided stated:

> We confirm that we are aware of the eurocurrency facility of US$ 5million which your Bank has granted to Spedley Securities Limited, which is a wholly-owned subsidiary of Spedley Holdings Limited.

> We acknowledge that the terms and conditions of the arrangements have been accepted with our knowledge and consent and state that it would not be our intention to reduce our shareholding in Spedley Holdings Limited from the current level of 45% during the currency of this facility. We would, however, provide your Bank with ninety (90) days notice of any subsequent decisions taken by us to dispose of this shareholding, and furthermore we acknowledge that, should any such notice be served on your Bank, you reserve the right to call for the repayment of all outstanding loans within thirty (30) days.

> We take this opportunity to confirm that it is our practice to ensure that our affiliate Spedley Securities Limited, will at all times be in a position to meet its financial obligation as they fall due. These financial obligations include repayment of all loans made by your Bank under the arrangements mentioned in this letter.

In due course the defendant did sell its shareholding without giving the appropriate notice **10.65** and did not ensure that the debtor was in a position to meet it financial obligations. The plaintiff then sought damages for breach of contract by the defendant. Rogers CJ determined that this letter, when read in light of the surrounding circumstances, in particular, the negotiations that led to this final version, did contain enforceable contractual promises. He saw the issue as turning on whether there was an intention to create legal relations and whether the terms were sufficiently promissory in nature. He said these were independent but related issues 'in that it is from the terms of the letter seen against the backdrop of surrounding circumstances that the parties' intention in both respects fall to be determined'.[171] When determining whether there was an intention to contract he noted that the whole reason for the financier being involved in the negotiations leading up to this letter was that it wanted some commitment and security to be given by the shareholder. The mere fact that the shareholder made it clear that it did not want to give a guarantee was not inconsistent with there being an intention to contract in respect to any promises given in the letter which would not make the shareholder liable for the debt but rather liable in damages.[172] When turning to discussing the presumption, he, at the same time, commenced his

---

undertaking by the holding company to use it best endeavours to see that the subsidiary would conduct its affairs in a responsible manner, maintain a sound financial condition and promptly meet its obligations).

[170] (1989) 21 NSWLR 502. Other cases where letters have been upheld include, *Gate Gourmet Australia Pty Ltd v Gate Gourmet Holding AG* [2004] NSWSC 149; *Bank of New Zealand v Ginivan* [1991] 1 NZLR 178. See also *Newtronics Pty Ltd v Atco Controls Pty Ltd* [2008] VSC 566. Cf *Hongkong & Shanghai Banking Corp Ltd v Jurong Engineering Ltd* [2000] 2 SLR 54.
[171] (1989) 21 NSWLR 502, 521.
[172] (1989) 21 NSWLR 502, 521–2. Query though the fact that liability under a guarantee is a liability to pay damages.

discussion as to whether the letter contained a promise. It is at this point his criticism of the reasoning in *Kleinwort Benson* began. In an important passage he said:[173]

> There should be no room in the proper flow of commerce for some purgatory where statements made by businessmen, after hard bargaining and made to induce another business person to enter into a business transaction would, without any express statement to that effect, reside in a twilight zone of merely honourable engagement. The whole thrust of the law today is to attempt to give proper effect to commercial transactions. It is for this reason that uncertainty, a concept so much loved by lawyers, has fallen into disfavour as a tool for striking down commercial bargains. If the statements are appropriately promissory in character, courts should enforce them when they are uttered in the course of business and there is no clear indication that they are not intended to be legally enforceable.

> If I may say, the judgments of Hirst J, at first instance in *Kleinwort Benson* [1988] 1 WLR 799; [1988] 1 All ER 714 and (Staughton J, whose unreported judgment in *Chemco Leasing SpA v Redifusion Plc* Staughton J, 19 July 1985, unreported) is extensively referred to by Hirst J, reflect the bias of experienced commercial judges to pay high regard to the fact that the comfort letters in issue before them came into existence as part and parcel of a commercial banking transaction and that the promises were an important feature of the letters.

> In the Court of Appeal in *Kleinwort Benson*, Ralph Gibson LJ held the principle in *Edwards v Skyways Ltd* inapplicable, saying that the presumption of intention only became significant when the words of the agreement were clearly promissory. The Court of Appeal pointed that, in a sense, the trial judge had been asked the incorrect question. The parties had conceded that one of the statements in the letter was a contractual promise and intended to have legal effect (at 790). The true question therefore was whether the statement sued upon was promissory in character. It was to this question that the Court of Appeal returned a negative answer.

> The Court of Appeal subjected the letters to minute textual analysis. Courts will become irrelevant in the resolution of commercial disputes if they allow this approach to dominate their consideration of commercial documents.

> Probably at the heart of the judgment delivered by Ralph Gibson LJ is the statement (at 792):

>> '... In my judgment, the defendants made a statement as to what their policy was, and did not in paragraph 3 of the comfort letters expressly promise that such policy would be continued in future.'

> That construction of the letter renders the document a scrap of paper. If the Lord Justice is correct, the writer has not expressed itself on anything relevant as a matter of honour.

10.66 After this statement Rogers CJ carried out, with respect, a very detailed contextual analysis of the letter and determined that it did contain contractual promises, one in relation to the maintaining of the shareholding, one as regards the notice provision and another as regards the shareholder's practice to ensure the debtor is in a position to meet its financial commitments.

10.67 A couple of points can be made about the supposed difference of approach in these cases. First, if an alleged agreement does not contain a promise then it cannot be a contract. Any discussion as to whether the presumption of an intention to contract applies in such a case because the parties are commercial parties is pointless and misplaced. Second, once it is

---

[173] (1989) 21 NSWLR 502, 523. See further Bernstein and Zekoll, 'The Gentleman's Agreement in Legal Theory and Modern Practice' (1998) 46 Am Jnl Comp Law, 87, 97.

determined the agreement contains a promise and it involves a commercial deal then it is suggested the presumption does apply. The decisions in *Kleinwort Benson* and *Banque Brussels* are *ad idem* on these two points. Third, whether or not a document does or does not contain a promise is a matter that opinions can and will legitimately differ on when the position is not clear. In deciding that issue courts will inevitably be compelled to look at the subject clause in context and both judgments engage in that contextual analysis. Moreover, both judgments, in deciding this issue, took into account what they thought was the appropriate factual matrix. All this is in line with general principles of construction.

There is therefore not much of a difference in approach in the judgments in these two cases **10.68** when it comes to the actual decision-making process.[174] There are, however, two further points to note. First, the court in *Kleinwort Benson* did suggest that in an appropriate case the document might be construed against the party drafting it. Rogers CJ does not directly comment on that point but one needs to try and make some sense of his criticism of the decision in *Kleinwort Benson*. As noted above, he was of the view that one must keep in mind that a court should strive to give effect to commercial transactions and recognize that these letters form an important part of financing transactions. That comment itself may suggest that he was against an application of the *contra proferentem* rule in this context. But strictly those comments were aimed at addressing the issue of intention to contract which, as he noted, was a separate issue from that of determining whether the letter contained a promise. But in that same passage he criticized the Court of Appeal in *Kleinwort Benson* for its minute contextual approach. So perhaps here he did merge the two issues and arguably this does, in the end, suggest that he would not be in favour of applying that rule of construction. But it still remains to determine whether this criticism was well founded. As noted, in the result, both courts carried out a contextual construction of the document in question and both looked at the factual matrix. Indeed, the differences in the results of the cases seem entirely correct given the different factual contexts. With respect there is nothing to suggest the English Court of Appeal was in any way ignoring the factual realities of the case before them, but they were dealing only with the facts before the court and this was entirely appropriate.[175] They were not dealing with a standard contract that is uniform within an industry where it may be relevant to take evidence of how the industry approaches those documents.[176] Therefore, it is suggested the criticism levelled at the decision by Rogers CJ was, with respect, misplaced.[177]

---

[174] See further McCamus, *The Law of Contracts* (Irwin Law, Toronto, 2005) 123–4; Burrows, Finn and Todd, *Law of Contract in New Zealand* (3rd edn, LexisNexis NZ Ltd, Wellington, 2007) para 5.4.2.

[175] It can certainly be argued that the court should have put more weight on those factors that the trial judge thought important (see above) but such a difference of opinion does not mean the court made an error of doctrine, see further Brown, 'The Letter of Comfort: Placebo or Promise?' [1990] JBL 281, 284.

[176] Cf *Beconwood Securities Pty Ltd v Australia and New Zealand Banking Group Limited* [2008] FCA 594.

[177] See further Giliker, 'Taking Comfort in Certainty: to Enforce or not to Enforce the Letter of Comfort' [2004] LMCLQ 219.

11

CERTAINTY AND COMPLETENESS

A. Introduction

Formation and the relevance of certainty and completeness

A contract is said to be void if it is uncertain or incomplete. Though true, this statement **11.01** hides more than it reveals. Initially issues regarding certainty and completeness are concerned with the certainty and completeness of the terms and promises contained in a contract. If a term is uncertain or incomplete then that term will be void. Whether or not such a void term will have the effect of avoiding the entire contract for uncertainty or incompleteness is the question that then follows that initial finding.[1] This latter issue is one of severance and turns on the intention of the parties. In rare cases even though it might be possible to give meaning to all the agreed terms, a transaction may still be held to be void for uncertainty or incompleteness.

Even the statement that for a contract to exist its *terms* must be certain and complete hides **11.02** much complexity. The statement assumes that any issues about certainty and completeness concern the 'terms' of a contract. Therefore, it appears to be an issue that is addressed after any issues as to whether or not the statements alleged to form the contract are or are not terms are decided. For a promissory term to be part of a contract the maker must guarantee

---

[1] *Life Insurance Co of Australia Ltd v Phillips* (1925) 36 CLR 60, 72 See also *Whitlock v Brew* (1968) 118 CLR 445, 461; *Prints for Pleasure Ltd v Oswald-Sealy (Overseas) Ltd* [1968] 3 NSWR 761.

its truth; this is determined from the position of a reasonable person in the position of the promisee. For other statements to become terms they must be incorporated by writing, notice or reference. However, arguably under the objective theory of contract there can be no legal agreement unless the terms are certain and complete. Without sufficient certainty and completeness there can be no meeting of the minds.[2] Thus, an 'offer' that is uncertain or incomplete is not an offer at all under the objective theory.[3] The objective theory does not entirely discount subjective intention.[4] For example, if it can be shown that the parties knew the meaning of a term that a reasonable person would have trouble understanding then the meaning attributed to it by the parties must prevail.[5] But it is not sufficient that one party knew the other party intended a term to have a particular meaning for it to have that meaning. It is necessary for the parties to have agreed that it have that meaning. Once a term is recognized as being incorporated into the contract it is taken to represent the intention of both parties and must be construed as such.[6]

11.03   There is a distinction between uncertainty and incompleteness although, on any given set of facts, a term or a contract can be void for both.[7] The requirement of certainty dictates that it must be possible to attribute meaning to the agreed terms. The need for a contract to be complete dictates that there must be agreement on all the essential terms of a contract. Completeness does not require the parties to have expressly dealt with every eventuality.[8] If it did there would be no need for the institution of the implied term or the doctrine of frustration. The modern approach is to leave it to the parties to determine what are the important terms.[9] The court generally does not concern itself with whether or not it thinks

---

[2] *G Scammell and Nephew Ltd v HC & JG Ouston* [1941] AC 251, 255.

[3] Thus, an offer is generally defined in terms of a statement which evidences an intention to contract on 'certain' terms without further negotiation. Of course if one read 'certain' here as meaning 'specific' rather than 'clear and understood by a reasonable person in the position of the parties', then it is possible to legitimately hold that an agreement has been reached which is then later held void for uncertainty. Some commentators prefer such a definition of an offer, see eg, Peel, *Treitel: The Law of Contract* (12th edn, Thomson, Sweet & Maxwell, London, 2007), para 2-002.n The latter approach does have the advantage that it easily allows for the need for certainty to be made out when the time for performance arrives rather than at the moment of formation, see *Greater London Council v Connolly* [1970] 2 QB 100, 109, see nn 58, 295. This then allows courts to respect the reality that in some contracts it is not possible to work out all the terms at the time of contract. However, this also results in certainty being more relevant to performance than formation except perhaps when it evidences a lack of an intention to contract. See further Farnsworth, *Farnsworth on Contracts* (3rd edn, Vol 1, Aspen Publishers, New York, 2004), § 3.27, p 418.

[4] See 1.09.

[5] *Bloom v Averbach* [1927] SCR 615, 3 DLR 721; *Kell v Harris* (1915) 15 SR (NSW) 473, 479; *Cameron v Wiggins* [1901] 1 KB 1. See also *Bank of New Zealand v Simpson* [1900] AC 182, 187.

[6] *Kell v Harris* (1915) 15 SR (NSW) 473.

[7] Eg *Whitlock v Brew* (1968) 118 CLR 445 (sale and lease back arrangement; the lease was to be 'upon such terms as commonly govern such a lease'; in addition to the uncertain and incomplete nature of that provision—there being no such external standard—the transaction was also incomplete as the parties had not agreed to the term of the lease or the rent payable); *G Scammell & Nephew Ltd v Ouston* [1941] AC 251 (sale 'on hire-purchase' terms uncertain as no standard terms existed and also incomplete, moreover, as the clause necessitated further agreement the contract was also void as an agreement to agree). See also Waddams, *The Law of Contracts* (5th edn, Canada Law Book, 2005), para 57.

[8] *Global Container Lines Ltd v State Black Sea Shipping Co* [1999] 1 Lloyd's Rep 127, 155–7.

[9] *Pagnan SpA v Feed products Ltd* [1987] 2 Lloyd's Rep 601, 619. See also *Broadcasting Corporation v XIVth Commonwealth Games Ltd* (1988) 18 NSWLR 540, 548 ('In many cases … there is a need for evidence in one form or another as to what subjects would be regarded as requiring agreement between the parties. *In this case the best evidence on that subject is to be found in the actual communications between the parties and, in particular, in the issues which they in fact addressed when they set about drafting their detailed contract.*') emphasis added.

the parties have agreed all the 'important' terms. The perspective in determining whether the parties have reached that point of agreeing the 'important' terms is that of a reasonable person in the position of the parties. It follows that the type of contract before the court will be a relevant matter.[10] In addition, the courts must exercise an overriding control of issues of certainty and completeness according to law. No matter what the parties may have agreed if a court cannot give it meaning in the sense of being able to enforce the contract by fashioning an appropriate remedy then the transaction or the term must necessarily be uncertain or incomplete. It is therefore necessary for there to be agreement on those terms required to enforce the contract. These may be called 'essential' terms but that word is ambiguous and may also be used to express those terms the parties think important.[11] Generally, what is essential in this enforcement sense will depend on the facts of the particular transaction but agreement (express or implied) on the parties and subject matter (which usually includes the price) are the basic essential terms for any contract.[12]

In matters of uncertainty and incompleteness, the onus of proof will lie with the party who raises the issue.[13] The resolution of some issue of uncertainty or incompleteness will often involve the application of contract law 'gap-filling' techniques. In addition, issues of uncertainty are often dealt with by interpreting and giving meaning to agreed terms and to this extent it is often said that whether or not a term of a contract is uncertain or incomplete is an issue of construction.[14] Similarly issues of incompleteness are initially dealt with by construction as this is the process that identifies any gap in the contract, but it can also be used to fill perceived gaps. Issues of construction are said to be issues of law rather than of fact.[15] Where an issue is one of construction, this necessarily means that the evidence available to determine meaning is governed by the principles of construction which limit the extent to which extrinsic evidence may be referred to.[16] Where extrinsic evidence is available to show a term in a contract was intended to have a meaning other than what might otherwise be its primary meaning, the search for that intention is an issue of fact.[17] More importantly, when the court turns its mind to determining whether the parties intended to contract in the face of some uncertainty or incompleteness that is a question of contract formation and is one of fact. Being a question of fact, extrinsic evidence is allowed to determine that question. It follows in theory that it is possible that on construction a term might be found to be uncertain but when the court then turns to consider whether that uncertainty impacts on intention to contract, extrinsic evidence may be taken to determine the intention of the parties on that issue which in turn might turn up evidence that resolves the uncertainty. Indeed being an issue of contract formation, conduct engaged in after the alleged moment of formation may be taken into account. This has led one commentator to suggest that in the case of ambiguity or vagueness (in contrast to when

11.04

---

[10] See *Parker v Manessis* [1974] WAR 54, 57.
[11] *Pagnan SpA v Feed Products Ltd* [1987] 2 Lloyd's Rep 601, 619. See 11.42.
[12] Eg *Whitlock v Brew* (1968) 118 CLR 445; *Bishop v Taylor* (1968) 118 CLR 518; *First City Investments Ltd v Fraser Arms Hotel Ltd* (1979) 13 BCLR 107, 104 DLR (3d) 617; *Australian and New Zealand Banking Group Ltd v Frost Holdings Pty Ltd* [1989] VR 695; *Custom Credit Corp Ltd v Gray* [1992] 1 VR 540.
[13] *Whitlock v Brew* (1968) 118 CLR 445, 454.
[14] *Whitlock v Brew* (1968) 118 CLR 445, 453. See also *Kell v Harris* (1915) 15 SR (NSW) 473, 479.
[15] *Hillas & Co Ltd v Arcos Ltd* (1932) 147 LT 503, 513–14 per Lord Wright.
[16] *Mercantile Credits Ltd v Harry* [1969] 2 NSWR 248, 249; *Re Nudgee Bakery Pty Ltd's Agreement* [1971] Qd R 24. See generally, *Investors Compensation Scheme Ltd v West Bromwich Building Society* [1998] 1 WLR 896; *Chartbrook Ltd v Persimmon Homes Ltd* [2009] 3 WLR 267.
[17] *Bruner v Moore* [1904] 1 Ch 305.

there is a lack of meaning) contracts should never be considered to be 'void' but rather ineffective 'for the time being, but capable of being rendered wholly effective by events subsequent to their conclusion'.[18] Having said that it needs to be pointed out that it has been held on numerous occasions that issues of severance are dealt with by construction.[19] That is, whether or not the contract can continue to operate despite some uncertainty or incompleteness is determined as a matter of construction. This is because issues of severance concern whether the parties intended to assume legal obligations; it is not merely an issue involving intention to contract.

Intention to contract

11.05 If the parties have not reached agreement on the essential terms of an agreement then that incompleteness may evidence a lack of an intention to contract.[20] Similarly it may be that uncertainty may evidence a lack of intention to contract.[21] For example, in *Brookhaven Housing Coalition v Solomon*[22] the employees at a new regional Internal Revenue Service (IRS) centre brought an action against the Town Board of Brookhaven seeking specific performance of an alleged agreement to implement a programme of low and moderate income housing for employees at the centre. Although the letter from the Town Board stated that the 'Town of Brookhaven will provide whatever programs would be necessary to meet the housing needs for all Federal employees which may develop as a result of the award of the project to the Town of Brookhaven', it did not define the programmes. The court dismissed the action on the ground that the provision was uncertain and in the circumstances there was no intention that the letter was intended to give rise to legal obligations because, if that were the intention, the town's obligations would have been specified with certainty as they were in respect of other aspects of the construction.

Overriding concern and principle

11.06 In any discussion about certainty and completeness it must be kept in mind that commercial courts are slow to draw the conclusion that a contract is void for uncertainty or incompleteness. This has long been the position and is also reflected in approaches to construction.[23] In recent years this approach has further developed and modern courts are particularly concerned with the expectation of the parties and in upholding contracts they seek to give effect to the reasonable expectations of the parties.[24] The modern approach was stated by

---

[18] Lücke, 'Illusory, Vague and Uncertain Contractual Terms' (1977) 6 Adel LR 1, 9.

[19] See 11.124.

[20] See *Clifton v Palumbo* [1944] 2 All ER 487, 499; *Barrier Wharfs Ltd v W Scott Fell & Co Ltd* (1908) 5 CLR 647, 666; *Farmer v Honan* (1919) 26 CLR 183; *Anaconda Nickel Ltd v Tarmoola Australia Pty Ltd* (2000) 22 WAR 101, 140–1.

[21] See further Restatement (2d) Contracts § 33(3).

[22] 583 F 2d 584 (1978).

[23] See McMeel, *The Construction of Contracts* (OUP, Oxford, 2007), paras 8.16ff.

[24] *Hillas & Co Ltd v Arcos Ltd* (1932) 147 LT 503, 512. This principle has been enunciated in many cases, eg, *Adamastos Shipping Co Ltd v Anglo-Saxon Petroleum Co Ltd* [1959] AC 133, 161 per Lord Morton; *Head v Kelk* [1962] NSWR 1363, 1370–1, 1378; *Prints for Pleasure Ltd v Oswald-Sealy (Overseas) Ltd* [1968] 3 NSWR 761, 765–6; *Amalgamated Television Services Pty Ltd v Television Corp Ltd* [1970] 3 NSWR 85; *Cudgen Rutile (No 2) Pty Ltd v Chalk* [1975] AC 520, 536; *Nea Agrex SA v Baltic Shipping Co Ltd* [1976] 1 QB 933, 948; *Meehan v Jones* (1982) 149 CLR 571, 589; *Biotechnology Australia Pty Ltd v Pace* (1988) 15 NSWLR 130, 135; *Hawthorn Football Club Ltd v Harding* [1988] VR 49; *Queensland Electricity Generating Board v New Hope Collieries Pty Ltd* [1989] 1 Lloyd's Rep 205, 210; *Anangel Atlas Compania Naviera SA v*

McHugh JA in *GR Securities Pty Ltd v Baulkham Hills Private Hospital Pty Ltd*[25] in the following terms:[26]

> [T]he decisive issue is always the intention of the parties which must be objectively ascertained from the terms of the document when read in the light of the surrounding circumstances ... If the terms of a document indicate that the parties intended to be bound immediately, effect must be given to that intention irrespective of the subject matter, magnitude or complexity of the transaction.

It is implicit in this passage that the courts' slowness to conclude an agreement void for uncertainty or incompleteness is limited to when the courts detect an intention to be bound[27] and the more uncertain or incomplete an agreement is the less likely that the parties intended to be bound.[28] It is of course possible for the parties to agree all of what they consider to be the essential terms and still not intend to be bound until some other terms are agreed or conditions satisfied.[29] It follows that the reference to an intention to be bound here refers to an intention to immediately assume legal obligations.[30] This approach dictates that courts do not require contracts to be 'worked out in meticulous detail'.[31] This is necessarily the case in a contract where it is not possible to predict how it is to be performed

11.07

Ishikawajima-Harima Heavy Industries Co Ltd (No 2) [1990] 2 Lloyd's Rep 526, 545; *Toyota Motor Corp Australia Ltd v Ken Morgan Motors Pty Ltd* [1994] 2 VR 106, 130 per Brooking J, 201 per JD Phillips J; *Homburg Houtimport BV v Agrosin Privtae Ltd (The Starsin)* [2004] 1 AC 715, 738, 749.

[25] (1986) 40 NSWLR 631. See also *Brown v Gould* [1972] Ch 53, 56, 58 per Megarry J ('the court is reluctant to hold void for uncertainty any provision that was intended to have legal effect'; 'only if the court is driven to it will it be held that a provision is void for uncertainty'). Indeed modern courts are more inclined to uphold a contract today even though historically the same facts were likely to result in the agreement being void for uncertainty or incompleteness, *Cudgen Rutile (No 2) Pty Ltd v Chalk* [1974] AC 520, 536; *Attorney-General v Barker Bros Ltd* [1976] 2 NZLR 495.

[26] (1986) 40 NSWLR 631, 634. This approach to formation goes hand in hand with modern principles of construction through principles such as a 'commercial construction' which strive to give meaning to terms 'which will preserve the validity of the contract', see *Meehan v Jones* (1982) 149 CLR 571, 589 per Mason J.

[27] See also *Hillas & Co Ltd v Arcos Ltd* (1932) 147 LT 503, 513 per Lord Thankerton; *G Scammell & Nephew Ltd v Ouston* [1941] AC 251, 268; *York Air Conditioning and Refrigeration (A'sia) Pty Ltd v Commonwealth* (1949) 80 CLR 11, 26; *Head v Kelk* [1962] NSWR 1363, 1370–1; *Brown v Gould* [1972] Ch 53; *AG v Barker Bros Ltd* [1976] 2 NZLR 495; *Sudbrook Trading Estate Ltd v Eggleton* [1983] 1 AC 444; *Money v Ven-Lu-Ree Ltd* [1988] 2 NZLR 414, [1989] 3 NZLR 129; *Biotechnology Australia Pty Ltd v Pace* (1988) 15 NSWLR 130.

[28] *Anaconda Nickel Ltd v Tarmoola Australia Pty Ltd* (2000) 22 WAR 101, 132–3 per Anderson J ('I think it is fair to say, speaking very generally, that where the parties intended to make a final and binding contract the approach of the courts to questions of uncertainty and incompleteness is rather different from the approach that is taken when the uncertainty or incompleteness goes to contractual intention. Where the parties intended to make an immediately binding agreement, and believe they have done so, the courts will strive to uphold it despite the omission of terms or lack of clarity ... However, the principle that courts should be the upholders and not the destroyers of bargains, which is the principle that underlies this approach, is not applicable where the issue to be decided is whether the parties intended to form a concluded bargain. In determining that issue, the court is not being asked to enforce a contract, but to decide whether or not the parties intended to make one. That inquiry need not be approached with any predisposition in favour of upholding anything. The question is whether there is anything to uphold.')

[29] *Fletcher Challenge Energy Ltd v Electricity Corporation of New Zealand Ltd* [2002] 2 NZLR 433, 443–4.

[30] *Milne v AG for the State of Tasmania* (1956) 95 CLR 460, 473. See 10.09.

[31] *Terrex Resources NL v Magnet Petroleum Pty Ltd* [1988] 1 WAR 144, 159 per Kennedy J. See also *Perry v Suffields Ltd* [1916] 2 Ch 187; *Storer v Manchester City Council* [1974] 1 WLR 1403; *Hancock v Wilson* [1956] St R Qd 266.

in the future.[32] Subject to what is said below, it is only necessary for the parties to have agreed on those essential terms that cannot otherwise be implied.[33]

11.08   As noted above there must be some overriding limits to the courts giving effect to such intention.[34] Thus, where the parties have expressed an intention to be bound but the terms agreed are so uncertain or incomplete that a court could not enforce the contract by granting a remedy then the agreement will be void. As Mahoney JA pointed out in *Air Great Lakes Pty Ltd v KS Easter (Holdings) Pty Ltd*,[35] in all cases it is necessary to ask, 'did the parties arrive at a consensus?; (if they did) was it such a consensus as was capable of forming a binding contract?; and (if it was) did the parties intend that the consensus at which they arrived should constitute a binding contract?'.[36] Perhaps today the order of questions two and three might be reversed but this does not deny the importance of question two.

11.09   In *Australian Broadcasting Corporation v XIVth Commonwealth Games Ltd*,[37] Gleeson CJ recognized a minimum legal requirement of certainty and completeness overriding the intention of the parties in the following terms:[38]

> It is to be noted that the question in a case such as the present is expressed in terms of the intention of the parties to make a concluded bargain ... That is not the same as, although in a given case it may be closely related to, the question whether the parties have reached agreement upon such terms as are, in the circumstances, *legally necessary* to constitute a contract. To say that parties to negotiations have agreed upon sufficient matters to produce the consequence that, perhaps by reference to implied terms or by resort to considerations of reasonableness, a court will treat their consensus as sufficiently comprehensive to be legally binding, is not the same thing as to say that a court will decide that they intended to make a concluded bargain.

11.10   This paragraph recognizes three issues. First, that the motivation for a court to uphold a bargain exists to the extent there is an intention to immediately assume legal obligations and not merely an intention to contract. Second, that intention to immediately assume legal obligations is distinct from a finding that the parties have agreed all what they consider to be the essential terms. Third, despite agreement by the parties on what they consider to

---

[32] *Fletcher Challenge Energy Ltd v Electricity Corporation of New Zealand Ltd* [2002] 2 NZLR 433, 443–4; *Ampol Ltd v Caltex Oil (Australia) Pty Ltd* (1986) 60 ALJR 225, 233.

[33] Coote, 'Contract Formation and the Implication of Terms' (1993) 6 JCL 51, 51–2. The reference to implied terms here reflects that it is possible to imply essential terms.

[34] See 11.03.

[35] (1985) 2 NSWLR 309. See also *Biotechnology Australia Pty Ltd v Pace* (1988) 15 NSWLR 130, 135, per Kirby P ('But the court will not do so, where, in effect, it is asked to spell out, to an unacceptable extent, that to which the parties have themselves failed to agree. Nor will the court clarify that which is irremediably obscure. Most particularly, the court will not accept for itself a discretion which the parties have, by their agreement, reserved to one or other of them. To do so would not be to effect the contract but to change it.')

[36] (1985) 2 NSWLR 309, 326.

[37] (1988) 18 NSWLR 540.

[38] (1988) 18 NSWLR 540, 548 (emphasis added). See also *Geebung Investments Pty Ltd v Varga Group Investments No 8 Pty Ltd* (1995) 7 BPR 14,551, 14,552 per Gleeson CJ, ('In a case such as the present, there are two, sometimes related, questions which require to be considered. The first is whether the parties to the putative contract intended to make a concluded agreement. The second is whether they succeeded in doing so. The answer to the second question may depend upon a number of factors, including whether the parties have reached agreement upon all the terms necessary, in the circumstances, to constitute a contract.') See further *Trollope & Colls Ltd v Atomic Power Constructions Ltd* [1963] 1 WLR 333, 337; *Fletcher Challenge Energy Ltd v Electricity Corporation of New Zealand Ltd* [2002] 2 NZLR 433, 443–4.

be the essential terms, there are overriding legal requirements of certainty and completeness which must be made out to a standard that allows a court to enforce the agreement.

It is important to emphasize these limits. It is possible to identify many statements in judgments to the effect that if the parties intend to contract and have agreed on all the 'essential' terms and those essential terms are certain, then the contract will not be held void for uncertainty or incompleteness.[39] If the view is adopted that whether or not a term is essential depends on the intention of the parties,[40] encapsulating those terms the parties believe to be important, then such statements on their face suggest that it is possible to enforce a contract that may be entirely unworkable. That cannot be correct and it follows that issues of certainty and completeness have a distinct legal role over and above agreement on such 'essential' terms. The law requires certain minimum standards of certainty and completeness to be reached so that if called upon the court can deal with any dispute. These might have been called 'essential' terms in the sense that the contract will not work without them.[41] Certainly the case can be made that, 'essential' should be limited to those terms necessary for enforcement by a court.[42] Nevertheless, it is a term that has been used to describe both those terms necessary for enforcement and those the parties believe to be important. It is always necessary to determine in what sense it is being used. Often in those cases where such statements are made the analysis that follows evidences the distinct legal role that investigations into certainty and completeness have; thus one sees conclusions that the parties had agreed all 'essential' terms but there is still a long analysis as to whether the terms agreed leave any uncertainty or incompleteness.[43]

11.11

It follows that courts will attempt to overcome problems that arise where terms have not been expressed in clear language or are not precise, particularly if deficiencies in drafting or the absence of terms were not considered by the parties as preventing a contract from coming into existence.[44] It also necessarily follows that clear acts of performance when carried out against a background of an intention to be bound will carry a lot of weight and rarely will a contract be held to be void for uncertainty or incompleteness if these are in evidence.[45]

11.12

---

[39] Eg *Anaconda Nickel Ltd v Tarmoola Australia Pty Ltd* (2000) 22 WAR 101, 112 per Ipp J, ('It does not follow that any omission will make a contract incomplete or uncertain in the sense of rendering it invalid. It is only the omission of an essential term that will have that effect'). See also *Sudbrook Trading Estate Ltd v Eggleton* [1983] AC 444, 478.

[40] *Pagnan SpA v Feed Products Ltd* [1987] 2 Lloyd's Rep 601, 619. See also *Ridgway v Wharton* (1857) 6 HLC 238, 304–5, 10 ER 1287, 1313.

[41] *Pagnan SpA v Feed Products Ltd* [1987] 2 Lloyd's Rep 601, 619, see also *Metal Scrap Trade Corp v Kate Shipping Ltd (The Gladys) (No 2)* [1994] 2 Lloyd's Rep 402. A typical example would be in the case of a lease where the parties have not agreed the commencement date; here it would not matter that the parties may have agreed all the terms they think are essential, a court will not enforce the agreement, see *Harvey v Pratt* [1965] 1 WLR 1025; *Brown v Gould* [1972] Ch 53, 61. See also *Bushwall Properties Ltd v Vortex Properties Ltd* [1976] 1 WLR 591. Cf *Jenkins v Harbour View Courts Ltd* [1966] NZLR 1 (lessee put into possession—see also as to rent when lessee is in possession *Meynell v Surtees* (1854) 3 Sm & G 101, 65 ER 581; (1854) 25 LJ Ch 257). As regards uncertainty in periodic leases and leases for life as opposed to fixed-term leases, see *Greco v Swinburne Ltd* [1991] 1 VR 304, 313–15, *Haslam v Money for Living (Aust) Pty Ltd* (2008) 250 ALR 419, 429.

[42] *Pagnan SpA v Feed Products Ltd* [1987] 2 Lloyd's Rep 601, 619. See 11.42.

[43] Eg see the analysis of Ipp J in *Anaconda Nickel Ltd v Tarmoola Australia Pty Ltd* (2000) 22 WAR 101, 110–28.

[44] *Vroon BV v Foster's Brewing Group Ltd* [1994] 2 VR 32, 68 per Ormiston J.

[45] *Vroon BV v Foster's Brewing Group Ltd* [1994] 2 VR 32, 71 per Ormiston J.

But the court has limited tools at its disposal to make a bargain.[46] Thus, although a court may be prepared to give much weight to an intention to be bound, the more complex the transaction the more likely that it may be found void for uncertainty or incompleteness. Moreover, the more omissions that exist in a bargain the more reason a court has 'to doubt that the parties have set down or expressed the whole of the terms upon which they wish to deal'.[47]

11.13 To sum up, it is suggested that the current position is as follows. If there is agreement on all the essential terms—being those terms the parties believed had to be settled before a contract could come into effect—and evidence of an intention to assume immediate legal obligations, then a court will be loath to hold that the agreement is void for uncertainty or incompleteness. However, that statement merely deals with motivation, it does not address legal doctrine. In terms of doctrine it is suggested that the position is that the law requires, in terms of completeness, for the parties to agree on all those 'essential' terms that they and only they can agree on.[48] 'Essential' here encapsulates those terms the parties considered necessary before a contract could come into effect and those that a court requires agreement on in order to enforce the contract. The reference to the need to only agree those terms the parties and only the parties can agree on acknowledges that the law can supply terms, even essential terms. These may be terms thought necessary for enforcement as well as terms the parties thought necessary. In terms of certainty, the law requires the terms to be sufficiently certain so that it is possible to apply them according to the intention of the parties.

B. Uncertainty

Introduction

11.14 A term will be uncertain if it totally lacks meaning or if a court cannot determine the meaning the parties intended.[49] Generally, a contract will be void for uncertainty if it is not possible to prescribe meaning to an essential term.[50] The requirement of certainty dictates that it must be possible to attribute meaning to the terms of a contract. That meaning must be found within certain perimeters, it must reflect the presumed intention of the parties. It is not enough that the court can give a term meaning, it must be able to attribute that meaning to the parties.[51] This rarely causes problems if a term has only one meaning but it

---

[46] *Trawl Industries of Australia Pty Ltd v Effem Foods Pty Ltd Trading as 'Uncle Bens of Australia'* (1992) 27 NSWLR 326, 333 per Kirby P.

[47] *Vroon BV v Foster's Brewing Group Ltd* [1994] 2 VR 32, 68 per Ormiston J.

[48] Coote, 'Contract Formation and the Implication of Terms' (1993) 6 JCL 51, 56.

[49] Eg *Mercantile Credits Ltd v Comblas* (1982) 40 ALR 65; *O'Callaghan v Olsen* [1948] SASR 123. See also *Stinchcombe v Thomas* [1957] VR 509 (promise to 'well reward' a housekeeper held to be uncertain). See further Farnsworth, *Farnsworth on Contracts* (3rd edn, Vol 1, Aspen Publishers, New York, 2004), §3.28, p 420.

[50] Eg *Re Vince, Ex parte Baxter* (1892) 2 QB 478.

[51] *G Scammell & Nephew Ltd v Ouston* [1941] AC 251, 268 per Lord Wright (a term or a contract will be uncertain if it is 'so obscure and so incapable of any definite or precise meaning that the court is unable to attribute to the parties any particular contractual intention'). See also *County Hotel and Wine Co Ltd v London and North Western Railway Co* [1918] 2 KB 251, 262–6; *Upper Hunter County District Council v Australian Chilling & Freezing Co Ltd* (1968) 118 CLR 429, 437; *Jaques v Lloyd D George & Partners Ltd* [1968] 1 WLR 625.

is in the nature of language to be ambiguous and the court usually must choose between different meanings. In some cases a term may be incapable of being given any meaning.

This necessarily raises the question as to what standard is required to be met before a term **11.15** will be held to be uncertain. Generally, the courts require a reasonable degree of certainty.[52] Courts must be able to construe an agreement so that they can enforce it. As regards promissory terms, the search for a reasonable degree of certainty is a search for an obligation that can give rise to a breach of contract and which will attract a remedy.[53] The degree of certainty required is linked to the remedy sought.[54] The Restatement (2d) Contracts, section 33(2) provides:[55]

> The terms of a contract are reasonably certain if they provide a basis for determining the existence of a breach and for giving an appropriate remedy.

Comment *b* to section 33(2) explains this rule in the following terms:[56] **11.16**

> The rule stated in Subsection (2) reflects the fundamental policy that contracts should be made by the parties, not by the courts, and hence that remedies for breach of contract must have a basis in the agreement of the parties. Where the parties have intended to make a contract and there is a reasonably certain basis for granting a remedy, the same policy supports the granting of the remedy ...
>
> [T]he degree of certainty required may be affected by the dispute which arises and by the remedy sought. Courts decide the disputes before them, not hypothetical disputes which might have arisen. It is less likely that a reasonably certain term will be supplied by construction as to a matter which has been the subject of controversy between the parties than as to one which is raised only as an afterthought. In some cases greater definiteness may be required for specific performance than for an award of damages; in others the impossibility of accurate assessment of damages may furnish a reason for specific relief. Partial relief may sometimes be granted when uncertainty prevents full-scale enforcement through normal remedies.[57]

The search for the meaning of a term is a search for the intention of the parties and is often **11.17** expressed as an issue of construction in a written contract or an issue of fact in an oral contract.[58] As most commercial contracts are written, the search for certainty involves an

---

[52] *G Scammell & Nephew Ltd v Ouston* [1941] AC 251, 255. See also Restatement (2d) Contracts § 33(1). See further *Candid Products Inc v International Skating Union* 530 F Supp 1330 (1982), 1333.

[53] See *Coal Cliff Collieries Pty Ltd v Sijehama Pty Ltd* (1991) 24 NSWLR 1, 21; *Summergreene v Parker* (1950) 80 CLR 304, 324–5. The alleged difficulty in assessing damages has been one reason for courts refusing to uphold an agreement to negotiate, see *Courtney & Fairbairn Ltd v Tolaini Brothers (Hotels) Ltd* [1975] 1 WLR 297, 301.

[54] *Foster v Wheeler* (1888) LR 38 Ch D 130, 133. See also Farnsworth, *Farnsworth on Contracts* (3rd edn, Vol 1, Aspen Publishers, New York, 2004), § 3.28, p 427. See further on the level of certainty required for specific performance, Spry, *Equitable Remedies* (8th edn, Thomson, Law Book Co, Sydney, 2010), 140.

[55] See also Uniform Commercial Code § 2-204(3).

[56] *Bettancourt v Gilroy Theatre Co* 120 Cal App 2d 364, 261 P 2d 351 (1953); *Hedges v Hurd* 47 Wash 2d 683, 289 P 2d 706 (1955). See also Farnsworth, *Farnsworth on Contracts* (3rd edn, Vol 1, Aspen Publishers, New York, 2004), § 3.28, p 421.

[57] This reasoning also suggests that the time for determining certainty is not the time of contract formation but the time of performance, see nn 3, 294, 11.50.

[58] *Summergreene v Parker* (1950) 80 CLR 304, 323; *Head v Kelk* [1962] NSWR 1363, 1377. See also *South Coast Oils (Qld and NSW) Pty Ltd v Look Enterprises Pty Ltd* [1988] 1 Qd R 680, 699; *Woodside Offshore Petroleum Pty Ltd v Atwood Oceanics Inc* [1986] WAR 253.

issue of construction.[59] The construction of a contract involves two aspects, one of finding the meaning of a term and the other its application (there is also the legal effect of a term such as when a term needs to be characterized under the tripartite classification of terms). A term may fail for uncertainty at either stage. It may be void for uncertainty because it is not possible to give it any meaning or because the application of any possible meaning makes no commercial sense and could not represent the intention of the parties.[60] It is also possible that words used in a contract may appear meaningless in a literal sense but take on meaning when applied to the facts.[61] Often a term may have multiple meanings but only one meaning when applied to the facts. For example, in *Timmerman v Nervina Industries (International) Pty Ltd*,[62] a contract contained a covenant for the vendor to repurchase certain property 'at cost plus CPI'. The expression 'CPI' (consumer price index) had multiple meanings as one existed for each capital city and varied with each metropolitan area. However, as the parties here were both Queensland residents and the contract a Queensland contract it was only possible to give the phrase one application which was the Brisbane All Groups Index.

11.18 A further aspect of 'application' is that a term may be found to have a number of reasonable applications but fail for uncertainty because it is not possible to determine which of those applications represents the intention of the parties.[63] For example, in the case of an ambiguity it may be possible to attribute multiple meanings and applications to a term but impossible to determine which application was intended by the parties. The classic example is that of *Raffles v Wichelhaus*.[64] This involved a contract to buy and sell cotton 'to arrive ex "*Peerless*"' from Bombay. However, there were two ships called Peerless sailing from Bombay, one left in October and one in December. The goods were shipped on the December ship and the buyer refused to accept them arguing that the contract required them to be on the October ship. The question that went before the court was whether the buyer was in breach of contract for failing to accept the tender of the December goods. The court gave judgment

---

[59] *Caltex Oil (Australia) Pty Ltd v Alderton and Knox* [1964] NSWR 456, 458.

[60] Generally, very clear evidence would be required before a court would conclude that a term is unreasonable in its operation.

[61] *R W Cameron & Co v L Slutzkin Pty Ltd* (1923) 32 CLR 81. Cf *Mercantile Credits Ltd v Harry* [1969] 2 NSWR 248. See also *Bank of New Zealand v Simpson* [1900] AC 182, 187 (extrinsic evidence may be taken 'not to contradict or vary the contract, but to apply it to the facts').

[62] [1983] 1 Qd R 1 (reversed on other grounds *Timmerman v Nervina Industries (International) Pty Ltd* [1983] 2 Qd R 261).

[63] *Mercantile Credits Ltd v Harry* [1969] 2 NSWR 248, 250 ('In cases where uncertainty is the basis of an argument the distinction between two classes of uncertainty must be considered. The first class is where through imprecision in the use of the English language the meaning intended by the authors of a written instrument is not revealed with certainty ... The second class is where the meaning of the words used in the written instrument is clear, but the operation of the instrument is not. In this class of case the uncertainty arises because either there is not any set of facts on which the agreement can operate at all ... or because, there being more than one set of facts that are within the words of the agreement, that instrument does not, by its provisions, define the set or sets of facts on which it is to operate.') See also *O'Callaghan v Olsen* [1948] SASR 123 (right to renewal of share-farming agreement 'with such variations as circumstances warrant' held uncertain). See further 11.21.

[64] (1864) 2 H & C 906, 159 ER 375. See Gilmore, *The Death of Contract* (Ohio State Uni Press, 1974), 35–44, Young Jr, 'Equivocation and the Making of Agreements' (1964) 64 Columbia L Rev 619; Birmingham, 'Holmes on "Peerless": *Raffles v Wichelhaus* and the Objective Theory of Contract' (1985) 47 U Pitt L Rev 183; Simpson, 'Contracts for Cotton to Arrive: The Case of the Two Ships Peerless' (1989) 11 Cardozo LR 287; Alarie, 'Mutual Misunderstanding in Contract (2009) Am Bus L Jnl 531. See further Restatement (2d) Contracts § 20 Reporter's Note.

for the buyer so the buyer was not in breach of contract. There are no reasons given for the decision in the report. One view might be that the buyer was correct and the goods should have been on the earlier vessel giving the buyer a right to sue for damages for breach of contract. The more accepted analysis of the facts is that it was not reasonably possible to determine the intention of the parties even though the limits of the ambiguity are clear, the goods were intended to be carried on one of the ships. Thus, in terms of literal meaning the contract was clear, the goods had to arrive on a ship called Peerless. But within the four corners of that contract there were two possible applications of that meaning; both applications were possible given the nature of the goods and the circumstances surrounding the contract which did not evidence any urgency in delivery. The contract was therefore void. However, counsel was stopped by the court and judgment given for the buyer just after a submission to the effect that there was no consensus *ad idem* because of the ambiguity, so it is not clear what the ultimate reasoning of the court was although in the result the court accepted the buyer's argument that he intended the goods to arrive on the October ship.

It follows from what has been said above that in practice both investigations overlap and it **11.19** can be difficult to distinguish the two issues. It is therefore necessary to carry out investigations as to both meaning and application and not cut short an investigation just because a clause makes no literal sense.[65] It follows that it is convenient to refer to the two processes together as the search for meaning and only distinguish them when necessary.

Uncertain terms and illusory terms[66]

As noted above, a contract term or a contract will be uncertain if it is meaningless or, if it **11.20** has meaning, the court cannot determine the meaning the parties intended it to have. A term, being a promissory term, will be illusory if the promisor retains an unfettered discretion whether or not to perform.[67] Issues concerning the illusory nature of a term are usually discussed in the context of consideration. If a promise made by a party is illusory then that promise will not constitute valuable consideration to support a contract.[68] It is

---

[65] See *Head v Kelk* [1962] NSWR 1363, 1371 ('Thus contracts which contained terms that the price was to be "reasonable", to "pay handsomely" for services, or to pay a commission on "the sum available for distribution" or a percentage of "the profits" of a business, in each case for services rendered, have been held to be enforceable according to the maxim *id certum est quod certum reddi potest*'). See also *Shire of Yea v Roberts* (1879) 5 VLR (E) 222.

[66] Lücke, 'Illusory, Vague and Uncertain Contractual Terms' (1977) 6 Adel LR 1.

[67] *Loftus v Roberts* (1902) 18 TLR 532, 534; *Beattie v Fine* [1925] VLR 363, 369; *Kennard v Bazzan* [1962] NSWR 1383; *Thorby v Goldberg* (1965) 112 CLR 597, 605, 605, 613; *Placer Development Ltd v The Commonwealth* (1969) 121 CLR 353, 359–60; *Lewandowski v Mead Carney-BCA Pty Ltd* [1973] 2 NSWLR 640; *Meehan v Jones* (1982) 149 CLR 571, 581; *Biotechnology Australia Pty Ltd v Pace* (1988) 15 NSWLR 130, 151; *Gregory v MAB Pty Ltd* (1989) 1 WAR 1; *Toyota Motor Corp Australia Ltd v Ken Morgan Motors Pty Ltd* [1994] 2 VR 106, 202. See also *Davis v General Foods Corp* 21 F Supp 445 (1937); *Smith v Chickamauga Cedar Company* 82 So 2d 200 (1955).

[68] Examples include, *Taylor v Brewer* (1813) 1 M & S 290, 105 ER 108 (work performed pursuant to a resolution of the employing committee that 'any service to be rendered by [the employee] should be taken into consideration, and such remuneration be made as should be deemed right'); *Roberts v Smith* (1859) 4 H & N 315, 157 ER 861 (promise to pay 'such sum of money as [the employer] may deem right as compensation for labour done'); *Kofi Sunkersette Obu v A Strauss & Co Ltd* [1951] AC 243 (commission payable to an agent was at the 'discretion of the' principal); *Placer Development Ltd v The Commonwealth* (1969) 121 CLR 353 (payment of a subsidy to be 'of an amount or at a rate determined by the Commonwealth from time to time'). Cf *Powell v Braun* [1954] 1 WLR 401.

clear that issues of meaning and discretion may overlap.[69] And just as in the case of uncertainty a court will not easily conclude a contract is illusory when there is a clear intention to be bound. A promise is not illusory merely because the promisor has some discretion in how or when its obligations are to be performed. It is only necessary that there be an obligation that the promise be performed and that the discretion is contained within defined parameters.[70] For example, a promise to pay a salary between £7,000 and £9,000 will be upheld with an obligation inferred to pay the lower figure if there is a dispute.[71]

Uncertainty and ambiguity[72]

11.21 A term can often have more than one meaning.[73] Such a term may be considered ambiguous in a strict sense. Usually in practice a term will not be held to be uncertain simply because it is ambiguous in this sense as it is usually possible to determine what application was intended by the parties.[74] Such ambiguity is resolved by construction. Most words appearing in a contract are capable of being ambiguous in terms of literary meaning as many words in the English language are capable of more than one meaning. When words are added together such as in a contract term the chance of such ambiguity is reduced because each word in the sentence will narrow down the possible meanings; in short the sentence gives context to the individual words, the clause gives context to the sentences contained in it and the contract as a whole gives context to the clauses contained in it. This is the process of construction and the court will choose that construction which it thinks represents the presumed intention of the parties using all the construction techniques that are available under the general law.[75] For example, in *Waldron v Tsimiklis*,[76] the parties

---

[69] *Biotechnology Australia Pty Ltd v Pace* (1988) 15 NSWLR 130 (promise to employee that he would have option to participate in an equity sharing scheme which he knew did not exist at time of contract was held by the majority to be uncertain because no external standard existed to give it meaning, a criterion of reasonableness could not be given any meaning when there was no evidence provided of similar packages in the marketplace, there was no intention to benchmark the scheme by reference to an external standard even if such a standard existed; it was also illusory as the employer had an unfettered discretion to create or not create such a scheme, there being no undertaking to do so).

[70] *Biotechnology Australia Pty Ltd v Pace* (1988) 15 NSWLR 130, 151. See also *Allcars Pty Ltd v Tweedle* [1937] VLR 35; *Thorby v Goldberg* (1964) 112 CLR 597; *Yaroomba Beach Development Co Pty Ltd v Coeur De Lion Investments Pty Ltd* (1989) 18 NSWLR 398, 404. See also *Tonelli v Komirra Pty Ltd* [1972] VR 737. See further, Restatement (2d) Contracts § 34(1); Uniform Commercial Code § 2-311.

[71] *Lewandowski v Mead Carney-BCA Pty Ltd* [1973] 2 NSWLR 640. See also *Hely v Sterling* [1982] VR 246.

[72] Young Jr, 'Equivocation in the Making of Agreements' (1964) 64 Col L Rev 619.

[73] A term may be ambiguous in terms of meaning or application. See 11.18.

[74] *Upper Hunter District Council v Australian Chilling and Freezing Co Ltd* (1968) 118 CLR 429, 436 per Barwick CJ; *Tailby v Official Receiver* (1888) 13 App Cas 523. See also *McDermott v Black* (1940) 63 CLR 161, 175 per Starke J, 188 per Dixon J; *Meehan v Jones* (1982) 149 CLR 571, 578 per Gibbs CJ; *Yaroomba Beach Development Co Pty Ltd v Coeur de Lion Investments Pty Ltd* (1989) 18 NSWLR 398, 405; *Trawl Industries of Australia Pty Ltd v Effem Foods Pty Ltd Trading as 'Uncle Bens of Australia'* (1992) 27 NSWLR 326, 344, CA; *Star Shipping AS v China National Foreign Trade Transportation Corp (The Star Texas)* [1993] 2 Lloyd's Rep 445, 452; *Carpenter v McGrath* (1996) 40 NSWLR 39, 57, 70.

[75] *Upper Hunter District Council v Australian Chilling and Freezing Co Ltd* (1968) 118 CLR 429, 436 per Barwick CJ. See also *Associated Alloys Pty Ltd v ACN 001 452 106 Pty Ltd (In Liq) (formerly Metropolitan Engineering and Fabrications Pty Ltd)* (2000) 202 CLR 588, 599; *Australian Football League v Carlton Football Club Ltd* [1998] 2 VR 546, 564.

[76] (1975) 12 SASR 48. See also *Three Rivers Trading Co Ltd v Gwinear & District Farmers Ltd* (1967) 111 Sol J 831; *Australian Energy Ltd v Lennard Oil NL* [1986] 2 Qd R 216 (relevance of meaning within an industry). The meaning of a term within an industry cannot contradict an express term of the contract, see *Dominion Coal Co Ltd v Dominion Iron & Steel Co Ltd* [1909] AC 293, 307.

entered into a contract of sale which was 'subject to the approval of all relevant authorities for the erection of a residential flat building on the subject land'. One question that went before the court was whether the term 'residential flat building' was uncertain. This was a case of ambiguity in the sense being discussed as everyone knows what a residential flat building is, the term is not therefore meaningless. The term would only be uncertain and the contract void if it was not possible to define the type of residential flat building contemplated, that is, if a specific meaning could not be attributed to the parties. The issue was resolved by construction, the clause was for the benefit of the buyer so the clause was held to be referring to a 'genuine flat project' which the buyer had decided upon and wished to proceed with.[77] Similarly, in *Upper Hunter County District Council v Australian Chilling and Freezing Co Ltd*,[78] it was noted that a term referring to the 'supplier's costs' was a matter that could give rise to various arguments as to its meaning in a particular case; that is, it did give rise to evidential uncertainty. But is was nevertheless capable of meaning because, 'the concept of a cost of doing something is certain in the sense that it provides a criterion by reference to which the rights of the parties may ultimately and logically be worked out'.[79]

11.22 Before moving on, it is important to note that a term will not in law be considered ambiguous simply because different judges come to different conclusions as to its meaning, each judge being certain that their understanding of the term is correct. Moreover, there has been a legal concept of ambiguity distinct from its meaning of a word or phrase capable of two or more meanings. In law the tendency has been to call a term 'ambiguous' only when it is incapable of meaning. That narrow meaning is breaking down and such a term today is more likely to be called 'uncertain'. For example, it is more common today for a court to determine that a term is ambiguous if it is capable of two or more meanings in order to access extrinsic evidence to determine its meaning or to attract a construction rule such as the *contra proferentem* rule.[80]

11.23 There are limits to resolving ambiguity. Although an ambiguous provision in the sense discussed in paragraph 11.21 above cannot be said to give rise to an absence of meaning, it can still be uncertain in its application. As the example of *Raffles v Wichelhaus*[81] discussed above shows, despite finding literal meaning and possible reasonable meanings in application it may still not be possible to determine which meaning or which application was intended by the parties. This is particularly the case where a term can have more than one application and those applications conflict so that either meaning is possible but not both. In such a case if the court is unable to attribute any of those meanings to the intention of the parties then the term will be uncertain.[82] For example in *Peter Lind & Co Ltd v Mersey Docks and Harbour Board*,[83] the plaintiff was asked to submit, and did submit, two tenders for the construction of a container freight terminal, one for a fixed price and the other at a variable price. The defendant wrote to the plaintiff stating that it accepts 'your tender'.

---

[77] (1975) 12 SASR 481, 483.
[78] (1968) 118 CLR 429.
[79] (1968) 118 CLR 429, 437 per Barwick CJ. See also *York Air Conditioning and Refrigeration (A'sia) Pty Ltd v The Commonwealth* (1949) 80 CLR 11.
[80] See generally, McMeel, *The Construction of Contracts* (OUP, Oxford, 2007), paras 1.84–1.90.
[81] (1864) 2 H & C 906, 159 ER 375. See 11.18. See also *Bishop v Taylor* (1968) 118 CLR 518 ('One-third share of crops' capable of multiple meanings but uncertain as to which meaning was intended).
[82] Although such absence of meaning might be traditionally termed 'ambiguous' in the sense discussed in 11.22 above.
[83] [1972] 2 Lloyd's Rep 234.

Cooke J held that a reasonable person in the position of the plaintiff would find such a communication ambiguous and ultimately the agreement was void as there was no way to resolve the ambiguity.

11.24 If the court can attribute both meanings to the intention of both parties then the application of those meanings still needs to determined, that is, can the contract work with both meanings. A more common finding is that a clause has two meanings, one of which has been adopted by one party and the other meaning by the other party.[84] This becomes an issue if there is a material difference in the meanings adopted by the parties.[85] Such a situation may mean there is no contract as there is no consensus *ad idem*, particularly if neither party is aware of the other's understanding[86] and even if both are aware of the other's understanding but have not assented to it. Section 20 of Restatement (2d) Contracts deals with this situation in American law. It provides:[87]

§20 Effect of Misunderstanding

(1) There is no manifestation of mutual assent to an exchange if the parties attach materially different meanings to their manifestations and[88]

(a) neither party knows or has reason to know the meaning attached by the other; or

(b) each party knows or each party has reason to know the meaning attached by the other.

11.25 Subsection (2) then goes on to deal with the situation of where one party only is aware of a conflict of meaning. It provides:

(2) The manifestations of the parties are operative in accordance with the meaning attached to them by one of the parties if

(a) that party does not know of any different meaning attached by the other, and the other knows the meaning attached by the first party; or

(b) that party has no reason to know of any different meaning attached by the other, and the other has reason to know the meaning attached by the first party.

11.26 The basic principle of subsection (1) is that 'no contract is formed if neither party is at fault or if both parties are equally at fault'.[89] Subsection (2) deals with a unilateral error.[90] The crucial question will invariably be whether either party knew, or had reason to know, of the meaning attributed by the other.[91]

---

[84] In such a case it is likely that a court will not be able to attribute any meaning to 'the parties', see *Raffles v Wichelhaus* (1864) 2 H & C 906, 159 ER 375.

[85] See Restatement (2d) Contracts § 20 comment *b* emphasizing that almost 'never are all the connotations of a bargain exactly identical for both parties; it is enough that there is a core of common meaning sufficient to determine their performances with reasonable certainty or to give a reasonably certain basis for an appropriate legal remedy'. See also Restatement (2d) Contracts § 33.

[86] *Raffles v Wichelhaus* (1864) 2 H & C 906, 159 ER 375.

[87] Some difficulties with this provision are traced in Speidel, 'Restatement Second: Omitted Terms and Contract Method' (1982) 67 Cornell L Rev 785, 800ff. See also Palmer, 'The Effect of Misunderstanding on Contract Formation and Reformation Under the Restatement of Contracts Second' (1966) 65 Mich L Rev 33.

[88] See Restatement (2d) Contracts §§ 18 and 19 for the meaning of a 'manifestation of mutual assent'.

[89] Comment *d* to § 20.

[90] This provision is in addition to any principle that might allow a party not at fault to avoid the contract by relying on a vitiating factor such as misrepresentation.

[91] It can be difficult to determine which provision should apply to the facts. For example in *Frigaliment Importing Co v BNS International Sales Corp* 190 F Supp 116 (1960) there was a misunderstanding over the term 'chicken' in a contract of sale. The seller had shipped stewing chicken but the buyer claimed that

It is also possible, particularly in the context of standard form contracts drafted for the   **11.27**
benefit of one party that a dispute involving ambiguity can be resolved by application of the
contra proferentem rule.[92] In *United States of America ex rel Union Building Materials Corp v
Haas and Haynie Corporation*,[93] Haas and Haynie Corporation (H & H) had secured a
contract to construct the United States Courthouse and Federal Office Building in
Honolulu and had entered into a subcontract with Union Building Materials Corporation
(UBM) for the acquisition and installation of padding and carpeting for the building. The
standard subcontract form normally used by H & H was used. UBM had been primarily
engaged in the sale of lumber products and was a newcomer to the market in carpet products. During the negotiations leading up to the signing of this contract, UBM repeatedly
stated that their financial position was not strong so that, for cash-flow reasons, they
required immediate payment from the project.

A dispute arose concerning payment terms and UBM claimed that payment for materials   **11.28**
delivered but not yet installed should include a proportion of the total overhead and profit
for the job, while H & H claimed that it should not. The contract was ambiguous on this
point since it merely specified that payment for materials delivered would only be made
after proof of quality and value had been presented without specifying how that value was
to be computed.

The court considered whether either party knew or had reason to know of the meaning   **11.29**
given to the contract by the other. H & H was judged to have had reason to know that
UBM expected recovery of some profit and overhead at the time of delivery of the material
because of UBM's repeated indications that it was important to them to receive such
expenses at an early stage. However, H & H argued that since the trade custom did not
allow for recovery of profit and overheads on the delivery of materials, UBM should be held
to have reason to know that such was the meaning attached by H & H. The court held that
UBM, being a newcomer to the field of carpet subcontracting, had no reason to know of
the trade custom and therefore should not be bound by it. The court went on to say, 'if only
one party knows or has reason to know of the conflict in meaning, the contract will be
interpreted in favour of the party who does not know of the conflict'.[94] Accordingly, the
meaning attributed to the agreement by UBM prevailed. The case also suggests that in the
United States trade usages may be utilized in appropriate cases to show that a party had
reason to know of a given meaning attributed to a particular term. Generally, for a person
to be bound by a trade usage they must have knowledge of that usage, or, if not, the usage

---

'chicken' meant young chicken suitable for broiling or frying. It was held that since the buyer's meaning was
not known to the seller and the seller had no reason to know of it, the seller's meaning prevailed. The seller's
subjective meaning was legitimate because it did coincide with an objective meaning of the word and was not
inconsistent with the terms of the contract. The buyer therefore carried the onus of proving that a narrower
meaning was adopted by the contract. Presumably that result, if it is to stand and not be caught by § 20(1)(a),
must be explained under § 20(2)(b) on the basis that the buyer had reason to know the meaning attached to
the term by the seller.

[92] See *Dann v Spurrier* (1803) 3 Bos & P 399, 404, 127 ER 218, 220, 221; *NSW Sports Club Ltd v Solomon*
(1914) 14 SR (NSW) 340. See further Restatement (2d) Contracts § 206.

[93] 577 F 2d 568 (1978).

[94] 577 F 2d 568, 573 (1978). The Court also considered that its decision was strengthened by an
examination of the conduct of the parties during performance. It pointed to the fact that H & H accepted an
invoice which included an amount for profit and overhead.

must be so well known that knowledge can be inferred[95] since the party in question must be in a position to know of the trade usage.[96]

C. Incompleteness

11.30   A court will not enforce an incomplete agreement or an incomplete term.[97] A term will be incomplete if it does not adequately deal with an issue that has arisen under the contract and which falls within its subject matter. A contract will be void for being incomplete if any incomplete term or terms are essential to the contract and cannot be supplied by some gap-filling technique;[98] here the courts often view the agreement as no more than an agreement to agree.[99] That analogy may not be correct in all cases, especially where the parties not only intend to be bound but where there is reliable evidence of their belief that the bargain is complete. Given that the importance of terms is determined by the intention of the parties,[100] it follows that whether or not an important term is missing is also informed by the intention of the parties.[101] However, the more important a term is in an objective sense then the more likely a court will conclude that the parties intended the contract to come into effect only after agreement has been reached on that term.[102]

11.31   In practice, a large proportion of everyday agreements made by business people are incomplete and few would satisfy a strict requirement of completeness. Business people are generally satisfied as long as there is agreement on the essential terms. They may be reluctant to spend much time negotiating the terms in meticulous detail.[103] In addition, in long-term

---

[95] *Frigaliment Importing Co Ltd v BNS International Sales Corp* 190 F Supp 116, (1960). See also Restatement (2d) Contracts § 222(3).

[96] See *Shamrock Steamship Co v Storey and Co* (1899) 81 LT 413. See also above n 92. In addition many contractual terms have built up an accepted meaning, eg *Rahcassi Shipping Co SA v Blue Star Line Ltd* [1969] 1 QB 173 (arbitration clause required arbitrators to be 'commercial men and not lawyers'; the phrase 'commercial men' had a long history and was not therefore uncertain). See also *Nea Agrex SA v Baltic Shipping Co Ltd* [1976] QB 933.

[97] *Rossiter v Miller* (1878) 3 App Cas 1124, 1151; *Booker Industries Pty Ltd v Wilson Parking (Qld) Pty Ltd* (1982) 149 CLR 600, 604.

[98] Eg *Eudunda Farmers Co-operative Society Ltd v Mattiske* [1920] SALR 309 (no agreement on rent); *Hempel v Robinson* [1924] SASR 288 (no agreement of lease term and no agreement of period of credit under credit contract); *Fong v Cilli* (1968) 11 FLR 495 (no dates set for repayment and no rate of interest set under a mortgage). See also *Randazzo v Goulding* [1968] Qd R 433; *Woodside Offshore Petroleum Pty Ltd v Atwood Oceanics Inc* [1986] WAR 253; *Australian and New Zealand Banking Group Ltd v Frost Holdings Pty Ltd* [1989] VR 695; *Colliers International (Singapore) Pte Ltd v Senekee Logistics Pte Ltd* [2007] SGHC 18, [2007] 2 SLR 230.

[99] For example in *G Scammell and Nephew Ltd v Ouston* [1941] AC 251 an order was made 'on the understanding that the balance of the purchase price can be had on hire-purchase terms'. As such terms come in various forms it was not possible to determine what the parties meant and therefore the agreement was incomplete requiring further negotiation and agreement. See also *May and Butcher Ltd v R* [1934] 2 KB 17n; *Summergreene v Parker* (1950) 80 CLR 304; *South Australia v Commonwealth* (1962) 108 CLR 130; *Stocks & Holdings (Constructors) Pty Ltd v Arrowsmith* (1964) 112 CLR 646; *Booker Industries Pty Ltd v Wilson Parking (Qld) Pty Ltd* (1982) 149 CLR 600, 604; *Fraser Edmiston Pty Ltd v AGT (Qld) Pty Ltd* [1988] 2 Qd R 1.

[100] See 11.03.

[101] *Ridgway v Wharton* (1857) 6 HLC 238, 304–5, 10 ER 1287, 1313.

[102] *Pagnan SPA v Feed Products Ltd* [1987] 2 Lloyd's Rep 601, 619.

[103] See Beale & Dugdale, 'Contracts between Businessmen: Planning and the Use of Contractual Remedies' (1975) 2 Brit J Law & Soc 45, 48–9 who found in their study that detailed negotiations were rare and stated that 'some details might be left vague, either consciously because the parties had decided that it was

contracts some terms, even terms considered ultimately essential by the parties, may not be capable of being fixed at the time of executing the contract. If, in all such cases, the courts were to deny the existence of a binding contract it would defeat the reasonable expectations of commercial parties and interfere with the efficiency and smooth running of business transactions.[104] It follows that courts will try hard to uphold a bargain even though it is not complete by using the techniques discussed later in this chapter. However, it may be noted here that the general approach to this issue was expressed by Lord Wright in *Hillas & Co Ltd v Arcos Ltd*, in the following terms:[105]

> Businessmen often record the most important agreements in crude and summary fashion … It is accordingly the duty of the Court to construe such documents fairly and broadly, without being too astute or subtle in finding defects; but, on the contrary, the Court should seek to apply the old maxim of English law, *verba ita sunt intelligenda ut res magis valeat quam pereat* [words are to be understood that the object may be carried out and not fail]. That maxim, however, does not mean that the Court is to make a contract for the parties, or to go outside the words they have used, except in so far as there are appropriate implications of law, as, for instance, the implication of what is just and reasonable to be ascertained by the Court as matter of machinery where the contractual intention is clear but the contract is silent on some detail.

Finally, it must be noted that even if the agreement is complete as regards what the parties **11.32** consider to be the essential terms, it may still be found to be void for being incomplete if gaps are such that a court cannot determine the existence of a breach of contract and fashion an appropriate remedy when approached by one of the parties. The courts must 'feel confident enough in their ability to fill in the gaps which the parties have left' before they will uphold an incomplete agreement that evidences an intention by the parties to be bound but which cannot operate on its agreed terms without the court filling the gaps.[106]

D. Agreements to Agree and Agreements to Negotiate

Agreements to agree[107]

The expression 'agreement to agree' can be used to mean different things in different con- **11.33** texts. For example, where all the terms of an agreement are settled but it is made 'subject to contract', a determination must be made, by reference to the intention of the parties, whether or not they intended the agreement to have immediate effect or was to come into effect when a formal contract was executed.[108] If the intention is that the agreement is not to be enforceable until a formal contract is executed then one could say that the 'agreement' is no more than an agreement to agree. But that conclusion does not of itself provide any reason as to why that result was reached. A related expression is a 'contract to contract'.

---

not worth negotiating certain areas of conflict, or unconsciously: managing directors might draw up "heads of agreement" unwittingly leaving many areas vague'.

[104] *Hillas & Co Ltd v Arcos Ltd* (1932) 147 LT 503, 514 per Lord Wright.
[105] [1932] 147 LT 503, 514.
[106] *Trawl Industries of Australia Pty Ltd v Effem Foods Pty Ltd* (1992) 27 NSWLR 326, 333.
[107] McLauchlan, 'Rethinking Agreements to Agree' (1998) 18 NZULR 77; McLauchlan, 'Some Further Thoughts on Agreements to Agree' (2001) 7 NZBLQ 156.
[108] See 9.15.

This too does not necessarily dictate a particular legal response. In *Chillingworth v Esche*,[109] Sargant LJ said of this expression:[110]

> In the strictest sense of the words the Court will often enforce a contract to make a contract. The specific performance of a formal agreement of purchase is the enforcement of a contract to make a contract; the ultimate conveyance being often in itself in many respects a contract. The same remarks apply to the specific performance of a clause in a lease giving the lessee an option to purchase the superior interest of the lessor, freehold or leasehold as the case may be. The true meaning of the phrase is that the Court will not enforce a contract to make a second contract part of the terms of which are indeterminate and have yet to be agreed, so that there is not any definite contract at all which can be enforced, but only an agreement for a contract some of the terms of which are not yet agreed.

11.34   Despite having no doctrinal force of its own, the expression 'agreement to agree' has long been used to denote a classification of negotiations that results in an agreement that is illusory, uncertain[111] and incomplete.[112] It has also been said that a true unenforceable agreement to agree lacks an intention to contract.[113] Whether an agreement is an agreement to agree has been said to be an issue of construction if the agreement is in writing and a question of fact if it is oral.[114] However, as noted, the words themselves are not conclusive and carry no legal implication.[115] It is possible for the parties to enter into a legally enforceable contract with an express or implied intention that further terms are still to be agreed.[116] What is relevant is whether or not the 'agreement' requires further consensus; a true 'agreement to agree' in the sense that it denotes a category of agreement, lacks the assent required for a contract.[117] The leading statement and example is contained in *May & Butcher Ltd v The King*.[118] In this case May & Butcher proposed to purchase 'tentage' from the Disposals

---

[109] [1924] 1 Ch 97.

[110] [1924] 1 Ch 97, 113–14.

[111] A contract will not be void if the agreement to agree is merely an alternative so that parties have agreed a set of terms that are to be applied unless they agree on other terms, see *Sidney Eastman Pty Ltd v Southern* [1963] SR (NSW) 815, 816, 817.

[112] *United Group Rail Services Ltd v Rail Corp New South Wales* [2009] NSWCA 177, [56].

[113] *Coal Cliff Collieries Pty Ltd v Sijehama Pty Ltd* (1991) 24 NSWLR 1, 4 per Kirby P.

[114] *Summergreene v Parker* (1950) 80 CLR 304, 323 (here an agreement on terms 'satisfactory' to one of the parties was held to constitute an agreement to agree).

[115] Eg *Smith v Morgan* [1971] 1 WLR 803 (contract for sale of land with first right of refusal being given to vendor contingent on purchaser deciding to sell; in such circumstances the purchaser was to offer the property to the vendor 'at a price to be agreed'; this was held not to be void as an agreement to agree but merely required the purchaser to offer to sell the property back to the vendor at 'the' price she was prepared to sell it for). See also *Re Empress Towers Ltd and Bank of Nova Scotia* (1990) 73 DLR (4th) 400.

[116] *Global Container Lines Ltd v State Black Sea Shipping Co* [1999] 1 Lloyd's Rep 127, 155–7.

[117] Farnsworth, *Farnsworth on Contracts* (3rd ed, Vol 1, Aspen Publishers, New York, 2004), § 3.27, p 419.

[118] [1934] 2 KB 17(n), 20 per Viscount Dunedin. See also *Ridgway v Wharton* (1857) 6 HLC 238, 305, 10 ER 1287, 1313; *Von Hatzfeldt-Wildenburg v Alexander* [1912] 1 Ch 284, 289; *Hempel v Robinson* [1924] SASR 288; *British Homophone Ltd v Kunz* (1935) 152 LT 589; *G Scammell and Nephew Ltd v HC & JG Ouston* [1941] AC 251, 269; *Re WG Apps & Sons Pty Ltd and Hurley* [1949] VLR 7; *Masters v Cameron* (1954) 91 CLR 353, 362; *Willetts v Ryan* [1968] NZLR 863; *Godecke v Kirwan* (1973) 129 CLR 629, 638–9; *Courtney & Fairbairn Ltd v Tolaini Brothers (Hotels) Ltd* [1975] 1 WLR 297, 301; *Mmecen SA v Inter Ro-Ro SA (The Samah and Lina V)* [1981] 1 Lloyd's Rep 40; *Booker Industries Pty Ltd v Wilson Parking (Qld) Pty Ltd* (1982) 149 CLR 600, 604; *Sudbrook Trading Estate Ltd v Eggleton* [1983] 1 AC 444, 476–7; *Cedar Trading Co Ltd v Transworld Oil Ltd (The Gudermes)* [1985] 2 Lloyd's Rep 623; *Woodside Offshore Petroleum Pty Ltd v Atwood Oceanics Inc* [1986] WAR 253; *Ratto v Trifid Pty Ltd* [1987] WAR 237; *Barrett v IBC International Ltd* [1995] 3 NZLR 170, CA; *Pratt Contractors Ltd v Palmerston North City Council* [1995] 1 NZLR 469.

Board (a body set up by the government to dispose of goods formerly required for war purposes). Tentage was a term used to describe a class of goods relating to the construction and equipment of tents. The Company received a number of letters from the Controller of the Board purporting to confirm the sale of 'the whole of the old tentage which may become available' up to 31 March 1923 upon terms which included the following:

> (3) The price or prices to be paid, and the date or dates on which payment is to be made by the purchasers to the Commission for such old tentage shall be agreed upon from time to time between the Commission and the purchasers as the quantities of the said old tentage become available for disposal, and are offered to the purchasers by the Commission …

> (10) It is understood that all disputes with reference to or arising out of this agreement will be submitted to arbitration in accordance with the provisions of the Arbitration Act, 1889.

There was a commercial reality to this transaction because the 'tentage' covered a variety of products of varying qualities and until the buyer viewed what was on offer it could not realistically determine its value. **11.35**

At one point May & Butcher made price proposals but these were refused by the Board. The Board then considered that it was no longer bound by the agreement on the ground that the price was never agreed. May & Butcher claimed first, that if the price was not agreed then the price was to be a reasonable price, and second, that even if the price was not agreed, the arbitration clause in the contract was intended to apply in the event of a dispute and arbitration could therefore be used to fix the price. **11.36**

The House of Lords held that since there was no agreement on these matters there could be no concluded contract. In his reasoning Lord Buckmaster made an unambiguous statement that an agreement to agree was void but on the same page he made the more equivocal statement that 'an agreement between two parties to enter into an agreement in which some critical part of the contract matter is left undetermined is no contract at all'.[119] **11.37**

Viscount Dunedin stated that:[120] **11.38**

> To be a good contract there must be a concluded bargain, and a concluded contract is one which settles everything that is necessary to be settled and leaves nothing to be settled by agreement between the parties. Of course it may leave something which still has to be determined, but then that determination must be a determination which does not depend upon the agreement between the parties … We are here dealing with sale, and undoubtedly price is one of the essentials of sale, and if it is left still to be agreed between the parties, then there is no contract. It may be left to the determination of a certain person, and if it was so left and that person either would not or could not act, there would be no contract because the price was to be settled in a certain way and it has become impossible to settle it in that way, and therefore there is no settlement. No doubt as to goods, the Sale of Goods Act, 1893, says that if the price is not mentioned and settled in the contract it is to be a reasonable price. The simple answer in this case is that the Sale of Goods Act provides for silence on the point and here there is no silence, because there is a provision that the two parties are to agree. As long as you have something certain it does not matter.

Lord Warrington similarly emphasized that the court could not imply a reasonable price because that would be at odds with the intention of the parties which was to agree a price. **11.39**

---

[119] [1934] 2 KB 17(n), 20.
[120] [1934] 2 KB 17(n), 21.

A term cannot be implied if it is inconsistent with an express term.[121] Thus, depending on the subject matter, a court can often resolve a case where there is agreement to pay a reasonable price but not an agreement to agree a price.[122]

11.40 As regards the arbitration provision, Lord Buckmaster thought the clause was not operative as it dealt with disputes arising out the 'agreement' and there was no agreement. Lord Warrington agreed, the lack of a binding contract meant the clause was not binding.[123] Lord Dunedin held that the clause dealt only with 'disputes' and this was not a dispute but a 'failure to agree'.[124]

11.41 Since this case there has been a continuing debate as to whether the courts should accord that much primacy to the intention of the parties to agree and therefore refuse to impose an obligation inconsistent with that intention. The alternative is that primacy should be given to an overall intention to be bound if it exists. For some a clear distinction should be drawn between an agreement to agree a contract which should be held illusory as the whole transaction is in a state of negotiation, and an agreement that contains an undertaking to agree a term. The latter often arises in a commercial context[125] and it is here that the courts are most likely to uphold the agreement unless the term to be agreed is an essential term.[126] Often parties enter into some preliminary agreement with an intention to contract and agree to agree the remainder of the terms. In many cases this is because it is not possible to determine all the rights and obligations at that time. There is a view that if there is a clear intention to be bound this should be given paramount importance so that if the courts can use the normal techniques to resolve any uncertainty or incompleteness then such agreements should not be struck down out of hand.[127] There is certainly a view in the modern law that those cases where an agreement to agree has been upheld can be explained by reference to the court being loath to hold a contract void for uncertainty and incompleteness if there is an intention to be bound and it is possible to give effect to the transaction.[128] The decision in *May & Butcher* itself has come in for some express criticism. In *Fletcher Challenge Energy Ltd v Electricity Corporation of New Zealand Ltd*[129] the court said the case 'is no longer to be regarded as authority for any wider proposition than that an "agreement" which omits an essential term ... or a means of determining such a term, does not amount to a contract. No longer should it be said ... if something essential is left to be agreed upon by the parties at a later time, there is no binding agreement'.[130] Arguably, given the analysis of the judgments in the case set out above, it was never intended to be authority for any broader proposition. The difficulty with the proposal suggested in *Fletcher Challenge* is to determine what was meant by the reference to 'essential' terms. It is suggested that the court

---

[121] [1934] 2 KB 17(n), 22. See also *Willis Management (Isle of Man) Ltd v Cable and Wireless Plc* [2005] 2 Lloyd's Rep 597; *Barrett v IBC International Ltd* [1995] 3 NZLR 170, CA. See further 11.118.

[122] See 11.51.

[123] [1934] 2 KB 17(n), 22.

[124] [1934] 2 KB 17(n), 22.

[125] Eg *American Airlines Inc v Hope* [1973] 1 Lloyd's Rep 233; *Tropwood AG of Zug v Jade Enterprises Ltd (The Tropwind)* [1982] 1 Lloyd's Rep 232.

[126] *Barrett v IBC International Ltd* [1995] 3 NZLR 170.

[127] *Sudbrook Trading Estate Ltd v Eggleton* [1983] 1 AC 444. See also the approach in Uniform Commercial Code § 2-305 and see Unidroit Principles of International Commercial Contracts, Art 2.1.14.

[128] See *Grow with US v Green Thumb (UK) Ltd* [2006] EWCA Civ 1201, [22], CA.

[129] [2002] 2 NZLR 433. See McLauchlan, 'Intention, Incompleteness and Uncertainty in the New Zealand Court of Appeal' (2002) 18 JCL 153.

[130] [2002] 2 NZLR 433, 446–7.

meant that the agreement could be enforced despite lacking terms the parties considered important but not those necessary for its enforcement.

As noted earlier, the word 'essential' in this context is ambiguous. The leading statement on **11.42** its meaning is that of Lloyd LJ in *Pagnan SpA v Feed Products Ltd*.[131] In this case Lloyd LJ suggested that an agreement to agree should be upheld unless what is agreed is unworkable or void for uncertainty. That is, it lacks terms necessary for its enforcement. As regards the meaning of 'essential' he said:[132]

> It is sometimes said that the parties must agree on the essential terms and that it is only matters of detail which can be left over. This may be misleading, since the word 'essential' in that context is ambiguous. If by 'essential' one means a term without which the contract cannot be enforced then the statement is true: the law cannot enforce an incomplete contract. If by 'essential' one means a term which the parties have agreed to be essential for the formation of a binding contract, then the statement is tautologous. If by 'essential' one means only a term which the court regards as important as opposed to a term which the court regards as less important or a matter of detail, the statement is untrue. It is for the parties to decide whether they wish to be bound and, if so, by what terms, whether important or unimportant.

Perhaps the most forceful commentator for upholding agreements to agree is McLauchlan **11.43** who also suggests that primacy be given to the intention to be bound so that even if a material term is left to be agreed the agreement should be upheld.[133] He writes:[134]

> [A]greements intended to be legally binding ought never to be rejected simply on the ground that a material term was deferred for future agreement between the parties. The fact that a term is designated as 'to be agreed' will often be simply an indication of the parties' understanding that the term is capable of being agreed in the future and that it is their intention to do so, not that there is to be no contract until such agreement is reached. Such an understanding is perfectly consistent with the existence of the further intention that, failing agreement, the gap is to be filled if possible by reference to the objective standard of what is reasonable in the circumstances.

It is interesting that there are some Australian cases that have adopted similar views[135] **11.44** because the decision of the High Court of Australia in *Masters v Cameron*[136] appears to be against such a proposition. That case is the authoritative Australian case on the meaning of 'subject to contract' which is dealt with in detail in another chapter.[137] However, the court suggested that the phrase may have one of three meanings, the parties may intend to be immediately bound and be required to perform, they may intend to be immediately bound

---

[131] [1987] 2 Lloyd's Rep 601. See also *Global Container Lines Ltd v State Black Sea Shipping Co* [1999] 1 Lloyd's Rep 127, 155.

[132] [1987] 2 Lloyd's Rep 601, 619.

[133] McLauchlan, 'In Defence of the Fourth Category of Preliminary Agreements: Or Are There Only Two?' (2005) 21 JCL 286; McLauchlan, 'Rethinking Agreements to Agree' (1988) 18 NZULR 77.

[134] McLauchlan, 'In Defence of the Fourth Category of Preliminary Agreements: Or Are There Only Two?' (2005) 21 JCL 286, 288.

[135] See *World Audio Ltd v GB Radio (Aust) Pty Ltd* [2003] NSWSC 855, [89]; *Capitol Theatre Management v Council of the City of Sydney* [2005] NSWSC 5, [45].

[136] (1954) 91 CLR 353.

[137] See 9.16ff.

but performance is suspended until the condition is fulfilled or they may intend not to be bound at all until the condition is fulfilled.[138] In explaining the third class they said:[139]

> Cases of the third class are fundamentally different. They are cases in which the terms of agreement are not intended to have, and therefore do not have, any binding effect of their own ... The parties may have so provided either because they have dealt only with major matters and contemplate that others will or may be regulated by provisions to be introduced into the formal document, as in *Summergreene v Parker* (1950) 80 CLR 304 or simply because they wish to reserve to themselves a right to withdraw at any time until the formal document is signed. These possibilities were both referred to in *Rossiter v Miller* (1878) 3 App Cas 1124. Lord O'Hagan said (1878) 3 App Cas 1124 at 1149: 'Undoubtedly, if any prospective contract, involving the possibility of new terms, or the modification of those already discussed, remains to be adopted, matters must be taken to be still in a train of negotiation, and a dissatisfied party may refuse to proceed. But when an agreement embracing all the particulars essential for finality and completeness, even though it may be desired to reduce it to shape by a solicitor, is such that those particulars must remain unchanged, it is not, in my mind, less coercive because of the technical formality which remains to be made'. And Lord Blackburn said (1878) 3 App Cas 1124 at 1152: 'parties often do enter into a negotiation meaning that, when they have (or think they have) come to one mind, the result shall be put into formal shape, and then (if on seeing the result in that shape they find they are agreed) signed and made binding; but that each party is to reserve to himself the right to retire from the contract, if, on looking at the formal contract, he finds that though it may represent what he said, it does not represent what he meant to say. Whenever, on the true construction of the evidence, this appears to be the intention, I think that the parties ought not to be held bound till they have executed the formal agreement'. So, as Parker J said in *Von Hatzfeldt-Wildenburg v Alexander* [1912] 1 Ch 284 at 289 in such a case there is no enforceable contract, either because the condition is unfulfilled or because the law does not recognise a contract to enter into a contract.

11.45   Although it might be possible to argue that these statements were made in the context of an agreement that lacked an intention to immediately assume legal obligations, in suggesting that there can be no contract when the parties 'have dealt only with major matters and contemplate that others will or may be regulated by provisions to be introduced into the formal document' the High Court has not left much if any room for upholding an agreement to agree even when what remains 'to be agreed' are some non-essential terms.[140] The High Court did recognize that when a formal document is executed it could contain further terms. That is the court recognized the efficacy of a case where 'the parties were content to be bound immediately and exclusively by the terms which they had agreed upon whilst expecting to make a further contract in substitution for the first contract, containing, by consent, additional terms'.[141] This must be correct, the parties are free to agree further terms which may take effect as a variation or re-negotiation. The essential point though is that there should be nothing in the original agreement that suggests a need to agree further terms for the operation of that agreement. In terms of certainty and completeness the original agreement must stand on its own feet. This, it is suggested, is the key the High Court's formulation of the principle. Where an 'agreement' evidences a need to agree further terms

---

[138] (1954) 91 CLR 353, 360.

[139] (1954) 91 CLR 353, 361–2.

[140] The term for 'agreement' on such terms traditionally inhibits the court using gap filling techniques as to do so is at odds with the intention of the parties.

[141] (1929) 43 CLR 310, 317–18.

in order for that 'agreement' to take effect then that evidences a lack of an intention to assume legal obligations.[142] The parties must have agreed all those terms that their own intention to be bound was contingent upon.[143] It is therefore possible for the parties to agree very few terms in a complex agreement and have that agreement enforced as long as they intend to immediately be bound and, in terms of certainty and completeness, the court does not require any further terms to enforce the agreement.[144]

The case usually put forward to evidence a contrasting approach to the *May & Butcher* case **11.46** is *Foley v Classique Coaches Ltd.*[145] Here the defendant entered into an agreement to buy land from the plaintiff to be used for the defendant's trailer park business for a certain price. In a separate agreement, executed at the same time, the defendant undertook to purchase all their petrol requirements from the plaintiff 'at a price to be agreed by the parties in writing and from time to time'. There was also an arbitration clause which was stated to be applicable to any dispute or difference arising over the subject matter or construction of the agreement. After the petrol sale agreement had been operating for three years at prices charged by the plaintiff, disputes arose and eventually the defendant repudiated the contract by informing the plaintiff of its intention to purchase petrol supplies elsewhere. The defendant claimed that no binding contract existed because there was no agreement as to price.

The Court of Appeal distinguished the *May & Butcher* case and held the agreement to be **11.47** valid and binding by implying a term that the petrol was to be supplied at a reasonable price; it should be noted that the result is arrived at by reference to an implied term rather than an imposed standard of reasonableness.[146] To get to that point the court had to determine where the line was drawn between the House of Lords decision in the *May & Butcher* case and the decision of the House of Lords in *Hillas & Co Ltd v Arcos Ltd.*[147] The facts of the *Hillas* case are dealt with later, it is not an express agreement to agree case but a case where the terms were not complete.[148] It is suffice to state here that the court in the *Foley* case said that the House of Lords in the *Hillas* case had made it clear that they were not laying down any general principles in the *May & Butcher* case and that each case turned on its own particular facts.

In the *Foley* case, in arriving at its decision that there was a contract, the court considered a **11.48** number of factors which were in addition to finding that an intention to contract existed. First, there was reliance, the parties had acted on the agreement for three years. Second, the price paid for the land was linked to the defendant's undertaking to purchase its petrol needs from the plaintiff. If at the time of contract that undertaking was not given, it was likely the plaintiff would either have negotiated for a higher price for the land or not agreed

---

[142] See 10.09.

[143] *CPC Consolidated Pool Carriers GMBH v CTM Cia Transmediterranea SA (The CPC Gallia)* [1994] 1 Lloyd's Rep 68.

[144] Eg *Perry v Suffields Ltd* [1916] 2 Ch 187; *Bigg v Boyd Gibbons Ltd* [1971] 1 WLR 913. Often a lack of agreement on detailed provisions in a complex contract will evidence a lack of intention to be bound, *Vroon BV v Foster's Brewing Group Ltd* [1994] 2 VR 32, 68 per Ormiston J.

[145] [1934] 2 KB 1. See also *Morton v Morton* [1942] 1 All ER 273; *Canada Square Corp Ltd v Versafood Services Ltd* (1981) 130 DLR (3d) 205.

[146] See 11.84ff. Cf *Voest Alpine Intertrading GmbH v Chevron International Oil Co Ltd* [1987] 2 Lloyd's Rep 547, 562.

[147] (1932) 147 LT 503.

[148] See 11.86.

to sell at all. Third, the provision for arbitration demonstrated that the parties were willing for prices to be fixed by some external method if they failed to agree.

11.49 How then do those factors allow the court to intervene when the parties had expressly agreed to agree? Scrutton LJ's reasons are quite brief. Essentially he said that the parties had intended to contract and the arbitration clause was there to deal with the situation that arose if they failed to agree. By drawing an analogy with principles governing tied houses[149] he said there was an implied term that the petrol would be supplied for a reasonable price and be of a reasonable quality. Greer LJ expressly recognized that a court cannot imply a term if to do so would be inconsistent with the intention of the parties but thought that here the implication would give effect to the intention of the parties.[150] Whether he was referring to the intention to contract as opposed to the intention to agree a price is not made clear.[151] In his judgment Maugham LJ said some weight, but not too much, could be placed on the intention to contract.[152] Indeed Maugham LJ, by focusing on the exclusive dealing arrangement aspect of the case—and by reference to an 'old-established rule in the case of tied houses'—was much clearer in expressing why this implication was not inconsistent with the intention of the parties, he said:[153]

> Are we to assume that both parties were so ignorant of business that no dispute as to price could possibly arise? Price is the very basis of this agreement, which surely does not mean that the company are not to purchase petrol from any other person or corporation if they are unable to agree in writing on the price or if the vendor chooses to fix a price above the commercial price which the company could possibly pay. If the clause were to be construed in that way it would be nonsense, and in my opinion it is necessary to imply … a proviso that so long as the vendor is able and willing to supply the company with sufficient petrol either at a price to be agreed … or at a fair and reasonable price if the price has not been so agreed, the company shall purchase it from him.

11.50 It would seem to follow from the above analysis that there may be three distinct approaches to overcoming incompleteness resulting from an agreement to agree all of which assume an intention to be bound. First, in some cases when the contract is construed as a whole it may not be inconsistent with the intention of the parties to agree a term for the court to imply a term if the parties fail to agree.[154] Second, there may be some recognition that it is possible to imply a term to fill a gap in the face of an agreement to agree that term when to do so gives effect to the overall expectation of the parties that the agreement should carry legal

---

[149] A tenant under a brewer's lease was required to only sell alcohol supplied by the landlord, this carried with it an implied obligation that the landlord will supply the alcohol at reasonable prices, see *Catt v Tourle* (1869) LR 4 Ch 654; *Courage & Co Ltd v Carpenter* [1910] 1 Ch 262.

[150] [1934] 2 KB 1, 12.

[151] Greer LJ went on to say that when the buyer repudiated the contract this relieved the seller of the obligation to discuss a price with the buyer, and, moreover, prevented the buyer from relying 'on the fact that the contract might have broken down in the future because of their refusal to pay a reasonable price or their possible refusal to accept what the seller said was a reasonable quality of petrol' [1934] 2 KB 1, 12. Here Greer LJ's language seems to place some weight on the misconduct of one of the parties. This might provide some, albeit weak, evidence that a court will not allow an agreement to fail if one of the parties has engaged in some form of unconscionable conduct.

[152] [1934] 2 KB 1, 13.

[153] Cf in the context of a building contract, *Courtney & Fairbairn Ltd v Tolaini Brothers (Hotels) Ltd* [1975] 1 WLR 297, 301.

[154] See further *Corson v Rhuddlan Borough Council* (1990) 59 P & CR 185, 193.

force.[155] Third, acts of performance and reliance may be resorted to not only to show an intention to be bound but to provide an insight into the meaning the parties intended and thus resolve any uncertainty and incompleteness; in this way it cannot be said reliance is being used to make a contract. There is a view that acts of performance or reliance are of themselves a reason for a court to either impose a standard of reasonableness or an implied term.[156] The use of such evidence is clearly legitimate if the issues of certainty and completeness are seen as going to contract formation. Use of such evidence is more problematic if issues of certainty and completeness are seen as issues of performance involving pure questions of construction.[157]

The first and second of these approaches is adopted in the United States under the Uniform **11.51** Commercial Code (UCC), which provides in section 2-204(3) that:[158] 'Even though one or more terms are left open a contract for sale does not fail for indefiniteness if the parties have intended to make a contract and there is a reasonably certain basis for giving an appropriate remedy.' Article 2-305 then specially deals with price and provides:

> (1) The parties if they so intend may conclude a contract for sale even if the price is not settled. In such a case the price is a reasonable price at the time for delivery if:
>> (a) nothing is said as to price;
>> (b) the price is left to be agreed by the parties and they fail to agree; or
>> (c) the price is to be fixed in terms of some agreed market or other standard as set or recorded by a third person or agency and it is not so set or recorded.[159]

Similarly, the Restatement (2d) Contracts, section 204, emphasizes the importance of **11.52** intention to contract. It provides:[160]

> When the parties to a bargain sufficiently defined to be a contract have not agreed with respect to a term which is essential to a determination of their rights and duties, a term which is reasonable in the circumstances is supplied by the court.

The effect of this section is to imply a term that is reasonable which is distinct from imply- **11.53** ing a term on the basis that it is reasonable to do so. Comment *d* to section 204 explains the application of the section as follows:

> The process of supplying an omitted term has sometimes been disguised as a literal or purposive reading of contract language directed to a situation other than the situation that arises. Sometimes it is said that the search is for the term the parties would have agreed to if the

---

[155] *Sudbrook Trading Estate Ltd v Eggleton* [1983] 1 AC 444, 483 (discussed at 11.107) suggesting that courts today are more willing to give effect to the overall expectation of the parties that their agreement would give rise to legal obligations and this approach can override the fact that a court imposed solution might be inconsistent with a particular term.

[156] See *Head v Kelk* [1962] NSWR 1363, 1370; *F & G Sykes (Wessex) Ltd v Fine Fare Ltd* [1967] 1 Lloyd's Rep 53; *Voest Alpine Intertrading GmbH v Chevron International Oil Co Ltd* [1987] 2 Lloyd's Rep 547, 561. See also Restatement (2d) Contracts §§ 34(2), (3). See further 11.84ff.

[157] Notes 3, 58, 204.

[158] The history of the American approach to 'agreements to agree' is traced in Speidel, 'Restatement Second: Omitted Terms and Contract Method' (1982) 67 Cornell L Rev 785, 790ff. A resurgence of a formalist position whereby agreements to agree will not be upheld is traced in Mooney, 'The New Conceptualism in Contract Law' (1995) 74 Oregon L Rev 1131.

[159] Where the parties do not intend to be bound unless the price is fixed or agreed, then there is no contract if the price is not fixed or agreed; § 2-305(4).

[160] This provision is not without its difficulties, see Speidel, 'Restatement Second: Omitted Terms and Contract Method' (1982) 67 Cornell L Rev 785.

question had been brought to their attention. Both the meaning of the words used and the probability that a particular term would have been used if the question had been raised may be factors in determining what term is reasonable in the circumstances. But where there is in fact no agreement, the court should supply a term which comports with community standards of fairness and policy rather than analyse a hypothetical model of the bargaining process.

11.54   Speidel notes that this approach to 'the problem of open price is carried over to other omitted terms in Article Two, Part Three of the UCC. If the parties "intend" to create a contract, if there is no agreement to the contrary, and if there is a reasonably certain basis for enforcement, the Code provides judicial "gap filling" standards for all terms thought essential to the bargain'.[161] There is certainly clear evidence that the courts draw on article 2-305 of the UCC for authority in non-sale and non-Code transactions,[162] on the basis that this provision illustrates 'the approach of the modern law, with its emphasis on reasonable commercial dealings and its rejection of technical requirements'.[163] In *Aycock v Vantage Management Co*,[164] the court held that, although article 2-305 was technically not applicable to leases of real estate, the principle expressed in that provision was sound and could apply so that a renewal provision was not held unenforceable simply because the rental was not specified. The renewal rent was to be based on a number of enumerated factors such as the then prevailing rental rates for properties of equivalent quality, size, utility and location. It was held, citing UCC, article 2-305(b), that the lessor was obliged to make a good faith determination consistent with these factors. The court was clearly keen to hold the parties to their evident intention to be bound by a provision that did not specify the exact rental.

11.55   In Anglo-Australian law the agreement to agree rent has been one of the textbook examples of an agreement to agree. There have been numerous cases over the years suggesting that a court cannot uphold an agreement for lease if the rent is to be agreed and there is no formula for its determination if there is a failure to agree.[165] Courts have been reluctant to apply a standard of reasonableness to such contracts.[166] In more recent years there has been some relaxing of that position which may evidence an adoption of the approach being discussed. One example of this relaxation was to distinguish between an agreement to agree

---

[161] Speidel, 'Restatement Second: Omitted Terms and Contract Method' (1982) 67 Cornell L Rev 785, 791.

[162] See further Knapp, 'Enforcing the Contract to Bargain' (1969) 44 NYU L Rev 673, 690–1.

[163] *Moolenaar v Co-Build Companies Inc* 354 F Supp 980, 984 (1973).

[164] 554 SW 2d 235 (1977). See also *Schmieder v Standard Oil Co of Indiana* 69 Wis 2d 419, 230 NW 2d 732 (1975) (contract giving defendants an option to purchase certain equipment 'at a price equal to Employee's costs, minus such depreciation as may be mutually agreed upon'; held that the contract was enforceable, and that a reasonable depreciation would be implied in the case where there was a failure to agree). Cf *Joseph Martin Jr Delicatessen Inc v Schumacher* 52 NY 2d 105, 417 NE 2d 541, 544 (1981).

[165] Eg *King's Motors (Oxford) Ltd v Lax* [1970] 1 WLR 426; *Brown v Gould* [1972] Ch 53, 58. See also *Eudunda Farmers Co-operative Society Ltd v Mattiske* [1920] SALR 309; *Trazray Pty Ltd v Russell Foundries Pty Ltd* (1988) 5 BPR 11,232; *Austotel Pty Ltd v Franklins Selfserve Pty Ltd* (1989) 16 NSWLR 582. It has been said that the rent figure must be certain at the time it becomes payable rather than the date of the lease, see *Greater London Council v Connolly* [1970] 2 QB 100, 109. This suggests that historically the need for certainty here had more to do with the landlord's remedy of distress for unpaid rent than with contract formation, see Gray and Gray, *Elements of Land Law* (5th edn, OUP, Oxford, 2009), para 4.1.29, cf para 4.1.31. Failure to agree on the term of the lease has also been held to be fatal, see *Bishop v Taylor* (1968) 118 CLR 518. See further *King v King* (1981) 41 P & CR 311, cf *Thomas Bates & Son Ltd v Wyndham's (Lingerie) Ltd* [1981] 1 WLR 505.

[166] Similarly a court will not imply an obligation that parties pay a reasonable price for the sale of land, see *Corser v Commonwealth General Assurance Corp Ltd* [1963] NSWR 225.

a lease, such as an option to take a lease where the rent is to be agreed and a rent review clause under an existing lease where the review clause states that the rent is to be agreed.[167] The latter could be upheld as there was a contract in existence while the former could not as it was nothing more than an agreement to agree. This is the distinction between an agreement to agree and an agreement to agree a term. However, even this distinction appears to have been rejected by the Court of Appeal in *Corson v Rhuddlan Borough Council*.[168] Here a lease provided for an option to renew 'at a rental to be agreed (but such rental shall not in any event exceed the rental hereby reserved)'. In upholding that provision the court made a number of important statements. First Ralph Gibson LJ (with whom Balcombe LJ agreed)[169] placed a lot of weight on the construction of the contract as a whole which clearly evidenced that the parties intended an obligation to flow from this agreement. He thought that if it was plain that the parties intended to contract a provision that the rent payable should be a fair rent could be implied.[170] He saw no reason to distinguish the principles that 'should be applicable to the construction, so far as concerns voidness for uncertainty, of a rent revision clause in an existing lease as contrasted with an option for a new lease or further lease in an existing lease'.[171] Staughton LJ agreed saying that one must first consider all the express and implied terms of a contract before holding it void for uncertainty.[172] He went on to say that the parties clearly intended a contract and if they were asked what would happen if they failed to agree would have answered that the court or an arbitrator would decide and the solution they would impose would be a fair rent. This result he said was grounded in the terms of the contract and surrounding circumstances.[173] It is therefore not a direct application of the approach under the Restatement (2d) Contracts § 204 discussed above. He did not think the parties would have expected the contract to fail if they failed to agree. There is an overriding importance attached the intention to be bound in his judgment.

There has also been some express acceptance of the third approach. For example, in *British Bank for Foreign Trade LD v Novinex LD*,[174] the Court of Appeal approved this statement of principle of the trial judge:[175]   **11.56**

> The principle to be deduced from the cases is that if there is an essential term which has yet to be agreed and there is no express or implied provision for its solution, the result in point of law is that there is no binding contract. In seeing whether there is an implied provision for its solution, however, there is a difference between an arrangement which is wholly executory on both sides, and one which has been executed on one side or the other. In the ordinary way, if there is an arrangement to supply goods at a price 'to be agreed' or to perform services on terms 'to be agreed', then although, while the matter is still executory, there may be no binding contract, nevertheless, if it is executed on one side, that is if the one does his part without having come to an agreement as to the price or the terms, then the law will say that there is

---

[167] *Beer v Bowden* [1981] 1 WLR 522.
[168] (1990) 59 P & CR 185.
[169] He thought that *King's Motors (Oxford) Ltd v Lax* [1970] 1 WLR 426 was not correctly decided despite the dictum of Goff LJ in *Beer v Bowden* [1981] 1 WLR 522, 525.
[170] (1990) 59 P & CR 185, 194.
[171] (1990) 59 P & CR 185, 194.
[172] (1990) 59 P & CR 185, 197.
[173] (1990) 59 P & CR 185, 198.
[174] [1949] 1 KB 623.
[175] [1949] 1 KB 623, 629–30.

necessarily implied, from the conduct of the parties, a contract that, in default of agreement, a reasonable sum is to be paid.[176]

11.57 This statement clearly adopts the view that by their conduct the parties may be taken to have agreed to pay a reasonable price. Despite this there are many cases that adopt a different view.[177] For example, in *British Electrical and Associated Industries (Cardiff) Ld v Patley*,[178] a sale was made 'subject to force majeure conditions that the government restricts the export of the material at the time of delivery'. This clause was held to be meaningless and McNair J added, 'notwithstanding that the parties may have thought and acted on the basis that a contract existed between them, no consensus ad idem will be held to exist where there still remains to be negotiated and agreed the exact form of the clauses or conditions referred to by the parties'.[179]

11.58 Finally, it needs to be stressed that there will be contracts where agreement on a term may be considered by the court to be so important that the court cannot consider there to be an intention to contract without agreement on that term. In such cases the court will not use its techniques to fill that gap. In *Courtney & Fairbairn Ltd v Tolaini Brothers (Hotels) Ltd*[180] a construction contract was expressed to be of such a nature. It is also possible for there to be agreement on what may be considered all the essential terms and for the parties still to evidence an intention not to contract until some further step is taken.[181]

Agreements to negotiate[182]

11.59 At present in Anglo-Australian law a simple agreement to negotiate is void.[183] It does not help to attempt to provide some standard for negotiation such as good faith by which to

---

[176] The importance of performance and reliance is also reflected in the Restatement (2d) Contracts § 34 which relevantly provides:

(2) Part performance under an agreement may remove uncertainty and establish that a contract enforceable as a bargain has been formed.

(3) Action in reliance on an agreement may make a contractual remedy appropriate even though uncertainty is not removed.

[177] For a survey of recent American authorities, see Mooney, 'The New Conceptualism in Contract Law' (1995) 74 Oregon L Rev 1131.

[178] [1953] 1 WLR 280.

[179] [1953] 1 WLR 280, 284.

[180] [1975] 1 WLR 297.

[181] *Fletcher Challenge Energy Ltd v Electricity Corporation of New Zealand Ltd* [2002] 2 NZLR 433, 443–4. See above 11.41.

[182] The relevance of the efficacy of such agreements to the development of pre-contractual liability is discussed at 12.77ff. See generally on this topic, Knapp, 'Enforcing the Contract to Bargain' (1969) NY Uni Law Rev 673; Farnsworth, 'Precontractual Liability and Preliminary Agreements: Fair Dealing and Failed Negotiations' (1987) 87 Columbia L Rev 217, 250ff. See also Kessler and Fine, 'Culpa In Contrahendo, Bargaining in Good Faith, and Freedom of Contract: A Comparative Study' (1964) 77 Harv L Rev 401; Hammond 'Contracts to Negotiate' [1976] 2 NZLJ 153.

[183] *Walford v Miles* [1992] 2 AC 128; *Coal Cliff Collieries Pty Ltd v Sijehama Pty Ltd* (1991) 24 NSWLR 1. See also *Carr v Brisbane City Council* [1956] QSR 402, 411; *Courtney & Fairbairn Ltd v Tolaini Bros (Hotels) Ltd* [1975] 1 WLR 297, 301 per Lord Denning MR, 302 per Lord Diplock; *Mallozzi v Carpelli SpA* [1976] 1 Lloyd's Rep 407; *Albion Sugar Co Ltd v Williams Tankers Ltd & Davies (The John S Derbyshire)* [1977] 2 Lloyd's Rep 457, 466; *Scandinavian Trading Tanker Co AB v Flota Petrolera Ecuatoriana (The Scaptrade)* [1981] 2 Lloyd's Rep 425, 432; *Itex Shipping Pte Ltd v China Ocean Shipping Co (The 'Jing Hong Hai')* [1989] 2 Lloyd's Rep 522, 526; *Surrey County Council v Bredero Homes Ltd* [1993] 1 WLR 1361, 1368; *Mamidoil-Jetoil Greek Petroleum Co SA v Okta Crude Oil Refinery AD* [2001] 2 Lloyd's Rep 76, 87. The contrary view expressed by

gauge the conduct of the parties and such a standard will generally not be implied.[184] The difficulty with such agreements is that they appear to be both incomplete and uncertain.[185] It is different if the agreement involves an undertaking not to negotiate with a third party—a lock-out agreement—which does not require the promisor to negotiate with the promisee[186] and rights of pre-emption which do not have to be exercised.[187] These are enforceable.[188]

The decision of the House of Lords in *Walford v Miles*[189] is the leading decision on simple   **11.60** agreements to negotiate. In this case the defendant/seller and the plaintiff/buyer entered into an oral 'agreement', under which the defendant agreed that if the plaintiff could provide a letter of comfort from its bank the defendant would 'terminate negotiations with any third party' in respect of the sale of certain property. That comfort letter was received and the defendant confirmed in writing, 'subject to contract' to sell the property to the plaintiff. In due course the defendant decided to sell the property to a third party and that sale was carried out. The case was initially pleaded on the basis of a lock-out agreement whereby the defendant promised to terminate negotiations with third parties in return for the provision of the comfort letter and the plaintiff's promise to continue negotiations, all this being 'subject to contract'. The pleadings were amended to argue that there was a term implied in fact into the agreement that the defendant would continue to negotiate in good faith with the plaintiff—the lock-in agreement; thus giving rise to the agreement to negotiate point. It was held that an agreement to negotiate was too uncertain to be enforceable. The addition of the standard of 'good faith' did not help bring certainty to the duty to negotiate because it was a standard that made no sense in the circumstances, those circumstances being the adversarial position of parties involved in negotiation.[190] Moreover, it was not

---

Lord Wright in *Hillas & Co Ltd v Arcos Ltd* (1932) 147 LT 503, 515, was disapproved in *Courtney & Fairbairn Ltd v Tolaini Bros (Hotels) Ltd* [1975] 1 WLR 297 and modern authorities have all agreed with this latter decision.

[184] See *Walford v Miles* [1992] 2 AC 128 where it was suggested that such a provision would be meaningless. Nor does a standard of negotiating 'with reasonable diligence' help; see *Antclizo Shipping Corp v Food Corp of India No 2 (The Antclizo)* [1992] 1 Lloyd's Rep 558, 569.

[185] Carter, *Carter on Contract* (Butterworths, Sydney), § 04.100. Cf Dugdale and Lowe, 'Contracts to Contract and Contracts to Negotiate' [1976] JBL 28. See further, Cohen, 'Pre-Contractual Duties: Two Freedoms and the Contract to Negotiate' in Beatson and Friedmann (eds) *Good Faith and Fault in Contract Law* (OUP, Oxford, 1995) Ch 2.

[186] See *Pitt v PHH Asset Management Ltd* [1994] 1 WLR 327, and the discussion in *Walford v Miles* [1992] 2 AC 128, 139, requiring the agreement to be for a specific time. See also Neill, 'A Key to Lock-Out Agreements?' (1992) 108 LQR 405; Jamieson, 'When Lock-Out Agreement Enforceable'[1992] LMCLQ 186.

[187] *ICT Pty Ltd v Sea Containers Ltd* (1995) 39 NSWLR 640, 663. On uncertainty and rights of pre-emption, see also *Brown v Gould* [1972] Ch 53, 58; *Nullagine Investments Pty Ltd v Western Australian Club Inc* (1993) 177 CLR 635, 649.

[188] Similarly agreements to conciliate or mediate disputes arising under a contract have been upheld in Australia if the process to be followed is clear, see *Hooper Bailie Associated Ltd v Natcon Group Pty Ltd* (1992) 28 NSWLR 194. Cf *Elizabeth Bay Developments Pty Ltd v Boral Building Services Pty Ltd* (1995) 36 NSWLR 709, 715. Contrast the position in England *Paul Smith Ltd v H & S International Holding Inc* [1991] 2 Lloyd's Rep 127, 131 per Steyn J (holding that such an agreement gave rise to no enforceable obligations).

[189] [1992] 2 AC 128. See also *Halifax Financial Services Ltd v Intuitive Systems Ltd* [1999] 1 All ER (Comm) 303; *Wellington City Council v Body Corporation 51702 (Wellington)* [2002] 3 NZLR 486. See further Cumberbatch, 'In Freedom's Cause: The Contract to Negotiate' (1992) 12 OJLS 587; Buckley, 'Walford v Miles: False Certainty About Uncertainty—An Australian Perspective' (1993) 6 JCL 58; Berg, 'Promises to Negotiate in Good Faith' (2003) 119 LQR 357.

[190] [1992] 2 AC 128, 138.

possible to apply such a duty because parties have a legal right to withdraw from negotiations whenever they choose.[191]

11.61 The court rejected the argument that an agreement to negotiate was synonymous with a promise to use 'best endeavours'[192] which was enforceable on the basis that it set a standard by which a court could judge whether or not there has been proper performance. Lord Ackner, with whom the other members of the court agreed said:[193]

> The reason why an agreement to negotiate, like an agreement to agree, is unenforceable, is simply because it lacks the necessary certainty. The same does not apply to an agreement to use best endeavours. This uncertainty is demonstrated in the instant case by the provision which it is said has to be implied in the agreement for the determination of the negotiations. How can a court be expected to decide whether, *subjectively*, a proper reason existed for the termination of negotiations? The answer suggested depends upon whether the negotiations have been determined 'in good faith'. However the concept of a duty to carry on negotiations in good faith is inherently repugnant to the adversarial position of the parties when involved in negotiations. Each party to the negotiations is entitled to pursue his (or her) own interest, so long as he avoids making misrepresentations. To advance that interest he must be entitled, if he thinks it appropriate, to threaten to withdraw from further negotiations or to withdraw in fact, in the hope that the opposite party may seek to reopen the negotiations by offering him improved terms. [Counsel for the plaintiff] accepts that the agreement upon which he relies does not contain a duty to complete the negotiations. But that still leaves the vital question—how is a vendor ever to know that he is entitled to withdraw from further negotiations? How is the court to police such an 'agreement?' A duty to negotiate in good faith is as unworkable in practice as it is inherently inconsistent with the position of a negotiating party. It is here that the uncertainty lies. In my judgment, while negotiations are in existence either party is entitled to withdraw from those negotiations, at any time and for any reason. There can be thus no obligation to continue to negotiate until there is a 'proper reason' to withdraw. Accordingly a bare agreement to negotiate has no legal content.

11.62 Often in practice parties do not enter into simple agreements to negotiate a contract. The parties may reach agreement on all the essential terms of the contract and expressly agree to negotiate the remaining terms.[194] As a general rule the efficacy of these agreements will depend on the general rules governing certainty and completeness.[195] If the jurisdiction

---

[191] [1992] 2 AC 128, 138.

[192] See generally, *Transfield Pty Ltd v Arlo International Ltd* (1979) 144 CLR 83; *Hospital Products Ltd v United States Surgical Corporation* (1984) 156 CLR 41, 64, 91–2; *Hawkins v Pender Bros Pty Ltd* [1990] 1 Qd R 135, 151; *Parland Pty Ltd v Mariposa Pty Ltd* (1995) 5 Tas R 121. See also *Queensland Electricity Generating Board v New Hope Collieries Pty Ltd* [1989] 1 Lloyd's Rep 205 (implied obligation to make reasonable endeavours to agree terms upheld). See further Lowcay, '"Best Endeavours" and "Reasonable Endeavours"' (1999) NZLJ 211.

[193] [1992] 2 AC 128, 138.

[194] The issue may be even more narrow, the 'agreement to negotiate' may be limited to negotiating the operation of a term, such a dispute resolution clause, here the issue may often be more one of performance and raise issues of good faith in the performance of contracts, see *AMCI (OI) Pty Ltd v Aquila Steel Pty Ltd* [2009] QSC 139; *United Group Rail Services Ltd v Rail Corp New South Wales* [2009] NSWCA 177. See also *Petromec Inc v Petro-Deep Societa Armamento Navi Appoggio SpA v Petroleo Brasileiro SA* [2006] 1 Lloyd's Rep 121, 153–4. See also Tochtermann, 'Agreements to Negotiate in the Transnational Context—Issues of Contract Law and effective Dispute Resolution' (2008) 13 Rev dr Unif 685.

[195] Even with an intention to be bound, an agreement on those terms that the parties consider essential without an agreement of the detailed provisions or specifications may make the agreement unworkable and incomplete, see *Bawitko Investments Ltd v Kernels Popcorn Ltd* (1991) 79 DLR (4th) 97.

does not enforce terms requiring negotiation of terms then that term will be void and the efficacy of the remainder of the agreement will depend on whether that term can be severed. Given the decision in *Walford v Miles*[196] this probably represents the position in England. It would generally then follow that if the essential terms are agreed the contract may be upheld unless there was a clear lack of intention to be bound until minor terms were also agreed. [197] In practice where the term for negotiation forms part of a preliminary agreement as opposed to an agreement that is intended to take effect as a final agreement, the issue of intention is more likely to be in issue.[198] Moreover, if there is no intention to be bound should negotiations break down then despite agreement on many terms the agreement is no more than a mere agreement to negotiate. The magnitude and complexity of the particular transaction will be an important indicator as to whether the parties intend to be bound while any part of the contract remains at the negotiation stage.[199]

It is also possible for the parties to enter into a preliminary agreement, or even what they **11.63** consider to be a final agreement, and leave an essential term to be negotiated. If there is an intention to be bound and if machinery exists within the contract to supply that provision should negotiations break down then there appears no good reason for not upholding the contract. Such provisions are often expressed in terms of an obligation to negotiate in good faith. In Australia there is some limited scope for upholding such agreements. The leading authority is *Coal Cliff Collieries Pty Ltd v Sijehama Pty Ltd*.[200] This case concerned negotiations between a number of companies to obtain ministerial approval for a coal mine and to carry out the necessary work when approval was given. The companies had executed a draft 'heads of agreement'. The preamble referred to the 'heads of agreement' as being a 'proposal ... subject to completion and implementation of agreements on the basis of [the] heads of agreement'. The 'heads of agreement' provided:

> This document will serve to record the terms and conditions subject to and upon which Coal Cliff Collieries Pty Ltd, Sijehama and Bulli Main agree to associate themselves ... The parties will forthwith proceed in good faith to consult together upon the formulation of a more comprehensive and detailed joint venture agreement ... which when approved and executed will take the place of these heads of agreement, but the action of the parties in so consulting and in negotiating on fresh or additional terms shall not in the meantime in any way prejudice the full and binding effect of what is now agreed.

The proposed joint venture agreement never eventuated. Negotiations broke down when **11.64** Coal Cliff Collieries (the appellant) varied its proposal from one of 'joint venture' to a 'share sale agreement'. This change was based upon the appellant's research which indicated, to it at least, that the joint venture was no longer viable. Sijehama (the respondent) treated this as a repudiation of the 'heads of agreement' and terminated the contract. The Court held that the agreement to 'proceed in good faith to consult together upon the formulation

---

[196] [1992] 2 AC 128.

[197] Eg *Granit SA v Benship International Inc* [1994] 1 Lloyd's Rep 526. See also *Ravinder Rohini Pty Ltd v Krizaic* (1991) 105 ALR 593, 603. Cf *Manatee Towing Co v Oceanbulk Maritime SA* [1999] 2 Lloyd's Rep 227.

[198] Farnsworth, 'Precontractual Liability and Preliminary Agreements: Fair Dealing and Failed Negotiations' (1987) 87 Columbia L Rev 217, 256.

[199] *Reprosystem BV v SCM Corp* 727 F 2d 257 (1984).

[200] (1991) 24 NSWLR 1. See also *United Group Rail Services Ltd v Rail Corp New South Wales* [2009] NSWCA 177; *Australis Media Holdings Pty Ltd v Telstra Corp Ltd* (1998) 43 NSWLR 104; *Aiton Australia Pty Ltd v Transfield Pty Ltd* (1999) 153 FLR 236; *Wellington City Council v Body Corporation 51702 (Wellington)* [2002] 3 NZLR 486.

of a more comprehensive and detailed joint venture agreement' was illusory, vague and therefore unenforceable.

11.65 Kirby P (Waddell AJA concurring) did, however, envisage that a promise to negotiate in good faith could in certain circumstances be enforceable.[201] He did not think the argument that such provisions should not be enforced because the court cannot fashion a remedy should be accepted. The court can award nominal damages if necessary or damages for loss of chance or damages for wasted expenditure.[202] Nor did he think that in upholding such provisions the courts were interfering with the right of a person to contract or not to contract; he said, 'it is the very exercise of the right to contract which has bound the parties to the negotiation in good faith that they promised … [T]o enforce that obligation is not to interfere in the freedom to contract, but to uphold it'.[203] In the result the efficacy of such a provision he thought depended on construction; there must be a present intention to contract and there must be sufficient certainty.[204] He thought that a clause that allowed a third party to settle uncertainties and ambiguities would evidence an intention to contract. However, even with such a provision he thought there would be some cases where the contract was still illusory or unacceptably uncertain.[205] In this case he thought the agreement could not be enforced. No arbitrator had been appointed. Many terms were yet to be agreed and a court was not equipped to fill in the spaces in such a complex transaction by reference to any objective standards or its own experience.[206]

11.66 Apart from expressing approval for Lord Wright's speech in *Hillas & Co Ltd v Arcos Ltd*,[207] Kirby P's comments seem to be limited to the enforcement of a provision for the good faith negotiation of remaining terms that is incorporated as a term of a contract. His comments arguably cannot be taken to be authority for upholding a mere contract to negotiate, that is, a form of process contract aimed at settling the terms of a principal agreement.[208] This seems to follow from his statement that such a promise will be enforceable 'depending on its precise terms … [and] … so long as the promise is clear and part of an undoubted agreement … The courts will not adopt a general principle that relief for the breach of such a

---

[201] Kirby P did not think that the agreement failed on the basis that it was no more than an agreement to agree, see (1991) 24 NSWLR 1, 18–21. It went beyond recording a mere stage in the negotiation process. The issue as he then saw it was whether or not the obligation to negotiate in good faith was one that upon default a court would remedy.

[202] (1991) 24 NSWLR 1, 25–6, 32.

[203] (1991) 24 NSWLR 1, 26.

[204] (1991) 24 NSWLR 1, 26. See also *United Group Rail Services Ltd v Rail Corp New South Wales* [2009] NSWCA 177, [43].

[205] (1991) 24 NSWLR1, 26. Perhaps this is a reference back to the beginning of his judgment where (at 4) he cites *Aotearoa International Ltd v Scancarriers A/S* [1985] 1 NZLR 513, 516 for the proposition that before a court will give authority to an agreement it must 'constitute a legally binding agreement'. Similarly (at 27) he again refers to his overriding concern that 'courts should hold back from giving effect to arrangements which the parties have not concluded'. The page reference of 516 is probably incorrect and should be to 556 where Lord Roskill made his famous remark that a court cannot imply a term into a contract until it has decided that there is a legally enforceable agreement. That statement is discussed in more detail below, but it may be that Kirby P is suggesting (depending on what he thought Lord Roskill meant) that either where the terms are unacceptably uncertain then an arbitration provision will not evidence an intention to contract or that such a third party cannot fashion essential terms.

[206] Cf *Carr v McDonald's Australia Ltd* (1994) 63 FCR 358, 370.

[207] (1932) 147 LT 503, 515.

[208] *Wellington City Council v Body Corporation 51702 (Wellington)* [2002] 3 NZLR 486, 491.

promise will be withheld.'[209] In the result Kirby P appeared to hold this agreement void for being incomplete whereas if he was intent on considering the efficacy of a simple agreement to negotiate one would expect the focus to be more on certainty.[210]

Handley JA dissented on this point. He found the joint venture agreement was in any event **11.67** subject to contract so any binding obligation, if it existed, was only binding 'in the meantime'.[211] He concluded that a 'contract to negotiate in good faith' was illusory as parties are free to pursue their own interests in negotiation, exercise their discretion to withdraw or continue negotiations and there was no identifiable criteria to determine the content of the obligation.[212] He suggested that an 'agreement to negotiate' was less likely to be upheld than an agreement to agree. His reasoning was, that an 'agreement to agree' would bind a promisor to act reasonably and to compromise in order to reach an agreement. Such an obligation he thought could not be implied into an 'agreement to negotiate'.[213] It followed that if an agreement to agree is not upheld under the current law an agreement to negotiate in good faith could be in no better position.[214] In respect of the enforceability of the terms of the 'heads of agreement' during the period of negotiation he found the 'heads of agreement' contradictory. To his Honour it appeared to be intended to be binding and subject to contract.[215] He thought that its concluding words which related to the agreement's 'full and binding effect' did not refer to the whole of the 'heads of agreement' but only to that which was 'now agreed'.[216] He noted that what was 'now agreed' was only to be binding 'in the meantime'[217] and since there would be no joint venture agreement until it was agreed, approved and executed,[218] then those provisions in the heads of agreement which were to be part of the joint venture were never binding even in the meantime. He said, 'only those provisions of the heads of agreement which contemplated or required performance in the period before the joint venture agreement was entered into were "now agreed" and were intended to be fully binding "in the meantime"'.[219] He did not think a contract would be struck down for incorporating such a provision as long as all the essential terms were agreed and the contract could operate on its agreed terms if negotiations broke down.[220] That is, it is possible to enter into an agreement that is subject to the agreement of further terms and for that original agreement to be enforceable if further terms are not agreed so long as it is certain and complete as regards the essential terms and intended to operate according to the terms agreed.[221]

It should be noted that Samuels JA of the New South Wales Court of Appeal in a later **11.68** case—*Trawl Industries of Australian v Effem Foods Pty Ltd Trading as 'Uncle Bens of*

---

[209] (1991) 24 NSWLR 1, 26.
[210] See *Wellington City Council v Body Corporation 51702 (Wellington)* [2002] 3 NZLR 486, 491. See also Liao, 'Good Faith: In Defence of WCC' [2008] NZLJ 190, 191.
[211] (1991) 24 NSWLR 1, 43.
[212] (1991) 24 NSWLR 1, 43.
[213] (1992) 24 NSWLR 1, 40–1.
[214] (1992) 24 NSWLR 1, 41.
[215] (1992) 24 NSWLR 1, 36.
[216] (1992) 24 NSWLR 1, 37.
[217] (1992) 24 NSWLR 1, 37.
[218] (1992) 24 NSWLR 1, 44–5.
[219] (1992) 24 NSWLR 1, 37.
[220] (1992) 24 NSWLR 1, 39, explaining the remarks of Kitto J in *Thorby v Goldberg* (1964) 112 CLR 597, 603.
[221] (1992) 24 NSWLR 1, 39.

Australia'[222]—suggested that the decision of Kirby P was at odds with the decision of the High Court of Australia in *Booker Industries Pty Ltd v Wilson Parking (Qld) Pty Ltd.*[223] Strictly, the reference here to *Booker Industries* is a reference to where the court said it would not uphold an incomplete agreement being no more than an agreement to agree. On its face this does categorize all incomplete agreements as unenforceable agreements to agree even though no express provision may appear in the contract to that effect. However, it does not necessarily dictate that the High Court was of the view that an agreement containing a provision for negotiation was necessarily incomplete. Recently in *United Group Rail Services Ltd v Rail Corp New South Wales*,[224] Allsop P made the point that the *Booker* case concerned incompleteness whereas the *Coal Cliff* case concerned uncertainty.[225]

11.69 Finally, there is as yet no clear statement as to the assessment of damages if in such a case one party breaches its obligation to negotiate. The damages may be assessed on the basis of a loss of chance but this may still result in a nominal sum being awarded.[226] Alternatively the damages could be assessed by reference to reliance loss.[227] As regards specific performance, the approach in *Coal Cliff Collieries* was not to hold the parties to their promise to negotiate but to determine the efficacy of the contract by reference to what a court can do to fill in the gaps if negotiations break down. Unless a court is prepared to recognize some basic standard for negotiations by, for example, giving some content to the concept of good faith, then it is doubtful that an order of specific performance would be granted.[228] Of course if the purpose of the proposed negotiation has become impossible the parties will be excused from the obligation to negotiate.[229]

11.70 In the United States there has long been accepted an obligation to perform a contract in good faith although there is still dispute over the meaning and application of that obligation. As regards the simple agreement to negotiate in good faith there is authority, consistent with that in England and Australia, that such an agreement would not be upheld. For example, *Candid Products Inc v International Skating Union*[230] concerned a series of contracts whereby the ISU (International Skating Union) granted Candid exclusive North American television rights to cover certain ice-skating events. The agreement reached between the parties referred to a right of first refusal to extend the rights and an agreement to negotiate in good faith. The relevant provision stated:

> The ISU hereby grants to Candid the right of first refusal to extend their exclusive North American television rights to the [European Championships or World Championships] for

[222] (1992) 27 NSWLR 326, 343.
[223] (1982) 149 CLR 600, 604.
[224] [2009] NSWCA 177, [50].
[225] Cf 11.66.
[226] See *Hillas & Co Ltd v Arcos Ltd* (1932) 147 LT 503, 515; *Coal Cliff Collieries Pty Ltd v Sijehama Pty Ltd* (1991) 24 NSWLR 1, 22–5.
[227] See Farnsworth, 'Precontractual Liability and Preliminary Agreements: Fair Dealing and Failed Negotiations' (1987) 87 Columbia L Rev 217, 263ff.
[228] See further *American Broadcasting Companies Inc v Wolf* 52 NY 2d 394, 420 NE 2d 363 (1981) (claim for injunctive relief refused).
[229] *Kirkby v Turner* [2009] NSWCA 131.
[230] 530 F Supp 1330 (1982). See also *Pinnacle Books Inc v Harlequin Enterprises Ltd* 519 F Supp 118 (1981); *Jilley Film Enterprises Inc v Home Box Office Inc* 593 F Supp 515 (1984); *Reprosystem BV v SCM Corp* 727 F 2d 257 (1984); *Ridgeway Coal Co Inc v FMC Corporation* 616 F Supp 404 (1985); *Bernstein v Felske* 533 NYS 2d 538 (1988).

an additional three year period. This right of first refusal shall work as follows: Candid and the ISU agree to negotiate in good faith the terms and conditions by which these rights shall be extended. If Candid and the ISU do not come to an agreement, the ISU shall then be free to offer these rights to a third party under the same terms and conditions last offered to Candid. The ISU agrees, however, that should it offer the rights under terms and conditions less favorable than those last offered to Candid, it will first offer the rights under the new terms and conditions to Candid who shall have thirty days in which to accept them. These offerings and acceptances shall be made in writing or by telegram to the respective offices of Candid and the ISU.

The right of first refusal was later deleted at the request of ISU and only the good faith **11.71** negotiation provision remained which read as follows: 'The ISU agrees that it will not negotiate any further contract for the rights for the World Championships after 1982 without first negotiating in good faith with Candid.'[231] In February 1980 discussions began concerning television rights for the World Championships after 1982 and ISU informed Candid that instead of contracting for a single event for a period of years, as it had in the past, it now wanted to structure the contract to cover all six ISU championships for a five-year period. However, Candid was not prepared to make an offer on these terms and, although there were further discussions, they did not result in an agreement.

During this same period Candid alleged that ISU had negotiated with CBS and granted it **11.72** the exclusive television broadcasting rights and that the ISU had thereby breached its good faith negotiation obligation. However, ISU argued that the good faith negotiation clause was so vague and uncertain that it was unenforceable. Candid relied on the decision in *DeLaurentiis v Cinematografica De Las Americas*[232] to support its assertion that the good faith negotiating clause was sufficiently certain. That case involved a contract to produce and distribute a motion picture and contained an undertaking to 'make every effort in good faith to cause to be created ... a story outline, screen treatment and final scenario acceptable to both' DeLaurentiis and the author of the book on which the picture was based. The court in the *Candid* case considered that the decision in *DeLaurentiis* did not assist *Candid* since in *DeLaurentiis* the purpose of the contract, namely the production and distribution of a motion picture, was 'clear and definite and provided a reference by which defendant's performance could be evaluated'.[233] In short the issue in *DeLaurentiis* concerned a more general issue of good faith in performance, rather than performance by way of negotiation with good faith operating as a standard of performance. It was said that the issue in *Candid* was not that of good faith, but 'whether the promise by ISU to negotiate is sufficiently certain, or can be made so, such that this Court can enforce it'.[234]

Candid therefore needed to show that the obligation to negotiate was sufficiently certain **11.73** and definite. It attempted to do this by arguing that the court should, as a requirement of good faith negotiation, imply various duties on the ISU, for example, 'to continue negotiations for a sufficient minimum period of time before signing with another to permit Candid a fair opportunity to overcome in all respects the comparative attractiveness of other proposals'. However, the Court rejected this argument on the basis that implying such terms

---

[231] There was also a similarly worded good faith negotiating clause governing rights to the European Championships after 1981.
[232] 9 NY 2d 503, 174 NE 2d 736 (1961).
[233] 530 F Supp 1330 (1982), 1334.
[234] 530 F Supp 1330 (1982), 1335.

would amount to making a contract for the parties rather than simply enforcing any bargain the parties themselves might have reached. The court also concluded that the parties' prior course of dealing could not be used to give meaning to the obligation to negotiate since the last negotiations were conducted under the dictates of a time limitation and a right of first refusal clause that was absent from this contract. Attention was drawn to the fact that the right of first refusal had recently been rejected by the ISU, and therefore it was concluded that it would be expressly contrary to the parties' intentions to imply such a term.

11.74 The court concluded that in this case there was not even an agreement to agree because all the material terms were left open. It was merely an agreement to negotiate. Accordingly, Weinfeld J concluded that: 'An agreement to negotiate in good faith is amorphous and nebulous, since it implicates so many factors that are themselves indefinite and uncertain that the intent of the parties can only be fathomed by conjecture and surmise.'[235] The court expressly referred to the possibility that during negotiations one party might state that it preferred not to do business with the other and questioned whether that meant that the court had the power to direct that party to continue negotiations despite its business judgment that it did not believe the negotiations to be in its best interests. The court had no difficulty in rejecting this possibility and concluding that '[a] commitment to good faith negotiations does not carry with it a surrender of one's right to decide not to enter into another contract with a party'.[236]

11.75 A further example is provided by the decision in *Necchi SPA v Necchi Sewing Machine Sales Corp*[237] which involved a claim by Necchi Sewing Machine Sales that Necchi had failed to negotiate with them in good faith for an extension of their distributorship agreement and claiming damages suffered as a result. The contractual provision required the parties 'to examine the possibility of executing a new ... long term distributorship agreement for the same territory and at such terms and conditions as will be then discussed and defined'. The court held that this did not impose any obligation on Necchi to grant a renewal of the distributorship and that made it impossible to say what relief would be appropriate where Necchi failed to examine the possibility of renewal. Marshall CJ (giving the opinion of the court) stated: 'It is impossible to assess any damages, as there is no way that anyone could foresee what would have come from examining the possibility of executing a new contract, even if this were done in the utmost good faith.'[238] He considered that it was not open to the court to write the terms of the renewal contract for the parties and that, in the absence of a clear definitive statement that the parties wished to litigate or arbitrate differences over the failure to engage in such discussions for renewal, 'the courts should hesitate before enforcing such a contract provision'.[239]

11.76 The case that is put forward to show a contrasting approach in the United States is *Itek Corp v Chicago Aerial Industries*.[240] This case concerned an asset sale agreement between the parties. The parties executed a letter of intent which confirmed the price and other terms of sale that had been agreed upon and then stated that the parties, 'shall make every reasonable

---

[235] 530 F Supp 1330, 1337, (1982).
[236] 530 F Supp 1330, 1337, (1982).
[237] 348 F 2d 693, (1965).
[238] 348 F 2d 693, 698, (1965).
[239] 348 F 2d 693, 698, (1965).
[240] 248 A 2d 625 (1968). See Farnsworth, 'Precontractual Liability and Preliminary Agreements: Fair Dealing and Failed Negotiations' (1987) 87 Columbia L Rev 217, 265.

effort to agree upon and have prepared ... a contract providing for the foregoing purchase ... embodying the above terms and such other terms and conditions as the parties shall agree upon. If the parties fail to agree upon and execute such a contract they shall be under no further obligation to one another'. The court concluded that it is 'apparent that the parties obligated themselves to "make every reasonable effort" to agree upon a formal contract, and only if such effort failed were they absolved from "further obligation" for having "failed" to agree upon and execute a formal contract ... [T]hese provisions ... obligated each side to attempt in good faith to reach final and formal agreement.'[241] Arguably the case is not concerned with a mere agreement to negotiate but was more akin to a preliminary agreement containing a clause under which the parties undertook to negotiate further terms and failing such successful negotiation the deal would fail for a lack of intention to contract. However, it is arguable that where such a preliminary agreement is intended to fail if negotiations break down then, despite all its agreed terms, that overriding intention dictates that it is no more than an agreement to negotiate.

A similar case is *Channel Home Centers v Grossman*.[242] This case involved a letter of intent **11.77** which was expressly made to induce the prospective tenant to enter into a lease with the lessor and contained a promise by the lessor to withdraw the property from the rental market and only negotiate with the prospective tenant. It also contained detailed provisions to be contained in the lease which covered most of the main topics covered in a lease. The lessor later withdrew from the negotiations and granted the lease to a third party. The Court of Appeals held that there was evidence of a valid contract to negotiate which obliged both parties to use their best efforts to negotiate in good faith in order to reach agreement. Again because of the detail contained in the letter of intent the case could be viewed as involving a preliminary agreement incorporating a negotiation clause; the letter could not be viewed as a binding lease. However, the case was successfully run on the basis that it was a valid agreement to negotiate.

E. Methods By Which the Courts and the Parties Resolve Uncertainty and Incompleteness

Introduction

Courts dealing with uncertainty and incompleteness have constantly emphasized the need **11.78** to take account of certain realities. First, commercial people do not always express themselves in clear terms yet it is necessary to give effect to their bargains if possible.[243] Second, and more relevant to incompleteness, in many contracts, particularly long-term contracts, it is not possible to predict and deal with every eventuality at the time of contract and it would be a harsh result if a contract which had been accepted and performed by the parties was later found to be void from its inception upon the happening of an event not dealt with by

---

[241] 248 A 2d 625, 629, (1968). The Court concluded that CAI had failed to negotiate in good faith so that in the breach of contract action by Itek, summary judgment in favour of CAI, as defendant, was not warranted.

[242] 795 F 2d 291 (1986). See also *Teachers Insurance and Annuity Association v Tribune Co* 670 F Supp 491 (1987); *Arnold Palmer Golf Co v Fuqua Indus* 541 F 2d 584 (1976). See generally Farnsworth, 'Precontractual Liability and Preliminary Agreements: Fair Dealing and Failed Negotiations' (1987) 87 Columbia L Rev 217.

[243] *Hillas & Co Ltd v Arcos Ltd* (1932) 147 LT 503, 514.

its terms.[244] Third, and clearly related to the second point, there is an imperative to uphold a bargain that has been partly performed.[245]

11.79   It follows that if a term is intended by the parties to have legal effect then a court will be loath to find it void for uncertainty.[246] Moreover, the modern law places a lot of weight on the overall intention to contract in the sense of intending to immediately assume legal obligations. This can result in the court using a technique to overcome uncertainty or incompleteness even though that might not accord with the intention of the parties with respect to a particular term. A simple example is that, traditionally, if the parties incorporate some mechanism into a contract to resolve an uncertainty that exists at the time of the contract and that mechanism breaks down, then the courts would not step in because to do so would not represent the intention of the parties which was to have their mechanism operate. Today if the court has available to it a technique to resolve the ambiguity the fact the contract mechanism has broken down will not prevent the court using that technique unless it is clear the parties did not intend to contract should the mechanism break down. In this way the overall expectation of the parties is respected.[247] The contract mechanism is, unless otherwise agreed, treated as a non-essential term.[248]

11.80   Although it is no doubt possible to find amongst the vast number of cases in this area examples and statements of where a court has upheld a bargain based on broad based policy considerations, the leading English authorities have always said that the quest is one of finding the intention of the parties. The court will use those legitimate techniques developed over many years to seek to find and give effect to the intention and expectation of the parties.

11.81   Prior to looking at the techniques used to overcome uncertainty and incompleteness it needs to be emphasized that the approach taken by the courts is not a narrow approach. The approach was explained in the following statement by Lord Wright in *G Scammell & Nephew Ltd v Ouston*:[249]

> The object of the court is to do justice between the parties, and the court will do its best, if satisfied that there was an ascertainable and determinate intention to contract, to give effect to that intention, looking at substance, and not mere form. It will not be deterred by mere difficulties of interpretation. Difficulty is not synonymous with ambiguity, so long as any definite meaning can be extracted. But the test of intention is to be found in the words used.

11.82   The approach therefore is commercial in nature. If it is possible to give a clause a reasonable meaning a court will generally do so.[250] In the search for that meaning the language is

---

[244] See *Prints for Pleasure Ltd v Oswald-Sealy (Overseas) Ltd* [1968] 3 NSWR 761, 766.

[245] *Vroon BV v Foster's Brewing Group Ltd* [1994] 2 VR 32 at 71 per Ormiston J. See above 11.46. See also Restatement (2d) Contracts § 34(2), (3).

[246] *Brown v Gould* [1972] Ch 53, 56; *Attorney-General v Barker Bros Ltd* [1976] 2 NZLR 495. See above 11.06.

[247] *Sudbrook Trading Estate Ltd v Eggleton* [1983] 1 AC 444, 483. Cf *Hall v Busst* (1960) 104 CLR 206. See further 11.107.

[248] *Sudbrook Trading Estate Ltd v Eggleton* [1983] 1 AC 444, 483. See further 11.107.

[249] [1941] AC 251, 268. This idea has also been expressed in terms of the search for intention not being 'narrow or pedantic', see *Council of the Upper Hunter County District v Australian Chilling and Freezing Co Ltd* (1968) 118 CLR 429, 437.

[250] *Brown v Gould* [1972] Ch 53, 57.

interpreted 'fairly and broadly' but without the court making the contract.[251] The court cannot go outside the contract except using the accepted techniques of implying terms and characterizing standards of performance.

Finally, because the search is for the intention of the parties it is a matter that opinions can **11.83** and will differ on. Many cases have dissenting opinions. It is therefore not helpful to provide endless examples of cases as each decision depends on its own facts. The concern here is with principle.

Standard of reasonableness

One technique used to resolve issues of uncertainty or incompleteness is by reference to a **11.84** standard of reasonableness.[252] It is necessary to explain how this technique operates at the level of legal doctrine. The use of standards of reasonableness is well documented in contract law. For example, if a contract is silent on the date for performance the law implies an obligation that performance must be within a reasonable time. That obligation may flow from a statute or an implied term; although the statutory provision may merely reflect the position that existed at law prior to the enactment of the statute.[253] Similarly there are many examples of where a contract is subject to some condition or contingency and where a party will be under an obligation to take reasonable steps to ensure that that event occurs.[254] The importance of recognizing that the standard operates as a term—whether express or implied—lies in the fact that for there to be an action for damages for breach of contract there must be a breach of a term. The term here is one of performing within a reasonable time and what then constitutes a reasonable time will depend on the circumstances of the case. The law here is not using a standard of reasonableness which then gives rise to a term to, for example, perform within two weeks. In this example, the term is one of a 'reasonable time'. English law does not imply terms on the basis of reasonableness.[255]

---

[251] See *Hillas & Co Ltd v Arcos Ltd* (1932) 147 LT 503, 514 (sale of goods). See also *Cohen v Mason* [1961] Qd R 518, 527, 528–9 (sale of land contract and terms of mortgage); *Hammond v Vam Ltd* [1972] 2 NSWLR 16, 18 (interest in mining operations); *Star Shipping AS v China National Foreign Trade Transportation Corp (The Star Texas)* [1993] 2 Lloyd's Rep 445 (arbitration clause).

[252] See generally Farnsworth, *Farnsworth on Contracts* (3rd edn, Vol 1, Aspen Publishers, New York, 2004), § 3.28, p 422ff.

[253] Eg Supply of Goods and Services Act 1982 (UK), s 14(1). See also Sale of Goods Act 1979 (UK), ss 29(3), and 37(1). See also *Manchester Diocesan Council for Education v Commercial & General Investments Ltd* [1970] 1 WLR 241, 247 (explaining the rule that an offer lapses after a reasonable time on the basis of an implied term). It may be noted that there is an argument that there is no need to resort to the concept of implied terms in this context, the obligation may be better explained on the basis of construction and thus constitute an express term, see Peden, *Good Faith in the Performance of Contracts* (Butterworths, Sydney, 2003) Ch 2; Peden, '"Cooperation" in English Contract Law—to Construe or Imply?' (2000) 16 JCL 56. There appears to be a general movement away from the use of the implied term concept, see *Attorney General of Belize v Belize Telecom Ltd* [2009] 2 All ER 1127 and see *Nielsen v Dysart Timbers Ltd* [2009] NZSC 43.

[254] Some examples are collected in *Himbleton Pty Ltd v Kumagai (NSW) Pty Ltd* (1991) 29 NSWLR 44, 61.

[255] See *BP Refinery (Westernport) Pty Ltd v Shire of Hastings* (1977) 180 CLR 266, 282–3; *Hospital Products Ltd v United States Surgical Corp* (1984) 156 CLR 41, 139. Cf *Byrne v Australian Airlines Ltd* (1995) 185 CLR 410, 422, 442, approving a test for implication in fact developed by Deane J (in *Hawkins v Clayton* (1988) 164 CLR 539, 573) under which reasonableness and business efficacy are alternatives for implication rather than cumulative requirements. This may signal in Australian law a break with attempting to merely give effect to the intention of the parties and recognize broader policy concerns. See also Restatement (2d) Contracts § 204 discussed above 11.52. There is also some English authority suggesting that an obligation might be implied on the basis of reasonableness, eg *Mamidoil-Jetoil Greek Petroleum Co SA v Okta Crude Oil Refinery*

For a term to be implied in law it must be necessary and for a term to be implied in fact it must be obvious and necessary for the business efficacy of the contract. Thus, in the example being discussed, reasonableness is the standard implied and not the reason for the implication. Being an implied term it is possible to take account of extrinsic evidence to imply the term and to determine whether the term has been breached.[256] Very few, if any, contractual obligations do not flow from a contractual term.[257]

11.85 If this standard of reasonableness technique is distinct from the implied term technique for resolving uncertainty and incompleteness (which is discussed below) then it must flow as a matter of construction from the other terms of the contract. It cannot 'come out of the ether' because such an approach would undermine the rule that terms cannot be implied solely on the basis of reasonableness. It also must be the case that the standard of reasonableness technique only applies where the application of that standard represents the presumed intention of the parties. Often this means that what is reasonable is drawn from the terms of the contract. But it is also possible that the standard of reasonableness may be an external standard. Such standards are discussed in more detail below. It is suffice here to note that for such a standard to be applied it must exist—in the sense that there are objective criteria that can be applied to determine what is reasonable[258]—and it must be referred to expressly or impliedly in the contract so as to represent the intention of the parties when applied.

11.86 The most well-known example of the application of this standard in the context of this chapter is that of *Hillas & Co Ltd v Arcos Ltd*.[259] This case involved a contract for the supply of '22,000 standards of softwood goods of fair specification over the 1930 season' together with an option in favour of the buyer which provided:

> Buyers shall also have the option of entering into a contract with sellers for the purchase of 100,000 standards for delivery during 1931. Such contract to stipulate that, whatever the conditions are, buyers shall obtain the goods on conditions and at prices which show to them

---

AD [2001] 2 Lloyd's Rep 76, 89–90; but this statement appears to be based on Lord Wright's speech in *Hillas & Co Ltd v Arcos Ltd* (1932) 147 LT 503, 517, which was in fact a reference to a standard of reasonableness.

[256] Stannard, *Delay in the Performance of Contractual Obligations* (OUP, Oxford, 2007), paras 1.11–1.34.

[257] Peden, *Good Faith in the Performance of Contracts* (Butterworths, Sydney, 2003), paras 1.5–1.10

[258] *Placer Development Ltd v The Commonwealth* (1969) 121 CLR 353, 372.

[259] (1932) 147 LT 503. Cf *Baird Textile Holdings Ltd v Marks & Spencer plc* [2002] 1 All ER (Comm) 737. See also *King v Ivanhoe Gold Corp Ltd* (1908) 7 CLR 617 (an offer of a 'handsome payment' for services; held that remuneration had to be a fair remuneration in ordinary circumstances plus an amount that was reasonable to make it a handsome payment); *Dominion Coal Co Ltd v Dominion Iron & Steel Co Ltd* [1909] AC 293, 310 (obligation of seller to supply coal 'reasonably' suitable for use in the buyer's business) *Bowes v Chaleyer* (1923) 32 CLR 159 (obligation to ship half the good orders 'as soon as possible' was thought by Issacs and Rich JJ (175) to mean 'as soon as reasonably practicable' and by Starke J (193) to mean 'within a reasonable time'); *Wenning v Robinson* [1964] NSWR 614 (agreement to sell stock 'at valuation' meant 'at a reasonable' value); *Sudbrook Trading Estate Ltd v Eggleton* [1983] 1 AC 444 (lessee given option to purchase freehold the price to be ascertained by parties appointing valuers; vendor failed to appoint valuer; held that the term to appoint a valuer evidenced, on construction, that the price was to be a fair and reasonable price). See further *Christison v Warren* [1903] St R Qd 186; *Powell v Braun* [1954] 1 WLR 401, 405; *Greater London Council v Connolly* [1970] 2 QB 100, 108; *Deta Nominees Pty Ltd v Viscount Plastic Products Pty Ltd* [1979] VR 167, 175, 188; *First City Investments Ltd v Fraser Arms Hotel Ltd* (1979) 104 DLR (3d) 617; *Meehan v Jones* (1982) 149 CLR 571, 589–90; *Biotechnology Australia Pty Ltd v Pace* (1988) 15 NSWLR 130, 145ff. Cf *Hall v Busst* (1960) 104 CLR 206 (but note the remarks of Kitto J at 227–8).

a reduction of 5 per cent on the fob value of the official price list at any time ruling during 1931. Such option to be declared before 1st January, 1931.

The 1930 agreement was duly performed but, when the buyers sought to exercise the **11.87** option for 1931 it was found that the sellers had already sold their entire production to a third party. The buyer sought damages claiming that there was a breach of contract. The sellers argued that there could be no contract for 1931 because the option was void for uncertainty in that it did not specify the type of goods to be supplied, the sizes or the quality. Nor did it specify the delivery dates. These were matters that required further agreement.

The House of Lords was able to fill these gaps by first implying the words 'of softwood **11.88** goods of fair specification' after the words '100,000 standards'. The reference to 'softwood goods' was a necessary implication to identify the subject matter of the contract. The words 'fair specification' were thought to be sufficiently certain having the same meaning that the phrase had in relation to the first contract, it was therefore a phrase capable of being rendered certain. Lord Tomlin advocated a negative approach to determining whether 'fair specification' was uncertain which was to see if no reasonable meaning of that term could represent the intention of the parties.[260] Indeed the sale conditions relating to the 22,000 standards were to be imported into the sale of 100,000 standards. Important to the reasoning of the court was the knowledge the parties had of the industry. Each had a lot of experience in the Russian softwood timber trade, they had carried out the initial purchase of 22,000 standards without incident and clearly intended the option to give rise to legal relations.[261] This formed part of the matrix of facts. The evidence showed that the nature of the business was such that it was not possible to predict in advance what kinds, qualities and sizes of timber would be available in the next season.

It was the fair specification implication that invoked a standard of reasonableness. That **11.89** standard could take effect as an implied term but that was not necessary as it flowed not merely from the matrix of facts that surrounded this option but the terms of the contract as the initial contract and option had to be construed together. The result therefore is grounded in construction. Lord Wright went on to set out how the standard operates. He said:[262]

> under such a description, the parties will work out the necessary adjustments by a process of give and take in order to arrive at an equitable or reasonable apportionment on the basis of the respondents' actual available output, according to kinds, qualities, sizes and scantlings; but if they fail to do so, the law can be invoked to determine what is reasonable in the way of specification, and thus the machinery is always available to give the necessary certainty … [It cannot be] objected that, though a fair and reasonable specification may not be impossible of ascertainment, the reasonable specification is impossible. The law, in determining what is reasonable, is not concerned with ideal truth, but with something much less ambitious, though more practical.

It is also possible for the parties to adopt an express standard of reasonableness. For exam- **11.90** ple, in *Corthell v Summit Thread Co*,[263] the plaintiff employee offered to sell some patents to his employer, the defendant. The parties entered into an agreement which, inter alia,

---

[260] (1932) 147 LT 503, 512.
[261] See also *Three Rivers Trading Co Ltd v Gwinear & District Farmers Ltd* (1967) 111 Sol J 831.
[262] (1932) 147 LT 503, 516.
[263] 132 Me 94, 167 A 79 (1933).

increased his salary for a five-year period, offered a payment for the existing patents and provided for 'reasonable recognition' in return for his promise to turn over his rights to future inventions to the company. The basis and amount of recognition was expressed to rest entirely with the employer. The contract also stated that its terms were 'to be interpreted in good faith on the basis of what is reasonable and intended and not technically'.

11.91 The plaintiff turned over his rights to other inventions in accordance with the terms of the contract but did not receive any compensation. In its defence to an action for breach of contract brought by the plaintiff, the defendant contended that although the words 'reasonable recognition' could be given meaning, when combined with the absolute discretion reserved to the defendant they were rendered vague and uncertain. However, the court laid stress on the last clause of the agreement which provided for an interpretation in accordance with what is reasonable and intended. This exhibited a clear intention to contract, the employer could not therefore decide to pay nothing and was required to pay reasonable compensation for the inventions. Here the reference to good faith was held to impose an obligation on the employing company 'to determine and pay the plaintiff the reasonable value of what it accepted from him'.[264]

11.92 There will be occasions where an express standard will fail. As with implied standards of reasonableness they can only operate if there is some criteria available to determine what is reasonable.[265] For example *Varney v Ditmars*[266] concerned an action by an employee against his employer alleging that the employer had agreed to pay the employee an extra $5 a week plus 'a fair share of my profits'. The court held that the words 'fair share' were uncertain and indefinite. The court went on to suggest that, had the word 'reasonable' been used in the place of 'fair', it would still not have been sufficiently certain.[267] In his judgment Chase J stated:[268]

> The question whether the words 'fair' and 'reasonable' have a definite and enforceable meaning when used in business transactions is dependent upon the intention of the parties in the use of such words and upon the subject matter to which they refer. In cases of merchandising and in the purchase and sale of chattels the parties may use the words 'fair and reasonable value' as synonymous with 'market value' ... The fair, reasonable, or market value of goods can be shown by direct testimony of those competent to give such testimony. The competency to speak grows out of experience and knowledge. The testimony of such witnesses does not rest upon conjecture ...

> The contract in question, so far as it relates to a share of the defendant's profits, is not only uncertain, but it is necessarily affected by so many other facts that are in themselves indefinite and uncertain that the intention of the parties is pure conjecture.

11.93 It should also be noted that unlike the situation in the *Corthell* case where the employee acted in reliance on the employer's promise, in the *Varney* case the employee's service subsequent to this promise amounted to no more than his normal duties as an employee.

---

264 132 Me 94, 167 A 79, 82 (1933).
265 *Baird Textile Holdings Ltd v Marks & Spencer plc* [2002] 1 All ER (Comm) 737.
266 217 NY 223, 111 NE 822 (1916). See also *Peters Ice Cream (Vic) Ltd v Todd* [1961] VR 485. Cf *Sinclair v Schildt* (1914) 16 WAR 100 (offer to pay 'a substantial sum' out of proceeds of sale upheld on the basis that the contract was partly executed). See further *Powell v Braun* [1954] 1 WLR 401; *Woodhouse v ADA Manufacturing Co Ltd* [1954] SASR 263; *Sandtara Pty Ltd v Longreach Group Ltd* [2008] NSWSC 373.
267 217 NY 223, 111 NE 822, 823–4 (1916).
268 217 NY 223, 111 NE 822, 823–4 (1916).

External standard

Where a term or terms of a contract are on their face uncertain or incomplete the courts **11.94**
may have regard to an 'external standard' in order to resolve that uncertainty or incompleteness. To a large extent the law on external standards to resolve uncertainty is linked to the
rules relating to the incorporation of terms by reference. Thus, for such a standard to apply
it must be expressly or impliedly incorporated into the contract by the parties. Very often
the reference will be to an external set of standard form terms that are intended to apply to
the extent that they are not inconsistent with express (specific) terms of the contract.[269]

Where an external standard is referred to, the issues that arise are, first, does the external **11.95**
standard exist; second, if more than one such standard exists can the court identify which
standard was intended to be adopted by the parties; third, assuming a standard can be
identified does it provide the certainty or completeness required. Where the standard does
not exist or if it is itself uncertain or does not complete the contract the issue will then
become one of severance to determine whether the certain agreed terms can stand on their
own.

Issues regarding the existence of a standard tend to arise where the parties attempt to incor- **11.96**
porate terms such as the 'usual terms' or 'reasonable terms'. For example, in *Whitlock v
Brew*[270] an agreement was entered into to lease certain land 'on such reasonable terms as
commonly govern such a lease'. No such terms existed. Moreover, the terms to be supplied
by the external standard were essential to the contract so the contract could not be upheld
without them.[271] Similarly in *Nicolene Ltd v Simmonds*[272] in a letter alleged to form part of
a contract for the sale of steel bars it was stated, 'I assume we are in agreement that the usual
conditions of acceptance apply'. It was held that that expression was meaningless as no such
terms existed. However, in this case it could be ignored. Denning LJ suggested that if a
clause is merely meaningless then often it can be ignored particularly if the party arguing
that the contract is void was the party who suggested the clause in the first place and the
clause is for the benefit of that party. He distinguished this from the situation that arises
where an essential term is yet to be agreed.

Where there are more than one set of such terms in existence, then the issue becomes **11.97**
whether it is possible to identify which, if any, were intended by the parties. For example

---

[269] Eg *Himbleton Pty Ltd v Kumagai (NSW) Pty Ltd* (1991) 29 NSWLR 44; *Trustees Executors & Agency Co
Ltd v Peters* (1960) 102 CLR 537.

[270] (1968) 118 CLR 445. Cf *Shamrock Steamship Co v Storey and Co* (1899) 81 LT 413. See also *Cumming
& Co Ltd v Hasell* (1920) 28 CLR 508 (cf *David T Boyd & Co Ltd v Louca* [1973] 1 Lloyd's Rep 209);
Summergreene v Parker (1950) 80 CLR 304; *Buyers v Begg* [1952] 1 DLR 313; *Peters Ice Cream (Vic) Ltd v Todd*
[1961] VR 485; *Myam Pty Ltd v Teskera* [1971] VR 725; *Deta Nominees Pty Ltd v Viscount Plastic Products Pty
Ltd* [1979] VR 167, 175, 188; *Foxtel Management Pty Ltd v Seven Cable Television Pty Ltd* (2000) 175 ALR
433, 479. See further *Hall v Busst* (1960) 104 CLR 206, 216 (note that in *Trawl Industries of Australia Pty Ltd
v Effem Foods Pty Ltd Trading and 'Uncle Bens Australian'* (1992) 27 NSWLR 326, 333, Kirby P suggested that
the law had moved on from the views expressed there).

[271] Compare the approach to non-existent standards under Unidroit Principles of International
Commercial Contracts (2004) Article 5.1.7(4). Cf Principles of European Contract Law Art 6:107. See
further Draft Common Frame of Reference II–9:107.

[272] [1953] 1 QB 543. See also *Fitzgerald v Masters* (1956) 95 CLR 420, 427 (severance possible as parties
had agreed all essential terms and the terms that were to be supplied by the non-existent external standard were
those which could be supplied by law). See further *Bosaid v Andry* [1963] VR 465.

G Scammell & Nephew Ltd v Ouston,[273] concerned an agreement to buy a motor-van with the balance of the purchase price being payable on hire-purchase terms. The reference to 'hire-purchase' terms is a reference to an external standard. The House of Lords held that there were a variety of hire-purchase agreements in existence and the language used did not sufficiently indicate which of these hire-purchase terms the parties intended. Again as in the *Whitlock* case, the terms to be supplied by the external standard were essential and the contract was therefore held to be void.

11.98 The above cases can be contrasted with *Allcars Pty Ltd v Tweedle*.[274] Here the defendant offered to take a car on 'on the terms of [the plaintiff's] usual hiring agreement or that of [the plaintiff's] nominee'. The plaintiff had no such usual terms but such terms did exist in the market and it was possible to make the terms certain by the plaintiff appointing a nominee who had such terms. In *Tonelli v Komirra Pty Ltd*,[275] in relation to a sale contract, interest payable on any outstanding part of the purchase price was to be one-quarter per cent above 'the current bank overdraft rate'. It was argued that this was uncertain as it referred to a current rate charged by any bank that the plaintiff might happen to approach for a loan which was open to negotiation between the bank and its customer. This was rejected, Smith J concluded that it did not refer 'to a rate of interest currently charged by banks for loans of a certain size or class, but [referred] to the only uniform rate that did exist, namely, the uniform maximum bank overdraft interest rate prescribed and published from time to time by the Reserve Bank'.[276]

11.99 In some cases resort to an external standard may not derive from incorporation by reference. Where a court determines that it falls within the intention of the parties to use a standard of reasonableness then what is reasonable may be determined by an external standard which is identified either by reference to relevant extrinsic evidence or because it falls within the matrix of facts.[277] The decision in *Bettancourt v Gilroy Theatre Co*[278] may be an example. Here vendors sold land on condition that the purchaser would erect a 'first class theatre ... as soon as materials, equipment, and furnishings were available at reasonable prices'. However, three years later, when the purchaser sold the land without having erected a theatre, the vendors sued for damages caused by the failure to enhance the value of the neighbouring land. The court held that the subject matter, namely a 'first class theatre', was sufficiently certain; there was reliable oral evidence as to the parties' understanding of what that meant, there was a frame of reference because the purchaser operated another theatre in the same city and to the city building code and fire laws prescribed minimum standards for theatre construction.

---

[273] [1941] AC 251. See also *Love & Stewart Ltd v S Instone & Co Ltd* (1917) 34 TLR 475; *Bishop & Baxter Ltd v Anglo-Eastern Trading & Industrial Co Ltd* [1944] 1 KB 12; *British Electrical & Associated Industries (Cardiff) Ltd v Patley Pressings Ltd* [1953] 1 WLR 280.

[274] [1937] VLR 35. See also *Webster v Higgin* [1948] 2 All ER 127, 128; *Hobbs Padgett & Co (Reinsurance) Ltd v J C Kirkland Ltd* [1969] 2 Lloyd's Rep 547.

[275] [1972] VR 737.

[276] [1972] VR 737, 741.

[277] See *Biotechnology Australia Pty Ltd v Pace* (1988) 15 NSWLR 130, 137; Cf *Peters Ice Cream (Vic) Ltd v Todd* [1961] VR 485, 489.

[278] 120 Cal App 2d 364, 261 P 2d 351 (1953).

Performance and reliance

The importance of performance and reliance has already been stressed in the above discussion on agreements to agree.[279] In *F & G Sykes (Wessex) Ltd v Fine Fare Ltd*[280] Lord Denning MR expressed the importance of performance and reliance in the following terms:[281]   **11.100**

> In a commercial agreement the further the parties have gone on with their contract, the more ready are the Courts to imply any reasonable term so as to give effect to their intentions. When much has been done, the Courts will do their best not to destroy the bargain. When nothing has been done, it is easier to say there is no agreement between the parties because the essential terms have not been agreed. But when an agreement has been acted upon and the parties, as here, have been put to great expense in implementing it, we ought to imply all reasonable terms so as to avoid any uncertainties.

Similarly in *G Percy Trentham Ltd v Archital Luxfer Ltd*[282] Steyn LJ commented generally on the significance of performance of an agreement when he stated that:[283]   **11.101**

> The fact that the transaction was performed on both sides will often make it unrealistic to argue that there was no intention to enter into legal relations. It will often make it difficult to submit that the contract is void for vagueness or uncertainty. Specifically, the fact that the transaction is executed makes it easier to imply a term resolving any uncertainty, or, alternatively, it may make it possible to treat a matter not finalised in negotiations as inessential.

What these statements show is that performance and reliance are important in determining whether or not an intention to be bound exists.[284] If it does, then as already noted the courts will be loath to hold the contract is void for uncertainty or incompleteness. The performance   **11.102**

---

[279] See 11.48ff.

[280] [1967] 1 Lloyd's Rep 53 (number of chickens to be supplied under contract after the first year to be agreed; held the figure should be a reasonable figure determined by an arbitrator under the arbitration provision contained in the contract).

[281] [1967] 1 Lloyd's Rep 53, 57–8. See also *Parker v Taswell* (1858) 2 De G & J 559, 571, 44 ER 1106, 1111; *Wilson v The West Hartlepool Railway Company* (1865) 2 De G J & S 475, 46 ER 459; *Hart v Hart* (1881) 18 Ch D 675, 685; *Re Galaxy Media Pty Ltd (in liq)* (2001) 167 FLR 149, 164–5; *British Bank for Foreign Trade Ltd v Novinex Ltd* [1949] 1 KB 623, 629–30; *Mamidoil-Jetoil Greek Petroleum Co SA v Okta Crude Oil Refinery AD* [2001] 2 Lloyd's Rep 76.

[282] [1993] 1 Lloyd's Rep 25. See also *Foxtel Management Pty Ltd v Seven Cable Television Pty Ltd* (2000) 175 ALR 433, 469.

[283] [1993] 1 Lloyd's Rep 25, 27. See also *York Air Conditioning & Refrigeration (A'sia) Pty Ltd v The Commonwealth* (1949) 80 CLR 11, 53 per Latham CJ ('When the parties have shown by their conduct that they understand and can apply the terms of a contract without difficulty, a court should be very reluctant indeed to pay no attention to such conduct by holding that the terms of the contract are unintelligible by reason of uncertainty.')

[284] *Barrier Wharfs Ltd v W Scott Fell & Co Ltd* (1908) 5 CLR 647, 669 per Griffith CJ stating that if the documents there disclosed a contract, 'the subsequent correspondence shows that it was not in the contemplation of either party that they were to be bound until all the essential preliminaries had been agreed to, nor until a formal contract had been drawn up embodying all the matters incidental to a transaction of such nature'; no point was taken as to the admissibility of this evidence, see at 654–5 per Higgins J). Acts of performance will not always overcome a perceived lack of an intention to contract, eg *Chillingworth v Esche* [1924] 1 Ch 97 (here in an agreement made 'subject to contract' the payment and acceptance of a sum of money prior to the formulation and execution of a formal contract did not overcome the intention that no contract was to come into existence prior to execution; moreover, as the court could reverse what had occurred by ordering the restitution of the sum no injustice resulted; the sum would have formed a deposit if the contract was signed and exchanged). See also *Sinclair Scott & Co Ltd v Naughton* (1929) 43 CLR 310; *Masters v Cameron* (1954) 91 CLR 353; *Marek v Australasian Conference Association Pty Ltd* [1994] 2 Qd R 521. Usually references to post formation conduct are made to affirm a finding that an intention to contract exists

or reliance may form the impetus for a court using one of its techniques to uphold the bargain. That technique might be the use of a standard of reasonableness or the implication of a term or even severance of an uncertain term on the basis that by their conduct the parties have shown that it is not essential.[285] However, it is still necessary to satisfy the requirements of those techniques which become more difficult if it is clear that essential terms have not been agreed.[286] Nevertheless, recourse to performance and reliance is a distinct method of resolving uncertainty.[287] It may evidence that the parties did have an understanding of a term of the contract that might otherwise be held to be uncertain.[288] The limit of this approach is that it is only relevant to when the parties have applied a provision.[289] Finally, to the extent that the issue before the court is seen as one of contract formation there is no problem in admitting that evidence as that is an issue of fact. There certainly appears to be a long history of accepting such evidence.[290] It would seem to follow that even if the issue is said to be one of construction, that is, an issue of law, a court will accept such evidence on the question of whether the parties intended to contract. For example, in *Anaconda Nickel Ltd v Tarmoola Australia Pty Ltd*[291] Ipp J (with whom Pidgeon J agreed) said:[292]

> Where parties have executed an instrument in writing but it is uncertain whether in so doing they intended to create legal relations, the court may have regard to all the relevant circumstances to determine, objectively, what the parties' intention was. 'Intention' in this sense means intention to contract, not what the parties intended by the terms of the contract. The relevant circumstances may include prior negotiations and subsequent conduct ... In accordance with the general rule, however, direct expressions of intent, made after the contract was arrived at, are not admissible.

11.103   In the same case Anderson J said: [293]

> It is well settled that, where the parties have reduced what they have agreed to writing, it is primarily a question of construction of the document as to whether or not the parties intended to make a binding contract at that point ...
>
> However, it is also clear that, on the question of intention to contract, extrinsic evidence may be admitted.
>
> As to what extrinsic evidence may be referred to, the evidence of the parties as to their subjective intent is, of course, not admissible but regard may be had to the conduct of and communications between the parties, both before and after the formation of an allegedly

---

or does not exist, see eg *Rossiter v Miller* (1878) 3 App Cas 1124, 1149 per Lord O'Hagan; *Allen v Carbone* (1975) 132 CLR 528, 533.

[285]   See *Carr v Brisbane City Council* [1956] St R Qd 402, 411.

[286]   *Stimson v Gray* [1929] 1 Ch 629.

[287]   *Sudbrook Trading Estate Ltd v Eggleton* [1983] 1 AC 444. See also Restatement (2d) Contracts § 34(2) and (3).

[288]   *York Air Conditioning and Refrigeration (A'sia) Pty Ltd v Commonwealth* (1949) 80 CLR 11, 53; *Hempel v Robinson* [1924] SASR 288, 292; *Integrated Computer Services Pty Ltd v Digital Equipment Corp (Aust) Pty Ltd* (1988) 5 BPR 11,110. See also *Re Galaxy Media Pty Ltd (in liq)* (2001) 167 FLR 149, 164–5, 168–9. See further *Oxford v Provand* (1868) LR 2 PC 135. The ability of have recourse to such conduct to find meaning may further suggest that certainty at the moment of formation is not crucial, see nn 3, 58, 11.50.

[289]   *Sportsvision Australia Pty Ltd v Tallglen Pty Ltd* (1998) 44 NSWLR 103, 111.

[290]   See *Howard Smith & Co Ltd v Varawa* (1907) 5 CLR 68, 78.

[291]   (2000) 22 WAR 101.

[292]   (2000) 22 WAR 101, 111.

[293]   (2000) 22 WAR 101, 133–4.

binding agreement for the purpose of determining, objectively, whether or not they intended to form a binding agreement. There are many authorities to the effect that a court may have regard to subsequent conduct and communications.

Terms of the contract

To the extent that the application of a standard of reasonableness or an external standard is dependent on the standard being incorporated into the contract and thus within the presumed intention of the parties, these techniques could be categorized as being applications of the terms of the contract. But what those techniques do is prove that there is no issue of uncertainty or incompleteness. There is a need to recognize another distinct technique which is labelled here 'terms of the contract'. Within this category fall contract mechanisms which resolve an issue of uncertainty or incompleteness rather than prove that no such issue exists.

11.104

The classic example is a provision that appoints one or more third parties to resolve the issue.[294] Such provisions usually appoint a third party as an expert—such as a valuer to value the subject matter of the contract or the solicitor[295] of one of the parties to settle the terms—or an arbitrator. Such provisions are infinite in their variety and can be used in those cases where at the time of contract it is impossible to predict such issues as the price of the subject matter of the contract. That is, they may be used to prevent the agreement being found to be an agreement to agree or otherwise void for uncertainty or incompleteness.[296] In terms of efficacy, it is necessary that the provision be certain and complete itself and as a matter of construction it must evidence that the third party is empowered to resolve the issue.[297] The key to the efficacy of such provisions lies in the contract not requiring any further agreement by the parties.[298] It is not sufficient if the third party is to agree terms with one of the parties to the contract.[299] It follows that theoretically the parties could leave to a third party the formulation of a term that the parties consider essential to the contract.[300] In such a case often there will be no intention to be bound until that term is formulated but it is also possible that the parties intend the contract to come into force immediately with only performance being suspended until that term is formulated.[301] Where the parties appoint a person to act as an expert, for example to value the subject matter of the contract in order to determine the price payable, then it is possible to simply

11.105

---

[294] There are numerous examples of such provisions appearing in the cases, see eg, *Foster v Wheeler* (1888) LR 38 Ch D 130; *Foley v Classique Coaches Ltd* [1934] 2 KB 1; *Upper Hunter County District Council v Australian Chilling & Freezing Co Ltd* (1968) 118 CLR 429; *Godecke v Kirwan* (1973) 129 CLR 629; *Booker Industries Pty Ltd v Wilson Parking (Qld) Pty Ltd* (1982) 149 CLR 600.

[295] Eg *Christison v Warren* [1903] St R Qd 186; *Axelsen v O'Brien* (1949) 80 CLR 219; *Suttor v Gundowda Pty Ltd* (1950) 81 CLR 418, 444–5; *Hancock v Wilson* [1956] St R Qd 266; *Godecke v Kirwan* (1973) 129 CLR 629, 645; *First City Investments Ltd v Fraser Arms Hotel Ltd* (1979) 104 DLR (3d) 617; *Meredith v Anthony* [1980] 2 NSWLR 784.

[296] Eg *Calvan Consolidated Oil & Gas Co Ltd v Manning* [1959] SCR 253, (1959) 17 DLR (2d) 1.

[297] *Foley v Classique Coaches Ltd* [1934] 2 KB 1. See also *May & Butcher Ltd v King* [1934] 2 KB 17n. As to the standard a valuer must exercise, see *Campbell v Edwards* [1976] 1 WLR 403, 407 and cf *WMC Resources Ltd v Leighton Contractors Pty Ltd* (1999) 20 WAR 489.

[298] *Axelsen v O'Brien* (1949) 80 CLR 219, 225.

[299] *Summergreene v Parker* (1950) 80 CLR 304, 316.

[300] *Godecke v Kirwan* (1973) 129 CLR 629, 645; *Booker Industries Pty Ltd v Wilson Parking (Qld) Pty Ltd* (1982) 149 CLR 600, 604. Cf *Sudbrook Trading Estate Ltd v Eggleton* [1983] 1 AC 444, 483–4.

[301] *Booker Industries Pty Ltd v Wilson Parking (Qld) Pty Ltd* (1982) 149 CLR 600, 605.

appoint that person and allow them to use their expertise to resolve the issue; no standard or yardstick need be provided in the contract although any decision would need to be reasonable and consistent with the contract.[302] However, often such a third party will be required to apply some pricing formula stated in the contract and here it is necessary that that clause be certain.[303]

11.106 One important issue concerns the approach of a court when the machinery set up under the contract to resolve some uncertainty breaks down. For example, the clause might require each party to appoint a third party to resolve the dispute. What then happens to the contract if one party, in breach of contract, refuses to appoint a third party? Similarly, what happens if a third party is appointed but he or she cannot or will not act to resolve the issue. In *Milnes v Gery*[304] a mechanism was incorporated into the agreement that the price was to be determined by two valuers, the parties appointing one each. If the valuers could not agree, then they were to appoint a third person whose decision would be final. As it turned out the valuers could not agree on a price but could also not agree on a third person to settle the dispute. Thus, the contract machinery broke down. Grant MR held that the court could not substitute its own machinery.[305] Much of his reasoning was based on the notion that a court will not make a contract for the parties and a court will not act inconsistently with the intention of the parties. He said:[306]

> The only agreement, into which the Defendant entered, was to purchase at a price, to be ascertained in a specified mode. No price having ever been fixed in that mode, the parties have not agreed upon any price. Where then is the complete and concluded contract, which this Court is called upon to execute? The price is of the essence of a contract of this sale. In this instance the parties have agreed upon a particular mode of ascertaining the price. The agreement, that the price shall be fixed in one specific manner, certainly does not afford an inference, that it is wholly indifferent, in what manner it is to be fixed. The Court, declaring,

---

[302] *Foster v Wheeler* (1888) 38 Ch D 130; *May & Butcher Ltd v King* [1934] 2 KB 17n; *Axelsen v O'Brien* (1949) 80 CLR 219, 225; *Himbleton Pty Ltd v Kumagai (NSW) Pty Ltd* (1991) 29 NSWLR 44, 63. Cf *Western Australian Trustees Ltd v Poon* (1991) 6 WAR 72 (suggesting a valuer's discretion cannot be unfettered).

[303] An additional problem is where a term, such as the price, is to be determined by a formula but there is no machinery provision provided to work out and apply that formula, see *Brown v Gould* [1972] 1 Ch 53. Suggested difficulties with such provisions have been raised where the parties appoint an arbitrator in the sense of a person appointed to resolve a dispute rather than preclude one, see *Collins v Collins* (1858) 26 Beav 306, 312–13, 53 ER 916, 918–19 and McPherson, 'Arbitration, Valuation and Certainty of Terms' (1986) 60 ALJ 8, 12. It is said that an arbitrator's standing is dependent on a contract being in place, McPherson, 'Arbitration, Valuation and Certainty of Terms' (1986) 60 ALJ 8, 13ff. Nevertheless, in many cases a standard of reasonableness can be implied to give effect to the contract, so that the price must be a reasonable price, and the arbitrator can give effect to that standard, see *F & G Sykes (Wessex) Ltd v Fine Fare Ltd* [1967] 1 Lloyd's Rep 53; *Mamidoil-Jetoil Greek Petroleum Co SA v Okta Crude Oil Refinery AD* [2001] 2 Lloyd's Rep 76, 89; *Vosper Thornycroft Ltd v Ministry of Defence* [1976] 1 Lloyd's Rep 58, 61. Moreover, generally where a third person is appointed to determine a matter based on their personal expertise then despite the use of the word 'arbitrator' it may be that they are being appointed as an independent expert and the contract will be construed in that way.

[304] (1807) 14 Yes 400, 33 ER 574. See also *Morgan v Milman* (1853) 3 De GM & G 24, 43 ER 10; *Vickers v Vickers* (1867) LR 4 Eq 529.

[305] As regards contracts for the sale of goods, if the price is to be fixed by a third party who in turn cannot or will not make the valuation, then the contract is avoided, see Sale of Goods Act 1979 (UK), s 9(1); Sale of Goods Act 1954 (ACT), s 14; Sale of Goods Act 1923 (NSW), s 14; Sale of Goods Act 1972 (NT), s 14; Sale of Goods Act 1896 (Qld) s 12; Sale of Goods Act 1895 (SA), s 9; Sale of Goods Act 1896 (Tas), s 14; Goods Act 1958 (Vic), s 14; Sale of Goods Act 1895 (WA), s 9. The buyer must however pay for those goods delivered to or appropriated by the buyer.

[306] (1807) 14 Yes 400, 406–7, 33 ER 574, 577.

that the one shall take, and the other shall give, a price fixed in any other manner, does not execute any agreement of theirs'; but makes an agreement for them ...

The case of an agreement to sell at a fair valuation is essentially different. In that case no particular means of ascertaining the value are pointed out: there is nothing therefore, precluding the Court from adopting any means, adapted to that purpose. The case, in which the Court has modified particular, subordinate, parts of an agreement, falls far short of the decree, that is now demanded.

This decision had been treated as settling the law on this point until *Sudbrook Trading* **11.107**
Estate Ltd v Eggleton.[307] Here an option clause provided that on the giving of notice the lessees were to become the purchasers of the reversion 'at such price not being less than £12,000 as may be agreed upon by two valuers one to be nominated by the lessor and the other by the lessees and in default of such agreement by an umpire appointed by the ... valuers ...'. The lessees exercised the option and nominated their own valuer. However, the lessors refused to nominate their valuer and claimed that the option was void for uncertainty.

The Court of Appeal followed the decision in *Milnes v Gery* holding that the court could **11.108**
not compel a party to appoint a valuer. The lessees appealed to the House of Lords, which decided that such a result would be remote from what parties normally intended and expected in including such a valuation clause, and was inconvenient in practice. The House of Lords held (Lord Russell dissenting) that on construction this was an agreement for sale at a fair and reasonable price and since the price was to be ascertained by machinery which was a subsidiary part of the contract, if that machinery broke down then the court would substitute its own machinery to ascertain that fair and reasonable price. Note that this approach is dependent on the machinery being construed as not being an essential term according to the intention of the parties.[308] This methodology gives effect to the expectation of the parties that legal relations were intended and less weight to the intention encapsulated in a single term to have a third party value some subject matter.[309] Lord Fraser stated:[310]

> I recognise the logic of the reasoning which has led to the courts' refusing to substitute their own machinery for the machinery which has been agreed upon by the parties. But the result to which it leads is so remote from that which parties normally intend and expect, and is so inconvenient in practice, that there must in my opinion be some defect in the reasoning. I think the defect lies in construing the provisions for the mode of ascertaining the value as an essential part of the agreement. That may have been perfectly true early in the 19th century, when the valuer's profession and the rules of valuation were less well established than they are now. But at the present day these provisions are only subsidiary to the main purpose of the agreement which is for sale and purchase of the property at a fair or reasonable value.

---

[307] [1983] 1 AC 444. See also *Re Malpass* [1985] Ch 42; *Didymi Corp v Atlantic Lines and Navigation Co Inc (The Didymi)* [1988] 2 Lloyd's Rep 108; *Queensland Electricity Generating Board v New Hope Collieries Pty Ltd* [1989] 1 Lloyd's Rep 205.
[308] [1983] 1 AC 444, 483–4. See also *Axelsen v O'Brien* (1949) 80 CLR 219, 226.
[309] See also *Queensland Electricity Generating Board v New Hope Collieries Pty Ltd* [1989] 1 Lloyd's Rep 205, 209–10.
[310] [1983] 1 AC 444, 483–4.

11.109   His Lordship concluded that:[311]

> where an agreement is made to sell at a price to be fixed by a valuer who is named, or ... who ... will have special knowledge relevant to the question of value, the prescribed mode may well be regarded as essential. Where, as here, the machinery consists of valuers and an umpire, none of whom is named or identified, it is in my opinion unrealistic to regard it as an essential term. If it breaks down there is no reason why the court should not substitute other machinery to carry out the main purpose of ascertaining the price in order that the agreement may be carried out.

11.110   Lord Fraser also noted that the principles in *Milnes v Gery* had been whittled away by the following exceptions: first, there were cases that did not apply it where the agreement was partly performed; second, there were cases that did not apply it where the machinery related to a subsidiary part of the contract and to apply it would result in the wider contract failing.[312] These comments again raise the importance of performance and reliance running through this area of law. A further example is the American case of *Tureman v Altman*.[313] The question here was whether the court had jurisdiction to value a property and fix the rent under the lease when the agreed mechanism failed. The lease in question provided for an annual rental of $6,000 for the first 15 years. Thereafter there was to be an appraisement 'to be made by three appraisers, one to be selected by each party ... and the third selected by the two appraisers so chosen'. The lease also specified that the annual rental for the five years after the first period of 15 years was to be 6% of the valuation so fixed. An agreement was not reached on valuation between the appraisers selected by the parties. The court held that it had jurisdiction to value the property and thereby fix a fair and reasonable rental. On the facts, the intervention could not be justified on the usual ground that the valuation provision in the lease was subsidiary or incidental to the main purpose of the contract because on these facts, due to the failure to agree, it had become the most vital part of the contract. The court noted the reluctance to generally order specific performance of arbitration provisions and noted an exception where the machinery provision was subsidiary to the main purpose of the contract. However, the court recognized that other reasons may exist allowing for the court to intervene. Performance and reliance were such reasons. Here the contract had been in place for 55 years, there had been part performance, the original parties did not expect the contract to fail if the rent review mechanism failed but rather expected a fair valuation to take place and a fair rent be payable.

11.111   In Australia the leading decision is that of *Booker Industries Pty Ltd v Wilson Parking (Qld) Pty Ltd*.[314] Here a lessee had an option to renew the lease with rental to be agreed between

---

[311] The naming of a specific individual may make it clear that the machinery provision is exclusive, see *Booker Industries Pty Ltd v Wilson Parking (Qld) Pty Ltd* (1982) 149 CLR 600, 614. However, the mere naming of a person such as a solicitor of itself may not be enough unless there is some reliance on the particular expertise of that solicitor. However, whether or not the formula or machinery are essential is a matter of construction, see *Gillatt v Sky Television Ltd* [2000] 1 All ER (Comm) 461.

[312] Cf *Booker Industries Pty Ltd v Wilson Parking (Qld) Pty Ltd* (1982) 149 CLR 600, 616 per Brennan J (disagreeing with the statement that these are exceptions, 'to a rule applicable where the contract lacks certainty or finality in an essential stipulation. Rather, these cases tend to show that where the express terms of a lease reveal an hiatus in the machinery for fixing the rent, the court will lean towards a construction of the lease which treats the machinery merely as a means of ascertaining what is capable of being ascertained objectively as a fair and reasonable rent and which thus avoids an hiatus in an essential stipulation').

[313] 361 Mo 1220, 239 SW 2d 304 (1951).

[314] (1982) 149 CLR 600.

the parties and failing agreement it was to be fixed by an arbitrator appointed under the terms of another provision in the contract. The lessee exercised the option and the lessor refused to grant the lessee a new lease. The question before the court was whether there was a concluded agreement between the parties. Gibbs CJ, Murphy and Wilson JJ after noting authorities that have held that a court will not decree specific performance of an agreement to appoint an arbitrator to fix a price, held:[315]

> If a lessor agrees to renew a lease at a rent to be fixed by a third party, and agrees (expressly or impliedly) to do all that is reasonably necessary to ensure that the rent is so fixed, it is not right to say there is no concluded contract until the rent is fixed. There is a contract which immediately binds the lessor to perform his obligations to do all that is reasonably necessary to ensure that the rent is fixed, although the performance of the further obligation to renew the lease is conditional upon the rent being fixed. There is no reason in justice or in law why the court should not make an appropriate order for specific performance in such a case, that is, an order that the lessor should do whatever is reasonably necessary to ensure that the rent is fixed, and if the rent is fixed, should renew the lease.

Thus, although an order for specific performance of the lease could not be granted prior to the rent being fixed the court could enforce the implied term that both parties would do that which was reasonably necessary to procure the nomination of an arbitrator.[316] **11.112**

The approach under the Uniform Commercial Code is similar to that in *Sudbrook Trading Estate Ltd v Eggleton*. The relevant provision is section 2-305(1)(c).[317] This provision deals with agreements to buy and sell goods where the price term is left open. The provision ignores such a gap in the contract if there is an overriding intention to contract. Where the price is to be fixed by a third person or agency and this does not occur, then if there is a clear intention to contract a reasonable price at the time of delivery will be payable despite the break down in the machinery. However, effect is given to the intention of the parties if in that circumstance there is no intention to contract; the provision does not make a contract. Comment 4 to this provision makes it clear that there may be instances where a particular third person's judgment is an essential condition to the making of the contract rather than intended 'as a barometer or index of a fair price'. The Comment uses a specific example of 'a known and trusted expert' who is to value a particular painting for which there is no market standard and compares this with a sale of cotton priced according to grade where the named expert is to determine that grade. Whereas in the first instance if the expert were unavailable it would support a finding that the parties did not intend to make a binding agreement, that would clearly not be the position if the expert in the latter case were unavailable. Where the price is to be fixed otherwise than by agreement by the parties and there is a failure in the mechanism through the fault of one of the parties, then the innocent party may either elect to cancel the contract or fix a reasonable price.[318] **11.113**

The last point above brings up the point of waiver. In *Sudbrook Trading Estate Ltd v Eggleton*,[319] Lord Diplock emphasized that the only reason the machinery broke down was **11.114**

---

[315] (1982) 149 CLR 600, 606.
[316] Cf (1982) 149 CLR 600, 617 per Brennan J.
[317] See also Unidroit Principles of International Commercial Contracts (2004) Art 5.1.7. Cf Principles of European Contract Law Arts 6:104 and 6:106. See further Draft Common Frame of Reference II–9:104 and II–9:106.
[318] § 2-305(3).
[319] [1983] 1 AC 444.

because one party breached the contract by failing to appoint. He did not think contract law should allow such a party to take advantage of its own wrong by effectively getting out of the contract. That party must be taken to have waived its right to have the price determined under the machinery provisions. On the facts the innocent party must also be taken to have waived its right to rely on the machinery provision.[320] He expressly left open the question whether the court would have power to appoint a valuer if the innocent party had not waived its right. On the other hand, the thrust of Lord Fraser's speech suggests that the court could enforce an agreement to value in any case except where the valuer was a named valuer or a particular person having particular expertise.

11.115 If all the essential terms are agreed it is possible to agree to leave the other terms to be formulated by one of the parties.[321] Thus, in *Sweet & Maxwell Ltd v Universal News Services Ltd*[322] where the parties agreed the rent and the term of the lease, it was possible to uphold the contract which contained a provision that the 'lease shall contain such other covenant and conditions as shall be reasonably required' by the lessor. Even without that provision, once those essential terms were agreed, the lease could be upheld on the basis that the court would insert the 'usual' covenants.[323] Interestingly, Pearson LJ appeared to suggest that the 'reasonableness' requirement was important as that stopped the agreement being no more than an agreement to agree.[324] This would be taking a very broad view of what constitutes an agreement to agree.[325] Perhaps he probably meant no more than that if the parties have not agreed all the terms of a contract but want to bring a contract into existence immediately then agreeing to other reasonable terms might be a way to do this as it gives the court a standard to fix terms should the parties fail to agree.[326] In any case if one party is given the power to fix the remaining terms such a standard is likely to be imposed.[327] In the result the key issue is whether or not the contract requires any further agreement of the parties.[328]

11.116 Difficulties arise where one party has power to settle an essential term. Here issues of illusory consideration may arise.[329] If such a party's discretion includes the power to refuse to

---

[320] [1983] 1 AC 444, 479.
[321] See Farnsworth, *Farnsworth on Contracts* (3rd edn, Vol 1, Aspen Publishers, New York, 2004), § 3.28, p 425–6.
[322] [1964] 2 QB 699. See also *Godecke v Kirwan* (1973) 129 CLR 629; *Yaroomba Beach Development Co Pty Ltd v Coeur De Lion Investments Pty Ltd* (1989) 18 NSWLR 398; *Money v Ven-Lu-Ree Ltd* [1988] 2 NZLR 414, CA, [1989] 3 NZLR 129.
[323] [1964] 2 QB 699, 726, 735.
[324] [1964] 2 QB 699, 733.
[325] See *Godecke v Kirwan* (1973) 129 CLR 629, 642–3.
[326] Cf *Godecke v Kirwan* (1973) 129 CLR 629, 647 per Gibbs J, critiquing a statement by Bray CJ in *Powell v Jones* (1968) SASR 394 where Bray CJ suggested that 'there is nothing in the *Sweet and Maxwell Case* to indicate that the Court of Appeal would have held the agreement to make the lease unenforceable if the word "reasonably" had been omitted'.
[327] See further Uniform Commercial Code §§ 2-305(2) (and see Comment 3) and 2-311(1); Unidroit Principles of International Commercial Contracts (2004) Art 5.1.7(2); Principles of European Contract Law Articles 6:105. See further Draft Common Frame of Reference II–9:105.
[328] *Godecke v Kirwan* (1973) 129 CLR 629, 641–2.
[329] See 11.20.

settle terms such that they make no promise to contract at all then no contract will exist. For Australian lawyers, Gibbs J in *Godecke v Kirwan*[330] gave the following warning:[331]

> I should perhaps make it clear that it does not necessarily follow from what I have said that an agreement which left further terms to be settled by one of the parties, rather than by his solicitors, would be treated as a concluded contract. In *May and Butcher Ltd v The King* [(1934) 2 KB 17n at p 21], Viscount Dunedin suggested that a sale of land which left the price to be settled by the buyer himself would be good. With great respect, it seems to me that there would be no binding contract in such a case, which would fall within the principle that 'where words which by themselves constitute a promise are accompanied by words which show that the promisor is to have a discretion or option as to whether he will carry out that which purports to be the promise, the result is that there is no contract on which an action can be brought': *Thorby v Goldberg* [(1964) 112 CLR 597, at p 605] ... [T]here can be no concluded bargain if a vital matter (such as price or rental) has been left to the determination of one of the parties ... Perhaps it may be different where agreement has been reached on all essential terms but the determination of subsidiary matters has been left to one of the parties.

The doctrinal point Gibbs J makes is sound in so far as it reflects the concept of illusory consideration. However, unless there is an express term to the contrary, it would be rare for a contract not to incorporate an obligation to carry out the subject act especially if there was an expectation that legal relations were intended to flow from the agreement. Moreover, there are many transactions in which an important term like the price cannot be determined at the time of contract and it may be left to be determined later and in some cases by one of the parties. These contracts would rarely today be struck down on the basis that they involved an illusory consideration.[332] It follows that it is possible to leave to one party the formulation of a term that the parties consider to be important. **11.117**

Terms to be implied in fact, law or custom

So long as the tests for implication in fact, law or custom are satisfied, a gap in a contract can be filled with an implied term. These are more appropriately dealt with in detail in standard works on contract law.[333] As regards resolving uncertainty and incompleteness perhaps the most well-known examples are the implication that performance occur within a reasonable time when no time is set for performance under the contract[334] and the implication of a term to pay a reasonable price for goods accepted by the buyer when no price is set under the contract.[335] Sometimes, rather than applying a standard of reasonableness the **11.118**

---

[330] (1973) 129 CLR 629.

[331] (1973) 129 CLR 629, 647. See further Howard, 'Terms to be Supplied by a Contracting Party' (1982) 56 ALJ 77.

[332] See Furmston, *Cheshire, Fifoot and Furmston's Law of Contract* (15th edn, OUP, Oxford, 2007), 58 discussing *Shell (UK) Ltd v Lostock Garage Ltd* [1977] 1 All ER 481.

[333] See eg Carter, *Carter on Contract* (Butterworths, Sydney) §§ 11-001–11-270; Furmston (ed), *The Law of Contract* (3rd edn, Butterworths, London, 2007), paras 3.19–3.25.

[334] See 11.39. See also *Parker v Manessis* [1974] WAR 54, 57 (implied term that settlement take place within a reasonable time in a contract for the sale of land). See further *York Air Conditioning and Refrigeration (A'sia) Pty Ltd v The Commonwealth* (1949) 80 CLR 11, 62; *W & J Investments Ltd v FCT* (1987) 16 FCR 314, 321; *Whitehouse Properties Pty Ltd v Bond Brewing (NSW) Ltd* (1992) 28 NSWLR 17, 21.

[335] Sale of Goods Act 1979 (UK), s 8 (and see Supply of Goods and Services Act 1982, s 15(1)). See also Sale of Goods Act 1954 (ACT), s 13; Sale of Goods Act 1923 (NSW), s 13; Sale of Goods Act 1972 (NT), s 13; Sale of Goods Act 1896 (Qld), s 11; Sale of Goods Act 1895 (SA), s 8; Sale of Goods Act 1896 (Tas), s 13;

courts use the language of implied terms to do that which is reasonable.[336] However, generally, the law has not up until now implied terms solely on the basis that it is reasonable to do so.[337] Moreover, up until now it has always been held that a term will not be implied if the implication is inconsistent with an express term of the contract. For example, the implication that the buyer must pay a reasonable price has traditionally only been available if the provision for the price has been left blank. If the price was expressed to be one which was to be agreed or negotiated by the parties the implication is not available.[338] In such a case the seller would need to look to one of the other techniques for overcoming uncertainty.[339] As already noted in this chapter there appears to be a view that in matters of uncertainty and incompleteness the courts should strive to uphold the contract when that would give effect to the overall expectation of the parties even if that is not entirely consistent with a term of the contract. However, that approach has not yet found its way into the tests for implication. Nevertheless, the courts have imposed a standard of reasonableness to pay a reasonable price in the face of an agreement to agree or negotiate a price.[340]

11.119 The one unresolved difficulty in using the implied term for the purpose of resolving uncertainty and incompleteness is the famous comment of Lord Roskill in *Aotearoa International Ltd v Scancarriers A/S*,[341] where he suggested that a court cannot imply a term into a contract until it has decided that there is a legally enforceable agreement. On its face that remark would appear to prevent the implied term concept being used to overcome uncertainty and incompleteness. Indeed some have taken that view.[342] Most commentators have taken the view that Lord Roskill could not have meant this but differ on what he did mean. One possibility is that he was only referring to terms implied in fact. That possibility must be set aside for the reasons put forward by Coote, viz:[343]

> Tidy though such a solution would be, it would be difficult to justify in principle. If, for example, one assumes an intention to contract and an agreement which is silent as to price or

---

Goods Act 1958 (Vic), s 13; Sale of Goods Act 1895 (WA), s 8. Although the action for a reasonable price is now a contractual action by virtue of the legislation, and would probably be implied in law in any case today, it was traditionally a restitutionary action. That restitutionary history would reflect the need to pay such a price for those goods that are accepted. To the extent that the action is now seen as contractual the obligation to pay for accepted goods would emphasize the importance of performance to overcoming uncertainty. Differing views have been expressed as to whether the general principles of implied terms would allow for such an implication in an executory contract of sale, see *Hall v Busst* (1960) 104 CLR 206, 222, cf *Australian and New Zealand Banking Group Ltd v Frost Holdings Pty Ltd* [1989] VR 695, 702. See also Coote, 'Contract Formation and the Implication of Terms' (1993) 6 JCL 51, 55. Such an implication will generally not be made in the context of land, see *Hall v Busst* (1960) 104 CLR 206; *Blazely v Whiley* (1995) 5 Tas LR 254.

[336] *Mamidoil-Jetoil Greek Petroleum Co SA v Okta Crude Oil Refinery AD* [2001] 2 Lloyd's Rep 76, 91.
[337] Cf 11.84.
[338] Eg *Mamidoil-Jetoil Greek Petroleum Co SA v Okta Crude Oil Refinery AD* [2001] 2 Lloyd's Rep 76, 91.
[339] *Hillas & Co Ltd v Arcos Ltd* (1932) 147 LT 503; *Foley v Classique Coaches Ltd* [1934] 2 KB 1; *Deta Nominees Pty Ltd v Viscount Plastic Products Pty Ltd* [1979] VR 167, 187; *Australian and New Zealand Banking Group Ltd v Frost Holdings Pty Ltd* [1989] VR 695.
[340] See the discussion in *Voest Alpine Intertrading GmbH v Chevron International Oil Co Ltd* [1987] 2 Lloyd's Rep 547, 561–2. See also Uniform Commercial Code § 2-305.
[341] [1985] 1 NZLR 513, 556. Cf *Trollope & Colls Ltd v Atomic Power Constructions Ltd* [1963] 1 WLR 333, 341.
[342] *Australian and New Zealand Banking Group Ltd v Frost Holdings Pty Ltd* [1989] VR 695, 702; *Money v Ven Lu Ree* [1988] 2 NZLR 414, 416–17 per Sir Robin Cooke (affirmed [1989] 3 NZLR 129, PC); *Marxen v Smith* [1990] 3 NZLR 585, 598.
[343] Coote, 'Contract Formation and the Implication of Terms' (1993) 6 JCL 51, 55 citing *Foley v Classique Coaches Ltd* [1934] 2 KB 1 and *Beer v Bowden* [1981] 1 WLR 522.

rental, the very fact of an intention to contract would point to the necessity of implying that a reasonable amount would be payable, even if there were no basis in custom or statute for implying such a term and even though, indeed simply because, without such an implication there would be no enforceable contract.

McLauchlan has suggested that Lord Roskill was in fact referring to the intention to con-   **11.120**
tract and when he said you cannot imply a term to find a 'legally binding bargain' those words are meant to be read 'contractual intention'.[344] Thus, one cannot imply a term in order to derive an intention to contract; if no intention to contract exists there is no point carrying on and trying to overcome any uncertainty in the bargain. As a doctrinal point this must be correct and may be a solution. However, the thrust of Lord Roskill's comment, and the context in which it was made, seems to suggest that the concern was that of uncertainty and incompleteness. In full he said:[345]

> It is not correct in principle, in order to determine there is a legally binding bargain, to add to those terms which alone the parties have expressed, further implied terms upon which they have not expressly agreed and then by adding the express terms and the implied terms together thereby create what would not otherwise be a legally binding bargain.

One observation that may be made is that Lord Roskill's statement is only concerned with   **11.121**
that level of uncertainty and incompleteness that would render the contract void. This would not prevent the implied term technique being used to overcome some uncertainty or incompleteness in relation to a term that would not otherwise affect the efficacy of the contract as a whole.[346] From this it would seem to follow that the implied term technique could not be used to provide an essential term.[347] But the implication of a price provision in a sale of goods contract would appear to do just that and although that implication is now dictated by statute, that statute does no more than reflect what would now be the common law position. Moreover, as has been pointed out, the law can imply an entire contract.[348] Indeed the more familiar a court is with the type of contract before it the more willing it is to fill any gaps by way of implication despite very open terms.[349]

Both Coote and Carter suggest a third interpretation both emphasizing that the point that   **11.122**
Lord Roskill was referring to was that a court will not make a contract for the parties, everything the court does must be consistent with what the parties intended. It is suggested that these reflect the better view. Coote states:[350]

> [T]he first question must always be whether any legally binding contract has been made. The answer to that first question depends not on whether the expressly agreed terms are sufficient in themselves to constitute a contract but on whether, given an intention to contract, the parties have specifically agreed all the terms which only they can decide. These ... may be

---

[344] McLauchlan, 'Offer and Acceptance in the Privy Council' [1989] NZLJ 136, 138–9.
[345] [1985] 1 NZLR 513, 556.
[346] Perhaps he did not see issues of uncertainty and incompleteness as being relevant to formation but performance as they need only be made out at the time for performance. However, whether or not an uncertain term can be severed or an incomplete agreement operate according to its agreed terms are more relevant to formation.
[347] As to the meaning of 'essential term' see 11.03.
[348] Coote, 'Contract Formation and the Implication of Terms' (1993) 6 JCL 51, 51–2.
[349] See *Cavallari v Premier Refrigeration Co Pty Ltd* (1952) 85 CLR 20, 25–6. See also *Coal Cliff Collieries Pty Ltd v Sijehama Pty Ltd* (1991) 24 NSWLR 1, 27.
[350] Coote, 'Contract Formation and the Implication of Terms' (1993) 6 JCL 51, 56.

very few indeed as in the case of a tenancy agreement or a contract of employment, for example, may be no more than the date of commencement, with all the rest being unstated but nevertheless, in the objective sense, 'intended' and capable of being deduced, inferred or implied.

On the other hand, in a complex matter where a range of matters have been settled which only the parties can agree, and only some of those matters have been agreed by them, there is no basis (other than second-guessing the parties) upon which the gaps can be filled by implication. That, it is submitted was the situation in the *Aotearoa* case, at least as the Privy Council perceived it ...

Perhaps the real truth is that Lord Roskill was saying rather less than he appeared to be. No court wants to be the destroyer or bargains but there has to be a bargain in the first place. On that point, the courts traditionally have insisted that they will not make contracts for the parties which the parties have not made for themselves.

11.123 Carter in discussing the reticence of courts to imply terms into complex contracts states:[351]

> The qualification in relation to complex commercial contracts reflects the absence of general implications for unique transactions. This may explain what otherwise appears to be an inconsistent proposition, namely, the law does not permit a court to imply terms for the purpose of making incomplete negotiations an enforceable contract. The proposition seems to be based on the view that in order for an implication to be made the parties must have finally agreed on a bargain. Accordingly, it is not sufficient for a court to be able to identify terms which, if they were implied, would complete an otherwise incomplete agreement. Instead, it must be possible to infer—under normal principles governing implication—that the parties impliedly agreed to the matter which has not been the subject of express provisions. Expressed in a slightly different way, where, for example, a contract is silent on a matter such as the price or quality of the subject matter of the contract, it must be possible to infer that the parties agreed to a particular standard which a court is capable of implying. Accordingly, an implication of a reasonable price or reasonable quality can only be made if that was the agreement. Mere consistency with the contract is not enough for the simple reason that a court cannot make a contract for the parties. ·

> On this basis, cases in which arguments for the implication of terms have succeeded are cases in which the parties have negotiated all essential terms, and agreed to a particular criterion omitted from their express agreement. Thus, in *Hillas & Co Ltd v Arcos Ltd* a buyer's option to take a further supply of goods did not specify kinds, sizes or quality or the dates and ports of shipment and discharge. However, the contract was upheld on the basis that in carrying out an initial part of the contract the parties attributed meaning to the agreement. It could therefore be implied that the contract required goods to be of a fair specification. Again, in *Foley v Classique Coaches Ltd*, where there was an agreement to purchase all petrol required at a price to be agreed by the parties from time to time, it was inferred that the parties intended to agree for the supply of reasonable quality petrol at a reasonable price. Cases in which arguments for the implication of terms have failed are cases in which the parties were still in the process of negotiating essential terms. Thus, in *May and Butcher Ltd v R* an agreement for the sale of goods at prices to be agreed upon was invalid because a vital term had still to be agreed. In the absence of agreement that a reasonable price would be paid no such term could be implied. More recently, in *Australian and New Zealand Banking Group Ltd v Frost Holdings Pty Ltd* there was held to be no enforceable contract where essential terms, including the

---

[351] Carter, *Carter on Contract* (Butterworths, Sydney) § 04-160 (footnotes omitted).

price, size, style and design of goods to be supplied was not agreed. The court would not imply terms to deal with these matters as there was, in the court's view, nothing to indicate the basis for implication.

Severance

Where all the above methods fail it may still be possible to sever an uncertain provision or **11.124** see if the contract can operate despite it being incomplete. Whether or not severance is possible is determined by reference to the intention of the parties.[352] It needs to be determined whether the parties envisaged that the subject provision could be severed or did they expect the whole contract to be void if the uncertainty could not be resolved.[353] The issue has been said to be one of construction which would prevent a court having recourse to extrinsic evidence.[354] It will generally be necessary to show that any severance will not affect the essential terms of the agreement. Moreover, severance will not be allowed if to do so would fundamentally change the nature of the agreement.[355] The contract must still be able to achieve its main purpose. For example, in a sale and leaseback arrangement, if the lease is void for uncertainty it would not then be commensurate with the intention of the parties to enforce the sale agreement.[356]

[352] *Life Insurance Co of Australia Ltd v Phillips* (1925) 36 CLR 60, 72; *Whitlock v Brew* (1968) 118 CLR 445, 461; *Update Constructions Pty Ltd v Rozelle Child Care Centre Ltd* (1990) 20 NSWLR 251, 278; *United Group Rail Services Ltd v Rail Corp New South Wales* [2009] NSWCA 177.
[353] Examples of where severance was ordered include *Fitzgerald v Masters* (1956) 95 CLR 420 (incorporation by reference of external standard form contract did not exist but could be severed as parties intended to contract despite this and all essential terms had been agreed); *Caltex Oil (Aust) Pty Ltd v Alderton* [1964–5] NSWR 456 (here a standard form limited guarantee was executed and did not state a limit; it was clear the parties had used the wrong document and had intended to enter into an unlimited guarantee; it was therefore possible to sever the irrelevant provisions). See also *David Jones Ltd v Lunn* (1969) 91 WN (NSW) 468; *Boult Enterprises Ltd v Bissett* (1985) 21 DLR (4th) 730; *Tern Minerals NL v Kalbara Mining NL* (1990) 3 WAR 486; *Glebe Island Terminals Pty Ltd v Continental Seagram Pty Ltd (The Antwerpen)* (1993) 40 NSWLR 206, 225–6. Examples where severance was not ordered include *Duggan v Barnes* [1923] VLR 27 (contract for sale of land requiring purchaser to lease property to any purchaser of the vendor's business; no terms of the proposed lease were set out; held the whole contract was void); *Whitlock v Brew* (1968) 118 CLR 445 (sale and lease back arrangement where terms of lease were uncertain; could not sever the lease aspect of the arrangement without fundamentally changing the nature of the contract). As regards the severance of meaningless terms, see *Nicolene Ltd v Simmonds* [1953] 1 QB 543; *Laybutt v Amoco Australia Pty Ltd* (1974) 132 CLR 57; *Spectra Pty Ltd v Pindari Pty Ltd* [1974] 2 NSWLR 617.
[354] *Whitlock v Brew* (1968) 118 CLR 445, 461; *David Jones Ltd v Lunn* (1969) 91 WN (NSW) 468.
[355] Eg *G Scammell & Nephew Ltd v Ouston* [1941] AC 251.
[356] *Whitlock v Brew* (1968) 118 CLR 445.

12

IS THERE A DUTY TO NEGOTIATE IN GOOD FAITH?

A. Introduction[1]

The issue

The account of the common law of contract formation given in the preceding chapters of this book has two apparent features which call for comment. One is that it looks rather formalistic. One could easily fall into the trap of treating the exercise as one of trying to fit the facts into a number of rather rigidly defined categories. Is this conduct an offer or is it only an invitation to treat? In practice, good judges treat the concepts robustly and use them as techniques to answer the question 'Is there a contract?'.[2]   **12.01**

A second feature presents more difficulties. In so far as there is a model of the negotiating process, it is one of buying a horse or nowadays a second-hand car; a transaction where the parties go from no relationship to completed contract in one negotiating stage carried out with all the unities demanded by classical drama. In fact, as we all know, many negotiations do not take this form but proceed through a series of meetings towards a complete agreement. In this scenario the parties typically make agreements at each stage, so negotiations between employers and unions might involve disagreements about the hourly rate; the number of hours to be worked; arrangements for holidays; arrangements for compulsory overtime, and so on. There will be a series of meetings and the parties will try to agree to the answers to a number of the problems at each of the meetings. In this type of negotiation,   **12.02**

---

[1] The chapter draws heavily on Carter and Furmston, 'Good Faith and Fairness in the Negotiation of Contracts' (1994) 8 JCL 1, 93 and the authors are grateful to John Carter for his ready agreement for the use of that material in this chapter.

[2] See Lord Wilberforce in *New Zealand Shipping Co Ltd v AM Satterthwaite & Co Ltd* [1975] 1 AC 154, 167.

although there is no complete agreement until the end of the series of meetings, most nego-
tiators most of the time would regard the interim agreements as in some sense binding.
Historically the common law has not found it easy to give legal effect to this perception. It
has tended to take the position that either there is a contract or there is not. This is obviously one of the reasons why there are so many difficulties in analysing the legal effect of
documents such as letters of intent. To some extent the common law has sought to address
this issue by having reference to extrinsic evidence in determining whether a contract exists.
But this does not apply to questions of construction which might arise when there are
documents and, moreover, it only seeks to determine and give effect to the intention of the
parties at the end of the negotiation process. One answer to this problem might be to treat
the parties as being under a duty to negotiate in good faith. This chapter is concerned with
the analysis of this possibility.

12.03 Many continental systems have adopted the notion that contracts should be performed in
good faith. This is explicitly stated, for instance, in the German Civil Code. Such a duty has
also been largely accepted by the American version of the common law. The Restatement
(2d) Contracts, section 205 provides:

> Every contract imposes upon each party a duty of good faith and fair dealing in its perfor-
> mance and enforcement.

12.04 Similarly section 1-203 of the Uniform Commercial Code provides:

> Every contract or duty within this Act imposes an obligation of good faith in its performance
> or enforcement.[3]

12.05 This acceptance of a duty to perform in good faith is a relatively recent development in the
American version of the common law and there is still much dispute as to exactly what
good faith performance involves. It is very much an open question whether other versions
of the common law will accept an obligation of this kind. The discussion has perhaps been
most explicit in Australia but rather sharply contrasting views have been expressed and the
High Court of Australia is yet to consider the issue.[4]

12.06 We shall say no more about good faith performance here, since the question we wish to
address is good faith in negotiation. In general, it would be fair to say that even civilian
systems which have long adopted notions of good faith performance have been much
slower to accept notions of good faith negotiation. So all over the world the question of
whether the parties should be under a duty to negotiate in good faith is very much at the
forefront of the debate.

---

[3] For a fuller discussion of good faith in American law see Burton and Anderson, *Contractual Good Faith*
(Little Brown & Company, New York, 1995). For a discussion of the position in England and Europe, see
Beatson and Friedman, *Good Faith and Fault in Contract Law* (Oxford University Press, Oxford, 1995);
Zimmermann and Whittaker (eds), *Good Faith in European Contract Law* (Cambridge University Press,
Cambridge, 2000). See also McCamus, *The Law of Contracts* (Irwin Law, Toronto, 2005), Ch 5.
[4] Priestley JA in *Renard Constructions (ME) Pty Ltd v Minister for Public Works* (1992) 26 NSWLR 234
and Gummow J in *Service State Association v Berg Bennett* (1993) 117 ALR 393. For a tantalizing glimpse
of English possibilities see *Phillips Electronique v B Sky B* [1995] EMLR 472. See further Carter and Peden,
'Good Faith in Australian Contract Law' (2003) 19 JCL 155.

The traditional view[5] is that there is no general duty of good faith in negotiation. From one **12.07**
perspective, the question whether our law currently recognizes a general duty of good faith
is an easy one, to which a straightforward and affirmative answer may be given. The common law concept of deceit imposes a duty on those who negotiate, perform or enforce
contracts to act in good faith. However, this is no more than a duty not to engage in fraudulent conduct. When contract lawyers speak of 'good faith' they take this aspect of the law
for granted: The good faith issue is both broader and narrower in its orientation.[6] It is
broader in the sense that the question is whether the law should recognize and apply—in a
wide variety of situations—a more onerous duty of good faith. It is narrower in the sense
that we are inquiring whether the current approach, under which the good faith concept is
inherent in a number of areas, should be made explicit in a general duty called 'good faith'.
For our purposes the good faith issue may be framed in the following way: accepting that
people must not act fraudulently, does the law require more than this? Again, there are
many who would say that the question is an easy one, to which a negative answer must be
given. However, in our view this dismissal is facile.[7]

In *Walford v Miles*,[8] Lord Ackner (with whom the other members of the House of Lords **12.08**
agreed) stated that 'the concept of a duty to carry on negotiations in good faith is inherently
repugnant to the adversarial position of the parties when involved in negotiations'.[9] There
is also a concern that adoption of a broad duty of good faith would unsettle the commercial
bargaining process, and that a court should not, in commercial matters, 'substitute law-
yerly conscience for the hard-headed decisions of business people'.[10] It has also been suggested that there is an economic justification in the current law, in promoting freedom of
competition by preserving the liberty to manoeuvre.[11] Few indeed would support a principle of good faith which required contracting parties to give up their negotiating advantages.[12] At the same time, however, in most contracting situations the parties have a
common interest in the successful completion of negotiations. There are also many cases,
such as joint ventures, where the parties enter into negotiations for a joint purpose, and
some special cases where a fiduciary relation between the parties requires the subordination
of self-interest. In these cases the adversarial justification makes little sense. In any event,
even if we accept an adversarial theory of contract negotiation—which is very much a

---

[5] See eg, Powell, 'Good Faith in Contracts' [1956] CLP 16, 25; Goode, 'England', in International
Chamber of Commerce, *Formation of Contracts and Precontractual Liability* (ICC Publishing Corp, New
York, 1990) 51; O'Connor, *Good Faith in English Law* (Dartmouth, Aldershot, 1990) 18. Cf Finn, *Equity and
Contract*, in Finn (ed), *Essays on Contract* (Law Book Co, Sydney, 1987), 104.

[6] Cf Powell's distinction between 'objective and subjective good faith' in Powell, 'Good Faith in Contracts'
[1956] CLP 16, 23.

[7] See also Brownsword, 'Two Conceptions of Good Faith' (1994) 7 JCL 197.

[8] [1992] 2 AC 128, 138.

[9] Cf Berg, 'Promises to Negotiate in Good Faith' (2003) 119 LQR 357.

[10] *Austotel Pty Ltd v Franklins Selfserve Pty Ltd* (1989) 16 NSWLR 582, 585 per Kirby P. See also *Woolworths
Ltd v Kelly* (1991) 22 NSWLR 189, 213; *Beneficial Finance Corp Ltd v Karavas* (1991) 23 NSWLR 256, 267.
Cf *Banque Brussels Lambert SA v Australian National Industries Ltd* (1989) 21 NSWLR 502, 523.

[11] See Fontaine, 'Concluding Report', in International Chamber of Commerce, *Formation of Contracts
and Precontractual Liability* (ICC Publishing Corp, New York, 1990), 343.

[12] A related problem is the disclosure of commercially valuable information. See Hertig, 'Transfer of
Technology Agreements; the Pharmaceutical Industry Example', in International Chamber of Commerce,
Formation of Contracts and Precontractual Liability (ICC Publishing Corp, New York, 1990), 215.

classical perspective—good faith may still have a role to play. At the least, we need to investigate both the extent to which the law promotes good faith and the extent to which the law requires the exercise of good faith.

12.09   Good faith is itself a flexible notion, which will take its meaning, in part, from its context. In particular the determination of good faith and negotiation involves different problems from that of determining good faith and performance, since in relation to the latter, provisions of the contract will have a good deal to say. This can be illustrated by the controversial American case of *Kham and Nate's Shoes No 2 v First Bank of Whiting*[13] where a bank granted a secured $300,000 line credit to a bankrupt Chicago shoe retailer, which was in reorganization. The contract provided for cancellation on five days' notice and added that 'nothing provided herein could constitute a waiver of the right of the bank to terminate financing at any time'. The bank terminated when $65,000 was outstanding and without giving reasons.[14] The trial judge held that the bank was in breach of its duty of good faith but the Court of Appeals reversed on the ground that the contract *pro tanto* ousted the duty of good faith. Clearly there is scope for different views as to whether the contractual language was sufficiently blunt to produce this result. Banks sometimes speak with forked tongues—nods and winks on the one hand; statements that all business is done on a demand basis on the other. It is not in principle unreasonable to suggest that sufficiently clear language might qualify its duty of good faith. A bank which heads its contract with statements in clear bold type 'Borrow from us at your peril. We often demand repayment at 24 hours' notice' would presumably improve its legal though perhaps not its commercial position.

The genesis of the duty of good faith

12.10   There is no need, indeed no point, in departing from the familiar techniques of the common law in investigating the existence and enforcement of good faith. In any situation a duty to act in good faith may be found in express terms, by construction of the contract as a whole or by the implication of a term. Recourse to these familiar concepts is both necessary and appropriate.

Good faith raises two closely related questions. The first is whether if the parties agree that they will negotiate in good faith, this is an obligation to which the law will attach substance. The second is whether there are circumstances in which, even in the absence of agreement by the parties, the law should impose a duty to negotiate in good faith. The extent to which good faith has been recognized in the various legal systems around the world varies considerably. English law is currently a prime example of one group which thinks that the answer to both the questions should be in the negative. The judicial influence on the issue means that there is no body of law analysed in the textbooks under the heading of good faith.

12.11   A second group of which the courts of the Australia and the United States may be members recognizes that if the parties agree that they will negotiate in good faith, this gives rise

---

[13] 908 F 2d 1351 (1990). Cf Patterson, 'Fable from the Seventh Circuit: Frank Easterbrook on Good Faith' (1991) 76 Iowa LR 503 for critical comment.
[14] Internal bank memoranda suggested that the bank's board 'did not think that [it] should be doing business on the south side of Chicago'.

at least in some cases to an obligation which can be enforced. Although we might gain the impression from reading the American literature and cases that there is a broad and general doctrine in many American jurisdictions, close examination reveals that this is not the position. The Uniform Commercial Code[15] and Restatement (2d) Contracts,[16] which have shaped many of the American principles of general contract law, both state obligations of good faith. However, in both, the obligation is stated in terms that every contract 'imposes an obligation of good faith in its performance' or 'enforcement'. When the Uniform Commercial Code speaks of 'Good faith and fair dealing' it presumably means both sides of this antithesis to bear different meanings, though it is worth noting that distinguished French lawyers insist that the correct French rendering of this expression is *bonne foi.* By implication, there is no such obligation in relation to the negotiation process itself.[17]

A third group goes further and imposes, at least in some circumstances, a duty to negotiate **12.12** in good faith. The Italian Civil Code expressly provides for such an obligation. The German Civil Code contains an express provision that the contract should be performed in good faith but no express provision that the parties have to negotiate in good faith. Nevertheless many civil law *systems* have developed the notion of *culpa in contrahendo*[18] though some civil lawyers have characterized this as a tortious rather than a contractual remedy. Although good faith therefore seems more in evidence in some civil law jurisdictions, there is no consistent approach and the content of the law appears to vary considerably.[19]

It is not surprising that when the United Nations Convention on Contracts for the **12.13** International Sale of Goods 1980 was drafted as a compromise between common law and civil law approaches to international sale transactions, it proved to be impossible to achieve a consensus for the imposition of a good faith duty.[20] On the other hand, the Unidroit Principles of International Commercial Contracts 2004 provide, in Article 2.1.15:

(1) A party is free to negotiate and is not liable for failure to reach an agreement.
(2) However, a party who negotiates or breaks off negotiations in bad faith is liable for the losses caused to the other party.

---

[15] § 1-201.

[16] § 205.

[17] Cf Restatement (2d) Contracts § 161 (duty of disclosure).

[18] See Kessler and Fine, 'Culpa in Contrahendo, Bargaining in Good Faith, and Freedom of Contract: A Comparative Study' (1964) 77 Harv L Rev 401.

[19] See also Cornelis, 'Belgium', in Hondius (ed), *Precontractual Liability* (Kluwer, Deventer, 1991), 63 (operation and role of good faith 'far from being settled'); Schmidt-Szalewski, 'France', in International Chamber of Commerce, *Formation of Contracts and Precontractual Liability* (ICC Publishing Corp, New York, 1990), 89 (promise to negotiate a contract is binding); Shalev, 'Israel', in Hondius (ed), *Precontractual Liability* (Kluwer, Deventer, 1991), 181 (statute requires person negotiating contract to act 'in customary manner and in good faith').

[20] Article 7(1) requires that, in the interpretation of the Convention, regard must be had to its international character and 'to the need to promote uniformity in its application and the observance of good faith in international trade'. The Convention already has the force of law in Australia, the US, Canada and many European countries, other than the UK. It remains to be seen how far Art 7 will operate to impose a good faith duty on parties to international sale transactions. See Bonell, 'Formation of Contracts and Precontractual Liability under the Vienna Convention on International Sale of Goods', in International Chamber of Commerce, *Formation of Contracts and Precontractual Liability* (ICC Publishing Corp, New York, 1990), 157.

(3) It is bad faith, in particular, for a party to enter into or continue negotiations when intending not to reach an agreement with the other party.

12.14 One reason why there is no general good faith duty is the robustness of the common law. It is very doctrinal—some say 'formalistic'—and relies heavily on principles based primarily on construction, that is, the will of the parties. Those espousing good faith then look, at least to practising lawyers, to be engaging in woolly thinking, relying on policy (rather than doctrine) and amorphous principles (rather than rules). However, in our view this confuses the content of the good faith duty with the application of an established doctrine of good faith. The former is, as a legal issue, as doctrinal as, say, the limits of the frustration doctrine. There is simply no reason to regard a concept of good faith as amounting to a licence to judges to do whatever they consider 'fair' in the context of a particular dispute.[21] In other words, as a common law concept, the content of good faith is not determined by judicial discretion. Its application does not amount to the exercise of a discretionary jurisdiction. Even if we allow for an equitable component, discretion will relate merely to the form of remedy. The plain fact is that, in the application of doctrine, English and Australian courts have promoted good faith and achieved results which are, for the most part, consistent with the operation of a general concept of that kind. Rule formulation is today less emphatic than in the 19th century, and rule application is more pragmatic. We do not draw from these features a conclusion that the doctrines constituted by the rules in question are therefore based on a foundation of judicial discretion. Criticism of the judicial approach may be made on this score only if the judging process is affected by a discretion which the court does not possess.[22]

Content of the duty

12.15 Reading between the lines in our case law, it appears that the courts are wary of good faith because they assume a greater content than it actually possesses. In other words, it may be that one reason for the reluctance of our courts to adopt a general good faith duty is the belief that it is an onerous duty, imposing an obligation on one person to act in the interests of another. Where the good faith issue arises in the context of contract negotiations this may be a conception that good faith means more than honesty in fact and must impose an obligation on each party engaged in the negotiations to subordinate its own interests to those of the other party. It may be that one reason why the academics who have argued in favour of good faith have been slow in convincing the courts of the viability of the concept is that they have not explained clearly what they mean when they speak of good faith.

12.16 Good faith certainly embraces 'honesty in fact', that is, the absence of fraud.[23] We have no difficulty in accepting this. Equally, it may be conceded that good faith must mean something more. Certainly, academics have a broader duty in mind. However, we must not

---

[21] Cf the rejection of 'idiosyncratic notions' of what is fair and just as a criterion in cases of estoppel and unjust enrichment in *Legione v Hateley* (1983) 152 CLR 406, 431 *Pavey & Matthews Pty Ltd v Paul* (1987) 162 CLR 221, 256; *Commonwealth of Australia v Verwayen* (1990) 170 CLR 394, 443.

[22] Cf Treitel, *Doctrine and Discretion in the Law of Contract* (Clarendon Press, Oxford, 1981).

[23] This is the basic criterion under the Uniform Commercial Code. See § 2-103(j). Cf § 1-201(20). See generally Farnsworth, 'Good Faith Performance and Commercial Reasonableness Under the Uniform Commercial Code' (1963) 30 U Chi L Rev 666; Burton, 'Breach of Contract and the Common Law Duty

confuse a duty of good faith with a fiduciary duty. The distinctive features of a fiduciary relation are that the fiduciary must not abuse his or her position and not allow interest and duty to conflict. The high standard guards against both actual and possible abuses of position, and requires the fiduciary to place the interests of the beneficiary above its own. Good faith is different. It is narrower. A breach of the duty of good faith may be established by showing that the party subject to the duty has acted for an ulterior motive or with an intention to injure the other party. Thus, Finn states[24] that there is a positive requirement to have regard to the legitimate interests of the other party. He rightly contrasts this with the more onerous duty of the fiduciary. Therefore, a person subject merely to a duty of good faith may take decisions which adversely affect the other party without being in breach of the duty.[25] Finn also emphasizes that while the existence of a fiduciary duty *denies* the right to act self-interestedly, good faith has a lesser effect and merely *curtails* the right to act self-interestedly.[26] Whether there is a good faith duty to have regard to the interests of another is therefore a different question, governed by different principles, from whether the parties to negotiations stand in a fiduciary relation.[27] From this we may conclude that a duty of good faith will generally embrace:

(a) a duty to act honestly; and
(b) a duty to have regard to the legitimate interests of the other party.

Given the possibility of the misconceptions noted, it seems important to point out that we are in fact all familiar with contracts containing duties more onerous than those of good faith, as defined above. Thus, express terms may, even in the context of contractual negotiations, create a duty to act both honestly and reasonably. Similarly, circumstances may (and often do) justify the implication of a duty to act both honestly and reasonably. Although we rationalize these situations by reference to the intention of the parties, this means no more than that our conception is of an internal (consensual or agreed) duty rather than an external (imposed or policy based) duty. This is just common law doctrine, it is not equity. Thus, Mr Justice Priestley has said that Australian law has reached the stage where terms may readily be implied having 'substantially the same effect as the good faith formulation in the United States'.[28] There are also limited cases, chiefly contracts *uberrimae fidei* and those between fiduciaries, where our law finds and enforces a duty to act in good faith merely on the basis of the kind of contract being negotiated or the relation between

12.17

---

to Perform in Good Faith' (1980) 94 Harv L Rev 369; Summers, 'The General Duty of Good Faith—Its Recognition and Conceptualization' (1982) 67 Cornell L Rev 810, 824–5.

[24] See Finn, 'The Fiduciary Principle', in TG Youdan (ed), *Equity, Fiduciaries and Trusts* (Carswell, Toronto, 1989), 4.

[25] See Finn, 'The Fiduciary Principle', in TG Youdan (ed), *Equity, Fiduciaries and Trusts* (Carswell, Toronto, 1989), 14.

[26] See Finn, 'Contract and the Fiduciary Principle' (1989) 12 UNSWLJ 76, 82–3. The object of what he describes as the 'fiduciary principle' is to secure the 'paramountcy' of an interest. That paramountcy may be of one party's interests in a relationship or of the parties' joint interest.

[27] See *Hospital Products Ltd v United States Surgical Corp* (1984) 156 CLR 41; *Noranda Australia Ltd v Lachlan Resources NL* (1988) 14 NSWLR 1, 18. See generally Lehane, 'Fiduciaries in a Commercial Context', in PD Finn (ed), *Essays in Equity* (Law Book Co Ltd, Sydney, 1985), 95.

[28] See Priestley, 'A Guide to a Comparison of Australian and United States Contract Law' (1989) 12 UNSWLJ 4, 23.

the parties. A duty going far beyond good faith is present where the parties to negotiations stand in a fiduciary relation or the terms of a contract create such a relation. Although the former is imposed and the latter agreed, the courts have been enforcing these duties for centuries. In all these cases there is a sound doctrinal basis for a duty to act in good faith. All in all, we are already very familiar with the existence of good faith duties.

B. The Role of Good Faith

Introduction

12.18   The relevance of good faith to contract is potentially very wide. This is because, as has already been mentioned, the concept may apply not only to the negotiation process but also to the parties' performance duties or their decisions on the enforcement of contractual rights. Although our principal concern is with the first of these—good faith in negotiations—it is difficult to ignore the other situations. Good faith may have at least two roles where one party alleges that negotiations have not reached the stage of a concluded bargain.

12.19   One role is to justify the enforcement of an obligation to continue negotiations, not in all cases but in those where the act of breaking off negotiations is capable of being characterized as an example of bad faith. The essence of this is that good faith has a 'preservation role': it provides a basis for upholding agreements. The other role relates to 'pre-contractual liability'.

12.20   The second role is therefore to provide a basis for relief. This has a number of aspects, including the following:

1. remedial consequences may attach where there is a breach of an express or implied (contractual) good faith duty;
2. breach of an imposed (non-contractual) duty of good faith may have remedial consequences;
3. reliance by one party on a promise that the other will contract or continue to negotiate may lead to a conclusion that the other party is bound by a promissory estoppel from which remedial consequences flow; and
4. a claim for restitution may be based on circumstances which include conduct which lacks good faith.

The preservative function

Introduction

12.21   The preservation function of good faith lies in the extent to which it operates to preserve a particular negotiating relationship. Of course, we start with the general rule that until negotiations are complete parties are free to withdraw without incurring liability for doing so. Until there is an agreement with legally recognized consideration, negotiations may, as a general rule, be broken off with impunity. So much flows from the approach to offer and acceptance, certainty of agreement, the interpretation of letters of intent and other preliminary agreements, the requirement of intention to contract and so on. Until the contract is formed the negotiating parties are presumed to be free to decide not to contract. Were the law otherwise we could not countenance what is an ordinary feature of the bargaining process, namely, the ability to negotiate in relation to a specific subject matter with a number of persons. The presumption is not rebutted merely by proof that a person has incurred expenditure in reliance on an expectation that a contract will be agreed. Contract negotiation always has a cost, and commercial people realize that the cost must, as a general rule, be recouped from contracts which result from successful negotiation. Negotiation expenses contribute to variable costs. There may be an intention to recoup individual transaction costs from a particular contract, but in all industries far more contracts are negotiated than are agreed, and even where the profit motive is a correct analysis, pricing structures reflect overall costs rather than individual transaction costs.

There is, however, an obvious tension in the law. It is not at all uncommon for negotiations   **12.22** to reach a stage where although there is arguably no contract, it can be seen that a decision to this effect will have harsh consequences. Although the conventional view is that there is no reliance theory in our contract law, the courts are naturally impressed by reliance and the result is a tension between the application of the formation rules and a desire to do justice. In the context of a situation in which negotiations have broken down prematurely, one party may be seen as deserving of assistance, or the court may wish to discourage a particular kind of conduct. The courts are both concerned to preserve doctrine and to promote good faith in bargaining. Similarly, the courts are both concerned to promote the economic (community) interest in the successful negotiation of contracts and to preserve the freedom not to contract. Again, the courts are concerned to promote fairness in negotiation and to conserve commercial advantages which may be exploited legitimately. The decisions therefore exhibit a certain ambivalence to the good faith issue.

There are three areas which, at least in the recent cases, illustrate the important role of good   **12.23** faith where negotiations are alleged to have broken down before agreement has been reached. First, the approach of the courts to the requirement of certainty of agreement.[29] Second, the current approach to 'subject to' clauses.[30] Third, but controversially, the approach to agreements to negotiate in good faith.[31]

Brief mention should also be made of the approach of the modern law to the agreement   **12.24** process, formalities and the presumptive approach to the question of intention to create legal relations. Offer and acceptance are now recognized as tools of analysis, rather than strict rules of agreement.[32] Therefore, although the rules of offer and acceptance still play a major role in the analysis of negotiations, we no longer attempt to force all commercial negotiations into that scheme. It is well known that certain commercial relations, for instance, those created by documentary credits, are enforced as a matter of commercial convenience without regard to the fact that consideration for the promisor's promise would

---

[29] Chapter 11.
[30] Chapter 9.
[31] See 11.59ff.
[32] Cf *Subdivisions Ltd v Payne* [1934] SASR 214, 220; *New Zealand Shipping Co Ltd v A M Satterthwaite & Co Ltd* [1975] AC 154, 167.

be very difficult to find. More generally, there are clear signs that in many contexts a pragmatic approach will be taken to the requirement of consideration.[33]

12.25   There is an element of good faith in the assumption that contracting parties will keep to their bargain even if it is merely verbal. The common law did not take the approach that only those agreements which have been certified by a public official are binding. The most that has been required is the presence of writing. The most famous example of this, the Statute of Frauds, did not go so far as to require a contract to be in writing. It was sufficient that written evidence could be established.[34] Most of the promises originally required to be so evidenced may now be enforced if purely oral. Moreover, courts of equity, in refusing to allow the statute to be an engine for fraud, engrafted a doctrine of part performance. In effect, parties were barred from pleading the statute where acts of part performance were sufficient to render this unconscientious.[35]

12.26   Although it is a necessary element in the formation of a contract that there is an intention to create a legally enforceable contract, this may be express or implied.[36] In commercial agreements there is a presumption that an agreement which has all the characteristics of a contract was intended to be legally enforceable. The onus of establishing that a commercial agreement did not create legal relations therefore rests on the party so contending. In part at least this may be explained by the view that to allow a person to deny legal effect would be to countenance bad faith. It is therefore rare for the conclusion to be drawn that the parties did not intend their agreement to be attended by legal consequences, and only in unusual circumstances will the presumption be rebutted.[37] Where an express exclusion of intention is relied on, the words used must be clear and unambiguous.[38]

---

[33] See *Williams v Roffey Bros & Nicholls (Contractors) Ltd* [1991] 1 QB 1. Of course, a bona fide belief of liability is a key factor in the question whether there is consideration for the compromise of a disputed claim. See eg, *Cook v Wright* (1861) 1 B & S 559, 569; 121 ER 822, 826; *Miles v New Zealand Alford Estate Co* (1886) 32 Ch D 266; *Wigan v Edwards* (1973) 47 ALJR 586, 594–5; *General Credits Ltd v Ebsworth* [1986] 2 Qd R 162, 166.

[34] See now, however, Law of Property (Miscellaneous Provisions) Act 1989, s 2 (repealing Law of Property Act 1925, s 40).

[35] The defendant was 'charged' upon the equities, and reliance on the faith of the agreement may be important. See *Maddison v Alderson* (1883) 8 App Cas 467, 475; *McBride v Sandland* (1918) 25 CLR 69, 77; *Ash Street Properties Pty Ltd v Pollnow* (1987) 9 NSWLR 80, 84, 101.

[36] See Chapter 10. See *Air Great Lakes Pty Ltd v KS Easter (Holdings) Pty Ltd* (1985) 2 NSWLR 309, 336; *Paul Wilson & Co A/S v Partenreederei Hannah Blumenthal* [1983] 1 AC 854, 917; *Australian Energy Ltd v Lennard Oil NL* [1986] 2 Qd R 216, 237; *Deutsche Schachtbau-zmd Tiefbohrgesellschaft mbH v Shell International Petroleum Co Ltd* [1990] AC 295, 315 (reversed on another point at 329). See Atiyah, 'The Hannah Blumenthal and Classical Contract Law' (1985) 102 LQR 363. Cf *Federal Commissioner of Taxation v Ranson* (1989) 90 ALR 533, 535, (1989) 25 FCR 57.

[37] See the letter of comfort cases: *Kleinwort Benson Ltd v Malaysia Mining Corp Berhad* [1989] 1 WLR 379; *Commonwealth Bank of Australia v TLI Management Pty Ltd* [1990] VR 510, 517; *Banque Brussels Lambert SA v Australian National Industries Ltd* (1989) 21 NSWLR 502.

[38] See eg, *Rose & Frank Co v JR Crompton & Bros Ltd* [1923] 2 KB 261, (reversed on other grounds [1925] AC 445) (honourable pledge clause). Contrast *Edwards v Skyways Ltd* [1964] 1 All ER 494 (words 'ex gratia' not sufficient to negative contractual intention); *Home Insurance Co v Administratia Asigurarilor de Stat* [1983] 2 Lloyd's Rep 674 ('honourable engagement treaty' did not negative contractual intent).

Certainty of agreement[39]

The general principle is that unless all the 'essential' terms of a contract have been agreed   **12.27**
the parties must still be in the process of negotiating the bargain and there is no contract.[40]
This is not an unreasonable stance for the courts to take. It is also, apparently, that which is
taken in many civil law jurisdictions.[41] On the other hand, where an allegation is made that
an agreement is uncertain or incomplete the decision will be based on the construction of
the agreement. If the agreement looks to be complete and certain, the allegation is one
which attracts little sympathy in the courts. On the basis of wishing to avoid the reproach
of being the destroyer of bargains,[42] the court will attempt to uphold the bargain.
Uncertainty of agreement is therefore a 'counsel of despair'.[43] On this basis the perspective
looks to be a detached one: the courts have not seized on good faith as a general basis for
preserving bargains. Of course, the commercial reality is that one party to the contract is
vigorously denying that the agreement is binding. That party would not reproach the
court. In effect, in applying the traditional doctrine that courts should adopt a construction which will preserve the validity of the contract,[44] courts deny to one of the parties what
is bad faith reliance on a legal principle.[45] This is achieved in various ways. One is the formulation of the rule of certainty itself. Because the rule is in terms that the 'essential' terms
must have been agreed, there will often be room for argument on what are the essential
terms, and this allows considerable scope in the rule application process.[46]

The most obvious (and familiar) preservation technique is the implication of terms. In a   **12.28**
commercial agreement the further the parties have gone with the contract, the more ready
are the courts to imply any reasonable term so as to give effect to the parties' intentions.[47]

---

[39] See Chapter 11.
[40] See eg, *G Scammell & Nephew Ltd v Ouston* [1941] AC 251; *Summergreene v Parker* (1950) 80 CLR
304; *South Australia v The Commonwealth* (1962) 108 CLR 131, 145; *Australian and New Zealand Banking
Group Ltd v Frost Holdings Pty Ltd* [1989] VR 695, 700.
[41] See eg, Dreyer, 'Switzerland', in International Chamber of Commerce, *Formation of Contracts and
Precontractual Liability* (ICC Publishing Corp, New York, 1990), 65 (court has no jurisdiction to complete
contract where essential ingredients not agreed); Hamza, 'Egypt', in International Chamber of Commerce,
Formation of Contracts and Precontractual Liability (ICC Publishing Corp, New York, 1990), 99 (preliminary
agreement binding only if all 'essential points of the contract' have been agreed).
[42] See *Hillas & Co Ltd v Arcos Ltd* (1932) 147 LT 503, 512. See generally *Head v Kelk* (1963) 63 SR
(NSW) 340, 344, 352; *Prints for Pleasure Ltd v Oswald-Sealy (Overseas) Ltd* [1968] 3 NSWR 761, 765–6;
Amalgamated Television Services Pty Ltd v Television Corp Ltd [1970] 3 NSWR 85; *Cudgen Rutile (No 2) Pty
Ltd v Chalk* [1975] AC 520; *Rowella Pty Ltd v Hoult* [1987] 1 Qd R 386, 393; *Hawthorn Football Club Ltd
v Harding* [1988] VR 49, 55; *Biotechnology Australia Pty Ltd v Pace* (1988) 15 NSWLR 130, 135; *Gregory
v MAB Pty Ltd* (1989) 1 WAR 1, 12; *Anangel Atlas Compania Naviera SA v Ishikawajima-Harima Heavy
Industries Co Ltd (No 2)* [1990] 2 Lloyd's Rep 526, 545.
[43] *Nea Agrax SA v Baltic Shipping Co Ltd* [1976] 1 QB 933, 948 per Goff LJ.
[44] See *Meehan v Jones* (1982) 149 CLR 571, 589; *Gregory v MAB Pty Ltd* (1989) 1 WAR 1, 12. See also
In re Roberts (1881) 19 Ch D 520, 529 (court should not repose on the easy pillow of saying that the whole
agreement is void for uncertainty).
[45] Cf *Didymi Corp v Atlantic Lines and Navigation Co Inc (The Didymi)* [1988] 2 Lloyd's Rep 108, in which
a provision that hire of a ship was to be equitably decreased in certain circumstances, by an amount to be
agreed by the parties, was held to refer to an objective standard and to relate to a subsidiary matter, with the
result that the obligation was enforceable.
[46] Cf. *Pagnan SpA v Feed Products Ltd* [1987] 2 Lloyd's Rep 601.
[47] Carter, Peden and Tolhurst, *Contract Law in Australia* (5th edn, Butterworths, Sydney, 2007),
para 4-12.

Thus, a contract which is prima facie incomplete may be upheld by the implication of terms, particularly where there has been substantial performance by a party (or both parties). The object is to avoid the injustice which would arise if a party who had performed was unable to enforce the contract. Similarly, when the parties have shown by their conduct that they understood the terms of a contract and can apply them without difficulty, a court will be reluctant to ignore such conduct by holding that the terms of the contract were uncertain or unintelligible.[48] A leading example is still *Hillas & Co Ltd v Arcos Ltd.*[49] A buyer's option to take a further supply of goods was upheld as requiring goods to be of fair specification, where the parties had in carrying out an initial part of the contract attributed meaning to the agreement, even though they had not expressly agreed various matters including sizes, quality or the dates and ports of shipment and discharge. The ability to uphold agreements extends to cases where the machinery established in the contract to determine an essential matter breaks down.[50] In *Oglebay Norton Co v Armco Inc*[51] the Supreme Court of Ohio ordered specific performance of an agreement to negotiate the price at which iron ore would be shipped. The agreement contained two price mechanisms. The first referred to a published price which ceased to be published during the currency of the contract. The second referred to a rate to be 'mutually agreed'. The contract was for a long term (over 50 years), and on the basis that the parties clearly intended the contract to have legal effect, the court directed that a mediator be appointed in the event of a breakdown in negotiations.

12.29 Whether all courts would go as far as the Ohio Supreme Court may be doubted, but the generous approach of the courts is essential today. The process of contract negotiation in the commercial context is vastly different from the processes of the 19th century. Informal letters of intent, heads of agreement and so on are common. These cannot be approached in a technical, and purely detached way. The complexity of many commercial agreements, including joint ventures, share purchase agreements and construction contracts is such that the documentation process is often slow and involved. The fact that forms of preliminary agreement are used, and that they now sometimes contain good faith provisions, raises the good faith issue in an acutely practical way. One challenge for courts today is whether good faith provisions are themselves too uncertain to be enforced.[52]

'Subject to' clauses

12.30 As we have seen, one of the major problems appears that the common law model of negotiation is simplistic. It assumes the parties moving from no agreement to total agreement as one step. Of course, in practice many negotiations are not of this form and involve the parties in making a series of agreements. In such situations if a party has agreed to points A,

---

[48] See *York Air Conditioning and Refrigeration (A'sia) Pty Ltd v The Commonwealth* (1949) 80 CLR 11, 53, per Latham CJ.

[49] (1932) 147 LT 503.

[50] See *Sudbrook Trading Estate Ltd v Eggleton* [1983] 1 AC 444, where a valuation procedure in an option to purchase broke down. Cf *Booker Industries Pty Ltd v Wilson Parking (Qld) Pty Ltd* (1982) 149 CLR 600 (no specific performance of provision for appointment of an arbitrator to be nominated by designated person who had not made the appointment).

[51] 52 Ohio St 3d 232; 556 NE 2d 515 (1990).

[52] See 11.59ff discussing the potential uncertainty of good faith negotiating clauses, and 12.77ff.

B and C it will often be thought unattractive behaviour to go back on these points in order to get a better deal on points X, Y and Z. The perception that this is in some way unfair clearly underlines the public discontent with the practice of gazumping. Of course the parties are not wholly without tools to defend themselves in this situation. In some circumstances they can proceed by making a series of contracts so that each separate negotiation becomes binding, but in other cases this would make no commercial sense unless further negotiations were actually fruitful. In some cases one could guard against change of mind by taking an option, but this is usually only helpful in rather clear-cut situations. In some cases the parties may make conditional contracts, dependent upon the satisfaction of some condition, such as the obtaining of planning permission. Thus, a very common form of clause is one stating that the agreement is 'subject to' the occurrence of a specified event, or one using words of similar import, that is, to indicate the parties' contemplation that some contingency must be fulfilled.[53]

In general terms the approach to such clauses is easy to state. The clauses create conditions **12.31** precedent or subsequent. Thus, the agreement itself, or the performance of the agreement, may be subject to the fulfilment of a condition precedent. When these clauses become the subject of litigation we often have the same scenario as in the uncertainty cases. One party alleges that there is no binding contract because the contingency has not been fulfilled. The other contends that the intention of the agreement was for the contingency merely to postpone performance. At one time it was possible to say that, in applying general construction principles, a court might well be persuaded that the non-fulfilment of the contingency meant that there was no contract.[54] However, nearly all these cases have been doubted or overruled in the more recent decisions.[55] Today, in virtually every case, the fulfilment of the contingency is treated as an element of contractual performance rather than the prerequisite to a binding contract.[56]

Although the courts have not found it necessary to refer to good faith as a justification for **12.32** their approach, the decisions have the effect of promoting good faith in the negotiation process. Indeed, it would be difficult to refute the argument of a realist that these cases are simply illustrations that, faced with a choice between two interpretations, a court chooses the one which has the effect of preventing withdrawal from negotiations on a ground not

---

[53] See Chapter 9.

[54] See eg, *Aberfoyle Plantations v Cheng* [1960] AC 115 (formation of contract of sale conditional on vendor obtaining renewal of leases); *Astra Trust Ltd v Adams* [1969] 1 Lloyd's Rep 81 (no binding contract until survey satisfactory to buyers had been obtained where sale of vessel was expressly subject to satisfactory survey); *Lee-Parker v Izzet (No 2)* [1972] 1 WLR 775 (formation of contract of sale conditional on purchaser obtaining satisfactory mortgage); *Myton Ltd v Schwab-Morris* [1974] 1 WLR 331 (failure to pay deposit prevented contract coming into existence).

[55] See eg, *Property and Bloodstock Ltd v Emerton* [1968] Ch 94, 116; *Perri v Coolangatta Investments Pty Ltd* (1982) 149 CLR 537, 542, 551, 557 (both doubting *Aberfoyle Plantations v Cheng* [1960] AC 115); *Varverakis v Compagnia de Navegacion Artico SA, The Merak* [1976] 2 Lloyd's Rep 250, 254 (doubting *Astra Trust Ltd v Adams* [1969] 1 Lloyd's Rep 81); *Damon Compania Naviera SA v Hapag Lloyd International SA, The Blankenstein* [1985] 1 WLR 435 (overruling *Myton Ltd v Schwab-Morris* [1974] 1 WLR 331, on this point); *Graham v Pitkin* [1993] 1 WLR 403 (doubting *Lee-Parker v Izzet (No 2)* [1972] 1 WLR 775) See further 9.94.

[56] The expression 'subject to contract' still occupies a special role, at least in conveyancing transactions. See *Chillingworth v Esche* [1924] 1 Ch 97; *Masters v Cameron* (1954) 91 CLR 353. See further 9.22.

related to the agreed event. In other words, the reality is that the courts, in choosing the interpretation which preserves the bargain, are not just promoting good faith in negotiation they are requiring it. Neither party is permitted to withdraw while the fulfilment of the contingency remains uncertain. The requirement is that each party have regard to the position of the other. The only answer that can be given to the realist is that the bargain is complete, since the event is not one which involves further negotiation. However, this answer to a large extent begs the question.

12.33 As we saw earlier in Chapter 9, two further aspects of the 'subject to' cases are important. First, these clauses sometimes raise issues of uncertainty. For example, at one time the expression 'subject to finance' was regarded as too uncertain, and agreements were struck down on that ground rather than on the basis that no binding contract exists until the contingency has been fulfilled. However, at least in Australia, it is now clear that prima facie such clauses are certain. Thus, in *Meehan v Jones*[57] the High Court of Australia, disapproving earlier contrary authority, held that a clause in a contract for sale of land (on which an oil refinery was built) stating that the agreement was executed 'subject to' the purchaser receiving approval for finance on satisfactory terms and conditions in an amount sufficient to complete the purchase, was not void for uncertainty.

12.34 The second aspect is that 'subject to' clauses commonly refer to a person's approval or satisfaction. Where there is no statement that the disapproval or dissatisfaction must be based on reasonable grounds it is open to a court to apply a subjective standard. Even under such an interpretation, the good faith criterion of honesty is necessarily implied.[58] The influence of good faith on the common law is also shown in similar cases where approval or satisfaction is required and the event involves or includes some course of conduct by one of the parties. Although there is no express promise, an implication will now often be made that there is some sort of obligation of reasonable endeavours or due diligence. For example, in *Meehan v Jones*[59] the clause stating that the agreement was executed 'subject to' the purchaser receiving approval for finance on satisfactory terms and conditions in an amount sufficient to complete the purchase was not illusory due to the absence of a promise to obtain finance. The High Court held that the purchaser had (at least) to act honestly and to take reasonable steps to find finance.[60] There is also support for the view that in *Meehan v Jones* the satisfaction criterion was objective, so that the purchaser's dissatisfaction had to

---

[57] (1982) 149 CLR 571. See Swanton, '"Subject to Finance" Clauses in Contracts For the Sale of Land' (1984) 58 ALJ 633. The recent trend in English authorities is along similar lines, see 9.68.

[58] See eg, *Astra Trust Ltd v Adams* [1969] 1 Lloyd's Rep 81, 87 (where contract for sale of vessel was subject to satisfactory survey; the word 'satisfactory' referred to the buyers' opinion and did not express an objective test so that proof of *bona fide* dissatisfaction was sufficient); *Albion Sugar Co Ltd v William Tankers Ltd, The John S Darbyshire* [1977] 2 Lloyd's Rep 457, 466 (*bona fide* dissatisfaction an implied requirement where acceptance of offer to carry goods was subject to satisfactory completion of trial voyages). Cf O'Connor, *Good Faith in English Law* (Dartmouth, Aldershot, 1990), 24.

[59] (1982) 149 CLR 571.

[60] See also *Butts v O'Dwyer* (1952) 87 CLR 267, 279–80 (if parties enter into agreement to transfer land subject to condition that it is not to become effective unless consent is obtained, an obligation is implied on the transferor to do all that is reasonable to ensure consent is obtained); *Kennedy v Vercoe* (1960) 105 CLR 521, 526, 529 (implied requirement, in sale of business subject to the purchaser being accepted as tenant by landlord, that purchaser would do whatever might reasonably be required to enable vendor to obtain landlord's consent); *Gregory v MAB Pty Ltd* (1989) 1 WAR 1, 15 (requirement of best endeavours to

be based on reasonable grounds.[61] This requirement will in all likelihood be a general implication in agreements where a 'subject to' clause refers to approval or satisfaction.

What stands out in the context of 'subject to' clauses is that the courts have in effect recognized a general term implied in law qualifying the express terms. The only debate likely to be raised in any case is the precise scope and content of the (good faith) implication. The courts will not always treat honest decisions as sufficient. Good faith merely requires that the other party's interest be considered. In many cases, more onerous obligations are implied.   **12.35**

Pre-contractual liability

General

Related to the preservation role is the willingness of courts to find liability following a decision to withdraw from negotiations. This is the remedial aspect of good faith. To what extent is good faith a useful rationalization of the law? The remedial aspect of good faith is usually discussed under the rubric of 'pre-contractual liability'. The law is here exceedingly complex in its structure and policy bases. The courts have not gone so far as to recognize good faith as a contractual duty applicable whenever two parties commence negotiations. Contractual duties of good faith must be found in agreements which have the force of contracts. It would, however, be irreconcilable with the doctrine of consideration to conceive of reliance by one party to negotiations on an understanding that the other will act in good faith as amounting to consideration. The general view is therefore that in order for breach of a duty of good faith to give rise to a contractual remedy, there must be a term of the contract imposing a duty to this effect. Where there is an express or implied term, in a single contract or a collateral contract, its breach may give rise to a liability in damages in contract.[62]   **12.36**

The duty of good faith, such as it already exists or may ultimately exist, need not be contractual. It may be tortious in character. There is, however, no tortious duty of good faith applicable to contractual negotiations separate from the law of deceit and negligent misstatement. Nevertheless, tort law is important since the remedy of damages is made available where loss or damage is suffered by reason of fraud, negligence amounting to the breach of a duty of care or the breach of a statutory duty.[63]   **12.37**

Other aspects of pre-contractual liability show that the requirement of good faith may be neither contractual nor tortious. Thus, in relation to insurance proposals, breach of the duty of disclosure entitles the insurer to rescind the contract, it does not give rise to a right to compensation. At best there is a right to restitution. This is of limited interest.[64] Again, in so far as there is a requirement of good faith in the process of term incorporation, the law   **12.38**

---

obtain development approval under agreement for the purchase of land). See Swanton, 'Failure of Condition Precedent—Uncertainty and Illusory Consideration' (1991) 4 JCL 152.

  [61] See (1982) 149 CLR 571, 588, 597.
  [62] See further n 124.
  [63] See further 12.41ff.
  [64] See, however, Waddams, 'Pre-contractual Duties of Disclosure', in Cane and Stapleton (eds), *Essays for Patrick Atiyah* (Clarendon Press, Oxford, 1991), 253–4.

is clear that breach of the duty merely has the effect of preventing incorporation of the term,[65] there is no liability to make compensation for breach of the duty. There is, however, some support for the view that lack of good faith may be the basis for a direct claim to restitution,[66] or a finding of promissory estoppel.[67]

Liability in tort

General

12.39 The law of tort, including breach of statutory duty, has, generally speaking, evolved without regard to good faith. Where good faith is relevant, as in the torts of deceit and negligent misstatement, the concern is broader than the negotiation of contracts. The tort of deceit does not depend on the tortfeasor being in a negotiating relationship with the other party. Therefore, although tort law often provides a pre-contractual remedy, relief does not depend on the conduct complained of operating in the context of contractual negotiations.

12.40 One reason why the common law concept of fraud cannot be equated with a duty of good faith may be traced to the general rules of freedom of contract and *caveat emptor*. For example, the mere fact of entering into contractual negotiations does not give rise to a duty of disclosure, only in specific contexts has such a duty been recognized. The law has developed in an ad hoc fashion. Of more immediate concern is the prospect that breach of the duty may itself confer a right to claim damages under tortious principles. Here there is an important question of policy in which our courts have not thus far shown much interest.

Fraud and other vitiating factors

12.41 Two features characterize the law on vitiating factors. First, the idea that a person who is induced to enter into a contract as a result of communicated misinformation or, broadly, unfair pressure, should have the right to rescind the contract or at least to approach the court for relief setting aside the contract. Second, there is the idea that a person who has a particular kind of culpability should be required to make compensation for losses suffered as a consequence of the culpable conduct.

12.42 The first feature is much broader than the second. Thus, courts of equity have always possessed a jurisdiction to relieve against every species of fraud.[68] The concept of equitable fraud is considerably broader than the common law concept of deceit, but its scope and the willingness of courts to exercise the jurisdiction have fluctuated.[69] Notwithstanding that equitable fraud is, in a sense, an embodiment of a duty of good faith, it has not been understood as such. Thus, the purpose of the conception of fraud in equity is to provide a jurisdiction to relieve against transactions affected by vitiating factors. The jurisdiction has little

---

[65] See *Interfoto Picture Library Ltd v Stiletto Visual Programmes Ltd* [1989] QB 433, 439.

[66] Modern writings on restitution emphasize unjust enrichment.

[67] The cases go no further than recognizing that promissory estoppel may be rationalized as promoting good faith.

[68] *Earl of Chesterfield v Janssen* (1751) 2 Ves Sen 125, 155, 28 ER 82, 100 per Lord Hardwicke (approved *Blomley v Ryan* (1956) 99 CLR 362, 385). See also *National Australia Bank Ltd v Nobile* (1988) 100 ALR 227, 229.

[69] However, at least in Australia, some forms of unconscionable conduct may be within this concept. See eg, *Taylor v Johnson* (1983) 151 CLR 422; *Commercial Bank of Australia Ltd v Amadio* (1983) 151 CLR 447.

to say about a good faith duty in respect of negotiations which break down. There is, moreover, no general right to compensation where equitable fraud is proved. No liability attaches for breaking off negotiations prematurely, except perhaps where there is bad faith in the specific context of a fiduciary relation existing independently of contract.[70]

The classic example of the culpable conduct required to give rise to a liability in damages is, **12.43** of course, fraud, that is, deceit at common law. There cannot be any doubt in principle that a plaintiff who can show that the defendant was fraudulent will have a remedy. Of course the defendant's fraud is usually a reason for the plaintiff having entered into the contract rather than for there being no contract but it is possible to imagine situations in which in principle there would be a remedy albeit with difficult problems of proof. Suppose for instance it can be shown that the defendant never intended to enter into a contract with the plaintiff and simply entered into negotiations in order to deflect the plaintiff from negotiating with somebody else. Granted that one's state of mind is a question of fact, this is capable of being a fraudulent representation.[71]

Twentieth century developments, such as the statutory recognition of damages claims for **12.44** innocent misrepresentation in some jurisdictions,[72] and the common law recognition of liability for negligent misstatement, are indicative of a community concern to increase the scope of our culpability concept. They also serve to require or promote good faith. However, the requirement element is narrow, and the promotion element controversial. As has already been said, it would be wrong to characterize the combination of these two elements as amounting to the recognition of a tortious duty of good faith.

As has also been mentioned, only in exceptional cases does the law impose a duty to disclose **12.45** facts to the other party to negotiations. This duty arises, generally, because only one of the two parties has knowledge of the material facts, as in the context of a proposal for insurance.[73] Outside these specific contexts there is no duty either to disclose facts or to disabuse a party of a misapprehension.[74] It is, of course, true that a duty to disclose a change in facts is not limited to cases of *uberrimae fidei*,[75] and also that although a contract of guarantee falls outside the class of contracts *uberrimae fidei*, the creditor is under a duty to disclose to the intending guarantor anything which is not naturally to be expected in the contractual

---

[70] Nor, so far as we are aware, has legislation in a common law jurisdiction, recognized a *right* to equitable compensation in lieu of rescission in the same way as there is a right to compensation in lieu of specific performance or an injunction. See eg, the discussion in *Munchies Management Pty Ltd v Belperio* (1988) 84 ALR 700.

[71] See *Richardson v Sylvester* (1873) LR 9 QB 34.

[72] See UK: Misrepresentation Act 1967; ACT: Law Reform (Misrepresentation) Act 1977; SA: Misrepresentation Act 1971.

[73] See eg, *Khoury v Government Insurance Office of New South Wales* (1984) 165 CLR 622; *Banque Financière de la Cité SA v Westgate Insurance Co Ltd* [1991] 2 AC 249; *Bank of Nova Scotia v Hellenic Mutual War Risks Association (Bermuda) Ltd, The Good Luck* [1992] 1 AC 233.

[74] See eg, *Smith v Hughes* (1871) LR 6 QB 597; *RW Cameron & Co v L Slutzkin Pty Ltd* (1923) 32 CLR 81, 90. The range of situations in which disclosure is required is, however, far from clear. See generally Finn, 'Good Faith and Nondisclosure', in Finn (ed), *Essays on Torts* (Law Book Co Ltd, Sydney, 1989), 150; Waddams, 'Pre-contractual Duties of Disclosure', in Cane and Stapleton (eds), *Essays for Patrick Atiyah* (Clarendon Press, Oxford, 1991), 237.

[75] See *With v O'Flanagan* [1936] Ch 575; *Jones v Dumbrell* [1981] VR 199.

relation,[76] but the paramountcy given to the freedom not to contract, and the reluctance of the courts to allow claims in tort for pure economic loss, are both inconsistent with the idea that a person must act in accordance with a broad duty of good faith when negotiating a contract.[77]

12.46   In this regard we should be wary of drawing comparisons with civil law jurisdictions in which a tortious duty of good faith has been developed in the specific context of pre-contractual negotiations, because this may have been influenced by a different approach to tortious liability.[78] Thus, it appears that the emergence of good faith in German law was prompted by the restrictions imposed on claims for breach of an alleged duty of care. In order to expand the scope of liability for negligence, the fact that parties were in a pre-contractual relationship was conceived as creating a duty of care.[79] It has not been found necessary to adopt this approach under English law, where the tort of negligence has been developed in an incremental way. Yet few would deny that our law is generous in its categorization of situations in which a duty of care may exist.

12.47   The tort of negligence has developed primarily under the guidance of the neighbour principle. It may be questioned whether we need a new tort, or need to widen the existing tort of negligent misstatement, to respond to what might be conceived as a lack of good faith.[80] However, in *Gibson v Parkes District Hospital*[81] an amendment to the plaintiff's statement of claim was upheld so as to permit an allegation of liability in tort for breach of a duty of good faith. It was held that such liability, which did not depend on the implication of a contractual term, could be based on a 'relationship brought about by contract'[82] in the context of workers' compensation insurance. But Badgery-Parker J decided no more than that the allegation was not so clearly untenable as to be liable to be struck out. In any event, given the approach of the common law, this seems a legislative question rather than a judicial issue.

12.48   Granted the development of modern law of misrepresentation it would seem that in principle there might be cases falling under the general ambit of *Hedley Byrne & Co Ltd v Heller*

---

[76] See *Hamilton v Watson* (1845) 12 Cl & Fin 109, 119, 8 ER 1339, 1343–4; *Commercial Bank of Australia Ltd v Amadio* (1983) 151 CLR 447, 454–8, 485; *Westpac Banking Corp v Robinson* (1993) 30 NSWLR 668.

[77] Claims for economic loss are 'special' in the sense that *they* usually involve reliance or the assumption of responsibility, or both: *Hawkins v Clayton* (1988) 164 CLR 539, 576 per Deane J. See also *Sutherland Shire Council v Heyman* (1985) 157 CLR 424, 479–80; *Yuen v A-G of Hong Kong* [1988] AC 175.

[78] The leading comparative study is still Kessler and Fine, 'Culpa in Contrahendo, Bargaining in Good Faith, and Freedom of Contract: A Comparative Study' (1964) 77 Harv L Rev 401. For recent surveys see International Chamber of Commerce, *Formation of Contracts and Precontractual Liability* (ICC Publishing Corp, New York, 1990); Hondius (ed), *Precontractual Liability* (Kluwer, Deventer, 1991); Collins, 'Good Faith in European Contract Law' (1994) 14 OJLS 229.

[79] See Ebke, 'Federal Republic of Germany', in International Chamber of Commerce, *Formation of Contracts and Precontractual Liability* (ICC Publishing Corp, New York, 1990), 35.

[80] There is some support for this in the US decisions and literature. See eg, Cohen, 'Restructuring Breach of the Implied Covenant of Good Faith and Fair Dealing as a Tort' (1985) 73 Cal L Rev 1291.

[81] (1991) 26 NSWLR 9. For commentary see Fleming, 'Insurer's Breach of Good Faith—A New Tort?' (1992) 108 LQR 357; Handford, 'A Good Faith Tort?' (1993) 1 Tort L Rev 87.

[82] (1991) 26 NSWLR 9, 35.

& Partners Ltd[83] where one party to the contract owes a duty of care to the other. A leading English case is *Esso Petroleum Co Ltd v Mardon*[84] where a contract resulted as a result of a careless representation by Esso executives. In the nature of things the duty of care must have existed before the contract and therefore in principle there must be cases where an action based on a duty of care can succeed even though no contract results. A possible example would be where a contractor is invited to tender for a major building project and asks a potential electrical subcontractor to give him an estimate. The contractor uses this estimate to build up the tender price and then one morning receives in the post two letters, one from the potential employer saying that the tender was successful and one from the potential electrical subcontractor saying that by an awful mistake the figure quoted for the work is $100,000 too low. We all know that as a matter of offer and acceptance the subcontractor is not bound. Normally this would not matter because if the subcontractor's price has been carefully put together the contractor would usually be able to find another subcontractor who will do the work at much the same price. But if the subcontractor has been careless and has produced a wholly erroneous price, clearly it will not be possible to recruit another subcontractor at that price. It does not seem absurd to argue that there is a duty of care in compiling the price in such circumstances since the subcontractor certainly knows that the contractor will rely on the price in putting forward the tender.

Breach of statutory prohibition

Section 52(1) of the Australian Trade Practices Act 1974 (Cth)[85] states that a 'corporation **12.49** shall not, in trade or commerce, engage in conduct that is misleading or deceptive or is likely to mislead or deceive'. There are also provisions in fair trading legislation in the Australian States and Territories reproducing this provision, with an important feature, expanding the relevance of the duty thus created, that the conduct need not be by a corporation.[86] These provisions are supplemented by others which create criminal offences.

There are even provisions, applicable to conduct in connection with the supply or possible **12.50** supply of goods or services of a kind ordinarily acquired for personal, domestic or household use or consumption, which prohibit conduct which is, in all the circumstances, 'unconscionable'.[87] As a result of very recent amendments, a more general provision is applicable to the conduct of a corporation in trade or commerce. This prohibits conduct which is 'within the meaning of the unwritten law, from time to time, of the States and Territories', 'unconscionable'.[88]

---

[83] [1964] AC 465. See also *L Shaddock & Associates Pty Ltd v Parramatta City Council* (1981) 150 CLR 225.
[84] [1976] QB 801.
[85] For proposals for reform see Australian Law Reform Commission, *Compliance with the Trade Practices Act*, Report No 68, 1994.
[86] See ACT: Fair Trading Act 1992, s 12(1); NSW: Fair Trading Act 1987, s 42(1); NT: Consumer Affairs and Fair Trading Act 1990, s 42(1); Qld: Fair Trading Act 1989, s 38(1); SA: Fair Trading Act 1987, s 56(1); Tas: Fair Trading Act 1990, s 14(1); Vic: Fair Trading Act 1999, s 9(1); WA: Fair Trading Act 1987, s 10(1).
[87] See Cth: Trade Practices Act 1974, s 51AB(1); ACT: Fair Trading Act 1992, s 13(1); NT: Consumer Affairs and Fair Trading Act 1990, s 43(1); NSW: Fair Trading Act 1987, s 43(1); Qld: Fair Trading Act 1989, s 39(1); SA: Fair Trading Act 1987, s 57(1); Tas: Fair Trading Act 1990, s 15(1); Vic: Fair Trading Act 1999, s 8; WA: Fair Trading Act 1987, s 11(1).
[88] See Cth: Trade Practices Act 1974, s 51AA(1).

12.51   The importance of the statutory duty not to engage in conduct which is misleading or deceptive or is likely to mislead or deceive is shown by the fact that a liability in damages attaches whenever the duty is breached and the plaintiff suffers loss or damage.[89] Although no such liability attaches where the prohibitions on unconscionable conduct are infringed, the court is empowered to make discretionary orders. These include an order directing the payment of the amount of loss or damage suffered to the person who suffered the loss or damage.[90]

12.52   By controlling misleading conduct, these provisions have a very significant impact on contractual negotiations. They operate, whether or not a contract results, to create a pre-contractual liability.[91] Although the provisions might be seen as 'consumer protection provisions', they have been used in the context of commercial transactions as well. Section 52, the key provision, although limited to conduct in trade or commerce, is not limited to the protection of consumers.[92] The provision will often be breached by conduct which does not conform to a requirement of good faith, even where there is merely an innocent misrepresentation. Moreover, in a procedurally significant section, it is provided that where a representation is made in relation to a future matter, the representation is misleading if there were no reasonable grounds for making it. The legislation deems this to be the position unless evidence to the contrary is adduced.[93]

12.53   The case law on these provisions is voluminous and diverse. There is no single theme and it would be an error to rationalize the law on the basis of a principle of good faith.[94] However, the duty extends, in some cases at least, to impose a disclosure requirement in cases where there is no direct analogue in either the common law or equitable conceptions of fraud.[95] For lawyers practising in Australia, the easiest way to formulate a set of pleadings which in

---

[89] See Cth: Trade Practices Act 1974, s 82; ACT: Fair Trading Act 1992, s 46; NSW: Fair Trading Act 1987, s 68; NT: Consumer Affairs and Fair Trading Act 1990, s 91; Qld: Fair Trading Act 1989, ss 99, 100; SA: Fair Trading Act 1987, s 84; Tas: Fair Trading Act 1990, s 37; Vic: Fair Trading Act 1999, s 159; WA: Fair Trading Act 1987, s 79. See generally JD Heydon, 'Damages Under the Trade Practices Act', in Finn (ed), *Essays on Damages* (Law Book Co Ltd, Sydney, 1992), 42 and note the important decision in *Sellars v Adelaide Petroleum NL* (1994) 179 CLR 332.

[90] See Cth: Trade Practices Act 1974, s 87(2); ACT: Fair Trading Act 1992, s 50(7); NSW: Fair Trading Act 1987, s 72(5); NT: Consumer Affairs and Fair Trading Act 1990, s 95(5); Qld: Fair Trading Act 1989, s 100(5); SA: Fair Trading Act 1987, s 85(5); Tas: Fair Trading Act 1990, s 41(5); Vic: Fair Trading Act 1999, s 158(2); WA: Fair Trading Act 1987, s 77(3).

[91] On the overlap between statutory and contract remedies see *Accounting Systems 2000 (Developments) Pty Ltd v CCH Australia Ltd* (1993) 114 ALR 355.

[92] See eg, *Hornsby Building Information Centre Pty Ltd v Sydney Building Information Centre Ltd* (1978) 140 CLR 216 For the meaning of 'in trade or commerce' see *Concrete Constructions (NSW) Pty Ltd v Nelson* (1990) 169 CLR 594. For the meaning of 'loss or damage' see *Demagogue Pty Ltd v Ramensky* (1992) 110 ALR 608.

[93] See Cth: Trade Practices Act 1974, s 51A; ACT: Fair Trading Act 1992, s 11; NSW: Fair Trading Act 1987, s 41; NT: Consumer Affairs and Fair Trading Act 1990, s 41; Qld: Fair Trading Act 1989, s 37; SA: Fair Trading Act 1987, s 54; Tas: Fair Trading Act 1990, s 11; WA: Fair Trading Act 1987, s 9.

[94] See eg, *Service Station Association Ltd v Berg Bennett & Associates Pty Ltd* (1993) 117 ALR 393. For a general survey see Harland, 'Misleading or Deceptive Conduct: The Breadth and Limitations of the Prohibition' (1991) 4 JCL 107. See also Terry, 'Misleading or Deceptive Conduct in Commercial Negotiations' (1988) 16 Aust Bus L Rev 189.

[95] See eg, *Demagogue Pty Ltd v Ramensky* (1992) 110 ALR 608. See also Skapinker, 'The Imposition of a Positive Duty of Disclosure under Section 52 of the Trade Practices Act 1974 (Cth)' (1991) 4 JCL 75.

effect seeks to impose a liability for bad faith discontinuation of negotiations is an allegation of misleading or deceptive conduct. To the extent that an obligation to pay damages may be imposed on a finding of contravention, Australian lawyers have been invoking a duty of good faith for some time.

Liability under estoppel

General

Few would deny that the doctrine of estoppel, even as applied in England, operates to promote good faith. Indeed, in *Jorden v Money*[96] itself, Lord Cranworth LC described estoppel by representation as 'a principle well known in the law, founded upon good faith and equity'. In *Waltons Stores (Interstate) Ltd v Maher*,[97] now the leading case in Australia, Deane J said that the underlying rationale of doctrines of estoppel is 'good conscience and fair dealing'. **12.54**

Promissory estoppel

Promissory estoppel (and the related concepts of waiver and election between rights) has traditionally been applied to non-contractual promises in the context of an existing contractual relation. A concept of fair dealing has been employed (and often described as such) to rationalize holding the parties in a commercial relationship to a particular course of conduct.[98] In these cases the concept is a basis for preventing reliance on contractual rights. *Waltons Stores (Interstate) Ltd v Maher*[99] freed promissory estoppel (at least in Australia) of the limitation of a pre-existing legal relationship, so that promissory estoppel could form the basis for pre-contractual liability in damages. Compensation was recovered where negotiations were broken off before a contract was concluded. However, the facts were rather striking. **12.55**

As part of a business expansion programme, Waltons proposed to lease property which the Mahers owned and which the Mahers were willing to develop. The Mahers were to demolish an old building on the land and to erect a new building, to specifications approved by Waltons. Certain proposed amendments to a draft agreement were discussed. Waltons' solicitors said that although they had not obtained their client's specific instructions to each amendment they believed that 'approval will be forthcoming', and said that they would let the Mahers know the next day if any of the amendments were not agreed. Although the Mahers had commenced demolition work, they were unwilling to complete this unless it was clear that the agreement would be signed. Documents executed by the Mahers were forwarded to Waltons' solicitors 'by way of exchange'. When construction of the new building was nearly half finished, Waltons were informed that the agreement had to be finalized within the next day or two or it would be impossible for the new building to be **12.56**

---

[96] (1854) 5 HLC 180, 10 ER 868.
[97] (1988) 164 CLR 387, 434. See also at 442.
[98] See eg, *Tankexpress A/S v Compagnie Financière Belge des Petroles SA, The Petrofina* [1949] AC 76, 98; *Plasticmoda Societa per Azioni v Davidsons (Manchester) Ltd* [1952] 1 Lloyd's Rep 527, 538; *Panchaud Frères SA v Etablissements General Grain Co* [1970] 1 Lloyd's Rep 53, 59. Cf *V Berg & Son Ltd v Vanden Avenne-Izegem PVBA* [1977] 1 Lloyd's Rep 499, 504. See also O'Connor, *Good Faith in English Law* (Dartmouth, Aldershot, 1990), 27–8, 38; Carter, 'Problems in Enforcement Part II' (1993) 6 JCL 1.
[99] (1988) 164 CLR 387.

completed in time. In the meantime, Waltons, who were well aware of what was happening, altered its retailing policy, and instructed its solicitors to 'go slow'. Ultimately, Waltons informed the Mahers that it did not intend to proceed with the proposed lease. Waltons (according to a majority of the court) made a promise that they would execute the lease document. The promise was not express: it was implied from conduct. It arose from the course which the negotiations with the Mahers had taken. The majority applied promissory estoppel to enforce the implied promise, which Waltons was therefore estopped from denying, to complete the transaction. The minority agreed with the result, but based their decision on common law estoppel, that is, an assumption that a binding contract existed.[100]

12.57 The High Court relied for its decision to award compensation on the enforcement of an 'equity' to have the agreement carried through to completion. In effect there are five steps in the reasoning. First, there was an implied promise relied upon by the Mahers. Second, it was unconscionable conduct for Waltons to deny its promise, once the Mahers had relied upon it in the way in which they did. Third, as a result an equity arose in the Mahers' favour. Fourth, the appropriate method for the enforcement of the equity would have been specific performance of the promise. However, specific performance was no longer available. Accordingly, there was a fifth step, namely, that damages could be awarded in equity in lieu of specific performance.[101]

12.58 Although there have been a number of further cases on promissory estoppel, the courts have not resolved the question of how far there is a right to direct enforcement of a promise supported not by consideration but by the satisfaction of the requirements of promissory estoppel. All these cases treat unconscionable conduct as the basis for the doctrine.[102] However, relief is governed by the extent of the *minimum equity* to which the plaintiff is entitled. Focusing on the factual connection between unconscionable conduct and detriment, it would appear that relief may be given either to prevent unconscionable conduct causing detriment, or to redress a detriment arising from unconscionable conduct following reliance. However, the scope and bases for relief are not as yet clear.[103]

12.59 To some extent these developments have parallels in English law.[104] However, the English courts may not be as ready as those in Australia to use promissory estoppel to control premature termination of negotiations for a contract, and the contrast between common law

---

[100] The High Court also held that a Statute of Frauds provision did not preclude the Mahers from obtaining relief.

[101] Apparently, under a local provision derived from the Chancery Amendment Act 1858 (21 & 22 Vic c 27), commonly referred to as Lord Cairns' Act. See *S & E Promotions Pty Ltd v Tobin Bros Pty Ltd* (1994) Unreported, FCA (FC), 24 May.

[102] See eg, *Silovi Pty Ltd v Barbaro* (1988) 13 NSWLR 466, 472; *Commonwealth of Australia v Verwayen* (1990) 170 CLR 394, 407ff, 431ff, 454, 500–1; *Metropolitan Transit Authority v Waverley Transit Pty Ltd* [1991] 1 VR 181; *Pascon Pty Ltd v San Marco in Lamis Co-operative Social Club Ltd* [1991] 2 VR 227, 233.

[103] Cf *Commonwealth of Australia v Verwayen* (1990) 170 CLR 394, 413, 415–16, 454, 487. See generally Lindgren, 'Estoppel in Contract' (1989) 12 UNSWLJ 153; Parkinson, 'Equitable Estoppel: Developments after *Waltons Stores (Interstate) Ltd v Maher*' (1990) 3 JCL 50; Priestley, 'Estoppel-Liability and Remedy', in Waters (ed), *Equity, Fiduciaries and Trusts* (Carswell, Thomson Professional Publishing Co, Ontario, 1993).

[104] See *Amalgamated Investment & Property Co Ltd v Texas Commerce International Bank Ltd* [1982] QB 84; *Taylors Fashions Ltd v Liverpool Trustees Co Ltd (1979)* [1982] QB 133n; *Norwegian American Cruises A/S*

estoppel and promissory estoppel is more significant in England than in Australia. Moreover, the terms of the proposed contract had been agreed in *Waltons Stores (Interstate) Ltd v Maher* and although the conveyancing procedure in New South Wales implied that the agreement for lease was 'subject to contract', there has been no case in which the doctrine has been applied to a case where important terms are still to be agreed. In *Attorney General (Hong Kong) v Humphreys Estate Ltd*[105] the Privy Council said that promissory estoppel did not apply where an agreement in principle had been reached for an exchange of property, and the agreement was 'subject to contract'. Lord Templeman did however suggest[106] that it was 'possible but unlikely' that a party to negotiations stated in a document to be expressly 'subject to contract' would be able to satisfy the court that 'some form of estoppel had arisen to prevent both parties from refusing to proceed with the transactions envisaged by the document'. On the other hand, in *Austotel Pty Ltd v Franklins Selfserve Pty Ltd*[107] Priestley JA concluded that, in an appropriate case, a plaintiff may be granted relief, often of a proprietary kind, even though there is no agreement on terms. In his view,[108] promissory estoppel may operate where the plaintiff legitimately assumes, from the defendant's conduct, that a contract will come into existence, that a promise will be performed or that an interest will be granted. There must be reliance by the plaintiff, and the departure from the assumption must be 'unconscionable'. Although Priestley JA dissented on the facts, Kirby P expressly agreed with this analysis.

The High Court in *Waltons Stores (Interstate) Ltd v Maher*, recognized the obvious link **12.60** between the doctrines of consideration and estoppel and regarded promissory estoppel as 'tending to occupy ground left vacant due to the constraints affecting consideration'.[109] It was also thought that consideration might be a broader concept in Australian law than in the United States. It should, however, be clear that the decision in *Waltons Stores* is not equivalent to an adoption of the principle in section 90 of the Restatement (2d) Contracts. Section 90(1) states:

> A promise which the promisor should reasonably expect to induce action or forbearance on the part of the promisee or a third person and which does induce such action or forbearance is binding if injustice can be avoided only by enforcement of the promise. The remedy granted for breach may be limited as justice requires.

The provision clearly allows for the direct enforcement of promises not supported by con- **12.61** sideration. The original section 90, in slightly narrower terms,[110] was initially interpreted by treating reliance as in effect a substitute for consideration.[111] It is no longer correct to regard the operation of section 90 as providing for enforcement on the basis that reliance is

---

v Paul Mundy Ltd, The Vistafjord [1988] 2 Lloyd's Rep 343; *Hiscox v Outhwaite* [1992] 1 AC 562, 583–4 (affirmed on other grounds, 585); *Kenneth Allison Ltd v AE Limehouse & Co* [1992] 2 AC 105, 127.

[105] [1987] 1 AC 114.
[106] [1987] 1 AC 114, 127–8.
[107] (1989) 16 NSWLR 582.
[108] (1989) 16 NSWLR 582, 610.
[109] (1988) 164 CLR 387, 402 per Mason CJ and Wilson J. Cf Atiyah, 'Contracts, Promises and the Law of Obligations' (1978) 94 LQR 193.
[110] See Restatement (2d) Contracts 1932 § 90.
[111] See eg *Drennan v Star Paving Inc* 51 Cal 2d 409 333 P 2d 757 (1958).

a substitute for consideration. The cases indicate that a promise which would not be sufficiently definite to constitute an offer may be enforced under section 90. The crucial factors emphasized are the reasonableness of reliance by the 'promisee'—which no longer has to be of a 'definite and substantial character'—and proof of injustice. A classic (although untypical) example is *Hoffman v Red Owl Stores Inc.*[112] The defendants were a franchising operation which over a period of time led Hoffman to believe that he stood an excellent chance of receiving a franchise if he took various steps to develop his business. As a result of this he sold one shop, acquired another shop, spent work on the development of the shop and so on. Eventually Red Owl Stores refused to grant a franchise and it was held that Hoffman had an action to recover his wasted expenditure.

Liability in restitution

General

12.62   It is clearly established that where negotiations for a contract break down after one party to the negotiations has conferred benefits on the other, the law of restitution may apply and provide a basis for the recovery of reasonable remuneration in respect of that benefit.[113] In the terminology of quasi-contract this is a claim for a *quantum meruit*.

12.63   Restitution certainly raises a number of important issues, not the least of which is the relation between restitutionary liability and the good faith issue. One element of uncertainty or controversy is a major one indeed, namely whether the conception of restitution, as applied in Anglo-Australian law, is limited to cases of unjust enrichment.

Unjust enrichment

12.64   Although the concept of unjust enrichment is recognized in English law,[114] its scope is still the subject of much debate. It is not yet clear to what extent unjust enrichment is determinative of the scope of restitutionary liability. However, much of the debate in relation to contracts which fail to materialize concerns how far claims for restitution may be justified by reference to the principle of unjust enrichment.[115]

---

[112] 26 Wis 2d 683, 133 NW 2d 267 (1965).

[113] See eg *British Steel Corp v Cleveland Bridge and Engineering Co Ltd* (1981) [1984] 1 All ER 504 (liability to pay *quantum meruit* equal to cost of supply where letter of intent was not effective as a construction contract but the work contemplated was executed); *Brenner v First Artists' Management Pty Ltd* [1993] 2 VR 221 (*quantum meruit* based on unjust enrichment for services rendered under contract void for lack of agreement on price). Cf *Marston Construction Co Ltd v Kigass Ltd* (1989) 46 BLR 109 (contractors awarded reasonable remuneration for work done in preparing designs and working drawings in anticipation of entry into a contract which never materialized, on the basis that the defendants obtained a realizable benefit); cf *Regalian Properties plc v London Dockland Development Corp* [1995] 1 All ER 1005. See also Wyvill, 'Enrichment, Restitution and the Collapsed Negotiations Cases' (1993) 11 Aust Bar Rev 93; Christensen, 'Recovery for Work Performed in Anticipation of Contract: Is Reliance an Element of Benefit?' (1993) 11 Aust Bar Rev 144.

[114] See generally *Lipkin Gorman v Karpnale Ltd* [1991] 2 AC 548; *Dimskal Shipping Co SA v International Transport Workers Federation, The Evia Luck* [1992] 2 AC 152; *Woolwich Building Society v IRC* [1993] AC 70. In Australia, see *Pavey & Matthews Pty Ltd v Paul* (1987) 162 CLR 221; *Australia and New Zealand Banking Group Ltd v Westpac Banking Corp* (1988) 164 CLR 662; *David Securities Pty Ltd v Commonwealth Bank of Australia* (1992) 175 CLR 353. Cf *Roxborough v Rothmans of Pall Mall Australia Ltd* (2001) 208 CLR 516; *Farah Constructions Pty Ltd v Say-Dee Pty Ltd* (2007) 230 CLR 89.

[115] See eg, Beatson, 'Benefit, Reliance and the Structure of Unjust Enrichment' [1987] CLP 71; Burrows, 'Free Acceptance in the Law of Restitution' (1988) 104 LQR 576.

The concept of unjust enrichment conditions recovery by reference to three elements. **12.65**
Recovery will be allowed if the defendant has obtained a *benefit*, at the plaintiff's *expense*, in
circumstances where it would be *unjust* to allow the enrichment of the defendant. The element of benefit is clearly satisfied in cases where there is an increase in the defendant's
assets. However, many of the cases concern the provision of services with no end product.
Because the scope of the concept of 'benefit' has not been fully determined, it is open to the
courts to conclude that the enrichment requirement is satisfied even if there is no benefit
other than the receipt of the plaintiff's services. This appears to be the position taken in
many United States decisions.[116] Equally, because the scope of restitutionary liability has
not as yet been held to be restricted to cases of unjust enrichment, it is open to the courts
to decide that restitution is not limited by that concept.[117] Finally, and most controversially, it might be held that in so far as they rely on a good faith concept, the cases in this
area in effect treat breach of a duty of good faith as justifying a remedial response of compensation assessed on a restitutionary basis.

Many of these ideas may be found, albeit in an undigested form, in the facts and analysis in **12.66**
Sabemo Pty Ltd v North Sydney Municipal Council.[118] Sabemo and the Council came into a
negotiating relationship for the purpose of entering into a contract to redevelop land owned
by the Council. It was contemplated that a building lease would be agreed, but there was
no promise to this effect. Sabemo did a great deal of planning work, ultimately to the complete satisfaction of the Council and regulatory bodies. Although it resolved to ask the
plaintiff to proceed with the redevelopment, and notwithstanding development approval,
the Council ultimately resolved not to proceed with any of the schemes proposed, leaving
Sabemo with the problem that it had no right to contractual remuneration in respect of its
account for $426,000 worth of professional services. Sheppard J in the Supreme Court of
New South Wales dealt solely with the general question of liability, that is, whether the
defendant had to pay for the work done. In holding that the Council was liable to make
'compensation or restitution',[119] Sheppard J rejected unjust enrichment as the basis for the
claim. He formulated[120] a general principle, applicable 'where two parties proceed upon
the joint assumption that a contract will be entered into between them'. Under this principle, liability attaches whenever one party to the negotiations 'does work beneficial for the
project, and thus in the interests of the two parties, which work he would not be expected,
in other circumstances, to do gratuitously' and 'the other party unilaterally decides to abandon the project, not for any reason associated with bona fide disagreement concerning the
terms of the contract to be entered into but for reasons which, however valid, pertain only

---

[116] See eg, *Earhart v William Low Co* 25 Cal.3d 503, 600 P 2d 1344 (1979), and generally Dawson,
'Restitution Without Enrichment' (1981) 61 Boston ULR 563; Farnsworth, 'Precontractual Liability and
Preliminary Agreements: Fair Dealing and Failed Negotiations' (1987) 87 Col L Rev 217.
[117] See Beatson, 'Benefit, Reliance and the Structure of Unjust Enrichment' [1987] CLP 71. Cf Birks,
Restitution—The Future (Federation Press, Sydney, 1992), 96–103; *Independent Grocers Co-operative Ltd v
Noble Lowndes Superannuation Consultants Ltd* (1993) 60 SASR 525.
[118] [1977] 2 NSWLR 880.
[119] Cf *Pavev & Matthews Pty Ltd v Paul* (1987) 162 CLR 221, 256 (restitutionary obligation to pay 'fair
and just compensation' for an accepted benefit). See also *Commonwealth of Australia v Amann Aviation Pty Ltd*
(1991) 174 CLR 64, 116.
[120] [1977] 2 NSWLR 880, 902–3.

to his own position and do not relate at all to that of the other party'. Applying this principle to the facts, it was concluded that the Council was liable.

12.67 Although facts of the kind considered in *Sabemo Pty Ltd v North Sydney Municipal Council* may be equally susceptible to analysis in terms of promissory estoppel, analysis in terms of restitution independently of unjust enrichment or analysis in terms of restitution based on a broad view of the benefit concept in unjust enrichment,[121] the principle which Sheppard J formulated and applied is manifestly one of good faith.[122] Whether intended or not, the words used, emphasizing the failure of the Council to have regard to the interests of Sabemo when making its decision to discontinue negotiations, are undoubtedly words which rely on the breach of a good faith duty. The decision therefore opens up for argument the possibility that a remedial response analogous to that available for waiver of tort is applied where there is a breach of a duty of good faith. Even so, we should not draw the inference that whenever two parties embark on contractual negotiations there is a duty of good faith. It is not the law that reliance on the prospect of entry into a contract places the other party in the position of having to pay a price if the negotiations fail due to a decision not to contract. Like the principle of promissory estoppel, the principle of *Sabemo Pty Ltd v North Sydney Municipal Council* assumes that negotiations have reached the stage where there is either a promise by the defendant to enter into a contract, or a fact situation in which it can legitimately be said that the plaintiff is, at the defendant's request, rendering services which will have to be paid for if negotiations break down. The decision of Rattee J in *Regalian Properties Plc v London Dockland Development Corporation*[123] involved facts rather similar to *Sabemo* and a decision to the opposite effect. It is clear that Rattee J did not regard the defendant as behaving in bad faith. He treated the situation as one in which both parties proceeded on the basis of each taking the commercial risk of the project not coming to fruition.

Liability in contract

General

12.68 If there is a duty to act in good faith, breach of the duty will not amount to a breach of contract sounding in damages unless it has a contractual character. Although the common law does sometimes admit the existence of a contractual duty without an express or implied term,[124] we may assume that there is no such liability except under an express or implied term creating the duty. Our concern is with good faith in negotiations, and the idea of an implied term creating a duty of good faith receives little support in the cases. We have already seen that there is more support for a tortious than a contractual duty.[125]

---

[121] See Jones, 'Claims Arising Out of Anticipated Contracts Which Do Not Materialize' (1980) 18 U W Ontario LR 447; Carter, 'Contract, Restitution and Promissory Estoppel' (1989) 12 UNSWLJ 30.
[122] See Mason and Gageler, 'The Contract' in Finn (ed), *Essays on Contract* (Law Book Co Ltd, Sydney, 1987), 15–16.
[123] [1995] 1 All ER 1005.
[124] Thus, at common law a customer owes a duty to take usual and reasonable precautions in drawing a cheque to prevent a fraudulent alteration which might occasion loss to the customer's banker. See *London Joint Stock Bank Ltd v Macmillan* [1918] AC 777; *Commonwealth Trading Bank of Australia v Sydney Wide Stores Pty Ltd* (1981) 148 CLR 304.
[125] See 12.41.

However, express terms of good faith are now regularly coming before the courts, and arguments for implied terms to the same effect are more common than in the past.

There are two main situations. First, a preliminary agreement may be intended to operate   **12.69**
as a contract to negotiate a second contract in good faith. Second, a single agreement may
be intended to operate as a contract to negotiate terms not yet agreed in good faith. Attempts
to enforce such agreements must be considered with proper regard to a proposition for
which there is authority of overwhelming weight, namely, that the law does not recognize
an agreement to enter into a contract as a binding contract.[126]

Although we have placed the discussion of these situations in the context of pre-contractual   **12.70**
liability, they could equally be regarded as part of the preservation issue, or even as an aspect
of good faith in performance. There are two reasons for locating the discussion here. First,
the validity of an agreement to negotiate in good faith is not fully established. Second, since
our assumption is that negotiations have broken down, the question is whether any liability
attaches. Moreover, most of the cases in which contractual liability has been imposed do
not involve enforcement of a promise to negotiate in good faith. They employ the more
familiar bases of collateral contract and implied contract. We should therefore first deal
briefly with these bases.

Collateral contract

The courts in Australia and England have shown much ingenuity in employing the concept   **12.71**
of a collateral contract to promote good faith by imposing—on the basis of the parties'
agreement—contractual liability for breaking off negotiations prematurely. Just as there
may be a contract the consideration for which is the making of some other contract,[127] so
there may also be a contract the consideration for which is some other circumstance within
the concept of consideration. Examples include contracts the consideration for which is
execution of work under a preliminary agreement,[128] or an agreement to accept the highest
bid made under a competitive tender. Thus, in *Harvela Investments Ltd v Royal Trust Co of
Canada (CI) Ltd*[129] the House of Lords held that the defendants, having invited tenders for
a block of shares and having promised to sell to the highest bidder, were bound to do so.
Although this was assumed to be the case by all of the judges in the three courts which
considered the matter, the most convincing explanation was that given by Lord Diplock
who analysed the situation in terms of two contracts, a contract to sell to the highest bidder

---

[126] See *Masters v Cameron* (1954) 91 CLR 353, 362 (approving *Von Hatzfeldt-Wildenburg v Alexander*
[1912] 1 Ch 284, 289); *Walford v Miles* [1992] 2 AC 128 (approving *Courtney & Fairbairn Ltd v Tolaini Bros
(Hotels) Ltd* [1975] 1 WLR 297). See also *Bosaid v Andry* [1963] VR 465, 477; *Godecke v Kirwan* (1973) 129
CLR 629, 639; *Booker Industries Pty Ltd v Wilson Parking (Qld) Pty Ltd* (1982) 149 CLR 600, 604; *Woodside
Offshore Petroleum Pty Ltd v Attwood Oceanics Inc* [1986] WAR 253, 258; *Biotechnology Australia Pty Ltd v Pace*
(1988) 15 NSWLR 130, 133; *Itex Shipping Pte Ltd v China Ocean Shipping Co, The Jing Hong Hai* [1989] 2
Lloyd's Rep 522, 525–6; *Paul Smith Ltd v H & S International Holdings Ltd* [1991] 2 Lloyd's Rep 127, 131.
[127] See *Heilbut Symons & Co v Buckleton* [1913] AC 30, 47 per Lord Moulton.
[128] See *Turriff Construction Ltd v Regalia Knitting Mills Ltd* [1972] EG (Dig) 257 (letter of intent regarded
as 'ancillary contract' in respect of preparatory work done during (abortive) negotiations for construction
contract). See also the discussion of the contractual significance of letters of intent in *British Steel Corp v
Cleveland Bridge and Engineering Co Ltd* (1981) [1984] 1 All ER 504 and generally Ball, 'Work Carried Out
in Pursuance of Letters of Intent—Contract or Restitution?' (1983) 99 LQR 572.
[129] [1986] 1 AC 207.

made binding by the submission of tenders and the principal contract for sale of the shares.

12.72 We have described the collateral contract device as illustrating the ingenuity of courts for two reasons. First, because the decisions use familiar doctrines to reach what is conceived as a 'sound' decision without having to consider whether we should adopt and apply a general duty of good faith. Second, they show that whether or not English courts ultimately embrace good faith, there is an inherent strength in the common law to police bad faith. Although this inherent strength should not be underestimated, we must be alive to the danger of decisions which have questionable reasoning. The danger lies not so much in the apparently uncompromising approach of our courts to good faith as the 'sedimentary' result of these decisions. Layer upon layer of complication in rule application places undue stress on the process of rule formulation. The law becomes overcomplicated, and the connection between the corpus of contract law and the commercial realities of contract negotiation becomes tenuous.

Implied contract

12.73 At one time, implied contracts were relatively common in the law. The fictitious examples—invented under quasi-contractual principles—are now obsolete. However, there is no reason why a contract should not be implied from conduct in the course of negotiations, even though one party claims that negotiations were discontinued prior to the complete agreement, and even if the parties contemplated execution of a formal document which has not been signed.

12.74 Thus, the terms under which payment for services is to be made may never have expressly been agreed. If there is found to be an intention to contract, and an obligation to pay a reasonable price for performance is present under an implied contract, there is a contractual obligation to pay the reasonable price. Thus, in *Way v Latilla*[130] the parties contemplated a contract under which the plaintiff would be given an interest in mining concessions as remuneration for his work in acquiring these for the defendant's benefit. However, that agreement was incomplete, due to the parties' failure to agree on price. The House of Lords considered that a contract of employment had been agreed, so that it was clear that the work done was to be remunerated by contract. Therefore, albeit on a different basis from that contemplated, there was a contractual right to payment for the work done. The fact that no express contract was agreed, and the enforcement of payment on a different basis from that contemplated, suggests that the whole contract was implied rather than express.

12.75 More recently, in *Blackpool and Fylde Aero Club v Blackpool Borough Council*[131] a contract was implied that the local authority would consider timely tenders even though the tenders were merely in response to invitations to negotiate. The Council had laid down careful and detailed rules for the submission of tenders to ensure anonymity and fair consideration. In particular it was said that tenders had to be submitted in sealed envelopes by noon on a

---

[130] [1937] 3 All ER 759. Cf *British Bank for Foreign Trade Ltd v Novinex* [1949] 1 KB 623 (implied obligation to pay reasonable commission on follow up contracts with party introduced by agent).

[131] [1990] 1 WLR 1195 (see Phang, 'Tenders and Uncertainty' (1991) 4 JCL 461. Cf *Fairclough Building Ltd v Port Talbot Borough Council* (1992) 33 Con LR 24.

named day. The plaintiff submitted their tender by 11am on the day in question but by mischance the letter box was not opened by the Council's employees and the tender was therefore treated as having been received on the following day and excluded from consideration. When the plaintiff discovered the error they sought to persuade the Council to reconsider but by this time the Council had entered into a binding contract with another tenderer. On these facts the English Court of Appeal held that the Council was in breach of an implied contract to consider all tenders duly submitted. For procedural reasons the Court of Appeal did not have to decide the amount of damages to be awarded. These would presumably have included the wasted costs of tendering which perhaps were not very large in this case but in many construction contracts are very substantial. Perhaps also the plaintiff might have been awarded damages to compensate them for the loss of the chance of being selected. Reading between the lines in the report of the case it appears that the plaintiff's tender was probably the largest and also covered the widest range of services.[132]

It is not always easy to distinguish these cases from those in which an express contract is formed by conduct, the classic example being *Brogden v Metropolitan Railway Co.*[133] A recent illustration is *Empirnall Holdings Pty Ltd v Machon Paull Partners Pty Ltd,*[134] where a contract by conduct was found in the acceptance of work done by the plaintiff, following the defendant's receipt of a printed offer which was never formally accepted by the defendant. Similarly, it is not always easy to distinguish cases of implied contracts from cases in which the parties purported to enter into an express contract and into which terms are implied, on the basis of intention, to cure incompleteness or uncertainty.[135] Again, there are some passages in the speeches in *Way v Latilla,* discussing *quantum meruit,* consistent with a restitutionary basis for liability. However, what is important is whether the implied contract cases are relevant to the good faith issue. They certainly serve to promote good faith, and it would be absurd to contend that a value judgment as to the fairness of the decision to break off negotiations plays no role in the court's decision to imply a contract. There is no need to put the matter any higher than this. However, it might be suggested that in so far as the implied contract analysis is a device for imposing pre-contractual liability, the growing maturity of restitution makes it less important today. Moreover, if the rationale of the decisions is a desire to police unfair conduct, the direct application of a good faith duty may be more compelling. **12.76**

---

[132] The reasoning in this case is similar to that of the well known American case of *Heyer Products v US* 140 F Supp 409 (1956) in which it was held that in principle the plaintiffs would have an action for their lost expenditure if they could show that, having tendered for a United States government contract they had been excluded from consideration because they had given evidence to a senate enquiry which was contrary to the perceived interests of the US Department of Ordnance.

[133] (1877) 2 App Cas 666 (supply of goods in accordance with draft contract was an acceptance of those terms by conduct).

[134] (1988) 14 NSWLR 523.

[135] Cf eg, *Foley v Classique Coaches Ltd* [1934] 2 KB 1 (where an agreement provided that all petrol required would be purchased at a price to be agreed by parties from time to time, a term was implied that reasonable quality petrol would be supplied at a reasonable price).

Express promise to negotiate in good faith

12.77   It is fair to say that there is no enforcement difficulty where there is an express good faith provision, or a term having a similar effect is present in an agreement which is clearly a contract.[136] For example, in *Hospital Products Ltd v United States Surgical Corp.*[137] an express term which stated that a distributor would devote its best efforts to distributing a company's products was clearly considered to be a valid term. There are in fact many examples in cases on consents, export and import licences and so on, where a duty of best endeavours is present and can be enforced.[138] However, in so far as these cases illustrate the enforcement of good faith duties they are cases on good faith in performance.[139]

12.78   There have been a number of cases investigating the existence and enforceability of a duty to negotiate in good faith. The starting point is, however, still the negative proposition that the law does not recognize as a contract an agreement to enter into a contract. Even accepting this as correct, the question may still be raised whether an express or implied duty to negotiate in good faith is enforceable. Because of the principle that a contract to enter into a contract is not valid, Lord Wright's well-known *dictum* in *Hillas & Co Ltd v Arcos Ltd,*[140] that a contract to negotiate may be enforceable if there is good consideration, has been rejected as unsound in the English cases.[141] However, it appears that Australian courts adopt a different attitude. In *Coal Cliff Collieries Pty Ltd v Sijehama Pty Ltd*[142] two members of the New South Wales Court of Appeal saw no difficulty in accepting the validity of Lord Wright's *dictum*. More recently in *United Group Rail Services Ltd v Rail Corporation New South Wales,*[143] the New South Wales Court of Appeal accepted the validity of an agreement to undertake genuine and good faith negotiations in a dispute resolution clause.

12.79   We could treat these conflicting views as amounting to no more than different interpretations of the general rule that an agreement to enter into a contract is not enforceable. Actually, the difference is more substantive.[144] Lord Wright clearly rejected the view that all agreements to enter into contracts are void. In his view that rule is restricted to agreements which do not amount to contracts. The House of Lords' approach is that any agreement to

---

[136] Cf *Insurance Co of Africa v Scor (UK) Reinsurance Co Ltd* [1985] 1 Lloyd's Rep 312 (claims cooperation clause).

[137] (1984) 156 CLR 41.

[138] See eg, *Re Anglo-Russian Merchant Traders Ltd* [1917] 2 KB 679; *Coloniale Import-Export v Loumidis Sons* [1978] 2 Lloyd's Rep 560; *Gregory v MAB Pty Ltd* (1989) 1 WAR 1, 15.

[139] See generally, Lücke, 'Good Faith and Contractual Performance' in Finn (ed), *Essays on Contract* (Law Book Co Ltd, Sydney, 1987), 155; Hunter, 'The Duty of Good Faith and Security of Performance' (1993) 6 JCL 19.

[140] (1932) 147 LT 503, 515.

[141] See *Courtney & Fairbairn Ltd v Tolaini Bros (Hotels) Ltd* [1975] 1 WLR 297; *Walford v Miles* [1992] 2 AC 128.

[142] (1991) 24 NSWLR 1 (see Tolhurst, 'Cliff Hanger Negotiations in the Supreme Court of New South Wales' (1994) 7 JCL 79). See also *Hughes Bros Pty Ltd v Trustees of the Roman Catholic Church for the Archdiocese of Sydney* (1993) 31 NSWLR 91.

[143] [2009] NSWCA 177.

[144] Cf, *Hooper Baille Associated Ltd v Natcon Group Pty Ltd* (1992) 28 NSWLR 194 where Giles J said an agreement to conciliate is in principle enforceable and held that the agreement in question could be enforced by a stay of arbitration proceedings. He disagreed with the views expressed by Steyn J in *Paul Smith Ltd v H & S International Holdings Ltd* [1991] 2 Lloyd's Rep 127.

enter into a contract, essential terms of which have not already been agreed, is itself necessarily void since the consideration for the agreement is merely illusory. This is an irreconcilable difference. Professor Farnsworth has said that there is a similar disagreement of principle in the United States.[145] He states that while some courts, like those in England, have refused to 'accord parties the freedom to impose this regime on themselves', Federal courts, applying New York law, 'have been most prominent in refusing on the ground of indefiniteness to enforce explicit agreements to negotiate whether expressed in terms of "good faith" or "best efforts"'. He finds no 'compelling justification' for the first line of cases and suggests that the 'burden lies on the party that would have the court refuse enforcement to show why enforcement should be denied'. He also explains that there have been 'intimations that such an obligation might be implied in law in the absence of any actual assent by the parties'.

In *Coal Cliff Collieries Pty Ltd v Sijehama Pty Ltd*[146] a document was executed by four compa- **12.80**
nies of which Coal Cliff Collieries (the first appellant) was a wholly owned subsidiary of
Kembla Coal and Coke (the second appellant) and Sijehama (the first respondent) was a
major shareholder in Bulli Main Colliery (the second respondent) which was the holder of
a coal mining authorization in respect of an area of land in New South Wales. Negotiations
for a joint venture between Coal Cliff and Bulli began as long ago as 1976 but were disrupted by three deaths in the Bowdler family, the controlling force in Sijehama. Negotiations
recommenced in the middle of 1980 and in October 1981 heads of agreement were executed by the four companies which envisaged the execution of a joint venture agreement
between the parties. Some 14 drafts of the joint venture agreement were prepared between
October 1981 and November 1985 when the negotiations were terminated by the appellants. In the course of these negotiations the parties reached agreement on many of the
outstanding questions between them. Basically the scheme involved Coal Cliff recovering
all the coal mined until the project had reached break even point. Break even point was
defined in relation to 'net profit before tax' but the parties were unable to agree on a definition of 'net profit before tax' which was clearly a key concept in the structure of any
agreement.

The heads of agreement which the parties reached in 1981 started with a statement: **12.81**

> This document will serve to record the terms and conditions subject to and upon which Coal
> Cliff Collieries Pty Ltd, Sijehama and Bulli Main agree to associate themselves in an unincorporated Joint Venture for the purpose of developing and exploiting the coal prospect currently the subject of authorisation application No A38. The parties will forthwith proceed in
> good faith to consult together upon the formulation of a more comprehensive and detailed
> joint venture agreement (and any associated agreements) which when approved and executed
> will take the place of these heads of agreement, but the action of the parties in so consulting

---

[145] See Farnsworth, 'Precontractual Liability and Preliminary Agreements: Fair Dealing and Failed Negotiations' (1987) 87 Col L Rev 217, 264. The passage is quoted in full by Kirby P in *Coal Cliff Collieries Pty Ltd v Sijehama Pty Ltd* (1991) 24 NSWLR 1, 24–5. See also Knapp, 'Enforcing the Contract to Bargain' (1969) 44 NYULR 673.

[146] (1991) 24 NSWLR 1, CA. See also *United Group Rail Services Ltd v Rail Corporation* [2009] NSWCA 177.

and in negotiating on fresh or additional terms shall not in the meantime in any way prejudice a full and binding effect of what is now agreed.

12.82   The agreements thus contemplated, relating to a coal mining joint venture, were never
executed. This was because the appellants withdrew from the negotiations. The contention
of the respondents was that this was a repudiation of the contractual obligations created by
the heads of agreement. They therefore purported to treat the contract as discharged and
claimed damages. The trial judge Clarke J held that this wording indicated that the parties
had assumed a binding obligation to negotiate in good faith and that the appellant had
been in breach of that obligation. The New South Wales Court of Appeal reversed this
holding but for differing grounds. Handley JA reasoned from the broad basis that 'a promise to negotiate in good faith is illusory and therefore cannot be binding'.[147] Kirby P, with
whom Waddell A-JA agreed said[148] the agreement came within a class of case in which the
promise to negotiate in good faith occurs in the context of an arrangement which indicates
clearly, by its 'nature, purpose, context, other provisions or otherwise', that it is unenforceable as being illusory, by reason of being too vague or uncertain. He reached this decision
reluctantly, agreeing with Lord Wright in *Hillas & Co Ltd v Arcos Ltd* that, in principle, parties who have bound themselves to negotiate or consult in good faith, 'should be held to
that promise'.[149] However, even on this view each case will depend on the precise terms of
the agreement alleged to be valid and enforceable. Thus, in the present case the agreement
to negotiate in good faith was not binding because it was too vague to be enforceable. It is
important to note that Kirby P also thought that even if there was an obligation to negotiate in good faith the appellants were not in breach of it and that the respondents were not
claiming wasted expenditure but for the loss of a chance of making a very profitable deal.

12.83   In *United Group Rail Services Ltd v Rail Corporation*[150] the decision of Kirby P in *Coal Cliff*
was affirmed. As noted above this case involved a 'genuine and good faith' negotiation provision within a dispute resolution clause. The case was not concerned with the efficacy of a
simple agreement to negotiate. As regards the efficacy of such a provision, Allsop P said:[151]

> An agreement to negotiate, if viewed as an agreement to behave in a particular way may be
> uncertain, but is not incomplete ... The relevant question is whether the clause has certain
> content.

> An obligation to undertake discussions about a subject in an honest and genuine attempt to
> reach an identified result is not incomplete. It may be referable to a standard concerned with
> conduct assessed by subjective standards, but that does not make the standard or compliance
> with the standard impossible of assessment. Honesty is such a standard ... Whether it is

---

[147] (1991) 24 NSWLR 1, 42. Cf *Trawl Industries of Australia Pty Ltd v Effem Foods Pty Ltd Trading as 'Uncle
Ben's' of Australia* (1992) 27 NSWLR 326, 343 where Samuels JA considered the conclusion of the majority
in *Coal Cliff* 'not to be wholly consistent' with *Booker Industries Pty Ltd v Wilson Parking (Qld) Pty Ltd* (1982)
149 CLR 600, 604. See generally Farnsworth, *Farnsworth on Contracts* (3rd edn, Aspen Publishers, New York,
2004), §§ 3.8, 3.8a, 3.8b, 3.8c, 3.26, 3.26a, 3.26b, 3.26c.
[148] (1991) 24 NSWLR 1, 27. Contrast *Ravinder Rohini Pty Ltd v Krizaic* (1991) 30 FCR 300 (relation,
antecedent to establishment of partnership, was enforceable as contract where the steps to be taken were
agreed).
[149] (1991) 24 NSWLR 1, 25.
[150] [2009] NSWCA 177.
[151] [2009] NSWCA 177, [64]–[73].

capable of assessment depends on whether there is a standard of behaviour that is capable of having legal content. Asserting its uncertainty does not answer the question. The assertion that each party has an unfettered right to have regard to any of its own interests on any basis begs the question as to what constraint the party may have imposed on itself by freely entering into a given contract. If what is required by the voluntarily assumed constraint is that a party negotiate honestly and genuinely with a view to resolution of a dispute with fidelity to the bargain, there is no inherent inconsistency with negotiation, so constrained …

What the phrase 'good faith' signifies in any particular context and contract will depend on that context and that contract. A number of things, however, can be said as to the place of good faith in the operation of the common law in Australia. The phrase does not, by its terms, necessarily import, or presumptively introduce, notions of fiduciary obligation familiar in equity or the law of trusts. Nor does it necessarily import any notion or requirement to act in the interests of the other party to the contract. The content and context here is a clearly worded dispute resolution clause of an engineering contract. It is to be anticipated at the time of entry into the contract that disputes and differences that may arise will be anchored to a finite body of rights and obligations capable of ascertainment and resolution by the chosen arbitral process (or, indeed, if the parties chose, by the Court). The negotiations (being the course of treaty or discussion) with a view to resolving the dispute will be anticipated not to be open-ended about a myriad of commercial interests to be bargained for from a self-interested perspective (as in *Coal Cliff*). Rather, they will be anticipated to involve or comprise a discussion of rights, entitlements and obligations said by the parties to arise from a finite and fixed legal framework about acts or omissions that will be said to have happened or not happened. The aim of the negotiations will be anticipated to be to resolve a dispute about an existing bargain and its performance. Honest and genuine differences of opinion may attend the parties' views of their rights and obligations. Such things as difficulties of proof and uncertainty as to fact or law may perfectly legitimately strike the parties differently. That accepted, honest business people who approach a dispute about an existing contract will often be able to settle it. This requires an honest and genuine attempt to resolve differences by discussion and, if thought to be reasonable and appropriate, by compromise, in the context of showing a faithfulness and fidelity to the existing bargain.

The phrase 'genuine and good faith' [as used in this clause] is, as I have said, a composite phrase. It is a phrase concerning an obligation to behave in a particular way in the conduct of an essentially self-interested commercial activity: the negotiation of a resolution of a commercial dispute. Given that context, the content of the phrase involves the notions of honesty and genuineness. Whilst the activity is of a self-interested character, the parties have not left its conduct unconstrained. They have promised to undertake negotiations in a genuine and good faith manner for a limited period (14 days). As a matter of language, the phrase 'genuine and good faith' in this context needs little explication: it connotes an honest and genuine approach to the task. This task, rooted as it is in the existing bargain, carries with it an honest and genuine commitment to the bargain (fidelity to the bargain) and to the process of negotiation for the designated purpose …

These are not empty obligations; nor do they represent empty rhetoric. An honest and genuine approach to settling a contractual dispute, giving fidelity to the existing bargain, does constrain a party. The constraint arises from the bargain the parties have willingly entered into. It requires the honest and genuine assessment of rights and obligations and it requires that a party negotiate by reference to such … It is sufficient to say that the standard required by the notion of genuineness and good faith within a process of otherwise tactical and self-interested behaviour (negotiation) is rooted in the honest and genuine views of the parties about their existing bargain and the controversy that has arisen in connection with it within the limits of a clause such as [that in question].

12.84   The House of Lords case is *Walford v Miles*.[152] The defendants, who were husband and wife, owned a photographic processing business which they were interested in selling. In 1985 there had been abortive negotiations with a company in which their accountants had a substantial interest. In late 1986 the plaintiffs, who were brothers, one of whom was a solicitor and the other an accountant, heard that the business might be for sale at about £2m and the plaintiffs were very anxious to buy at this price which they regarded as a bargain. In March 1987 the plaintiffs agreed 'subject to contract' to buy the business. On 18 March 1987 there was an oral agreement between one of the plaintiffs and Mr Miles, that if the plaintiffs obtained a comfort letter from their bankers, confirming that they were prepared to provide the finance of £2m the defendants would terminate negotiations with any third party. The comfort letter from the bank was provided, but on 30 March the defendants' solicitors wrote to the plaintiffs stating that the defendants had decided to sell the business to the company in which their accountants were interested. The plaintiffs claimed that, although there was no binding contract for the sale of the business, there was a binding preliminary contract. The argument was that in return for the provision of the comfort letter the defendants had bound themselves to a 'lock-out' agreement, that is an agreement which would give the plaintiffs an exclusive opportunity to come to terms with the defendants. The House of Lords did not doubt that it was in principle possible to make a binding lock-out agreement.[153] However, in order to make any commercial sense such an agreement would have to have an express or implied time limit. If all that A does is to promise not to negotiate with anyone other than B, that in itself does not impose a legal obligation to negotiate with B; still less to reach an agreement with B. But, of course, if A had agreed not to negotiate with anyone but B for six months, this would put A under some commercial pressure, which may in some cases be very great, to make a serious attempt to reach agreement with B. The agreement in this case had no express time limit. The plaintiffs argued that it was subject to an implied term that the defendants 'would continue to negotiate in good faith with the plaintiffs'. The trial judge held that there was a breach of a collateral contract. However, a majority of the English Court of Appeal reversed this decision on the ground that there was no more than an agreement to negotiate which was not enforceable under English law. The House of Lords affirmed this decision. One answer to the claim would be that no such term would be implied. However, the answer given by the House of Lords was that even if such a term was implied it would not help the plaintiffs because a duty to negotiate in good faith was meaningless and without content. In addition, any sale agreement was 'subject to contract', so that there was complete freedom to break off negotiations until a formal document was signed.

12.85   Putting to one side the 'subject to contract' complication in cases such as *Walford v Miles*, it is difficult to see who benefits from the decision to apply the rule that an agreement to negotiate is not in law an effective contract, in cases where there is consideration for the promise. If businesspeople are prepared to reach such agreements, why should the law not

---

[152] [1992] 2 AC 128.
[153] See now *Pitt v PHH Asset Management Lid* [1994] 1 WLR 327 (see MacMillan, [1993] CLJ 392).

enforce them?[154] In *Walford v Miles* Lord Ackner, with whom the other members of the House of Lords agreed, said[155] that a duty to negotiate in good faith is 'unworkable in practice as it is inherently inconsistent with the position of a negotiating party'. No one would suggest that specific performance is available in respect of such agreements. The only available remedies are damages and injunction. The prospect of an injunction would certainly cause some alarm. If we assume negotiations in relation to specific property, the delay caused by defending the proceedings could well be very prejudicial on a falling market. Any decision to sell the property prior to the expiry of the term for negotiation would be made at the vendor's peril. On the other hand, this is essentially the position with an option, the only difference being that the terms of the sale are already known. In other words, there is always a risk inherent in a contract the effect of which is to qualify the liberty to contract. Business people are well aware of this. They understand, or ought to understand, both that the agreement must not subject them to commercially unacceptable risks and that the consideration for the promise must be commercially adequate. In this regard, just as an agreement subject to finance should require the purchaser to undertake some obligation in relation to the pursuit of finance, so the imposition of an obligation of good faith may well be seen by the commercial community as part of the consideration appropriate as the price of relinquishing freedom to contract elsewhere.

One might object to a duty to negotiate in good faith on the grounds that it is very difficult to tell whether parties are negotiating in good or bad faith. This objection cannot be dismissed out of hand. Certainly the leading American textbook[156] contains a lengthy discussion of the complex case law on where the line is to be drawn. Nevertheless it may be plausibly argued that distinguishing between good and bad faith is precisely the kind of job for which judges are appointed. Certainly of all the countries in the world it is hard to believe that England has judges least well equipped for tasks of this kind. **12.86**

It seems more probable that Lord Ackner is not saying that it is difficult to distinguish between good faith and bad faith but that a duty to negotiate did not involve any duty to reach a complete contract. This may be readily conceded. Nevertheless, the House of Lords was perfectly prepared to admit that a contract not to negotiate with anyone else for good consideration would be binding. Similarly, the House of Lords regarded an agreement to use best endeavours to reach an agreement as in principle binding. Although the distinction between negotiating in good faith and using best endeavours to reach an agreement may be regarded as over sharp, those who know the case law would obviously be well **12.87**

---

[154] Predictably, academic reaction to the decision has been critical. See eg, Cumberbatch, 'In Freedom's Cause: The Contract to Negotiate' (1992) 12 OJLS 587; Neill, 'A Key to Lock-Out Agreements?' (1992) 108 LQR 405; Jamieson, 'When Lock-Out Agreement Enforceable' [1992] LMCLQ 186; McDonald and Swanton, 'Contract Law: Agreement to Negotiate, Deal, Consult or Confer' (1992) 66 ALJ 744; Buckley, '*Walford v Miles*: False Certainty About Uncertainty—An Australian Perspective' (1993) 6 JCL 58. Cf Peel, '"Locking Out" and "Locking In": The Enforceability of Agreements to Negotiate' [1992] CLJ 211. Similarly, the cases approved had previously been criticized. See eg, Hammond, 'Contracts to Negotiate' [1976] NZLJ 153.
[155] [1992] 2 AC 128, 138.
[156] See Farnsworth, *Farnsworth on Contracts* (3rd edn, Vol I, Aspen Publishers, New York, 1990), §§ 3.26, 3.26a–c (see also 7.17b–c).

advised to take advantage of this distinction. Of course this does not mean that the House of Lords should not one day seriously reconsider *Walford v Miles*, since to expect all businessmen to be familiar with the nuances of the case law is unrealistic.

12.88 The essential point which appears to be overlooked in the judgment of the House of Lords is that loss can be inflicted by bad faith negotiations irrespective of whether a contract is ever reached. The natural loss in most cases is the wasted expenditure of conducting negotiations with somebody who is not negotiating in good faith. This was also overlooked by the plaintiffs, who claimed that the property was in fact worth £3m and that therefore they had lost in effect at least £1m because they had expected to buy for £2m. It is difficult to see how in any view this could possibly be right. The damages liability under an agreement to negotiate in good faith is quite different from that which is likely to be imposed on a party who breaches the obligations created by an option to purchase. Even if there had been a binding contract to negotiate in good faith or not to negotiate with anyone other than the plaintiffs, this would not have guaranteed that a contract to sell at £2m would have been the end result, because the defendants might at any time have woken up to the real value of the business, and asked a price which came closer to it. This would not have been a breach either of an agreement to negotiate in good faith or of an agreement not to negotiate with anyone else. What the plaintiffs had in fact lost as a result of the abortive negotiations was a loss of much more modest size, made up of the value of their own wasted time and the wasted fees of their professional advisers. In fact, a sum had been awarded for some such losses in the lower courts and was not the subject of an appeal.[157]

12.89 The claim in *Walford v Miles* was misconceived. There was no real prospect of loss of bargain damages being awarded against the vendor of the property. In both *Coal Cliff Collieries Pty Ltd v Sijehama Pty Ltd*[158] and *Hillas & Co Ltd v Arcos Ltd*[159] it was recognized that damages may be awarded on the basis of loss of a chance, and that the award might be for nominal damages only. It is hard to feel that the House of Lords produced really conclusive reasons why parties who wish to assume mutual obligations to negotiate in good faith should be denied the court's support in such a perfectly reasonable endeavour. It is suggested that there is no sufficient reason for the courts to refuse enforceability to agreements to negotiate in good faith. There may be specific cases in which a court cannot give effect to such a commitment, or where the damages are only nominal, but it is over simplistic to assume all cases are of this kind.

Implied duty to negotiate in good faith

12.90 Whether the courts should impose on the parties a duty to negotiate in good faith is a more difficult question. It does appear however that there are cases where a person may reasonably complain that he or she has been 'led up the garden path' and should recover the reasonable costs of being so misled and where at least the existing English law might find this difficult. Most of the discussion of an implied good faith duty has been in the context of

---

[157] The majority in the Court of Appeal upheld the award as damage for the defendants' misrepresentation of intention.
[158] (1991) 24 NSWLR 1, 25.
[159] (1932) 147 LT 503, 515.

good faith in performance. Often the focus is on how far reasonable or fair conduct should be implied as an element in the decision-making process in relation to post-contractual conduct. The difficulty of implying terms into contracts, particularly detailed commercial contracts is well known. Most difficult of all is the argument that an additional duty (contractual or tortious) should be implied to increase the obligations created by the express terms of the agreement or tortious principles.[160]

Implication of a good faith term in an agreement which is clearly a contract is quite different from implication of a duty of good faith in the context of contractual negotiations. We are, of course, very familiar with the implication of a requirement of reasonableness where particular terms have not been agreed. It is also clear that where terms are to be added before execution of an otherwise complete agreement it will be implied that the terms are reasonable and consistent with the bargain as a whole.[161] Given the approach to the so-called 'contract to contract', it is believed that the main situations where there might be an implication of a good faith term are where there is a preliminary agreement, such as a letter of intent, or an agreement to renew or extend an existing contract. As the law currently stands, the approach of the courts will be from the perspective of the preservation function of good faith.[162] In other words, where there is an argument that the preliminary agreement, or agreement to renew or extend, is too uncertain, courts will search for a means of upholding the agreement. On the other hand, as we have seen,[163] some courts, particularly in the United States, have approached the issue more generally, so as to preserve the bargain and to impose a liability for breach of the good faith duty.

12.91

C. Conclusion

We have not sought to argue either for or against the existence of a duty of good faith in relation to the negotiation of a contract. The traditional view, that there is no general duty of good faith in the bargaining process remains valid. We have also been content in the analysis to investigate how far good faith requires particular courses of conduct. A contrary view is that good faith merely operates to exclude certain kinds of conduct. This is a contrast between, on the one hand, a normative role of requiring conduct to reach a particular

12.92

---

[160] See generally *Tai Hing Cotton Mill Ltd v Liu Chong Hing Bank Ltd* [1986] AC 80; *Hawkins v Clayton* (1988) 164 CLR 539; *Johnson v Perez* (1988) 166 CLR 351, 363; *Reid v Rush and Tompkins Group plc* [1990] 1 WLR 212; *Banque Keyser Ullmann SA v Skandia (UK) Insurance Co Ltd* [1990] 1 QB 665 (affirmed on other grounds *sub nom Banque Financière de la Cité SA v Westgate Insurance Co. Ltd* [1991] 2 AC 249); *Bank of Nova Scotia v Hellenic Mutual War Risks Association (Bermuda) Ltd, The Good Luck* [1992] 1 AC 233; *Johnstone v Bloomsbury Health Authority* [1992] 1 QB 333; *Scally v Southern Health and Social Services Board* [1992] 1 AC 294.

[161] See *Godecke v Kirwan* (1973) 129 CLR 629 (clause in land contract referring to execution of further agreement which was to contain terms already agreed and further terms reasonably required by vendor's solicitors was valid but probably restricted to formal matters).

[162] See, however, *Blackpool and Fylde Aero Club v Blackpool Borough Council* [1990] 1 WLR 1195, 1204, where the implied contract included a term that the local authority decision to reject a timely tender would be made in good faith. Cf *Ravinder Rohini Pty Ltd v Krizaic* (1991) 30 FCR 300.

[163] See 11.59ff.

community standard, and, on the other, a role of prohibiting certain conduct which is recognized as not being acceptable to the community.[164]

12.93   What is clear is that the doctrinal principles applied in England and Australia very frequently serve to promote good faith. Indeed, we would be surprised if the position were otherwise. Contract is an inherently moral institution.[165] The former Chief Justice of Australia, Sir Anthony Mason has, however, suggested (extrajudicially) that the quality of 'Australian commercial life could only profit from an infusion of good faith'.[166] Whether the courts should do this by the introduction of a good faith principle is a difficult question on which differing views may legitimately be expressed. The promotion of good faith is not the same thing as the formulation and application of a rule of law.[167]

12.94   It follows from the disparate list of bases for liability that there is no general good faith principle synthesizing the law on pre-contractual liability. Rather, in particular situations, liability may attach by virtue of the satisfaction of the requirements of a particular concept, doctrine or statutory rule. Many of these operate outside the general law of contract. We have seen that, apart from cases of fraud—where a court considers a (narrow) requirement of good faith is appropriate—negotiation in bad faith does not give rise to a liability to pay compensation. Putting breach of a statutory prohibition to one side, for commercial parties today the two principal bases for pre-contractual liability are promissory estoppel and restitution. The remedial consequences of promissory estoppel are as much open to debate as whether the operation of the concept signifies the enforcement of a duty analogous to good faith. The law on restitution still has some very controversial components. But there is no support for a general restitutionary liability based on conduct which shows a lack of good faith.

12.95   The most that can be said in favour of a tort of bad faith negotiation is that it might have the very useful function of simplifying some relevant aspects of the law on negligence, estoppel and restitution. It is now common for pleadings alleging pre-contractual liability to roam through negligent misstatement, promissory estoppel and restitution. This all adds to the expense of litigation, without any obvious benefit being obtained. Perhaps we should act more directly on this in the interests of simplification. In Australia, breach of the statutory prohibition on misleading or deceptive conduct is also added, almost as a matter of course. While not couched in terms of good faith, the prohibition does amount—as would a general duty of good faith—to the imposition of a norm of conduct. It has not simplified the law. It has not led to greater certainty. We have no empirical evidence that it

---

[164] The question whether good faith is an 'excluder' is discussed by·Priestley JA, with reference to the academic literature. in *Renard Constructions (ME) Pty Ltd v Minister for Public Works* (1992) 26 NSWLR 234, 266–7.

[165] On the implications of this for good faith see eg, Reiter, 'Good Faith in Contracts' (1983) 17 Valparaiso Univ Law Rev 705; Bridge, 'Does Anglo-Canadian Contract Law Need A Doctrine of Good Faith?' (1984) 98 Can Bus L Journal 385; Steyn, 'The Role of Good Faith and Fair Dealing in Contract Law: A Hair-Shirt Philosophy?' [1991] Denning Law Journal 131.

[166] See Mason 'Foreword' (1989) 12 UNSWLJ 1, 2–3. See also Angel, 'Some Reflections on Privity, Consideration, Estoppel and Good Faith' (1992) 66 ALJ 484.

[167] See Waddams, 'Pre-contractual Duties of Disclosure' in Cane and Stapleton (eds), *Essays for Patrick Atiyah* (Clarendon Press, Oxford, 1991), 255.

has changed the course of commercial conduct.[168] Clearly, developments in many of the areas of pre-contractual liability indicate that those negotiating contracts will frequently be found to have qualified their liberty to break off negotiations even though there is no contract. It would, to say the least, be difficult for Australian lawyers to accept Lord Ackner's suggestion in *Walford v Miles*[169] that the duty of a party engaged in negotiations is limited to the avoidance of 'making misrepresentations'. Whether it squares with the English law on estoppel, and the overall approach of the courts to pre-contractual liability, is a matter of some importance for English contract lawyers.

Those who wish to argue for a general rule of good faith, contractual or tortious, can cer-   **12.96** tainly find support in some of the cases considered. It cannot, however, be argued that the mere fact of entering into negotiations creates such a duty. The negotiations must at least have reached the stage of establishing a relation between the parties in which one may legitimately rely on the conduct of the other.[170] The relational feature of contracts is not well developed in England. The tendency is still to regard individual unit contracts of sale as the paradigm. Accordingly, the prospect of giving effect to a negotiating relation as a species of contract is fairly remote.

---

[168] Cf *Banque Brussels Lambert SA v Australian National Industries Ltd* (1989) 21 NSWLR 502, 505 per Rogers CJ Comm D (whether the development of the equitable doctrine of estoppel and the prohibition against misleading or deceptive conduct have 'succeeded in bringing legal obligation into closer alignment with the call of commercial morality').

[169] [1992] 2 AC 128, 138.

[170] See Murphy and Speidel, *Studies in Contract Law* (4th edn, Foundation Press, New York, 1991), 477–8. Cf O'Connor, *Good Faith in English Law* (Dartmouth, Aldershot, 1990), 100.

13

PRE-CONTRACTUAL LIABILITY[1]

This Chapter considers situations where the parties set out to make a contract but do not complete the course and make that contract. It considers whether one party may be liable to the other and in what circumstances. As the contract making process has become longer and more complex this has become an increasingly important area of law and one which is still in active development. There are a number of possibilities. **13.01**

A. Liability in Contract

It may seem paradoxical to start with contract as a head of pre-contractual liability but on this journey there are many stops before the destination. So in the two-contract analysis which is an important feature of the law relating to auctions and tenders the first contract will come into existence even if the second does not.[2] Similarly in the Letter of Intent situations discussed in Chapters 7 and 8 there will often be a contract even though the parties have never made the contract they started out to make. A good example is *Emcor Drake & Scull v Sir Robert McAlpine*[3] where the parties set out to make a contract worth £34.25m but ended up doing work which produced a contract for £14m. **13.02**

It is quite common for parties to start or even to finish the intended works before they have completed the formalities of the contract making process. In practice the further they have got the more likely it is that there will be held to be a contract. An instructive case is *G. Percy Trentham Ltd v Archital Luxfer Ltd.*[4] Here Trentham were the main contractors for the **13.03**

---

[1] Farnsworth, 'Pre-contractual Liability and Preliminary Agreements: Fair Dealing and Failed Negotiations' (1987) 87 Columbia LR217; Jones, 'Claims Arising out of Anticipated Contracts which do not Materialize' (1979) U of Western Ontario LR 447; Goff and Jones, *Restitution* (7th edn, Sweet & Maxwell, 2007) Ch 26; McLure in Degeling and Edelman *Unjust Enrichment in Commercial Law* (Law Book Co, 2008) Ch 11; Hayne in Degeling and Edelman *Unjust Enrichment in Commercial Law* Ch 12.

[2] See discussion in Chapter 5.

[3] (2004) 98 Con LR 1, Section 7.50.

[4] [1993] 1 Lloyd's Rep 25.

design and build of two industrial units. There were two main contracts, each of which contained provision for aluminum window works. There was no doubt that the window works had been carried out by Archital Luxfer and that they had been paid for the works. The negotiations for the contract had never been carried through to the stage of signing subcontracts. There were alleged defects in the windows and Trentham sued. Archital Luxfer argued that there was no contract. The Court of Appeal held that there was a contract. Steyn LJ said:

> The third matter is the impact of the fact that the transaction is executed rather than executory. It is a consideration of the first importance on a number of levels. See *British Bank for Foreign Trade Ltd v Novinex*, [1949] 1 KB 628, at p 630. The fact that the transaction was performed on both sides will often make it unrealistic to argue that there was no intention to enter into legal relations. It will often make it difficult to submit that the contract is void for vagueness or uncertainty, or, alternatively, it may make it possible to treat a matter not finalised in negotiations as inessential. In this case fully executed transactions are under consideration. Clearly, similar considerations may sometimes be relevant in partly executed transactions.

13.04 An important case is the decision of the House of Lords in *Way v Latilla*.[5] In this case Mr Way was appointed as manager of a gold mine in the Gold Coast (now Ghana). While in England he had a meeting with Mr Latilla who asked him to explore the possibility of other concessions on his behalf and intimated that he would give Mr Way a share in anything that was found. Mr Way did this and procured concessions for Mr Latilla and for companies controlled by Mr Latilla which generated very substantial returns. Mr Latilla refused to give Mr Way any interest in the proceeds. Lord Atkin said:

> There certainly was no concluded contract between the parties as to the amount of the share or interest that Mr Way was to receive, and it appears to me impossible for the court to complete the contract for them. If the parties had proceeded on the terms of a written contract, with a materials clause that the remuneration was to be a percentage of the gross returns, but with the figure left blank, the court could not supply the figure. The judge relied upon the decision of this House in *Hillas & Co Ltd v Arcos Ltd*. But in that case this House was able to find, in the contract to give an option for the purchase of timber in a future year, an intention to be bound contractually, and all the elements necessary to form a concluded contract. There is no material in the present case upon which any court would decide what was the share which the parties must be taken to have agreed. But, while there is, therefore, no concluded contract as to the remuneration, it is plain that there existed between the parties a contract of employment under which Mr Way was engaged to do work for Mr Latilla in circumstances which clearly indicated that the work was not to be gratuitous. Mr Way, therefore, is entitled to a reasonable remuneration on the implied contract to pay him quantum meruit.

He thought £5,000 a reasonable figure for Mr Way's services.

B. Quantum Meruit

13.05 Lord Atkin described Mr Way's claim as being on a quantum meruit. There is no doubt that in this case the claim was on a genuine implied contract. It is equally clear that not all quantum meruit claims are genuinely contractual but include claims which we should now

---

[5] [1937] 3 All ER 759.

regard as restitutionary. A good starting point is the decision of Barry J in *William Lacey (Hounslow) Ltd v Davis*.[6]

In this case Davis, the defendant, was the owner of certain premises which had suffered war damage. He invited three builders, one of whom was the plaintiff, to tender for rebuilding the premises as a shop with residential flats above. The plaintiff submitted the lowest tender and was led to believe that he would get the contract. The plaintiff was then asked to do very substantial work in connection with Davis's claim to the war damage commission in relation to damage to the building. This resulted in a substantially improved claim.

Barry J held that there was no concluded contract between the parties but that apart from **13.06** the work on the original tender, the plaintiff should be paid for the other work he had done which was of a kind which was not normally done without payment. Barry J said:

> This, at first sight, is a somewhat formidable argument which, if well founded, would wholly defeat the plaintiffs' alternative claim. If such were the law it would, I think, amount to a denial of justice to the plaintiffs in the present case, and legal propositions which have that apparent effect must always be scrutinised with some care. In truth, I think that Mr. Lawson's proposition is founded upon too narrow a view of the modern action for quantum meruit. In its early history it was no doubt a genuine action in contract, based upon a real promise to pay, although that promise had not been expressed in words, and the amount of the payment had not been agreed. Subsequent developments have, however, considerably widened the scope of this form of action, and in many cases the action is now founded upon what is known as quasi-contract, similar, in some ways, to the action for money had and received. In these quasi-contractual cases the court will look at the true facts and ascertain from them whether or not a promise to pay should be implied, irrespective of the actual views or intentions of the parties at the time when the work was done or the services rendered.

It is clear that terminology has changed. In 1957 few talked of restitution and unjust **13.07** enrichment. In 2009 no one talks of quasi-contract. Today the language of Barry J has a somewhat dated air but his decision seems correct. The work the plaintiff did after the original tender was not work which he intended to do for nothing for it was clearly well outside the sort of work which a builder might do as a follow up of a tender. The work in support of the defendant's war damage claim was of a quite different sort.

Nevertheless there are clearly problems of drawing the line. A case which seems to be on the **13.08** other side of the line is *Regalian Properties Plc v London Docklands Development Corporation*.[7] The claimants were a firm of developers who were interested in building houses on land in the former London docks. The defendants were a public body charged with promoting such development. It was also the planning body and owned much but not all of the relevant land. In 1986 the plaintiff tendered a sum of £18.6m for development of the land 'subject to contract'. Between 1986 and 1988 there were extensive negotiations and much work on plans. The defendant had to secure vacant possession of parts of the land which caused delay. Eventually in November 1988 the project was abandoned because of moves in the property market. By this time the plaintiffs had spent some £3m which they sought to recover from the defendants. Rattee J held the action failed. He thought that the plaintiff

---

[6] [1957] 2 All ER 712.
[7] [1995] 1 All ER 1005; [1995] 1 WLR 212; Mannolini (1996) 59 MLR 111.

knew that there was no contract though they hoped there would be one and had taken the risk involved in the expenditure. The defendant had not received any benefit from the expenditure nor were they in anyway responsible for the collapse of the project.

13.09   Rattee J agreed with the result in *Lacey v Davis* though he did not agreed with all the reasoning.[8] He was pressed with the rather similar Australian case of *Sabemo Pty Ltd v North Sydney Municipal Council*.[9] In this case the defendant council owned land which it wished to have redeveloped. The plaintiff proposed a solution which the defendant accepted. This did not create a contract but the plaintiff then undertook a substantial amount of work. As regards one part of the work there was a specific agreement about payment but there was no agreement to pay for any of the other work. The defendant abandoned the project. Sheppard J held that the plaintiff could recover the cost of the work it had done. He said:

> In a judgment of this kind it would be most unwise, and in any event impossible, to fix the limitations which should circumscribe the extent of the right to recover. It is enough for me to say that I think that there is one circumstance here which leads to the conclusion that the plaintiff is entitled to succeed. That circumstance is the fact that the defendant deliberately decided to drop the proposal. It may have had good reasons for doing so, but they had nothing to do with the plaintiff, which in good faith over a period exceeding three years had worked assiduously towards the day when it would take a building lease of the land and erect thereon the Civic Centre which the defendant during that long period had so earnestly desired. In the *William Lacey* case ((73)) too, the defendant made a unilateral decision not to go on, but to sell its land instead.

13.10   This would of course provide a ground of distinction between the *Regalian* and *Sabemo* cases. It is clear however that Rattee J did not rely on this difference for his refusal to give judgment for the plaintiff. The relevance of one party breaking off the negotiations was also considered in the earlier case of *Brewer Street Investments v Barclays Woollen Co Ltd*.[10] In this case the defendants, who were prospective tenants, were in negotiation with the plaintiff landlords about the terms of a lease. The defendants asked the plaintiff to make alterations which the plaintiffs carried out. It was clear that the defendants would pay if the lease resulted. The negotiation for the lease broke down. The Court of Appeal held that the defendant should pay for the alteration. Somervell and Romer LJJ both thought that as the defendants had asked for the improvement and as the negotiations had not gone off because of anything done by the plaintiffs the defendants should pay. Denning LJ put a similar point slightly differently. He said:

> I do not think, however, that in the present case it can be said that either party was really at fault. Neither party sought to alter the rent or any other point which had been agreed upon. They fell out on a point which had not been agreed at all. From the very beginning the prospective tenants wanted an option to purchase, whereas the landlords were only ready to give them the first refusal. Each of them in the course of the negotiations sought on this point to get more favorable terms—the prospective tenants to get a firm option to purchase, the landlords to give a first refusal of little value—but their moves in the negotiations can hardly be considered a default by one or other.

---

[8] He disagreed with the result in *Marston Construction Co. Ltd v Kigass Ltd* (1989) 15 Con LR 116.
[9] [1977] 2 NSWLR 880.
[10] [1954] 1 QB 428. See also *Jennings and Chapman v Woodman Matthiews & Co* [1952] 2 TLR 409.

What then, is the position when the negotiations go off without the default of either? On whom should the risk fall? In my opinion the prospective tenants ought to pay all the costs thrown away. The work was done to meet their special requirements and was prima facie for their benefit and not for the benefit of the landlords. If and in so far as the work is shown to have been of benefit to the landlord credit should be given in such sum as may be just. Subject to such credit, the prospective tenants ought to pay the cost of the work, because they in the first place agreed to take responsibility for it; and when the matter goes off without the default of either side, they should pay the costs thrown away. There is no finding here that the work was of any benefit to the landlords, and in the circumstances the prospective tenants should, I think, pay the amount claimed.

There is a useful summary of the present state of the authorities in *MSM Consulting Ltd v* **13.11** *United Republic of Tanzania*[11] where Christopher Clarke J said:

I regard this as a helpful analysis of the authorities from which I also derive the following propositions:

(a) Although the older authorities use the language of implied contract the modern approach is to determine whether or not the circumstances are such that the law should, as a matter of justice, impose upon the defendant an obligation to make payment of an amount which he deserved to be paid (quantum meruit): Lacey; for that reason it does not seem to me that section 18 of the Estate Agents Act 1989 has any application to this claim;

(b) Generally speaking a person who seeks to enter into a contract with another cannot claim to be paid the cost of estimating what it will cost him, or of deciding on a price, or bidding for the contract. Nor can he claim the cost of showing the other party his capability or skills even though, if there was a contract or retainer, he would be paid for them. The solicitor who enters a 'beauty contest' in the course of which he expresses some preliminary views about the client's prospects cannot, ordinarily expect to charge for them. If another firm is retained; he runs the risk of being unrewarded if unsuccessful in his pitch.

(c) The court is likely to impose such an obligation where the defendant has received an incontrovertible benefit (e.g. an immediate financial gain or saving of expense) as a result of the claimant's services; or where the defendant has requested the claimant to provide services or accepted them (having the ability to refuse them) when offered, in the knowledge that the services were not intended to be given freely;

(d) But the court may not regard it as just to impose an obligation to make payment if the claimant took the risk that he or she would only be reimbursed for his expenditure if there was a concluded contract; or if the court concludes that, in all the circumstances the risk should fall on the claimant: *Jennings & Chapman*;

(e) The court may well regard it as just to impose such an obligation if the defendant who has received the benefit has behaved unconscionably in declining to pay for it

C. Estoppel

In some circumstances, particularly in transactions involving land, an incomplete transac- **13.12** tion may give rise to an estoppel which has the effect of carrying the transaction to completion. An important early case is *Dillwyn v Llewelyn*.[12] A father wished to provide for a

---

[11] (2009) 123 Con LR 154. See also *Easet Antennas Ltd v Racal Defect Electronics Ltd* (2002) Hart J Chancery Division unreported and *Country Communication Ltd v ICL Pathway Ltd* [2000] CLC 324.
[12] (1862) 4 DeGF&J 517.

younger son and intending to transfer land, signed a memorandum, not under seal: 'For the purpose of furnishing himself with a dwelling house.' The son spent a great deal of money building a house on the land. When the father died the elder brother claimed the house. Lord Westbury LC held that the younger son should have a fee simple. This is really a case of an imperfect gift but Lord Westbury said it was analogous to the doctrine of part performance in contracts for sale of land inadequately evidenced.

13.13   In *Plimmer v Wellington Corporation*[13] Plimmer held a landing place and jetty on licence from the government who in pursuance of their policy of stimulating immigrants to New Zealand, encouraged Plimmer to develop the jetty. It was held that they could not revoke the licence.

13.14   In *AG of Hong Kong v Humphreys Estates*[14] there were dealings between the Hong Kong government and the plaintiff company which envisaged an exchange of 83 flats owned by the plaintiffs for the grant of a crown lease of government property. All the dealings were 'subject to contract'. The exchange had been carried out and the plaintiff had paid the Hong Kong government a sum representing the agreed difference in value of the two premises. It was held that the plaintiff group was not estopped from withdrawing from the transactions. Lord Templeman said:

> Their Lordships accept that the government acted to their detriment and to the knowledge of HKL in the hope that HKL would not withdraw from the agreement in principle. But in order to found an estoppel the government must go further. First the government must show that HKL created or encouraged a belief or expectation on the part of the government that HKL would not withdraw from the agreement in principle. Secondly the government must show that the government relied on that belief or expectation. Their Lordships agree with the Courts of Hong Kong that the government fail on both counts.
>
> Mr. Morritt submitted that every action of the government and every action of HKL after the date of the agreement in principle served to create or encourage a belief and expectation in the government that the agreement in principle would be carried into effect and that HKL would not withdraw. HKL allowed the government to take possession of Tregunter, to fit out the flats, to re-house senior civil servants and to dispose of their former residences. HKL prevailed on the government to allow HKL to enter upon and to destroy the buildings comprised in Queen's Gardens and adjacent sites and HKL paid in full the price for taking over Queen's Gardens. It was impossible for the government to go back and unthinkable that HKL would not go forward. It was unconscionable for HKL to seek to exercise their legal right to withdraw from the agreement in principle.
>
> Their Lordships accept that there is no doubt that the government acted in the confident and not unreasonable hope that the agreement in principle would come into effect. As time passed and more and more actions were undertaken in conformity with the proposals contained in the agreement in principle, the government's hopes were strengthened. It became more and more unlikely that either the government or HKL would have a change of heart and would withdraw from the agreement in principle. But at no time did HKL indicate expressly or by implication that they had surrendered their right to change their mind and to withdraw. That right, expressly reserved and conferred by the government, was to withdraw

---

[13]   (1884) 9 App Cas 699.
[14]   [1987] 1 AC 114; see also *Pridean Ltd v Forest Taverns Ltd* (1998) 75 P&CR 447.

at any time before 'document or documents necessary to give legal effect to this transaction are executed and registered'. HKL did not encourage or allow a belief or expectation on the part of the government that HKL would not withdraw. HKL proceeded in accordance with the proposals contained in the agreement in principle but at the same time they continued to negotiate the exact provisions of the documents which were necessary to be executed before the parties could become bound.

13.15 It is clear that this is a very important decision. Here many acts had been done in the hope that a contract would be made but nothing had ever been said to abandon the right not to enter into a contract. This was fatal to the estoppel claim. This is also the position in the latest and most important case in the chain *Cobbe v Yeoman's Row Management Ltd*.[15] In this case Mr Cobbe was an experienced property developer. He entered into an arrangement with the first defendant, a property company, and the third defendant, Mrs Lisle-Mainwaring, the only director of the first defendant. The arrangement was at all times said to be binding in honour only. Under it Mr Cobbe was to seek to obtain planning permission for the demolition of a block of flats owned by the company and its conversion into a very expensive set of town houses. It was agreed that if planning permission were obtained Mr Cobbe would buy the block for £12m, carry through the development and that the parties would share equally the gross proceeds over £24m. Mr Cobbe devoted much time and skill to the project. On the day on which planning permission was obtained, Mrs Lisle-Mainwaring announced that the price had gone up to £20m and a 40% share of the gross proceeds over £40m. It seems clear that this change of mind had taken place earlier but that Mrs Lisle-Mainwaring had continued to encourage Mr Cobbe.

13.16 Etherton J held that Mrs Lisle-Mainwaring's behaviour was unconscionable and that claims in proprietary estoppel and constructive trust succeeded. The Court of Appeal agreed but the House of Lords did not. They thought that it was not sufficient that Mrs Lisle-Mainwaring's behaviour was unconscionable, which they thought it was but that to succeed Mr Cobbe had to propose a proprietary claim which she was estopped from denying and that there was no such claim.

13.17 Reasoned speeches were delivered by Lord Scott and Lord Walker. Lord Scott said:

> Both Etherton J and Mummery LJ regarded the proprietary estoppel conclusion as justified by the unconscionability of Mrs Lisle-Mainwaring's conduct. My Lords, unconscionability of conduct may well lead to a remedy but, in my opinion, proprietary estoppel cannot be the route to it unless the ingredients for a proprietary estoppel are present. These ingredients should include, in principle, a proprietary claim made by a claimant and an answer to that claim based on some fact, or some point of mixed fact and law, that the person against whom the claim is made can be estopped from asserting. To treat a 'proprietary estoppel equity' as requiring neither a proprietary claim by the claimant nor an estoppel against the defendant but simply unconscionable behaviour is, in my respectful opinion, a recipe for confusion.
>
> Let it be supposed that Mrs Lisle-Mainwaring were to be held estopped from denying that the core financial terms of the second agreement were the financial terms on which Mr Cobbe was entitled to purchase the property. How would that help Mr Cobbe? He still

---

[15] [2008] 1 WLR 1752; [2008] UKHL 55; Macfarlane and Robertson, 'The Death of Proprietary Estoppel' (2009) Lloyds MCLQ 449.

would not have a complete agreement. Suppose Mrs Lisle-Mainwaring had simply said she had changed her mind and did not want the property to be sold after all. What would she be estopped from denying? Proprietary estoppel requires, in my opinion, clarity as to what it is that the object of the estoppel is to be estopped from denying, or asserting, and clarity as to the interest in the property in question that that denial, or assertion, would otherwise defeat. If these requirements are not recognised, proprietary estoppel will lose contact with its roots and risk becoming unprincipled and therefore unpredictable, if it has not already become so. This is not, in my opinion, a case in which a remedy can be granted to Mr Cobbe on the basis of proprietary estoppel.

13.18   Lord Walker said:

When examined in that way, Mr Cobbe's case seems to me to fail on the simple but funda-mental point that, as persons experienced in the property world, both parties knew that there was no legally binding contract, and that either was therefore free to discontinue the negotia-tions without legal liability—that is, liability in equity as well as at law, to echo the words of Lord Cranworth LC in *Ramsden v Dyson* LR 1 HL 129, 145–146 quoted in para 53 above. Mr Cobbe was therefore running a risk, but he stood to make a handsome profit if the deal went ahead, and the market stayed favourable. He may have thought that any attempt to get Mrs Lisle-Mainwaring to enter into a written contract before the grant of planning permis-sion would be counter-productive. Whatever his reasons for doing so, the fact is that he ran a commercial risk, with his eyes open, and the outcome has proved unfortunate for him. It is true that he did not expressly state, at the time, that he was relying solely on Mrs Lisle-Mainwaring's sense of honour, but to draw that sort of distinction in a commercial context would be as unrealistic, in my opinion, as to draw a firm distinction depending on whether the formula 'subject to contract' had or had not actually been used.

13.19   The House of Lords did however support a personal claim by Mr Cobbe. This is dealt with very briefly by Lord Scott and not at all by Lord Walker. The question appears to be treated as straightforward. One suspects that this may reflect the way the appellants presented the case in the House of Lords. They may have thought that to argue too strenuously that Mr Cobbe should get nothing would be forensically counter productive. The Proprietary claim was worth £2m, the personal claim perhaps £150,000.

Lord Scott said:

It seems to me plain that Mr Cobbe is entitled to a quantum meruit payment for his services in obtaining the planning permission. He did not intend to provide his services gratuitously, nor did Mrs Lisle-Mainwaring understand the contrary. She knew he was providing his ser-vices in the expectation of becoming the purchaser of the property under an enforceable contract. So no fee was agreed. In the event the expected contract did not materialise but a quantum meruit for his services is a common law remedy to which Mr Cobbe is entitled. The quantum meruit should include his outgoings in applying for and obtaining the planning permission, which should be taken to be reasonably incurred unless Mrs Lisle-Mainwaring can show otherwise, and a fee for his services assessed at the rate appropriate for an experi-enced developer. To the extent, of course, that Mr Cobbe's outgoings included the fees of planning consultants whom he employed, there must not be double counting. The amount of the quantum meruit for Mr Cobbe's services would, in my opinion, represent the extent of the unjust enrichment for which the defendant company should be held accountable to Mr Cobbe.

13.20   Obviously it would have been very hard if Mr Cobbe had left court with nothing but the decision is not without difficulties. The reliance that if he succeeded in getting planning permission he would not go unrewarded was precisely the same reliance that he could not lean on for the purpose of estoppel. Mr Cobbe never expected to do the work for a fee. Any professional asked to do such work for a fee on the basis that he would not be paid if unsuccessful would certainly ask for substantially more than his standard fee. The reasoning of the House of Lords as to how Mr Way should be rewarded in *Way v Latilla* would be relevant here.

INDEX